Resistance and Support

Resistance and Support

Contact Improvisation @ 50

Edited by
Ann Cooper Albright

Oxford University Press is a department of the University of Oxford.
It furthers the University's objective of excellence in research, scholarship,
and education by publishing worldwide. Oxford is a registered trade mark of
Oxford University Press in the UK and in certain other countries.

Published in the United States of America by Oxford University Press
198 Madison Avenue, New York, NY 10016, United States of America.

© Oxford University Press 2024

All rights reserved. No part of this publication may be reproduced, stored in
a retrieval system, or transmitted, in any form or by any means, without the prior
permission in writing of Oxford University Press, or as expressly permitted
by law, by license or under terms agreed with the appropriate reprographics
rights organization. Inquiries concerning reproduction outside the scope of the
above should be sent to the Rights Department, Oxford University Press, at the
address above.

You must not circulate this work in any other form
and you must impose this same condition on any acquirer

CIP data is on file at the Library of Congress

ISBN 9780197776278 (pbk.)
ISBN 9780197776261 (hbk.)

DOI: 10.1093/9780197776308.001.0001

Paperback printed by Marquis Book Printing, Canada
Hardback printed by Bridgeport National Bindery, Inc., United States of America

Contents

Acknowledgments vii
List of Contributors ix

Introduction 1
Ann Cooper Albright

Productive Tensions 13
Ann Cooper Albright

1 Mindfully Rocking and Rolling: Contact Improvisation as a Feminist
Practice in the Turbulent 1970s 19
Dena Davida

2 Getting There from Here: A Road Map for Safer Brave Open Jams 37
Michele Beaulieux

3 Gender, Power, and Equity in Contact Improvisation 61
Kristin Horrigan

4 Not: Not Contact Improvisation 80
Joy Mariama Smith, edited by Asimina Chremos

5 Doing It Wrong: Contact's Counter Countercultures 105
Emma Bigé and Paul Singh

6 Tracing the Natural Body for More Inclusive and Equitable CI Futures 122
Robin Raven Prichard

7 Underscoring Nancy Stark Smith's Legacy: Definitions and Disruptions 139
Sarah Young

Responsive Touch 153
Ann Cooper Albright

8 The Small Dances of Listening 159
Lesley Greco

9 Listening Touch 177
Rosalind Holgate Smith

10 Therapeutic Applications of Contact Improvisation 194
Aaron Brandes (Brando) and Gabrielle Revlock

11 XCI: Intimacy in Contact Improvisation 212
Aramo Olaya

12 Rolling and Knowing: Reflections on the Endurance of the CI Event 226
Brian Schultis

vi Contents

13 **Something We Touch or That Touches Us: A Newcomer Locating Themselves in Contact** 237
Lisa Claire Greene

14 **The Religious Function of Contact Improvisation** 245
Carol Laursen

Local Communities/Global Contexts 259
Ann Cooper Albright

15 **Resistances and Horizons: EPIICO, Community, and Self-Organization** 263
EPIICO: Ariadna Franco Martínez, Esmeralda Padilla García, Elisa Romero Morato, Mariana Torres Juárez, and Laura Villeda Aguirre; translated by Caroline Tracey

16 **Making Contact: Practicing and Creating Spaces of Contact Improvisation in India** 276
Guru Suraj and Adrianna Michalska

17 **Contact Improvisation in China and Taiwan** 291
Roundtable discussion with Ming-Shen Ku, Shuyi (Candy) Liao, Xiao Zhang, Huichao (Dew) Ge; introduction by Ge; transcription and translation by Yuting (Elsie) Wang

18 **Deviant Bodies: Improvising Survival in Brazil** 303
Ana Carolina Bezerra Teixeira

19 **Queering Contact Improvisation with Sara Ahmed (and the Wheelchair)** 311
Mª Paz Brozas Polo

20 **Intensive Curiosity: A Dialogue about Teaching CI** 328
Joseph Dumit and Dorte Bjerre Jensen

Index 343

Acknowledgments

The vision for this book began in the fall of 2019 when I jokingly told the first years in my Contact Improvisation (CI) class at Oberlin College that they would graduate the summer of CI @ 50. Having hosted CI 25 at Oberlin College in 1997, I felt it would make sense to host the 50th anniversary celebration here as well. My desire was to sponsor an event that included not only workshops and performances by select seasoned teachers, but also to invite proposals from anyone interested in participating. In addition, I wanted to incorporate historical discussions and panels focused on critical issues in CI in the twenty-first century. Interested in the ideas embedded in the form and its impact on people's lives, I envisioned a writing workshop at the conclusion of the festival in which folks would come together to share ideas and perspectives, as well as drafts of their writing, with one another. The year-long series of events that became *Critical Mass* acquired a sense of urgency with the passing of Nancy Stark Smith in May 2020 and the subsequent demise of *Contact Quarterly* as a regularly published journal.

Critical Mass: CI @ 50 took place at Oberlin College, July 7–11, 2022, immediately followed by a three-day writing workshop. I am immensely grateful to the participants in that workshop, as well as to all the contributors to this volume—most, but not all, of whom were involved in *Critical Mass*. Their interest, fortitude, and patience with the different stages and multiple revisions has made corralling 20 different writings into a coherent collection wonderfully satisfying.

It has been my great pleasure to teach at Oberlin College. Over the years my students have sustained my passion for dancing in contact with others, as well as my interest in thinking about the cultural implications of our dancing. I am deeply indebted to all my Contact students for keeping me engaged and curious about how this potent form of creative movement navigates the cultural tides of our lives. I thank Rebecca Janovic (OC 2018) for coming back to Oberlin College after COVID lockdowns and joining me as a teaching assistant and the *Critical Mass* project coordinator. It was her support, both physical and administrative (so many emails!), that helped me keep it together during that very intense year of multiple community jams, exhibitions, and an international dance festival. As I was pulling this manuscript together, Alana Reibstein (OC 2016) provided essential editorial support. I am so grateful for her willingness to step into this project as it gathered its own momentum. Thanks also to Sophie Bransfield, who graduated in 2022, stayed to volunteer at *CI @ 50*, and then spent a year dancing Contact in Berkeley, California. This past fall she returned to be my teaching assistant and helped me revitalize my dancing. Her enthusiasm for CI and her belief that it offers important life lessons for a younger generation has encouraged my work in bringing these essays into an accessible format.

Finally, I want to thank the team at OUP. I very much appreciate the time that Norm Hirschy (acquisitions editor) and Laura Santo (production editor, who also happens to be Rebecca Janovic's cousin—small world) took to talk with me about the cover design in New York last January. Hema Arumugam has been superb as the project manager, and

viii Acknowledgments

I appreciate the care that Dorothy Bauhoff took as the copyeditor. Thanks also to the two outside readers for their insightful comments.

As always, this book is grounded in a multitude of interconnected dancing networks, both local and international, physical and intellectual. The inspiration I receive when teaching and dancing with others sponsors my profound sense that Contact Improvisation has the potential to make our world a better place in which to breathe, live, and move together.

Contributors

Ann Cooper Albright

A dancer and a scholar, Ann Cooper Albright is Professor of Dance at Oberlin College. Her 2019 book, *How to Land: Finding Ground in an Unstable World*, uses Contact Improvisation practices to offer ways of thinking about and dealing with the uncertainty of our contemporary lives. Her other books include *Simone Forti: Improvising a Life*, *Engaging Bodies: The Politics and Poetics of Corporeality*; *Traces of Light: Absence and Presence in the work of Loie Fuller*, *Choreographing Difference: the Body and Identity in Contemporary Dance*. She is co-editor, with David Gere, of *Taken by Surprise: Improvisation in Dance and Mind*. Albright is a veteran practitioner of Contact Improvisation, teaches internationally, and directed *Critical Mass: CI @ 50* which brought 300 dancers from across the world to learn, talk, and dance together in celebration of the 50th anniversary of this extraordinary form. The book *Encounters with Contact Improvisation* is the product of one of her adventures in writing and dancing and dancing and writing with others.

Michele Beaulieux

Michele Beaulieux is an independent scholar, consent culture advocate, marketing communications consultant, liturgical dancer, and identical twin. Her writing on preventing boundary violations and creating safer brave spaces at Contact Improvisation jams has appeared in *Contact Quarterly*, the *CQ Contact Improvisation Newsletter*, and on her blog, ReservoirOfHope.blog. Except for a few brief forays, she has lived her entire life within walking distance of Lake Michigan. In the summers, she swims daily in her waters. Michele recently returned to her hometown of Milwaukee and is looking forward to dancing Contact there.

Emma Bigé

Emma Bigé studies, writes, translates, and improvises with contemporary experimental dances and queer & trans* feminist theories. Holding a PhD in philosophy, she irregularly drag-impersonates the positions of dancer, curator, and epistemology professor in visual art and dance schools and contexts. Co-editor of several anthologies on improvisation (*Steve Paxton: Drafting Interior Techniques*, 2019; *La perspective de la pomme. Histoires, politiques et pratiques du Contact Improvisation*, 2021) and author of a monograph on dance and ecology (*Mouvementements. Écopolitiques de la danse*, 2023), she is currently working on a book at the intersection of trans* studies, ecoactivism, and somatics. The rest of the time, she lives near a forest in the Périgord vert (Dordogne, France), and, in the lookout for ways of living otherwise, she rolls on the ground.

Aaron Brandes

Aaron Brandes (aka Brando), MSW, M.ED, is a founding member of the improvisational dance company Set GO and teaches and performs internationally. His dance videos have collected over a half million views and can be viewed via his website, BodyandBeing.net. In 2009, Brando established CI Ground Research, an annual conference for the pedagogical and embodied research of Contact Improvisation. He continues to host a bi-weekly CI event in Northampton which explores the relationship between improvised music and dance. Brando is a licensed psychotherapist, a nationally certified Structural Integration bodyworker, and a certified Kripalu Yoga teacher.

x Contributors

He has integrated aspects of bodywork, movement, and clinical social work in his therapeutic practice.

Mª Paz Brozas Polo

Paz Brozas Polo is a scholar and a dancer based in Spain, who also moves in neighboring countries. She has a degree in Education and Physical Education and a PhD in Theater Studies. She is dedicated to teaching Body Expression and Dance and other subjects related to the performing arts at the University of León. She is interested in the practices of diversity and of body communication. The Contact Improvisation is at the core of her artistic research and her recent publications. Paz is the cofounder of El Aula de Artes del cuerpo that offers CI, dance, circus, improvisation practices, and other creative experiences for the community: https://blogs.unileon.es/danzaule/.

Dena Davida

Dena Davida, artivist dancer, educator and scholar, has practiced and written about postmodern dance for over 50 years. Immigrating from the United States to Canada in 1977, she taught Montréal's first classes in Contact Improvisation, instigated the Catpoto Dance Collective, and created three CI-infused dance works. She also cofounded and co-curated Montréal's first dance festival and presenting space. While teaching CI, LMA, dance composition and theory at the Université du Québec à Montréal (1979–2010), she completed a doctoral dissertation (2006) in dance ethnography. Her writings on dance, culture, and live arts curation have been published in magazines, journals, and as book chapters. She conceived two anthologies, *Fields in Motion: Ethnography in the Worlds of Dance* (2012) and *Curating Live Arts: Critical Perspectives, Essays and Conversations in Theory and Practice* (2018). In 2022 she cofounded and is currently managing editor of *TURBA: The Journal for Global Practices in Live Arts Curation*.

Joseph Dumit

Joseph Dumit is an anthropologist of passions, performances, brains, games, bodies, drugs, and facts. He is chair of Performance Studies, and Professor of Science & Technology Studies, and Anthropology at University of California Davis, and Professor of Interdisciplinary Data Collaborations at the Interacting Minds Centre, Aarhus University, Denmark. He is author of *Picturing Personhood: Brain Scans and Biomedical America* (Princeton, 2004), *Drugs for Life: How Pharmaceutical Companies Define Our Health* (Duke, 2012). He works with neuroscientists, artists, makers, and improvisers in Europe and the United States on multimedia workshops and playful installations for social learning and togetherness. http://dumit.net.

Ariadna Franco

Performer, psychotherapist, and Contact Improvisation practitioner. She lives in Mexico City. Since 2008 she has made artistic work with the body as the center of the work and with the dissolution of creator-spectator roles. Through dance therapy, Contact Improvisation, and somatics, she has carried out Encounters and workshops for all bodies, confirming that dance belongs to all of us. Her current research in CI (and in life) is collective creation, community work, caring for the land, and social justice. She has been with EPIICO since 2013.

Huichao (Dew) Ge

Founder of Body On&On, producer of performing arts, curator, cofounder of Touch Contact Improvisation Festival China, International Visitor Leadership Program 2022 alumna, European Festival Academy alumna. As the founder of Body On&On, Dew is a leading figure of inclusive arts in China. In 2019, oriented to the core of "body, inclusion, and art," she founded the Luminous Festival, the first international inclusive arts festival in China. It has become a global platform for disabled artists, the creative aging, and minority groups to display and communicate.

Lesley Greco

With backgrounds in osteopathy, movement and voice, Lesley's work is interdisciplinary. Rooted in practice research, drawing on a principles of Contact Improvisation (CI) and integrating osteopathic concepts, Lesley investigates attention, perception, and movement principles in the context of listening and responding in relationship. CI and has been a strong influence since being introduced to it in Tkaronto/Toronto in 2001. For her, CI is a puzzle, a wilderness, a moving laboratory, a weird difficult love affair, a way to learn from disorientation and a companion that colours every part of her life.

Lisa Claire Greene

Lisa Claire Greene is a Chicago-based interdisciplinary artist. Their work explores the intersection of mind, body, and spirit through disciplined physical practice, in order to visually represent direct and abstract experience. Shaped by queerness and growing up with severe behavioral disorders, they intentionally weave drawing, writing, and performance to communicate a human experience that is both shaped by and entirely separate from identity groups. They have shown work at music venues, nightclubs, DIY spaces, and galleries. In 2016, they curated their first show, *Things Are Like This*, with site-specific installations by eight artists. In 2022, they had an essay about Contact Improvisation and the body published in *Stillpoint Magazine*'s February Supporter's Issue. Also in 2022, they co-curated their second exhibition, *Draw Showing*, at No Nation Art Lab which featured work from over 60 artists, including video programming via Colombia by artists from around the world.

Rosalind Holgate Smith

Rosalind Holgate Smith (UK) is a Dance Artist and Choreographer based in Berlin. She creates performances, immersive installations, and art that investigates intimate experiences between people, place, and the environment. Rosalind develops her work through practices of touch, training the senses, and dancing outdoors, on land and in water. She has trained in somatic practices including Body Mind Centering®, Authentic Movement, Skinner Release Technique, and The Axis Syllabus, and has taught Contact Improvisation for over 10 years. Teaching forms a significant part of her practice and she has also worked in UK universities and has delivered dance and performance programs with diverse groups including children, disabled adults, and older people. Rosalind completed a Foundation Diploma in Art & Design at DeMontfort University, a BA (hons) in Fine Art & Choreography at Dartington College of Arts, and a Masters in Dance at Trinity Laban. Her PhD, based at Kingston University in London, investigates how Touch makes possible encounters with Otherness and the vocabulary of touch that is used in Contact Improvisation. Her essay included in this collection reflects some of the findings of this touch-focused research project. https://rosalindholgate-smith.com/.

Kristin Horrigan

Kristin Horrigan is an improviser, choreographer, scholar, and educator who serves as an Associate Professor of Dance at Emerson College in Boston, Massachusetts. She has been researching and practicing Contact Improvisation for 25 years, teaching in the United States and internationally. For the past decade, she has been studying the ways that embodied ideas about gender influence dance practice and performance, with particular focus on Contact Improvisation. She also writes on questions of consent, equity, and access in dance education. Her writing has been published in the *Journal of Dance Education*, *Dance Education in Practice*, and *Contact Quarterly*.

Dorte Bjerre Jensen

Dorte Bjerre Jensen is a Copenhagen-based director, creator, choreographer, performer, and Contact Improvisation teacher for 25 years. Dorte's work is anchored in an evolving artistic inquiry into multisensory relations of ecological attention through movement, manifested as performance, participatory performative scores, live art installations, workshops, and writing. As a researcher she develops windows into basic processes of interaction, togetherness, perspective taking, and surprise, using art-science collaborations with the Interacting Minds Centre, Aarhus University.

Ming-Shen Ku

Taiwan-based artist; founder of Ku and Dancers, a strong improvisational dance company, which has just reached its 30-year anniversary, and has set its footprint all over the world. After teaching for 25 years, Ming-Shen Ku retired as the Dean of the Dance School of Taipei National University of the Arts. She received the Wu San Lien award, a lifetime achievement award in 2009, and the National Award for Arts in 2020.

Carol Laursen

Carol Laursen graduated from Reed College, earning an interdisciplinary BA in math and biology while taking all the dance classes they offered. After some years of travel, odd jobs, Contact jams, and theater intensives, she earned an MFA in Acting from Ohio University. Guided by a deep interest in the way inner life interfaces with outer forms, she has joined several religious communities. Carol is a long-time member

xii Contributors

of Cleveland Friends Meeting and has taken vows for lay ordination with a teacher at the San Francisco Zen Center. She is married with two adult children and one toddler.

Shuyi (Candy) Liao

CI and Feldenkrais Method teacher, theater director, Beijing Contact Improvisation (BJCI)/ "Touch Contact Improvisation Art Festival" co-founder. Her exploration as a CI practitioner began in 2009, and she learned CI from different generations, including participating in Nancy Stark Smith's January Intensives in 2017 and 2018. In recent years, she has developed materials with her Lab group partners, performing and teaching regularly in the community and public. Also as a theater director, she works with people from different communities, focusing on how somatic experience could interact with social issues. Her main works include "Still Here"; "MissUnderstanding"; "Moving without a Background"; among others.

Adrianna Michalska

Adrianna is a Contact Improvisation dancer, facilitator, performer, and independent artist from Poland, with a background in Contact Improvisation, somatics, and various improvisation methods studied across the globe. Adrianna graduated with a Dance and Culture degree from University of Surrey, United Kingdom, and is a certified DanceAbility teacher. Currently Adrianna is collaborating with Contact Improv India and InContact—organizations that foster the development of the Contact Improvisation scene in India through movement arts residencies, workshops, and performances. Adrianna is interested in embracing artistic practices from different cultures into a creative process, and looking at the transdisciplinary potential when working with text, image, sound, and movement.

Aramo Olaya

Aramo Olaya is a dancer-researcher on Contact Improvisation and tango, somatics, and queer touch practices and sexualities. They have studied CI at Formación de Contact Improvisación Madrid. They have facilitated numerous embodied philosophy workshops in Europe, the United States, and Latin America. Aramo holds a BA in Philosophy, a PhD in the Sociology of Gender, and is currently part of the PhD in Performance Studies at University of California Davis.

Esmeralda Padilla

Anthropologist, movement researcher and CI practitioner. Her interests are in somatic movement practice and improvisation, in both traditional and contemporary dance. She is an itinerant part of EPIICO.

Robin Raven Prichard

Robin Raven Prichard is a scholar/artist working between the worlds of contemporary Western dance and Indigenous dance. In her First Act, she danced throughout the United States and Australia for award-winning choreographers, Opera Australia, and created her own award-winning choreography. In her Second Act, she was a professor of dance for two decades at universities in the United States and Australia. She has published in JODE, DEiP, and in several books on dance education and history. She has won two Fulbright Fellowships (2002 and 2023) to research Indigenous dance in Australia and New Zealand. Now in her Third Act, she is pursuing dance studies, where she writes about inscrutable, unruly dancing bodies, both in Western and Indigenous dance.

Gabrielle Revlock

Gabrielle Revlock is an internationally touring postmodern choreographer and the creator of Restorative Contact, a partner mindfulness practice where touch is the primary anchor. As a practitioner of CI for over 20 years, she has led workshops and talks on Restorative Contact and CI at *CI @ 50*, the Embodiment Conference, Dance & Somatics Conference, Smith College, Future of CI, School for Contemporary Dance & Thought, Philadelphia Dance Projects, Earthdance, and Movement Research. As a dancer she has performed for Lucinda Childs, Makini (Jumatatu Poe), Susan Rethorst, Leah Stein, David Gordon, Bebe Miller & Angie Hauser, Christopher Williams, Vicky Shick, Bill Young, Jane Comfort, and Susan Marshall. Revlock is a recipient of a New York Dance and Performance "Bessie" Award and received an MFA in Dance from Smith College.

Elisa Romero Morato

Dancer, performer, somatic movement educator in formation and CI practitioner. She resides in México City. Since 2017 she has performed and shared movement practices in collective and community projects. For the past six years she has been a member of EPIICO Collective, focused on practice, research, and the transmission of Contact Improvisation in México City. She is interested in the sensitive body and how it relates with other living beings.

Brian Schultis

Brian Schultis, PhD, CLMA (b. 1986), explores movement in relation to human and nonhuman partners, environments, and materials in practice and theory. An avid Contact Improvisor in Northern Ohio, he participated in the six-month Oberlin College residency leading to the *Critical Mass: CI @ 50* event at Oberlin College. He has published in *The Unfamiliar* and *Performance Philosophy* and has taught courses at Kent State University, The University of Kent (UK), and the University of Akron. He lives in Oberlin, Ohio.

Paul Singh

Paul Singh (he/him) is a dance artist, choreographer, and educator living in New York City. He earned his BFA in dance from the University of Illinois. He has danced for Gerald Casel, Risa Jaroslow, Will Rawls, Phantom Limb Company, Stephanie Batten Bland, Peter Pleyer, Douglas Dunn, Christopher Williams, Kathy Westwater, Faye Driscoll, and was featured in the inaugural cast of Punchdrunk's New York debut of *Sleep No More*. Singh has had his own work shown at multiple venues in New York City and Berlin, and in 2004 his solo piece *Stutter* was presented at the Kennedy Center. He has taught Contact Improvisation (CI) around the world, and currently teaches varied technique classes for Movement Research at The Juilliard School. In 2021, he began his role as Program Manager at Baryshnikov Arts.

Joy Mariama Smith

A performer, installation, and movement artist, as well as an educator, Joy Mariama Smith focuses on issues related to visibility, projected identities, and self-representation in different contexts, and investigates the interplay between the body and its cultural, social, and physical environment. In their* dance, performances, and installations, they create spaces in which the distinction between spectator and participant becomes blurred and visitors are encouraged to reflect on the ways in which they deal with space. When they facilitate, they actively try to uphold inclusive spaces. * they/them/their: used as a first-person gender-neutral pronoun in English.

Guru Suraj

Guru Suraj is an Indian artist with a background in visual and movement arts, dedicated to facilitating, researching, organizing, and performing Contact Improvisation at the cross-section with different art forms. He has a Bachelor's degree in Painting and a Master's degree in Philosophy of Yoga. Together with other first Indian teachers of Contact Improvisation, he founded Contact Improv India (CII) and InContact— organizations that focus on teaching and performing CI throughout India. In his teachings he bridges both the radical and the traditional. He investigates how to strengthen creativity, discipline curiosity, and learn by sharing different modes of communication.

Ana Carolina Bezerra Teixeira

Carolina Teixeira is a Brazilian cis woman, dancer, choreographer and art educator, based in the Northeast of Brazil. Her works concern disability as an aesthetic experience and cripple arts. She has a PhD in Performing Arts at the Federal University of Bahia. Currently she is an Assistant Professor at the Dance Department at the Federal University of Paraiba and consultant in Aesthetical Accessibility in public institutions. Carolina has lived through the experience of a brain stroke since 1988.

Mariana Torres Juárez

Performer, somatic and Contact Improvisation practitioner. She is interested in exploring freedom of movement-voice in daily life. Within CI, her approach is as a tool for social fabric and identity. Mariana has taken workshops at international festivals and in México. Since 2014 she has been part of EPIICO, as a platform for the research, spread, and practice of CI in México City.

Laura Villeda Aguirre

Laura is a Mexican dancer based in México City, with a martial arts somatic background; she has a major in Communication Science. As a performer, somatic educator, and CI practitioner, she has facilitated classes and has participated in local encounters and festivals. Since 2013,

xiv Contributors

with EPIICO collective, she has co-organized and managed spaces to investigate, practice, and diffuse Contact Improvisation in México City. In her CI practice she is interested in moving/dancing questions about public space, community, internal and relational space, colonialism, extractivism, and bodily autonomy.

Sarah Young

Sarah Young has co-coordinated the Global Underscore since 2020, has been part of the Underscore +/− Group, Northampton, Massachusetts, since 2013, and took part in GLIMPSE 2, New York City, in 2014. She is a former Director of Earthdance Creative Living Project, a Guild Certified Feldenkrais® Practitioner, returned Peace Corps Volunteer/Morocco, and has a BFA in Dance from the University of Illinois, Urbana-Champaign. She has collaborated with dancemakers Nancy Stark Smith, Chris Aiken, David Dorfman, Jill Sigman, Hilary Easton, Stephan Koplowitz, Alexx Shilling & Ann Robideaux, Dana Salisbury, and the Treehouse Shakers. She lives in Northampton, Massachusetts, and Stolzenhagen, Germany.

Yuting (Elsie) Wang

Graduate of Oberlin College; dancer, CI practitioner, educator. Other than CI, Elsie also practices various Asian martial and performing arts, including Noh, Kunqu, and Aikido. As an educator, Elsie has designed a series of curricula aimed at bringing embodied research into the education of teenagers. Her workshops cover topics such as identity, gender performativity, the boundary of self and other, and the relationship between the body and space.

Xiao Zhang

Independent dancer and photographer, CI researcher and practitioner, experimental theater creator, interdisciplinary researcher and artist, primarily working with the mediums of the body, photography, and literature. Starting in 2016, Zhang began studying Contact Improvisation and currently promotes the local development of CI in Hangzhou through workshops, performances, and daily jams. Zhang's research focuses on the inner connections between improvisation and the physical body, naturality, and Zen, aiming at cultivating the indigenous, artful aspects of Chinese daily life. Zhang's experimental theater works include "Outside the Game," "Daydream," and "Nothing is Nothing," which mostly point to the subtle and delicate sensations of life, revealing the fragility and sentimentality of life that cannot be directly confronted.

Introduction

Ann Cooper Albright

Resistance as Support

I am sitting in one corner of Warner Main Space, the big old wooden gymnasium turned dance studio at Oberlin College. This is the site of Steve Paxton's 1972 *Magnesium* performance, a seminal work in the history of Contact Improvisation (CI). This is also where we held the twenty-fifth anniversary "jubilee" celebration of CI in June 1997, and where the opening circle of *Critical Mass: CI @ 50* took place in July 2022. It is a magical place, filled with the ghosts of decades of Contact classes and public jams. I have often joked that in the three decades I have been teaching in the space, I have rolled over every square inch of this wonderfully responsive floor. Usually with someone else. Most days there are 25–30 people dancing CI in this studio; occasionally there are several hundred. Today the studio is empty, the floor reflecting the sunlight streaming through the windows. Closing my eyes, I can feel the reverberations of these dancing histories seep into my bones. A former student, Nick Thompson, describes a similar experience when he writes:

> We were on our backs on the floor doing the imagery exercise. Ann started to embrace the history of contact in Warner Main and explain how she feels that the experience of each dance coats the floors and walls of the space. I started to feel for the first time how loaded that room is, thinking of *Magnesium* being in the floor beneath me, of the injuries, of the joy, and of all the classes that have experienced the expansion I have been feeling all semester. I started to envision Warner Main as an ancient wooden cup or grail, that is only used during its specific ritual and ceremony of dance. We are, and they have been, the wine or the nectar that swirls in the cup, and after it is emptied, its essence and flavor remain, shaded into the grain of wood, so that it can never be washed away. (Thompson 2010, 41)

Resistance and Support: Contact Improvisation @ 50 reflects on the many powerful conversations about continuity and change that came out of the *Critical Mass* celebration of the 50th anniversary of Contact Improvisation held at Oberlin College from July 7 to 11, 2022. This collection of essays is not meant to be either comprehensive or exhaustive in its range of topics. It does not document the complete history of CI, nor does it chart all the different approaches to this wildly inventive dance form. It does, however, include perspectives from many people from different places, providing a wonderfully rich tapestry of voices and experiences from across the world. When I first conceived of an anthology coming out of *Critical Mass*, my goal was to cultivate thoughtful discussions that took the form seriously enough to be critical of it. I wanted to introduce a new kind of writing from within the dancing—one

2 Resistance and Support

that didn't just wax poetic about its many pleasures, but could provoke challenging discussions, ultimately inspiring more intentional dancing.

Most of these writings came out of a three-day workshop that took place immediately after *CI @ 50*. Twenty of us from different generations, countries, and experiences moved together, read one another's drafts, and talked about what had just transpired during the festival. Later, we had many more conversations over Zoom and exchanges of drafts back and forth over the course of the past year. The essays gathered here are the result of this combination of editorial resistance and support—resistance as support. The writers were all wonderfully responsive to mine and each other's feedback, and I am indebted to everyone for believing in the importance of creating a critical literacy around this most ineffable form of improvised dancing. I am also grateful to the writers who contributed to this collection who were not able to attend this extraordinary event. Their perspectives expanded these discussions of the issues at stake in dancing CI today.

As a form of contemporary partner dancing, CI has its sources in the cultural revolutions of the 1960s and 1970s. During these decades, the United States experienced unprecedented social and artistic changes. Together, a new generation of Americans challenged the status quo and fought for civil rights, women's rights, and gay rights. They took part in massive public antiwar demonstrations, celebrated the Black Arts movement (including the immense popularity of jazz and African American musical forms), and constructed hippie countercultures in an attempt to free themselves from the conventions of bourgeois society. These influences were dynamic forces shaping the experimental dance scene at the time. In her book on the improvised choreography of Richard Bull, Susan Foster charts the multiplicity of influences on the practice of improvisation in the 1960s and 1970s. She references Brenda Dixon Gottschild's critique of histories of postmodern dance which elide the seminal influence of Africanisms and African American culture but expands the African American legacy of influence to include a hybridity of forms.

> The calm suggested in Asian practices coincided with the detached cool of Black art. These powerful aesthetic stances also mingled with a Latino aesthetic of spontaneity, [. . . and] Native American artistic practices and theorization of spirit-world-person integration as inspiration and justification for their work. (Foster 2002, 37)

These scholars and others have rightly pointed out the exclusionary and racist biases (conscious or not) of much mid-twentieth-century dance.

Eschewing the monumental gestures and narrative arcs of modern dance styles at that time, young dancers envisioned a new way of moving and living together—casual, relaxed, connected. In addition, these young dancers were interested in shifting the hierarchical dynamic of traditional dance companies working under one master choreographer. They forged artistic collectives, seeking to democratize their process of making and producing dance. Groups such as Judson Dance Theater and its antecedent, the improvisational collective Grand Union, blurred the distinction between art and life, framing pedestrian experiences such as walking, talking, sitting, and lying down as performance. As it emerged in the environment of the late 1960s and early 1970s, movement improvisation transformed from being a method of generating innovative material for choreography to being a valid investigation on its own.

Besides the development of CI, there were many dancers working improvisationally with musicians, as well as within the context of dance theater. In discussing this exciting creative milieu, veteran improviser and *Contact Quarterly* co-editor Lisa Nelson claims:

> There was a lot to develop in the early seventies, there were so many different efforts with improvisation in dance, it was like a virus, Judith Dunn-Bill Dixon, Grand Union, Dianne McIntyre's Sounds in Motion, Daniel Nagrin's Workgroup, all were happening at the same time. It was like an explosion of activity and some of those efforts continued for many, many years. (cited in Bigé 2019, 168)

In New York City, downtown artists appropriated as radical or experimental practices that which had been a core part of African American aesthetics for years, including the profound influence of jazz music on the avant-garde art scene. Certainly, the use of the term "jam" to indicate an open session of improvisational dancing in CI was part of this trend. This was also a time when many Americans began to study East Asian movement traditions, including Tai Chi and Aikido, two forms that were deeply implicated in Paxton's own physical training.

When Steve Paxton created *Magnesium* at Oberlin College in January 1972, he had come as part of a month-long Grand Union residency whose members taught movement classes and composed dances on students.[1] Paxton's dance for 12 men alternated between the bombastic crashing of bodies falling toward one another and onto the floor and a more meditative standing while feeling the subtle forces of gravity and air on the body. Paxton has said the impetus for this movement score arose from a solo he was working on where he tried to launch his body into the air and not care so much how he would land. Later that summer, Paxton invited various dancers (including Nancy Stark Smith and Curt Siddall from Oberlin College and Nita Little from Bennington College) to investigate these adrenalized states of falling and catching, as well as focus on internal sensation in the form of standing that would come to be known as "the small dance." These all-day open rehearsals were called "Contact Improvisations" and the form has developed and spread from those early roots.[2]

In January 1973, a group of dancers, including Paxton, Smith, Siddall, Little, and Karen Radler (another Bennington College student) toured the West Coast. They taught workshops and demonstrated their evolving practice in a series of performances aptly called "You come. We'll show you what we do." These casual showings of free-flowing movement and risky physical exchange left the audiences enthralled. According to those present, the audience members would often stick around after the show and proceed to jump on the performers and roll with each other. As the original members moved to different locations, more and more people became exposed to the burgeoning form. Pockets of practitioners developed across the country, including in San Francisco, California, and Minneapolis, Minnesota. Smith, Siddall, and Little all moved to California in the mid-1970s and began to share the work with their housemates and larger communities. The ethos was open and friendly; folks with an appetite for these movement exchanges would start teaching others, experimenting with new possibilities along the way. As Cynthia Novack notes in *Sharing the Dance*, her 1990 ethnographic study of the development of CI, the form attracted both "dancers" and

[1] For more details about this historic residency, see Wendy Perron's (2020) book *The Grand Union: Accidental Anarchists of Downtown Dance, 1970–1976* (Middletown, CT: Wesleyan University Press), pp. 139–151.

[2] For a thorough account of the beginnings of CI, see Cynthia Novack's book *Sharing the Dance: Contact Improvisation and American Culture* (Madison: University of Wisconsin Press, 1990).

4 Resistance and Support

"non-dancers." "It drew people oriented towards performing who sought a new approach and people oriented towards recreational and therapeutic participation" (1990, 74). These two populations would continue to explore the form side by side over the next 50 years.

Eventually, however, a core group of dancers became committed to developing the form, traveling beyond their own communities, teaching and sharing the physical skills needed to survive the dancing. They created a loose network of professionals that developed into highly skilled practitioners. The dancers who came together for a "ReUnion" tour in 1975 (including Paxton, Smith, Little, Siddall, and David Woodberry) recognized that this movement form spoke to a deep cultural desire. Concerned that some folks were getting injured in classes and jams taught by amateurs without much movement background, the group parsed different organizational possibilities, including a brief discussion about patenting the form or trademarking the name. Instead of policing the dissemination of CI, however, they opted for creating a newsletter to exchange information and teaching practices. Nancy Stark Smith (who had been working as an assistant for writer Diane di Prima) became the official news gatherer and editor, and in November 1975 she published the first *Contact Newsletter*. This informal collection of reports about CI in different parts of the United States and Canada would eventually become *Contact Quarterly: A Vehicle for Moving Ideas*. Later, Smith was joined by Lisa Nelson as co-editor, and their labor sustained the journal through 45 years of coverage of CI and the somatic and artistic practices that influenced its development. By writing about the form as it emerged and by creating an international "contacts" list that facilitated folks finding other CI dancers across the globe, *Contact Quarterly* helped consolidate the form as a major force in contemporary dance.

Almost 50 years after the initial experiments in 1972, Contact Improvisation is now an umbrella term for many diverse interpretations of the play with touch and weight between one or more partners. CI continues to be practiced by professional dancers and recreational movers alike, although there can be tensions between different expectations. Some dancers regard CI as a serious and skilled movement technique, while some others see it primarily as a form of social gathering to dance. Then, too, there are people who use the intimate contact with others as a deeply therapeutic engagement with the world. Certainly, CI has morphed over time as it has traveled through different communities. Nonetheless, there are enough common kinesthetic approaches and skills such that dancers from different countries, languages, and cultural backgrounds can gather at festivals and dance with one another without any formal introductions. These include tuning into internal sensation and touch, an awareness of peripheral vision, falling, rolling, continuing to move in the midst of spatial disorientation, feeling one's weight, and using gravity and momentum to play with speed and force. The radical openness to different kinds of bodies (including those with mobility restrictions or visual impairments) is one of the hallmarks of the form. CI is less about learning movements per se, and more about cultivating a certain way of being embodied in the world—one that is open to falling off balance, engaging other bodies across conflict and intimacy, as well as releasing into the support of the earth.

Sitting in Warner Main brings me back to the summer of 2020, when I first began organizing *Critical Mass: CI @ 50*. Gazing up at the massive rafters above me, I linger in the memory of those hot days when I set up a desk in one corner of this magnificent space. This was the time when we were in lockdown due to COVID-19 restrictions. Spurred on by my incorrigible optimism (and faith in the promise of a vaccine), I emailed possible collaborators, sketched out an international festival that would include dancing as well as discussing, and applied for grants to help fund my vision. Most folks I spoke with that summer thought I was out of my mind to imagine the possibility of a celebration of a dance form predicated on close physical contact at a moment when we were advised to stay 6–10 feet away from everyone not in our immediate family or friend pod. Admittedly, it was a scary time to think about the future; no one knew what the world would be like in two years. As I drew on my improvisational practice of facing the unknown, I began to envision a year-long series of events that included two archival exhibitions, regional jams, and a variety of guest artists residencies—all capped by an international festival and conference celebrating the 50th anniversary of Contact Improvisation. This last five-day event in July 2022 would grow to include classes, workshops, panels, performances, open jams, and a curated evening of films.

The summer of 2020 was also a time when many of us were mourning the untimely death of Nancy Stark Smith (1952–2020). Nancy had been a major presence in the development of CI, teaching and performing internationally and founding and co-editing *Contact Quarterly* for 45 years. An Oberlin College dance and creative writing major (OC 1974), she had offered many workshops at Oberlin over that time as well. She produced "The College Issue" of *Contact Quarterly* while in residence during the January 1983 winter term. I still have the original "glyphs" she made as part of her 2010 talk-through of the Underscore, a comprehensive group format for extended dancing that she crafted from her years spent teaching workshops and guiding longer jams. Compounding this real sense of loss was the news that *Contact Quarterly* would stop publishing regularly, eventually transitioning to an online, open-source archive of past issues. Throughout the summer, I heard some naysayers suggest that perhaps an era had ended, that maybe Contact Improvisation had run its course, and that it was no longer relevant in this twenty-first-century age of online communities such as TikTok.

Fortunately, that was not the attitude of my students, who regularly fill the CI classes that I offer. Perhaps it is the magic of Warner Main Space, but in the 30-odd years that I have been teaching Contact at Oberlin College, I have found that students readily embrace this form of improvised dancing. In fact, if you go to any CI jam in most major cities, chances are good you will find several generations of former Oberlin students rolling across the floor.[3] Many of my CI students are not exclusively dance majors, and they bring valuable insights from other majors such as neuroscience, or politics, or gender, sexuality, and feminist studies to bear on our practice together. This makes for a rich mix of ideas connecting our dancing with what is happening in the world outside the studio. These students have both affirmed my deep investment in this form of dance and resisted my assumptions about its universality.[4]

Which brings me to the title *Critical Mass: CI @ 50.* I chose this play on words to register the extent to which Contact Improvisation has become a global phenomenon—we have reached critical mass (CI currently exists in every continent except Antarctica), as well as to indicate that it was time not only to celebrate, but also to critique and unpack many of the

---

[3] In the fall of 2018, when I was introducing the form to a new class, I mentioned to the first years in the room that they would be graduating in 2022, CI's 50th anniversary year. Sure enough, several took the bait and stayed engaged with the form. They included students such as Kate Fishman (OC 2021) and Gabe Gomez (OC 2022), who continued with my Varsity Contact class and became my student assistants, helping build and launch the *Critical Mass* website and Rebecca Janovic (OC 2019) who returned to work as my teaching assistant and program coordinator. Gabe's Contact story is featured on the Dance Department's website. See https://www.oberlin.edu/arts-and-scien ces/departments/dance/contact-improvisation.

[4] In 2010, my Varsity Contact students and I published *Encounters with Contact*, a wonderful collection of over 70 shorts writings about learning and teaching Contact Improvisation in colleges and universities around the country.

6 Resistance and Support

assumptions regarding the form's inherent inclusion and accessibility. I wanted to pierce the veneer of egalitarianism (anyone can come to our jams) and gender equity (men lift women and women also lift men) that had been circulating as a central tenet of CI in the late twentieth century. Over the course of the twenty-first century, and particularly over the past decade, this "democratic" ethos has been fiercely challenged and debated. Given that many Contact jams are casual social spaces that are often only loosely regulated, discussions of consent have become increasingly important, as have the calls for reckoning with the implicit structures of racism that affect how we come together. These are fraught issues; but to pretend that we do not have to address them is to negate the power of this form as a vehicle for social change. In creating a year-long series of events for the 50th anniversary of Contact Improvisation, I wanted to celebrate and challenge; to honor history without nostalgia; to embrace the form without worshipping it.

In the time between the summer of 2020 when I started this process and July 2022 when the final five-day festival took place, there was a virtual conference provocatively titled *The Future of Contact Improvisation*. This important event was instigated by Kristin Horrigan (a dance professor at Emerson College and former board member at Earthdance) with the institutional support of Earthdance, a retreat center in western Massachusetts which has a long history of producing CI workshops and jams (including Nancy Stark Smith's annual January intensive for advanced dancers). Taking advantage of the pause in most people's dancing enforced by the pandemic, this three-day series of online workshops, panels, and discussions was specifically designed to address issues of social justice, articulate the often-ignored power dynamics around gender and sexuality, and center the voices of BIPOC (Black, Indigenous, and People of Color) dancers—all within a global context. The organizational team included Sze-Wei Chan (Singapore), Ariadna Franco (Mexico), Diana Thielen (Germany), and Kristin Horrigan (U.S.), with early contributions from Jolyn Arisman and India Harville. With presentations and panels such as "Envisioning Fair Festivals," "Questioning CI," "Recognizing Whiteness," "CI as Political Practice?" as well as opportunities for affinity spaces for BIPOC dancers, the conference brought to the surface discussions of implicit bias, equity and access, historical hierarchies, and the harm suffered by countless people who felt both violated in their experiences dancing and unsupported by the organizers of jams and festivals.

These issues had been bubbling up from time to time on the sidelines of events and more recently in the pages of *Contact Quarterly*, but this was the first time that they were the explicit focus of an event.[5] The fact that *The Future of Contact Improvisation* was online (with times to accommodate folks across the world) and had an open call for proposals made the conference infinitely more accessible than an in-person conference would have been. It also demonstrated to the community that many dancers were ready to engage with difficult conversations around the ongoing legacies of racism and the need for establishing guidelines for consent if we were going to truly dance together. Some aspects of the conference were quite contentious, and conversations could get heated. Yet by the end of those three days, it had become clear that as a community of dancers moving in the twenty-first century, Contact Improvisers could no longer pretend that this form was openly available and experienced similarly by all people. If we believed in shifting the power dynamics (some of which were quite toxic), we needed to be proactive and thoughtful about the next steps.

---

[5] My student assistants Kate Fishman and Gabe Gomez and I were able to attend the majority of the sessions.

Like *The Future of Contact Improvisation* conference, *Critical Mass: CI @ 50* issued an open call for proposals (including workshops, panels, presentations, performances, and films). The convention of open calls is used regularly for academic conferences and other kinds of somatic gatherings such as the Body Mind Centering annual conference. However, in the CI world, very often the teachers and performers are chosen by a selected group of curators, often organized in collaboration with Nancy Stark Smith before she passed. Certainly, this was the case for the CI 25 and CI 36 celebrations. This "curation" creates an in-house casting system tending toward a group of "tried and true" teachers and performers. In her editor's note after the CI 36 event at Juniata College, Pennsylvania, in June 2008, Nancy Stark Smith expresses an ambivalence about this sense of "founder's lineage," while simultaneously reaffirming it. At first, she declares: "I agree that it's high time to extend our historical gaze beyond the founding generation of contactors to the many significant developments of this work brought about by other people, in other time periods and locations throughout CI's thirty-six-year history." But interestingly, in the very next sentence she hedges: "At the same time, I was deeply relieved to have Steve Paxton's voice and view back in the mix among all of us present during his talk at CI36 . . ." (2009, 3).

As the director of *CI @ 50*, I tried to be sensitive to the delicate balance of honoring our "dancestors" while also expanding the opportunities for new people to teach and perform. An open call helps to even the playing field, so to speak, allowing for people to contribute and for possibilities to emerge that were previously unknown. At the same time, given that Nancy Stark Smith had passed two years earlier during the pandemic, I sought a way to honor her immense contributions to the form by creating an archival exhibition focused on *Contact Quarterly* and the Underscore in the library—a way to highlight both the dance form and an important dance alumna from the college for the broader public.

Throughout the 2021–2022 academic year, I crafted different dancing opportunities that were open to the public. Although it is in a small town in the Midwest, Oberlin College has always been a very porous place. This was true in 1972 as well as 2022. Bringing in folks from the broader Contact community is a wonderful way to expose students to other dancers, as well as to help build momentum for our July festival. In November 2021, we held a three-day regional/alumni jam. I was astonished when 70 people showed up from all around the Midwest, as well as places further away, such as Philadelphia and Durham, North Carolina. It was good to measure people's interest in dancing together again and to plant the seeds for them to come back in July. In January, we also invited Slovenian artist Jurij Konjar to guest teach a three-week Winter Term Intensive exploring the physicality behind Steve Paxton's original concept for *Magnesium*. Jurij had worked extensively with Steve, re-enacting some of his early solos for Steve's retrospective at Dia Beacon in New York, and Steve had gifted him his Goldberg Variations solo.

This was also the time when we were joined by 12 international guest artists who moved to Oberlin for six months—participating in classes and workshops and conducting their own research labs. It was an amazing experience to host a group of experienced dancers and teachers from Argentina, Poland, India, and Slovenia, as well as from all over the United States. These folks were instrumental in helping to organize the final festival, and many of them took on the immense labor of crafting community guidelines and creating a "response team" to manage any issues that might arise during that event.[6] Another special guest artist

---

[6] These wonderful people included: Rebecca Janovic (project coordinator), Teresa Więcko, Gabi Torta, Yusa Jacobo, Brian Schultis, Adrianna Michalska, Guru Suraj, Anya Yermakova, Cara Graninger, Michal Schorsch, Autumn LeBank, Jaqueline de Melo Silva, Nicholas Travers, and Charlotte Andrews, in addition to Jurij Konjar.

8 Resistance and Support

who joined us for a week in the spring was mayfield brooks, who shared their artistic work and facilitated our dancing together. In early May, we launched the memorial exhibition on Nancy Stark Smith with a weekend jam in which we staged Smith's the Underscore with the help of Sarah Young, a colleague of Nancy's and member of the Global Underscore team.

Oberlin College hosted *Critical Mass: CI @ 50*, a multifaceted international dance conference and festival that included 42 workshops, 4 panels, 8 performances, 3 public jams, and a curated film showing. One of the larger goals of this event was not only to celebrate the 50th anniversary of this unique dance form, but also to take stock of its past, present, and future. *Critical Mass* brought close to 300 dancers from all over the world to Oberlin, Ohio. Many guest artists participated in this festival, some of whom were funded by a National Endowment for the Arts (NEA) grant. In addition to the library exhibit on Smith, this five-day series of events also included an archival exhibition at the Allen Memorial Art Museum entitled *Collective Gestures: Experimental Performance at Oberlin College in the 1970s*, that documented, among other art happenings, Grand Union's 1972 winter term residency.

As the first major international gathering of Contact Improvisers after the global shutdowns caused by the COVID pandemic, there was amazing interest and enthusiasm for the event—so much so that the initial registration filled up in less than 10 hours and we had to make more spaces available so that folks across the globe could also participate. For many, it was the first time they had danced in physical contact with other people in almost three years. Given the precarious nature of the pandemic and the fact that so many people were traveling some distance to attend, we were rigorous about vaccine mandates and required indoor masking. (In each session, we had volunteers in purple T-shirts enforcing this requirement.) The festival was attended by an international group of dancers and teachers, including people from Taiwan, China, India, Sweden, Canada, Poland, Slovenia, Argentina, Mexico, Germany, France, Spain, England, the Netherlands, Russia, and Ukraine, as well as the United States.

During these days, we honored our elders, embraced the present moment, and thought seriously about the ways in which Contact Improvisation was an ever-evolving dance form with its own blind spots and inevitable failings. As part of the festival, there were roundtables presenting early experiences developing the form, as well as panels interrogating the exclusionary history of the postmodern dance scene in which it was born. There were also over 40 different workshops taught by participants, as well as performances (at 7 and 9 p.m. Friday and Sunday evenings), a staging of the Underscore on Saturday evening, and a curated evening of films Thursday evening at the historic Apollo movie theater in town. We also produced a daily "zine" in paper with poetic tidbits, critical discussions, and comments about the classes and reflections on people's experiences dancing. In addition, we partnered with the Jerome Robbins Dance Research Collection in the New York Public Library at Lincoln Center to conduct a series of oral history interviews and create an archive of the festival (including the website, videos of the performances, and assorted ephemera). After the main festival was over, I led a three-day writing workshop for participants who were interested in writing thoughtfully and at some length about their perspectives on Contact Improvisation.

The July 2022 celebration was both joyous and messy. The dancing was terrific, the performances inspiring, and the weather was lovely. There were tensions, however, among people's expectations. Interestingly, our daily paper zine reflected that continuum of experiences. Entitled */sharing weight/* the first day's zine presented the format and offered guidance by the editorial crew (Brian Schultis, Sophie Bransfield, Adrianna Michalska, and Lola Chalmers-Dribbell) for submissions:

Framed as an anniversary and set in one of the important locations for the founding of Contact Improvisation, this event will often look to the past. We are all concerned about the future, of our personal lives, of our society, and of this form we love. For the zine, though, we'd like to follow Lisa Nelson's score from the opening circle and think about the present. Here we are together, to dance, to discuss, to share. What happened? How was it? These zines are published daily and are short, so there isn't time or space for too much analysis—for putting together what it all means. That's ok. We're also not trying to "capture" everything. There's way too much. What we can do is share the moments that feel important to us, the impressions that linger.

What folks shared on the whiteboards placed throughout the spaces and in the zines published every morning were the range of experiences of deep pleasure in dancing with others again, as well as questions about how power gets distributed in dancing communities. In Friday's zine, for instance, Rythea Lee writes:

The years of the pandemic seemed to create a loss of pathways in my body and I felt them receding and could not hold onto them. It felt like parts of me were drying up and my waterways were emptying. . . . Today, here, back with my dancing people, the tributaries are opening again with small and big rushes of muscle memory. The pathways are remembering themselves and it's so similar to oxygen flowing into my veins!

Across the page, Adrianna Michalska questions:

When the international CI community gathers, how can we co-exist? How can we improvise with each other outside of the dance floor? With our words, our terms, our concepts, our culture, our expressions. Who gets to speak and who needs to adjust?

Coming 15 months after *The Future of Contact Improvisation* online conference, *Critical Mass* took up many of the same issues debated earlier and included multiple panels on consent and diversity.[7] In addition, we strove to support the presence of BIPOC dancers in many different ways, not the least of which were seven BIPOC travel grants funded by the Office of the President of Oberlin College, which helped (among others) EPIICO, a feminist collective from Mexico, to participate.[8] We also arranged for various affinity jam spaces such that BIPOC dancers could experience moving together in peace and solidarity. Given the histories of racial violence in the United States, it has become more common to create exclusive spaces for Queer and BIPOC folks to dance together. This subject can be highly charged in ways that may have surprised many of the international dancers coming from countries where issues of class or caste are more urgent.

For instance, I remember overhearing an intriguing conversation between two male dancers, one American and the other Canadian. The U.S.-based dancer was asking the other why they didn't come to the BIPOC affinity jam, enthusiastically relating how wonderful it was to be in a space with other Black, Latinx, and Asian "brothers and sisters." His colleague replied

---

[7] For a full list of the various panels and workshops, see the conference program archived at: https://sites.google.com/oberlin.edu/criticalmassci50?pli=1.

[8] EPIICO performed, and gave a talk at Critical Mass, which is the basis of their essay in this volume.

10 Resistance and Support

that he was happy for the other person, but personally he wasn't interested in that kind of exclusionary setting. He didn't feel that he needed to dance in a segregated jam space just because he was Black. These two different perspectives were indicative of a range of viewpoints among the participants that coexisted and led to interesting discussions. Sometimes these perspectives clashed, which also led to necessary—if more challenging—discussions. For instance, the attitude that white European ethnicity necessarily equals settler colonialism brought some pushback from participants from Eastern European countries that had been subjected to imperial conquest and whose families were persecuted in a variety of ways. Histories are complex. Naming can be tricky. But there was something about being able to dance with these issues that felt important. We may not agree, but we can find ways to move side by side, dancing in the midst of this friction, rather than ignoring it.

Another event that elicited mixed reactions was the Saturday evening enactment of Nancy Stark Smith's the Underscore. Traditionally, the Underscore has been accompanied by live improvised music (very often by composer Mike Vargas, Nancy Stark Smith's partner of many years) that combines acoustic and electronic sounds and has its grounding in the new music of the 1960s and 1970s. Often comprising longer, sustained tones, this kind of ambient composition intends to create a sonic environment that functions as a backdrop to the moving without influencing it unduly. Frankly, I believe that this type of abstract ambient music with no real rhythm is one of the ways that a certain kind of middle-class, white ethos pervades the dancing experience in many Contact spaces. So, when one of the invited accompanists who is a DJ decided to liven things up a bit by playing a different kind of dance music—club music with a serious downbeat—some dancers were super excited and happy to dance along, while others were put off by the sudden shift of sonic atmosphere. Folks complained that it was too early in the evening for such dynamic music, and that people were still moving through the preliminary stages of the score, which calls first for "arriving," "bonding with the earth," and then slowly evolving to more complex interactions in the space. Zine #4 captured some late-night comments from the whiteboard, including: "Please don't call that an underscore" and "Change keeps traditions alive!" and the dueling "I agree!" and "I disagree!" (For a more detailed explanation of this event, see Sarah Young's Chapter 7, at the end of the first section of the volume, Productive Tensions.)

I decided to title this collection *Resistance and Support: Contact Improvisation @ 50* because those terms effectively represent the wonderful mix of pushback and sincere commitment to making this form live up to its potential for inspiring social change that was a prevailing ethos during *Critical Mass*. Now that we are starting to emerge from most pandemic restrictions and given the surge of alienation and sense of loneliness so many people have experienced in the early 2020s, Contact Improvisation has the possibility to create space for joyous, physical, and thoughtful connections between people. Even in the year since we produced *Critical Mass*, Contact communities have begun to flourish again in cities large and small. But this is not a return to the "good old days" of playful noodling around together. Rather, younger dancers (for whom conversations about consent have always been a given) are joining older dancers to create guidelines and jam protocols that recognize the ways that implicit racism and (hetero)sexism can impact people's ability to be truly present. Yes, it means that we are asking folks to show up on time for the opening circle introductions and jam protocols. Yes, we are making it clear this is not a space to hook up with that person with whom you just had a great dance. Yes, we are asking that you not show up under the influence of whatever might affect your responsiveness to the immediate moment. Yes, we are sometimes recognizing and respecting a strategic essentialism that might call for affinity jams in the middle of a festival or workshop, and no, they will not be marginalized to the basement studio—they will be in the big, glorious, sun-filled space, right where they belong.

For me, there is another meaning to the words *resistance* and *support*. When I teach skills, such as giving and receiving weight from a partner, I often say "resistance is support"—meaning that when I resist your weight, I am, in fact, supporting you. Feeling that support allows your partner to keep going, to feel safe giving more of their weight. I then make an analogy between the physical and the metaphysical by talking about how it is important to be able to feel intellectual resistance as support as well. When I push back on your ideas in a responsive and not a reactive manner, it is as a kind of support, not a negation or dismissal of them. This exchange can then move back and forth, beginning an improvisation, the trajectory of which has not previously been imagined.

The chapters which follow are organized in three sections: Productive Tensions, Responsive Touch, and Local Communities/Global Contexts. As organizing categories, these sections are fairly porous—the ideas and insights from one might well relate to an essay in another section. For instance, one can read about issues of consensual touch in both the Productive Tensions section as well as the Responsive Touch section. Even within one section, the essays often propose different, sometimes conflicting, facets of the issue at stake. Instead of introducing all the essays here, I have chosen to enumerate their interconnections in brief prefaces to each section such that the reader can approach the different themes in any order they desire. Taken as a whole, this collection interweaves somatics and politics, realizing the potent interconnectedness of body and mind—of moving together—that is the past, present and future of Contact Improvisation.

Critical Mass: CI @ 50 was both joyous and contentious, immensely healing and deeply provocative. There were multiple and sometimes conflicting expectations about what should happen. Fortunately, Warner Main Space is big enough to hold all our different energies, the vibrations of which I can still feel in the floor, two years later. I am proud of what we created together in those days as I am proud of the essays that developed out of that extraordinary moment. These writings represent a dynamic engagement with a dance form that has now weathered half a century and whose future is ours to make.

References

Albright, Ann Cooper, editor (with Katie Barkley, Kai Evans, Jan Trumbauer, David Brown, and Rachel Wortman). *Encounters with Contact: Dancing Contact Improvisation*.

Bigé, Romain (Emma) (ed.). *Steve Paxton: Drafting Interior Techniques*. Lisbon, Portugal: Culturgest, 2019.

Foster, Susan. *Dances That Describe Themselves: The Improvised Choreography of Richard Bull*. Middletown, CT: Wesleyan University Press, 2002.

Smith, Nancy Stark. "Editor's Note." *Contact Quarterly*, 34.1, Winter/Spring 2009, p. 3.

Thompson, Nick. "Journal notes," in *Encounters with Contact*. Oberlin, OH: Oberlin College Theater and Dance Program, 2010, 41.

Productive Tensions

Ann Cooper Albright

For a long time, Contact Improvisers prided themselves on "going with the flow." One of the unspoken measures of a dancer's skill was the ability to blend their energies with another person's movement. At the end of the twentieth century, most Contacters learned to release into the support of gravity and follow the point of contact as it rolled across our bodies and through the space. Aikido rolls helped us fall with grace, and the ease with which dancers were lifted onto a shoulder was an enviable quality of the most virtuosic dancing.

The shadow side of this smooth, effortless flow, however, could be a manipulative pressure to conform with the status quo. Unstated assumptions about one's psychic and physical pliability had different resonances with different bodies. Resistance, tension, anger, and effort were often disparaged. Feminist killjoys were accused of not embracing their full sensual, sexual selves. Women who refused to be lifted were less "fun" to dance with. Although it is true that one of the hallmarks of early CI was the startling fact that women could lift men and there was no leader or follower role assigned on the basis of gender, that theoretical openness could easily get lost in the midst of a crowded jam where it is not unusual to see large men lifting smaller women on their shoulders as if they were prized game. Similarly, the social dynamics of being available to all kinds of physical contact can feel downright invasive for some people. BIPOC folks were an anomaly in the largely white postmodern dance context in which CI was cultivated. The sense of ease and flow in one's dancing is built on largely unacknowledged gendered and racial privilege. Not all bodies feel equally safe in jam situations.

Entitled "Productive Tensions," this section takes up critical discussions across the themes of feminist and queer interventions, racial reckonings, and contested histories. The past decade has brought issues of racial violence, embodied class privilege, and sexual harassment (highlighted by the impact of the #MeToo movement) to people's attention, piercing the veneer of that "democratic" and "egalitarian" ethos of CI. This reckoning with unspoken power dynamics has had a profound impact on the return to dancing post-pandemic, and many of the essays in this section elaborate the implications of these issues within CI communities. The essays included here all embrace that critical edge, sharing a belief that resistance is valuable and tensions can be productive.

The first essay in this section, Chapter 1, is Dena Davida's "Mindfully Rocking and Rolling: Contact Improvisation as a Feminist Practice in the Turbulent 1970s." In her autobiographical discussion of the confluence of feminist ideals and early training in CI, Davida charts how she moved from dance as a form of artistic expression to dancing as a consciously activist pursuit. Recounting her experience with the women's collective Catpoto (1977–1980), Davida describes how female dancing bodies became "emblems of equality and empowerment" at that time. Davida attests to the very real embodied sense of liberation that she experienced when she asserts that CI "profoundly changed my life's trajectory as a woman, vocational dancer, and global citizen." However, instead of leaving her essay as a tidy

14 Resistance and Support

historical recounting, Davida continues into the present moment, parsing her own experiences with more recent interrogations of the form at several 50th anniversary celebrations, including *Critical Mass* and a similar event held in Montreal (November 2022).

If Davida's essay evokes the liberatory aspects of CI for women, Michele Beaulieux's Chapter 2, "Getting There from Here: A Road Map for Safer Brave Open Jams," delves into the myriad problems with a dance form predicated on intimate touch, especially in the casual public jam situations where few are willing to regulate unwanted sexual behavior. Beaulieux is one of the clearest voices calling for such group accountability in jam situations. In her essay, she persuasively argues for discussions about physical safety to engage a broader conversation about consent and well-being. Her vision of a "safer brave space" moves us past the individualistic sensibility of so many CI spaces (first take care of yourself) to acknowledge the critical importance of a group ethos of responsibility and accountability (care for others in the space as well).

As any survivor of unwanted sexual contact will tell you, the issue is never simply a violation of physical boundaries, but also a question of what happens next. In 2014, Beaulieux encountered a man at the weekly Chicago jam who violated her boundaries. The deeper harm, however, was the inability of those facilitating the jam to do anything about it when she complained, even though this person had a history of unwanted sexual contact with others. Thus began a years-long work to educate the wider Contact Improvisation communities about what we need to do to make our spaces accountable to all bodies. In her essay, Beaulieux articulates her concept of what consent culture could look like, detailing "The Beaulieu Test" as "a quick yardstick for assessing whether an event recognizes that safety is a community responsibility." She calls on Contact communities to understand the inherent dynamics of so-called democratic spaces—if leadership is casual, then we will be necessarily reinforcing existing power dynamics. By contrast, clear guidelines provide transparency that allows people to be part of a larger conversation about safety and community. Ultimately, Beaulieux's hope is that these conversations will facilitate a deeper, more engaged dancing where everyone can feel truly welcome.[1]

In Chapter 3, "Gender, Power, and Equity in Contact Improvisation," Kristin Horrigan also challenges the notion that bodies in CI are somehow "neutral," enumerating the many ways that gendered identities and identity-based power dynamics enter our dancing with one another. Horrigan echoes Beaulieux's call for attentiveness to these dynamics, underscoring how the refusal to acknowledge power dynamics simply reinforces social privilege. Given how often twentieth-century discussions of gender in Contact Improvisation extolled the seeming equality of men and women both lifting and being lifted by one another, Horrigan's interrogation is a much-needed intervention. Indeed, in the 1990s, I remember even hearing some dancers suggest that gender doesn't exist in CI (this at a time when well-known male teachers would routinely enter into liaisons with their students).

Drawing on feminist and queer cultural theory, Horrigan's essay begins by laying out key concepts such as gender identity, gender expression, and gender socialization to demonstrate how these different threads of history, experience, and desire interweave throughout our dancing. Alongside her more theoretical points is a personal narrative that illustrates the physical implications of working to resist certain aspects of her own embodiment. Like Davida, Horrigan describes the ways in which CI first helped her move past her gendered

---

[1] Michele Beaulieux was one of several people offering invaluable counsel as the *Critical Mass* team drew up their community guidelines.

socialization as a young woman to embrace the physical possibilities that more fully aligned with her growing feminist disposition. Through training in CI, she writes, she learned to "push back, support weight, and calm my reflexive response to pain. I delighted in lifting my partners as an equal and knowing how to organize my body for strength and action." One of the wonderful things about CI is the possibility embedded in its improvisational impulse. To that end, Horrigan introduces the delightful concept of "secret scores" in which dancers consciously decide to limit one kind of movement habit in order to explore a less common or comfortable one, extending the limits of their own somatic identity. She suggests that these intentional experiments can create a queer sense of play, opening the space up to a continuum of embodied genders.

Self-identified queer, nonbinary, femme, and Black educator and movement artist living in Amsterdam, Joy Mariama Smith invites their reader to "dance" with the written text of Chapter 4, "Not: Not Contact Improvisation." Their writing is a performance, rather than standard academic discourse, and the double refusal of its title—the "Not CI" and yet "Not: Not CI"—slyly teases our imagination as it slips through our intellectual categories. We are in limbo, true, but nonetheless still in motion, partnering with a textual vocalization that alternately whispers and cajoles, declares, and shouts. Warmly welcomed into the party, we are asked to consider a series of "what ifs?": "What kind of container is needed to host a space of discomfort? What sort of space fosters community building, what is an affirming space, what is a space for introverts, for researchers, for refugees, for critical thinking and critical feeling?" Smith affirms the somatic and communal potential of Contact Improvisation but prods us to re/consider our perspective when entering the dancing. "What happens when we take the core principles of CI and layer in varying socialcultural perspectives, somatic intelligences, and experiences of people of color, of queers, of krips . . . ?"

These questions embrace a politics of disorientation and fluidity as well as one of rest and connection. For Smith, it's a *CCAAT* thing, and they provide examples of the ways we can build *C*ommunication, *C*onsent, *A*gency, *A*ccountability, and *T*rust, recognizing that consent is the essential precondition for any gathering of people connecting across true vulnerability in the flesh. With a nod to Denise Ferreira da Silva, Smith highlights the etymology of the word consent, *con-sentire*, which literally translates to feeling or sensing together. What would Contact Improvisation look like if we were to bring the BIPOC, queer, krip folks to the center of our worlds? Before ending with a final (wish)list of #CIFuturisms, Smith invites us once again to dance with their text—encouraging us this time to refresh our Contact flow with a bit more Free Style.

One of the myriad questions that Smith asks in their piece is "What happens when we do the form 'wrong' as a radical act of protest against 'rightness' (read: whiteness)?" This is also a driving inquiry in Chapter 5, "Doing It Wrong: Contact's Counter Countercultures," the textual and textured conversation between Emma Bigé and Paul Singh. Instead of beginning in 1972 with the Weber Gallery performances in New York City, their essay's historical overview begins with another time and place—a performance by Fred Holland and Ishmael Houston-Jones. This punky, playful, tough love duet was programmed as part of the "Contact at 10th and 2nd" retrospective at St. Marks Place, New York City, in June 1983. This series of performances celebrated a decade plus of Contact Improvisation and was memorialized in a video compilation distributed through *Contact Quarterly*. By coincidence, I saw Holland and Houston-Jones's duet dance in Philadelphia months later. It was the first time I had ever seen CI performed in a theater, and it immediately appealed to my punk proclivities and the

16   Resistance and Support

pleasures of seeing physical connections at once fierce and erotic. What I didn't know then, but what Bigé and Singh's discussion makes clear, is that this duet was set to a secret score, "Wrong Contact Manifesto," whose first line is: "We are Black." Wearing street clothes and construction boots, these two young Black men slammed into one another, pulled, pushed, and dragged each other's bodies across the floor, and embraced with an odd mixture of effort and urgency. Another line from their manifesto: "We will fuck with flow and intentionally interrupt one another and ourselves."

This opening duet sets up the authors' dialogic back-and-forth, as academic references to classic works by Sara Ahmed, Fred Moten, and mayfield brooks (among others) are mediated by accounts of personal experiences of racism and exclusion. These two artist/thinkers push and pull their way across the historical and contemporary landscapes of CI, unpacking the assumptions of whiteness in the form by questioning what origin stories get told and retold. Their initial conversation took place during the pandemic, and in his comments, Singh marks this moment of suspension as a useful re-set for the form, asking what is different now, 50 years after the initial experiments by "a couple of white guys standing in a room, and running towards each other and jumping, and wondering what was going to happen." Once again, the readers are encouraged to seize the opportunity to "fuck with flow," critique our own complacency, embrace a poetics of refusal in order to see what other dancing choices we can make.

Chapter 6, "Tracing the Natural Body for More Inclusive and Equitable CI Futures," also unpacks the racial, class, and gendered biases of the cultural roots of CI. But instead of starting in the mid-twentieth century, as in "Doing It Wrong," in this essay Robin Raven Prichard takes us all the way back to early modern dance and the beginnings of somatic theory. Critiquing the rhetoric of the natural body in both Isadora Duncan and F. M. Alexander, Prichard highlights how these figures used a particular brand of American aesthetic puritanism to reify the natural body as both physically liberating and morally uplifting. Following in the footsteps of feminist dance scholars such as Ann Daly, Prichard demonstrates the complex way Duncan was able to pull the natural body away from its position as the antithesis of the rational, enlightened body by drawing on popular Hellenism, casting Classical Greece as the foundation of Western culture. Duncan represented her own (white) body as "chaste" and spiritual by drawing on racist tropes that positioned popular African American dances such as the Charleston as overly sensual and sexual. Her movement inspiration came from the solar plexus, not the hips.

Moving from Duncan through Martha Graham and Merce Cunningham to the 1960s and 1970s, Prichard traces how the natural body morphs into a neutral body, all the while maintaining many of the same "silent carriers" of Eurocentric biases. She also notes how somatic practitioners begin to provide scientific terminology that adds to the conceptualization of a neutral body that lends itself to universality but, in fact, is always coded as "white." Prichard analyzes how these discourses covered over the cultural specificity of different bodies by focusing on the neutrality of mass, weight, momentum, and muscle tone, instead of more social-psychological referents implicated in cultural identities. She then turns to the twenty-first century to articulate how these unmarked terms have recently been disrupted by artists such as mayfield brooks in their seminal article "Improvising While Black." Prichard points to events such as *Critical Mass* in positing the potential of improvisation to shake up the physical and metaphysical roots of Contact and move us into a more inclusive practice.

Chapter 7, the final essay in the "Productive Tensions" section, brings questions of history and legacy back to the present moment. Sarah Young's "Underscoring Nancy Stark Smith's Legacy: Definitions and Disruptions" discusses three very different examples of enactments of the Underscore, a finely articulated framework for group improvisation that Smith had been developing and refining for the last two decades of her life. Comparing her experiences with an ongoing Underscore group that meets weekly in Northampton, Massachusetts (and included Smith until she died), and two events at Oberlin College in 2022 (each situated differently within the frame of the 50th anniversary of CI), Young parses a question that Smith herself once posed: "What is the range in which something can still be what it is?"

Of course, the Underscore has always been an evolving practice, both in language and its interpretation—even while Smith was alive. For instance, Smith's original terminology for the moment of bringing the group together at the beginning was "Pow-wow." This immediately prompted pushback for its appropriation of a Native American word, and after much discussion Smith decided to change it to "Gathering." But given Smith's untimely death, the question for Young is how to keep enough of the Underscore intact to be recognizable as Smith's legacy, while at the same time allowing for change. What Young realizes over the course of writing this reflection is that Smith's true legacy may be less about correctly following the details of her score and more about following her example as a teacher and facilitator. As Young writes: "The Underscore is a framework that Nancy Stark Smith held closely while also constantly giving it away." Perhaps this can be a model for more general concerns about legacy in Contact Improvisation—that we can simultaneously hold histories close while giving them a new future.

1

Mindfully Rocking and Rolling

Contact Improvisation as a Feminist Practice in the Turbulent 1970s

Dena Davida

> Along with the rock music of [the late 1960s and early 1970s], dancing both reinforced and crystallized an image of the self: independent yet communal, free, sensual, daring . . . also associated with contemporary social movements and practices such as the civil rights movement, youth culture, and drug-taking, and with values such as rebellion, expressiveness, and individualism within a loving community of peers. Dancing encoded these ideas in a flexible and multi-layered text, its kinesthetic and structural characteristics laden with social implications and associations. (Novack 1990, 38)

Drawn passionately into the vortex of this revolutionary youth movement 50 years ago, along with so many of my North American (and Global North) peers, I recall how we danced together fervently but also purposefully. We were dancing in clubs, gymnasiums, theaters, and galleries, in the streets, parks, our homes, and at outdoor rock concerts. Our way of moving "freely," alone and together, was imbued with a constellation of meanings: heralding a new era of liberties, embarking on social experiments, and not the least, promoting world peace. Going back to nature, we lived in rural enclaves, envisioned a "natural food" movement with health and environmental concerns. We imagined ourselves enacting the lives of countercultural rebels, attempted communal lifestyles in which we experimented with open relationships (now called polyamorous). For second wave feminists of my generation, both our psychedelic social dance events and the postmodern dance movement in the arts, the latter germinated by the choreographers associated with the Judson Dance Group (see Banes 1980b), offered opportunities to affirm both women's strengths and sensuality. We danced to advance our "self-realization" and express self-affirmation, intending to create a more meaningful, sustainable, and humane future for our democratic society and planetary survival. Pushing up against the strictures of previous social conventions and stereotypes, we determined to shape our dancing bodies into emblems of equality and empowerment. These were some of the values and ideologies that formed the fertile terrain for the conception of Contact Improvisation (CI), quite soon to be "invented" by Steve Paxton.

Laying the Ground

To position myself with transparency, at the dawn of those 1970s I was a 21-year-old white, heterosexual, middle-class woman raised by a single mother on the Western and Eastern

Dena Davida, *Mindfully Rocking and Rolling* In: *Resistance and Support.* Edited by: Ann Cooper Albright, Oxford University Press.
© Oxford University Press 2024. DOI: 10.1093/9780197776308.003.0002

20 Resistance and Support

coasts of the United States. The progeny of Hollywood and Broadway actors, writers, film directors and producers of Lithuanian and Georgian Jewish lineage, my art world family most certainly inspired and encouraged my choice of an artistic vocation. The year was 1970 when, as a fresh dance and theater Bachelor of the Arts from the University of California at Irvine, I was ready to enter the wider world of professional arts. With cat in carrying case and $200 in my backpack, a burgeoning dancer and actress replete with optimism, I hitched a ride up the California Pacific Coast Highway, drawn to the vibrancy of the youth movement in San Francisco. So began my young adult life in the revolutionary 1970s. I joined an artists' commune, performed Shakespeare in the Streets, and studied modern dance, at the beginning of the aftermath of the Summer of Love. These West Coast adventures would indelibly mark my lifelong worldview and propel future artworld journeys as I moved away from the rigors of modern dance training toward the freedoms of Contact Improvising.

Like my mother and under her influence, I have self-identified as a feminist for as long as I can remember. Born over a century ago in 1920 in Massachusetts, she was a free-spirited bohemian and post–World War II feminist. It cannot be overstated that despite all good intentions and a few exceptions, this phase (as was the first!) of the women's liberation movement was largely predominated by white, middle and upper class women, and those who were of color were largely marginalized. It was given momentum by the determined entrance of newly empowered women moving into the workforce after the war, entering university studies, and becoming prominent in political life.

This essay is penned in the outlook and context of that earlier era of the late 1970s and the early 1980s, recounting how and why Contact Improvisation became a crucial force in shaping my life's trajectory and that of others as a feminist dancer, and ultimately my way of being in the world. At the same time, it is essential at the onset of this chapter to acknowledge insights that have been evoked by so many through the lens of the current sociopolitical landscape in 2024 who are pressing for profound changes in the ethical foundations of CI. Among them are Keith Hennessey, who has done so resoundingly through his challenging zine *Questioning Contact Improvisation* (2018), and Royona Mitra in her new essay "Unmaking Contact: Choreographic Touch at the Intersection of Race, Caste, and Gender" (2021). Unmistakably, in its early history, Contact Improvisation provided groundbreaking opportunities for women in dance to take the unconventional role of supporting, carrying, and "leading" men, uprooting and rethinking Western gender conventions, and reopening the limits and perceptions we had previously held concerning our body's strength and robustness. I am thinking here of the conventions of "partner work" in most artistic dance forms, and how cultural dance forms had long practiced gender-specific ways of moving in relationship to male and female morphologies and societal conventions.

Contact Improvisation, throughout its 50-year history, has offered a vital space for corporeal expressivity, body-to-body physical connections, and movement exploration for those who are, as we now say, "differently abled," including neuroatypical, physically challenged, and aging bodies of all shapes and sizes. But it has also led some CI participants to feelings of exclusion for various reasons, and certain cultural communities have not been drawn to its way of moving together by sharing weight through a point of contact. It is also true that its practice can and sometimes does violate boundaries of what is perceived as respectful, welcome touching and intimacy. Concerning uncomfortable physical contact in CI jams and classes, in her analysis of ethnographic fieldwork with Contact Improvisors in Montréal and a study in which I was an "informant," researcher and CI practitioner Claire

Vionnet reminds us with frankness how indeed "[t]he physical closeness creates a vagueness around boundaries . . . creates a blurriness between a dance touch and an erotic caress" (2021, 332). To be able to dance in this way with psychosomatic comfort and pleasure, it is necessary to set personal touch boundaries and to heighten awareness of when and how we extend unwelcome touching to others and fail to define our own. In a recent workshop at *CI @ 50* in Oberlin College, guided by Keith Hennessey, we practiced "touching consent" in duets, in echo to the #MeToo movement, methodically asking verbally if our partner would accept (or not) the placing of certain of our body parts on specific areas of their bodies. It was indeed revealing, as I discovered that I have few—but *do* have some—limits to what kind of touching I find comfortable. There have in fact been many kinds of challenges to the safe and pleasurable practice of CI. Certain aspects of these current-day contemporary politics will be expanded toward the end of this chapter and are also deeply examined in other chapters of this anthology.

Returning again to the 1970s, for myself and so many friends and colleagues, artistic and social dancing had become so much more than simply an irrepressible urge to express exuberant physicality, a modern mating ritual, or even the subject of study for a university degree program leading to professional career options. In the folds of the rebellious postmodern dance movement that was flourishing in the context of North America and beyond, in the midst of these new collective ways of dancing-making and improvising, forming dance groups and dancing together were emblematic of what Banes aptly characterized as "democracy's body" in the title of her published dissertation on the day-to-day workings of the Judson Dance Theater (1980b). Her thesis bears witness to the burgeoning ethos of collective processes and sociopolitical investigation through movement exploration. In the eyes of Banes, Judson dancers' work became a vehicle for progressive social change.[1] To my mind at the time, CI was a subspecies of postmodern dancing that provided a vibrant model for forging a feminist dance practice within the collective fold of a caring and playful community of like-minded dancers. We determined to create what we thought might be a model "community of experience," as Novack (1990) characterized it.

Full-time devotion to the vocation of dancer soon became my profession. For the next half century I navigated various sectors of the North American artistic dance world, assuming the roles of dance interpreter, improvisor, occasional choreographer. I later became a community and university educator, academic researcher, writer, anthropologist and curator, and finally editor of anthologies of artistic dance ethnography (Davida 2012) and live arts curation (Davida 2019).[2] But it was in the early days of my engagement with Contact Improvisers that grounds were laid for my orientation as an "artivist" (artist + activist), caught up in the tides of shifting geopolitics.

In the guise of a feminist auto-ethnographer crafting an analytical narrative through self-reflection and in cultural context, I'll take you in this chapter through my shift from modern to postmodern dancer while living in San Francisco, initiation into the newly forged Minnesota CI community, teaching a community CI class in Québec, to finally becoming a university teacher of CI in my adopted home of Montréal. Next, I'll open a window into the herstory of our all-women's dance collective Catpoto and, finally, revisit *Each Man for Herself*, my first efforts at crafting a "Contact-infused feminist choreography."

---

[1] It is worth recalling that in 2024, at the moment this book is being published, we are experiencing (once again) a critical moment for global societies in which the concept of democracy is being heatedly debated and facing threats to its viability and future existence in the midst of rising theocracies and populist movements.

[2] My latest project is the conception and management of *TURBA*, a journal for live arts curators with a global reach and decolonial aspirations (Davida 2022).

22 Resistance and Support

Perhaps it is serendipity to be called on to reflect on the meaning of one's youthful exploits as a septuagenarian, while memory still serves, and the accumulation of life experiences offers temporal distance and a matured perspective. And now, surrounded by artifacts and archives of my life in the CI community—photos, handwritten notes, posters, and digital folders—the story is ready to begin.

Discovering Artivism

Wandering the streets and parks of the Haight-Ashbury district of San Francisco in the early 1970s, I became a proponent of an American "alternative culture." A self-identified "child of the New Age," I was indeed a "seeker" who wore flowers in her hair. But it wasn't until I experienced a new kind of sensual, free-flowing, and high-touch dance class in Minnesota called Contact Improvisation that I understood how a dance form might embody the ethos of my marching-in-the-streets activism. Body-to-body, we shared a point of contact and base of support, moving mindfully together in duets (and trios) in mutual support. Our bodies were relaxed, attentive to inner sensation and allowing the interplay of physical forces to guide us. We felt/thought that dancing this way might promote the kind of progressive, egalitarian and communal ways of interacting that augured a more peaceful and cooperative future for humanity.

But before entering the Contact community in 1976, my daily practice in San Francisco as an aspiring Nikolais modern dancer and Physical Theater actress (think Grotowski and Iowa Theater Lab) remained secluded from my social life as an activist in the women's and peace movements and as a community volunteer in food cooperatives. My work as an actress and dancer had thus far been dictated by authoritarian, if charismatic, choreographers and theater directors. With their absolute power directing my every move and breath, so-called creative work had not proved a democratic process. In another vein, walking into the calm of a dance studio when training alone, turning my attention to breathing, stretching, and strengthening in predetermined movement sequences, provided refuge from the adrenalized political marches. But ironically, it was when demonstrating, shouting, singing, and gesturing publicly in the streets of the city that my body/mind felt empowered to impact social change, resonating with kinesthetic empathy when enveloped in a pulsating sea of other protesting bodies.

It was through dance training sessions that my body became gradually injured. A decade of regimented modern dance classes and ballet barres had left my knees, hips, and spine aching, as I fruitlessly strived for the impossible, "ideal" dancer's body. In the Western dance world of that era, injury was common and debilitating, often leading to leaving the profession. The damage to joints and tissues intensified over years from this kind of rigorous physical skill-building. I wondered: would I ever be able to bear the demands of dancing in a professional company? And then one day in 1969, when attempting to absorb the impact of catching a large man jumping up into my arms in a university theater production, the sudden compression of the vertebra of my lower lumbar spine provided an existential challenge to my intended career. A forced arabesque was no longer in question, so how could I continue dancing? It wasn't until several years later, moving from San Francisco to Minnesota, in the midst of Mary Cerny's CI class, that this transition toward a postmodern dance ethos would change the course of my professional dance life. It was then, with a literal sigh of relief, that

I left behind the struggle to "open my hip joints" in the futile effort to acquire the iconic 180• split stretch. The promise of ease afforded by this way of improvisation, along with the American postmodern dance embrace of the "everyday" and "released" body, provided new grounds on which to begin dancing again.

The late American dance teacher and choreographer Mary Fulkerson penned a revelatory herstoric essay in 1996 within the pages of the CI community's seminal magazine the *Contact Quarterly*, articulating her personal understanding of postmodern dance's sociopolitical philosophy and how it had democratized the dance profession at the end of the twentieth century. Like Novack and Banes, Fulkerson deftly seized, although from another angle, the *zeitgeist* of the dance-as-politics moment as I experienced it, when she wrote:

> The post-modernist search for the real person in dance, the whole person, the holistic act of performing, and the non-manipulative approach to the audience, paralleled closely developments in the art world at that time . . . By the end of the '60s, the experimental forefront of the dance had become democratic, personal, human scale, individual, idiosyncratic, and less presentational. (Fulkerson 1996, 40)

And so, casting aside my hard-earned modern dance technique, I stepped into this egalitarian and democratized dance practice, one which favored collective work and creation, and which provided the intellectual and kinesthetic laboratory for Steve Paxton's (and others') original research from which CI emerged in 1972. Fulkerson further elucidated the impact of this new mode of dance-making, as articulated by Judson instigator Yvonne Rainer in her Minimalist "No Manifesto" (1974, 62–63):

> Her essential message was "No" to all forms of social dominance or intimidation within performance and practice of dance . . . dancers of the group Grand Union inherited her social charter and with it a desire to resolve the problem of how to create dance work which put its ideas into practice. (Fulkerson 1996, 40)

Reading about the legacy of Rainer's *Trio A* and "No Manifesto," and workshopping with members of Judson's progeny Grand Union (of which Paxton was a cofounder in 1970), crystallized the imperative of her minimalist proclamation that all movements might be seen as dance, from balletic arabesques to ordinary head-scratching (Rainer 1974, 62–63). We had moved beyond the technical vocabularies of a handful of modern dance styles; everything now seemed possible.

First Contact in Minnesota

Picking up the first archival album sparks the recollection of my first CI class in 1973 (see Figure 1.1). Here are two women, dance educator Wendy Oliver and me (on the left), smiling playfully while immersed in an almost symmetrical counterpull during Mary Cerny's first CI course at Nancy Hauser's modern dance studio in Minnesota. Our two tense modern dance–trained bodies were fully outstretched, precariously seeking a stable balancing point in our counter-pull. We had not yet grasped the novel idea that it was a "released," destabilized body that would best mobilize our Contact duet. Cerny, one of the early protagonists

Figure 1.1 Wendy Oliver (at left) and the author (at right) attempting a first exercise in counter-pulling in Mary Cerny's initial CI class in Minneapolis, Minnesota, in 1973 at Nancy Hauser's Modern Dance Studio. Printed with permission from Dena Davida. Photographer unknown.

of Contact Improvisation, was teaching the dance form in Minnesota. In the course of her class, we explored the principles of what were becoming some of the agreed-upon components of its pedagogy. This was still an exploratory phase of forming a teaching technique. Contacters had early on adopted Paxton's idea of a relaxed stance, called "the small dance," one that allowed the interplay of physical forces to guide the movements of our destabilized bodies. By learning how to (safely) literally cede control of our bodies, these Contact classes turned the dance studio into a laboratory-playground.

I soon grasped that sharing weight through a rolling point (or surface) of contact would require an openness to a kind of intimate, sustained full-body touching rarely shared among strangers. These were also the early days of our feminist "sexual revolution," one which included women's investigation of their sexuality, and CI provided a new landscape for the exploration of sensorial touch—not only as an exercise in pleasure, but also as a form of communication and movement research. As a woman who had experienced sexual aggression a decade earlier, it was in Cerny's class that I rediscovered a place for sensuality and intimacy that felt (almost but not always) nurturing and non-threatening. Continuing throughout life to seek a gentle and caring kind of human intimacy, I preferred (and still do) the lighter touch of skin-to-skin, rather than bone-to-bone, weight, and pressure sharing in my Contact dances. I was rapidly smitten by the joy, freedom, and sheer pleasure that emerged from CI inter/play. The space separating social dancing and artistic dance practice dissolved.

Introducing *Improvisation en Contact* in Québec

I entered Canada as a landed immigrant in 1977. Choosing to leave the place of my birth, in part because of the unbearable violence that the United States was inflicting on the people of Vietnam, came with a sense of relief that I would be entering the relative (if imperfect) calm of a peacekeeping country. Forty-seven years later, I remain grateful to be living in a stable democracy with a strong social safety net. The island of Montréal became my home for its beauty, cosmopolitanism, safety, and the sheer vibrancy of its mix of North American, Québécois, and European societies and multitude of world cultures.[3] The effervescent local artistic dance milieu, but for a few exceptions, seemed to embrace my desire to introduce new ideas to their world.

On my arrival, the Québec Ministry of Culture had just launched public consultations in view of distributing new funds to initiate their support to foster professional dance and pedagogy (see Davida and Lavoie Marcus 2012). There were a handful of dance studios in the city and throughout smaller towns in the province, a rich but a little-known dance historiography yet to be written, and a few dance companies founded by modernist choreographers. Yet to materialize were the multiple festivals and presenting organizations, university programs and professional dance academy, the scores of choreographers and hundreds of performers that now form our dance ecosystem. In 1980, inside a small second-floor walk-up loft downtown, I cofounded Tangente with three colleagues—Howard Abrams, Louis Guillemette, and

---

[3] I arrived in *La Belle Province* of Québec in a turbulent societal moment that was the outcome of The Quiet Revolution (*La revolution tranquille*) of the 1960s, in which the Québécois were striving to define and consolidate their endangered cultural identity as French-speaking North Americans, supporting a movement for the succession of Québec from Canada, experiencing themselves as "an island of French in a sea of English," as they would say. Language was at the heart of these identity politics, and the First Nations peoples of Québec were not yet in the forefront (as they have become today) of these political battles. In these circumstances, Québécois artists were cherished and relatively well funded, seen as the shapers of a distinct Québécois habitus.

26   Resistance and Support

Silvy Panet-Raymond—a seminal dance-presenting venue for which I remained artistic director and curator until 2019.[4]

A few days after arriving in Montréal, I came across a poster announcing Montréal's first Contact Improvisation workshop with Andrew Harwood, a second-generation CI dancer originally from Montréal, who was then living in Vancouver, where he was teaching and performing CI mostly on Canada's West Coast. As the workshop ended, he encouraged me to teach, and his sister Carol Harwood, along with other workshop participants, joined my first community classes in the downtown feminist gallery Powerhouse. Judson Dance Theater aficionado Vicky Tansy had just moved south near the U.S. border in Abercorn to build her country dance retreat. It was her inner-city students who populated my first CI class, certainly drawn by the promise of "improvisation," the basis of Tansy's own teachings: an idiosyncratic mix of dance and theater techniques. As so many others who had become captivated by Contact Improvisation, I also began a multi-year pilgrimage to numerous intensive Contact workshops and gatherings across North America.

In those formative years, the Euro-American Contact community was immersed in formulating a framework for teaching the emerging practice. The *Contact Quarterly* served as a vital forum for discussions among teachers and other practitioners. As I traveled throughout various workshops and other kinds of CI gatherings, it seemed that a consensus was gradually arising over certain basic ideas, activities, exercises, and principles, although with various viewpoints on precisely how they needed to be implemented, that might form the components of a "Contact pedagogy." From my handwritten notes: "I spent August [1977] at the Vermont Contact Conference [where] I first became aware of the differing styles, philosophies, and approaches people were developing in their Contact work" (Davida 1977). As witnessed during the *CI @ 50* celebration at Oberlin College in Ohio, a core question remains debated to this day: What might be identified as Contact Improvisation per se in the face of the variations and permutations of the form that have been proposed, leading it away from Paxton's original intention of creating a "purely" physical dance research practice? I am thinking here, for example, of early proposals to invite live musicians to play in the previously silent jams and Contact collective Mangrove's inclusion of vocal theatricalized dancing.

As I began facilitating those first CI classes in Montréal in the late 1970s, I recall introducing students to what was then an agreed-upon group of skills and principles. Drawing from my first class plans, these included, among others: nurturing a responsive and relaxed body through inner-focused attention to one's weight and the pull of gravity; awareness of the subtleties of the relaxed standing "small dance" with its orientation to off-balance and the play of physical forces; learning to fall safely by fine-tuning one's attention to descending and landing and impact-absorbing rolling and "sloughing" off one another's bodies; counter-pulling and pushing with various body parts, but not favoring grasping with the hands; practicing spiral rolling patterns alone and together across the floor; opening one's peripheral vision through a "soft focus" of the eyes; practicing an inner-focused somatic attention to one's skin, bones and joints, muscles, fascia, and weight. It was in particular the "carrying and riding" exercises for supporting a partner's weight by offering "ledges" on one's hips, thighs, arms, backs, and shoulders, for both men and women alike, that aroused my feminist sensibilities. Contact's egalitarian guidelines allowed for possibilities of all kinds of movements, each according to their abilities and with no restrictions based on gender, body type, ability, or age.

---

[4] I eventually presented duet performances at Tangente by Steve Paxton and Lisa Nelson, and later Lisa Nelson and Nancy Stark Smith.

The Catpoto Dance Collective (1977–1980)

Following a common sequence of events in the wider CI milieu, my initial community classes in 1977 soon gave birth to a "working group" of 10 students interested in devoting more time and effort to developing their Contact practice, and so to meeting two or three times a week. By fall of that first year, three of the working group members, all white women, were meeting with me regularly and also, like myself, traveling to attend workshops. We soon formed a dance collective which, in January 1978, we named Catpoto (meaning "old buddies" in vernacular Québécois). We were: Carol Harwood (a dancer), Gurney Bolster (a new recruit), Evelyn Ginzburg (already a Contact aficionado), and myself. We were later joined for a time by Sylvie Saint-Laurent (a gymnast) and Lisette Poisson. All of us were young, white, well-educated women and like-minded peers; you might call us a sorority of common experience.[5] We all felt the calling to proliferate this groundbreaking dance practice, one we thought might encourage new potentials for our local dance community by embracing female dancers' strength, proposing novel choreographic possibilities, and presenting a feminist challenge to traditional male-female duets.

Our dance collective progressed rapidly, and we soon were teaching three classes a week to 40 students of mixed skill levels. We spent several months forging and negotiating the distinct character of our CI collective, working assiduously to integrate and resolve our differing aesthetic outlooks. Our work sessions included an extended dance marathon, skill sharing, and an invitation to outside dance colleagues to observe our work and offer commentary. Into our Contact practice we introduced elements from our various backgrounds in Laban Movement Analysis and theatrical techniques. We also integrated components that were less common in CI, such as "shape awareness, the opening of space between dancers, solo development, working with contrasts and blending, exploring the emotional textures inherent in our dancing" (Davida 1978). Carol Harwood and I reminisced recently, agreeing that our dancing was marked by a frisky playfulness and a gentle sensibility. We were caring and supportive, but did challenge each other's physical capabilities. That we were all women allowed us to explore the full extent of our capacities as supporters, lifters, and carriers, and ultimately became a distinguishing characteristic of our group identity.

We were burgeoning with the excitement of entering the local experimental arts scene, keen to spread our fervor throughout different cultural and educational communities,[6] accepting invitations to perform in museums and at dance events. We began almost immediately by presenting our dancing in the public spheres of parks and cafés. In the cultural context of Montréal in 1977, what we were doing appeared rather strange because it was unfamiliar to most onlookers. I took note of this expression of surprise from a nearby customer at our first café demonstration, as we navigated the spaces in between tables and chairs. He exclaimed out loud, "*On se touche beaucoup, eh?!*" which roughly translates as "You sure are touching a lot!" It wasn't long before we were invited to join the programming of local cultural institutions, and to perform and teach in elementary schools, community colleges, and universities.

---

[5] Many thanks to reader Neil Schotsky for this insightful observation.

[6] A new dance program was just being formed in 1979 at the Université de Québec de Montréal, and department founder Françoise Riopelle offered me a *charge de cours* (a course in dance improvisation) in which to offer Contact Improvisation to theater students, and soon after to dance and non-dance students within the new undergraduate program for dance majors. This position as a "part-time lecturer" at the university was to span 23 years.

28 Resistance and Support

We rented and renovated a studio for ourselves in a spacious room with a sprung wood floor at the back of Café Les Entretiens on Rue Laurier. It housed our practice sessions, open community CI jams, public workshops, and eventually informal public performances. Our dance space in Montréal became a destination for nomadic Contact teachers and performers traveling in North America. Throughout our existence, as was the case for other Contact groups and individuals, we became local impresarios for workshops and performances by Contact Improvisors on tour.[7] This collegial "Contact touring network" offered Catpoto a reciprocal North American tour in 1978.[8]

About the dynamics of this cooperative interconnectedness across an increasingly international CI community, Banes wryly observed, "Like the food co-op movement that flourished in the same decade, and motivated by the same populist spirit, Contact Improvisation sets up a network for distribution (of dance rather than vegetables) outside the big business of the dance world" (1980a, 68). As a community of dancers and audiences, we came from various social classes, age groups, and educational backgrounds and vocations, and it was common to have families with young children witnessing the dance presentations. Sometimes these informal performances were called "You come, we'll show you what we do," a title that caught the spirit of continuity between movers and watchers. This desire to circumvent the capitalistic so-called cultural industries by creating nonprofit organizations was the precursor to my cofounding the Tangente dance-presenting space in Montréal with an artists' collective in 1980.

We were invited to perform in a series of performances in 1978 at the Musée des beaux-arts de Montréal, the museum's visual arts curators having classified us as a newly forged genre of performance artist. Curators at the Musée du Québec in Québec City then invited us into their galleries to improvise within an exhibit of tactile art. This proved a judicious match of aesthetic forms, as we leaned into and climbed through the artworks on display. We were also presented at artist-run visual arts centers Articule in Montréal and La Chambre Blanche in Québec City, adapting ourselves to any and all art spaces with a sprung wood floor. And so it was that we entered the institutional, nonprofit visual arts world, swirling and rolling through galleries as visitors walked gingerly around and among us. This was a formative period for the live arts, beginning with performance artists, to enter into museum and gallery spaces.

As for the fledgling professional Québécois dance community, they soon viewed us as an experimental dance company, and we were frequently invited to join the program for their dance evenings and multimedia events. As for Montréal dance critics and writers, they announced our new company in local newspaper and magazine articles (in this pre–social media era) enthusiastically through interviews, attempting to describe and explain Contact Improvisation to their neophyte readers. It is interesting to note that while variously describing our dancing as lying somewhere between sport, dance, and (in one headline) "group cuddle," these journalists perceived Catpoto's Contact Improvisations as being playful rather than political artistry.

---

[7] Our Contact dance-presenting activities at the Laurier Street studio began in 1977 with Jerry Zientara and Melanie Hedlund, then Byron Brown and Steve Paxton. We later hosted Mangrove, Fulcrum, Andrew Harwood with Helen Clark, and in a third cycle Michael Linehan, Kris Wheeler, Nancy Stark Smith, Lisa Nelson, Mary Cerny, Jim Tyler, and John Gamble.

[8] Catpoto's 1978 tour included workshops and presentations in Toronto (at the Women's Gallery, hosted by Carol Shaeffer), Ann Arbor (at Mirage), Chicago (at Link's Hall, hosted by Bob Eisen), Cleveland (hosted by Bob Martin), Minneapolis (Wendy Oliver), Portland (Bert Weiss), and Peterborough (at Public Energy, hosted by Bill Kimball).

An inflection point in our feminist trajectory came in the spring of 1978 when we became a foil for the high-spirited and athletic all-male Contact collective Mangrove, composed in this iteration of Byron Brown, John LeFan, Curt Siddall, and James Tyler. We organized their residency in Montréal as they traveled on tour from their home base in California, an event which included a shared evening among our two collectives in our Montréal studio. For that occasion, we deliberately set into motion ideas about the performance of gender. We structured the evening in view of each group presenting a separate set of scored improvisations, then ended the program by dancing together in an open set. At the audience talk afterward, we posed penetrating political questions. Do biological gender identities imply aesthetic destinies? What were the possibilities and limits of women's strength and capacity to lift, carry, and catch each other? What are men's capacities to be "riders" with female partners? Did characteristics arise in the dancing that might be seen as gender-specific?

Over time, certain Montréal choreographers became curious about CI, drawn to the unusual movement aesthetics of relaxed, falling bodies, and while watching dancers moving with so-called non-skilled (really non-dance-trained) bodies in performance. They were particularly intrigued, they told us, by the novel choreographic possibilities afforded by this dance form. As with all movement systems, schools, techniques and practices, Contact Improvisation—despite its status as open-ended movement research—to my mind, at the time, had given rise to a distinctive, recognizable aesthetics of released bodies in off-balance and free-flowing motion. During the last phase of our dance collective in 1979, Catpoto's burgeoning interest in "contact-infused choreography" led us to invite Canadian choreographers Marie Chouinard and Paula Ravitz to build structured improvisations for the collective. They shaped our dancing into poetic, metaphoric "compositions." As each of us finally turned our attention to other pursuits and our company disbanded, these initial choreographic explorations became the touchstone for my next dance world chapter: a decade of feminist performance works.

The Woman Question: *Each Man for Herself* (1983–1985) with Daniel Godbout

> Royona Mitra: Do you think touch within choreography can be used as a political tool? . . .
> Steve Paxton: I do think that at the very beginning of contact in its earliest years, what was considered extraordinary about it was that women supported men. And in all dance prior to that, that I had experienced—ballet, modern dance, folk, etc.—there was always this relationship of men supporting women, and women being in need to be supported by men. So yes . . . (Mitra 2018, 14)

Those early days of Contact Improvisation had always been for me, as a feminist, both a sociopolitical *and* a physics experiment. As Paxton later confirmed in this interview with Mitra, women's abilities as lifters and carriers that had been developed through CI practices were an extraordinary phenomenon in the professional Euro-American dance world at that time (see Figure 1.2). Our temporary gatherings at jams provided grounds for reimagining, among other things, women's roles in postmodern dance. It was finally within the CI community, in which no limits were set by gender-assigned vocabularies and dynamics, that I was able to

30 Resistance and Support

Figure 1.2 A portrait of Mark Lewis Tompkins and Dena Davida in an informal CI duet in a public square in Aix-en-Provence. This presentation was presented during the tour of *Each Man for Herself* in 1985, organized by Tompkins with French CI group Atelier Contact. Printed with permission from Dena Davida. Photographer: Christiane Robin.

explore my full physical capacities and the possibilities of "dancing equality" with male partners. My goal was not necessarily to cultivate displays of female bravado and muscularity, although I later choreographed a study of female bodybuilders, *Pièce de résistance*, but rather to acquire the skills for an efficient use of weight, momentum, counterbalance, tensile strength, leverage, and other physical forces that would expand my capacities.

Through the late 1970s and early 1980s, as I devoted increasing time to Contact dancing, I became progressively more proficient at lifting, carrying, counterbalancing, and otherwise supporting the weight of male-presenting Contact partners as they rolled and balanced on top of me, pulled and propelled themselves upward onto my body. Despite my early back injury, largely healed in later life, my skeletal structure was proving robust, for I had always danced with somatic awareness and careful attention to my weaknesses, avoiding pain and seeking efficiency.

One day in 1981, I "fell into sync" with a most sympatico Contact partner: Daniel Godbout. From our initial touch, it was clear that we shared an affinity for fluidity, lightness, spiraling, and ease of motion. We were soon jamming together regularly and facilitating workshops in a countryside retreat. As innate a "rider" as I had determined to be a "carrier," Daniel relished being airborne, and so a collaborative performance work that featured a woman who loves to lift and carry men sprang to life between us. In her accolade to the empowering expression of female athleticism, Contacter and choreographer Jo Kreiter would affirm a decade later, in the pages of the *Contact Quarterly*, what I had discovered through this compositional process with Godbout:

> As a pivotal movement form within postmodern dance, contact improvisation has given me to the tools to test [the] assumption [that] dance-making which embraces women's physical strength also embraces the possibility of transcending the legacy of social forces that have asked women to be second to men . . . [It] is founded on principles of egalitarian participation. (Kreiter 1996, 41)

We imagined this composition as an ode to gender role-reversal, and a feminist platform from which to challenge traditional male-female partnering in our professional dance world. Together, we forged a choreographic "vocabulary" of Contact duets, demonstrating the capacity of a female performer to maneuver the weight of her male counterpart.

With the idea of inviting 10 male guest performers to join us onstage in each city, I then chose the mischievous title *Each Man for Herself: A pas de douze for one woman and eleven men*. Godbout and I took these performances on tour in small-scale artist-run spaces across Canada, situating our presentation in the interstice between dance and performance art, as had Catpoto. The dance composition alternated three scenarios of scored material: our live duet dancing, images captured on slides of a public performance in a shopping center, and a series of simple support-and-carry improvisations with each of the 10 local male participants.

As the audience entered the gallery at each performance, they came upon a semi-circle of chairs upstage occupied by 10 anxious, seated, "non-dancing" men. They were of varying sizes and ages. These willing volunteers were recruited locally by each art space's curators, and in one of the venues they were drawn entirely from the gallery's board of directors. Their lack of performance experience and dance training was of the essence, bringing poignancy to their uneasy presence and tentative actions as they waited at/tentatively for their turn to be called into action. I offered them simple instructions only minutes before the performances, while insisting on no rehearsal beforehand: requesting that they wait until, at various improvised junctures, I would direct my attention to each of them in turn by literally reaching my arms out to them invitingly. They were then to rise and walk toward me at center stage, and search for some way to climb up onto my standing body so that they might be supported, held, and carried by me back to their seats. I remember what ensued as a novel form of the male gaze, as each one studied my body for possibilities of supporting the weight of their arms, legs, pelvis, and spine. By bending and extending my thighs, lower back, hips, forearms, and shoulders, I offered shelf-like surfaces for them to cling and hook onto, as they transferred their weight gingerly onto my firmly planted physical frame. Once they were fully off the ground, I carried them gently back to their chairs. Their vulnerability is imprinted in my memory.

In other sections of *Each Man for Herself* we projected a series of slides (the sophisticated technology of the 1980s) onto a large upstage screen. We had ourselves photographed while performing gender-reversed Contact lifts in the massive central atrium of the Complexe Desjardins office building, just as it was filling up with a found audience of workers and shoppers during the noon lunch break in downtown Montréal. Dressed in conservative and business clothing, Daniel was outfitted in a dapper suit and tie, while I wore a tailored, business-like skirt and jacket with low-heeled shoes (posing a playful challenge to stability and balance). We imagined ourselves in unconventional roles: as a couple of business associates working on a new kind of CI fitness routine. Standing my ground with a concentrated and determined demeanor, I thought it must have been clear to onlookers that I was a woman in charge of maneuvering my male colleague, and that I was inclined to breaking metaphoric glass ceilings.

Interspersed throughout the performance composition, the third sequence offered a series of live Contact duets which featured my role as carrier/lifter and Daniel as the lifted and carried partner. His lithe and fluid athletic body (he's a swimmer and lifeguard by trade) was prone to supple spiral pathways and ever-so-sensuous in its relishing of flight and lightness, as he rolled up my body and spiraled around my shoulders. After a couple of years of CI jamming and teaching together, we were able to navigate improvised duets with skillful ease, along with a deep, subtle knowledge of each other's somas and movement tendencies. Although we never became life partners or lovers, our dancing always emanated camaraderie, pleasure, and joy.

All three scenarios were alternated in short segments in the space of an hour-long performance, with both audience and volunteer performers seated in a semi-circular formation in the intimate art galleries. This multilayered and meditative study of female strength, support, and caring also put on display male tenderness and sensuality.

Rocking and Rolling, Ever More Mindfully: Contact Improvising in the Contentious 2020s

Moving through a two-year writing process in conceiving this Contact memoir, I have become keenly aware of how complex a task it is to balance past and present perspectives. The challenge has been to learn how to write with attention to both in mind, without diminishing the impact of this story of feminist empowerment from the past century and in light of its necessary reckoning with the sociopolitical climate of the new millennium.

Encountering the global Contact community once again in 2022 after a long hiatus, during the *CI @ 50* celebration at Oberlin College, proved revelatory if challenging. Thorny discussions and debates on politics and ethics seemed to surface from the outset and at every turn and roll on the dance floor. It was also true that the sheer volume of participants gathered from throughout the world and the vibrancy of this gathering bore witness to CI's persistence and renewal. A few months later in October, during the Dance Studies Association (DSA) annual conference "Dancing Resilience: Dance Studies and Activism in a Global Age" in Vancouver, I encountered Mitra's challenging essay on "unmaking" Contact Improvisation. In it she suggests how problematic the intimate touching in Contact Improvisation might be when considered from the vantage point of her Indian culture in which a social caste persists which is called "the untouchables." She recounts how her society literally doesn't permit public touching between men and women, and in which dance traditions have long favored solo dancing. Echoed by others who attended *CI @ 50* and the DSA conference, she contended in her paper that:

> although its healing, generative, and connective properties have been celebrated in dance studies, there is still an unmet need to identify and examine choreographic touch, especially as it shapes CI, as a discriminatory practice, through the intersectional lenses of race, caste, and gender politics. This is a necessary corrective to the body of work on CI and contact-driven choreography, in order to challenge 1960s/1970s Global North dance attitudes that have equated its touching bodies with counterculture liberation. (Mitra 2021, 9)

To her point, and along with knowledge gained during my doctoral studies in dance anthropology, a dance form based on physical touch and moving about "freely" (improvising) cannot easily be transplanted indiscriminately from one cultural context to another without attention to local mores, economies, and dance traditions. As my late muse, dance anthropologist Joann Kealiinomoku, declared so categorically, all dances are ethnic (1969/1970). My understanding of how CI is becoming adapted and transformed in countries such as India, Mexico, and China was clearly enriched during the panel presentation and audience discussion "Global and Local: Facilitating Contact in Different Communities," one which I was tasked with hosting during *CI @ 50* in Oberlin. This brings me to reflect once again on the CI community that we had fostered in Montréal in the 1970s and 1980s. In that particular cultural context, whiteness was in fact predominant among participants in classes and jams, despite Canada's proud cultivation of a multiculturalism that we call here the "cultural mosaic" (a term not universally appreciated by BIPOC Canadians). I can now only wonder: might I have been more aware of this, done more to make my Contact classes and our Montréal jams into more welcome places for all? There are no easy answers.

In view of the recent #MeToo movement and my lifelong engagement with feminism, when beginning to teach Contact Improvisation in 1977, I was conscious that nonconsensual, discomforting touch might threaten to surface. And so, in conversations with my students, I never insisted that CI was a desirable dance activity for everyone because of its basis in sustained, intimate physical touch. It was also important for me to remind them how they might respectfully pull away from an unwanted dance, and true to my word, I always assumed control of my personal boundaries with resolve as I danced in workshops and jams. As dance researcher Vionnet further clarifies in her study, it is a matter of "how intimate boundaries are redefined under circumstances of close proximity and how subjective the feeling of intimacy might be" (2021, 324). In my case, it was when Contact improvising that I had finally rediscovered a place for sensual and intimate touch, but have been quick to walk away from duets that caused me discomfort and dis-ease.

34 Resistance and Support

Coda: Moving Forward, Keep on Dancing

> How do we historicize, imagine, and mobilize CI into the present and future? (Cloud and Shafffman 2022)

It is now 60 years after the Judson Dance Theater convened in Judson Memorial Church, New York City, to shift the direction of Euro-American artistic dance. And it is now more than half a century since the genesis of Contact Improvisation in 1972 with Steve Paxton's informal workshop presentation of *Magnesium* in the Oberlin College gymnasium in Ohio and the first public performances at the John Weber Gallery in New York.

Tracing my own story within the communities of these postmodern dance worlds has sparked the memory of how this revolutionary dance movement had profoundly changed my life's trajectory as a woman, vocational dancer, and global citizen. If not the quintessence of freedom for everybody—as it was for me—Contact Improvisation certainly affirmed a new kind of democratic, egalitarian, and collective form of dancing and dance gathering that stood in stark contrast to modern dance's dominance of the art dance world by a handful of charismatic and autocratic choreographers.

For the Montréal dance community, the movement possibilities arising within Contact Improvisation classes, jams, and public presentations have become integrated over time into the local choreographic lexicon. For many (if not all), this infiltration of CI into the professional dance world at large has all but eliminated the exclusivity of traditional gender roles, and so it seems, has also opened more space for gender fluidity in local dance-making.

A gathering of our local Contact community last November to mark the 50th anniversary of CI, organized by Stéphanie Gaudreau, reminded me of how we had created our "temporary communities of experience" in the late 1970s. At the same time, it bore witness to the profound effects of current-day politics on how the local CI community was dancing together now. The assembly of Contacters at this celebratory gathering was markedly more culturally diverse than in the first jams. Taped to the wall were charts with new guidelines, forged over the years, encouraging safe and respectful behavior. We shared a vegetarian buffet, looked through a comprehensive collection of *Contact Quarterly* and other publications, photos, posters, and diverse historic artifacts, and Gaudreau had us build an intergenerational timeline about the progress of CI in Québec since that first class and workshop in 1977.

Consequent to this local event, feeling the weight of the historian, I began compiling a bibliography of CI writing, research articles, dissertations, and websites. I discovered the wealth of research projects and writing from Contact Improvisors around the world, who continue to build a multitude of new resources: informational and archival websites, global and local networks, symposiums and research projects, culture-sensitive community guidelines for local jams, and specialized study groups. These are impacting important changes in the culture of Contact. Among the research projects, it was astonishing to unearth such vast resources, emanating from so many fields of study in the sciences and humanities, ranging from physiology to psychology. It was evident that CI continues to expand and remain relevant, as cultural variations and mutations of the practice have emerged in so many countries and continents.

Even as it contributed to my identity as a feminist dancer and choreographer, my decades-long immersion in Contact Improvisation has left indelible traces in my body and psyche. As early as 1980, Banes observed, "For the Contactors, the form is a part of daily life, a way of using the body and becoming constantly aware of the body that permeates all activity and that is fed by other jobs, arts, sports, readings, social concerns" (1980a, 68). It is manifest in every step I take. My daily walk has long been a meditation on the pattern of the weight shift between my foot soles and the ground's surface. I still carry a hefty backpack, strapped high up onto my shoulders, with the hip belt distributing some of the weight onto my pelvis, thus continually strengthening my body as a supporting structure. The ability to sink into a deep squat, acquired through Contact dancing, remains the cornerstone of my claim to suppleness. I would even venture to say that the kind of released, fluid, and sensitive body I acquired in CI has become my ideal signature "movement identity," a way of moving through the day within my house and throughout the world.

From my first small dances, fallings, liftings, and carryings, counterbalances and rolling points of contact, as a resolute feminist, I have always felt kin to Contact Improvisation's sensuous community. However idealistic, I sincerely believed then—as I still do today—that by dancing together in this way, we are fostering a more humane and sustainable world through our "touch revolution" (Nelson 1996, 65).

Acknowledgments

Many thanks to Ann Cooper Albright for instigating this writing project and keeping my focus clear and steady. A debt of gratitude is also owed to multiple outside readers who scrutinized and questioned previous versions of this essay, much to its benefit: Michele Beaulieux, Aurore Biry, Carol Harwood, Sarah Mininsohn, María Pax Brozas Polo, Neil Schotsky, and Régine Wagnac. Thanks also to Lisa Clark, Flora Campise, and Meldy IJpelaar from the "feedback group" of our writing workshop at *CI @ 50* for their provocative and productive critique of an early draft of this chapter. My heartfelt appreciation to Lisa Nelson, and the late Steve Paxton and Nancy Stark Smith, Contact scholars and writers, and all of my Contact teachers and partners, in opening my body to this impactful dance world of dance exploration and communication.

References

Banes, Sally. 1980a. *Terpsichore in Sneakers: Post-Modern Dance*. Boston: Houghton Mifflin.
Banes, Sally. 1980b. *Democracy's Body: Judson Dance Theater 1962–1964*. Ann Arbor, MI: UMI Research Press.
Bull, Cynthia Jean Cohen (aka Cynthia J. Novack). 1999. "Sense, Meaning and Perception in Three Dance Cultures." In Jane Desmond, ed., *Meaning in Motion: New Cultural Studies of Dance*. Durham, NC, and London: Duke University Press, 269–287.
Cloud, Anya, and Karen Shaffman. March 2022. "Think Gravity–Dance Tank" research project symposium, ATLAS Institute, University of Colorado Boulder. Quotation taken from the *CI @ 50* program notes in May 2022.
Davida, Dena. 1977–1979. Personal handwritten notes from Catpoto meetings.
Davida, Dena, ed. 2012. *Fields in Motion: Ethnography in the Worlds of Dance*. Waterloo, ON: Wilfred Laurier Press.
Davida, Dena, ed. 2019. *Curating Live Arts: Critical Perspectives, Essays and Interviews in Theory and Practice*. New York: Berghahn Press.

36 Resistance and Support

Davida, Dena, ed. 2022–2024. *TURBA: The Journal for Global Practices in Live Arts Curation*. New York: Berghahn Journals. Davida, Dena, and Catherine Lavoie-Marcus. 2012. "Like Cactuses in the Desert: The Flourishing of Dance in Montréal Universities in the 1970s." In Allana Lindgren and Kaija Pepper, eds., *Renegade Bodies: Dance in Canada in the 1970s*. Toronto: Dance Collection Danse Press/es, 155–170.

Fulkerson, Mary. 1996. "Taking the Glove without the Hand." In Lisa Nelson and Nancy Stark Smith, eds., *Contact Quarterly* 21/1 (Winter/Spring). "Focus on Sexuality and Identity": 40–42.

Hennessy, Keith. 2018. *Questioning Contact Improvisation*. San Francisco: Circo Zero.

Kealiinohomoku, Joann. 1969/1970. "An Anthropologist Looks at Ballet as a Form of Ethnic Dance." *Impulse* 20: 24–33.

Kreiter, Jo. 1996. "Athletics, Power and Feminism." In Lisa Nelson and Nancy Stark Smith, eds., *Contact Quarterly* 21/2 (Summer/Fall), "Focus on Sexuality and Identity 2": 36–39.

Mitra, Royona. 2021. "Unmaking Contact: Choreographic Touch at the Intersection of Race, Caste, and Gender." *Dance Research Journal* 53/3 (December): 6–24.

Mitra, Royona. 2018. "Talking Politics of Contact Improvisation with Steve Paxton." *Dance Research Journal* 50/3 (December): 6–19.

Nelson, Karen. 1996. "Touch Revolution: Giving Dance." *Contact Quarterly* 21/1 (Winter/Spring), "Focus on Sexuality and Identity": 65–67.

Novack, Cynthia J. 1990. *Sharing the Dance: Contact Improvisation and American Dance*. Madison: University of Wisconsin Press.

Rainer, Yvonne, ed. 1974. "A Quasi Survey of Some 'Minimalist' Tendencies in the Quantitatively Minimal Dance Activity Midst the Plethora or an Analysis of *Trio A*." In *Work 1961–1974*. New York: The Press of the Nova Scotia College of Art and Design; New York University Press.

Vionnet, Claire. 2021 "Touch in Contact Improvisation: Proximity/Distance under Intimate Circumstances." *The Senses and Society* 16/3: 320–338.

2

Getting There from Here

A Road Map for Safer Brave Open Jams

Michele Beaulieux

Introduction

Let's take a deep breath together. Imagine any time you felt safe. If you are a Contact Improviser, recall a time you felt safe in a jam. Get comfortable. Put yourself at ease. Loosen up. Shake it all out. Relax. Let go. Now think about a time you felt brave. You took a risk. Stretched to do something scary. Reached out to someone and were glad you did. You asked, offered, listened. The person responded, accepting your invitation. The exchange might have been fast and fun, or soft and tender, or something else entirely. You might have been rolling on the floor or flying through the air. It was mutual, and it was beautiful.

I danced Contact Improvisation for years without consciously thinking about safety and bravery . . . until one day I realized what I had taken for granted. In November 2014 in the Chicago Sunday Contact Improvisation jam, I was in a clump of people in the middle of the dance floor when a man started to try to dry hump me. I extracted myself from that dance, had some words with him, and told the jam leaders.

Here is my memoir chronicling what happened next, my manifesto for change, and a manual on creating "safer brave spaces"—spaces that consciously support a culture of consent and work to make being brave safer, especially for marginalized people. My focus is open Contact Improvisation (CI) jams—gatherings open to the public for dancing—but the concept of safer brave space has much wider applicability. It is relevant for many other types of gatherings and get-togethers in which people participate voluntarily and risk vulnerability, especially situations involving touch. It may be adapted for gatherings practicing other dance forms—such as Ecstatic Dance, Touch & Play, and social dances—as well as other performing arts and contact sports.

Over the eight years following the violation, I combined my knowledge of sexual violence prevention and small-group democratic governance to advocate for safer brave space in the Chicago weekly CI jam, and I developed tools for assessing and creating such spaces. I processed what happened through the lens of sexual violence prevention theory, which emphasizes the importance of community. After a fellow student raped me in college, I had become an independent scholar and advocate for consent culture. I also brought my understanding of democratic group governance from my undergraduate studies in political science. I had studied small-group interactions and the concept of the common good.

Michele Beaulieux, *Getting There from Here* In: *Resistance and Support*. Edited by: Ann Cooper Albright, Oxford University Press.
© Oxford University Press 2024. DOI: 10.1093/9780197776308.003.0003

I came to understand that where we are now is often grounded in rape culture—a culture that normalizes all types of sexual violence, from harassment to rape. I envisioned a culture of consent—a culture that normalizes consent—where I—and many others—would like to be. For many reasons, getting from here to there can be challenging, so I developed some tips and tools for facilitating the transition.

In 2017, three years after the violation I experienced, the #MeToo movement brought greater awareness of the toll of sexual violations, and practicing consent became more normalized as people began observing six-foot social distancing due to the COVID-19 pandemic. As a result of a variety of factors, including new, dedicated leaders and my advocacy, the Chicago CI jam evolved into a much safer brave space.

As a well-educated, white, U.S.-born and raised, able-bodied, 60-plus, cisgender woman, I am aware that I have many privileges, even if I do not always recognize how they manifest. Having experienced unwelcome sexualized touch in a CI jam, my lens is sexual safety. I am also committed to working intersectionally, addressing physical, emotional, and spiritual safety. Many of the concepts I discuss may be relevant beyond the white female sexual violence lens that I am using and may apply to other types of violence, including but not limited to racial, ethnic, physical, emotional and psychological, and socioeconomic violence. All these types of violence may compound each other, creating and supporting a culture of coercion.

My lens is North American, and more specifically, most of my CI experience is in Chicago, Illinois, in the United States. These issues may play out differently in other countries and cultures.

After celebrating 50 years of CI in 2022, let's take stock and rebuild.

Here and There in CI

CI relies on touch boundaries and personal space much more intimate than those acceptable in society at large, and so it has its own social norms around touch. My focus is on open jams of at least a dozen people where people may be touching people they know, as well as people they don't. Some jams are ongoing weekly events, and some are annual weeklong festivals. Jam dynamics are distinct from classes and performance groups, which have leaders— teachers and choreographers—who are typically paid and responsible for holding the space and which may prohibit romantic relationships. In contrast, jams are recreational, people participate voluntarily, and organizers are typically volunteers. Sometimes they are paid nominally. While jams often discourage people from specifically searching for sexual partners at jams, romantic partners sometimes meet at jams or attend together.

Open jams each have their own norms and culture, and that culture can range from rape culture to consent culture. Many open jams still follow an individualistic "take care of yourself" approach, but other jams, including the current Chicago Sunday CI jam, are working toward creating a culture of consent. Table 2.1 illustrates the phases of individual freedom—ignoring and reacting—that support rape culture, and the facets of safer brave space—planning, creating, and sustaining—that support consent culture. In 2020, referring to a similar table, CI teacher and commentator Richard Kim said, "Most CI communities are between Ignoring and Reacting" (2020). In other words, most jams were still firmly embedded in rape culture.

Table 2.1 The Shift from Rape Culture to Consent Culture in Open CI Jams

		Rape Culture Phases of Individual Freedom		Consent Culture Facets of Safer Brave Space		
		Ignoring	Reacting	Planning	Creating	Sustaining
Stated values	Community vision	We don't have violations here.	If we decide a violation is bad enough, we will confront the person.	Violations happen and are dealt with in a reliable and systematic way.	Violations don't have to happen.	We want everyone to feel safe enough to dance bravely, if they so choose.
	Participant guidelines	We have no rules. No guidelines. Just dance!	We only have one rule: Take care of yourself; say "No."	We prioritize listening for "Yes" over saying "No."	We explain what to expect at our jam.	We expect active co-strugglers and jam citizens.
Community practices	Who is welcome	Everyone is welcome.	We have banned people after multiple well-substantiated complaints of egregious behavior.	We welcome people who follow our participant guidelines.	We require participants to agree to our publicly available guidelines before participating.	We reach out to participants who stop attending and consult with other groups about paused people.[a]
	Group governance	We do what works.	We see no need for formal structure.	We share and/or rotate leadership.	We hold leaders accountable and can remove them.	We distribute authority, resources, and information.
	Organizer responsibilities	We are leaderless.	Organizers respond to problems on an as needed basis.	Organizers set expectations; assure circles are well run.	Organizers make sure people with less privilege are represented.	Organizers rely on active citizens; improve continuously.
Accountability commitments	Receiving reports of violations	We haven't gotten reports. (Whisper networks tell who to avoid.)	We take reports ad hoc. We don't track them.	We solicit and track reports regardless of source or severity.	We welcome reports and provide multiple ways to report.	We seek out reports from people with less privilege.
	Responses to reports	We expect the "harmed" to take responsibility for their role. Our focus is the rights of the accused.	We try to soothe those claiming harm and ask for complete details.	We start by believing reports. We acknowledge microaggressions and intersectionality.	We provide timely, predictable, proportional consequences with opportunities to learn and repair harm.	We prioritize the safe and comfortable participation of those who have been harmed.

Adapted from Emerson, Megan, and the Portland Country Dance Community. (2018). *The Stages of Consent Culture for Dance Communities* (Portland, OR: Megan Emerson).

[a] The participation of people who violate group guidelines is paused contingent on fulfilling specified requirements.

We can see the continuum from rape culture to consent culture along three components: a jam's values, how it lives into its values, and what it does when the values aren't upheld. A group's stated values show in its community vision and participant guidelines; its community practices in whom it welcomes, its group governance, and organizer responsibilities; and its accountability commitments in how it tracks and responds to reports of violations.

Here: Current Contact Improvisation Culture

The "here"—where many groups are now—features the mistakes and transgressions of rape culture as well as seeds of truth and a foundation for growth. CI is a form based on egalitarian ideals on which we can build. CI, however, can attract people to jams who misinterpret the physical closeness as sexual intimacy and act inappropriately, violating personal boundaries. In addition, anyone—experienced CI dancers included—can violate others' boundaries. Some nonconsensual interactions are intentional, and others are unintentional. Some may be accidental one-offs by fumbling newcomers. Others may be part of a pattern of serial violations by well-known teachers whose status enables them to abuse more easily. Some consent violations are sexual violations, others are personal space violations, and still others relate to physical limitations, safety, and bodily comfort. Boundary violations at jams come in many variations: a person who is lifted might not want to be lifted, a hand might linger a little too long on a breast, touch might be overly enthusiastic, a person might be uncomfortably close, or a comment might suggest an unwelcome sexual liaison. Such unwelcome attention and sexualized touching may be uncomfortable, traumatizing, and illegal. Laws vary from country to country and state to state, but suffice it to say that society recognizes that these breaches can be serious.

Rape Culture

Sexual violence is a crime of power. CI leaders espouse egalitarian values, yet often fail to recognize that CI is operating within a broader rape culture with unequal power dynamics that inevitably seep into jams. CI leaders have had a baffling inability to address the risks of sexual violation inherent in a form based on touch within a society of inherent inequality. CI founder Steve Paxton admonished that CI is "physics, not chemistry" and is not a "gland game" (Novack 1990, 164). His distinction tacitly conceded that unwanted chemistry and gland games can be a problem, but he did not discuss how to prevent violations and what to do if they happened. Maddeningly, many CI leaders often still do not explicitly address how to prevent nonconsensual interactions. This "not seeing" is the ignoring phase of rape culture.

Fortunately, the form is evolving from this obliviousness (Kim 2020). Women's experiences being violated in jams are now well documented (Yardley 2017). Jams are recognizing the need to address violations, but they often put the onus on potential victims to defend themselves, rather than recognizing the problem as a community responsibility. Jams are moving from ignoring to reacting, but are still operating in rape culture.

Rape culture in CI has led women and other marginalized people to opt out. CI teacher Martin Keogh inadvertently acknowledged this unfortunate reality when summing up his

Table 2.2 Components of Rape Culture

	Organizational Elements	Individual Roles
Stated values	Individual responsibility	Free individuals
Community practices	Tyranny of structurelessness	Inactive citizens
Accountability commitments	Accountability of the harmed	Disrespected reporters

recounting of the true story of "Roland," a man who made women sexually uncomfortable in jams. He concluded that, since Roland ended up reforming and staying in the group, "it worked out well for both Roland and the group," even though he also stated that during the process of reining Roland in, "[m]any . . . women were never seen at the jam again." (Keogh, 62). Based simply on the numbers, Keogh's cost-benefit calculation is off. The price of keeping one persistent man who consistently violated women's boundaries in the group was the loss of many uncounted and unnamed women (Beaulieux 2019b). This absence of women and other marginalized people has shaped the form in ways we may not ever know.

I see rape culture here in CI comprising three cultural components, as shown in Table 2.2: stated values, living into values through community practices, and accountability commitments, or what we do when we don't live into values. In CI, a value of individual responsibility, a community practice of organizational structurelessness, and accountability required of people who have been harmed, rather than of those who have harmed, all point to rape culture. Individuals have freedom and no organizational responsibilities, and they are not respected for bringing issues forward.

Stated Value of Individual Responsibility

In keeping with a rape culture mentality, safety solutions in CI have unfortunately been individualistic and directed at those who have been or could be harmed, rather than the community and those who might harm. In 1994, in response to someone repeatedly offending at multiple jams, renowned CI teacher Karen Nelson prioritized self-care: "One needs to maintain the defenses of one's personal safety that one uses in the real world" (1994, 76). Likewise, a 1997 New York City safety flier advises dancers to "[b]e alert and sensitive to yourself and others" and reminds them: "You have the ultimate responsibility for your own well-being and enjoyment" (Marx and Mosey 1997). And in an attempt to address the issue of sexual violations, the 2018 WcciJam organizers "committed to empowering dancers to maintain healthy boundaries, to cultivate self-care and agency in their dance relationships" (Dancers Group 2018).

These individualistic solutions became codified as the "first rule" of Contact Improvisation (Beaulieux 2019). In some places, when people came to a jam, they were told that there was just one rule to follow: "take care of yourself." In many jams, participants are still told that. Let's put that neoliberal instruction in context. There is a difference between the "real world" and a community that is coming together for a common purpose. In a CI jam, we are inviting people, often strangers, to participate in a highly vulnerable dance form that is based

42   Resistance and Support

on touch. The form relies on connecting with and trusting other human beings. Do we want the first message we tell people to be: "take care of yourself"? That's essentially saying: "it's dangerous here and you're on your own. We won't help." That advice might be valid for a friend taking a solo trip to the arctic tundra, but how is it an appropriate message from a group sponsoring an event in which people touch each other? The group and leaders are essentially throwing up their hands, abdicating responsibility. Telling people to take care of themselves is putting the onus on them not to get harmed. A talent and skill in fending off sexual advances should not be a prerequisite for participating in CI.

The first rule attempts to stop violations at a jam by putting the responsibility on marginalized people to avoid getting harmed, rather than on trying to prevent people from harming in the first place. This first-rule thinking is part of rape culture. It is sad and telling that women find being told to "take care of yourself" so empowering. Our boundaries are ignored and we want to learn to defend them so badly that we rejoice and revel in the permission to say "no."

Don't get me wrong. Taking care of yourself is a good thing. It is a necessary and useful element of a comprehensive safety strategy. But on its own, it's insufficient. It's a backup strategy, an unfortunate last resort, not a good primary strategy. It's not the first thing I want to hear when I join a new group, especially one predicated on touching strangers. As the first or only rule, the first rule is actively harmful. If we want to talk in terms of rules, I support making the first rule the second rule.

At the time that the man attempted a sexual act with me in the Chicago jam, the first sentence of the Chicago Sunday jam website guidelines after "Welcome to the Chicago Sunday Contact Improvisation Jam," was a variation of the first rule: "You are responsible for your own safety." Like many people, it had not occurred to me to look at the guidelines before I went to the jam. If I had, I'd like to think I wouldn't have gone. But truth be told, I don't know that I would have recognized the emphasis on personal safety as the red flag that I now know that it is. If I had, I would have been right: the primacy of personal responsibility pervaded the group ethos.

The Tyranny of Structurelessness in Community Practices

Many CI jams mimic the free-form format of the form and have little formal organizational structure, but that doesn't mean they have no structure. Structure exists whether we consciously create it or not. Leaderless jams experience what political scientist Jo Freeman dubbed "the tyranny of structurelessness" (1973). Without formal structure, leadership is informal and cannot be easily challenged. Groups' unconscious structures often reflect and perpetuate our toxic societal norms. When we don't formalize organizational structure, we reinforce existing power dynamics. Groups that are supposedly structureless enable elites to dominate (1973).

The long-time de facto leader of the Chicago jam, a middle-aged, able-bodied, white cisgender man, led the group for more than two decades. His long tenure violated the principle of shared and rotating leadership crucial to democratic governance that I had naively hoped would be valued in a dance form espousing egalitarian principles. His first rule thinking was at odds with most group members, but he was very dedicated and did a lot for the group, so participants left decision-making authority to him. His power was informal. Participants did not have a vehicle for expressing their concerns with his leadership. Decision-making was not transparent. It also was not clear how people became part of the leadership collective or how teachers were chosen.

Accountability of the Harmed

In rape culture, processes that hold people who have harmed accountable are nonexistent or ad hoc. Instead, people are considered responsible for avoiding getting violated. When violations inevitably occur, people who are harmed are expected to step forward—even though no one else does—to rectify the situation. In #MeToo protests in 2018, CI dancers who had experienced consent violations resorted to disrupting jams in order to educate participants about boundary violations and to demand change and accountability (Harrist 2019). People who report problems are given derogatory titles. Sara Ahmed explores the frustrating fates of those who complain (2021). In rape culture, it may take years before their valuable contributions are recognized. Both the initial, primary violations and the secondary violations that people who were harmed experience as they seek help can cause lasting harm and trauma (Williams 1999). CI participants experience organizational betrayal when a jam group fails to prevent or respond supportively to wrongdoings that occur within the group when participants could reasonably expect protection (Freyd 2022).

In Keogh's example, two women who were uncomfortable with Roland asked the organizer of a jam "to do something about him," but the organizer instead encouraged the women to talk to Roland directly. Unsurprisingly, the tactic was ineffective: Roland was soon at it again. A man abusing power is unlikely to listen to people with less power whom he was abusing. The women had wisely asked leadership to intervene, but they were operating within a rape culture that did not recognize the power inequities enabling and perpetuating the abuse.

In another example, in an accountability process in 2018 about a long-time CI teacher's consent violations, the teacher did not fulfill the agreement to "work on a list of personal guidelines, shifts in behavior, and practices, especially in CI spaces" (Kingwill 2018,). He continues to teach and promote CI events (Frost n.d.), and it continues to fall on women to avoid him (Rea 2019). Rape culture continues in CI. By not insisting on accountability, the CI community enables abuse.

The man who attempted to violate me during the Chicago jam had been behaving inappropriately with multiple women before I complained. When the jam leader learned what happened, he was at loose ends about what to do. He told me that this incident was "only" the third time in all his years leading the jam that a violation had been reported to him. I was incredulous. Even though he was aware that dancers had previously been violated (and if he was aware of three incidents, there were likely many more unreported ones), he started trying to figure out what to do to prevent violations from happening again only after I publicly reported what I had experienced. If he had acted earlier, perhaps what happened to me wouldn't have happened.

The leader told me that it would be best for me not to come to the jam until he had spoken to the man. In my view, though, if the jam wasn't safe for me, it wasn't safe for anyone. If he couldn't stop the man from attending, then he should cancel the jam until he could figure out what to do. So I went to the jam the next week. The man was not there. The leader was surprised to see me. As the pre-jam class ended and more people were arriving for the jam, the leader, who was leading the class and jam that day, did not stop to have an opening circle as was standard, but started flowing into the jam. I, however, wanted participants to know what had happened, so I loudly announced that I had been violated in the jam the week before. People stopped dancing, sat in circle, and discussed the situation.

In the flurry of emails that followed between the jam leaders and me, it became clear that they had no protocol for responding to reports of harm. I suggested that we form a committee to address safety issues. I was not traumatized by the incident, but I didn't want to have to deal with the possibility of it happening again and I didn't think I, or anyone else, should have to. In January 2015, several leaders, jam members, and I met with the goal of establishing preventive measures, but nothing came of it. I didn't have the energy to keep fighting what was clearly an uphill battle, so I stopped attending the jam. I couldn't trust and so didn't want to touch people who weren't prioritizing safety.

I consoled myself that at least the man wasn't attending the jam anymore. Four years after I left the jam, however, I learned that my assumption was inaccurate. In the intervening years, the jam leaders had allowed the man to return to the jam without my knowledge, much less an accountability process with me and others he had harmed. His participation did have stipulations, such as attending the class before the jam. Unsurprisingly, he violated even more women's boundaries, and multiple women complained, insisting that the man be asked to leave. After much lobbying, the jam leader asked him not to come back to the jam ever again.

When the man attempted to dry hump me in 2014, I had only recently returned to CI. When I was originally attending the jam in the early 1990s, a man and I met there and became involved. After a difficult breakup with him, I stopped going to the jam. Being in the same room with him was too painful for me. He had no problem being in the same room as me, however, so he saw no need to negotiate a mutually satisfactory compromise. Because I did not have a way to negotiate a rotating participation agreement with him, I stopped going. While not all support teams would consider disagreements among consenting adults to be a responsibility under their purview, the power inequities in rape culture impact who stays when such conflicts occur. Support teams can enable people who might not otherwise feel comfortable participating, including women, marginalized people, and people who have been harmed, to participate, thereby creating a more equitable space.

There: Safer Brave Space

In CI, touch that normally would not be welcome is welcome. Other activities, such as BDSM, and contact sports such as boxing and wrestling, also expand the boundaries of socially acceptable touch. In these contexts, consent is critical. There are many definitions of consent. For CI, the derivation of the word "consent," from the Latin *consentir*—which means "to feel together"—is particularly instructive. Mutuality is key. Other chapters in this volume address the specifics of touch and consent. My focus is on the community and organizational structures that support a culture of consent, rather than the specifics of touch and consent.

Consent Culture

What happened to me in the Chicago CI jam did not happen in a vacuum. A strong community can play a crucial role in preventing and responding to all kinds of violence, including sexual violence. The following violence prevention and response paradigms identify three elements in violence: a person who causes harm, a person who experiences harm, and a community or lack thereof:

- **Routine activities theory**, a traditional theory of crime, posits that crimes occur when three factors are present: a likely offender, a suitable target, and the absence of a capable guardian. The community, for example, can be a capable guardian.
- **Community accountability theory** supports people who have been harmed while holding both the person doing harm and the community accountable. Community accountability seeks social change through collectivity. *The Creative Interventions Toolkit* expands the concept of accountability beyond individuals to communities: "We believe that violence is not an individual problem and that solutions also cannot be individual. It takes all of us to end violence" (Creative Interventions 2021, Section 2, 12).
- **The ecological model** posits that preventing violence requires acting across multiple levels at the same time—individual, relationship, community, and society—which it represents as concentric circles (Krug 2002). The U.S. Centers for Disease Control and Prevention subscribe to the ecological model prevention framework, which expands beyond the other two models by adding an additional layer beyond community. The final level, the societal, impacts us in ways that we might not even be aware of.

Rape culture focuses on individuals, tasking them with finding solutions, rather than looking at the larger systemic context. In contrast, these theories posit that responsibility for violations goes beyond the person who caused the harm. They suggest that preventing violations requires prioritizing community responsibility. Routine activity theory uses the language of guardianship to describe community responsibility. Community accountability recognizes the community role as critical. And the ecological model names the community, as well as societal, levels in its prevention paradigm.

In consent culture, mutual consent in interpersonal relations and respect for each other's choices is the norm (Cliff 2012). In such a culture, people ask, wait, and listen. They respect the answers they receive. They understand that everyone has the right to personal and bodily autonomy. For CI, that means that dancers come to agreement before and while dancing together and accept when someone expresses disinterest.

The Beaulieu Test

After the violation I experienced, I advocated for reforms. As the discussions bogged down into details, I realized that debating name tags and sign-in sheets was useless if we didn't agree on the basic assumptions necessary to create a culture of consent. I developed a simple test to evaluate whether participant guidelines start with the fundamental value of looking after each other and the group. Inspired by the Bechdel Test for women's representation in movies that cartoonist Alison Bechdel created, CI community member Charlie Halpern-Hamu suggested calling it the "Beaulieux Test." "Beau lieu" means beautiful place in French, which seemed an apt name for a test with the goal of creating consensual places. (For the test, I corrected the misspelled French of my last name.)

The Beaulieu Test, shown in Box 2.1, gives potential participants a quick yardstick for assessing whether an event recognizes that safety is a community responsibility. It looks to see whether the participant guidelines for a voluntary event, such as a CI jam, assign the responsibility for violations to the group and those who have violated, rather than those who have been violated. That is, it evaluates whether group guidelines follow the first rule or not.

46 Resistance and Support

Box 2.1 The Beaulieu Test: A Quick Test for Safer Brave Space

1. Does the event have publicly available participant guidelines?
2. Do the guidelines have more words about respecting and caring for each other and the group (and listening for "yes") than about taking care of oneself (and saying "no")?
3. Do the words about the former come before the words about the latter?

A "yes" answer to all three questions in the Beaulieu Test means a jam passes the test and is likely to provide a culture of consent that asks people to recognize their own power and privilege and listen for yes. CI jam guidelines that pass the Beaulieu Test are starred in the Compendium of CI Jam Guidelines and provide good starting points for jams looking to create or update guidelines (Pierce n.d.). So while each jam has its own needs and the process of discussing guidelines is valuable, jams don't have to start from scratch.

At the time of this writing, half the guidelines in the Compendium passed the test, and many have lovely expressions of community. The Contact Improvisation Twin Cities' values and guidelines start by saying, "Together, we are creating opportunities to: share, connect, dance, enjoy! CITC values care for others—care defined as respect, empathy, and compassion. We encourage and challenge you to deeply listen to the dances and interactions you cultivate" (n.d.). And the Philadelphia Thursday Jam guidelines begin by answering the question, "How is Contact Improvisation practiced at this jam?" by stating "(1) We listen to and respect our partners" (2021).

The Vision: Safer Brave Space

In a "forum theatre" exercise at a Theatre of the Oppressed workshop that I attended, we first acted out a story of oppression from the news and then we tried it again, this time improvising alternatives (Boal 2021). What might people do to change the outcome? Seeing this plethora of possibilities, this transformation from despair to hope inspired me to consider what CI might be like with safer brave spaces. I envisioned CI spaces where I (and others) could risk vulnerability and dance. We take care when we touch each other, and the touch that occurs is welcome and consensual. We relax into the moment, conscious of one another and the group as a whole. The movement ebbs and flows within this collective awareness and understanding of our dance.

No space will ever be completely safe for everyone, but some spaces can be safer than others. Some people object to the concept of safe, or even safer, spaces as not supporting risk-taking and have suggested the term "brave space" as an alternative. Brave spaces support people in taking risks (Arao and Clemens 2013), but may not recognize that marginalized people often must summon disproportionate bravery to do things that come easily to others (Verduzco-Baker 2018).

I propose "safer brave spaces" as spaces that consciously work to make being brave safer especially for marginalized people. Safety is a lack of danger and, therefore, the potential for harm. Bravery is strength and courage in the face of difficulty, danger, or fear. We're more likely to take risks when we feel both safe and brave. Safer brave spaces are spaces that are as safe as possible, enabling people to be brave, but that also recognize that bravery may be more challenging for some people than for others. In a safer brave space, we can more safely relax, let go, be vulnerable, and take risks; we can be brave without fear of unwanted advances and boundary violations.

Safer brave spaces recognize that power differentials can make withholding consent more difficult for some people than for others, so they not only uphold the norm of consent, but also have structures that support it. In safer brave spaces, if people do not take responsibility after they have violated others, the community may seek accountability in coordination with the people who have been violated. Safer brave spaces welcome people who look out for the health of the community, restrict participation of those who violate group norms until they take responsibility, and proactively support marginalized people who are more likely to be violated. They develop and implement prevention and repair measures with the input of people, especially marginalized people, who have been or are more likely to be harmed. Safer brave spaces recognize that when we actively institutionalize the unacceptability of sexual and other types of violence, people who were violated or feel in danger of being violated are more likely to choose to participate, and we are a richer, more vibrant community with their contributions.

The Beaulieu Assessment

As a guide for creating safer brave spaces, the Beaulieu Test, I realized, was limited: it only assesses a jam's values. While passing the Beaulieu Test is necessary, it is not sufficient. To create a safer brave space, a jam also needs to operationalize the communal values of interpersonal and community care that are assessed by the Beaulieu Test. It must have structures to uphold the guidelines that it asks participants to follow.

I developed the 12-question Beaulieu Assessment for Safer Brave Space to evaluate jams on their stated values; how they live into their values; and how they handle situations when their values aren't upheld. Just as in rape culture, each component manifests in organizational elements and individual roles. In safer brave spaces, however, as Table 2.3 shows, jams value community accountability and respectful partners and co-strugglers, democratic governance and active citizens, and sensitive response processes and respect for reporters.

Table 2.3 Components of Safer Brave Space

	Organizational Elements	Individual Roles
Stated values	Community accountability	Respectful partners, co-strugglers (and roles below)
Community practices	Democratic governance	Active citizens
Accountability commitments	Sensitive response processes	Respected reporters

48   Resistance and Support

Box 2.2 Beaulieu Assessment Questions for Stated Values

- Do the publicly available participant guidelines pass the Beaulieu Test, name who is responsible, and explain what to expect?
- Does the group have values—such as equity, transparency, community accountability for preventing harm, and continuous improvement—that support respecting and caring for each other and the group?
- Do the publicly available guidelines for leaders (event facilitators, online moderators, teachers, etc.) include agreeing with, actively modeling, and promoting the group values?
- Are participants expected to be respectful partners and, to the extent they are able, to be co-strugglers, engaged group citizens, and reporters?

Stated Values of Group Care

Safer brave spaces state their values, and participants co-struggle to live into them. In a safer brave space, people respect and care for each other, publicly establishing a community of care. Box 2.2 provides questions for assessing a group's stated values.

Jams providing safer brave spaces are transparent about their values, and their foundational value is respect and care for each other and the group. In other words, their public guidelines pass the Beaulieu Test. By clearly and publicly stating what people can expect (Rea n.d.) in writing and/or orally either live and/or on video, their guidelines help newcomers make informed decisions about participating and set expectations for participants and leaders.

In safer brave spaces, participants are expected to be sensitive dance partners and co-strugglers as well as active citizens and reporters. I follow Black thought leaders, including Mariame Kaba, in using the term "co-struggler" (Russo 2019, 27). They urge people to go beyond being allies—merely supporting people who have been harmed—to take the struggle on as their own. Ta-Nehisi Coates said, "one has to even abandon the phrase 'ally' and understand that you are not helping someone in a particular struggle; the fight is yours" (Gay 2015). Co-strugglers step up to inequities, recognizing that there is no such thing as neutrality, that silence equals violence. In Keogh's story of Roland, male members of the community finally intervened. Only then did Roland reform. The men, acting as "co-strugglers," succeed in creating safer brave space for the community (Beaulieux 2019b).

In 2014, after the Chicago jam sat in a circle after I announced what had happened to me the week before, a woman who was a professor of disability studies came up to me and validated my desire to make change. She supported my contention that changes made to accommodate me in the jam would also help other people likely to be recipients of unwanted attention (Blackwell 2017). Her co-struggling sustained me.

In 2021, the Chicago Contact Improvisation Jam finally took down its first-rule-based guidelines from its website. The jam's current guidelines support a sense of community and pass the Beaulieu Test. Its stated values come from the principles of the form: creating a container, resisting, sharing weight, and consent (n.d.).

> ### Box 2.3 Beaulieu Assessment Questions for Community Practices
>
> - Are people required to agree to the participant or leader guidelines before participating or leading?
> - Is the group democratically structured as outlined in the "Tyranny of Structurelessness," including sharing and rotating leadership (Freeman 1972)?
> - Are people with less power and privilege represented fairly in decision making?
> - Are there community practices, such as well-facilitated opening and closing circles involving all participants, that frame and hold events as safer brave spaces?

Democratic Community Practices

If we want to create a culture of consent, we can't just dance. Instead, I suggest we become active jam citizens and govern our groups democratically in safer brave spaces (Beaulieux 2020). Creating a safer brave space requires more than just having communal values, it requires community practices that integrate, live, and breathe those values. Box 2.3 provides questions for assessing a group's community practices.

Sexual and other forms of violence thrive in power imbalances. Maintaining a democratic community in which everyone has a voice flattens power disparities, counteracting rape culture and preventing abuse. By democratic governance, I mean an organizational structure supporting equal representation. In small groups, decisions may be made by consensus, voting, or another method in which all people can be represented. Groups work to make sure that people with less power and privilege are represented fairly in decision-making. Formal and transparent democratic governance enables groups to create safer brave spaces. As Jo Freeman explains:

> For everyone to have the opportunity to be involved in a given group and to participate in its activities, the structure must be explicit, not implicit. The rules of decision-making must be open and available to everyone, and this can happen only if they are formalized. . . .
> Having an established process for decision-making ensures that everyone can participate in it to some extent. (n.d.)

Well-facilitated opening and closing circles that involve all participants frame and hold events as safer brave spaces by providing time for verbally sharing group guidelines and expectations, as well as reflections and announcements. The CI structure, the "Underscore," supports the democratic practices of opening circles, which it calls "Assembly," and closing circles, which it calls "Sharing/Thanksgiving" (Koteen and Smith 2021).

A safer brave jam welcomes people who agree to the community agreements and expects participants to be active citizens and reporters to the extent that they are able. Functional, responsive organizations depend on active citizens to prevent violations and to address fairly the harm that unfortunately does occur. They recognize that safety is everyone's responsibility, not just leaders'. Citizens have rights, responsibilities, and privileges as members of a community with a governance structure that provides them vehicles for input. The traditional responsibilities of citizens apply in CI: citizens participate in decision-making, often by voting; pay taxes or participation fees; obey the law or guidelines of the group; serve on juries for accountability processes; and fill out censuses. Citizens also respect differences and help others.

Rebuilding coming out of the pandemic in 2021, the Chicago CI Jam restructured its governance and worked to prevent such violations from occurring in the first place.

By 2022, the jam had instituted community practices that supported safer brave space, and the leadership collective spread out decision-making (2022b). Given these changes, I decided to attend one Sunday. In the opening circle, the jam support members introduced themselves in their roles as welcomers for newcomers, feedback takers, and generally available co-strugglers. They were actively engaged citizens of the group, encouraging us to be so as well. They stated the jam's values. Their tone was caring and warm.

Community Accountability Commitments

While harm will be less likely in safer brave spaces, it will still occur, so having protocols in place to receive reports and address the harm shows a commitment to accountability. Box 2.4 provides questions for assessing a group's commitments to group accountability.

We all make mistakes, and there is always room for improvement. Safer brave spaces embrace the problems that occur as learning opportunities and have response processes for dealing with them. Drawing from restorative and transformative justice paradigms, some CI groups have conducted accountability processes for individuals who violated boundaries (Pierce, n.d.). These processes can be time consuming and messy, and people who harm can manipulate them, but we are learning, fumbling towards repair (Kaba and Hassan 2019).

Box 2.4 Beaulieu Assessment Questions for Accountability Commitments

- Does the group provide multiple ways to give feedback and report harm and does it solicit input from those who have left and/or have less power and privilege?
- Does the group start by believing (End Violence Against Women International n.d.) and listening (Burke 2018) to those who report harm and/or request support and, if harm is established, does the response center their input?
- Does the group's response to reports of harm prioritize the safe and comfortable participation of those who experienced harm over the participation of those who have harmed and the comfort of the community?
- Are the group's responses to reports of harm caused by participants, leaders, and/or the group—including the consequences for causing that harm—timely, predictable, and proportional with opportunities for the group and the individual(s) who caused the harm to learn, take responsibility, and make repairs?

Accountability processes can address organizational and leadership wrongs as well as interpersonal violations. Consent culture is imperfect. The processes may need to address situations in which leaders violate boundaries themselves and also when they enable violations or support conditions that allow such behavior to occur.

In addition to co-strugglers and active citizens, safer brave spaces need reporters: people who call the group to accountability. Reporters can be especially important in situations in which the leaders are not fulfilling their obligations. Often reporting falls on people who have been harmed, but in safer brave spaces, co-strugglers step up to the responsibility, too. In safer brave spaces, people who call out problems are heard and respected.

In 2019, Chicago jam members enthusiastically shared on Facebook my articles inspired by what happened in the jam. Jam leaders also referred to the Beaulieu Assessment while developing their next steps.

In 2022, the Chicago jam developed a comprehensive harm-response process to use in addressing harms such as those I had experienced (Schaffer and Chicago Contact Improvisation 2022).

From Here to There

As it turns out, envisioning and outlining the characteristics of safer brave spaces is the easy part. The challenge is getting there from here.

Why Getting There from Here Is So Tough

Change can be difficult. Social norms, which support group cohesion, are strong. Rape culture is entrenched. Even in groups in which people have the knowledge and vision and desire to create safer brave spaces, the groups may fail to make the transition.

People often don't advocate for change or stand up for people who have been harmed. They may determine that going against the status quo is not worth the risk. They are often making rational decisions. Costs can be immediate and significant and the benefits distant and obtuse. They could potentially be singled out, retaliated against, and labeled hypocritical. For CI jams, the costs are largely social: reporters can lose friends and social standing. They may also lose their community and no longer feel comfortable going to jams. Sometimes, advocacy can have financial ramifications. Reporters can lose teaching jobs and performing gigs.

Three different sociological "effects" help explain why so few people overcome their psychological inhibitions in order to object and report, and thus why groups have trouble transitioning out of the dysfunction of rape culture.

- **Threshold effect:** Most people will step forward only after others have. A person's threshold is the number of people doing an activity before the person agrees to join them. Whistleblowers have a threshold of zero. Others will act once a whistleblower speaks. And still others have an even higher threshold. More and more will follow after more and more come forward (Granovetter 1978). Broader cultural shifts, like the

52 Resistance and Support

growing awareness of sexual violence as a result of the #MeToo movement, can lower people's thresholds so that they step up sooner than they might have previously.

- **Bystander effect**: Potential co-strugglers assume that others will act, so they don't. Because of the bystander effect, individuals are less likely to intervene the greater the number of people around. The presence of others diffuses the responsibility, making people more comfortable not helping someone in need: Someone else will take care of it (Blagg 2023).
- **Snowball effect**: Once a quarter of people support a change, then it may snowball and gather momentum. Under the right conditions, 25 percent of people coming forward can be the critical mass required for social change. The first to adapt are people on the periphery without a lot of social capital and without much to lose. Popular people aren't generally first movers (Centola 2021).

These inhibiting effects are compounded for situations of sexual violence, which has its own psychological inhibitions. Rape culture norms often shroud sexual violence in silence and shame. People who have been harmed often don't come forward, and those who do come forward often aren't believed. As a result, people who have been harmed often think they're alone, when, in fact, they may be part of a pattern of abuse by a particular person or in a community. Because people who have been harmed often understandably don't speak out, potential co-strugglers might not even be aware of the situation. With fewer people coming forward, the problem becomes less likely to meet people's thresholds to act and is less likely to snowball. As a result, abuse is not addressed, and an unhealthy culture persists.

I am an activist. I have a low threshold. I am comfortable speaking my mind and calling out problems. Others have higher thresholds. Eventually, however, the Chicago jam did reach the 25 percent tipping point and started to focus in earnest on creating a safer brave space.

Initiating the Shift from Here to There

A precipitating event, such as an egregious violation or the discovery of a pattern of harm, is typically the catalyst for a jam to address its culture and start transitioning from valuing individual freedom to creating safer brave space. It can no longer ignore the seriousness of the harm that its rape culture enables. The value of transitioning into a culture of consent becomes apparent.

I danced Contact Improvisation for years without thinking about the potential for abuse and the need for safety protocols. Then, I was violated in a jam. The incident was jarring, awakening my awareness and sparking my drive to make sure no one else experienced what I did.

A combination of outside pressure and inside wherewithal can shift an organization from supporting rape culture to creating a culture of consent. To move a group into a culture of consent, safer brave space advocates can propagate new social norms. They can do this by starting on the fringes of social networks and building redundancy into their communications (Centola 2021). The repetition means that people hear the same message from multiple people in their social networks. They validate the message, and it becomes more and more compelling. To change the CI culture and group norms, co-strugglers can begin by objecting to behaviors that support rape culture (Rea 2020). They can take small steps that show support, such as offering a smile or a few kind words, or "liking" comments on social media.

From the Outside

People outside of a group can address what is going on without the social pressure to conform to group norms. They have a lower threshold for action. Outsiders don't face the same social costs for speaking out that those within a group do. They can more easily shine a light on bad situations and thereby make stepping up and intervening more attractive for insiders. Outside pressure can weaken the social pressure to conform, changing the social benefit calculus and lowering the thresholds of insiders who are hesitant to take a stand.

Outside pressure comes in many forms. The media can shine a light on improprieties. Outside activist groups might lobby for change. Former participants and people from other groups within the form might also fulfill the role of reporters. Outside organizations, such as the media, government, independent agencies, and certifying associations, can evaluate situations without the vested interests that people involved in a community have. In the amorphous CI world, intervention from outside the form, however, is uncommon: CI jams garner little media or government attention and there is no central governing body.

When I went to the Chicago jam in 2014, I was essentially an outsider. I had not participated in the jam for about two decades, but I knew and loved the form. In the early 1990s, I was a regular participant in the Chicago Sunday Contact Improvisation jam. We were a small ragtag group of mostly dancers. We kept the cash we collected for the rent hidden in a closet in the dance studio until the week the envelope was stolen. Often, whoever had the key to open the space was late. As this was before cell phones, the rest of us would wait outside on the sidewalk in front of the studio, hoping the person hadn't forgotten. I had wonderful dances in the jam. I did not experience any nonconsensual sexual touch in the jam and had not considered that this type of unwanted touch might happen, much less how the group or I would deal with it.

When I returned after a two-decade hiatus, the group had changed a lot. There were more people. Still mostly white. The new de facto leader was not a trained dancer. Volunteer teachers taught classes before every jam. Very few of the dancers I knew previously were still participating. I had been to the jam less than half a dozen times when the man violated me. I did not have much social capital in the current group. I was essentially an outsider, so being a reporter was easy. I didn't have a lot to lose by complaining. It is also my natural disposition to advocate for justice.

After the jam did not make changes that would move it toward safer brave space after the attempted violation, and I then stopped participating, I became even more of an outsider, but I didn't go away. I continued monitoring and reporting. I occasionally looked at the jam's Facebook page and a few times I posted, calling the group to accountability and calling for reforms, including the resignation of the leader. I was not the only person frustrated with him. A few people supported me. Often the people who liked my Facebook posts were similarly on the periphery of the group. I connected with a few other people, some who had had bad experiences in the jam and others who were outside the jam and easily recognized the manifestations of rape culture. At the same time, many people defended the status quo.

I wanted to go back to the jam but I was concerned, for starters, that the first rule guidelines were still up on the group's website. I was told that the jam practiced consensual interactions in person and the guidelines on the website were irrelevant. If, however, the group couldn't manage the simple one-minute task of taking the old guidelines down, I questioned the foundation on which the jam's in-person consent lessons were built.

And the Inside

It can be difficult for insiders to develop momentum on their own to make change. A precipitating event and outside pressure for accountability can create urgency for insiders to act. Active citizens inside a group can build organizational structure and protocols in response to the demands that reporters call out.

From my outside view, I can only surmise what happened on the inside of the Chicago jam group to result in the reinvigorated jam support team (Chicago Contact Improvisation Jam, n.d.b) and protocols (Chicago Contact Improvisation Jam 2022). I imagine that inside advocates were instrumental in pushing for the changes and that my occasional badgering helped keep the group on track.

Facing Past Harm

While it might be tempting to try to move forward without addressing trauma, the reality is that there is no escaping it. It's embodied. So if there's been trauma in a jam, it's in the jam. We can find and feel past trauma in a current jam just by being with people in that jam (carroll 2020).

Creating a New "Here"

When a jam ignores and does not process trauma, it affects the jam and who participates in the jam. Rather than remain loyal or try to reform an existing group, those who have been harmed may exercise their option to exit (Hirschman 1970). They may leave a jam or leave CI altogether, or if they want to keep dancing, they may opt to start a new jam that will support safer brave space. People have started their own jams because, for example, they wanted stricter COVID-19 protocols. Building new from the ground up allows them to set up new expectations and guidelines for safer brave space from the get-go.

When I was advocating for change in the Chicago CI jam, many people suggested that I start another Chicago jam, but given that I had been away from CI for decades and didn't know current CI dancers, trying to start a new jam didn't seem realistic. I did imagine such a fresh start for the women who dealt with "Roland," the man whom Keogh described as continuing to violate women's boundaries. I wrote a story in which the women, frustrated with the leadership's failure to address the situation, started their own democratically governed jam to support a safer brave space (Beaulieux 2022).

Going Back in Order to Get There

To create safer brave spaces, jams might consider delving deeper into the accountability commitments component of safer brave space to deal with unaddressed past harms. CI has not done well addressing violations on a case-by-case basis as disparate issues between the person harmed and the person who harmed. Predatory teachers, for example, continue to teach. Addressing violations systematically means not only that individuals who violate take responsibility and make amends to those harmed, but also that the community examines and takes responsibility for its role in enabling the initial harm and, in many cases, for an inadequate or insensitive initial response.

If a group decides to institute new preventive measures as a remedy for past harm, then it might also consider retroactive repair. Reckoning with past harms requires not just developing processes to prevent the same thing from happening again, but also rectifying the past mistakes, which may involve reaching out to people who were harmed. Even newly forming groups may find it necessary to address harms in their leaders' pasts and in the form's history. Such repair enables inclusion. It allows people who were harmed in the past (and people who are like them) to trust the good intentions.

CI may be wise to look to transitional justice models, which address widespread patterns of wrongdoing. Transitional justice provides useful tools to address historical injustices: truth and reconciliation commissions, memorials, reparations, institutional reforms, prosecution, and commemoration. Transitional processes seek out people who no longer participate in order to learn why (Lu 2021).

The Chicago jam's repair process for past harms is the only documented process of which I am aware that is repairing the harm caused by a jam's past response to consent violations. The only other documented process seeking to repair past harms in CI that I could find addressed racist harms. In 2019, the CI retreat center Earthdance conducted a truth and reconciliation process to address the patterns of racism it had perpetrated; afterward, the Earthdance Board of Directors issued an acknowledgment of past transgressions (n.d.). While the process was groundbreaking for CI, many BIPOC were not satisfied and called for sunsetting the organization. Some argued that the process did more harm than good. Steps toward repairing harm can be imperfect and, indeed, damaging, but I would argue that it is important to try if we are to move into a culture of consent in CI. We are new at this. We are learning, developing models and protocols.

And in celebrating 50 years, the form is reckoning with its past. The *Critical Mass: CI @ 50 at Oberlin* mission statement "committed to examining the culture of Contact Improvisation and acknowledging its history of nonconsensual transgressions, inequity, ableism, sexism, and racism, and recognizing the ways these power imbalances continue to influence the spaces we co-create" (*Critical Mass: CI @ 50* n.d.). Publicly acknowledging the form's past harms at its fiftieth anniversary was a significant step forward for healing in the form. May it provide a platform for repair moving forward in support of safer brave space at open CI jams.

In 2021, seven years after the man attempted a sexual act with me in the middle of the Chicago jam, things finally started to shift. The jam collective offered me a meek apology for its poor handling of what happened to me in 2014 and its subsequent failures to address jam safety. While the apology commended my courage, it misrepresented my demands and defended the leader who allowed the man who had tried to dry hump me to return (Schaffer 2021).

Then, facing other complaints in addition to mine, the leader finally resigned from jam leadership, opening up opportunities for new, younger leaders to take the reins (Halkin 2021). The jam put out a general call for volunteers, input, and feedback (Schaffer 2021).

I had multiple meetings with Sarah Schaffer, the coordinator of the Chicago CI Jam Response Protocol Working Group. Sarah asked me what I wanted, and I said that I would like the leadership collective to take down the old first-rule-based guidelines. I also wanted a public apology on the Chicago Jam Facebook page for keeping the old guidelines up and allowing a man who had sexually violated women's personal boundaries to return to the jam without accountability for his past harms, much less the knowledge of the women he had harmed. I also wanted the collective to score the jam on the Beaulieu Assessment since I had developed it with the Chicago Jam in mind. I noted that the jam leader's decades-long tenure did not sync with the democratic principle of rotation of leadership, and his repeated prioritization of people who had harmed did not sync with prioritizing people who had been harmed (Beaulieux 2021). An apology and a commitment that the former group leader would not be welcome back without a process was critical for me to consider coming back. Since his resignation contained a victim-blaming non-apology apology (Halkin 2021), I wanted an actual one before I could feel comfortable dancing in the same room with him.

In September 2022, the Sunday Ci Jam at Links Hall posted the following updated apology on Facebook:

> *As organizers of the Chicago Jam, we would like to apologize for the lack of a cohesive response to harm as well as a culture of victim-blaming that has hurt many of us over the years. This is a culture we have both inherited and participated in and take responsibility for transforming.*
>
> *It took Michele Beaulieux's immense vulnerability and courage to bring attention to the violation she experienced at the jam eight years ago, and then again when it was handled with inadequate transparency, expediency, and care. We are sorry to all survivors of harm who, like Michele, have borne the burden to bring about accountability. We are still working to do our part to shoulder this burden.*
>
> *For these reasons, we have reorganized into a new Collective Governance, articulated our values, voted on new Community Agreements for participants and facilitators, established a Protocol for Responding to Harm, and trained a new group of Jam Support – volunteer jamgoers who seek to foster a culture of consent and accessibility. We regret that it has taken as long as it has to put these pieces in place and are committed to creating a culture that supports us all to listen to one another and act with care. (2022)*

The jam organizers had publicly apologized. The jam support group also started discussions with former leaders to reflect on my and others' experiences of harm. They committed to facilitate conversations between the former leaders and me.

The resignation of the Chicago jam leader, new leaders committed to establishing a culture of consent, my advocacy, and the growing awareness inspired by the #MeToo movement led to the jam reopening after COVID with new community agreements, a protocol for responding to harm, and jam support volunteers. These steps toward safer brave spaces were good, and with discussions with former leaders in process, I went to the jam for the first time in eight years. On a Sunday at the end of October 2022, I found myself in the CI class that took place before the Chicago Sunday jam. The teacher asked us to choose a partner and instructed us in an exercise. One partner was to lie on the floor and the other was to firmly brush their partner's body with their hands outward from their partner's core to their hands and feet. The idea was that we would be enlivening our partner's bodies, but I felt like that movement would dissipate my energy and I needed all my resources in order to deal with being back in the space. But then I reframed it. My partner, Sarah Schaffer, lay on the floor first. As I brushed outward from Sarah's core, I thought of how much she and so many others working together in the leadership collective and jam support group had gifted the space, and I sent those gifts into the space. When it was my turn to lie down, I released the trauma back into the space and also gave what I'd learned to the space.

In 2023, as part of the repair process, Jam Support facilitated individual conversations with three former female leaders and me. Two expressed remorse for their role and one did not. While the lack of remorse was distressing, it was good information to have for interacting with this former leader in the future. While not ideal, I was satisfied. After all, the perfect is the enemy of the good. The former male leaders, however, were not willing to sit down and talk with me in a facilitated conversation, and Jam Support was not requiring such a conversation. Jam Support was willing to facilitate ways that the former leaders who did not want to talk to me and I could avoid dancing together, but I didn't want to be avoiding them. I wanted to resolve the situation. As a result, I opted not to return to the jam because I do not want to dance in a jam where people do not want to talk to me.

While my past harm was not repaired such that I felt comfortable returning to the jam, the jam has done a lot to create a safer brave space for others moving forward and I am happy and grateful for that. A frequenter of CI spaces who first came to the Chicago jam in 2022 said,

> _The procedures and curation of the Chicago Jam were very clearly the product of a reckoning, meaning those aspects of the Chicago Jam are intentional, clear, and starkly different from other jam spaces I've been in. Usually difference and transformation like that don't happen without a huge upheaval. It is one of the things that keeps me coming back to the Chicago Jam, the fact that it has changed, and can change, for the better, even if I don't know all the details._
> _(Anonymous 2023)_

References

Ahmed, Sara. 2021. *Complaint!* Durham, NC: Duke University Press.

Anonymous. 2023. Private email correspondence.

Arao, Brian, and Kristi Clemens. 2013. *The Art of Effective Facilitation: Reflections From Social Justice Educators*. Sterling, VA: Stylus.

Beaulieux, Michele. 2019. "How the First Rule Brought #MeToo to Contact Improvisation." *Contact Quarterly* 44, no. 1 (Winter/Spring): 46–50. https://contactquarterly.com/cq/article-gallery/view/how-the-first-rule-brought-metoo-to-contact-improvisation#.

Beaulieux, Michele. 2019b. "Starting by Believing Maria: Responding to Sexual Violence in Safer Brave Contact Improvisation Spaces." *CQ Contact Improvisation Newsletter* 44, no. 2 (Summer/Fall). https://contactquarterly.com/contact-improvisation/newsletter/view/starting-by-believing-maria.

Beaulieux, Michele. 2020. "Can't We Just Dance?: Not if We Want to Create Safer Brave Contact Improvisation Spaces." *CQ Contact Improvisation Newsletter* 45, no. 1 (Winter/Spring). https://contactquarterly.com/contact-improvisation/newsletter/#view=cant-we-just-dance.

Beaulieux, Michele. 2021. "Comment on Post Announcing Zoom Jam." Chicago Contact Improvisation Facebook page. https://www.facebook.com/groups/chicagocontactimprov/posts/4015001421897633/?comment_id=4015160195215089.

Beaulieux, Michele. 2022. "Can't We Just Dance? A Counterstory." *Reservoir of Hope*. http://reservoirofhope.home.blog/2019/10/10/cantwejustdance/.

Blackwell, A. G. 2016. "The Curb-Cut Effect." *Stanford Social Innovation Review*, 15, no. 1: 28–33. https://doi.org/10.48558/YVMS-CC96

Blagg, Robert D. 2023. "Bystander Effect: Diffusion of Responsibility." *Britannica*. https://www.britannica.com/topic/bystander-effect/Diffusion-of-responsibility.

58 Resistance and Support

Boal, Augusto. 2021. *Games for Actors and Non-Actors*. Milton Park, UK: Taylor & Francis.

Burke, Tarana. 2018. "Me Too Founder on the Path Forward after Harvey's Arrest." *Variety*, (May). https://variety.com/2018/film/opinion/harvey-weinstein-arrest-tarana-burke-column-120 2823662/.

carroll, rosemary. 2020. "Dialogue Recorded: White People, Consent, and Contact Improvisation." *Contact Quarterly*. https://contactquarterly.com/cq/rolling-edition/view/consent-and-cont act-improvisation-dialogue

Centola, Damon. 2021. *Change: How to Make Big Things Happen*. New York: Little, Brown Spark.

Chicago Contact Improvisation Jam. 2022. "Protocol for Responding to Harm." Chicago Contact Improvisation Jam. https://sites.google.com/site/chicagocontactimprov/about-the-jam/proto col-for-responding-to-harm.

Chicago Contact Improvisation Jam. 2022b. "Collective Governance." Chicago Contact Improvisation Jam. https://sites.google.com/site/chicagocontactimprov/about-the-jam/collect ive-governance

Chicago Contact Improvisation Jam. n.d. "Community Agreements & Values." Chicago Contact Improvisation Jam. Accessed July 5, 2024. https://sites.google.com/site/chicagocontactimprov/ about-the-jam/community-agreements-values

Chicago Contact Improvisation Jam. n.d.b "Jam Support." Chicago Contact Improvisation Jam. Accessed November 18, 2022. https://sites.google.com/site/chicagocontactimprov/about-the-jam/jam-support.

Cliff, Pervocracy. 2012. "Consent Culture." *The Pervocracy*. https://pervocracy.blogspot.com/ 2012/01/consent-culture.html?

Contact Improvisation Twin Cities. n.d. "About." CITC. Accessed October 10, 2022. https://www. citwincities.com/about-1.

Creative Interventions. 2021. *Creative Interventions Toolkit: A Practical Guide to Stop Interpersonal Violence*. Chicago: AK Press.

Critical Mass: CI @ 50. n.d. "Critical Mass: CI @ 50: Oberlin." Accessed April 18, 2023. https:// sites.google.com/oberlin.edu/criticalmassci50

Dancers' Group. 2018. "Contact Improvisers Consider #MeToo." *In Dance* (June), 5. https://dance rsgroup.org/2018/06/contact-improvisers-consider-metoo/.

Earthdance. n.d. "Equity and Access Initiatives." Accessed October 30, 2022. https://www.earthda nce.net/EquityandAccess.

Emerson, Megan. 2018. "The Stages of Consent Culture for Dance Communities." Google Docs. https://docs.google.com/document/d/1jqkWdUlDkhVOWd-wNxRf1wvvC3bIkKVlfI_ehB_ mksU/edit

End Violence Against Women International. n.d. "Start by Believing." Accessed October 28, 2022. https://startbybelieving.org/home/.

Freeman, Jo. "The Tyranny of Structurelessness." https://www.jofreeman.com/joreen/tyranny. htm. Accessed October 29, 2023.

Freyd, Jennifer J. 2022. "Institutional Betrayal Research Home Page." Freyd Dynamics Lab. https:// dynamic.uoregon.edu/jjf/institutionalbetrayal/index.html.

Frost, Karl. n.d. Karl Frost Transparency site. Accessed October 11, 2022. https://kftransparency.site/.

Gay, Roxane. 2015. "The Charge to Be Fair: Ta-Nehisi Coates and Roxane Gay in Conversation." *B&N Reads* (August). https://www.barnesandnoble.com/blog/the-charge-to-be-fair-ta-nehisi-coates-and-roxane-gay-in-conversation/.

Granovetter, Mark. 1978. "Threshold Models of Collective Behavior." *American Journal of Sociology* 83 (6): 1420–1443. http://www.jstor.org/stable/2778111.

Halkin, Daniel. 2021. "Untitled post, August 9, 2021." Chicago Contact Improvisation Facebook page. https://www.facebook.com/groups/chicagocontactimprov/posts/4510511915679912/.

Harrist, Cookie. 2019. "#MeToo DISRUPTION at the 2018 West Coast Contact Improvisation Jam." *Contact Quarterly* 44, no. 1 (Winter/Spring): 50.

Hirschman, Albert O. 1970. *Exit, Voice, and Loyalty.* Cambridge, MA: Harvard University Press.

Kaba, Mariame, and Shira Hassan. 2019. *Fumbling towards Repair: A Workbook for Community Accountability Facilitators.* N.p.: Project NIA.

Keogh, Martin. 2003. "101 Ways to Say No to Contact Improvisation: Boundaries and Trust." *Contact Quarterly* 28, no. 2 (Summer/Fall): 61–64.

Kim, Richard. 2020. "Write It Down! A Retrospective and Call to Action with Richard Kim." https://www.youtube.com/watch?v=DG6dBM8kh5w.

Kingwill, Amy. 2018. "Report on Community Meeting with Karl Frost." San Francisco Bay Area Contact Improvisation Facebook Group. https://www.facebook.com/groups/bayarea.ci/posts/10155024189262614

Koteen, David, and Nancy S. Smith. 2021. *Caught Falling: The Confluence of Contact Improvisation, Nancy Stark Smith, and Other Moving Ideas.* N.p.: Contact Editions.

Krug, E. G. et al., eds. 2002. "Violence: A Global Public Health Problem." *World Report on Violence and Health*, World Health Organization, 1–21. https://apps.who.int/iris/bitstream/handle/10665/42495/9241545615_eng.pdf

Lu, Christina. 2021. "Does America Need a Truth and Reconciliation Commission?" *Foreign Policy.* (April) https://foreignpolicy.com/2021/04/29/united-states-transitional-justice-truth-reconciliation-commission/.

Marx, Katherine, and Charlie Mosey. 1997. "Community Safety Report." *Contact Quarterly* 22, no. 2 (Summer/Fall): 75.

Nelson, Karen. 1994. "Dear CQ." *Contact Quarterly* 19, no. 1 (Winter/Spring): 76.

Novack, Cynthia J. 1990. *Sharing the Dance: Contact Improvisation and American Culture.* Madison: University of Wisconsin Press.

Philadelphia Thursday Jam. 2021. "Welcome Dancer!" https://www.cis.upenn.edu/~bcpierce/ci/WelcomeDocument.pdf.

Pierce, Benjamin. n.d. "Compendium of CI Guidelines from around the World." Accessed October 3, 2022. https://docs.google.com/document/d/1Os8c2ukZRS5cnJhJv0SuBX5MrpGKAMZk6U3i-Pbfezk/edit#heading=h.axpp7s2sk9zp.

Rea, Kathleen. 2019. "Twenty Years of Coming to Terms: Shifting from Disempowerment to Activism and Systemic Thinking." *Contact Improv Consent Culture.* https://contactimprovconsentculture.com/2019/08/11/twenty-years-of-coming-to-terms-shifting-from-disempowerment-to-activism-and-systemic-thinking/.

Rea, Kathleen. 2020. "Moving from Bystander to Action: How Communities Can Respond When Witnessing DARVO, Gaslighting and Other Abusive Tactics." *Contact Improv Consent Culture.* https://contactimprovconsentculture.com/2020/10/03/how-contact-improvisation-communities-can-move-from-bystander-to-action-when-witnessing-darvo-gaslighting-and-other-abusive-tactics/.

Rea, Kathleen. n.d. "RDD Dance Jams." *REAson d'etre dance.* Accessed November 22, 2022. https://reasondetre.com/downloads.

Russo, A. 2018. *Feminist Accountability: Disrupting Violence and Transforming Power*. New York: NYU Press.

Schaffer, Sarah. 2021. "Untitled, March 13, 2021." Chicago Contact Improvisation Facebook page. https://www.facebook.com/groups/chicagocontactimprov/posts/4076044615793313/.

Schaffer, Sarah. 2021b. "Untitled, September 7, 2021." Chicago Contact Improvisation Facebook Page. https://www.facebook.com/groups/chicagocontactimprov/posts/4597183207012782/.

Schaffer, Sarah, and Chicago Contact Improvisation. 2022. "Chicago CI Sunday Jam Virtual Town Hall." Facebook. https://www.facebook.com/events/1462405794209075/.

Sunday Ci Jam at Links Hall. 2022. "Untitled, September 24, 2022." Chicago Contact Improvisation Facebook page. https://www.facebook.com/groups/chicagocontactimprov/posts/5772046036193154/.

Verduzco-Baker, Lynn. 2018. "Modified Brave Spaces: Calling in Brave Instructors." *Sociology of Race and Ethnicity* 4, no. 4: 585–592. journals.sagepub.com/doi/full/10.1177/2332649218763696

Williams, Joyce E. 1999. "Secondary Victimization: Confronting Public Attitudes about Rape." *Victimology* 9, no. 1: 66–81.

Yardley, Brooks. 2017. "Respecting Boundaries/Coexisting Genders: A Zine about Women's Experiences of Feeling Unsafe in Contact Improv." *Contact Quarterly CI Newsletter* 42, no. 2 (Summer/Fall). https://contactquarterly.com/contact-improvisation/newsletter/index.php#view=respecting-boundaries-coexisting-genders.

3

Gender, Power, and Equity in Contact Improvisation

Kristin Horrigan

Introduction

A dancer perches on their partner's back, balanced on the side of their hip, their legs and arms slightly bent and floating in the air. Their body wafts a little bit one way and another, while their partner shifts beneath them to sustain the balance. The suspended dancer releases their spine, pours their weight toward their head, and rolls off their partner's back, nimbly catching the floor with first hands and then feet. As they descend, the under-dancer extends a leg, offering a surface for their partner to slide down, slowing their tumble toward the ground, maintaining connection. With this supportive leg, they nudge the fallen dancer into a roll and kneel on them to take a small hop. Twisting around the rolling point of contact, both dancers press into one another and rise to standing, walking and then running through the space—one beast with four legs. One dancer shifts behind the other, wraps their arms around their partner, and lifts.

One of the beauties of Contact Improvisation (CI) is that, in this scene, the dancers could be almost anyone—people of any gender, culture, race, class, age, sexual orientation, profession—anyone who is able-bodied in the ways the movement describes.[1] Some might even say that the dancers' identities do not matter: what matters is just what is happening between their two bodies in the rhythms of support and supporting, rising and falling, initiating and responding. And yet, as Robin Raven Prichard argues in Chapter 6, these dancers are not just neutral bodies. They have multiple intersecting identities—some visible and some invisible—and rich life histories that inform the ways they respond to the world around them.

Do these two dancers experience each other simply as bodies? Let us try a thought experiment and imagine for a moment that one dancer is a 24-year-old Indian, cisgendered, queer woman and the other is a 55-year-old white, German, cisgendered, straight man. What do these dancers experience of their own genders and their (projections of their) partner's genders as they dance? How are their movement choices shaped by the gendered, raced, aged, and other ways they've learned to take up space, organize their bodies, and respond to their environments? Do the dancers have to stretch far beyond the values they were raised with in order to roll on a dancer of a different gender, color, and culture? Does the woman take a feminist joy in lifting the man, rather than only being lifted by him? Does the man enjoy the opportunity to embody softness in a way he doesn't always feel allowed to inhabit? Do the young woman's experiences with older men and/or white people lead her to take a protective stance in the dance? Does the older white man unconsciously sexualize and/or exoticize the

---

[1] It is critical to note that Contact Improvisation does not require athletic movement and that anyone with the ability to move in some way can dance a version of CI.

Kristin Horrigan, *Gender, Power, and Equity in Contact Improvisation* In: *Resistance and Support*. Edited by: Ann Cooper Albright, Oxford University Press. © Oxford University Press 2024. DOI: 10.1093/9780197776308.003.0004

young, brown, female dancer? Does the male dancer do more than an equal share of initiating movement? Who lifts whom at the end of the duet? Does it mean something different if the male dancer turns the female dancer around and grabs her from behind for a lift than if she does the same to him? And what if the young Indian dancer is instead a transman? Does the cis-male dancer misgender him as female and project heteronormative dynamics onto him? Has the trans dancer been the recipient of violence perpetrated by cisgender men, and if so, is he able to relax into touch with this unknown cis-man?

This thought experiment shows some of the many ways that identity and identity-based power dynamics can enter into CI dancing. It illustrates how patterns of oppression from our larger society can affect dancers' movement choices, internal experience, and interactions with others. Moreover, it reveals the emotional labor that some dancers must expend to navigate these oppressive power dynamics on the dance floor.

Although we often treat them as such in CI, human beings and their bodies are not neutral, unmarked surfaces to roll upon. Our patterns of moving, relating to others, and inhabiting our bodies are deeply conditioned by our lived experience and embodied identities. We are socialized to respond to other people based on who we perceive them to be and what power we think they may hold—responses that are shaped by oppressive power dynamics such as sexism, homophobia, heteronormativity, transphobia, racism, ableism, xenophobia, ageism, and classism. Our responses are often not conscious, operating beneath the surface or at the level of reflex. A refusal to acknowledge that identity-based power dynamics exist will privilege those with more systemic power. Those with less systemic power may need to expend significant energy protecting themselves in CI.

This chapter argues that gendered power dynamics in CI negatively impact the experience of some dancers more than others, inequitably limiting access to full participation. To establish this claim, I first lay out many of the ways that gender and gendered power dynamics show up in CI dancing. I also identify aspects of CI that make it easy for dancers to replicate oppressive patterns from society. Together, these approaches illustrate the significant gap between inclusive ideals of CI and the exclusions that happen in practice—delineating the ways some dancers must work harder than others to navigate identity-based power dynamics when dancing CI. The chapter also identifies aspects of CI that help dancers resist replicating daily social hierarchies in their dancing and proposes a series of practices to begin working toward a more equitable and inclusive CI.

The writing that follows here addresses the CI community—not only dancers who already have an interest in gender's many roles in CI, but also those for whom it is new to think about gender, identity, and equity in dancing. It works to generate dialogue, deepen our collective understanding, and make the inner workings of gender- and identity-based limitations in CI more common knowledge among dancers, teachers, and organizers. It also serves as a call to CI dancers to use this knowledge to make change, both in their own dancing and in their communities.

Gender and Other Definitions

In this chapter, gender is defined as a socially constructed set of ideas about what behaviors and attitudes are expected of people based on their assigned sex—ideas that vary based on culture, age, class, and other aspects of identity. The number of genders recognized and the traits ascribed to each differ significantly across time and place, though for the past few centuries the European/colonial binary gender system of male and female has had broad influence around the world (O'Sullivan 2021). More recently, trans and nonbinary gender identities have been gaining wider recognition in many places where a binary concept of gender previously held precedence, (re-)opening the field of gender. This change is happening rapidly—though many would argue not rapidly enough—and it poses a significant learning curve for those raised to understand gender as binary, biological, and unchanging.

Gender is something we do (Butler 1990). It lives in the gestures, postures, fashion statements, and interactions that mark us as gendered in the eyes of others. In those daily choices and habits, we fit ourselves into (or align ourselves against) the systems of gender in the world around us. Since nearly all movement qualities, attitudes, and patterns are gender-coded in most societies, it is difficult to escape doing gender, especially when dancing.

Some other gender-related concepts that will be helpful in this chapter include: gender identity, gender expression, and gender socialization. *Gender identity* describes an individual's internal felt sense of their own gender, which may or may not align with societal expectations. *Gender expression* refers to the many ways gender is performed in the world—through gesture, posture, interactions, clothing choices, hairstyles, and so on. *Gender socialization* is the process by which a person is taught the prevailing beliefs about gender in their society and is given specific expectations for their own presumed gender (based on sex assigned at birth). The socialization process includes direct messages (e.g., "Boys don't cry!" or "Be a good young lady and smile") and indirect modeling by family members, teachers, friends, media, religion, education, sports training, and more.

Gender is a complex, multilayered, and multifaceted negotiation that we make throughout our lives. At minimum, there is the continual entanglement of our own gender identity and the ideas about gender put upon us from outside. The gender socialization we received in our youth is often particularly deeply embedded in our physicality, shaping the ways we organize our bodies, respond to our environment, and relate to the space around us. It can emerge in our improvisation even when these habits don't reflect our current gender identity. At the same time, our dance choices are shaped by our true felt-sense of our gender identity and the values, beliefs, postures, gestures, and relational dynamics that constitute it. This can happen subconsciously through the habits we have formed, or actively as we practice attributes we wish to reinforce.

As a child, I learned to be delicate, graceful, and small like my mother—making me easily pushed aside, crushed, or hurt. As a young adult with an emerging queer, feminist consciousness, I began to resist the physical patterns of delicacy that were so deeply embedded in me. I was troubled by the ways my movement and postures did not reflect my beliefs about women's capability or right to take up space. Over time, I learned new ways of being in my body that better aligned with my values. Beginning to dance CI was helpful, as I learned to push back, support weight, and calm my reflexive response to pain. I delighted in lifting my partners as an equal and knowing how to organize my body for strength and action. I carried this new empowered embodiment with me on and off the dance floor, but the old patterns still emerge at times. Even in dancing CI, I sometimes find myself folding in to take up less space, disconnecting from a body organized for power, or being crushed by a moment of unexpected weight.

We also vary our gender expression depending on the age, race, culture, or class of the people with whom we are interacting. For example, queer folks often act differently with other queer folks than they would in a group of cis-straight people—sharing in-group body

64 Resistance and Support

language, speech, and jokes, and perhaps relaxing some protective tension carried around non-queer folks. Similarly, one's gender expression with people of one's own race or culture may be different than one's gender expression around those of other races or cultures. At times, this "code-switching" can be a survival strategy. For those outside of dominant power structures, acting in ways that comfort those in power may be a pathway to safety or acceptance.

How many dancers need to code-switch to step into the CI spaces in your community? Do dancers have to shift their gender expression to the dominant racial, class, or cultural norms in the room to feel safe and welcome? Are minority-identity dancers who don't code-switch still seen to "belong"? Are dancers in your CI community given more or less opportunities to dance based on their conformity to prevailing (raced, classed, etc.) gender norms?

CI technique also creates its own norms of gender expression, adding another layer to the genders we carry in our bodies. For example, everyone in CI gives weight to their dance partners, even those whose gender expression normally involves hiding or denying that their body has weight. To bear weight and find stability, most CI dancers adopt wide stances, spreading their legs and extending their pelvis out behind them, even though a narrower stance is more consistent with some types of femininity and an upright posture more consistent with some racial, class, or religious norms. Practicing CI also requires some degree of softening and yielding that may be rejected in the day-to-day gender expression of some masculine folks, as well as some feminine and nonbinary folks who resist heteronormative scripts of femininity. Although we may not think of it in terms of gender, dancing CI involves expanding our range of movement qualities, postures, and relationships to others, and may include some ways of being that are outside our normal gender expression.

Are there ways the technique of CI shifts your gender expression and maybe even your sense of your own gender while you dance? Do you allow yourself to embody qualities of movement, postures, positions, or relationships to other genders that are excluded from or even contrary to your daily gender expression off the dance floor? Which aspects of your gender identity come out most strongly in CI and which recede? Do you have a CI gender that is different from your daily gender? (Similarly, one could ask if dancers have a tango gender, a ballet gender, or a hip hop gender. How much do dance techniques ask dancers to take on a particular notion of gender while dancing?) How much do you take on the gender embodiment of your CI teachers as part of CI technique? How much have CI originators Steve Paxton and Nancy Stark Smith's gender expressions permeated the movement conventions of CI?

We come into CI carrying the gender models we were taught and the gender identities we became, the genders we are trying on and the genders we are trying to exorcise, the genders of the dominant group and the genders of our subgroups, our daily gender and our "CI gender," genders we want to present and genders we want to contradict, the gendered embodiment of our CI teachers, and the various raced/classed/aged/cultured genders that correspond to the many aspects of our identity.

Before leaving this section on definitions, let us turn our attention to one more term: *intersectionality*. First coined by Kimberlé Crenshaw in 1989, the term *intersectionality* was originally used to highlight the interconnection between gender and race. Over time, it has expanded to encompass many more aspects of identity and their associated layers of privilege and oppression. White, Western, middle-class, cisgender scholars have long ignored the intersectional nature of gender, writing about gender in ways that fail to speak to the lives of those who do not share the writers' racial, class, or cisgender privilege. As a white, Western, middle-class, cisgender person, I too have fallen into this harmful pattern at times.

While this chapter does not take an entirely intersectional approach—equally centering race and gender—it holds an intersectional consciousness, considering how gender is interwoven with race, culture, class, age, sexual orientation, role in society, and ability/disability. It recognizes that there are multiple masculinities, femininities, queer, and nonbinary gender identities in each culture and context, and provides opportunities for the reader to consider how gender is constructed in their community. When there is a need to get specific about how gender manifests in movement, I offer examples from my own embodied experience and supply readers with questions and exercises to help them analyze their own.

In the spirit of intersectionality, let me take a moment to further situate my own voice. I have already stated that I am white, queer, cisgendered, small-bodied, middle class, socialized as female, and a CI dancer since early adulthood. To flesh out that description, I would add that I am female-identified, U.S. American, and teaching dance in a university. I have been dancing CI for 25 years, all of my adult life, and teaching CI for much of that time as well. Dancing and teaching have taken me many places across the United States and around the world. My understanding of CI is deeply informed by conversations and collaborations with friends of many identities beyond my own. At the same time, my views are also shaped by my particular set of lived experiences.

Situating CI's Relationship to Gender

In its core principles, CI rejects gender roles. And yet, as this chapter will demonstrate, in practice, ideas about gender influence and limit CI dancing in many ways. This tension between apparent gender freedom and actual gender limitation forms the context for studying gender in CI.

Wearing the long hair, T-shirts, and loose pants popular in U.S. counterculture of the time, dancers in the film CHUTE (filmed at the first performances of CI in New York's Weber Gallery in 1972) appear androgynous. In their dancing, they tumble and roll without distinguishing between genders—in rough collisions and falls, as well as intimate moments of sensing weight. Dancers with breasts roll under and over dancers with beards, supporting weight and being supported. Two dancers with beards dance slowly and sensitively, facing one another, hands lightly touching.

As Dena Davida highlights in Chapter 1, Contact Improvisation was quite gender-progressive for its time when it emerged in the 1970s, and it was celebrated for being one of the few partnered dance forms without prescribed gender roles. It echoed some of the (largely white, middle-class) feminist values gaining prominence in the United States in the 1960s and 1970s which promoted equality of the sexes, advocating for women to have the same rights and privileges as men. Although Steve Paxton's original experiments toward the creation of CI (e.g., *Magnesium* in 1971) included only men, once female-identified dancers such as Nancy Stark Smith and Nita Little convinced Paxton to open the experiments to women, they remained an integral part of the practice. Dating back at least to the Weber Gallery residency where Contact Improvisation was first presented, weight-bearing and risky movements (such as jumps, catches, and falls) were not limited by gender, and neither were pairings between dance partners.

66 Resistance and Support

About 10 years ago, I was teaching Contact Improvisation at a small college on a mountain in Vermont. For the first time, I had a substantial number of out trans and nonbinary students in my class. Several of them reflected to me that CI class offered the greatest space of gender freedom that they had ever encountered—a space without assigned gender roles or pressure to conform to them. This was possible in part because our class was a closed container, outside the larger world of CI, and like Guru Suraj and Adrianna Michalska in Chapter 16, I closed the space to sexual exploration. This context limited dynamics around partner-seeking that pervade many CI jam spaces and that draw attention to gender.

Arguably, CI is quite a queer (and nonbinary) proposition—queer in being outside heteronormative and cisgender dynamics (Hennessy 2019; Horrigan 2017; Papineau and Engelman 2019)—and tremendous possibility exists in the way CI allows us to play outside the gender lines of our societies. Through play, we practice new relationships to others and ourselves—a powerful process for expanding our ways of being in the world and dreaming into possible futures. Space exists within CI to make gender-affirming choices, enacting the qualities one wishes to claim for one's gender. Many find this healing and empowering, especially if their choices are outside of traditionally defined gender roles in their society. A female-identified dancer who has faced expectations to be delicate and fragile can cultivate strength and integration of her body. A male-identified dancer who has been denied the right to embody "feminine"-assigned qualities in daily life can explore sensing, listening, and gentleness. A nonbinary dancer can express the full bouquet of qualities they identify with, with less pressure than in daily life to fit into others' binary boxes. Anyone who chafes at the restrictions of heteronormative concepts of gender can move outside these lines.

However, in daily practice, gender norms and gendered power dynamics often do enter CI dancing, coming in on the wings of sexual desire and partner-seeking. This is especially true in the looser container of jam settings—as opposed to classes—for jams serve some people as social gatherings, and they are often very open spaces with little facilitation. Many dancers attend jams exclusively and rarely, if ever, go to CI classes. That said, jam settings are not the only place where gender dynamics enter CI. There are aspects of the physical practice of CI itself that invite in gender norms, power dynamics, and oppressive patterns.

Quick decision-making, visual apprehension of identity, the intimacy of bodily contact, and even the encouragement to follow our own interests are all aspects of CI that open the door to gendered patterns and power dynamics. When making instantaneous decisions, we cannot consciously choose every part of our bodily response, so we are forced to draw somewhat on habits and embodied patterns. Familiar ways of organizing our bodies—including the ways we express our gender, culture, race, and so on—come into the dance. As visual cues give us ideas about our partner's identity, social scripts about how to treat people—based on their gender, age, culture, race, and so on—can shape our choices about how much weight to give, whom to engage in a dance, and what dynamics of play are appropriate or desirable. This brings in relational power dynamics from our societies—patterns such as gender roles, sexism, heteropatriarchy, and homophobia—that we may propagate by habit even if we do not actively believe in them. And of course, since we often do not truly know each other's identities in CI, our reactions to others' identities are often projections. Within all of this, we are intimately close with other bodies, which for some awakens sexual desire and brings attention to gender. Additionally, many CI teachers, myself included, encourage dancers to notice and follow their interests moment-to-moment within the dance. While this practice cultivates presence, curiosity, and play, taken to its extreme, it can foster a kind of self-interest that disregards the needs and experience of others. Desires that reflect social roles, hierarchies, or power dynamics may be mapped onto other dancers without consideration for how they may be affected.

Fortunately, there are also aspects of CI that support us to work against repeating gendered patterns and oppressive power dynamics. The awareness we cultivate in CI helps us to sense both habitual pathways and new possibilities, and the ethos of CI encourages us to explore the unknown. Together, these aspects of CI give us tools to identify and move away from patterns that we bring into our dancing. The spirit of play in CI allows for the trying on of possibilities, the making and remaking of worlds. Contact Improvisation is also a deep practice of collaboration—one that invites trust and reciprocity and gives us a profound physical experience of our partners' humanity. We can build upon this care for one another to address the ways our patterns and social scripts oppress one another. CI gives us practice in working across difference, finding points of connection, and listening to one another. Reciprocity—mutually beneficial exchange of support—in CI is not only a kindness, but also a necessary technical skill. Through some new forms of reciprocity, we may act in greater solidarity with one another, reducing the ways we unintentionally limit one another's dancing.

The above paradoxes are the context in which the rest of this chapter unfolds. Contact Improvisation offers tremendous freedom from the constraints of gender, and at the same time, it often replicates gendered patterns and power dynamics from daily life. CI dancing contains both mechanisms that bring in gender dynamics and tools for resisting these habits and patterns.

I invite you to join me embracing the painful aspects of CI along with the joys, denying neither, holding complexity with generosity. Let us cultivate the skills to better acknowledge the power dynamics in our spaces, listen to each other's experiences, and develop personal and community solidarity practices. And may we be mindful of our own potential to wander into self-interest that fails to account for others' experiences.

Gender Habits Limit CI Technique

Most constructions of gender are inherently limiting, and practicing a set of limitations in our CI dancing, especially if we're doing so unknowingly, can have a negative effect—both on ourselves and on those we dance with. This is especially true because CI is a dance that values openness to possibility.

The habits of gender limit many dancers' CI technique. Coming into CI, each person has more practice with some of the needed skills: those that are already part of their gender expression and other intersectional aspects of their identity, and those shaped by their past movement activities. Likewise, they have less practice with skills that have not been part of their previous movement patterns. Of course, in learning CI, each person works to build those skills that are less familiar to them. Nonetheless, often significant gaps remain unnoticed, dramatically limiting an individual's possibilities in their CI dancing. Gender-related habits are one of the factors that shape those unseen limitations.

A few years into studying the embodiment of gender, I noticed that when supporting my partner's full weight in CI, I often felt like an object or a piece of furniture—I would brace my body and wait for my partner to finish their dance on top of me. I also noticed that I felt like an object while being lifted, waiting for my partner to decide when to put me down. Iris Marion Young's article "Throwing like a Girl" (1980) was very helpful to me in thinking about my lack of agency in these moments. She wrote about the way women in her time and place (white, Western, middle-class society of the 1970s–1980s) were treated more as objects to be viewed or acted upon than subjects with agency to act in the world. As a product of the time and culture she wrote about, I found that my physical experience resonated deeply with many of her ideas about "feminine" embodiment in this patriarchal society. Although I do not embrace "objecthood" as part of my gender identity, I saw myself behaving as an object to be acted upon. Wishing to find more of a sense of subjecthood in lifting and being lifted, I gave myself the score of keeping some motion in my body while supporting or being supported. This opened new opportunities in my dancing and improved my facility with this part of CI technique.

As a teacher of CI, I'm now more aware of the ways that gender socialization may be limiting my students. A person socialized to treat their body as a collection of parts to be sexualized and evaluated—as many female-socialized folks are—may have difficulty organizing their body into one unit for action. This limits their ability to launch into and roll through lifts. I can help such dancers by including exercises and images that help integrate their bodies before teaching bigger lofts and rolls. In another example, a person expected to lead because of their gender may bring strong skills in initiating movement, but find that (at least initially) they're not as skilled in sensing what their partner is wanting and following where their shared dance is going. For such dancers, I might include more work on embodied consent practices, teaching skills for checking-in nonverbally about how much weight is okay or whether a lift is desired.

Individual dancers can also interrogate their relationship to gender as part of developing their CI technique. While gender theorists can offer insight into some patterns of gender performance in a particular culture, each person's lived experiences and intersectional identities make their experience of gender unique. A teacher may be able to address some of the technical limitations in your dancing, but there's a layer to unwinding gendered embodiment that you must do for yourself. To shift gendered patterns in your own technique, you can observe yourself, reflect on your patterns of movement and interaction, and consider what ideas and attitudes have shaped those patterns. Then you can create strategies to help you shift your habits. Facilitated practices of introspection and exploration can provide community support to this process. Embarking on this work in community also raises the collective level of awareness about gender expression, gender oppression, and gendered power dynamics, allows a platform for people to share their stories, and invites greater understanding and solidarity between dancers.

These questions and exercises can help you discover how you embody and express gender: What qualities are valued in "men," "women," and other genders in the society where you live now? What gendered expectations were placed on your behavior, posture, capabilities, preferences, desires, fears, and relationships with others when you were growing up? Can you identify specific ways that these expectations shaped the ways you stand, sit, occupy space, handle objects, navigate social situations, or assess what you can or cannot do?

Try an experiment. Move your body (any dancing or simple action will do) and then exaggerate gender. Add more femininity for a few minutes—or I should say, femininities, as there are many ways to be feminine!—then more masculinities, then more queerness. Notice what changes in your movement each time, and then articulate the embodied ideas about gender and gender stereotypes that emerge.

Which ways of moving feel familiar? And do the familiar patterns resonate with your present sense of gender? Or with gender ideals that you learned in the past? This solo dance experiment can be very helpful in finding your own set of gender patterns to address in your CI dancing.

Creating "secret scores" for our dancing is a way we can re-pattern our movement choices. A "secret score" is a set of rules or guidelines for improvisation that you can practice in a jam setting without needing to tell others. Using scores to shift our habits is an extension of the re-patterning of instincts and reflexes we all go through in learning to dance CI. For example, as beginning CI dancers, we learned to embrace disorientation and to quiet the righting reflex that seeks to pull our heads back to vertical. We learned how to roll across bodies as surfaces while still maintaining some social boundaries (e.g., keeping our fingers out of others' ears/mouths). We can retrain around gendered patterns of embodiment as well, as in the example at the beginning of this section, where I created a score to shift my pattern of acting like an object when lifting or being lifted.

After doing the self-analysis exercise above, set a secret score that subverts one of the gendered embodiment patterns you noticed in yourself. Observe yourself so that you can notice when the pattern is occurring or about to occur. Decide how you'll respond. Will you replace the old pattern with a new pattern? Will you direct yourself away from the old pattern each time it arises, turning toward new possibilities?

Gendered Dynamics Limit Others' Dancing

Gendered patterns of action and behavior not only limit our own dancing, but also can limit the dancing of those we partner with. Those on the low end of power imbalances are likely to be most negatively affected. This section explores how what we offer to a dance partner and what we expect of them can be conditioned by ideas about our own gender and about our dance partners' genders.

Shared language for thinking about the intersection of gender identities and power will be helpful in exploring these arguments further. *Heteronormativity* is a point of view that assumes heterosexuality as a given, instead of one of many possibilities. Implicit in this ideological system is a binary construction of gender, which is strictly linked to biological sex. Transgender, gender fluid, genderqueer, gay, bisexual, pansexual, asexual, and intersex folks are all "othered" within this understanding of the world. *Cisgender* describes people whose gender corresponds to their biological sex, while *transgender* describes people whose gender is different from their sex as assigned at birth. Homophobia and transphobia are other structures that function to maintain the dominance of heteronormativity. The term *homophobia* describes a range of negative, adverse, and/or hostile reactions to homosexuality and/or gay/lesbian/bisexual/pansexual people. *Transphobia* describes negative thoughts or feelings or discriminatory actions toward transgender people and others who do not occupy binary gender roles. *Patriarchy* (and its close relative, sexism) is a system which places men in power over all others. Through the lens of patriarchy, men are viewed as natural leaders, their points of view are given more weight than those of other genders, and they are entrusted with greater decision-making power over their communities.

One of the first ways we respond to other dancers in CI jams and classes is deciding whom to dance with. While sometimes we select dance partners based on proximity or movement style, other times we may be influenced by dancers' (perceived) identity and

70 Resistance and Support

our attendant ideas about their desirability as a dance partner. In the most obvious example, some dancers are drawn to dancing with those of the gender, age, and body type they find attractive. At the least, this brings a focus on gender into the dancing, and at the worst it brings objectification, inappropriate sexual touching, or other sexual misconduct. Some are also drawn to particular genders (or races, ages, etc.) based on assumptions about ability or what kind of dance will be offered. Conversely, some dancers avoid those whom they perceive as different or undesirable. Older friends, especially women, have talked with me about feeling passed over on the dance floor, and then hearing surprise from dance partners when they are discovered to be more capable than expected. Some older men have reflected to me that they have been seen as predatory for dancing with younger women, even when they do not bring sexual intent to the dancing. A dark-skinned Black male friend observed to me that people at majority-white jams often avoid partnering with him. Gay male friends have noted that many male-identified dancers avoid them on the dance floor. And some trans dancers have reflected to me similar patterns of avoidance when in spaces dominated by cisgender dancers. At least some of the time, these aversions to difference are likely informed by patterns of sexism, ageism, racism, homophobia, and transphobia.

In writing about the 2007 Freiburg Festival, Andreas Hechler observed, "Even at the blind jam—which offers the possibility to get in contact with dancers one might otherwise not get in contact with—many contacters first touched each other's hair to find out the gender of their counterpart. Men suddenly touching a bald head dropped back. . . ." (Hechler 2007). Heteronormative partner choices (and homophobic responses to same-gender partnerings) are part of what make CI spaces less accessible for those who do not identify with binary genders and heteronormative gender roles.

For straight folks—Do you avoid partners of the same gender out of fear of how your dance will be perceived, either by your partner or by others in the room? If you have a slow, sensual dance with someone of the same gender, do you worry that you will be perceived as gay, or that your partner will think you are making sexual advances?

For queer folks—Do you avoid partners who are likely to perceive your dance as a heterosexual pairing? If you partner with someone who sees themselves as "the opposite" gender, are you concerned that they will try to get you to enact heteronormative gender roles?

Another way we respond to identity in CI is in deciding *how* we will dance with a given person—how much weight we will give, how much trust we will offer, what roles we will take in the dance, and what forms of play we will engage. While it is possible to determine these things through the dancing itself, sometimes people make assumptions about their partner's strengths, interests, or abilities before the dance even begins. Based on these assumptions, dancers offer different kinds of dances to different people.

For a simple example, consider Hechler's (2007) further observations from the Freiburg Festival: "(heterosexual) men seem to dance differently according to the gender of their partner—sensual and sensitive with a woman, rather technical with a man." Here Hechler observed that some men change the style of dance they offered their partner based on their perception of that partner's gender. Furthermore, Hechler proposes that these male dancers' heterosexuality shaped their dance style, following desires to create sensual intimacy with female dancers, while focusing purely on dance technique with men. The patterns that Hechler observed may be operating consciously or unconsciously, and they are likely informed by a range of desires and fears—sexual desire, desire for homosocial bonding, fear of

Gender, Power, and Equity in Contact Improvisation **71**

being perceived as having homosexual desire or intent, fear of hurting a (presumed) weaker partner, and so on.

I have used the following exercise to help dancers access a physical experience of their own reactions to a partner's identity:

> *Begin a dance with a new partner. As you dance, observe what choices you are making and what choices your partner is making. Notice patterns in who initiates lifts, who shifts the tempo or style of the dance, who manipulates or directs, who accepts or rejects, and so on. Ask yourself what you feel willing to offer this partner and what (if anything) you are avoiding offering. Tune in to the energy between you and think about how you would describe it. Is it relaxed, charged, tense, playful, warm, cool, flirtatious, bored, competitive, sensuous?*
>
> *Now, pause your dancing and, staying in contact with your partner, envision your partner with a new identity—a different gender, and perhaps a different sexual orientation, race, or age. Be very clear and specific in imagining this new identity. Resume dancing while imagining your partner in this new way. Observe if your physical impulses or attitudes in the dance shift in response to this new identity. Do you offer any new opportunities? Do you feel more or less safe? Does the energy in the dance shift?*

In my experience teaching this exercise, not everyone is able to effectively imagine a new identity for their partner (or convince their bodies of that new reality), but for those who can adopt the illusion, many interesting discoveries emerge. For example, practicing this exercise once while teaching, I experienced that I was much more guarded and resistant to being lifted in my initial dance with a partner I perceived to be a young cis-male, than in the second round, when I imagined my partner to be a butch lesbian.

Assessing our partners' identities in a CI jam or class is often an act of projection, which adds further complication. Nonverbal cues such as hair color and texture, skin color and texture, clothing style and condition, personal grooming choices (hair styles, makeup, shaving patterns, body odors/scents), movement facility and limitations, posture, body shape, and social behaviors shape our impressions about a dancer's age, gender, race, class, sexual orientation, and so on. However, without talking to someone about the subject explicitly, we can't be sure that we know their identity, including their gender. Gender identity cannot be reliably apprehended based on secondary sex characteristics (breasts, facial hair, etc.) and gender expression (clothing, hairstyle, posture, etc.), as this approach risks excluding trans and nonbinary dancers, as well as cisgender folks who do not conform to gender norms. For example, not all dancers with breasts identify as female, and not all people who identify as female have breasts. A person with a beard may wear a dress, and that person may be a transwoman, a person with a nonbinary gender, or a simply a cisgender man wearing a dress.

Gender projection can easily lead to misgendering. One of the most common modes of misgendering involves projecting heteronormative interpersonal dynamics and cisgender identity onto dancers who are queer. However, cis-straight people can be misgendered as well, if they are placed into roles that don't suit their particular masculine or feminine gender identity.

One common heteronormative dynamic in CI projects binary gender onto those seen as "women" through manipulation and control, replicating a "doer" and "done to" sexual dynamic. In this pattern, heterosexual male-identified dancers repeatedly lift, lower, and steer "female" dancers, whether or not their partner is cooperating with these changes of direction.

72 Resistance and Support

While some dancers enjoy this gendered dynamic, many feel frustrated and/or angered by it—resenting the control over their bodies, the limitations placed on the dance, and/or the gender role they're being placed in. For some, this is also a misgendering because they either don't identify as female (they are nonbinary or trans), or they don't identify with this model of heteronormative femininity.[2]

For another example, a dancer (of any gender) may perceive that their partner has a beard, decide they are male, and therefore assume they are interested in a rowdy, athletic dance. This assumption limits the range of the dance and may be harmful if the dancer in question is (a) not male-identified (and experiences the boisterous dancing as a misgendering); (b) not interested in a muscular, athletic dance at the moment (whether or not they identify as male); and/or (c) frustrated at having a heteronormative concept of gender projected onto them. The above assumptions are sometimes further shaded by racial stereotypes, ageism, or ableism. Few people enjoy being misidentified or stereotyped, and these actions are especially harmful to people whose identities are regularly threatened, erased, or vilified.

A score to resist projection: Leading a warm-up for the annual jam in Burlington, Vermont one year, I was asked by the organizers to embrace their theme, which said in part: "All bodies are part of the whole. All bodies hold stories. Listen." At the start of the jam, I asked the dancers to alternate between stillness and moving slowly. I then invited pairs to create a point of contact between a moving dancer and a still dancer with an "asking" level of pressure. The still dancer had the choice of whether or not to "answer" this pressure. If they did answer by pushing back into the touch, the two could begin a short, slow duet. I encouraged them to repeat the asking and answering pattern moment-to-moment, as a way to stay curious and to avoid diving into habitual patterns or assumptions. Tying into the theme, I urged the dancers not to assume that they know the story this person holds—based either on their appearance or on past experiences—and to be open to "hearing" the range of stories present in the jam today. For at least a few minutes, held in the inclusive container of the organizers' theme and the structured curiosity of the warm-up, people showed a broad willingness to meet one another across dimensions of difference—in ways that stretched beyond the dynamics of partner selection and identity-informed engagement that often dominate a recreational jamming space.

When we become more aware of our propensity to make identity-based assumptions and project stereotypes, we take a step toward making the shifts in behavior that can foster a more equitable and inclusive environment in CI. These assumptions and projections are some of the key mechanisms through which societal oppressions are enacted in CI, and some of the less obvious. Uncovering our own patterns in responding to dancers of different identities requires significant personal reflection, and communities of CI dancers can work together to support one another in the reflection process.

As this section demonstrates, everyone can be negatively affected by gendered power dynamics, but those more likely to be misgendered or excluded from dancing are most affected. For queer and/or trans dancers, it can be especially invisibilizing, exhausting, triggering, or otherwise unwelcoming to be misgendered, touched with unwelcome (hetero)sexual intent, or placed into heteronormative roles on the dance floor. Concerns about homophobic or transphobic interactions increase the risk that queer folks must undertake when entering into touch with strangers. The fact that gender assumptions in CI are often based on visual apprehension

---

[2] It is worth noting that dancers of any gender or sexuality may enjoy the power play of lead/follow or active/passive dynamics, without the constraint of the presumptive gender roles in the above example.

can be further off-putting and anxiety-provoking for trans or nonbinary folks, particularly in a space dominated by cisgender and heterosexual dancers. Furthermore, unintentional micro-aggressions in a class, opening circle, or even casual conversation affect the degree to which queer and trans folks feel welcome in the space—for example, use of binary gender language to address the group, assumption of a person's gender based on bodily characteristics, or even references to birth/infancy/developmental movement (the time when trans folks were first misgendered). Even casual conversations about partnerships or "jam crushes" that assume heterosexuality can be alienating. Those perceived as women also experience gender discrimination, in and out of CI. As the artists of EPIICO explore in Chapter 15, while CI as a dance form does not espouse hierarchical gender roles, patriarchal ideas absorbed throughout our lives can manifest in our dancing and in our management of our CI communities.

Objectification and Sexual Predation in CI

Some people take advantage of the physically intimate dancing in CI to pursue sexual desires nonconsensually—objectifying, soliciting, and sometimes assaulting other dancers. This behavior can be a side effect of dancers following their interests and desires, as we are taught to do in CI. However, even if sexual boundary-crossing is unconscious or unintentional, that does not diminish the negative impact it has on those affected.

Objectification can take the form of unwanted comments on appearance, partner selection based in desire to touch someone's body, overemphasis on sexualized body parts in the dancing, ogling dancers' bodies, or gratuitous stroking, squeezing, or fondling during a dance. Any dancer can objectify any other dancer whom they find attractive or whom they fetishize for some reason—gender, race, culture, ability. Objectification is not limited to heterosexual folks, and unwanted objectifying attention can make the dance space quite unwelcoming for any recipient. However, a great deal of the objectification that happens in CI spaces is directed at people perceived as female, especially those who are young and who fit conventional heteronormative beauty standards.

Zara Hannaford writes poignantly about her experiences with heteronormative objectification:

> When I dance, . . . I can truly find a place of single-minded focus, of extreme awareness of life and sensation and of beingness. It is a feeling that transmutes into a reciprocal feeling of flow and mutual connection to the moment when I dance with another. These feelings, I know now, are permeable to thievery in the form of the man who stands, as if on the sidelines of a match, as if greedily watching a performance that isn't for him. This moment, which would have previously been reserved for my own self to relish the stoppage of time, the ease of clean breath, or to practice speaking in the one-of-a-kind language that can only be spoken in the space between two bodies meeting, these moments, are dulled for the influx of uncalled-for attention. This man is not one man, but is the amalgamated creation of every man who has ever stood there, languid in his contentment to watch without listening, to gaze without seeing. His feet are still, wide apart and planted in unapologetic certainty that his belonging is decided, his position is sure and this looking is just fine. If he could see, if I could make him see, he would note with chagrin the selfishness of his incursion, and he would turn his gaze down and away. (cited in Yardley 2016, 37)

The man in this story objectifies the female dancer by persistently studying her body as she dances, failing to recognize that the pleasure he takes is not freely given and that his gaze negatively affects the dancer's ability to be present in her dance.

Unsurprisingly, objectification often includes or leads to sexual boundary-crossing. Touch that sexualizes a dance partner's body or that seeks sexual pleasure from a dancer's body without their permission violates the trust central to Contact Improvisation. While there are contexts in which people are experimenting with deliberately welcoming sexual touch into Contact Improvisation (e.g., Touch and Play festivals, and Aramo Olaya's XCI described in Chapter 11), in most CI classes and jams, a shared agreement to not pursue sexual intent is foundational to allowing for full-body contact. The fact that this agreement is often tacit rather than explicit is certainly problematic. Similarly, the complete exclusion of sexuality from CI is unrealistic, given the way physical intimacy inevitably brings up attraction/arousal in some moments. Nonetheless, it is taken as a foundational premise here that CI dancers have a right to not be sexually engaged without consent.

Sexual boundary-crossing disproportionately affects those perceived as female, limiting their ability to dance without vigilance against sexual predation. As Kathleen Rea notes, "When a young lady comes into the room for her first jam, there is sometimes a lineup of men ready to try her out and throw her around or see how far she will go in terms of sensual expression" (2017, n.p.). Similarly, the 2016 Montreal-based zine *Respecting Boundaries/ Co-existing Genders* relates a disturbing array of stories of men inappropriately stroking, fondling, or kissing those perceived as women in CI, and even pushing them into sexual positions to observe their breasts and crotches. While clearly outside the project of Contact Improvisation, such behavior is not particularly surprising given the heteronormative trope that eroticizes "taking" and "being taken"—romanticizing nonconsensual touch as a script of seduction. Also, as Vivek Patel points out, those with privilege often receive the implicit message that they do not have to honor (or even listen for) the consent of those "below" them in social hierarchy (2020). This dynamic can play out heteronormatively between those who identify as men and those who are perceived as women, along racist lines between (in a U.S. context) those who are white and those who are non-white, along ableist lines between those who are able-bodied and those with disabilities—disproportionately affecting those with multiple unprivileged intersecting identities.

Sexual predation is a well-documented problem throughout the history of Contact Improvisation. For his 2020 talk at the online Consent Culture in CI Symposium, Richard Kim reviewed decades of published accounts of sexual misconduct in CI (2020a). His video lecture and extensive bibliography are available online, and while his research is limited to resources he could find available in English, it indicates a clear pattern (Kim 2020a, b). Even Steve Paxton, who had often avoided making pronouncements about what CI is or is not, took a stand on this issue. In a 1996 *Contact Quarterly* article, he shared that although he was not closed to sexuality in CI, "anyone using CI to cruise is a predator, and the prey-predator relationship is not CI" (51).

Male dancers may not realize that dancers perceived as female—particularly young dancers—often navigate unwanted sexual energy, dynamics, and touch on a daily basis in CI. Even if one is lucky enough to avoid blatantly abusive touch, the extra petting, attempts to cuddle, unasked-for backrubs and CI "lessons," and the icky feeling of someone taking pleasure in your body without permission take a toll over time. Managing or avoiding these encounters takes energy and attention away from dancing.

Sexual predation creates inequitable conditions for dancers assumed to be female and limits who participates in CI. Additionally, those who already feel uncertain or unsafe in a CI setting because of class, race, sexual orientation, culture, age, or ability are made to feel even more unwelcome when their dancing is co-opted by a sexual predator. The degree to which sexual predation limits who participates in CI is difficult to quantify because it is counted in the bodies of all the dancers who choose to never return to CI jams and classes.

A number of dynamics in CI and CI culture create the conditions that allow sexual misconduct to continue. As Robin Raven Prichard argues in Chapter 6, dancers can have a hard time recognizing and speaking up about sexual misconduct in Contact Improvisation, because sexuality is "not supposed to be there." In this way, the framing of Contact Improvisation as non-sexual does a disservice to those on the receiving end of unwanted sexual energy. Rythea Lee points out that trauma histories can further limit a person's ability to assert boundaries against sexual predation in CI, as some develop a "freezing" or "fawning" reaction when confronted with a potential aggressor—responding to unwanted sexual advances by shutting down or by acting in ways that attempt to soothe those with the power to harm them (2020). And of course, the idea that is the receiver's job to resist unwanted sexual attention is in itself heteronormative and inequitable. Michele Beaulieux shows that this idea is deeply ingrained in Contact Improvisation through highlighting the "first rule"—the idea that contact improvisers must take responsibility for themselves before others (2019). Many are beginning to question this premise, as it privileges those who have little reason to fear transgression to dance as they please and leaves those whose boundaries are often transgressed to dance defensively.

Sexual predation is perpetrated by individuals, but communities can take action to intervene and help prevent violations and to hold accountable those who enact sexually inappropriate behavior. As explained more fully by Michele Beaulieux in Chapter 2, many communities have instituted jam guidelines to communicate clearly that nonconsensual sexual advances and touch are unwelcome in the dance space. However, these guidelines hold little power if they are not paired with practices of accountability (Beaulieux 2022). Having a care team who can listen to those who have experienced unwanted sexual attention and who support processes of harm repair is a helpful first step, especially when paired with second-level approaches such as skilled support for more serious violations and an accountability process for perpetrators.

Another step that teachers and community organizers can take to help reduce sexual boundary crossing in CI is to teach and advocate for more embodied consent practices in dancing. This means going beyond the take-care-of-yourself-first approach, which focuses on skills like dancing defensively, avoiding unwanted touch, communicating "no" with one's body, and getting out of undesirable situations. All dancers can learn better how to ask for consent moment-to-moment in the dance through movement—and also verbally when needed—and listen for the answers. As teachers and dancers, we can normalize asking nonverbally for consent in weight sharing, lifting, jumping/catching, and other deeply physical interactions—for example, pressing in slowly and waiting to see if your dance partner meets your weight before giving more, and repeating this a number of times at the start of a dance to give your partner a chance to show how much weight they want to take. These kinds of strategies distribute the responsibility for minding everyone's boundaries, rather than burdening only those who feel they need to protect themselves on the dance floor. For all the reasons shared in this chapter, many dancers would like to know that the privilege to touch,

76 Resistance and Support

give weight, or lift, will be asked for rather than assumed and that "no" will be an acceptable answer.

Gender, Self-Protection, and Access in CI

A number of dancers find their access to CI impeded by the amount of effort it takes to protect themselves from identity-based power dynamics on the dance floor—including misgendering, objectification, stereotyping, sexual misconduct, and bias. Avoiding and mitigating experiences of these power dynamics are active processes that take energy and focus away from dancing. In this way, CI spaces are more dangerous and exhausting for some dancers than others. As Royona Mitra so clearly asserts, "In reality . . . not everyone can improvise freely without the fear of how power might enact on and harm our bodies in and through our CI partner's relational social positionings" (2021, 10).

As we think about ways to decrease identity-based oppression in CI, it is also important to remember that some patterns of identity-based response in CI are needed for self-protection, and asking dancers who carry such protective patterns to set them aside may in fact make CI less accessible to them. There is no responsibility for those facing systemic oppression to fully relinquish their caution around those with privilege and power. For example, a transwoman may avoid cisgender dancers if she has experienced transphobic violence at the hands of cis folks in the past. A small AFAB (assigned female at birth) nonbinary dancer may be especially cautious around large cis-men, as she/they have experienced that men do not always take "no" for an answer and that those with greater muscular strength have the power to force their desires on the dance. A Black man may be wary of dancing with white women (at least in the U.S.) given the violent history of false accusations that have often made such contact unsafe for Black men.

A practice of solidarity: Consider how your presence might affect those around you in the space. Whose identity might feel empowered or supported by your presence? Who might experience your identity as a threat?

Is your identity in a position of power relative to some others in the space? How might that power dynamic affect consent in your dances? How is the work of self-protection inequitably distributed in your CI spaces? If you are doing less work than others, how could you step up to disrupt harmful dynamics or modulate your own presence to require less protective behavior from others?

An example: A dancer who, at that time, identified as a straight cis-man showed up as an ally to a queer-centered CI class/jam that I was helping to facilitate. They reflected that they felt a heightened awareness of the amount of physical space that their bold and energetic dancing can take up and how privileged they are to feel safe initiating dances. In the queer-centered space, they actively modulated these aspects of their dancing, choosing to scale back the "volume" of their presence in the space and letting others approach if they desired.

Gathering by identity group—especially in affinity spaces exclusively for members of that group—can lower the amount of attention devoted to self-protection and to increase ingroup solidarity. With regard to gender, there have been an increasing number of CI events specifically for queer folks and/or women in the United States and Europe, in Mexico (as described in Chapter 15), and beyond. These spaces can reduce the power dynamics around gender in the room and allow dancers to devote more of their mental and physical energy toward their practice of CI, particularly when the spaces are closed containers (exclusive of allies). In the United States, more multi-day jams and festivals are including queer and/or BIPOC affinity spaces as part of their events. A number of communities also have ongoing affinity jams. For example, at the time of this writing, there is a bi-weekly queer CI jam in Amsterdam, a bi-weekly BIPOC jam in Berkley, California, and a monthly BIPOC jam in New York City.

Conclusion: Carving New Pathways

Contact Improvisation is a richer and more varied practice because of the differences among us. The diversity of our individual characteristics allows for a great range of dances to emerge. One of the most beautiful aspects of dancing CI is that it offers us the opportunity to build reciprocal connections with a wide range of people, finding ways to connect with and support each other. To fully embrace this beauty, we need to make space for a wide range of people to be present.

As the interventions sprinkled throughout this chapter demonstrate, there is much we can do as individuals, teachers, communities, and organizers to change gender-based limiting patterns and reduce their power to exclude. Individuals and lab groups can undertake self-reflection, beginning with some of the practices and exercises shared here. As they build self-awareness, they can create scores to shift their patterns. Teachers can include exercises that help students retrain their social impulses in ways that counteract the oppressive dynamics we carry into the space—sexism, racism, ageism, and so on. We can retrain habits of mind, just as we do habits of the body. Teachers can also develop their pedagogy around embodied consent practices and include such practices regularly in classes and jam warm-ups. Organizers can support care teams, accountability processes, and affinity spaces, and have conversations in their own communities to locate the particular dynamics of exclusion operating within the intersectional identities of their area. We can all normalize learning about the range of identity-based needs in our CI communities and responding collectively to them.

While embracing the potential for growth in CI, we can also support artists who are imagining new containers for dancing that address some of the shortcomings of CI. For example, Andrew Suseno has instigated the creation of Moving Rasa, a BIPOC-centered, site-specific, inclusive, and cooperative improvisational movement practice that draws on some practices from Contact Improvisation. mayfield brooks's body of work, Improvising While Black, uses improvisational dance practices—including some from CI— as resistance to systems of anti-Blackness and settler-colonial logic and a way of dreaming new futures (2016). Aramo Oloya's XCI, described in Chapter 11 of this book, repurposes aspects of CI in a new dance practice that explores queer sexuality.

Envisioning possible futures, we can take some inspiration from Sara Ahmed's metaphorical use of the concept of "desire lines":

[I]n landscape architecture they use the term "desire lines" to describe unofficial paths, those marks left on the ground that show everyday comings and goings, where people deviate from the paths they are supposed to follow. Deviation leaves its own marks on the ground, which can even help generate alternative lines, which cross the ground in unexpected ways. (2006, 19–20)

78 Resistance and Support

Although Ahmed uses this concept to talk about the new life paths carved by living as a lesbian, the metaphor of desire lines could easily be applied to the ways our desires shape the paths of action we follow in CI. This chapter has laid out how gendered habits and (hetero) sexual desires have carved deep lines into the practice of this ungendered, not-explicitly-sexual dance form. And yet with awareness, desire for change, and conscious action, Contact dancers, teachers, and organizers can create new lines. Each time we make a specifically anti-patriarchal, anti-heteronormative, anti-racist, anti-classist, and/or anti-ableist action or policy, we carve a new path toward a more accessible and equitable practice of CI. As individuals and communities, we have the power to cultivate new habits, new ways of relating, new forms and containers for dancing, new structures of support, care, and accountability. As more and more feet (and wheels!) travel the new paths we lay, those paths grow wider, drawing traffic from the old, well-worn routes.

Descending from the lift, one dancer's arms release the other's center and the two spiral away from one another. Will the dance continue or end?

The dancers choose to approach one another again. When their shoulders meet, they press into one another for a long, sustained moment, a stillness alive with sensation and possibility. Will they slip back into the patterns of what came before, or co-create something new?

References

Ahmed, Sara. 2006. *Queer Phenomenology: Orientations, Objects, Others.* Durham, NC: Duke University Press.

B., Lori, and Steve Paxton. 1996. "The Sex Issue." *Contact Quarterly* 21(1): 43–51.

Beaulieux, Michele. 2019. "How the First Rule Brought #metoo to Contact Improvisation." *Contact Quarterly* 44(1): 46–50.

Beaulieux, Michele. 2020. "The Beaulieu Tools for Creating Safer Brave Spaces." *Reservoir of Hope.* Revised October 31, 2022. https://reservoirofhope.home.blog/2019/10/01/beaulieu-test/.

brooks, mayfield. 2016. "IWB = Improvising While Black: Writings, Interventions, Interruptions, Questions." *Contact Quarterly* 41(1): 33–39.

Butler, Judith. 1990. *Gender Trouble: Feminism and the Subversion of Identity.* New York: Routledge.

Chute. 1979. Script/narration by Steve Paxton. Editing by Steve Christiansen, Lisa Nelson, Steve Paxton, and Nancy Stark Smith. Videoda. https://contactquarterly.com/ contact-editions/index.php?fbclid= IwZXh0bgNhZW0CMTAAAR3EBzkuJdFY7KF06M5A9W0IfICXCRBqIMPw1n1TYoDk-MGhoMst9LYZrEf4_ aem_5bFs0vFSCfZIu Nzu3s3aRw#title=chute-(1979)

Crenshaw, Kimberlé, 1989. "Demarginalizing the Intersection of Race and Sex: A Black Feminist Critique of Antidiscrimination Doctrine, Feminist Theory and Antiracist Politics." *University of Chicago Legal Forum* 1989(1): pp. 139–167.

Hechler, Andreas. 2007. "Heteronormativity in Contact Improvisation." Accessed May 25, 2022. http://www.contactfestival.de/Bilder/text/07_HeteronormativityinCI_hechler.pdf.

Hennessy, Keith. 2019. "Questioning Contact Improvisation." *In Dance.* October 1, 2019. https:// dancersgroup.org/2019/10/questioning-contact-improvisation/.

Horrigan, Kristin. 2017. "Queering Contact Improvisation: Addressing Gender in CI Practice and Community." *Contact Quarterly* 42(1): 39–43.

Kim, Richard. 2020a. "Write It Down! A Retrospective and Call to Action." Consent Culture in CI Symposium. April 2020. https://www.youtube.com/watch?v=DG6dBM8kh5w&t=1124s.

Kim, Richard. 2020b. "Write It Down! Resources and Citations." Contact Improv Blog. April 2020. https://contactimprovblog.com/consent-talk.

Lee, Rythea. 2020. "Trauma Informed CI: A Way into Understanding Consent." Consent Culture in CI Symposium. April 2020.

Mitra, Royona, 2021. "Unmaking Contact: Choreographic Touch at the Intersections of Race, Caste, and Gender." *Dance Research Journal* 53(3): 6–24.

O'Sullivan, Sandy. 2021. "The Colonial Project of Gender (and Everything Else)." *Genealogy* 5(3): 67–75.

Papineau, Em, and Sofia Engelman. 2019. "Creating Space for Queer Contact Improvisation." *Contact Quarterly* 44(1). https://contactquarterly.com/contact-improvisation/newsletter/view/creating-space-for-queer-contact-improvisation#$.

Patel, Vivek. 2020. "Pleased to Meet You. I'm Human Too." Consent Culture in CI Symposium. April 2020.

Rea, Kathleen. 2017. "'That Lady': The Story of What Happened When a Woman Put Up a Boundary in the Contact Improv World." Contact Improv Consent Culture. December 3, 2017. https://contactimprovconsentculture.com/2017/12/03/first-blog-post/.

Suseno, Andrew. Accessed 2023. Moving Rasa. https://movingrasa.com.

Yardley, Brooks (ed.). 2016. *Respecting Boundaries/Coexisting Genders: Women's Experiences Feeling Unsafe in Contact Improvisation*. Zine. http://contactimprov.ca/doc/ci_en6_web.pdf.

Young, Iris Marion. 1980. "Throwing like a Girl." *Human Studies* 3: 137–156.

4

Not

Not Contact Improvisation

Joy Mariama Smith, edited by Asimina Chremos

~~You are~~ Y'r Welcome

You are welcome to dance with this text. Eyes may receive the letters, the color of the ink on the page. Ears may hear the sound of text-to-speech; ~~this could~~ could this be written in braille, in which case you are feeling, touching each letter or word. From my body/mind (in 2022 in Amsterdam the Netherlands) to yours, across/space. Your body and this text body, in a dance, in an improvisation, discovering: What . . . is . . . real . . . right . . . now? Despite our baggage, we've never been here before, have we?

So many ways to read: to search, to absorb, to soak in, to reject, to critique, to judge, to learn, to wonder, to discover, to experience new sensations, to find harmony, feel dissonance . . . consider this a Contact duet, an improvisation through touch. The text one skin, and your organ of perception (sight or hearing or haptic) another? Or a trio: Two minds (human and non-human) and a text? The selves multiply as we count and list the elements of any encounter. As do the absences. . . . I'm writing in English, a polyglot system of communication that continues to evolve through centuries of colonization. A silver lining of this mindset: thinking one owns everything makes it easy to pick up new terms and ditch old habits that do not serve you. Maybe English is not your familiar language—what then to make of this? Maybe language is not your language.

You'll find a lot of questions in this text. This is because my jam as a dramaturg, facilitator, educator is "thinking with." I can tell you what I think, but that's only half of our dance. I want to think with you. However, we're in an asynchronous relationship here. If the questions make you pause, stop, reflect—good. You can "think with" this text by writing in your journal or just taking mental notes.

Each of us has been to many other places before we got here. We are on a path shaped by what came before. We have some momentum, as well as places where we're stalling. Let's get moving, let's get this party started.

* * *

What Type of Party Is This?

This is not an academic text. This is also not an academic text. There will be little to no academic conventions. Engage with this text in any way that you see fit. Sit with this text as you would with a dear friend, or a lover. Be with this text as if it were a piece of music, or architecture. Or even a dance partner. Just be in relation to the text, understand the text as your partner for the next little while. There is the space of the text and there is the space you are in, and there is the space between you and this text. You and this text are in a *dynamic field of relation* (ref: *Dramaturgy in Motion: At Work on Dance and Movement Performance*).

As you sit with this text and get deeper or further into it, you may notice some things, you may also have some desires. Please do attend to those, and also know that you can leave the text at any point,

unfinished

of sequence   out

whatever suits you.

I will do my best to provide you with breadcrumbs to help you along the way and give you some insights, but also backgrounds, inspirations, and support. There will be resources that you can use should you want to go down a rabbit hole that I have been down in order to get here. You will see *content in italics* (ref: in parentheses) that relates to a resource list at the end of this text.

No but Really, What Type of Party Is This?

It's the type of party that has already started. Here is what you walked into:

There is soft multicolored lighting, warm in some places, and cool in others. Turquoise, pink (closer to magenta or fuchsia even), and purple party lights swirl around on the ceiling and walls. Green pinpoint laser lights speckle the walls and floor, like some sci-fi femme supernova light design; in other words, party lighting. There is smoke or a haze, not from a machine but from the burning of a cleansing and medicinal herb for smudging: sage, juniper, cedar, sweetgrass, lavender.

The air is wet. There is the smell of sweet sweat in the air, and some muskiness, but the good kind.

It's early, you're sober, or your senses are heightened. How do you know this? You salivate, your smell sharpens, your heart quickens, the little hairs on your ears stand up, maybe you have goosebumps, your pupils are dilated because it's dark. Your spine is liberated, you (unconsciously) feel sound vibrating in your pelvis, sternum, wrist, ankles, jaw . . .

. . . you're already dancing.

You've realized you are there to warm up the party. This is the best part. It's almost empty.

There are only 4–5 people on the dance floor, so you finally have space, enough to dance. BIG DANCE. Get weird, take up space, take a deep breath, take a deep breath, bust out all your sweet moves, see what you can do. DANCE. Dance in order to grieve, praise, heal, feel, be angry, survive, thrive, to live, to forgive, to honor, to respect, to connect, to tap into the flow, to stop thinking, to turn into fire, to protest, to rest, to manifest, to talk to your ancestors, to be possessed, to channel, to perform, to become invisible, to see, to lose, to lose time, to lose

82 Resistance and Support

track, to get loose, to time travel, to start over, to be accountable, to build community . . . to just get in a solid hour of good cardio.

Oh! and what's that there?! A shimmering moving image moving toward you (is it me?). A figure, a person, an energy, a unicorn, a black unicorn (but is it me?). A smile and a wink . . .

> *"Hello, welcome, you're right on time..."*
> *"I'm really glad you are here, thank you for coming . . . "*
> *"Relax, no rush, we are just softly arriving . . . "*
> *"I'm Joy or Black Joy, your gracious host."*

In the background you hear/feel the base that just became consciously audible and has been coursing through your bloodstream the whole time (((BOOM BOOM MMM MMM MM BOOM BOOM MMM MMM MM)))

mmmmultiple subwoofers, surround-sound . . .

Electric blue eye make-up, eye liner art, a touch of biodegradable glitter, flawless agender/genderfluid fashion, breath as minty fresh as the beats.

No it's not that at all.

Ideally, this party is a container that allows us to work with our discomfort. It's an affirming space that allows for community building and welcomes introverts, researchers, and refugees. It's a place for critical thinking and critical feeling, a party where accountability is hip, a space that can even embrace placelessness. It's a space where care is one of the foundational/support structures.

It's a party where celebrants can explore questions like:

- Where does the space start and end?
- How do I/we enter and exit the space?
- How is everyone contributing and knowingly implicated in the creating of this space?
- Who invited us/you?
- Why are we/you here?
- Who do I want to dance with?

I ~~will begin with Starting with~~ acknowledge and am grateful to my DANCEstors, all the bodies I passed through, carried, brushed up against, tried on, traded and exchanged with . . . bodies that I touched and were touched by, that knowingly and unwittingly led me to this moment I am in right now. How I got here. Right/Write here, in this place at this desk where I am writing as an act of honoring myself, and thinking/feeling through the inception moment for Not Contact Improvisation (NCI hereafter) and why I/we need NCI. I am asking what happens when we strip CI of the white cisgendered heterosexual and ontological expansive (read: colonial) perspective, and move into an anti-colonial analysis.

"Form" does not equal "culture." There is the form of Contact Improvisation and there is the culture in which it is embedded. Some of the culture that I have experienced in CI contexts was unwelcoming to my own culture, meaning I could not fully be myself while practicing the form.

I believe this calls for a cultural shift. The practice of NCI is an open invitation to practice the principles (form) of CI without certain aspects of the culture of CI. I named NCI due to the observation that the culture of CI marginalizes the very people I want to dance with.

I wanted to understand why a dance rooted in improvisation looks the same across cultures and continents, and I took this as a sign that something needs to change. I'd like to see what happens when we take the core principles of CI, and layer in varying social-cultural perspectives, somatic intelligences, and experiences of people of color, queers, and krips. Let's give this practice to those who have been systematically oppressed. Let's playfully do the form "wrong" (as a radical act of protest against "rightness" (read: whiteness).

You're invited to an analysis and critical thinking/feeling through how the core concepts and foundations of CI—movement, momentum, gravity, weight-sharing—lead to a more accessible, more inviting, and less harmful way into the dance for anyone/everyone.

I want to share principles and themes of NCI, as well as some somatic exercises that can lead us/me back to why we are all here: because of the dancing. I am here because of the dancing and I want to get back to the dancing. What do we need in order to create space, to gather, to dance?

* * *

> *Dance Break: Breathing to Shift . . .*
> *Take a deep breath.*
> *(now if you didn't take a deep breath, consider why you didn't)*
> *You can take another one, and as you do that, slide your hand across a part of your body that needs care/attention/touch. Let that route lead you to a place of tension (your neck, the top of your left/right shoulder, your lower back) and give that area a little massage.*
> *Are you comfortable? If not, what do you need to do to get more comfort?*
> *(None of this is existential, none of this is mandatory, you don't have to do it. Take it or leave it.) Back to that breath. When you circle back and think about why you did or did not take a breath when invited to, don't worry about it. Maybe you noticed something, maybe you didn't. This text isn't going to close or have some dramatic moment about the breath in the conclusion. What this text will do is invite you to change and shift perspective, to sit in discomfort, to reorient and recalibrate. This text will ask you to be in relation with—with you, with it, with me, This text will encourage you to lean into thinking while feeling. What is feeling together? What is feeling with?*
> *What if we assume that everyone's body is highly, deeply, expansively intelligent?*

Now that we're at the party, there is space, there is time, there is intention, there is curiosity, there is commitment, there is access. NCI is a community-based practice. It comes from community, it's for the community and it builds community.

I like to dance in places where I am explicitly invited. And not an "all welcome" invitation, but a BIPOC to the front, QUEERS to the front, femmes to the front, _____ (specific minoritarian identity named explicitly here) to the front, YOU to the front. This is for you. I like to know what might happen, or what material might be worked on. I like to know what the values are or what we will build together. I also like a space where I can speak freely and be as supported in a rigorous line of inquiry as I am in learning from inevitable mistakes. A space that is working toward safety but is transparent in not being entirely safe.

84   Resistance and Support

NCI is a praxis space. The parameters of the space are set up by me, the practitioner, and the needs I have at the time. Right now, I need a separatist space of people of color, that has queers, trans,* neurodiverse folx, people with disabilities, immigrants, and locals, people that speak different languages, and maybe not everybody shares the same common language. I like a space where the music is already playing and the tea has already been brewed as if the guests are expected; hospitable. Dance experience not necessary, a desire to be there is a must.

Acknowledgments

Thank you, Jonathan David Jackson, Ishmael Houston Jones, Keith Hennessy, and Ann Cooper Albright, Asimina Chremos, Ancestors and Descendants.

* * *

Some Thoughts (Sauce) Still Here

When I think about how to structure NCI—the practices, themes, and exercises I want to move through—I find it necessary (as with most inquiries) to start with myself. With this body. This body with its particular histories and intersections. From there, as with any praxis I engage in, I start with either one of two questions:

> *What do I need now?*
> Or
> *What didn't I get when I did this before?*

I'm not sure if these questions come from a place of selfishness, or a deep desire to survive and thrive. Of course *it can be both/and instead of either/or* (ref: *White Supremacy Culture-Still Here*). Over the years, I have realized that most people don't know how to answer the first question. Here's how I do it:

> Right now, we are talking about thinking/feeling through the legacy and potential of CI. What do I need to do that? In order for me to do that, I have to look back. OK, what do I need, to do this looking back? I have to look back, maybe not all the way back, but look at some key moments in my personal history and relationship with dance and improvisation. So: Being the only Black body in a room where a dance technique was being taught did not first happen in the context of CI. Imagine being a young Black kid with a parent/Mother who cared enough to put me in ballet/tap/jazz classes (a common trio of dance techniques in which pre-pubescent girls who are socialized as female are trained into forms that are meant to be looked at by an audience). I was the only Black kid in so many contexts that it seemed normal. I am aware that there is no "normal," and like most things, "normalcy" is one of many social constructs but in the 1980s being the one chocolate chip in the cookie was really common. So common that I took that experience for granted.

This text is not an entry point into my own personal therapy or a reason to enter into the trauma Olympics with you or anyone else. I am just trying to make a point that those experiences shaped me. So when I was *the only Black person in CI*, initially I was not busy with it (ref: *Improvising While Black*). Until I was.

The experience of everyone knowing who I was, of everyone knowing my name, of being othered, of standing out, of being the only this-that-or-the-other, became so common that I was able to experience it like background noise. If/when I started with the base question of What do I need? or What didn't I get?, my answer is that I needed to not be the only Black person in the room. I didn't get to dance with other *bodies of color* (ref: *A working definition of PoC/bodies of color*). I didn't get to honor my ancestry and the ancestry of others through the dance. I didn't get to bring my social-cultural dances to the table; my social dances didn't have value. The many moments in my social life, in my family life, with my folx my peeps my kin, when we were touching and moving—and experiencing joy—I didn't get to bring that in. I was too busy blending in while sticking out like a sore thumb.

My experience is personal, but also indicative of a broader cultural situation about the field of dance. We know that CI sits in areas that border of both performance (dance as a form to be learned and looked at) and social practice (dance as experience for the dancers). So what I see is that NCI has to be a PoC centered practice. Sometimes it needs to be exclusively PoC, sometimes we (and by we, I mean the non-white bodies) need separatist spaces to heal and thrive. And that is abso-fucking-lutely ok.

Having space to dance where maybe it's a majority PoC space: this changes the dance, informs the dance, expands the dance.

But why?

I never authentically, honestly inhabited a homogenous utopic space of CI. I never self-identified as a hippie (no shade). I do identify as a person who loves to dance, I love to move, I love to research through movement, I need to dance as if my life depended on it. Because I really believe my life does depend on it.

Beware/Be aware: When CI starts to look the same everywhere you go—no matter what country or context or continent—start to question why that is. Is it because there are a set of codes, tropes, rules, behaviors? Has something been taken for granted—like for instance the concept of improvisation. Have certain modalities of dancing/meeting/touching become dominant and therefore have non-dominant ways been erased? What and where is space for improvisation, and how do we feel safe enough to improvise? It's improvisation. It's improvisation in as much as when, in the early 1980s in my cousin's living room while listening to DEVO's *Whip It*, she taught me how to pop and lock. Now I can bring that into my dancing CI. Why not?

To put it another way: There is a reason there are offshoots of CI that build in a negation of the form. It's because of the homogenous white spaces that CI takes up, it's because of the history of alienation, assimilation, exclusion, and more; a history that not only needs to be acknowledged but also talked about. If I want to teach a class in Contact Improvisation, the first thing I do is **not** call it Contact Improvisation. If I call it Contact Improvisation, I automatically push people to the margins, it marginalizes and alienates ~~people~~ the people I want to work with.

It's the people from the margins that I fucking want to center and work with! PoC to the front, krips to the front, femmes to the front, trans to the front, queers to the front! It has another side too: Because we already know there is a legacy of PoC dancers that have been practicing CI since the beginning (Bless you). By naming NCI, the non-white bodies that practice CI can also come and feel welcome and say "NCI . . . hmm, what is that? I know CI already. . . ."

So from where I'm sitting NCI is a win-win.

* * *

Y'r Practice

The Individual Work of NCI

As contact improvisors, it's important to know that when we step into a room, before we touch another body, that room is not just one room. It's a multilayered space. Your work as a member of the NCI community resides in inquiring:

- How you locate your Self, your individual identity in the space
- Naming the real and conceptual spaces as well as the categories you bring with you
- Noting: who is here, who is not
- Doing the self-examination to understand how you locate the bodies that are "not my body"
- Naming in what real and conceptual spaces and in what categories you place those bodies that are "not my body"
- Determining what invisible rules and guidelines are located in this space that may be brought by you or others
- Identifying the un/spoken invitations
- Identifying the un/spoken prohibitions.

The C.C.A.A.T. Breakdown

Are you a cat person or a dog person?

Well regardless, get into C.C.A.A.T.! It's an acronym I made that was meant to be an easy take away from NCI practice. It's simple:

C. C. A. A. T, is for Communication ~~or consent,~~ Agency, Accountability, Trust.
Not that NCI is a pillar-oriented practice, but if it were, these would be the five pillars.

"C" is for Consent

Whether the first "C" is for ~~consent or~~ communication ~~I haven't landed on yet. But I'm inclined to have it be "communication" because~~ consent is already—or I hope it is—the foundation of NCI. And if we run with the architectural metaphor where C.A.A.T. are the pillars, they would stand on a foundation which would be consent. *Unfortunately I do not observe that consent culture is the basis of CI as it is historically and usually practiced.*

In my opinion, consent ~~must be~~ has to be present in the room, part of the discourse, part of the foundation. You should not be doing this form or teaching this form if you are not coming from a place where you are actively bolstering a consent-based culture. I'm serious, because if you are not, then the space you are creating could be really harmful. I still don't understand why consent is not a part of dance education, why it's not part of a choreographic pedagogical approach, why conversations on consent are missing from the room. A lot of harm has been done under the guise of practicing CI. This is precisely why I don't practice the form, because consent is missing.

Figure 4.1. "C" is for Communication. QTBIPOC artists gather to talk and listen in the opening circle of Color Block 2023, an annual retreat at Ponderosa (an art-centered place in the German countryside) for artists of color to share space and community. Joy Mariama Smith is the founding artist of Color Block. Photographer: Tom O'Doherty.

Here in 2023 I am asking, why is consent not the stated basis of this practice? And what are the implications of that, and where do you locate yourself in those implications? What would consent being the universally acknowledged basis of this practice look like?

"C" is for Communication

I mean explicitly verbal communication *first*—which, in my personal experience, is a "no-no" in CI. I have been in jam spaces and classes or workshops where talking has been discouraged, where using one's voice has been discouraged and frowned upon. I understand that in this work those that practice are busy with cultivating nonverbal communication, and listening beyond the ears and getting into understanding and building an exchange and vocabulary via movement. But before we go quiet, we need to be able to *talk*.

I like to start a class or jam with checking in. So we all know what emotional and physical states are in the room. So that we share a collective responsibility for understanding what is in the room. You can't build a safer space without intention and verbal, multimodal communication. Later in a class or jam, I find that it is really helpful to create space and time for discourse/discussion. *Not to intellectualize the NCI practice or even the concepts we are doing. But to process together and alone what we may be feeling and what the implications are.* If we are going to touch each other and then trust each other to take risks together, we need to talk first. Part of emotional and somatic intelligence is being able to verbally articulate how you are feeling, emotionally and physically.

NCI is also a practice in relating, a practice in intimacy, a practice in boundaries and more. At the start of all of those things is communication. It doesn't matter what you are busy with in your everyday life, in the space of NCI we are going to talk. It's not a space for silence or silencing. If you need to say something, say it. We do this until we don't need to do it. We need to get to know each other. We need to understand our differences and intersections, as a way to support each other in understanding each other's bodies, their capacities and availabilities.

If we talk first, it could be that it provides more potential for not talking later. There is space for verbal expressions of fear, insecurities, curiosities, doubts, affirmations, objections, confusion, enthusiasm, and more. *Either way we bring those into the dance.* I am just saying, make space to name it and talk about it. Maybe talking about it gives more space to think/feel for other things. And talking about how you are feeling is one of many practices for communicating in interpersonal relationships outside of the studio.

"A" is for Agency

You are your own agent. The practice of NCI ~~will not work~~ isn't working if people don't understand and know that there should always be potential for them to shift their experience of the practice because they always, always have agency. When working/teaching/facilitating in international settings, often there is not a direct translation of the word "agency." And that in and of itself is valuable information. So we walk it back and talk about the concept of agency. Of being your own agent.

Agency can be defined in many ways depending on your discipline. I like to frame it as the body having rights and choices. The idea that your body has the right to "do" or "not-do." Moreover, your body has the right and ability to choose. You need to feel like you have power, or control over your own body and what happens to it. Including the right to give up that control. Not having any agency does not feel good. Part of the work is ensuring that each person feels like they have a sense of agency, but also to be able to name when they do not. Not everyone is going to be comfortable all the time!

Conversations around power often have some discomfort. But we have to be able to talk about power, privilege, access, intersections, and so on, when talking about agency. We need to understand that not everyone has the same relationship to this term, so that we can work toward equanimity, or a more equitable (not equal) environment when dancing/practicing in terms of our individual and collective understanding of agency. *Why does it feel like agency is not a core principle of CI pedagogy?*

"A" is for Accountability

Accountability may be seen as the other side of the coin of agency. Both principles need to be in the room and a part of the culture. I have been in CI settings where the introduction to the space starts with some assumptions. A most common one being that you are responsible for your own safety and well-being, so this somehow relinquishes the collective from the responsibility of caring for the individual: if something happens, well, it's your fault because you are responsible for yourself. Accountability requires community. Even if it's just the temporary community of the dance studio for that moment.

If you're facilitating a class or jam, practice NCI by introducing the space with language articulating that *individuals are responsible for their own safety and well-being (agency) as well as the safety and well-being of others.* We want to create a culture where individuals are responsible (accountable to the collective for the effects of their individual actions on others. This is not a rule or announcement, but the start of a conversation that includes us talking about what stops us from being accountable. This conversation can include talking about how to strive toward a "shame and blame"–free space so we can dance together.

Harm will happen, conflicts will happen. This is part of being together. Mistakes will happen. There is no shortage of creepy dudes, creepy women, creepy people, or abuse of power in CI. There is no shortage of cancel culture either, but that doesn't actually solve anything. All of this is an opportunity to learn. Practice and learn how to say, "Oh my bad, my mistake, I did that thing that made you uncomfortable," or "I'm sorry." Accountability culture is the opposite of cancel culture. Get into it.

"T" is for Trust

Oh, trust. I was just binge watching *The Nevers* (an American science fiction drama television series) and there was an interesting statement about trust:

> *"A friend is the one you trust to trust you back."*

Again, let's talk about it. NCI offers a space where we can explore trust both nonverbally and by talking. We can learn to define trust for ourselves, and learn how to build it. We can explore the relationship between having trust and the ability to take physical and emotional risks and creating the space to be vulnerable. Dancing and moving together in a practice that involves touch is a ripe ground for discovering just what ingredients we may need, individually and collectively, to cultivate trust. Consider the following: honesty, reliability, accuracy, confidence, care, respect—none of these things are black and white and maybe all exist on a spectrum. We must address trust before we get to defying gravity and all that jazz of semi-acrobatic shoulder-lifts and so on that are so dramatic and thrilling.

> *"I wouldn't trust you as far as I could throw you."*
> What does that mean?

> *"Moving at the speed of trust"*
> That is the basis from which we start.

* * *

90   Resistance and Support

The Eight Limbs of NCI

1. Invitation

Maybe you have noticed while watching cartoons that the warm steamy aroma of food is animated as a kind of vaporous figure. It dances around the room, and then after a lengthy meander it concludes its journey by pausing underneath someone's nose, and then, forming the shape of a tickling little finger, beckons a bystander by the nose. Is that an invitation?

> *Dance Break: Subtle sensing . . .*
>
> *What can you smell in the background right now?*
>
> *What sounds do you hear in the background?*
>
> *Is there anything that is enticing to any of your senses?*
>
> *Maybe you didn't notice it yet, maybe it's subtle.*

I am curious how you felt invited to this text. What led you to it, did someone give it to you, are you reading it for work, pleasure, or both? Something more? Something else?

I like my invitations to be clear and direct. Unambiguous. This clarity and directness—which is helpful in consent-based practices but not always available—can be reached in a variety of ways. The basis of an invitation is that there must be an open line of communication and some trust and vulnerability. The communication does not need to be only verbal, or only nonverbal, or monolithic in any way. It does not need to be sensical. It can happen in many ways in many registers and maybe the route is simply just trying to lead to a connection. ~~Is it not the same with dancing?~~ It is the same with dancing. A bottom line for the structure of an invitation is that there always needs to be space for the invitee to say "no." It is our responsibility as practitioners to hold space for the "no" and to invite others into our "no" practice.

Exploring modes of invitation is also a great way to work on our boundaries. And I am curious where this point (boundaries) is in the legacy of CI. Where is the discourse on boundaries and boundary work? What is the understanding of how different people in different circumstances and contexts relate and process levels of intimacy? Sharing intimacy could also be another tangent in terms of discourse on CI.

Questions for Developing Your NCI Invitation Practice:

- What do you need to feel invited into a space?
- What is the way you feel comfortable ~~and safe~~ to enter a space, I mean feel invited and comfortable?
- Would you want to be invited into a space where you knowingly would feel unsafe?
- Would you want to be invited into a space that is potentially dangerous, or harmful for you?
- Do you want to be invited into a space where there is care and attention anticipating what you specifically would need to enter that space?
- What about being invited into a space where you know that when you leave, you will leave an impact, the space of your absence, behind?
- What does a space of care, understanding, growth, development, and supportiveness feel like?
- What is the opposite of an invitation?
- Alienation, rejection, isolation: How do those things feel?

- How does a warm and thoughtful invitation feel to give, and how does it feel to receive?
- How does an invitation heal and repair and help us to feel seen and heard and maybe even special?
- How does being invited give us a sense of self while simultaneously giving us a sense of agency?
- How do we cultivate a healthy "no"?
- When or where in your education, research, life, upbringing, socialization were you taught about how to say "no"?

* * *

2. Approach

There are so many things that you notice can occur prior to touching.

I remember a while ago I made a little diagram in my notebook, to try to categorize and scale the different types of touch. Ranging from incidental and accidental, to clinical or medicalized, all the way to familial, sensual, and intimate touch (not explicitly sexual). If there are many options for types of touch, then it stands to reason that there are also many different ways to approach touching. There is so much information in the moment prior to a physical encounter, notions of proximity, and also exchange, and also meeting. There is a whole dance to be had just in the approach.

Once contact is made, there is a glorious attribute of touch, in that it is a sense where reciprocity is integral and built in: what you touch touches you back. Acknowledging this reciprocity facilitates consent. In my conversations with Denise (ref: Denise Ferreira da Silva)—she blows my mind as we are trying to conceptualize the experience of consent. Like the word nerds we both are—no, okay, I speak for myself—like the word nerd I am, I go back to the etymology of the word and take it apart: *con* + *sentire* = feeling/sensing *together*.

Also check this out, I discovered by talking with Denise that all or most of the senses can be framed through the experience of touch. The eyes see because light touches rods and cones in our eyes, the nose smells because molecules touch the membranes inside our nose, we taste . . . and so on. Not only does this expand possibilities for understanding consent, which is a key principle of NCI, it also expands the notion of touch. Descriptions of CI often include something about touch because we are talking about being in contact. But as I continue to practice, "contact" includes this more expansive understanding of touch.

Questions for Practicing NCI Approach:

- How do we approach each other?
- Can an approach include elements of well wishing, of good intention, of care, of empathetic gaze, of kinship, of nurturance culture, of consent culture . . . of trust?
- Can a dance start with a high five, or a shout across the room? Can a dance start with call and response, an embrace, or a look askance?
- Can a dance include those who are not physically present in the room?
- Do you want to be touched right now?
- How do you want to be touched right now?
- Is there a certain way you want to be touched?
- What is touching?
- Am I touching you right now? Can you feel me?

* * *

Figure 4.2. Working with our discomfort during Not Contact Improvisation (NCI) practice at Color Block 2023. Pictured: Amelia Uzategui Bonilla in red jacket, Joy Mariama Smith in blanket. Photographer: Tom O'Doherty.

3. Dis-Orientation/Dis-Identification/Dis-Association

I come from a generation where the word "dis" came to mean "insult" ("They dissed me. . ."). I think that this sense of disparagement is part of the lines of thinking put forth by Munoz, Tempest, and Wallenhorst in their writings about dis-orientation, dis-identification, and dis-association. To my mind the prefix has the potential to empower non-dominant ways of navigating, living, surviving that center (or value) doing the opposite of, or deprive of, or exclude. Dis-orienta/identifica/associate-tion is a radical skill to cultivate.

Some of us were never comfortably oriented, identified, or coherently associating to begin with, so to live in and feel discomfort is not a large step for us, and absolutely gives us access to other ways of being and adapting. It would be really easy to talk about power and privilege, but I'd rather talk about the link between modes of perception and shifting perspectives.

If you've done CI, you've probably had moments with eyes closed, upside down, backward, and/or spinning around. Disorientation, not unlike confusion, is a generative state. Being disoriented allows for cracks to emerge and creates space for new ways of thinking and/or navigating from between those cracks. Moments of disorientation allow for adaptation and also allow for something new to emerge. Sit in the discomfort. Or don't. Or do something else entirely.

It's about perception and perspective. Moving in and out of orientation, identity, and association/disassociation shifts your perspective, and when our perspective changes, we may see a new or different set of opportunities. Moreover, if we practice the "dis," we can move further away from the fear associated with the unknown.

Questions for Developing Your NCI Dis-Practice:

- How do you locate your desires from a place of disorientation?
- What do you need in order to sit in a place of discomfort?
- How do you locate your desires from a place of disorientation? And how do we (as practitioners) cultivate that skill?
- What are the things, systems, tools, circumstances, that you encounter and find yourself disoriented?
- What do you use to orientate? Or is it your super power to thrive within disorientated states?
- What happens if the dominant culture thrives for order, sense-making, connectedness, homogeneity, monodirectional-unilateral thinking/feeling: What of the normative, what of the assimilated, what of the integrated?
- Perception versus perspective: What is the difference?
- How do you/we navigate this through dancing?
- How do you relate to disorientation?
- How do you relate to dis-identification?
- How do you relate to dissociation?
- Are these dis-states states of liberation?
- How can dis-_____ inform and cultivate skills in both how we sense or become aware of things while at the same time understanding the importance and uniqueness of our point of view?
- When you are disoriented, what do you use to orient yourself?
- Do you need to know where you are doing, or do you get a thrill when you move from the unknown?
- What is a reason one would need to dis-identify with a culture?
- For what reason would we dissociate, does that reason need to be a bad thing, and can you release some judgment here?
- What about the feeling of being tossed about in the ocean as a big wave crashes over you, and you surrender, and you relax and . . . what happens next?
- Did you ever spin around as a child to try and get dizzy, was it fun?

* * *

4. Fluids

Fluid is an integral part of NCI research. In mayfield brooks's work, the fluid in the inner ear is of particular interest. They explore how to start a dance with a heightened awareness of the fluid in an ear and meet other bodies ear to ear not only to listen but to move. Many feel that there is a link between the percentage of our body's composition that is made up of water and the percentage of water in the earth. The percentage of water in the human body is 60 percent, the percentage of water on the earth is 70 percent. Attending fluidly connects us to our collective human identity as earth-beings.

Water will always find the cracks; water finds the path of least resistance. It can change states, from solid, to liquid, to gas, and back again. It can take on the shape of the vessel it is in. Water travels, can affect things, can influence things, can nurture things. There are large

94 Resistance and Support

and small bodies of it. We are of it and from it; it can move in waves. Sound passes through it differently than through air; it reflects and refracts light. We can learn a lot from this.

Blood, saliva, tears, sweat, semen, mucus, urine, vaginal, synovial, spinal, amniotic, endolymphatic, perilymphatic, gender, sexuality—water goes in, water goes out. There are so many different types of fluid in our bodies and they have so many functions. Some are for balance, some regulate toxins and remove impurities . . . some lubricate. Some are viscous, some are not.

"Fluidity" and "flow" are also words that we use to describe states of being and consciousness. Psychologist Mihaly Csikszentmihalyi coined the term "flow state," and I invite a line of somatic inquiry about this as well.

Exercises for Working with Fluids:

With a partner

With a buddy, or with yourself if no one is around, begin to understand yourself as a body of water. If you are near a body of water (a lake, a river, the sea, an ocean) and you can hear it in the background, use that as your soundscape. If you don't have access or are not near a body of water, you can generate sounds of water creatively, or you can play a recording of some watery sounds (rain, waves, washing machine, bathtub sounds).

If you are working with a buddy or partner, lay down on the floor. You can face up or down, whichever is the most comfortable for you. Close your eyes if you feel comfortable and safe enough to do so. Listen to the sounds of water as a texture in the background.

Your buddy/partner will put their hands on you and gently start to shake your body back and forth, at the same time they are speaking to you in a calm/soft/low tone. They remind you that you are made of water: "Your head is made of water, your eyes are made of water, your ears are made of water. . . ." Et cetera. The gentle shaking is to act as somatic support in reminding the body of the water that is already present. If you are working alone, you can act as your own buddy, talking to yourself, giving yourself gentle reminders and shaking parts of your body or your entire body as a whole.

In a group

We name the different types of fluid in the body and then just free-associate and name any fluid we can think of is a useful exercise: honey, molasses, water, tea, olive oil, wax. . . . What can you take in your carry-on bag when you fly? What constitutes a fluid? When we name and identify qualities of fluid, then we can begin to describe what those qualities mean. From there we can choose to adopt, embody, or inhabit certain qualities.

Questions for Practicing with Fluids:

- What are my everyday practices of fluidity?
- What strategies have I developed as a moving body when I try to adopt the qualities of water?
- What are the qualities of water?
- What is the relationship between fluid, fluidity, and improvisation?
- Can one improvise without fluidity?
- How much fluidity is needed to enter a flow state?
- What amount of trust is needed, how much intimacy, how much risk-taking, how much adaptation, how much instinct, intuition, calculation, intention, surrender, reverence, et cetera, is needed to flow?

- How do we identify and experience fluidity and flow?
- How do we embody fluidity and/or flow?

* * *

5. The Force(s)

There are forces that are at play when we dance. We can identify and conceptualize them. If you are science-y, then maybe you are thinking of the mathematical equation "force equals mass times acceleration." And if you are not science-y, then let's simply say that mass and acceleration, along with momentum, are things to be considered. But there are lots of forces: forces of nature, forces of attraction, normal force, gravitational, magnetic, centrifugal. . . .

Tensegrity and *propinquity* are words that I like to use when I offer up exercises in understanding forces that are both concrete and abstract. Tensegrity and propinquity are both action-based, or dynamic relations. With both of these somatic concepts you can start to practice spatial relationships. What are you in relation with, and how. Another way to look at it is: How do these notions play into the idea of contact and being in contact?

Tensegrity . . . what the what? Well, here it is as I understand it: Imagine you are standing, or even sitting. Or, can you think of the mechanics of walking? What is tension, what is compression, catch-and-release, and how do these things relate to force? I think of sticks, I think of rubber bands. But before we think, what are we doing? How are you in the position you are in right now? And what if you think/feel of *tension* and *compression* as a set of somatic parameters for relating?

Propinquity . . . may be more complex. It may have many elements, but you can check which of them feels easier to embody. Propinquity is a spatial relationship based on not just distance but also kinship or affinity. It is the idea that if you like something you would try to be near it, or next to it, or close to it. Not just that, but with this idea, see how you also *do* it. When do you do the opposite?

Questions for Exploring Forces:

- Is force another mode of understanding motivation? Of impulse?
- Can you think of "fixedlessness"?
- What does it feel like to be far away from something you really like? Is that a state of tension or compression?
- What happens when an unstoppable immovable force meets an immovable object?
- What goes up must come down. How do we embody that in the dance?
- What happens if I push you?
- What is adversity?
- What is resistance?
- What is oppression?
- What if I press into your skin?
- What is too much pressure?
- When dancing in contact, what do forces have to do with empathy and consent?
- Of any of the forces we can name or conceptualize, how can we realize them in our dance on a practical level?

* * *

Figure 4.3. Rest is one of the Eight Limbs of NCI. Joy Mariama Smith (seated on green ball) guides participants in NCI at Ponderosa in 2023. Photographer: Tom O'Doherty.

6. Rest

Notions of rest are embedded within the practice of NCI. The viewpoint is one of rest as resistance, supportive and generative practice, a basic human right, and as a path to equanimity, among other things. I'm interested in exploring the territory between rest and cultural and/or ancestral trauma. In my daily life practice of resisting the binary—which actively includes providing alternatives to the constant monetization of labor—I see work and rest not as polar opposites, but as necessary ways of relating to the world. I constantly ask myself how I experience "rest" and "work." I try to see if I can uncouple these concepts from capitalism; and wonder if that intentional uncoupling is a form of work, or perhaps a release/relief.

> *Dance Break: Rest . . .*
> *Take a break.*
> *Take a breath.*
> *Pay attention to your body, it has some information for you.*
> *Stillness is always an option.*
> *How are you feeling right now? Are you sitting, standing, lying down? Are you multitasking? Are you holding on to tension in your body where you don't need it? Can you relax? Can you relax more?*
> *Is relaxing intimate infinite? Have you ever had the feeling that you can relax more?*
> *Can you, right now, make a link between rest and resilience; and can that link be a somatic link instead of an intellectual link?*

I realized quite recently that my relationship and understanding of rest comes—like most things for me—via an understanding and experience of ~~three~~ multidimensional space. Rest not only generates space, but also requires spaciousness. When I am aiming to get to a space of bodily relaxation, I often visualize more space. More space in my joints, or more space for my organs, space in the roof of my mouth, space between my ears, space between the many small bones in my ankles, space in my nostrils, space for my thoughts, space for my energy.

I want to have the same level of inquiry around rest as I do with movement as a creative practice. I was thinking about the moments when I am not-doing, when I am not active, when I am not reactive, or productive, or trying to accomplish something. I remember how I think/feel when I'm fucking around or dicking around, being idle, being aimless, not having a goal, not trying to accomplish something. At the same time, I also think of the privilege and the labor of resting. For me to arrive at a state of rest I need to be in relation with myself and others and examine my relation to work.

Rest is not only an individual practice, even if you come from or are working in an individualist culture. You can make space for collective rest. This is imperative. Support each other. Invite each other to rest.

Say less.
Do less.
Do nothing.
Take a load off.

Questions for Exploring Rest:

- Can you take a day off?
- When was the last time you had a day off?
- What is a day off?
- If you take a day off, is your tendency to schedule things to do?
- What are your patterns and tendencies around rest?
- Do you experience/have resistance when you have "free" time?
- When do you make space for aimlessness, laziness, anti-productivity, daydreaming, spacing-out, dissociation?
- If there is space, can something emerge and/or does something need to emerge?
- What does rest look like for you?
- Do you feel like your rest needs to look the same as everyone else's rest?
- Do you have the capacity to rest without judgment? If not, where does that judgment come from?
- How is rest a necessary part of the dance?
- Do you have a memory of stepping into a warm bath, or floating in a body of water?
- What is rest about, is it about reaching a certain state in the nervous system?
- What of the parasympathetic nervous system?
- How is your brain/mind functioning when you are resting?
- How does your body feel when it's resting? What about your spirit?
- Have you experienced restlessness?
- What is rest, and why rest?
- What is the link between rest and white supremacy culture?
- What about receptivity, confusion, adaptation, inspiration, empathy, listening, compassion: Can these things emerge from a place of rest?

* * *

98   Resistance and Support

7. Connection

Are we (you and I) connecting right now via this text? Connection is a type of relation, it is dynamic and it can be sensed. Take care not to conflate "contact" with "connection."

In the practice of NCI, we recognize that connection can be a radical act for some of us. The oldest trick in the book is "divide and conquer," which is the opposite of connection. In ~~non-white~~ BIPOC dance spaces, it is possible that there are different access needs and access routes around connecting. We need to consider this and discover what taking this into consideration would look like.

NCI invites us to think/feel through states of connection or connectivity without centering the eyes. The eyes do not need to be the center of attention nor the locus of information-getting. Connecting can be as simple as creating a link between one thing and another thing or things: a bridge, a joint, a point, a feeling, a state. The experience of connection is not linear. The experience of connection is multi-nodal and multidirectional. Multidimensional?!

I imagine that people will have various associations with the word "connection." Some that come to my mind are energy, ideas, technology, the internet, fiber optics, mechanics, dial-up modems, telephones, transportation, communication, and access. Then there is the matter of what we are connecting with, or through, such as the earth, the land, nature, spirit, ancestors, universe, and/or the multiverse. I think also of reflections or twists on connection: alienation, separation, isolation, codependence, interdependence, intradependence, entanglement, quantum physics, and importantly for NCI: diaspora.

I think about something that is called "the look back"—when you see someone or you pass someone on the street, and you feel an attraction or an affinity or a kinship or a connection with them. But you don't know them and you are on your way and they are on their way. And you pass each other, the moment is gone, time has passed, and you both carry on. But then, there is a little tug, something, a pull—a small feeling that compels you to look back in that person's direction. And the joy, if as you look back at them, you find they are also looking back at you!

One of my friends uses the term "link-up" when we meet. They also say whenever we spend time together things like "it was great to reconnect." In my mind this always makes me chuckle. Because I never thought that we were not connected, so how would we be reconnecting? If a connection was established, then the connection is not lost. Being out of contact does not mean being outside of connection.

Has anyone ever asked you, "Are you reading my mind?" Have you ever been thinking of a loved one and in that moment they send you a text message: "I was just thinking about you"? What does that feel like in the body? What sensations arise?

Stay curious.
About connection.

Questions for Exploring Connection:

- What is connection?
- How do you connect without using your eyes?
- What's the story of "connection" versus "contact"?
- What is the opposite of "divide and conquer"?
- When does connection start, and what connects us?
- Is/can connection exist independent of identity?
- Is it a set of shared lived experiences, is it being in the same place, in the same room?
- Is it touch, listening to the same music together, or moving together?
- How does it feel when you are connected?
- What is the interplay between connection and trauma?
- What about connecting with the nonhuman, with ancestors, with unseen spirits; what type of connection is this?
- What does it mean to work on connection as part of a movement practice?
- How is it that we practice cultivating connectivity while dancing; and what skills are we using and strengthening?
- What does it mean to connect?
- How can you become more aware of the connective tissue in the body?
- How do you define, calibrate, embody, experience connection?
- What do you need to feel connected in life?
- What do you need to feel connected in the dance?

* * *

Figure 4.4. Resisting homogeneity in improvisation, participants of Color Block 2023 engage in movement research during NCI practice. Photographer: Tom O'Doherty.

100 Resistance and Support

8. Free Style

An NCI protest slogan: *RESIST HOMOGENEITY IN IMPROVISATION*

One of my major pet peeves in CI is the fact that in the dominant (read: white) CI culture, the dances tend to look the same. No matter what, no matter where, in different corners of the earth you can go to a Contact jam and somehow the tempo, aesthetics, and movement patterns all seem to look the same. I am specifically talking about jams and jam culture, and not performance. The basis of improvisation is doing—whatever—extemporaneously, so then that would include spontaneity, and variety. Not homogeneity.

If I take a closer look, things that come up naturally have to do with various colonial histories, white supremacy culture, and the result of these things, namely cultural erasure, racialized aesthetics, and othering—things that are most visible when one is not operating from the perspective of the normative (read: ~~dominant~~ white) Contact Improvisation culture. This is also why there are branches, ruptures, or fractures/offshoots of Contact Improvisation whose names include an inherent negation of the form (e.g., NCI).

Improvisation was not invented and has no point of origin, neither does touching while moving.

In a more inclusive and equitable Contact Improvisational practice, space is made—no not made, but asserted and necessary—for social and cultural dances and honoring our ancestors. They are allowed and actively welcomed into the dance. Our movements contain history, stories, melodies, memories and more.

RESIST HOMOGENEITY IN IMPROVISATION

In order to catalyze improvised dance moves that are not milk toast (milquetoast) or rote, the strategy I use in NCI is a gentle but impactful reframing: enter "free style." For example, as a counterpoint for the round robin (the really common CI improvisational structure), in NCI we practice social dance structures like the cypher and/or the soul train. Inviting social and cultural dances into the space provides an opening. Bring in the vogue and ballroom, bring in the popping and locking, bring in your ancestral dances, bring in other genres and meet each other in the dance.

I spoke with a person of color recently who practiced Contact Improvisation on another continent and they shared with me (or us, because we were in a PoC only separatist dance space and these spaces are much-needed spaces and please do consider why) that they stopped dancing/practicing CI because they were often policed or shamed when they entered the dance space because their energy was "too much," too sporadic, it didn't "match" the energy of everyone else, so no one would want to dance with them.

A Key Strategy for Facilitating NCI

If someone new to the form is dancing with a skilled CI practitioner, they should not have to change or shift how they are dancing. A skilled CI practitioner will be able to listen and adapt.

Free. Style. Rather than talk about the complexities of the Free (freedom and who gets to experience it), I want to reflect on notions of Style. Style as in fashion, style as in movement quality, style as in a way of being. All of these are part of the dance. It is very easy for me to visualize a certain era and a certain time period when I think of being a student at Oberlin college in the mid- to late 1990s, learning Contact Improvisation. When I recall that time period—and all the sights, sites, sounds, colors, smells, and tastes—I can very easily see:

The Trope of the "Contact Improvisation dancer"

Dance pants:
> A drop crotch pant or low crotch pant that is tied at the waist, either cotton or linen, maybe hemp

Warm/autumnal color palette:
> Burnt siennas, greens, muted (or dull, meaning faded) blues, neutrals . . . nothing too bright.

In general:
> Loose clothing
> Knee pads
> Patchouli (the cheap kind)
> Body odor
> Whiteness and with that a level of cultural appropriation
> Rough and/or calloused feet, bare feet

Now back then, this aesthetic was called "crunchie," a kind of hippie update. There was a certain overlap with hippies and CI. And I was not a hippie. So in looking at the above list of ingredients, what if I start crossing those things off and/or changing these things. For example, practice CI while wearing _____. Notice what changes about the dance based on what you are wearing. Wear street clothes or high heeled shoes or. . . . Style is an opportunity to do something or wear something in a particular way, to provide an opportunity or distinction. To distinguish oneself from the other. To not assimilate.

RESIST HOMOGENEITY IN IMPROVISATION

Another element of free style or having the liberty to express oneself and continuously and constantly reinvent oneself is adapting, transforming, shape shifting, adopting. You can make a riff. You can engage in call and response. The idea that I can see/taste a dance move and try it on and allow it to pass through me while at the same time having it inform my next move(s) is part of free style. I can take something and then make it my own. This is the opposite of assimilation.

Basic practices of CI, "listening" and "responding," should point us to placing a high value on malleability, flexibility, responsiveness, and adaptability in-the-moment. By placing the responsibility on OGs to welcome and adapt to new bodies in the space and allowing newbies to be themselves, we create a situation in which skilled practitioners will constantly expand their neuro-physical-cultural-emotional plasticity, while newbies can feel welcome and valued, especially for the richness and new information they are bringing into the communal space, keeping the overall form alive, shifting, and evolving away from its specific roots in white postmodernist dance and into a more global and diverse reality.

Questions:
- If the basis of CI is improvisation, then how can homogeneity be? Why is this?
- What happens when you let various movement forms and/or styles pass through you, as if trying on a series of jackets to see which one fits?
- What are the social dances of your community/ancestors/culture/locality?
- What are you wearing?

* * *

The Take Away: NCI Strategies and Beyond

Only then, when we lean into the discomfort of diverse and divergent realities, will we truly improvise. Only then will the form start to open and flourish. Let's move toward the dynamic and multiple potentialities this form truly has and dance continuously toward what this form can be.

NCI is a radical act of communal care. The dance is just that. What this means and looks like is that my personal practice of NCI came from a desire to practice a wonderful dance form but/and to uncouple that form from the inherent ~~white supremacy culture, patriarchal, colonial, cisgendered, heteronormative, assimilationist, homogenous~~ oppressive elements and spaces that are harmful to me. By negating those things, practicing the form while explicitly naming the things I do not want to practice, and also explicitly naming alternative ways to practice and inviting people in, I (finally) have the space to again find the joy in the dance and reacquaint myself with dancing.

I am not saying that all CI has these oppressive elements, or that all CI practitioners do these harmful things. What I am saying is that for me, this form (NCI) developed from personal need based on personal experience. When I took the time to reflect on my needs and validate them and attend to the healing of the harm(s) and then share that as a practice, my dancing became richer.

One of the beautiful things about CI in its "purest" form is that it is a dance that is queer, radical, not-ableist, feminist, revolutionary, and more. But who is in control of this dance? Who gets to change it?

What is the dance of resistance, the dance of grief, the dance of avoidance, of rage, of frustration, of queerness*, of transness*, of blackness*? What is the dance of the other? How can we make space for that? Who do you/we need to invite in and how? What is the dance of the introvert, the rebel, the outsider? What is the dance of consent, of trust, of agency, of accountability, of accessibility?

What is the dance of critical thinking? Critical feeling? Critical sensing?

Here is where I start.

I think about whom I want to dance with, and I invite them in. I invert the formula. I center the people in the margins and I learn from them by dancing.

This is not, Not Contact Improvisation. Now here, you and me and this text, we are doing it.

~~Conclusion~~ The Future of CI

#CIFuturisms   For Ish and Keith—Black Joy CI @ 50

CI is for queers*
CI is for witches
CI is for krips
CI is for gyps
CI is for bitches
CI is for switches
CI is for broken
CI is for token(s)
CI is for wheelchairs

CI is for blank stares
CI is for femmes*
CI is for thems
CI is for thugs
CI is for drugs
CI is for heels/heals
CI is for feelz
CI is for boots
CI is for old coots
CI is for freaks
CI is for geeks
CI is for drunks
CI is for punks
CI is for clowns
CI is for gowns
CI is for queens
CI is for hos
CI is for moms
CI is for Dom/mes
CI is for Blacks
CI is for cracks

References, Things to Catalyze Thoughts, Future Dance Partners

Denise Ferreira da Silva is an artist and scholar addressing ethical questions of the global present. She is Professor and Director of the Institute for Gender, Race, Sexuality and Social Justice at the University of British Columbia, Vancouver. She is also a Visiting Professor at the School of Law at Birkbeck, University of London. I first heard the term "anti-colonial" while in her class. I admire her philosophy around coloniality and race.

ECCO stands for "Expanded Choreographies of Consent," is a limited edition 'zine that I wrote that also includes the transcript of a conversation with Denise. Contact me for a copy.

A working definition of PoC/bodies of color: Race is a social construct and the experience of being racialized may differ based on your cultural context. We define PoC as: Those who are descended (through one or more parents) from anywhere in Africa, Asia, the Middle East, Indigenous peoples of Australasia, the Americas, the Caribbean, Indian Pacific, and Roma, Sinti (and) Travelers and people of mixed ancestry/origin. (This does not include descendants of Europeans who migrated to Africa, Asia, or the Americas for occupational/colonial reasons or white European migrants.) Our group includes people with varied ancestry, origin, and ethnicity. We understand that race is a social construct and racialized experiences can vary, depending on context. Mixed background? We encourage your presence regardless of how you self-identify, but have a look at this link: http://weareallmixedup.tumblr.com/FAQ. This definition is based on experiences and it reflects our realities in the U.S. and European context. This definition is a work in progress and is open to critique and updates. Please contact us colorblock00@gmail.com.

104 Resistance and Support

Ten Theses on Touch by Hypatia Vourloumis and *Who Touched Me?* by Fred Moten/Wu Tsang: These are two publications on touch that I read to support my thinking about touch.

Improvising While Black: A text by mayfield brooks that I provide for people to read when I invite them to practice NCI.

Ishmael Houston-Jones: This: https://vimeo.com/114657723q.

Jonathan David Jackson: One of my CI teachers in Philadelphia while he was studying at Temple University looking at Vogueing. He wrote a scholarly article, "Improvisation in African American Vernacular Dancing," https://www.jstor.org/stable/1477803. This article opens up improvisation and helps my thinking in connecting vernacular dancing with CI.

Dramaturgy in Motion: At Work on Dance and Movement Performance: The part of Katherine Profeta's book I find relevant to NCI is the essay "Doing What We Know," which articulates how relating is always dynamic.

For the Wild: I love this podcast, especially this episode: https://forthewild.world/listen/tricia-hersey-on-rest-as-resistance-185?rq=tricia.

The Spell of the Sensuous: While I find this book by David Abram to be mostly annoying, it contains some interesting writing around sensing, synesthesia, and so on, and it helped me think more deeply about touch as a means of perception.

On Connection: Kae Tempest's profound book found me: It was recommended to me by a fellow participant at CI @ 50.

White Supremacy Culture—Still Here: Tema Okun and others name either/or thinking as a tenet of white supremacy culture. Everyone has a worldview that affects the way they understand things. Learn more: https://www.dismantlingracism.org/uploads/4/3/5/7/43579015/white_supremacy_culture_-_still_here.pdf.

Trans Aesthetics: Read this! I've never read anything like it before: https://www.e-flux.com/journal/117/385637/like-a-real-veil-like-a-bad-analogy-dissociative-style-and-trans-aesthetics/.

Quantum Listening is Pauline Oliveros's book, a manifesto for listening as activism.

Shimmering Images Trans Cinema, Embodiment and the Aesthetics of Change is Eliza Steinbock on aesthetics of change in cinema.

The Clearing is a book by JJJJJerome Ellis that inspires me to also engage in refusal, dysfluency, and more, and can shift and open up other ways of relating (it's also an album).

Disidentifications, Queers of Color and the Performance of Politics is a book I have read so much that it's tattered and torn. It helped me find my way in performance.

Rest Is Resistance: A Manifesto by Tricia Hersey is a book that changed my relation to rest and oriented me toward "serious leisure."

Space as Atmosphere, *Floating in a Molecular Bath* is a chapter in the book *Slow Spatial Reader: Chronicles of Radical Affection*. This chapter really supported me in thinking about sensing space.

5

Doing It Wrong

Contact's Counter Countercultures

Emma Bigé and Paul Singh

> [A] call to action to heat up, aerate, moisten, activate and decompose the world we live in.
>
> —mayfield brooks, *Viewing Hours*

> Can we evoke the idea of a counter culture without also participating in a desire to cut into something, to slash into a territory, to form an aesthetic of resistance as a form of empire building?
>
> —Jeanne Vaccaro, " 'Judson Loves Transsexuals' "

To start somewhere, let us not begin our story with a "hot muggy New York City day" in an art gallery in Soho, where were held the first performances of what was then called (in the plural) Contact Improvisations. Instead, let's "begin in the middle," with a performance, 11 years later—a duet by Ishmael Houston-Jones and Fred Holland in St. Mark's Church, in lower Manhattan, in 1983. The piece—which has now gained a certain currency within the stories that Contact Improvisation tells about itself—remained quite forgotten until Ishmael Houston-Jones reposted an excerpt of it online in 2014. Untitled, but also sometimes referred to as Oo-Ga-La, it was improvised to a score—a secret Wrong Contact Manifesto—*a piece of writing that would only surface 31 years later, with the recirculated video (Houston-Jones & Holland [1983] 2014). The* Manifesto, *as posted in 2014, reads:*

> We are Black.
> We will wear our "street" clothes (as opposed to sweats).
> We will wear heavy shoes, Fred, construction boots / Ishmael, Army.
> We will talk to one another while dancing.
> We will fuck with flow and intentionally interrupt one another and ourselves.
> We will use a recorded music score—loud looping of sounds from Kung Fu movies by
>   Mark Allen Larson.
> We will stay out of physical contact much of the time.

The dance resulting from this manifesto was presented on the eleventh anniversary of the creation of Contact Improvisation, at an event called Contact at 10th and 2nd—*a reference to the location of St Mark's Church's Performance Space on the New York grid, where the gathering took place. The scene is that of a reunion: the "family," the then-emergent "community" of Contact Improvisation, is called into gathering to celebrate its own existence—and here are*

Emma Bigé and Paul Singh, *Doing It Wrong* In: *Resistance and Support*. Edited by: Ann Cooper Albright, Oxford University Press.
© Oxford University Press 2024. DOI: 10.1093/9780197776308.003.0006

two dancers who accept the invitation, but propose to play the role of killjoys (secretly, for them-selves, without even telling the others): they are going to practice Contact badly, in a way that is not in expected, or seemingly appropriate.

To speak of the Wrong Contact Manifesto *as a killjoy intervention within the history of Contact Improvisation is to think with Sara Ahmed's essay, "Feminist Killjoys (And Other Willful Subjects)." Of the killjoy and her relationship to (happy) family reunions as a technology of disappearance, Ahmed writes:*

> The family gathers around the table; these are supposed to be happy occasions. How hard we work to keep the occasion happy, to keep the surface of the table polished so that it can reflect back a good image of the family. So much you are not supposed to say, to do, to be, in order to preserve that image. If you say, or do, or be anything that does not reflect the image of the happy family back to itself, the world becomes distorted. You become the cause of a distortion. You are the distortion you cause. Another dinner, ruined. To become alienated from a picture can allow you to see what that picture does not and will not reflect. (2010, 1)

Contact Improvisation is often referred to as a "community," a family of sorts, with its favored histories, its hegemonic self-representations, its (anti)heroes, and sometimes, its compulsory hap-piness. Throughout its history, there have been members of the CI community who have sought to disagree, to agitate, to put themselves in the way of things. How do those killjoy interventions play in the history of Contact? How are they contributing to its developments, ramifications, and fur-thering? And—could it be that these interruptions, these Wrong Contact manifestos, are a condi-tion for a practice of Contact? Taken to task and inspired by mayfield brook's IWB = Improvising While Black *(brooks 2018; brooks and Nelson 2016), by Keith Hennessy's* Questioning Contact Improvisation *(Hennessy 2019), and by many more efforts to look at Contact Improvisation through the diffractive lenses of race and activism (Barber 2018; Nelson 2018; Rabah-Konaté 2021 Sengco 2016; Suseno 2019; Will 2018; Will, Kim, Heydon, and Bryant 2020), the following conversation took place in January 2021 and was rewritten in the course of 2022. It was con-ducted then within the context of starting an archive of the wayward and activist legacies of Contact Improvisation,[1] and was transcribed and rewritten for the purpose of this volume.*

We wonder, from our situated queer/white/brown/cis/trans/European/North American per-spectives, not only as dancers, but also as cultural theorists and curators (Emma dedicated her PhD in philosophy to Contact Improvisation, while Paul now holds an administrative position in an art center in NYC): How does the current cultural currency open the possibility to artic-ulate Contact Improvisation's underrepresented relation to the aesthetics and poetics of black-ness? And—what kind of gestures are made possible, and what kind of gestures are hindered when the haptics of race come to the fore?

Surviving This Crisis, and the Next

EMMA BIGÉ — Let's start from where we are, in the belly of the beast. In the times of COVID-19, capitalism emphasizes, maybe more than ever, a crucial and paradoxical lesson

---

[1] For more information about the W-Archive of Contact Improvisation, a project initiated in 2019 by Emma Bigé, Defne Erdur, and Dieter Heitkamp, go to wrongcontact.zone/about.

in improvisation: the skill of adapting and creating with limited resources. However, capitalism's interpretation of this *forced state of improvisation* leans toward an individualistic and solitary approach to survival. On the contrary, I imagine Contact Improvisation's focus to be on collaborative forms of improvisation, rooted in mutual dependence and mutual support. Especially for those of us who "were never meant to survive" (Lorde 1978 [2019], 33), what are the survivals skills engaged in Contact Improvisation informing us about?

PAUL SINGH — I think it is crucial to insist that, if Contact Improvisation is about witnessing survival mechanisms (in me, in us), it's less about individual resourcefulness and more about our collective ability to navigate unexpected situations together. This approach has deep historical ties to BIPOC, feminist, and queer resistance against white supremacy (Norman 1977; Spade 2020). Throughout history, marginalized communities have thrived by helping each other, evident in endeavors like the Underground Railroad and COVID-19 mutual aid groups. It's frustrating to witness the prevailing fear of mutualism in our country, often mislabeled as socialism to discredit it, perpetuating a reluctance to acknowledge our interconnected lives.

In the context of a still raging pandemic, losing Contact Improvisation is an incredibly painful thought to me, yet I have this uncanny ability to project beyond terrible circumstances. A severe car accident in my youth that should have killed me, going blind for two weeks in my late 20s—each time in these tragic moments, I've been able to project beyond and through to a place of ease. It's a strange resilience that propels me forward. However, I worry more deeply when it comes to returning to Contact Improvisation. This one is harder for me to be envision. Will I remain stagnant, unchanged? Will I be the same person from before instead of accepting that the world demands we listen? I want to evolve, not just re-enact previous experiences.

The future landscape poses new inquiries about Contact Improvisation. The initial narrative depicted white individuals exploring physicality and interaction. Yet, today, we're confronting different questions. As two people made up of many different cultural backgrounds approach each other in a room, what nuances emerge compared to the 1970s? How have the physical inquiries transformed?

The path of Contact Improvisation's evolution is not ours to choose. It's continually redefined and questioned across different contexts and regions. In some countries, the challenge of the practice is eschewing complacency. In others, the overemphasis on "flow" can start to create so many repeated patterns that the improvisation part of Contact Improvisation starts to disappear. Some teachers revisit the origins of the form (in its most wild state), while some students enter with rigid expectations. And I want to know: what are the lenses we will have to equip ourselves with when we try to redefine the form?

Since the inception of the United States, racism has existed in various forms. The shift today is the transparency and acknowledgment of this issue. In this context, how does Contact evolve? Should it change? Should it stay the same? Should it dissolve? These are some of the questions that were rightfully being considered by the Future of Contact conference that Sze-Wei Chan, Kristin Horrigan, Diana Thielen, and Ariadna Franco organized for the spring of 2021. What matters most is observing how people grapple with these questions physically. And in the end, to address how race and Contact Improvisation collide, what I crave is a multiplicity—an array of colors, bodies, thoughts, and movements in our encounters.

The Resistance of the Object

PAUL SINGH — Okay, from there, let's return to 1983, to *Oo-Ga-La Dance* and the *Wrong Contact Manifesto*, yes? The day before Ishmael-Houston Jones and Fred Holland performed their duet, there was a sort of "jam as performance" event, in the same venue, at *Contact at 10th and 2nd*. Images of this performance (not the ones from Jones and Holland's performance) were then commodified and circulated through *Contact Quarterly*'s video documentation of the event (Nelson, Svane, and Weis 1983), so we can still see the amazing people that were there: Lisa Nelson, and Christina Svane and Cathy Weis filming, and Nancy Stark Smith, Steve Paxton, and a very young Kirstie Simson dancing along with David Appel, Peter Ryan, Alan Ptashek, and Robin Feld. As I think about this assembly, a question arises: What apprehensions or fears led to their selection of white people and exclusion of others? This thought nags at me.

When Ishmael Houston-Jones and Fred Holland reconceived Contact Improvisation, they engaged in a deliberate counter to Contact's counterculture. Through "Wrong Contact Improvisation," they introduced unconventional elements—wearing shoes, constant speech, minimal physical contact. They confronted the very notion of being "wrong" within the context, acknowledging their presence as Black individuals in a space that had traditionally perpetuated whiteness. This dynamic countercounter approach critiques and evolves Contact's role, challenging what is taken for granted. (It's brilliant to imagine them rediscovering the counter counterculture of the 1970s and instilling it through the political act of Contact in the early 1980s.)

EMMA BIGÉ — Steve Paxton, in a postcard addressed to Ishmael Houston-Jones a few days after the performance, describes *Oo-Ga-La Dance* (the "Wrong Contact Manifesto" dance) as "a maze of images woven effortlessly, evoked from air, earth+fire, carried on a fluid lighter than water. I was much moved" (Paxton 1983, n.p.). Undoubtedly intended as praise, the effortlessness evoked runs contrary to the intent which Houston-Jones recalls as:

> to purposely show the effort of Contact. Like not to pretend that we were weightless and that we could actually fly, but actually to show the muscularity and sometimes allowing things to fail, really embracing failure. (Houston-Jones in Houston-Jones et al. 2021, n.p.)

This gesture of interrupting the flow (a flow that had become the expected form of Contact Improvisation) stands in contrast with the sort of lightness, ease, and athletic perfection of the flowy moves that were performed as "Contact Improvisation" the night before, by an all-white group of dancers in sweatpants and bright-colored T-shirts. Nancy Stark Smith, a few years later, aptly described "the kinetic pleasures and soothing rhythms of time-in-flow" as "hypnotic" and "often go[ing] unchallenged in Contact" (Stark Smith 1986, 3). She continues:

> Why rock the boat now that we've finally gotten it steadied. As I've said, I've always loved "doing flow" and still do, but the time came when I began to wonder what else was possible. What other kinds of time could be played out in the dancing, and where might that take us? What I am finding is that it is there, in the departures from the established time frame, that new aspects of the dancers' personalities emerge and new risks are taken. Taking the lid off the flow container, time can move in new ways, reflecting not only the dancers' mutuality, but their singularity, in time and in space.

What happens when we "take the lid off the flow container"?, asks Nancy Stark Smith. And Ishmael Houston-Jones and Fred Holland respond in their own way, by making the work visible: "showing the muscularity" and "embracing failure." Making the work visible, not erasing the effort, is a classical aesthetico-political Marxist move: it consists in the refusal of what Marx called commodity fetishism—that is, the fetishist forgetfulness that behind every commodity or spectacle displayed, there is labor being extracted. Talking while dancing, interrupting each other mid-dance, Houston-Jones and Holland perform a movement-against-the-flow— flow of Contact/flow of the fetish of commodity—that is akin to what poet and philosopher Fred Moten calls the "resistance of the object" (Moten 2003, 5). That is, a certain refusal of the total access that is fantasized by logistics, which would like nothing else than the perfect uninterrupted flow of resources, labor, and commodities, each one dreamed as ruled by the same principle of permanent availability and permanent reconfigurability = "fungibility."

PAUL SINGH — Avoidance frustrates me deeply. I don't advocate for confrontation, but I'm perturbed by the passive act of ignoring issues or averting our gaze. I wonder about the institutional racism woven into Contact's roots—does it persist due to unchallenged assumptions? I believe no one intended to dismiss or ignore others consciously, but passivity permitted it, concealing a larger societal context.

Contact's legacy seems to foster toxic environments by selectively ignoring certain aspects, failing to extend invitations. Regardless of my proficiency in the form—requiring a redefinition of "proficiency"—I often feel like I don't have value in the room. The notion that one must exert twice the effort to achieve half the recognition resonates, paralleling a long-standing sentiment in the Black community: "You have to work twice as hard to earn half as much."

What interests me in Contact Improvisation is the raw essence of it, and often I wonder what the initiators of the form think of it now, and the way these very energetic forms of unknowing have turned into these very tender and listening forms of unknowing. If I say: Emma, close your eyes, and imagine a Contact Improvisation dance, what comes to your mind?

In New York City in most of the classes, you will be taught Contact Improvisation choreography: you will be on all fours, receiving someone else's back, you will have people going up on other people's shoulders, and so on. And I'd want everyone to write down: what they see Contact Improvisation IS (how it's being taught, how it's being performed at jams, etc.), and what they want it TO BE. You know, I love hearing the stories of how Steve refused ownership of Contact Improvisation, and said something to the effect of "take it and run with it," but then that does require we go for the grab, and own it, not in the proprietary sense, but really in the sense of making the effort to inflect it with our desires, and become responsible for what we do and don't do, what we reveal and what we mask.

White Histories of Contact Improvisation

EMMA BIGÉ — There's a remarkable paper by Ann Cooper Albright, "Open Bodies: (X) changes of Identity in Capoeira and Contact Improvisation," in which Contact is introduced as "a dance form developed in the early 1970s by a group of people who were interested in exploring the dancing produced by the exchange of weight between two (or more) people,"

110 Resistance and Support

embodying "many of the issues about self, independence, community, and change that were emblematic of the 1960s," while, strikingly, Capoeira is presented as a form of Afro-Brazilian martial dance that emerged during the colonial era, when white settlers started to displace people from the regions of Angola and Kongo to enslave them to their plantations (Albright [2001] 2013, 221). Reading these two presentations, I wonder what it would look like to offer a description of the origins of Contact Improvisation which, like for Capoeira, would center around the racial dynamics that presided over its initiatory gesture?

Contact Improvisation could, for instance, be described as *a form of white North American artsport that emerged during the United States' (post)colonial era,* or *as a dance form that was first investigated in the majority-white milieu of settler-colonial elite U.S. academia, and was further developed in the (counter)cultural milieus of dance, art, and neo-rural alternative spaces.* Much like the presentation of Capoeira as "an Afro-Brazilian dance from the colonial era," such a presentation of Contact as "a white North American artsport from the postcolonial era" is not a definition—it is not a delineation or delimitation of what Contact Improvisation can be and has indeed become. Rather, it is an acknowledgment of origins. It is a way of saying that the initial setting for Contact Improvisation is the world of what philosopher Sylvia Wynter designates as "the white bourgeois ethnoclass called 'Man'" (Wynter 2003, 260)—a legacy which, in some important ways, Contacters have endeavored to counteract through the kinds of movement and relationality they foreground: refusing the privilege of the upright posture, ungendering the relation to weight and lifting weight, elaborating a *genre* of the human as mass rather than sexed, classed, racialized, or abled.

That, in its forms, Contact Improvisation can and should be construed as looking for an antidote to universal Man and its overrepresentation is what many cultural theorists and practitioners have noted and celebrated as its "practice of freedom" (Goldman 2010), its contribution to "finding ground in an unstable world" (Albright 2019). But the question remains: How do we—practitioners and cultural theorists of the form—come to terms and render ourselves response-able vis-à-vis its original and ongoing milieu of deployment?

It seems "white guilt" has long protected Contact Improvisation from naming itself as white, at least in origins. But following Audre Lorde—"I have no creative use for guilt, yours or my own" (Lorde 1981, 9)—and Eula Biss—suggesting the necessity to transform "white guilt" into "white debt" (Biss 2015), we could ask: How do we become capable of responding to the very shitty forms of unequal distribution of power, wealth, and access to culture that allowed for the development of Contact Improvisation?

One direction for such a process in response-ability might lie in considering once again the context in which Contact Improvisation emerged and the stories told about that context, and specifically, in considering how Black U.S. history is obfuscated or erased from these stories. Rearticulating this Black history is part of a more general counter-hegemonic project of decentering the narratives that Contact Improvisation possesses about itself. It is only one part, and it certainly needs to be complexified with an acknowledgment of other forms of silenced influences and debts, ranging—to name only a few of those who have already been clearly formulated in Contact Improvisation's own forum, *Contact Quarterly*—from disabled and crip critiques of ableist visions of what a bodymind can do (Bartley 2020; Curtis and Ptashek 1988), to feminist critiques of the social division of powers and movement potentials (Albright 1989, 1990), and to queer critiques of heteronormative forms of pleasure and erotic containment (Hennessy 1996, 2014; Horrigan 2017).

The usual context that is foregrounded in the stories Contact Improvisation tells about itself concerns the protests against the Vietnam War, as well as the "sexual liberation" and hippie counterculture of the 1960s—all of which took place approximately at the same time as the civil rights movement, and which, for its part, is almost never mentioned. This is not to say that Contact Improvisation equates itself with the white (countercultural) movement culture that precedes and surrounds it. In actuality, most initiators of the form present it as occupying a *counter* countercultural space. For instance, Karen Nelson talks about Contact Improvisation as a "touch revolution," and specifies this revolution as offering a critical stance vis-à-vis the limited modes this tactile revolution took shape, understood solely in the form of the sexually promiscuous (Nelson 1996). Or, Steve Paxton talks about Contact as presenting antidotes to the most shallow aspects of the countercultural movement (Paxton, cited in Cvejić and Laberenz 2013). Or, Nancy Stark Smith figures Contact as a "portal" that "seemed to connect 'me' to an experience of the body as part of a much bigger system of life and movement and communication than just my immediate 'civilization,' however I defined that" (Stark Smith 2015, 3). This refusalist stance vis-à-vis the "immediate civilization" is often articulated to a radical involvement with practices born in Asia and imported to the United States. In her classical anthropology that stages Contact within the backdrop of a rather hegemonically white "American movement culture," Cynthia Novack (1990) thus refers to the legacies of non-Western practices, such as Yoga and Aikido and Zen Buddhism, pointing to movement cultures that unsettled the hegemony of the individual mover, a fantasy that remains central to the settler-colonial U.S. culture and its mythologies of the pioneer, the automobile, the self-reliant, and self-made.

But for all these countercultural and counter countercultural gestures, none of these authors and makers refers to a closer (geographically) and yet at the same time apparently further (symbolically) range of political and aesthetic practices, namely those of the history of Black arts and politics. This forgetfulness gets perpetuated by most cultural theorists of Contact Improvisation. I, for one, have been thinking alongside Contact Improvisation for about 10 years, and I have contributed to this same containment in the stories that I've told, or obediently repeated, about the origins of the form. For instance, in 2017, I edited a folio in *Contact Quarterly* dedicated to "improvisation and philosophy," where all the thinkers assembled and quoted were white European or North American thinkers, effectively conflating (improvisation) philosophy to whiteness and empire. These are stories and viewpoints I inherited, and that didn't appear as questionable, in part because of their capacity to ensure my own making sense and being an appropriate/not-questionable (white) body in the lineage these stories were establishing.

Other stories were and still are available. For instance, in *Dances That Describe Themselves*, Susan Leigh Foster (2002) traces the genealogies of North American dance improvisation in the 1960s through its debt to the aesthetics of the Black radical tradition (Moten 2003; Robinson 1983)—notably offering searing critiques of the hegemony of whiteness in dance's postmodernity. In a remarkable passage, Foster (2002, 42–44) describes how dance improvisation in majority-white contexts figures itself as demarking oneself from preexisting traditions. Following the ruptural logic of (modernist) avant-garde, *improvising-while-white figures itself as a practice of renouncing one's predecessors while simultaneously investigating materials as a way to express a universal human experience.* By contrast, the white gaze or the white scene contains the racialized body to expressing its purportedly associated culture or ethnicity, barring it from the avant-garde position of rupture with predecessors and

112   Resistance and Support

from universalist claims about the human. In other words, what gets in the way of the possibility of recognizing non-white influences is the fact that non-white bodies are considered to be standing for ethnically marked and separated streams of culture. Blackness thus containerized—or contained—bears no mark onto the (white) culture of universal Man. And it is the work of cultural theorists, such as Foster, to undo this unmarkability—which she does.

One of the intriguing things about *Dances That Describe Themselves* is that it was started by dancer and anthropologist Cynthia Jean Cohen Bull—who died of cancer in 1996 before she got to finish it, leaving her friend Susan Leigh Foster to take up her notes and make the book. Cynthia Bull is better known, in the world of Contact Improvisation, as Cynthia Novack, the anthropologist and dancer who published the first monograph on CI, *Sharing the Dance: Contact Improvisation and American Culture*, in 1990. While in *Sharing the Dance*, Novack participated in the (white) containment of the stories that Contact tells about itself, seldom referring it to the African American political and aesthetic cultures, in *Dances That Describe Themselves*, she was trying to bridge the gap in her scholarly work, most notably by way of her relation with choreographer and improviser Richard Bull (her husband) who, himself, stood between those worlds of jazz and experimental dance improvisations. Her book, which she never got to publish because of her untimely death, never became part of the set of books that are sold by *Contact Quarterly*, a set which contributes to define the bibliographical resources for Contact Improvisers, especially beginners. It fell out of the bookshelf of CI, a gap in the stories we tell about Contact—the revision that Novack (could have) offered to her own framing of "American" movement culture in *Sharing the Dance*. What would happen if we were to follow some of the suggestions of Novack/Foster and envisage the ways the aesthetics and poetics of the Black radical tradition have contributed to shape the context in which Contact Improvisation was developed?

Poetics of Refusal

EMMA BIGÉ — One of the most obvious lexical and conceptual debts that Contact contracted toward the aesthetic of the Black radical tradition lies in the adoption of free jazz's concept of *jam*. Jams are the most prevalent form of Contact Improvisation's spaces—a space dedicated to the meeting of strangers, the improvised sense of not-knowing each other and yet having to come up with ways of communicating and figuring it out together.[2]

Some remarkable descriptions of jam sessions in jazz speak of contacts, as this text by Ralph Ellison, where he talks of:

> the give and take, the subtle rhythmical shaping and blending of idea, tone and imagination demanded of group improvisation. The delicate balance struck between strong individual personality and the group during those early jam sessions was a marvel of social organization. . . . Life could be harsh, loud and wrong if it wished, but they lived it fully, and when

---

[2] In 2019, I interviewed Lisa Nelson as she was giving a workshop of the Tuning Scores at Performance Space—we were walking in the streets of lower Manhattan and I asked her about jazz and its influence on her growth as a dancer—and her response was to the effect of: "In New York jazz was like the air you breathed". And she added something along the line of: "We didn't talk about it, and yet it was so much a part of the everyday experience of living in the City". And so there you have something like a key, I think, to understand the simultaneous influence and erasure of jazz, which operates like the proverbial water the fish can't see because they are so immersed in it, but at the same time is so defining of their mode of moving and imagining movement.

they expressed their attitude toward the world, it was with a fluid style that reduced the chaos of living to form. (Ellison [1955] 2002, 6)

In this early description of jamming, improvisation is figured as an emergent form of sociality that consists in not-knowing what we are going to do with each other, and surviving together this unknowing. The recording industry complexified and partially captured what Fred Moten (2003) calls, after W. E. B. DuBois, the "sociology hesitant" of improvisation—hesitant because it doesn't know in advance *who* or *what* the *socius* is made of. The technological capture of improvisation simultaneously contributed to its recognition qua artform, and back-dropped its micropolitical value in inventing ways of being together otherwise—meaning: otherwise than under the rule of the hegemonic and the pre-decided (Muyumba 2009). On the contrary, jazz's unrehearsed negotiations attune to the "the prefatory dance" that precedes but is an integral part of the music. "Preparation is the playing," Moten writes, "the trace of another organizing" (Moten 2003, 46).

These are, importantly, values one can find (or look for) in Contact Improvisation's spaces, and that accounts of the Black radical tradition aptly describe. In fact, these analyses were mobilized in the pages of *Contact Quarterly*: through the words of mayfield brooks and what they say about their practice, IWB = Improvising While Black. In an interview published by *CQ* in 2016, brooks articulates IWB as a certain way of refusing and evading capture in (white) spaces of improvisation. Following Fred Moten, brooks conceives of blackness as "an expressive entity . . . that lives in a place that's not stable" (brooks & Nelson 2016, 34–35), a "sociopoetic force" that evades easy identification to an ethnicity, a class of people, or even a culture (Moten and Harney 2013, 19; Wynter 1976).

This fugitive sociopoetics is directly connected to the history of maroonage, of escaping the plantation and building lives "outside," at the border of (colonial) culture, but it is also connected, in another sense, to the history of jazz and the recording industry, and the problematic movement through which improvisation came to be seen as art, but also sold as art in the society of spectacle and the world of images-commodities, and sometimes at risk of losing its improvisational and sociopoetic force. Indeed, as mayfield brooks further elaborates, blackness's "place that's not stable" (a place that's oppositional or appositional to the society of spectacle and its desires for stable identities and stabilized practices) comes into contrast with what happens often in Contact jams, where

assumptions might be made that everybody is in the same energy or state. Folks may be moving in a similar way, and when someone starts moving in a different way, it shifts the energy of the jam. I've had really exciting experiences like that. But I think, in general, people want to be comfortable in jams. There is a default jam feeling that relies on softness and sensing that can be beautiful. I also like when that is challenged and people bring in sound or rhythm, interrupting the comfy, soft place. (brooks 2018, 37)

mayfield brook's concept of blackness, mediated through Fred Moten's, thus allows for an interrogation of a certain sense of comfort and stability, a certain capture of improvisation by the tired habits of tepid maneuvers. It opens for an insistence to improvise in a way that doesn't rest on the already established and codified, and in a way that doesn't presuppose an equal access to rest and ease and comfort and consent.

Conversely, and again crucially, it happens that Fred Moten, in his turn, thinks with contact improvisation (not capitalized), imbuing the practice of improvising in contact with the sense of providing an antidote, or rather, an antedote (the presence of preceding and recessive

114 Resistance and Support

traits) to the brutal modes and the brutal an/aesthetics forged by the Middle Passage and that remain ongoing in the course of modernity/coloniality.

In the few passages where contact improvisation is conjured in Moten's work, it is thus said to be "how we survive genocide": an "animation in and of the maternal ecology—Michael Brown's innovation, as contact, in improvisation" (Moten and Harney 2021, 49). If Contact Improvisation is survival to genocide, it is not in the sense of its rehearsing of modes of surviving falling, speed, and high athletics through somatic techniques of releasing tension in the face of danger—as is argued by Danielle Goldman in her essay on Contact Improvisation and nonviolent protest (Goldman 2007). Rather, Contact Improvisation survives genocide by virtue of its rehearsing ways of being "more than my damned self" (Moten and Harney 2021, 45), that is: by attuning consensually to a certain proximity of skins that allows for leaving behind the obsessive notion of an individuated, recognizable, manageable, capitalizable self. Contact improvisation is "how we survive genocide" because improvising in Contact is how we train and experience "consent not to be a single being," a phrase coined by Édouard Glissant (Diawara 2009), which Moten (2015) revisits recursively in his oeuvre as a sort of ethical dilemma: if it's true that blackness has been refused individuation, if it's true that Black people have been denied the right to personhood, does that mean that becoming an individual is desirable? What if what was missing was not individuation, but the possibility to "consent not to be a single being"? What if what was missing was the possibility to refuse what had been refused? Contact Improvisation is seen as one example of what's at stake in this refusal of what has been refused: a place where pre-individuated (non)selves get to flesh together, become no-body, refuse the capture of life within the confines of the individual.

Fred Moten's contact improvisation, which is not Contact Improvisation but which Contact Improvisation visits and encounters, is associated with that excessive ani*mater*iality that spills over, which Black feminism has called the flesh (Spillers 1987), this no-thing that surfaces "if you're ready to be less and more than human, to be nobody, to have no body, to claim the nothingness that surpasses understanding" (Moten 2015). This "non-compliance [with Man's desire to humanize us] is contact improvisation," says Moten. Understand: a contact improvisation is where we get to study and share in the flesh what exceeds the containerized sense of ourselves, the identifiable, the nameable, the ascribable. Importantly, flesh is not an enviable no-thing to be assigned to, and what Spillers has described as its hieroglyphics are inscribed through the most brutal modes of subjection. And yet, flesh can also become a "centrifugal factor" (Weheliye 2014, 52) and serve as an expropriative force that counteracts the mythologies of the individuated and autocratic mover, in favor of an unsurpassable sociogeny of movement.

A condition for this, says mayfield brooks in "touching myself: a refusal of contact improvisation," is to "never assume that people want to be touched." And brooks continues:

> As a black person constantly dealing with anti-black violence, I understand trauma as a prerequisite to my very existence or—more aptly put—non-existence. This colors the way I interact with Contact Improvisation and is part of my refusal to fully embrace CI as a practice. . . . I challenge myself to practice refusal. I make noise, disrupt comfort cuddle zones, and keep dancing, touching myself and other objects, asking permission to touch others, and doing CI (see I/eye) on my own terms. (brooks 2018, 39)

Placing a poetics of refusal at the heart of touch is what makes room for a "consent not to be a single being"; without this insistent practice of disruption, the brutal modes of inclusion (however gently disguised under the chant of "every body's welcome") resurface. Again: noncompliance as contact improvisation.

On Being Included

> When our appointments and promotions are taken up as signs of organizational commitment to equality and diversity, we are in trouble. Any success is read as a sign of an overcoming of institutional whiteness. "Look, you're here!" . . . This very structural position of being the guest, or the stranger, the one who receives hospitality, allows an act of inclusion to maintain the form of exclusion. (Ahmed 2012, 43)

PAUL SINGH — Undoubtedly, there's a paradoxical trend outlined eloquently by Sara Ahmed in the opening quote of this section—an insidious way for exclusion to persist through the guise of inclusion and diversity. My current inclusion in numerous conversations (including this one) reflects this phenomenon. I, along with Brian Evans, a fellow person of color in the Contact dance world, have seemingly become tokens, added to discussions to project diversity. This quick fix, attempting to remedy the imbalance by tossing diversity into a mix steeped in racism, is insufficient. (We see it all the time, in a different method, with academic institutions requiring incoming dance teachers to have Afro-Caribbean dance forms in their teaching practice to quickly fill the void.) Brian and I chuckle about our newfound role as talking points—aware that we're being tokenized. However, we're compelled to say, "I see what you're doing by using us as tokens, but I also need to be in the room to call it out, shed light on it, and provide insights."

This is my understanding of why the counter countercultural gesture remains vital. The racial lens is increasingly undeniable. The George Floyd trial in the United States, ongoing as we speak, serves as a stark reminder of the issues unaddressed since the inception of Contact in the 1970s. The evasion, dismissal, and pretense regarding these issues persist today, just as they did then.

If you tap back into Steve Paxton in a gymnasium at Oberlin College in 1972, what you have is him gathering a group of white men, asking the question of unknowing: "How do we get to a place where we don't know what's going to happen?" And, apparently, it had to be men, it had to be full-on—almost violent—running, jumping, and seeing what happens.

And now it seems we are asking: What are different ways (other than violently running toward another human) through which we may become capable of unlearning each other? But we're surrounded by the knowledge that we are surrounded by violence already. And then if we put color into the room: What if it's no longer two white men, but a white and a Brown person running toward each other? What sort of unknowing will be implied there? And will violence, or high energy that could cause harm, be the tool used to unknow these relations?

Regarding your question about the civil rights movement, my perspective is colored by my unique background. As a first-generation American with roots in India and the West Indies, I find myself color-switching all the time. My skin tone often leads to assumptions— sometimes being mistaken for Black, at other times for Iranian, Pakistani, or Hispanic,

116 Resistance and Support

depending on facial hair and other factors. But at the end of the day, it shouldn't matter what color my skin is if I have the skills and the knowledge to practice the form and communicate. But sadly, this is not always the case. Sadly, we are not always shielded from the biases ingrained in societal systems.

My mother has worked in hospitals her whole life as a registered nurse, working on people who do not want a person of color working on them, regardless of her skills and knowledge to do so. When Obama was elected, my mom said: "Mark my words, you are going to see an undercurrent of racism come to the surface, quickly when he first comes into office, and again more deeply when he leaves office. I lived it when I moved to this country, and I'm going to see it again." And she was right. I can listen to studies from all the best social scientists in the world, but hearing her saying it, and the gravity with which she said it after living it, that was something else.

And so, I am disheartened by the way this country has repeatedly pretended that racism vanished after the civil rights movement or with Obama's election. This delusion persists, and I'm pessimistic that Contact will avoid the same fate unless we continue to address these issues head-on. Though we're currently on hiatus, jam sessions will resume at some point, prompting the question of how we'll address consent, predatory touch, and racism in the space. The good work of those raising these pertinent questions is commendable, but I'm unsure if significant change will happen. Personally, I've prepared for this crisis within Contact since I first encountered the form—finding ways to navigate predominantly white spaces, showcasing skills for recognition, and maneuvering between silence and leaving the room.

Somactivism and Racial Haptics

EMMA BIGÉ — Contact Improvisation is a unique creature because it has relentlessly over the years been a context for a sort of haptic study of all sorts of disciplines. You just have to look at the many "special issues" of *Contact Quarterly* to see that all sorts of dimensions have been considered to be key aspects to be interrogated in order to become more capable to practice Contact Improvisation: there's a focus on Groups, on Healing, on Sports, on Documentation, on Perception, on Sexuality & Identity, on Activism & Community; there's a College Issue, a Children's Issue, a Space/Time Issue, a Music and Sound Issue, a Dancing with Different Populations Issue. There's even an Issues Issue. But, there hasn't been an "Issue of Blackness," or "the Issue of Whiteness," or a "Race Issue"—as has happened, for instance, in other journals and quarterlies I read, like the *Transgender Studies Quarterly* (2017), or *GLQ: A Journal of Lesbian and Gay Studies* (2012), or the *Women Studies Quarterly* (1986). But it seems that this special issue of *Contact Quarterly* that hasn't been written is currently writing itself in different parts of Contact Improvisation's cultures, wondering: How is Contact Improvisation concerned by the study of these racial haptics? And how couldn't it be?

PAUL SINGH — I spend a lot of time imagining dances with other bodies of color. I want you to imagine having a conversation with people of color. People that you see in news reports, that you see in marches, people that you are rarely near, because that's not what your life's affording you. I'm not saying that imagining is better than doing. But when your jam is predominantly white, I believe it's important to start dreaming into a diverse space so it's not such a shock to the physicality when you do get to be in contact with a body of color. So it's not something you shy away from. I think it's about manifesting things, in your consciousness, that you want in the universe. And I always am wanting more people of color in the jams, so I must start imagining it, and then doing it—inviting people, practicing the practice. I think this is very important to practice for people that have racism in their bodies, which is all of us.

I have this example of somatics meeting activism that recently happened. There was a trans*-led march in Brooklyn during the height of the pandemic. It was in support of trans* Black people, and it got 15,000 people to show up. And the people leading it were somatic practitioners, though they used the term "creative workers," knowing that the word "somatics" can be an unwelcome, unfamiliar term. But in truth they were somatic practitioners specializing in racial diversity and anger management/physical altercation. The police were prepared with batons to take physical action, if necessary, but it never happened. The practitioners moved the people in such a way that they corralled the police and had them surrounded, and the police never got a chance to get angry because they did not understand what was happening. It was like peaceful confusion. These trans* Black activists had asked the practitioners, who were mostly dancers, to imagine the pathways of the crowd, and how to keep space and lines of communication open. They also asked the speakers with mics to remind people to drink water, to harmonize their bodies ("touching the belly," like Resma Menaakem says): they had people physically ready to allow strong, hard things to be said without inciting violence toward them. Somatic practices were behind the curtain of how this march was able to maintain peace—even when resistance and intensity were the factors necessary to enact listening/change.

When I said earlier that we artists and dancers are the kind of people that might have the knowledge to deal with crises, I meant it. The thing is that no one wants to hear from us really. They want to hear from specialists in the field, sociologists, and political scientists, people who have codified knowledge. Fuck that. Because we are the ones who really know how to walk that walk. And so, the problem is: How do we get heard?

So how does that translate for this specific milieu of Contact Improvisation? I must say first that we are lucky, somehow, that the jams tend to attract people that are rather well-rounded, that are open-minded, and so I don't have to practice too much getting people being comfortable around me because I have brown skin. What I don't know is what happens when I travel to other countries and how my skin color is affecting the room. I don't know how many people avoid me because of the way I look—because they aren't comfortable or don't have a lot of history being in contact with darker skins. I don't know how much of that is actually happening, but I have to project it into the room, so that I can keep a certain guardedness and a safety.

So, there's this physical stiffening, a physical harshness that I might find multiplying in unknown environments, and yes: I can soften in the skills of Contact, soften the stiffness of my guard. But the duality of being guarded while also softening is exhausting.

I once went to CMC ["Contact Meets Contemporary", in Goettingen, Germany] and had a fantastic time at the festival. However, on my flight home these two older women were enraged because a person of color (me) was in the seat next to them. The flight attendant did her best to quell them and actually burst into tears, with other passengers telling me, "We're so sorry; we hope you get moved to first class." I ended up saying to the flight attendant, "if they don't want to sit next to me, I don't want to sit next to them, is there another seat on the flight?" The only other seat on the flight was the last seat on the last row, next to the bathroom at the back of the plane—and I'm like: "What the fuck just happened?" Also: "Why am I sitting here consoling this flight attendant for crying when I am the one who is getting burdened?" My point is that I will have to travel again, and can hope for a different circumstance, but I will most likely hold the apprehension of what happened from before. And this will exhaust me.

And so, somatically, how do we approach these challenges? I think we are going to need a landing space of 30 minutes before every jam. I think we are going to need bodies of color teaching (and not just as students being told what to do).

Improvisation is never vague, never imprecise; it's always making choice after choice. All the ways you move are a constant reflection of what you are divorcing from and, simultaneously, of all the things you are embracing. So, the question we need to keep asking ourselves collectively, is: *Who are we making ourselves capable to dance with?*

References

Ahmed, Sara. 2006. *Queer Phenomenology: Orientations, Objects, Others*. Durham, NC: Duke University Press.

Ahmed, Sara. 2010. "Feminist Killjoys (and Other Willful Subjects)." *The Scholar and Feminist Online* 8.3; available at http://sfonline.barnard.edu/polyphonic/ahmed_01.htm.

Ahmed, Sara. 2012. *On Being Included. Racism and Diversity in Institutional Life*. Durham, NC: Duke University Press.

Albright, Ann Cooper. 1989. "Writing the Moving Body: Nancy Stark Smith and the Hieroglyphs." *Frontiers: A Journal of Women Studies* 10.3, pp. 36–51.

Albright, Ann Cooper. 1990. "Mining the Dancefield: Spectacle, Moving Subjects, & Feminist Theory." *Contact Quarterly* 15.2, Spring/Summer, pp. 32–40.

Albright, Ann Cooper. 2001. "Open Bodies: (X)changes of Identity in Capoeira and Contact Improvisation." Reprinted in *Engaging Bodies: The Politics and Poetics of Corporeality*. Middletown, CT: Wesleyan University Press, 2013, pp. 218–229.

Albright, Ann Cooper. *How To Land: Finding Ground in An Unstable World*. Oxford: Oxford University Press, 2019.

Barber, Tiffany E. 2018. "Us, *THEM*, and High-Risk Dancing." *InVisible Culture: An Electronic Journal for Visual Culture* 29; available at https://ivc.lib.rochester.edu/us-them-and-high-risk-dancing/.

Barbour, Floyd B. (ed.) 1968. *Black Power Revolt*. Manchester, NH: Extending Horizons.

Bartley, Colleen. 2020. "On Being an Introvert, Neuro-diversity, and Contact Improvisation: Being Truly Inclusive." *Contact Quarterly* 45.1, Winter/Spring; available at https://contactquarterly.com/contact-improvisation/newsletter/index.php#view=on-being-an-introvert-neuro-divers ity-and-contact-improvisation.

Biss, Eula. 2015. "White Debt." *New York Times Magazine*, December 6. https://www.nytimes.com/2015/12/06/magazine/white-debt.html.

brooks, mayfield. 2018. "Touching Myself: A Refusal of Contact Improvisation." *Contact Quarterly* 43.2, Summer/Fall; available at https://contactquarterly.com/cq/article-gallery/view/ci-inters ections.pdf.

brooks, mayfield, and Karen Nelson. 2016. "IWB = Improvising While Black." *Contact Quarterly* 41.4, Winter/Spring, pp. 33–39.

Chan, Sze-Wei, Kristin Horrigan, Diana Thielen, and Ariadna Franco. 2021. *The Future of CI: A 3-Day International Online Conference*, Earthdance, MA, April 23–25.

Christiansen, Steve, Lisa Nelson, Nancy Stark Smith, and Steve Paxton. 1987. *Fall after Newton.* Videoda, 22′45″.

Curtis, Bruce, and Alan Ptashek. 1988. "Exposed to Gravity: Two Accounts of Dancing with Physical Disabilities." *Contact Quarterly* 13.3, Fall, pp. 18–24.

Cvejić, Bojana, and Lennart Laberenz. 2013. *. . . in a non-wimpy way / steve paxton.* Available on vimeo.com/76095626, 18′01″.

DeFrantz, Thomas F., and Anita Gonzalez. 2014. "Introduction." In *Black Performance Theory.* Durham, NC: Duke University Press, pp. 1–16.

Diawara, Manthia. 2009. *Édouard Glissant: One World in Relation*, K'a Yéléma Productions, 48 min.

Ellison, Ralph. [1955]. "Living with Music." Reprinted in *Living with Music.* New York: Modern Library, 2002, pp. 3–14.

Felber, Christian. 2015. "Contact vs. Capitalism: At the Contactfestival Freiburg, curated by Daniela Schwartz with responses by Adrian Russi, Eckhard Müller, Sara Shelton Mann, Steve Paxton, Daniel Lepkoff, Nita Little, and Nancy Stark Smith." In *Contact Quarterly*, Unbound; available at https://contactquarterly.com/cq/unbound/index.php#view=contact-vs-capitalism.

Fischlin, Daniel, Ajay Heble, and George Lipsitz. *The Fierce Urgency of Now: Improvisation, Rights, and the Ethics of Cocreation.* Durham, NC: Duke University Press, 2013.

Foster, Susan Leigh. 2002. *Dances That Describe Themselves: The Improvised Choreography of Richard Bull.* Middletown, CT: Wesleyan University Press.

Goldman, Danielle. 2007. "Bodies on the Line: Contact Improvisation and Techniques of Nonviolent Protest." *Dance Research Journal* 39.1, pp. 60–74.

Goldman, Danielle. 2010. *I Want To Be Ready: Improvised Dance as a Practice of Freedom.* Ann Arbor: University of Michigan Press.

Hennessy, Keith. 1996. "Love and Sex, Touch and Weight: 11 Notes on Sexuality, Sex, Gender, Community & Contact Improvisation." *Contact Quarterly* 21.1, Winter/Spring, pp. 68–70.

Hennessy, Keith. 2014. "848 Community Space: Queer, Sex, Performance and Contact Improvisation in 1990s San Francisco." *Contact Quarterly* 39.1, Winter/Spring, pp. 36–38.

Hennessy, Keith. 2019. *Questioning Contact Improvisation.* San Francisco, CA: Circo Zero.

Horrigan, Kristin. 2017. "Queering Contact Improvisation. Addressing Gender in CI Practice and Community." *Contact Quarterly* 42.1, Winter/Spring, pp. 39–43.

Houston-Jones, Ishmael, and Keith Hennessy. 2017. "Our Own AIDS Time: Keith Hennessy and Ishmael Houston-Jones in Conversation." *Open Space SF Moma.* Available on openspace.sfmoma.org/2017/02/our-own-aids-time-keith-hennessy-and-ishmael-houston-jones-in-conversation/, February 9.

Houston-Jones, Ishmael, and Fred Holland. 1983. "'Wrong' Contact Manifesto." In *Fred Holland & Ishmael Houston-Jones, 1983. Contact at 2nd & 10th.* Video by Cathy Weis. Available on vimeo.com/114657723, posted on December 16, 2014.

Houston-Jones, Ishmael, Nita Little, Keith Hennessey, and Ann Cooper Albright. 2021. "Panel—Long View: CI as a Political Practice?" In Sze-Wei Chan, Kristin Horrigan, Diana Thielen, and Ariadna Franco. *The Future of CI: A 3-Day International Online Conference.* Earthdance, MA: April 23.

Lorde, Audre. 1978 [2019]. *Black Unicorn.* London: Penguin Classics.

Lorde, Audre. 1981. "The Uses of Anger." *Women's Studies Quarterly* 9:3, pp. 278–285.

Moten, Fred. 2003. *In The Break: The Aesthetics of the Black Radical Tradition.* Minneapolis: University of Minnesota Press.

Moten, Fred. 2015. "Amuse-bouche." In Claudia La Rocco and Judy Hussie-Taylor (eds.), *Dancers, Buildings and People in the Streets*. New York: Danspace Project. Available on https://danspaceproject.org/2018/04/13/fred-moten-amuse-bouche/.

Moten, Fred, and Stefano Harney. 2013. *The Undercommons: Fugitive Planning and Black Study*. London; New York: Minor Compositions.

Moten, Fred, and Stefano Harney. 2021. *All Incomplete*. London; New York: Minor Compositions.

Moten, Fred, and Wu Ingrid Tsang. 2018. *Who Touched Me?* Amsterdam: If I Can't Dance.

Muyumba, Walton M. 2009. *The Shadow and the Act: Black Intellectual Practice, Jazz Improvisation, and Philosophical Pragmatism*. Chicago: University of Chicago Press.

Nelson, Lisa, Christina Svane, and Cathy Weis. 1983. *Contact at 10th & 2nd*. VideoDa & Contact Quarterly.

Nelson, Karen. 1996. "Touch Revolution." *Contact Quarterly*, 21.1, Winter/Spring, pp. 65–67.

Nelson, Karen. 2018. "CI (Embodied) Interrogates Its Own History." *Contact Quarterly* 43.1, Winter/Spring, pp. 39–43.

Norman, Alex J. 1977. "Mutual Aid: A Key to Survival for Black Americans." *The Black Scholar* 9.4, pp. 44–49.

Novack, Cynthia J. 1990. *Sharing the Dance: Contact Improvisation and American Culture*. Madison: University of Wisconsin Press.

Paxton, Steve. 1983. "Dear Ishmael." June 29. Available at www.ishmaelhouston-jones.com/photos.

Paxton, Steve. 1987. "Improvisation Is...." *Contact Quarterly* 12.2, Spring/Summer, pp. 15–19.

Paxton, Steve. 1993. "Drafting Interior Techniques." *Contact Quarterly* 18.1, Winter/Spring, pp. 61–68.

Paxton, Steve. 2009. "Talk at CI36 (transcript)." *Contact Quarterly* 34.1, Winter/Spring, pp. 11–15.

Rabah-Konaté, Myriam. 2021. "Race et corporéité dans le Contact Improvisation. Une perspective noire entre Europe et Maroc." In *La perspective de la pomme. Histoires, politiques et pratiques du Contact Improvisation*. Rome: Piretti, pp. 189–198.

Robinson, Cedric J. [1983] 2021. *Black Marxism: The Making of the Black Radical Tradition*. London: Penguin.

Sengco, Joseph. 2016. "A Response to 'Leave Your Identity at the Door?'" *Contact Quarterly* 41.1, Winter/Spring; available at https://contactquarterly.com/contact-improvisation/newsletter/index.php#view=a-response-to-leave-your-identity-at-the-door.

Spade, Dean. 2020. "Solidarity Not Charity: Mutual Aid for Mobilization and Survival." *Social Text* 38.1, pp. 131–151.

Spillers, Hortense J. 1987. "Mama's Baby, Papa's Maybe: An American Grammar Book." *Diacritics* 17.2, Summer, pp. 64–81.

Stark Smith, Nancy. 1986. "Back in Time." *Contact Quarterly* 11.1, Winter, p. 3.

Stark Smith, Nancy. 2006. "Harvest: One History of Contact Improvisation." *Contact Quarterly* 31.1, Summer/Fall, pp. 46–54.

Stark Smith, Nancy. 2015. "Sensation as Portal: Worlds within Worlds within Words." *Contact Quarterly* 40.1, Winter/Spring, p. 3.

Suseno, Andrew. 2019. "My Story about People of Color's Contact Improvisation (POC CI) Jams and Parcon Resilience" in *CQ Unbound* online; available at [https://contactquarterly.com/cq/unbound/view/my-story-about-people-of-colors-contact-improvisation-poc-ci-jams-and-parcon-resilience#$]

Weheliye, Alexander G. *Habeas Viscus: Racializing Assemblages, Biopolitics, And Black Feminist Theories of the Human*. Durham, NC: Duke University Press, 2014.

Will, Taja. 2018. "Inclusion or Invisibility for POC in CI." in *Contact Quarterly*, vol. 43.2, Summer/Fall, p. 39.

Will, Taja, Richard Kim, Leslie Heydon, and Rebecca Bryant. 2020. "Race in Contact Improvisation." www.bridgeproject.art/interview-race-in-contact-improvisation, Interview conducted on September 15, 2020.

Wynter, Sylvia. 1976. "Ethno or Sociopoetics." *Alcheringa: Ethnopoetics* 2.2, pp. 78–94.

Wynter, Sylvia. 2003. "Unsettling the Coloniality of Being/Power/Truth/Freedom: Towards the Human, after Man, Its Overrepresentation—An Argument." *CR: The New Centennial Review* 3.3, pp. 257–337.

Epigraph

brooks, mayfield. 2019. *Viewing Hours*. New York: The Kitchen; https://www.printedmatter.org/catalog/56364.

Vaccaro, Jeanne. 2018. "'Judson Loves Transsexuals': Tracing a Genealogy of Identity and Dance." In Lou Cantor and Katherine Rochester (eds.), *Intersubjectivity*, vol. 2: *Scripting the Human*. Berlin: Sternberg, pp. 99–105.

6
Tracing the Natural Body for More Inclusive and Equitable CI Futures

Robin Raven Prichard

It is 2010, and I am at a two-week Contact Improvisation (CI) workshop taught by two highly respected CI teachers. One participant shows a video of a friend's new baby alone in a crib and waving her limbs. Among the oohs and ahhs, the teacher says: "That is the most perfect example of Contact dance. If only we could be like that baby again." I think to myself—wow, that's not at all what I am trying to do when I dance CI. As the workshop continues, we roll, root, and fly, we lean, fall, and press, we suspend, shift, and catch, in solos, twos, threes, or twelves. We receive quixotic instructions, such as "remember being starfish." I recognize that many of the instructions we are given match the rhetoric of early modern dancers, like language reminiscent of Isadora Duncan: "be a vessel for something greater than yourself," and "dance training is actually untraining." In many exercises, we work through various stages of biological evolution, and it is implicitly understood that many of these stages are preferable to the cultural, contemporary world in which we live and dance. How odd, I think, that 100 years later, two dance forms that feel and look completely different from each other share similar, fundamental ideas about the body. Yet their principles diverge, and both visually portray the culture and time period in which they developed, much more so than any unified aesthetic of the body. The implication exists in both that an untrained or de-trained body, unattenuated by culture or learning—a "natural body"—underlies good dancing. I wonder why my "natural body" needs so much training.

It is not an accident that CI and the pre-modern dance of Isadora Duncan share a fundamental belief about the natural body as a pure place separated from culture. Ideas from the early twentieth century permeate the past 100 years of dance and somatics training, including CI; yet because the concepts can remain unrecognized, they act on individuals in subtle ways that are not always known. Ideas about the natural body can also be the silent carriers of the biases of the nineteenth and early twentieth centuries, including racism, misogyny, classism, and heterosexism. While the values that result from the nineteenth- and early-twentieth-century ideas and practices have been discarded, often the biases are conveyed forward through invisibilized norms.

In this essay, I aim to demonstrate that the natural body and natural movement are sets of aesthetic choices bound by culture, like any aesthetic or artistic practice. Through the legacies of somatics and modern dance, CI has adopted Eurocentric biases about what is assumed to be a neutral, natural body, and these concepts have negatively impacted inclusion and equity in CI. Thus, by analyzing and challenging the natural body, CI can address its past and make equitable and inclusive choices for the future.

This essay traces the natural body through the developments of modern dance and somatics, two strands that weave together particularly toward the latter twentieth century, and strikingly so in CI. The natural body co-constitutes and transmits ideas of race, gender, class,

Robin Raven Prichard, *Tracing the Natural Body for More Inclusive and Equitable CI Futures* In: *Resistance and Support.* Edited by: Ann Cooper Albright, Oxford University Press. © Oxford University Press 2024. DOI: 10.1093/9780197776308.003.0007

and notions of freedom and liberation, transforms into the neutral body through somatics and release techniques, and thus continues to assert influence on CI as a "secret skeleton." I identify ways in which CI both reinforces and repudiates conceptions of the natural body, illuminating the ways in which the natural/neutral body is both validated and challenged within improvisational movement practices. The fundamental question this investigation leads to is: How can the exclusion and inequity that are caused by conceptions of the natural body be attenuated, negotiated, and ultimately changed?

Both the practices and teachings of CI are important, the everydayness as well as the deliberate transmissions. CI is not one monolithic practice or a set of hierarchically controlled ideas, and CI manifests in multiple ways in multiple sites. The practices and concepts that I trace reoccur through time and in various sites, but it is impossible to account for the wide diversity of CI practices or its worldwide dispersion. One failure of this chapter is its American-centeredness. While this is appropriate in terms of the early development of CI, I acknowledge that CI has developed differently in multiple places and situations. I hope others will write the histories of CI in other locations, as the authors in the third part of this book, Local Communities/Global Contexts, have done.

What Is the Natural Body?

The natural body is an ideologically constructed binary of Western metaphysical philosophy. Nature exists in opposition to culture, and one cannot exist without the other. Nor could they exist without the foundational mind/body binary in which culture and the mind align under a privileged valence, while body and nature exist together as unprivileged sites. Culture/nature also align with other binaries, such as male/female, rational/emotional, white/nonwhite, ultimately aligning a natural body with femaleness, emotionality, and the earth. The natural body is a construct in which a biological body exists outside of and prior to culture. In simple twentieth-century terms, a natural body is the nature side of the nature/nurture dichotomy: a timeless body unaffected by culture.

Early Twentieth Century Ideas about the Body

As the twentieth century began, social upheavals and anxieties of modern life caused people to long nostalgically for the past and for stability, both of which the natural body seemed to offer. People believed that modern society threatened men's masculinity and women's connection with their natural bodies. In gendered responses, men played "savage" by pretending to be Native Americans, joining the Boy Scouts, or becoming survivalists; women endeavored to dance and move naturally, gaining direction from classical Greek sculpture and pottery and Delsarte training. In these gendered ways, men and women compensated for the unhealthy effects of modern living. Natural movement and dance, therefore, became an antidote for the insecurities of a modern, industrial life.

Recapitulation theory provides a key to understanding how white subjects, particularly men, could utilize the return to nature without being permanently polluted by it or stuck within a lower evolutionary stage. Dependent on social evolution, recapitulation theory posits that children relive stages of social evolutionary development on their way to adulthood.

124 Resistance and Support

Specifically colonial, racist, and classist, recapitulation theory imagined that only white men were able to make it through all the evolutionary stages; Indigenous, Black, other racialized people, and even working-class Europeans were biologically inhibited from reaching full civilization (Morgenson 2016). Paradoxically, primitive people were lucky to still possess this direct connection to nature, while they were denied access to the privileged realm of the mind, rationality, and advancement. White boys and men, however, could absorb primitiveness temporarily through enacting indigeneity, without relinquishing their civilized status. The concept that only certain people could regress temporarily to primitiveness and then advance back to civilization becomes important in modernism's justification as to who can access the universal body in the development of dance in the twentieth century.

Modern Dance Legacies

Isadora Duncan endures as an iconic figure of early-twentieth-century dancing and the most well-known progenitor of the natural dancing body. Even now, in the twenty-first century, she claims a place in the popular imagination as well as the annals of dance history as a symbol of spontaneity and freedom. Scholar Ann Daly details how Duncan, through claiming nature as her only teacher, nostalgically traced the natural body back to classical Greece, which represented the romantic values that modernity threatened to destroy. Daly shows how nature signified order, unity, comfort, and stability, and provided the means for the right individual (white and middle-class) to transcend the self and harness the cosmos—in other words, the ability to claim a "universal body." Duncan considered culture the dominant inhibitor and contaminator of individuals, and she believed that the natural body led to freedom and liberation from culturally imposed inhibitions and loss. By claiming a natural body, Duncan posited a free expression that accessed a bodily interior where truth, nature, and stability resided.

Duncan danced out the natural body in gendered, racialized, and classed ways that posited dance in the early twentieth century as white, female, and middle-class. Ann Daly argues that in order to differentiate it from the skirt dancing, vaudeville acts, and ballet—all of which were considered sexualized displays of the female body—Duncan had to align nature with culture, whiteness, and middle-classness. Duncan did this by using the cultural capital of both classical Greece and the nineteenth-century romantic poets (Daly 1995). Presenting a chaste female body, she was able to connect the body to spiritual wellsprings in which her body acted as a natural conduit: "I did not invent my dance, it existed before me; but it was slumbering and I awoke it" (cited in Franco 1995, 5). Further, she connected the natural body to the mind by using the ideas and words of great thinkers of late romanticism. Duncan's construction of the natural body was "an artistic transformation of 'Nature' into 'Culture'" (Daly 1995, 112).

Duncan's dance rearranged the binaries of nature/culture in that she was able to align the natural dancing body with culture, taste, and high art, and she accomplished this elevation and cultural legitimacy through exclusion. She claimed the natural body for herself and for American dance by differentiating it from Black and Native American dances, for which she held only derision. Her vision of American dance had no "tottering, ape-like convulsions of the Charleston," no jazz influences, and, in fact, "no rhythm from the waist down" (Duncan 1927, 42). Moreover, she claimed an innocent, spiritual body for herself by opposing it to the sexualized bodies of Blacks: "this dance will have nothing in it of the co-quetry of ballet or the sensual convulsion of the negro. It will be clean" (Duncan 1927, 43). Lastly, she claimed middle-classness by distinguishing her dance as a higher calling than the wage labor of ballet and vaudeville dancers (Franco 1995). By excluding unwanted connections, Duncan created a pristine status for her white, middle-class dance to express her version of the natural body.

The Primitive Body

Duncan was clear to differentiate the natural body from the primitive body. Here, recapitulation theory becomes important, and the ability to choose becomes an important distinction between the natural body and the primitive body. In modernist art-making, primitiveness must be a temporary choice; if one is relegated by race, gender, or class to primitiveness, then one could not advance past primitiveness to access the civilizing forces of Euro-Western aesthetics. Moreover, those confined to lower evolutionary points could not express human universals since they could not access all points of humanity. Thus, recapitulation theory explains one modernist justification of how race, class, gender, and sexuality bind some to the inability to access universality in modernism.

In contrast to the natural body, the primitive body was non-white, oversexed, lower-class, and unevolved. Non-whites were considered to inhabit a natural physical freedom and to be already bodily liberated, particularly in terms of sexuality. The white imagination imbued primitive people with a troublesome bodily liberation that justified white surveillance and control (Franko 1995).

Women were often consigned to a position in the early twentieth century in which they were incapable of separating from the biology of their bodies. Duncan was able to create a natural body in which the female body could join with nature, yet also transcend it to join with the mind, making women fully evolved—not a given in the early twentieth century. This constituted a major move on which modern dance was based (Daly 1995). Thus, Duncan removed white women from the confines of the primitive body.

As the natural and primitive bodies evolved in the next generation of dance artists, the primitive became useful as source material for white, Western art forms, and many artists pursued "authenticity" through both the unconscious and the primitive. Martha Graham, Ted Shawn, and other early modern dancers were able to descend through evolution temporarily, accessing the primitive body by choice and leveraging it into use value, from which they extracted "newness" and innovation. Yet newness requires the destruction of competing items: "the creation of novelty as commodity, as a salable experience of newness, requires a kind of exclusivity that necessitates [a] practice of elimination" (Rikfin 2017, 169). In order for modern dance choreographers to position their work as new and unique, their source material had to be eliminated as a competing item. Thus, Graham's, Shawn's, and other's temporary use of the primitive body overwrote and disappeared the bodies of those from whom they extracted use value—primarily the Native Americans and African Americans with whom they shared the spaces of American culture and competed with to represent "American dance."

As we trace the natural body into the next generation, it seems to disappear temporarily. The subsequent generation of modern dancers, often epitomized by choreographer Merce

126   Resistance and Support

Cunningham, is usually regarded as a repudiation of the natural body, expressiveness, and interior voyages of primitiveness (Copeland 1995; Foulkes 2002; Morris 2006). Yet the Cunningham generation's rejection of past dance practices and previously conceived notions of the natural body did not question the racist, sexist, classist, or heterosexist traditions implicit in the natural body. Indeed, Cunningham couched his opposition to expressivism and the natural body in gendered terms, simultaneously questioning women's leadership of the field. Cunningham employed masculinist cues in his language to associate expression and emotion with the feminine, and objectivism and action with masculinity (Morris 2006). This was not new to modern dance; Ted Shawn expressed the underlying Euro-Western idea of action as male when he argued for male domination in dance by contending that "men have always done big things, the important things in life, being quite willing to let embroideries and ornamentation be the work of women" (1926, 93). By associating the natural body with women, male choreographers leveraged their privileged position and their associations with action and culture to gain a superior position in dance—by denigrating the feminine and the natural in order to elevate themselves.

Further, Cunningham's chance procedures never resulted in a duet in which women partnered women or men partnered men; his partnering remained an expression of compulsory heterosexuality (Johnston 1998). Nor were Cunningham's casts more racially inclusive (Morris 2006): objectivist modernism was a project of universal white bodies, leaving the gendered, racist, classist, heterosexist inheritances from the earlier era untouched.

Legacies from Somatics

Twentieth-century somatics emerged from the bodily anxieties about modern industrial society, its continuous upheavals, and its lack of consistency or reliability. These anxieties manifested as nostalgia for simplicity, which an earlier, less developed, society was thought to have embodied. Meant as a return to an Edenic state before any human or cultural influences, somatics' fundamental belief was based on the theory that bodies exist in perfect harmony when not influenced by outside forces. Peace, calm, and healing depended on returning to a natural, precultural state in which harm only enters from the outside.

Somatic practitioners' beliefs depended on biological and social evolution as progress of humanity. Early-twentieth-century somaticians intended to retrieve ways of moving that were lost due to modern life—once again, regressing down the evolutionary chain to retrieve the simplicity, stability, and health that the natural body was thought to possess. However, although "primitive peoples" were the most in touch with their natural bodies, they were thought to not have the properties of a rational mind to conjoin it with.

F. M. Alexander is frequently touted as being revolutionary in considering the mind and body not as two separate entities but as working together to bring about the efficient functioning of both. Most accounts remove the fact that Alexander believed that this was available only to whites. "Man's Supreme Inheritance," which was needed for Alexander technique, could only be embodied by white subjects (Alexander 1918). Alexander also justified colonial rule based on his belief that non-whites failed to bring natural instincts under conscious control. He believed that non-whites' physical evolution extended beyond their mental capacity and that they lacked a moral consciousness. Moreover, Alexander believed that lower-class whites had reverted to nature and had thereby lost their higher mental capacity.

Alexander was closely connected to the eugenics movement; in fact, eugenics propagandist Caleb Williams Saleeby, head of the Eugenics Education Society, funded and helped publish Alexander's first book, *Man's Supreme Inheritance*. Alexander equated Africans to animals that rely on base instincts:

> The controlling and guiding forces in savage four-footed animals and in the savage black races are practically the same; and this serves to show that from the evolutionary standpoint the mental progress of these races has not kept pace with their physical evolution from the plane of the savage animal to that of the savage human. (Alexander 1918, 72)

Moreover, Alexander projected negative moral qualities onto African Americans, such as lack of courage: "when confronted with the unusual [African Americans] quaked like cowards, and fled, panic-stricken, from the unaccustomed, as in the case of the negroes in the Southern States of America when the men of the Ku-Klux Klan pursued them on horseback dressed in white" (1918, 161). The Alexander technique thus hails directly from racist and classist ideas of human evolution and eugenics, put into action as movement therapy.

The evolution from animal plane to human plane (anatomically, from the transverse plane to the sagittal plane) was not metaphorical for Alexander; the position of the head on the spine indicated how evolved a person was and what place they should have in society. Alexander's focus on the head reflected social evolutionary ideas that the head, under primary and conscious control, reaching toward heaven, was morally good; habit, base instincts, unconscious control, and poor head posture, was morally bad. Many generations of somaticians adopted the idea that good posture was how a person could reach their "greatest height of attainment in any field" (Sweigard 1974, 202). Improving posture through mental exercises rather than physical ones has remained a core component of somatics and dance training through Alexander technique, Ideokinesis, Irene Dowd, and other forms of visualization techniques.

Alexander's argument that posture was a universal constant and a source for human salvation influenced movement educator Margaret H'Doubler (Huxley 2012). A significant figure straddling the modern dance and somatics areas, H'Doubler established the first university dance major in the United States at the University of Wisconsin, and she influenced generations of students who would go on to teach and establish their own dance programs. Her teachings depended on a conflation of the "correct" with the "natural," and she believed that the first step was to "train back to the natural or correct way of moving" (Ross 2000, xxiv). She constructed a natural body that was non-sexual, moral, and upper-class by creating oppositions to people of color, the lower classes, and particularly African American movement (George 2020). In order to do this, following many others of her time, she projected dubious morals onto raced and classed others. "Sexual display" was projected onto the working class; she considered jazz, for example, as wild and unartistic (Ross 2000). African American movement was savage, overly sexual, and belonged nowhere in a university curriculum. Moreover, freedom should be also limited to white, middle-class people. Thus, H'Doubler strived for a construction of the natural body that was pure and non-sexualized; a body that reflected whiteness, morality, and middle-class values led to liberation and was meant to represent neutrality and universality.

Resistance and Support

Mabel Todd's book, *The Thinking Body*, published originally in 1937 with the most updated printing in 2008, was a study of human physiology that utilized biomechanics, anatomy, and kinesiology, in order to bring about movement re-education (2008). Todd's project focused a great deal on mechanical balance, utilizing postural alignment to increase efficiency and find ease. She taught her course "Structural Hygiene" at Teacher's College, Columbia University, where she influenced generations of teachers, including Lulu Sweigard, the developer of Ideokinesis. As the name suggests, Structural Hygiene equated uprightness with moral goodness; it symbolized positive progress and was grounded in a conflation of biological and social evolution. It also equated beauty with progress: efficient movement produced "more pleasing upright figures" (Todd 2008, ix). Upright posture indexed rational thinking, morality, and evolved consciousness. She stated, "watch any man as he walks down the avenue, and you can determine his status in life . . . the explorer and pioneer stand up; the prisoner and the slave crouch; the saint leans forward, the overseer and magnate lean back" (2008, 1–2).

Todd's work relied on concepts of a primitive mind and body that an advanced mind and body worked to overcome; freedom and volition were only available to the fully evolved. She believed that body efficiency depended on accessing the movement patterns of lower phylogenic species that remained as remnants in the human body due to evolution (George 2020). Students were emulating the evolutionary struggle, the object of which was to obtain the full evolutionary uprightness of a white, middle-class, morally good individual. Todd depended upon a biological body that was objective, pure, and non-sexual, yet presumed to be heterosexual. Here, a natural body transforms into a neutral body—a body described through anatomical language that is supposedly unaffected by culture and can be utilized as a universal body.

All three somatic teachers used science to create a body that was biological, pre-cultural, and "natural," as well as covertly white, middle-class, and non-sexual. Also evident within these three somaticians is a transition from a natural body to a neutral body: a universal body under natural physical forces. Somaticians and dance teachers utilized anatomy and kinesiology to enact a universal body, forwarding assumptions of neutrality as valenced with whiteness, middle-classness, and a purity that implied cisgenderedness and heterosexuality.

Early Contact Improvisation

CI both enacts and reflects a full transition from a natural body to a neutral body. As a generic and scientifically knowable body, the neutral body defaults to white, upper-class, sanitized, and de-sexualized valences without an overt realization of their presences. This completes the transition from the earlier romantic Duncan body and the early modern dance body à la Graham, which were mysterious, ineffable locations in touch with infinite natural forces that could never be fully known. One might be in touch with these natural forces for a short time, even channel them through the conduit of the body, but they were never fully knowable. Through CI, Paxton reverses this valence; the neutral body becomes fully knowable through science, observation, and experience, whereas elements of race, class, as well as psychology and spirituality, become the true unknowables, expunged temporarily from the practice. Thus, Paxton did not disavow a cultural body; rather, he regarded it as an impediment to a truly neutral body and thus not relevant to the concerns of early CI.

Physical, Aesthetic, and Political Freedoms of the Neutral Body

Paxton heavily relied on descriptions of forces such as weight, momentum, friction, and investigations of space, time, and mass: all scientific physical concepts that are key to CI, somatics, and early modern dance. Both Duncan and Paxton depended on the physical force of gravity and the assumption that ideas could be explained "directly to the body" (Paxton 2003, 179). Paxton heralds an early use of such specific scientific language with dance, prefiguring uses of the neutral body that release techniques and modern dance technique would later fully adopt. In particular, Paxton uses the sciences of physics and anatomy to describe the organism in its environment and its response to planetary forces. Paxton's generic person, "a simple imaginary person with no physical, sensorial, or social inhibitions," or even more favorably, a child (1993, 64), could find the neutral body by attending to the way the body reflexively interacts with its environment.

Reflecting back on the beginnings of CI, in 1993, Paxton remembers:

> Once things were relatively simple. I thought I knew how this then-nameless work should not be described. It was to be about improvisation without any ambiguous appeals to the imagination, because I did not know precisely what "the imagination" was. . . . For the same reason I would omit mention of sexuality, psychology, spirituality. These I would leave in the hands of the experts, and proceed with what seemed more immediate: the senses and the physical body. (2003, 176)

Paxton did not use the binary language of mind and body (or nature/culture); nevertheless, he delineated between a neutral body and a social body, using complex and scientifically oriented language. As Bob Turner notes, Paxton's explicit and detailed physiological discussions relied on and reinforced conceptual binaries of mind/body and culture/nature through the "repeated opposition of the 'reflex' and 'bodily,' on the one hand, to mere 'habit,' 'culture,' and 'consciousness,' on the other" (2010, 131).

Paxton and early CI hold the same relation to freedom and liberation vis-à-vis the physical body as early modern dance and somatics in which the physical body is a site of liberation and potential freedom, while oppressive forces lie in society. Paxton's focus was on what the culture had "physically suppressed or selected out" and "what might be reclaimed" (1993, 64). CI's physiological claims to freedom and its scientific aspects become, as explained by Cynthia Novack, "a neutral value, a part of natural law rather than an aesthetic (cultural) overlay" (1990, 68).

Importantly, though, Paxton does not claim that dance is any freer of disciplinary procedures on the body than any other cultural production; rather, in dance, "repression of possibilities is the general rule, mirroring social forms" (1972, 133). He does, however, locate freedom within improvisational potentialities, the physical body, and in particular, the reflexes. Without consciousness as an obstacle, the body could be free, spontaneous, and uninhibited, much like Duncan's natural dancing.

Like the preceding artists in the lineage of modern dance, Paxton also positions CI as a realm of aesthetic freedom, disrupting what he had inherited from the previous generation to create new models of artistic possibilities. Paxton's aesthetic freedom was intimately tied to eliminating the constraints of the technical and organizational rule of both dance and

130 Resistance and Support

society. Paxton's aesthetic freedom would result from returning decision-making to dancers and anyone who moved: "the weighty theatrical tradition of subjecting one's self to another person's aesthetic of time-space-effort manipulation is ignored in favor of the attempt to be emancipated without confining or restricting others" (2003, 131). Paxton rebelled as well from Cunningham's impersonal practices; CI would be directed by the sensations of the movers, not rules and codes that produced proper performance. By removing cultural constraints that produced inhibitions, CI would free the consciousness from cultural influences, which Paxton conceptualized as block and gaps in conscious awareness. Thus, any person could excavate a natural, unfettered body by removing the layers of culture that adhered to the neutral body.

Paxton, like Duncan and other early modern dancers, proclaimed the potential political freedom of CI. However, while most modern dancers considered that the political realm existed within the content of the dances as social critique—that is, the message—Paxton located the political in the power relations in the studio and the physical relationships between improvisors. CI would not just reform the movement of dance, but the structure and hierarchy of the dance studio as well: "In modern dance (Graham, Limón, Lang, et al.), the same social form was used except magicians rather than monarchs held sway. Post-modern dancers (Cunningham, Marsicano, Waring) maintained alchemical dictatorships, turning ordinary materials into gold, but continuing to draw from classical and modern-classical sources of dance company organization" (Paxton 1992, 131).

Paxton saw within CI the potential to impact not only the individual or the world of choreographic performance, but larger political structures as well. Bob Turner offers the idea that CI's potential, both then and now, is in encouraging a

> radically participatory, active subject—capable of acting assertively and attentively in determining its own life, liberty, and happiness. . . . CI's interior techniques could encourage us individually and collectively to act more directly, to take increasingly active responsibility— through our liberal political and societal institutions, or if necessary through other means— in the determination of our own lives. (2010, 129)

Yet Turner also notes that CI has largely abandoned the political ideals and possibilities of CI and has narrowed concerns to primarily the individual and their body. In so doing, Turner criticizes the turn CI has taken that aligns it with American liberal cultural practices, where CI becomes a celebration of the individual, personal aesthetics, and a spiritual experience through metaphor. Turner attributes this to the way that Paxton's physiological discussions rely on pre-established oppositional categories already integrated into society's understandings of the body in culture. In other words, while using the preexisting categories of the natural and neutral body, Paxton both reinforces the categories as well as challenges them. However, Paxton's heirs, according to Turner, have focused almost exclusively on the ways that CI reinforces the binary categories; "thus CI [became] an activity of the body and the soul; the body itself became spiritual, and one needed to be free from the mind" (2010, 130). For Post-Paxton CI dancers, the body's pre-cultural status excluded the need to address the cultural production of a body. In this, CI has a political potential that has yet to be realized. I argue that this political potential must be reorganized around diversity, equity, and inclusion to reform the white body supremacist, sexist, and queerblind codes that underlie the tacit acceptance of a generic, neutral body.

Training the Neutral Body

Because CI is improvisational and determined in the moment by each individual, some have asserted that CI has no dominating aesthetic; release technique teachers and somaticians often claim the same, while asserting that their forms should be used as a universal training system. By making a claim to natural law, objectivity, and planetary forces, CI dancers and others ignore the existence of cultural foundations that any practice—artistic or pedestrian—necessarily contains. Their claim to the neutral is nothing less than an entitlement to an objectivity that no one else can access—a universal that belongs only to them.

While the natural body dancing in the 1900s looks very different than the natural body dancing in the twenty-first century, an underlying precept in the training of the natural/neutral body is that training is often untraining. If adults can undo all the cultural habits, responses, and inhibitions that they have accreted, then the neutral body can be excavated. Training should return one to a natural state before any learning; in fact, children and animals are to be emulated since they have fewer layers of cultural sediment. Thus, a baby in a crib, while doing nothing related to CI, can be considered the perfect CI dancer. Harm in the neutral body is conceptualized as coming from the outside world, which is chaotic and damaging; the inside, or the pure neutral body, is ordered, calm, and comforting. Therefore, the unlearning that CI and other forms achieve will lead to a naturally derived harmony and ease.

The pursuit of this ease determines the aesthetic preferences of CI, even when no aesthetics are predetermined or given within the initial form. In their history of the natural body, Doran George illuminates how CI has developed a preference for ways of moving that reject great effort. Muscular force, for example, is negative, equating to the ego; it is an example of the mind overtaking the body (George 2020). This does not signify that CI, somatics, and dance will not use muscles, but that muscles are de-prioritized: as little muscle use as is possible becomes the measurement of good dancing. Instead, momentum, initiation, and flow are prioritized; muscles follow secondarily and rarely need to be consciously considered. This non-muscular, non-ego-driven movement leads to ease that allows both psychological release and safeguards injury. Effort, on the other hand, causes emotional repression and potential injurious harm to the body. Overworking is a "retrogressive, psychological habit tied up with willful bodily control" (George 2020, 41).

The dominant CI aesthetics prefers physical looseness and unpredictability, both of which are equated with freedom. Indirectness and yielding are privileged, as direct movement and force can be a result of mindful striving. And of course, non-muscular use of a body that chooses momentum, flow, and sequential articulation leads to a neutral, unencumbered self.

These aesthetic priorities are not just the aesthetics of CI and release techniques; through the genealogical inheritance outlined above, they are valenced with white, middle-class, heterosexualized bodies. Further, ease is connected to white, upper- and middle-classness through an imposed opposition to the African American aesthetic of high, boundless energy, and the working-class aesthetics of ribald sexuality and lack of restraint. Moreover, the choice to do non-physical work has historically been limited to the white upper classes: the choice to move with ease has been a privileged one. Movement in general has not equaled freedom; but the conscious choice of when and how to move and the option to move with ease have equated to a full humanity and liberation.

CI's entanglement with somatics indicates that ideas of the evolution of the species have a stronghold within the teaching and development of CI. For example, Bonnie Bainbridge Cohen's Body-Mind Centering (BMC) was published in *Contact Quarterly* from 1980 to 1992 and demonstrates a strong entanglement between BMC and CI. Cohen also acknowledged Mabel Todd as an influence in her work (Cohen 1993), and BMC's use of accessing the lower phylogenic patterns locked in the human body due to evolution reveals Todd's lineage. BMC is an integrated and embodied approach to movement and consciousness undertaken to discover ease that underlies transformation (Cohen 1993). One of BMC's fundamental procedures is to integrate the re-patterning of developmental movement patterns, in a practice that follows the theory of "ontogeny recapitulates phylogeny": the biological growth of an individual replays the evolution of its species. Originating in 1866, this concept was once taken as natural law and taught as fact; now it is regarded as a theory with limited applicability. BMC is recapitulation theory in action: Cohen systematically takes a mover through the evolutionary stages from single-cell organism, through the navel radiation phase of starfish, through to human development. Cohen also utilizes the reflexes and movement patterns of developing infants and children. If a person can adequately go through all stages, according to Cohen, they will be whole, unstuck, and transform into ease (1993). In BMC, a mover will, in essence, return to a neutral body by working scientifically through evolutionary processes, thereby freeing the body from sedimented layers of culture that inhibit one from accessing developmental patterns and bodily wisdom. Only by going backward evolutionarily can we truly be liberated.

Here what is meant to be anatomical or scientific cueing can become mystical imagery for some. The instruction mentioned in the introduction—"remember being starfish"—for those in the know is shorthand for naval radiation: a pattern of six limbs moving inward toward or outward from the navel in synchronicity with each other. This is a pattern that, according to Cohen, must proceed standing upright and the contralateral pattern of walking. Thus, BMC participates in an evolution-based teleological grand narrative for the human species and movement. For those not in the know, however, it is a quixotic instruction that can only be taken imagistically, and many have taken it in a quasi-spiritual, mystical way. As Turner argues, the original physiological focus of early CI is now taught and described through metaphor and poetry, a spiritual endeavor concerned with " 'getting at the soul of our dance' by means of metaphor" (2010, 129).

Why Is the Neutral Body White, Queerblind, and Modest?

Neutral, with all its codes and attachments, is still constructed in opposition to characteristics that have been determined in the twentieth century to be African American and Latinx: commercial, sexually explicit, overly showy, rhythmic, and affective. It is not happenstance that the main aesthetics in CI are non-sexual, not ostentatious or pretentious, contain little in the way of counts or rhythm, repudiate marketability and profitability, and are non-affect driven. The aesthetics of CI and the neutral body are as much a reaction and repudiation of African American aesthetics as they are an embrace of preferred characteristics. The neutral body is white, queerblind, and modest by design.

CI has exhibited an enormous ability to overlook African American contributions to American dance and to the fact that improvisation itself is an originary African American form and technique. A quote from *Contact Quarterly* in 1977 elucidates this obfuscation, proclaiming that CI "is the closest thing that dance has to jazz" (Woodward 1977, 16). In order to assert this, one has to have erased over 70 years of dance that occurred in tandem with jazz music, from ragtime to concert jazz.

Colorblindess, Queerblindness, Genderblindness

Colorblindness is a term that indicates a form of racism in which one professes to be unable to see race. This claim seemingly protects the speaker from charges of racism; in reality, the "inability" to see race means that a person is unable to confront racial biases when they happen (Bonilla-Silva 2013). The claim of colorblindness implies that the problem is in talking about and bringing up race, and it asserts equality by denying racial and cultural differences. This is the general strategy that CI, release techniques, and much dance training held for many decades (Prichard 2019).

Doran George asserts that downtown dance and CI erased the cultural sources of their forms by claiming that the forms were pre-cultural (2020). By claiming natural sources for aesthetics, white downtown dancers and CI practitioners could claim improvisation as their own without acknowledging African American or Asian American cultural influences. As George details, mid-century American somaticians and artists extracted ideals from Eastern cultures, then removed the culture's ownership by proclaiming them natural, pre-cultural, and transhistorical. Positioning Eastern philosophy and artistic practices as universal crafted the circumstances in which Western artists and somaticians had equal authority to use Zen and Eastern epistemologies. Thus, release technique and somatics contain similar ideologies to Asian art forms, but crucially, the role of culture has been removed and replaced with nature. The same is true of the way that Africanist forms and influences were erased. Thus, the Western rhetoric of the natural body claims authority over all existence everywhere through a universal natural body and essential bodily truths.

Genderblindness was also embraced in the early years of CI, and asserting that both genders should be trained the same was radical in the dance world in the 1970s. CI accomplished liberation in many ways for many dancers through its non-gendered approach to movement. Women lifting other dancers was liberating for women stuck inside feminine codes of moving, and men lifting other men was equally radical in allowing men to inhabit roles that resisted masculinist codes. Without downplaying the liberation that existed and still exists for many in the non-gendered teaching of CI, the assumed genderblindness of CI can, once again, be a place in which the oppression through gender is unseen, unacknowledged, and therefore assumed not to exist. When one is trained not to consider gender roles and to think of a practice as genderless, one can become blind when gender normativity reasserts itself.

The performed modesty of the neutral body creates its own challenges, in asserting both a queerblind practice and a heteronormative sexlessness. This makes it difficult to identify an assumed heterosexuality or the ways in which gendered and sexed codes are inherent in the neutral body. In a sanitized, supposedly non-sexual form, dancers will have a harder time recognizing gender and sex oppression and their associated power differentials. When sexuality is ignored because it is regarded as absent or inconsequential, it makes dancers less able to recognize in the moment when sexuality is playing a role in a partner's dancing. It also made it difficult to complain about unwanted sexualized touch, as people within CI were not

134   Resistance and Support

practiced in issues of consent or sexuality. By sanitizing sexuality out of the body, several generations of CI dancers were trained to ignore sexuality in the practice, which led to distrusting and second-guessing themselves when put into a sexualized position by a partner. Sadly, this created generations of "perfect victims," who were trained to ignore sexual possibilities rather than identify and block unwanted sexual contact.

Late Twentieth-Century and Twenty-First-Century Natural/Neutral Bodies

In what ways is the natural/neutral body being embraced or repudiated? What aesthetics are being proposed in forms that ostensibly contain no aesthetics? Currently, some assert release techniques as the universal location in which the human body exists free of aesthetics, signaling release techniques as the current carriers of the natural body. Wendell Beavers delivered a good example of this when he wrote of his release technique as consisting of developmental/evolutionary principles, ranging "freely through pre-history toward the forward edge of the future," and transcending the industrial revolution through uncovering, undoing, and not doing (2008, 125). He described the foundation of his technique as basic, primitive patterns, as a process of de-evolution, and of unlearning and returning to zero. His specific mention of the industrial revolution reveals his ties to early somatics and late-nineteenth-century ideas of nature, how nature dwells within the body and is threatened by human culture, and his notions of unlearning mirror the philosophies of Duncan and other progenitors of natural dancing. Beavers presumed the neutrality of his technique and other release techniques when he suggested that somatics could be used to enter a new dance era of World Dance. According to Beavers, American modern dance has an aesthetic bias; somatics, by contrast, is aesthetic-free and thus can be used to "break down the barriers between existing cultural forms" and establish a new foundation for modern dance (2008, 132). Beavers unwittingly demonstrates how the release body is a restatement of the early twentieth century's natural body, with scientific and anatomical terms occluding its cultural specificities in order to claim a universal, objective body.

Many release technique teachers and some CI teachers still depend on Todd's 1937 anatomy book, even though scientific ideas have changed a great deal in the past 80 years, and Todd's outdated ideas are obvious and numerous. If these teachers recognize the outdated scientific elements or the problematic race and class elements, they give no indication of doing so. The only bias recognized and discussed in these teachers' work is the "muscle/bone bias of Western dance" (Beavers 2008, 131). Although the terms of the conversation derive from anatomy and science, the transmissions of ideas and information echo a cult following, passed down by oral history and unencumbered by the scientific method. Thus, the troubling racial and class oppression of Todd and other progenitors is quietly secreted away and the proclaimed universality looms within their techniques.

Twenty-first-century somatics may currently pose the largest potential to challenge the natural/neutral body through theories of inherited trauma as conceptualized by Bessel van Der Kolk (2015) and Resma Menakem (2017). Addressing how trauma impacts physiology and kinesiology, the notion of retreating to or even uncovering an Edenic, precultural body recedes as a possibility; instead, as individuals work somatically, they uncover stored harm induced by societal relations. Moreover, physiology can be changed by these harms and passed on to succeeding generations. Can a natural/neutral body still be accessed? Neither Menakem nor Van der Kolk address this; however, changes to an individual's physiology through cultural impacts indicates that an arrival at a natural/neutral body might be deferred indefinitely. The question remains: Do ideas about inherited trauma challenge the fundamental concept of a natural body, or does it just defer its access through many more steps of recovery? Either way, harm to the body and self is still societal, but through being embodied, stored, and passed on, physical trauma also becomes part of the inside bodily system. While this does not completely disrupt the idea that bodily trauma is imposed from the outside and onto an innocent, peaceful natural self, it does modify this system in that individuals now carry societal harm inside themselves. Therefore, harm can come from both inside or outside: somatics does not necessarily lead to a recovery of primordial states of wholeness.

mayfield brooks's Improvising While Black (IWB) workshops both utilize and contest the natural body. Rather than uncovering reactions to pure physical forces, brooks utilizes improvisation to uncover cultural impacts and explore cultural power. Brooks's workshops challenge somatics' claims to universal humanity in its attempts to find a one-size-fits-all healing (Bibler 2022). Rather, brooks asserts the irrevocable "racial profiling of performance" and the reality that "the body becomes hypervisible and the human inside it becomes invisible" (brooks and Nelson 2016, 38). Brooks uses disorientation to expose anti-Black regimes of perception, and disorientation becomes a method for exploring alternate positions in society. Brooks associates verticality with straight, white, body supremacy; therefore, brooks utilizes CI exercises that employ leaning, falling, rolling, and off-balance in order to find alternate spaces. Because brooks uses familiar exercises from CI and other improvisatory practices, the context in which the exercises are used is what allows the practices to contribute to anti-racism, rather than some inherent property of the exercises themselves.

Improvising While Black does not challenge existing bodily tropes, and it retains the conventional, Western meanings attributed to movement and space: verticality remains a purview of whiteness, backspace symbolizes the past, leading from the head equates to vision, whiteness, and truth. Thus, IWB reinforces the interpretations and meanings of bodily movement and space provided by white supremacy and the hegemonic order; it could be inferred that these associations are naturalized within the practice. Brooks vacates the space that white supremacy claims for itself and, in a move that shows their desire for the marginal, claims alternative spaces. In doing so, IWB retains and strengthens the given binaries and works to privilege alternative spaces, rather than to challenge the system that creates the binaries and exclusion. In this way, brooks's work is content to stay in the margins and abdicate the mainstream to dominant powers. But there is power to staying in the margins: disorientation will not become oriented, fracturedness will not become whole, instability will not become steady, and none of it can become commoditized. Thus, while brooks denaturalizes a universal humanity, they reify tropes of bodily movement and space.

Where Are We Now?

In CI, we see a movement form reckoning with its legacy and endeavoring to rid itself of the natural/neutral body in order to be emancipated from its tacit, oppressive, twentieth-century codes. But will ridding ourselves of the natural/neutral body liberate us from oppression? Or will humans continue to create ways to quickly read and categorize people so as to eliminate

136 Resistance and Support

complexity in relating to others? Will the ideas that replace the natural body set us free from rigid and limiting categories? Or will we continue to find new ways to interpellate individuals before they are even born? As mayfield brooks articulates, in the hypervisibility of the body, will the person *inside* become invisible?

The progressivist ideas of the 2020s are ruthlessly constructionist—a necessary antidote to the earlier tacit oppression of biologism. The natural body and the limitations of race, gender, and sexuality imposed by biology are increasingly disappearing. Within many academic discourses, the body is reduced to only a blank sheet on which society writes itself, generally in the form of depressingly deterministic regulations (Albright 1997; Dempster 2010). With the natural banished, only culture remains. When Ann Cooper Albright writes of "the slippage of outside and inside, of reading the surface of the body as if it were a window to the soul (or at least an 'inner self)" (1997, 42), she speaks of a pervasive identarian approach that limits the reading of the self and others to surface characteristics. Perhaps the inside no longer exists? And if the inside is no longer, is that good news, or bad news? Will the absence of a natural/neutral body liberate us from the oppressive codes of white body supremacy, heteronormativity, and cisgenderism, or will a blank body simply be a place for new, restrictive constructionist codes of discipline to develop?

At *Critical Mass: CI @ 50*, a global CI community gathered in Oberlin, Ohio, to celebrate, reckon with, and unsettle the histories of CI and to imaginatively construct new directions for a much beloved form. Two prevalent strategies for orienting CI toward justice, equity, and inclusion emerged: operating with active consent, and disrupting normative language and practice. What emerged in *CI @ 50* was the incompatibility of consent and disruption. Disruption by design cannot ask for or require consent; and while it only takes one person to disrupt, it takes an entire group to consent. Moreover, in American contexts, disruption is often the container for righteousness, as well as the pathway through which righteousness acts, and righteousness by design finds all other issues less imperative than its own cause, making consent a trivial issue. The closing circle showed the extent to which disruption had exhausted those whose main concerns were not fulfilled through the actions of disruption and the extent to which agreement, wholeness, and unity were desired, as participants struggled even in the last moments to define the rules and processes of closing the conference. This culminates in a looming question: Can consent and disruption exist within the same space at the same time? And if CI demands both, can they negotiate a coexistence?

CI @ 50 was an open platform in which community members were encouraged to offer classes, workshops, discussions, forums, or other assemblies for CI. No proposal was denied. Thus, the festival endeavored to reflect CI communities and was meant to produce a radical inclusion. Yet even a forum meant for maximum inclusion that materialized through the offerings of the participants could not hold every identity, need, or idea about the body. Deeply held beliefs about raced, gendered, classed, and sexed bodies conflicted, occasionally opposing each other in ways that meant that they could not coexist together. Moreover, an American hegemony asserted itself, and many international participants felt run over by American-centric conceptions of raced, gendered, classed, and sexed bodies. This prompted the question of how multiple streams of raced, gendered, classed, and sexed bodies can coexist without disappearing within a hegemonic display of identity.

CI @ 50 showed undeniably that the question for twenty-first-century CI communities is no longer *if* movement contains the oppressive, restrictive codes of culture, but *how*, and by what means they can be challenged and uprooted. *CI @ 50* sought to provide a pathway through the Scylla and Charybdis of body, identity, and culture by acknowledging that the realities of moving bodies, their choices, and processes are the non-negotiables in reforming outmoded, oppressive codes. For some, CI negotiates the places between the blank body and the overly determined cultural self to find more satisfying power distributions and group relations. For others, asserting an identity stream within the form is the most crucial. *CI @ 50* exposed that the inquiries are urgent and passionate, with an intensity of feeling and reaction belying a relevance and timeliness requiring vital attention. Ultimately, if CI can accustom practitioners to making conscious choices in uncertain territory, redistributing power along lines of justice and equity, then CI will become a practice pointing us toward a more just future.

References

Albright, Ann Cooper. 1997. *Choreographing Difference: The Body and Identity in Contemporary Dance.* Hanover, NH; London: Wesleyan University Press.

Alexander, F. Mattias. 1918. *Man's Supreme Inheritance: Conscious Guidance and Control in Relation to Human Movement in Civilization.* New York: E. P. Dutton.

Beavers, Wendell. 2008. "Re-Locating Technique." In *The Body Eclectic: Evolving Practices in Dance Training,* edited by Melanie Bales and Rebecca Nettl-Fiol. Urbana; Chicago: University of Illinois Press, 126–133.

Bibler, Zena. 2022. "Disorientation as Critical Practice: Confronting Anti-Black Perceptual Regimes and Activating the Otherwise in mayfield brooks' Improvising While Black Pedagogy." *Dance Research Journal* 54(1): 30–49. https://doi.org/10.1017/S0149767722000055.

Bonilla-Silva, Eduardo. 2013. *Racism without Racists: Color-Blind Racism and the Persistence of Racial Inequality in the United States.* Lanham, MD: Rowan & Littlefield.

brooks, mayfield, and Karen Nelson. 2016. "Improvising While Black: Writings, Interventions, Interruptions, Questions." *Contact Quarterly* 41(1) (Winter/Spring): 33–39.

Cohen, Bonnie Bainbridge. 1993. *Sensing, Feeling, and Action.* Northampton, MA: Contact Editions. https://www.bodymindcentering.com/about/.

Copeland, Roger. 1995. "Beyond Expressionism: Merce Cunningham's Critique of 'the Natural.'" In *Dance History, An Introduction.* 2nd ed., edited by Janet Adshead-Lansdale and June Layson, 182–197. London; New York: Routledge.

Daly, Ann. 1995. *Done into Dance: Isadora Duncan in America.* Middletown, CT: Wesleyan University Press.

Dempster, Elizabeth. 2010. "Women Writing the Body: Let's Watch a Little How She Dances." In *The Routledge Dance Studies Reader*, edited by Alexandra Carter and Janet O'Shea, 229–235. London; New York: Routledge.

Duncan, Isadora. 1927. *My Life.* Garden City, NY: Garden City Publishing.

Foulkes, Julia. 2002. *Modern Bodies: Dance and American Modernism from Martha Graham to Alvin Ailey.* Chapel Hill; London: University of North Carolina Press.

Franko, Mark. 1995. *Dancing Modernism/Performing Politics.* Bloomington; Indianapolis: Indiana University Press.

George, Doran. 2020. *The Natural Body in Somatics Dance Training*, edited by Susan Leigh Foster. New York: Oxford University Press.

Huxley, Michael. 2012. "F. Matthias Alexander and Mabel Elsworth Todd: Proximities, Practices and the Psycho-Physical." *Journal of Dance and Somatic Practices* 3(1–2): 25–42.

138 Resistance and Support

Johnston, Jill. 1998. *Marmalade Me.* Hanover, NH; London: Wesleyan University Press.

Menakem, Resma. 2017. *My Grandmother's Hands: Racialized Trauma and the Pathway to Mending Our Hearts and Bodies.* Las Vegas, NV: Central Recovery Press.

Morgenson, Scott L. 2015. "Cutting to the Roots of Colonial Masculinity." In *Indigenous Men and Masculinities,* edited by Robert Alexander Innes and Kin Anderson, 38–61. Winnipeg: University of Manitoba Press.

Morris, Gay. 2006. *A Game for Dancers: Performing Modernism in the Postwar Years, 1945–1960.* Middletown, CT: Wesleyan University Press.

Novack, Cynthia, 1990. *Sharing the Dance: Contact Improvisation and American Culture.* Madison: University of Wisconsin Press.

Paxton, Steve. 1972. "The Grand Union." *TDR: The Drama Review* 16(3) (T55): 128–34.

Paxton, Steve. 1993. "Drafting Interior Techniques." *Contact Quarterly* 18(1): 64–78.

Paxton, Steve. 2003. "Drafting Interior Techniques." In *Taken by Surprise: A Dance Improvisation Reader*, edited by Ann Cooper Albright and David Gere, 175–84. Middletown, CT: Wesleyan University Press.

Prichard, Robin. 2019. "From Color-Blind to Color-Conscious: Advancing Racial Discourse in Dance Education." *Journal of Dance Education* 19(4): 168–177. doi:10.1080/15290824.2018.1532570.

Rifkin, Mark. 2017. *Beyond Settler Time: Temporal Sovereignty and Indigenous Self-Determination.* Durham, NC: Duke University Press.

Ross, Janice 2000. *Moving Lessons: Margaret H'Doubler and the Beginning of Dance in American Education.* Gainesville: University of Florida Press.

Shawn, Ted. 1926. *The American Ballet.* New York: H. Holt.

Sweigard, Lulu. 1978. *Human Movement Potential: Its Ideokinetic Facilitation.* New York: Harper and Row.

Todd, Mabel. 2008 [1937]. *The Thinking Body.* Princeton, NJ: Dance Horizons.

Turner, Robert. 2010. "Steve Paxton's 'Interior Techniques': Contact Improvisation and Political Power." *TDR: The Drama Review* 54(3): 123–135.

Van der Kolk, Bessel. 2015. *The Body Keeps the Score: Brain, Mind, and Body in the Healing of Trauma.* New York: Penguin.

Woodward, Stephanie. 1977. "Writing Moving." *Contact Quarterly* 2(3): 16.

7

Underscoring Nancy Stark Smith's Legacy

Definitions and Disruptions

Sarah Young

What is the range in which something can still be what it is?

—Nancy

Introduction

The Underscore was originally developed in 1990 by Nancy Stark Smith (1952–2020) as a framework for practicing and researching dance improvisation. The format evolved out of the multidimensional questions and observations she was tracking through her role teaching and performing Contact Improvisation (CI), as well as co-editing *Contact Quarterly*, an international dance and improvisation journal. The Underscore is a "score" (inspired by the musical term) with twenty-some phases, outlined with simple words and corresponding figurative "gylphs" (see Figures 7.1 and 7.2 below). These chart the stages of solo and group improvisation, starting from arriving, to attuning the body to gravity, to moving in an open score, then a final moment of "harvesting" everyone's reflections. The Underscore usually takes about 3–4 hours and draws on a focused commitment to increasing perception in movement improvisation. It sets up an attention toward experiencing multiple states—physically, mentally, energetically—and a responsiveness to the changing of these states and how they affect the overall composition in the room. Although there is often a progressive arc to the Underscore, Nancy did not consider it linear. I smile each time I think of her saying, "This is a hologram, not a railroad track." Each time it is practiced, it is created anew. Yet, I wonder: How far can the practice morph from its original intentions before it is no longer recognizable as Nancy Stark Smith's legacy?

Each June, around the solstice, 70+ sites worldwide practice the Underscore simultaneously. As a facilitator of this Global Underscore, I have seen how the score itself offers a guidepost for how various groups approach CI and share it in their communities and among their students and collaborators. It is a useful tool, inspiring improvisation through its form, language, structure, ritual, and practice. Inherent in the Underscore is the insistence to keep exploring our options, questioning our choices, and testing its range of possibilities. Yet even with this openness of the Underscore's format, last summer I co-led a version that stretched my assumptions about the Underscore. I recognized that what we had facilitated was *not* how Nancy Stark Smith would have facilitated it. Questions arose: How did it relate to Nancy's vision? Was it respectfully challenging? Or somehow rebuking our elder?

Sarah Young, *Underscoring Nancy Stark Smith's Legacy* In: *Resistance and Support*. Edited by: Ann Cooper Albright, Oxford University Press. © Oxford University Press 2024. DOI: 10.1093/9780197776308.003.0008

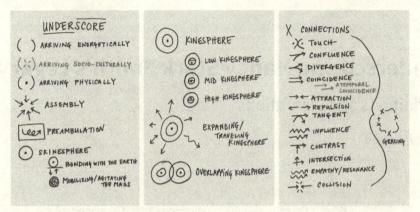

Figure 7.1. The Underscore words and glyphs are written out on five pages during a "talk-through," then posted in the studio during the Underscore practice. Aspects listed in gray are additions suggested in recent years. Many facilitators experiment with variations, prompting discussion and adaptation. Drawings by Sarah Young.

I am committed to perpetuating the Underscore as something that has enough integrity to be recognizable as Nancy Stark Smith's legacy. Simultaneously, times change, bodies change, interests change, and, even in the small group that met weekly with Nancy in Northampton, Massachusetts, we had not arrived at a score that was "finished." So, compounded by Nancy's passing on May 1, 2020, questions of legacy continue to swirl: How can the form evolve and still maintain its connection to the many arenas Nancy had tended with open-ended curiosity? Where do my curiosities lie? I offer here three of my experiences with the Underscore as I explore these questions.

Underscore +/– at the Blue Guitar: Dropping the Bone

From the mechanics of CI to the art of group facilitation, Nancy Stark Smith was an influential mentor of mine. My studies of her work began before I had met her—through her influence on Chris Aiken, my first CI teacher and the person who introduced me to *Contact Quarterly* and early videos of CI while at the University of Illinois, Urbana-Champaign, in 2004. Around 2011, I began crossing paths with Nancy in New York City and at the Bates Dance Festival. Then, starting in 2013, I had the privilege of engaging with Nancy more directly, as I was then the director of Earthdance in Plainfield, Massachusetts, while she was co-editing *Contact Quarterly* nearby in Florence, Massachusetts.[1] We regularly discussed leadership, organization, programming—and CI. It was during these years that I began practicing weekly with Nancy in the Underscore +/– group in Northampton, Massachusetts. We have continued to practice the Underscore since her passing. We have done the Underscore with many variations, including backward and, practically, inside-out. We've extended it

---

[1] Earthdance is an arts, dance, and movement organization and retreat center with a focus on Contact Improvisation (CI) established in 1986 in western Massachusetts in large part due to the proximity to *Contact Quarterly*, www.earthdance.net; *Contact Quarterly* (CQ), a vehicle for moving ideas, has been an international journal of dance, improvisation, performance, and contemporary movement arts since 1975, with Nancy Stark Smith and Lisa Nelson being primary engines. It is the longest-running, independent, artist-made, reader-supported journal devoted to the dancer's voice in the field of contemporary dance and improvisation and is an invaluable archive, www.contactquarterly.com.

Underscoring Nancy Stark Smith's Legacy   141

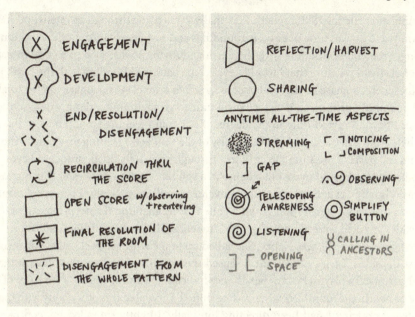

Figure 7.2. The Underscore words and glyphs are written out on five pages during a "talk-through," then posted in the studio during the Underscore practice. Aspects listed in gray are additions suggested in recent years. Many facilitators experiment with variations, prompting discussion and adaptation. Drawings by Sarah Young.

over 24 hours and have moved different phases around every which way, with Sharing at the very beginning, Skinesphere skipped entirely, Assembly during the Open Score, and so on.[2]

Having a regular practice of the Underscore with a committed group creates an environment in which we can play with the structure together, riffing on themes and ideas as they arise over hours, weeks, months, and even years. This also provides a net such that each person can yield to the state that they find themselves in on any given day because the form is permissive enough, the group tolerant enough, and the weekly practice resilient enough to not only handle, but benefit from fluctuations in states and conditions. Among our group of mostly white educated middle-aged Americans, there is a lot of crossover in ethics around CI, though we all have our individual habits and preferences. We have years of practice negotiating touch and consent together, and many years with a shared history of learning together. Through our awareness, we increase our agency to disrupt, interrupt, bulk, and/or amplify our own choices and those of others. Through the repetition and familiarity, we can also fall into fail-safe patterns and deepen into our preferences.

One evening in 2015 at the Blue Guitar, Christie Svane's dance studio at the time, we Arrived Physically and Energetically, then sat in a circle for Assembly. One by one, we shared our needs and curiosities for that particular practice; then we moved through

---

[2] A description of the Underscore, including this terminology and accompanying "glyphs," as well as a bit of history and practice notes, can be found in *Caught Falling: The Confluence of Contact Improvisation, Nancy Stark Smith, and Other Moving Ideas* (Northampton, MA: Contact Editions, 2008) by David Koteen and Nancy Stark Smith. Also a resource: www.nancystarksmith.com/underscore/. Typically, the Assembly occurs near the beginning of the Underscore, with the group specifying their inspirations and parameters for that particular practice. Skinesphere also happens early in the practice as a time for settling individually. After a period of orienting to the space, oneself, and the other dancers, the Open Score unfolds, with more compositional awareness arising in the improvisation. During Sharing, dancers verbally describe "snapshots" of their experience.

142 Resistance and Support

Preambulation and into Skinesphere. Personally, I was going through an intense period, and all I wanted to do was tune out my surroundings and rest deeply into subtle sensation. That evening, I remember Bonding with the Earth and diving so deeply into a parasympathetic rabbit hole that I was sure that I would never come back out! Bonding with the Earth is part of Skinesphere, a phase of the Underscore in which attention is primarily given to all that happens within our skin, so it was a logical time to go spelunking into my own sensations. I noticed beyond myself only to the degree that I could feel the smoothness of the dance floor below me and the cold, hard verticality of the wall I was leaning up against. The other dancers and parts of the studio were blurry through my barely open, unfocused eyes. Then, in my hazy view, I could make out a figure in a soft blue cashmere sweater starting to come my way. Visually, I caught the color and movement, and energetically, I perceived a state and attention that contrasted with my own. While I didn't abandon the deep-sea exploration of my insides, my cells were already beginning to reorganize to the shifting conditions.

The figure, of course, was Nancy. She sidled up to me with her back—that soft sweater—against my shins. I felt her warmth. I sensed the rhythm of her breath, different than my own. I perceived a playful kind of persistence indicating without words, "Come out of there! Come be here in the room!" Slowly, my state shifted. I accepted this other body with the same heightened noticing I had been directing internally. I lightly extended my consciousness and incrementally met her tone. I took this as a bridge into the world beyond my skin—into Overlapping Kinesphere.

Kinesphere is a term Nancy describes in *Caught Falling* as "the sphere or bubble of space around the body through which one can reach and move one's limbs without changing the placement of one's center" (2008, 92). Then, Overlapping Kinesphere is when people dance within their own space while their spheres share the same space with others. I nudged myself—just a little—to lean in a bit more, take a sliver more weight, to unambitiously let my focus take me in a new direction. I was in relationship with this other person through individual choices of attention, weight, and speed.

Like that, I was "in." Nancy would talk about "dropping the bone," often around the timing of when Skinesphere gives way to Kinesphere. It's a process of releasing or shifting tone, perhaps physical or mental, that often starts with noticing. It could be something like, "Oh, I'm still thinking about what happened on my way here. My awareness isn't sticking with anything in this present moment. So, how do I *drop the bone*?" Like a dog unwilling to give up that bone in his mouth, you are compromised. You can't really do anything with it until you let it go.

When I share this story with others in our group, I often get a nod of recognition. Many have had similar experiences with Nancy as an implicit part of doing the Underscore with her. She would bring us back into the room. It wasn't as if I was doing anything wrong, *and* the proportions of where we put our attention matter—whether it's more internally or externally focused, in more of the social realm, in memory, in judgment, and so on. So, physically, nonverbally, with awareness and care, she made a prescriptive attempt to adjust the dials. This became a tether for me, a possible option that was more available because of her close proximity. I was more likely to expand my awareness beyond the confines of my skin. I centered my attention more equally internally and externally, noticing the space was potentiated by active movers and witnesses.

The values enacted that day at the Blue Guitar remain an integral part of my Underscore practice. I check myself: Are my thoughts continually drifting out of the room? Are frequent judgments surfacing? Am I separating from or avoiding people in the space?

I consider Nancy's care and attentiveness toward priming connection in others as part of the Underscore. This means being attentive to others as people, perpetuating the score forward without leaving anyone (too far) behind. (It's part of Human Skills, one of the "pods" of Nancy's States of Grace.) When I am facilitating an Underscore, I pay attention to clues from the group to notice if anyone may be having some difficulty. I listen during Assembly: How are they feeling? What has happened during their day that might impact their focus in the dancing? On occasion, I toy with Nancy's strategy of sidling up to someone who's "in the sticks." I observe how that choice can cause a change in my own state and may or may not shift something for the other person and/or the room. In the Underscore, Nancy figured out a way to organize her understanding and embed her values into a shareable rubric. It was not devised or perpetuated in isolation. She shared it. A lot. She gave away as much of it as possible while being fantastically consistent, adhering to meanings and language, approaches and perspectives that she articulated through dance and conversation with others over years—immersed within the context of the larger form of CI. And, while the whole world came in *through* the research, the primacy was always the dancing. This, for me, is an important part of her legacy.

Saturday Night Underscore at *Critical Mass: CI @ 50*, July 2022

In July 2022, I co-led a version of the Underscore that pushed at the seams of the form. It was Saturday night, the crest of the five-day event, *Critical Mass: CI @ 50*, in which a large group of people gathered at Oberlin College, charged with celebrating 50 years since the inception of the form of CI. The temperament, energy, and attention during the Underscore mirrored the vibrating, treading toward polarizing, zeitgeist of the event and the times. The conditions of this particular Underscore were different from any of the other Underscore experiences that I have had. Some people said later that what we did wasn't even an Underscore. Before I describe what happened, let me begin with the two different Underscore-focused sessions offered in the afternoon before the big event. The sessions' facilitators had studied directly with Nancy, and both sourced the aspects, phases, and connections of the Underscore that Nancy had taught.

The first session, *Agitating the Underscore*, led by Jun Akiyama and Ronja Ver, was set up in a way reminiscent of the talk-through format Nancy had used—with the glyphs written out and posted on large pages, each word and drawing explained. As participants, we were listening and taking notes. Jun and Ronja voiced their concerns with various terms of the Underscore, including the historical use of the words "Pow Wow" as appropriative of the Native American gathering and the harm done during the 25+ years it took for Nancy to change the wording to "Assembly." They described the additions of glyphs not originated by Nancy, including "Socio-Cultural Arrival" that they had been in ongoing dialogue with her about. In describing Kinesphere, a term Nancy used, coined by Rudolf Laban, they highlighted a connection of Laban to Nazi Germany. At this, there was a shift in the tone and format—the focus stayed on this topic as people expressed concerns in a group dialogue. There was a charge to better understand and consider the implications and impacts of the history, actions, and affiliations of those who developed the form of CI—and of those who had influenced these early CI originators.

144 Resistance and Support

Jun and Ronja practiced the Underscore with Nancy for many years. In their session's description,[3] they noted:

> We share our work based on over a decade of researching, performing, interrogating, arguing and practicing the Underscore with Nancy Stark Smith and others. Our work together has been applying a decolonial, intersectional lens to Nancy Stark Smith's score and evolving it toward a decidedly anti-racist practice, in conversation with NSS [Nancy Stark Smith].

I presume their work with Nancy would still be ongoing and unfinished if she were still alive today. Nancy would bring into our Thursday night practices seeds from topics that Jun and Ronja had instigated.

Underscore Unwound,[4] led by Kellyn Jackson and me, was the next Underscore-focused session offered. It was a nonlinear structure with self-chosen stations set up throughout the space, akin to a kindergarten classroom. Participants were able to engage with, observe, and influence various proposed activities for considering the Underscore. It was experiential with a live musician, dancing, writing, reading, talking, and listening. There were resources for perusing such as *Caught Falling*, video footage of Nancy describing Streaming (the continuity of your life force energy), and Harvests from Global Underscores. Approaches to talk-throughs and ways of presenting the glyphs were posted on the walls. The session proved successful in the ways the environment encouraged people to seek out and dance their questions. We set up a playful laboratory with focused yet open-ended scenarios, which scratched an essential itch for Kellyn and me in our investigations of the format of the talk-through. It was a departure from what's been instructively typical and seems to have created something new in and of itself.

I see these two sessions as part of a larger experiment. Both lived up to their session titles. Neither was done as Nancy would have done it. They each had unique value in their further

---

[3] An excerpt from the session description for *Agitating the Underscore*, led by Jun Akiyama and Ronja Ver at *Critical Mass: CI @ 50*: "I'm very curious to learn more about what you're longing for with the anti-racist lens and how/where it might be integrated in the Underscore. Maybe it's not so much a phase or glyph but either an Anytime or in another category of foundational principles for the practice. Like: All in, All the Time. [. . .] To me it is a crucial and powerful aspect of the Underscore. More and more I realize how important this is in manifesting the kind of inclusive, awake, varied individual and collective improvisation that we find so extraordinary. It's kind of funny that things like that aren't in fact 'written' into the Underscore exactly." Nancy Stark Smith, in an email to Ronja in July 2019.

Ronja Ver, native to Finland, lives on unceded land of the Lisjan Ohlone nation. They are a dancer, dance maker, teacher, and organizer. A perpetual student of performance as a way of participating in community, they are deeply inspired by physical, social and mass movement, and its capacity to create meaningful impact on a personal and global scale. Ver is a graduate of Moving On Center and holds an MFA in Dance from Hollins University.
Jun Akiyama currently lives on the unceded territories of the Ute, Cheyenne, and Arapaho people. He is a voluntary immigrant from Japan, a practitioner of the Japanese martial art of Aikido, and an improvisational artist working in the mediums of movement, performance, and photography. He has performed with Nancy Stark Smith and others in San Francisco, New York, and Seattle in the Glimpse project.

[4] Session description for *Underscore Unwound*, led by Sarah Young and Kellyn Jackson at *Critical Mass: CI @ 50*: Like visiting a museum, designing a science experiment, or playing your favorite board game, this will be an interactive way of engaging with the aspects, phases, and states of the Underscore, a long-form dance improvisation structure developed by Nancy Stark Smith. Through overlapping instances, simultaneous scores, and nonsequential Anytime-All-the-Time interactions, you'll observe, influence, and choose various proposed vantage points for considering the Underscore. Kids with an adult are welcome to join.
Kellyn Jackson is a dance artist, contact improviser, and dance/movement therapist. She attended Nancy Stark Smith's January Workshop in 2020 and spent the pandemic figuring out ways to continue making contact in a contactless world. She has facilitated talk-throughs and experimented with the Underscore in a variety of contexts— from her graduate research to the Chicago Contact Improvisation Jam, from parks/busy streets to the inside of her apartment, and in mysterious virtual lands.

consideration of the Underscore, Nancy's legacy, and where we go from here. Neither was a comprehensive base-level introduction for anyone who had never participated in the Underscore before, which, I think, had an impact on the practice later in the evening.

The Underscore was held in Warner Main, a big, beautiful studio with a lovely wooden floor and balcony from which spilled in the warm summer evening. The New York City Public Library film crew was set up to capture the experience for the archives. I felt the fervor of the swirling topics of discussion and debate and the resonance of the teachings of the day and was awestruck by this never-before-experienced combination of individuals in this moment, particularly after a hiatus for many of gathering in large groups due to COVID-19.

After Arrival, we Assembled, hearing each voice in a crowd of 150+ people. Then, we Preambulated, moving through the space to orient to one another and to the environment. Adjacent to Warner Main, there was another dance studio, with big windows and high ceilings, for spillover of our large group. I chose to ground myself in this quieter, more sparsely populated studio, to Bond with the Earth by standing quietly, then laying down. After some minutes, I Grazed back over to Warner Main, where I was met with a wave of pulsating movers, influenced by the rhythmic beats chosen by the DJ, elle hong. The pronounced beat and increasing volume came strongly into my awareness. The music was highly influential. Claudio Garrido, who has been part of the Northampton Underscore +/– group since its beginnings in 2010, shared his account of the Underscore at CI @ 50: "I laid down on the floor for Skinesphere, as I often do, allowing my body to surrender to gravity. Then, the pulsating beat of the music began. I was surprised! Normally, we do this in silence." Claudio continued to lie on the ground for a few moments longer, then rose to standing, deciding he was "in." "To improvise, we have to adapt."

Most often, as a facilitator, I choose to ask the musician to remain quiet during Skinesphere. (Mike Vargas, Nancy's longtime partner and collaborator, said that he would challenge himself to play at a volume that only he could hear at this point.) The reason is that a person can close their eyes to lessen visual stimulation; it's harder to close one's ears. I try to prioritize an environment that allows for different states of the nervous system to quiet and settle and that is conducive to participants' directing their awareness toward internal sensations and to calibrating to the ambient sounds in the environment. I typically choose not to have a particular person, such as the music, have a larger proportion of external influence at this early point in the practice. So, the prominent sound during this Skinesphere was an uncommon experience for me.

My impression was that Bonding with the Earth did not happen for many people in that room. This could have been for many reasons: They didn't know that it was "supposed" to happen because they had not attended a talk-through or Underscore before. It was difficult to achieve at the level of the nervous system because their conditioned response to such musical stimuli reactively activated their attention externally more than it drew their awareness internally. They simply didn't want to Bond with the Earth by lying or standing quietly, choosing instead to follow impulses in confluence with the music. Later that evening, I spoke to another dancer who did not find a way to engage in the dancing. The disorientation of the dissonance between what they had expected and what was present was overwhelming to a point that they chose to leave the space.

When certain elements are missing from an Underscore, or a part is uncomfortable, or there is so much going on that tracking the phenomena is difficult, or if the experience is different from any other Underscore that came before, I consider these as phenomena that one

146 Resistance and Support

might reasonably encounter in a practice of the Underscore. The absence of an aspect and the experience of elements in extreme proportions are not reasons to dismiss an Underscore. We can talk about "that part" in which the high-volume, pulsating music with explicit lyrics occurred during a period of time when there might otherwise be ambient sounds—in the way the Underscore is currently practiced in many places. We can reflect on the strong impulse by the group at-large to move their bodies in relation to that sound rather than to contrast that influence by being relatively still and quietly standing or lying on the floor. Would that same choice have been made had the music started 10 minutes later? Or if there were far fewer people in the room? Or if every single person in the room had a regular Underscore practice? Or even had each person attended a talk-through?

We can take such a highly complex situation, such as 150+ people in a room, from multiple backgrounds with a wide range of experience in CI and a broad range of familiarity, expectation, understanding, and experience with this particular score, and we can analyze it. We have language for this thing that we did together on Saturday, July 9, 2022, at Oberlin College. Some people liked it; some didn't. Some people think "this" went wrong and some liked when "that" happened. Some didn't know what was going on, so they either went with it, made up their own stories about it, stopped dancing, tried to control it, or gravitated toward something that felt safe and grounded. Some spent their time in the Gap (a temporary absence of reference). And I'm writing about it. Even as I write about it, my relationship to that moment is shifting and will continue to shift.

Often people would ask Nancy for a definition of Contact Improvisation.[5] She would suggest, rather than define CI, to consider, "What is the core proposition of CI?" To that, Nancy described it as "the frame and the empty middle." There was a beautiful way that Nancy had conducted her frame and the "empty middle." She embedded her values and beliefs, creating a culture, in the ways she described, shared, repeated, performed, and practiced the Underscore. There was ritual in the passing of it along, in the inquiry, in the preparation for it, and the manifestation of it. There is intention in the chewing over it. But she also would say, "We can't let that frame get too thick."

Nancy Stark Smith writes in *Caught Falling*,

> During the [Underscore] *harvest*, it can be interesting to reflect on actions that were experienced by you or others as being out of the frame of this practice and why. Discernment of all kinds is constantly functioning, but it's an unnecessary waste of energy to worry if you're doing it right while it's going on. Assume that you are. (2008, 98)

I do regret not having a clearer charge that people completed a pragmatic talk-through prior to participating in this Underscore. I can imagine this shared orientation could have lent context, grounding, choice, and, perhaps, more avenues to stay available to the improvisation when overstimulation, confusion, or judgment set in for people.

Overall, I felt joy. At the end, I felt satisfied. Our co-facilitation team of Jun Akiyama, Patrick Crowley, Prema Kelley, Rythea Lee, Saliq Savage, Ronja Ver, and myself had worked hard to take risks. We tested out directions according to our interests and values. We worked

---

[5] Nancy Stark Smith shared this during the 2020 January Workshop at Earthdance, Plainfield, MA. In addition, she offered that Steve Paxton responded with "Do under others as you would have them do under you." She then commented that Paxton's brilliance was in his ability to keep making a space for others to figure out how to fill in.

within the framework in such a way that I could see the influences of our choices on the various inputs (i.e., schedule, timing, music, spaces, posting glyphs, filming). We did it. We did the *ucking Underscore with a bunch of people with big opinions who hold CI dear in a range of ways. We followed the charge of Jun and prioritized musicians of color. We honored Ronja's request of hearing names and access needs at Assembly. Some people left. Some people complained. And I was okay with not pleasing everyone.

There is further to go in facilitating an environment in which we recognize that we are wearing glasses tinted by our history, acculturation, and habituation, and to ensure we come equipped with strategies and compassion for how to calibrate toward equity, given the impacts of our tinted views. As facilitators, we are charged with heightening our listening to perceive the ways in which another person's lenses are categorically different from our own because the dance floor, the improvisation itself, is not an "empty middle." There are many blocks and obstacles that some of us see, feel, and are impacted by, while others are oblivious. So, as facilitators and practitioners, we are charged with building the frame to navigate those barriers with transparency. This is difficult if the form is continuously practiced in the same way it's always been done, or only in the way our mentor taught us.

May 2022 Underscore at Oberlin College: A Time to Honor Nancy Stark Smith

On May 13, 2022, two months prior to the large Underscore at *Critical Mass: CI @ 50* just described, 40 undergraduate students and artists-in-residence gathered in Warner Main, the same studio at Oberlin College, for an Underscore talk-through. This was in preparation for an Underscore practice to follow the next day. I had been invited by Ann Cooper Albright, Oberlin Professor of Dance, to lead an Underscore as part of a series of events aligned around the anniversary of Nancy Stark Smith's death and the 50th anniversary of the inception of CI.

Oberlin College, with one of the longest-running academic programs for the study, practice, and development of CI,[6] was hosting an exhibit in the college's Mary Church Terrell Main Library about Nancy Stark Smith, an Oberlin graduate. The exhibit illustrated her early efforts in the organizing of CI as it was forming, early correspondences of *Contact Quarterly*, and posters of the Underscore. There was also an exhibit at the college's Allen Memorial Art Museum, which paired notes and videos from the early days of CI with visual art of the same period, called *Collective Gestures: The Impact of Experimental Performance at Oberlin in the 1970s*. For my part, facilitating a talk-through and Underscore was an opportunity to honor Nancy by referencing how I had witnessed her holding the practice.

An Underscore talk-through is a phenomenon, in and of itself, of passing on knowledge and investigating language to discover what's meaningful and influential in the dance. It can be done in a multitude of languages. It can be done online. Or outside. It's best done with storytelling and meanderings, whimsical musings and jokes, with snacks during, and maybe even dinner and wine afterward. For this talk-through, there was a mixture of people; some had never attended a single talk-though or heard of the Underscore before. A couple of people had attended many talk-throughs and Underscores. Most were somewhere in

---

[6] https://www.oberlin.edu/news/oberlin-dance-department-celebrates-50-years-contact-improv.

148   Resistance and Support

between. I had my notes and references laid out within my reach as the group gathered together to begin.

Each time I write out the glyphs and talk through the score, I immediately feel Nancy's presence, as I did on this occasion. I recalled vividly her practiced, clear way of writing out each of the five pages, beginning with "Underscore" written at the very top of the first blank page, with a line below "Under" and above "score." I drew out the glyphs as I talked through the phases, aspects, and connections, underpinning the definitions with stories, questions, and examples, as I had heard Nancy do many times. I relayed conversations I had been part of or heard secondhand from Nancy, for example, about how Yen-Fang Yu in Taipei, Taiwan, discovered a translation of "Gap" in Chinese that revealed a new way of perceiving the concept.[7] As people drew the glyphs in their notebooks, they asked to dig deeper into various points, and, after an hour and a half, they left with more nuanced questions than they had when they entered the space. Luckily, they had some time to integrate the information prior to doing the Underscore.

The next morning, we returned to the same studio—this time to fully practice the Underscore. Ann had thoughtfully laid out paper and writing utensils for "real-time Harvesting," and a bouquet of lilacs, a favorite flower of Nancy's, in a sunlit corner of the studio. We gathered in a circle for Assembly, which included a Land Acknowledgment. This, as well as our discussion during the talk-through about "Calling in Ancestors,"[8] prompted one participant, Shireen Hamza, to ask us to consider whose ancestors, for various reasons of non-inclusion, were passively excluded from early developments of the Underscore and to also recognize that some of our ancestors caused past harms and to be responsible and conscientious about how we bring them in. I imagined Nancy nodding thoughtfully.

Anya Yermakova provided the soundscape. Leading up to this Underscore, Anya and I had many conversations about rhythm, contrast, duration, balance between atmospheric and generated sound, and the fluctuating relationship between dancing and instrumentation. She began introducing sound once most people were shifting from Skinesphere into Kinesphere. Then, she created an overlapping patchwork of qualities and dynamics. There was even an interplay of past and present: that same studio, Warner Main, is the place where Steve Paxton demonstrated *Magnesium*, his initial experiment with CI in 1972, and the mechanism of the studio's sprung floor still remains as it was 50 years ago. Anya experimented with this by recording the sounds produced by our movements as relayed to the floorboards and picked up with floor mics. This original spring of the floor is sonically resonant, making it easily audible. She played the charango and melodica, overlapping the sounds. Then, further layering these sounds and histories, she played pre-recorded whale

---

[7] The Gap is an Underscore aspect described in English as a temporary absence of reference. Yen-Fang Yu of Taipei, Taiwan, shared, "This Chinese character I picked to translate Gap [ ] is a word can be separated into two parts: 門 means door; it looks like a door as well. 日, means the sun. Together it can mean place, space in between two spaces, two people, two states. In Buddhism, it also means the state/space between life and death. During the Global Underscore 2021 In-Depth Talk-Through, I got a chance to look at it through the participants' eyes, A real look at my own native language. Just realize that it's a sun coming through the space between doors. I love it even more now."

[8] "Calling in Ancestors" was proposed by Andrew Suseno at the 2019 wcciJAM with a glyph drawn by Jun Akiyama resembling a DNA strand—and Nancy's long braided hair. Nancy began adding it to the pages of Underscore as one of the Anytime All-the-Time Aspects, writing it in purple pen (instead of the usual black ink) to distinguish it as a new element to consider.

sounds, inspired by mayfield brooks's *Whale Fall* Cycle.[9] (mayfield had just been in residency at Oberlin a few weeks prior.) The soundscape faded to silence by Final Resolution.

So, we moved through the structure during the agreed-upon time frame, and it was both a complex and a simple experience. The light through the windows shifted over the duration of the practice. The room cooled during Bonding with the Earth and heated up during Open Score. The dancers stirred the space with multiple engagements, each with their own dynamic changes, varying from slow, quiet, and contemplative to robust, lively, and physically risky dancing. Many observed at times from within and from the perimeter of the space. As we gathered back into a circle afterward for quiet, individual Reflection and Harvest through writing, resting, stretching, and drawing, I brought out the heaping bowls of watermelon and figs with fresh mint and lime juice that I had prepared that morning. We snacked as we described our reflections and discoveries to each other. I remember some melancholy being shared. I felt an intimacy and vulnerability among the group. During the Sharing, my sense was that people were comfortable and confident enough to be present in these more tender states. Many of the students were at the apex of the semester, dense with projects, rehearsals, and schoolwork. And while a majority of the people in the room had not known Nancy, there were a few of us who had known her for years, and the sense of loss was present.

In the end, we ate every last piece of watermelon. We offered our gratitude to the space, the dancers, the musician, the organizers, and to Nancy. It was spacious. We completed the practice with a "clamshell," in which we all opened our arms wide like the shell of a giant clam, then slowly brought our arms together, closing them with synchronicity as a group. I felt balanced and easeful in my body, with a stirring of ideas and reflections for contemplation. This particular Underscore carried an intention to honor Nancy and her deep contributions to so many through her sustained practice and development of dance improvisation. Buoyed by my gratitude, I guided the Underscore in ways that have become familiar, inspiring, and dear to me. I offered facilitation reminiscent of the person who invented it in the practical, organizational, social, spatial, physical, creative ways that I was able to recognize and recreate: There was a rigor of questioning—with curiosity superseding the demand for an answer. There was a proactive tending to the conditions of the space and for the people. Within the balance of the dialogue between movement, space, and sound, there was opportunity for changing states, awareness, and modulation of tone, noting and experimenting with influence, and moments of silence and contrasting sound. I enjoy looking for clues through Nancy's ways of guiding to discover why and how she set up the conditions and proportions as she did, while simultaneously taking my own responsibility for it, claiming ownership of it, and following personal interests and intrigues. She would say, "Be careful what you teach," in the January Workshops. Where and how am I directing my attention in the facilitation of the Underscore, and why? What are the impacts of this steering and of the score itself on the dance and on who's dancing? What are the impacts of what I do and say, and what I *don't* do and say?

---

[9] *Whale Fall* Cycle is a series of written, digital, and live provocations by mayfield brooks. Brooks brings to the fore the Black body throughout history through parallels with the death and decomposition cycles of whales. "Brooks was inspired by a whale fall, a term that describes how a whale, after it dies, sinks to the ocean floor; there, its carcass supplies deepwater creatures with nutrients, so that even in death, it feeds the ocean." Excerpt from "A Choreographer Diving into Grief Looks to Whales," *New York Times*, April 14, 2021, https://www.nytimes.com/2021/04/14/arts/dance/mayfield-brooks-whale-fall.html; https://danspaceproject.org/2022/06/09/sensoria-brooks-drum/.

Ongoing Questions

The Underscore is a framework that Nancy Stark Smith held closely while also constantly giving it away. There is great value in *how* she organized, expressed, and shared her ideas. There are many of us who have pages of notes on what Nancy has taught us, likely mixed in with questions and revelations of our own, inspired by her words, comments made by others, and reflections on the dances that transpired. We consider and discuss the significance and the impacts of the various aspects of the Underscore, as they're being added to, modified, and reinterpreted in many different contexts. It's an ongoing question—an infinite game—as to what provides coherence. What combinations of the elements of the Underscore and in what proportions meet the conditions of any given practice? This question arises each time a new group comes together for the Underscore.

The legacy of Nancy Stark Smith—and of the Underscore—is in initiating a form where there hadn't been one, one that resonates enough with enough people that it perpetuates. Its resiliency is in its dependability and recognizability, as much as in its fluidity and adaptability. In 2008, when *Caught Falling* was published, the Underscore was less than 20 years into its development. Nancy wrote then, "The Underscore is a form of play and research, not the law. I hope you will approach it in this spirit" (2008, 90). While there is a simple idealism in the words, Nancy was also quite diligent in her questioning and tuning of the parameters of the score. She goes on to write in "The Practice Notes":

> Though the focus is definitely on movement (with the welcome inclusion of Contact Improvisation), each participating group will determine what materials they are interested in including while staying true to *the intention of the Underscore, as they understand it*. There are, of course, limits, but we have to reach them to discover them. The form is still too young to know what they all are and why. And who sets those limits? Me? Or do the people who are currently in the room, practicing the score, setting the limits? Probably, and ideally, it will be a combination of both. (Stark Smith/Koteen 2008, 97; emphasis added)

There is a probing into the "how" of the form's development, which is a root shared with CI at-large. These kinds of questions are highlighted during these recent years following her death (and, again, mirrored within the larger context of CI at 50 years).

In Nancy's absence, who's the "me"? Who are the "we"? What is the process for adding to, omitting from, and evolving the score? To what degree can it change and still be considered the Underscore? When, where, and by whom are these determinations made? Is it, literally, myself and others who continue to engage deeply with the Underscore who decide? Collectively and individually? Do we carry forward Nancy's teachings, her writings, her ways of conveying the score as primary for perpetuity? How would we do that when our own preferences, biases, tendencies distort our memories and mimicry? How is someone who's never heard of Nancy Stark Smith engaging with the Underscore? I emphasize the importance of a talk-through to be passed along, person-to-person, but, also, can't someone just go online or pick up a *Caught Falling* and organize their own Underscore?

I do not want to be an arbiter of what has enough integrity to be ascribed to Nancy Stark Smith's legacy, of the right way to approach the Underscore. I am curious to ask:

Why do people keep doing the Underscore?
What is it serving for people and for improvisation?
How many different ways can it evolve?
Where will we arrive in 50 years from now?

The Underscore is a beautiful holographic object that continues to be recognizable as the form that Nancy Stark Smith shared with us—*with and because of* all the adaptations, evolutions, and varied expressions of it. Built into its structure is the permission and encouragement to take initiative and to take it apart—which we have learned to do with discernment, curiosity, and care. There are even plenty of "escape" routes that allow us to *change* what we've so carefully built, word by word, glyph by glyph. This is what allows it, or something entirely different, to evolve when the present version no longer serves.

Nancy encouraged us to name the appearances of things and to articulate how we experience and perceive our existence and surroundings through movement improvisation. These investigations—through dancing—offer us an exploratory space at the intersection of our self and our experience and, also, between our self and our own witnessing of our experience. The evolution of the Underscore is entangled with a response-ability to play and to attend to this entanglement of us, our experience, and our witnessing of experience. Through this, I think, we are tasked with continuously illuminating what's most obvious and basic about the score—in the presence of novelty—to see where it goes. This is relative to the conditions of each moment as it happens and as we each perceive it and every iteration. And then do that again. And again.

I am satiated by the Underscore and all that it stirs—through adherence and agitation. It's one of my favorite ways of being with others—in focused, spherical, nonlinear, physical connection. I find it often to be a mirror of what's already happening in a larger context. Amidst the backdrop of a global pandemic that both stifled and expanded possibilities for engaging in CI and dance improvisation, the reach and depth of the Black Lives Matter movement, the overturn of *Roe v. Wade*, and the imminence of our global climate crisis, this moment in the wake of Nancy's passing offers a unique opportunity to observe the transmission of her tone, focus, movement, concepts, references, and details. What happens next?

Responsive Touch

Ann Cooper Albright

This section parses the question of what it means to touch and be touched—literally as well as figuratively. The discussions that follow are expansive in nature; they describe the myriad ways that haptic perception and tactile sensation bring us into relationship with others. Their focus is on somatic states of being in Contact Improvisation, the implications of which are always evolving. Interestingly, several of these essays refer to Steve Paxton's use of the Stand (and the related concept of the small dance) as a foundational practice of paying attention to the subtle shifts of one's body as we experience the pull of gravity on our structure and the flow of air on our skin. These practices are important for training our dancing bodies for the unknown for sure, but they are also deeply relevant in our everyday encounters with the forces—cultural, political, environmental—that shape our worlds. Moving from neurobiological perspectives on listening and balance, to practices of attunement with natural environments and the challenging histories of land ownership, through therapeutic touch and explorations of queer intimacy, to philosophical discussions of embodied knowing and spiritual traditions, to the impact of CI on neurodivergent sensibilities, these essays attempt to articulate the ineffable experience of moving in contact with others in the world. Little wonder, then, that the writing in this section often takes on a lyrical quality in which critical analyses are partnered with poetic evocations of dancing. To touch in a truly responsive manner, one first trains one's attention, engaging awareness of those physical exchanges of weight and energy as a form of communication that, while it is sometimes troubling, can be ultimately healing as well.

Chapter 8, Lesley Greco's "The Small Dances of Listening," brings composer Pauline Oliveros's notion of "deep listening" into conversation with Steve Paxton's practice of the Stand. Both are meditations that engage our physical attentiveness. Listening to and playing with the forces of gravity through our proprioceptive sensing brings us into an awareness of the nonvisual forces—giving us a portal to the mysteries of the unseen world. Listening is a common trope in CI. I have heard teachers offer the poetic image of the pores of our skin being like thousands of little ears with which to attune to our partners. As an osteopathic practitioner, Greco integrates her discussions of our vestibular system with her reflections on gravity as a kinesthetic form of Eros, the god of attraction. Listening, for Greco, is a form of active connection.

Neurobiology teaches us that the physical is real. Dancing with another person teaches us that touch has metaphysical implications. They are reciprocal sensibilities. In a powerful example taken from her own life, Greco explains how the process of recovery from a concussion made her fearful of falling. Her physical tensing up when feeling off-balance became habitual, even once she had fully recovered from the injury. Thus, she had to consciously retrain her body to be willing to experience being off-balance. Paxton's Stand was key to this training, helping her distinguish between "being in the eye of the storm rather than being

154   Resistance and Support

blown around in the hurricane." This recognition, in turn, led her to reflect on the reciprocal exchange of stability and mobility. Eventually, she learned how to discern the difference between being uncomfortable and being unsafe while navigating the thrill of moving with another person. Listening to both her own desires and the sounds of their mutual motion, Greco hears the resonance of their shared humanity.

Rosalind Holgate Smith, in Chapter 9, "Listening Touch," also invokes listening as critical for Contact Improvisation, but she extends the implications of this skill past dancing to include a bodily engagement with relationships of history to memory. The issue in listening is not *what* one hears, but *how* one hears. In her essay, Smith situates listening touch as a haptic practice that facilitates encounters with Otherness. This is not to say that it makes those encounters easy, but rather that it helps us experience those challenges without shying away or trying to cover over, excuse, or distract ourselves from the horrific environmental realities of the Anthropocene. Smith interweaves somatic practices of attention, such as Paxton's the Stand, Body-Mind Centering's concept of Cellular Touch, and witnessing in Authentic Movement with the new materialist theories of Karen Barad and Jane Bennett. Another important conceptual influence is Leah Bassel's notion of stewardship (as opposed to ownership) of the land. While these thinkers invoke the importance of ethical relations across people and lands, Smith crafts embodied practices that prepare us for such encounters. Drawing from her case study researching touch with a group of dancers in Berlin, as well as her own deeply powerful experience listening to the colonialist legacies embedded in the desecrated logging site in Big Pats Creek, Australia, she proposes three techniques: *hovering*, *accompanying*, and *listening in action*.

One of the most complex issues around touching, particularly when using the hands, is the negotiation of power between the toucher and the receiver of touch. Most Contact dancers are clear that they prefer a "touch that is not asking or expecting anything." However, as Smith points out, alongside CI are modalities of bodywork in which one person takes on the role of caregiver. These unequal legacies of touching and being touched, whether directly violent (abuse) or patronizing (care) have compelled her to shift dynamics of fraught encounters. What would it mean to listen before touching? Waiting, witnessing, hovering are intentional practices that extend these moments of suspension. Pausing before touching creates a more expansive situation in which to explore new possibilities of being with an Other. Listening with our bodies, we feel the existential reverberations of kinesthetic practices—from the studio into the world.

Several essays in this collection speak to the influences of somatics and bodywork on the movement qualities common to many Contact Improvisation dancers. Aaron Brandes and Gabrielle Revlock reverse this current of influence, focusing on how CI directly influences their therapeutic practices. In Chapter 10, "Therapeutic Applications of Contact Improvisation," these two authors explore various techniques of physical bonding which, when introduced with thoughtfulness and the full consent of the client, can have a powerful impact. As one therapist quipped about a client who had trouble advocating for herself, "We can talk over the reasons why, or I can just teach her how to push back." Sometimes, the most direct route to a behavioral change is through the body.

Brandes is a licensed psychotherapist who refers to his work as "Body & Being Psychotherapy," and Revlock is a professional dancer and educator who developed "Restorative Contact," a partnered, touch-based mindfulness practice. Their stories underscore how valuable the kind of full-body engagement can be for folks who are not interested in dance per se, but may benefit from the kind of non-sexual touch that CI specializes in. Revlock speaks of using a combination of slow movement and moments of stillness, emphasizing the power of breathing together. Brandes experiments with introducing Contact exercises such as full-body compression as client and therapist slowly roll over and under each other. Rather than shunning therapeutic touch because of its troublesome history of abusive encounters, these two dancer/practitioners encourage its intentional and strategic applications. So often counseling happens face to face, where one's public persona is engaged. It can provide deep relief then to just sit back-to-back, feeling the support of someone else's spine and the subtle movement of their breath. Bodies can communicate trust, connection, and a sense of positive intimacy simply by holding space with one another.

Positive intimacy is also important for Aramo Olaya, whose Chapter 11, "XCI: Intimacy in Contact Improvisation," explores the movement language of CI with the context of queer sexuality. Once again, we find the lessons about responsive touching seeded in CI growing into new areas of inquiry. Olaya took part in the feminist/queer anarchist social movements in Spain in the first decade of the new millennium, but was disappointed (like so many of us) that this body-centered discourse failed to take seriously embodied practices of transformation. Delving into the worlds of Queer Tango and Contact Improvisation, as taught at Espacio Formación Contact Improvisación Madrid, they studied moving and entangled bodies with an eye to how gendered norms are unconsciously reproduced or intentionally resisted. Olaya was interested in a non-heteronormative exchange that cultivated queer, nonviolent intimacy that was neither devoid of sexual energy nor focused exclusively on genital sex. They began researching practices of intimate touch, which they jokingly referred to as XCI, where X stands for "the unknown in the interstitial space between queer sexuality and CI."

Olaya's essay reports on the findings of their 2021 research with Ilda Freire, a close colleague, articulating the layers of improvisational meaning in their moving together. What they found crucial was what Cristiane Boullosa and Diana Bonilla (who direct Espacio FCI) call "non-intentionality." This term (which no doubt loses something in translation from the Spanish *no intencionalidad*) does not mean unintentional, but rather suggests an open witnessing attitude toward touch and movement, one that is not focused on a goal or specific outcome of the duet. This is similar to what Smith's own research group referred to as "unwanting touch" or "touch that is not expecting anything." Olaya recognizes that their project is aspirational. Nonetheless, they document an important distinction between *consent* and *co-sense*. Inspired by the work of Caro Nouvella, this concept of co-sensing offers a complement to consensual practices, bringing bodies into an attunement in which a moving intimacy can help us imagine previously unknown desires.

Brian Schultis's Chapter 12, "Rolling and Knowing: Reflections on the Endurance of the CI Event," begins with a lyrical evocation of rolling on the grass with a partner. His writing conjures two duets with the same person in the same place, separated by a year of intensive dancing. How do we articulate the embodied knowledge at the heart of these intertwined sensations once we surface from the dancing? How can language capture the flow of two bodies around a moving point of contact? Spiraling around an axis that is always changing its relation to the ground, these bodies refuse the usual mapping of points in space or memories of the past. This is Schultis's project, an inquiry into the metaphysical nature of that special matrix of interconnectedness we call Contact Improvisation.

As his writing traces the contours of ribs, pelvis, spine, and the soft tissue of belly, his reflections become entangled with the philosophical musings of Tim Ingold, Gilles Deleuze,

156 Resistance and Support

and Félix Guattari. Terms such as Ingold's "the logic of inversion" and Deleuze's and Guattari's notion of "intensity" are reinterpreted within the fleshy logic of rolling together. This dis/junction produces a world that is enacted through the orientation to another body—a never-ending mobius strip of spirals. This space is not objective; it is established only by moving through it. Schultis tries to trace the contours of that world, calling forth its poetic resonance in words that seek to honor "the ephemeral unfolding of the dancing in its own time." Refusing the omniscient gaze of objective thinking, Schultis gives us a perspective from the fleshy middle, rolling the physical and the conceptual, presence and absence, life and memory into one moving improvisation.

Lisa Claire Greene only started dancing Contact Improvisation in the fall of 2021, but right away they took a deep plunge into the form. They began by joining jams in Chicago and then ventured over to Oberlin College for periods of more intensive study, including participating in the January 2022 intensive with Jurij Konjar and *Critical Mass: CI @ 50* that July. Their Chapter 13, "Something We Touch or That Touches Us: A Newcomer Locating Themselves in Contact," begins charting their CI journey by reflecting on those first moments of intoxication with the dancing. Particularly important for Greene was the power of feeling accepted right away by a group of peers, something they had previously struggled with. This recognition of "the personal transformative potential" of Contact led them to consider the ways in which CI offers pathways for neurodivergent folks to engage with social interactions. Greene describes how over the course of a year dancing, their habitual anxiety toward new situations lessened.

A central theme in the essay is the similarity between CI and cognitive behavioral therapy (CBT). So many of the somatic underpinnings of CI involve attention to our perceptual systems, particularly ones that are underutilized in our contemporary culture. In Greene's experience, the physical mindfulness training in tactile-sensation, three-dimensional space, as well as the invisible forces of gravity and air, is particularly valuable for supporting behavioral changes. Diving headlong into CI was a powerful awakening for Greene, but their initial euphoria was tempered by the recognition that CI was not as inviting to everyone. The challenging discussions during *Critical Mass* about Contact's history and the whiteness of that downtown New York City scene that nurtured its early years provoked this realization. These discussions continued to reverberate within Chicago jams the following year. Working to establish a sense of community that welcomed new participants, Greene came to view CI as less of a movement technique and more of a continual questioning of its own premises. While working on their contribution to this collection, Greene revived an art practice of drawing that focused on states of mutual embodiment and deep listening, helping them grapple with the contradictions implicit in the evolution of this powerful, yet imperfect, form.

The last essay in this section is Carol Laursen's Chapter 14, "The Religious Function of Contact Improvisation." In this heart-felt personal and poetic reflection, Laursen details her journey through various religious traditions, including Aikido, Quakerism, and Buddhism. Intriguingly, her appetite for an open and embodied form of communion was whetted by early experiences with CI in college. She found something wonderfully mysterious and even spiritual about dancers coming together at jams to explore improvisational possibilities in community. In these situations, she found that touch can be transformative, especially if it is accompanied by deep listening. Like Greene's essay, Laursen begins with a discussion of her Aikido practice, comparing the partners in CI with the interchangeable roles of *uke* (attacker) and *nage* (attacked). The martial training in Aikido focuses on circular movements.

The point is to meet force with a soft generosity. Laursen notes that Steve Paxton was an avid student of Aikido when he was beginning to experiment with Contact. Cultivating a responsive body and learning to fall well by spreading the impact of the descent over a greater area of the body are physical concepts integral to both forms. The connections between CI and Aikido have been well documented. Laursen intends to push that conversation further by highlighting the spiritual dimensions of this Asian martial art. *Ki* (like "chi" in Tai Chi) means life force. As she suggests, Contacters also follow invisible lines of energy and connect with their partner center-to-center, *Ki* to *Ki*.

Moving on to Quakerism, Laursen notes the way that the round robin format in CI is like the Quaker meeting structure; both begin with what she describes as an "expectant waiting." This is a responsive listening that affords members the patience to move beyond the initial manifestations of ego. What might arise if we resist expectations of what a dance or enlightenment should look or feel like and instead expand our curiosity? Laursen's last example is Buddhism, specifically the practice of Soto Zen. She compares the communal gathering of sitting meditation in a group setting with Nancy Stark Smith's Underscore. Laursen interprets the willingness of Contact dancers to face the unknown as similar to the Zen practitioner's confrontation with the uncertainty of change. Collectively, each group calls forth a vital sense of community that can also manifest in a sense of sacred Presence.

8
The Small Dances of Listening

Lesley Greco

The light in the studio is low and the door to the fire escape is wide. I'm watching someone—they've been standing, quietly facing the door for quite some time. Their body, like an ocean, is swooning and rolling just under the skin. I move to stand nearby and we sway together in this slow-moving river of night air. Behind me and to my left, a third person joins. I don't see them, but I recognize them. They are unmistakable, full of gravity and lightning. We three are standing in the spaces of our own bodies in this loose triangle at the edge of the studio. Three bodies grown in different soils at different times in history.

Each of us are made up of similar parts yet vastly different in composition and expression. If we look at the way our spines have been shaped, we can easily see that the parts are similar but the ways that they move together as a whole is entirely original. Take, for example, the way as babies we tilted our head toward our caregivers, who tilted their heads in their own peculiar ways; the food made in the homes we grew up in, in the cultures we were born to that nourished our growing bodies; the fall from the bed, the love of climbing trees, or playing basketball, or reading books, or studying snails; the nature of the people who surrounded us, who shaded us, or who allowed us certain kinds of light.[1]

We are ecosystems. We would have to draw on multiple ways of perceiving to take in the shape of these three spines and the bodies they move within as we stand here listening together tonight within the gravity that holds us to this planet. *There are at least 8 billion ways to listen.*

Standing and Listening

The Stand, also known as the small dance,[2] is a form of meditation[3] described by Steve Paxton and the pioneers of Contact Improvisation (CI) in the early 1970s. In a talk at the 2014 Breitenbush Jam in Oregon, Paxton spoke about the Stand as a means of training physical awareness, attending to balance and reflexes, quieting habits of thought, and witnessing events in the body happening in this ongoing dialogue with gravity. He stated that one

[1] Analogy shared by Rollin Becker D.O. in his book *Life in Motion* (R. E. Brooks, 1997).
[2] While this essay is focused on standing meditation as a traditional CI practice, the concepts being explored here are as applicable to bodies that cannot stand as it is to bodies that can. I like to make a distinction between the Stand and the small dance. The small dance of the physiology organizing in gravity happens in all physical configurations—standing is one way of many. The small dance in various positions is a concept explored by Joerg Hassmann in the article *Explorations within the Small Dance* published in *CQ Unbound* in 2015.
[3] Forms of standing meditation are found within styles of Chinese and Japanese martial arts and in some yogic lineages. Historians of standing meditation contemporarily known as Zhan Zhuang estimate the practice to be more than 2,700 years old. Standing meditations are described in several of the Chinese internal arts, in Taijiquan, Qigong, Baguazhang, and Xingyiquan, such as Wuji standing meditation and Yiquan standing meditation (Dudeja 2019).

Lesley Greco, *The Small Dances of Listening* In: *Resistance and Support*. Edited by: Ann Cooper Albright, Oxford University Press.
© Oxford University Press 2024. DOI: 10.1093/9780197776308.003.0009

reason for incorporating the Stand in the early days of CI was that he had hope of mitigating the physical danger the dancers navigate when moving at high speeds and with momentum (Nelson 2015). Paxton points to the Stand as an opportunity to expand our perception of subtlety and nuance in motion, thereby refining our ability to move securely and intimately with one another. Fifty years on, the Stand is still around, albeit sparsely. It's a different world now than it was in the 1970s. Amid the amplification of countless global, ecological, social, personal, and interpersonal crises, the fight for our attention has become extraordinarily sophisticated—we appear to be in a crisis of perception. Stabilizing and sustaining attention are challenging for many of us, particularly considering trauma histories, neurodiversities, and more recent accelerations of screen use. The ability to stabilize our attention enough to receive present moment sensory information is increasingly challenged, yet remains a critical foundational skill in CI.[4]

Looking back to transcribed verbal facilitation of the Stand given by Paxton in 1977 (Manheimer 2020) we find an emphasis on directing attention to internal physical experiences (or the development of *interoceptive awareness*). He describes attending to the micro reflexes—the rapid contractions and relaxations of muscle that typically happen below conscious awareness. Paxton feeds the listener's imagination with modest descriptions of eye sockets, sensations of ribs, lungs, diaphragm and motions of breathing, the reflexes, sensations of mass, weight of pelvis, upthrust of bone. The descriptions are spare and full of pause. The unfolding of the listening takes time. Without force or interference, physical events emerge within awareness in the ongoing dialogue with the gravity holding us to this earth. Paxton's curiosity about gravity is a legacy to CI.

Each time I return to Paxton's reading of his book *Gravity* (2020), I hear something I hadn't heard before, my learning is unfolding in layers. I'm reading again through some of Nancy Stark Smith's (1979, 1987) descriptions of befriending gravity, learning to stay awake inside disorientation and falling. I'm studying the work of French dancer and researcher Hubert Godard and relationships between gravity, standing practice, and CI as explored in a dialogue between Godard and Emma Bigé (2019). I'm learning about gravity in relation to the flowing forms of nature through the insightful research of Theodore Schwenk (1996) and reverence for the Intelligence of Nature in Rachel Carson's writings (2003), and in Robin Wall Kimmerer's generous teaching (2013), and in the remarkable work of Tyson Yunkaporta (2020). There is something common I'm noticing among these curious minds across different fields of research: the questions they ask are uncommon. The unknowns that they hold are substantial, and it is their listening sensibility that is most palpable to me—listening to understand things *as they are*. They seem to have this in common: a capacity to soften habits of perception enough to humbly learn directly from nature. I find it thrilling and entirely countercultural. The Stand might be considered as a dialogue with gravity. How do we refine the quality of our attention in ways that invite gravity to teach us, rather than exclusively imposing our ideas on it? What does that even mean? How do we soften what we think we know, and learn to listen directly for what gravity and our own bodies have to say?

---

[4] Gratitude to the Oberlin CI residents of 2022 for participating in a practice of the Stand over a two-week period of time and helping me gather information about how the Stand is being understood, practiced, and experienced by this small but dedicated sample of practitioners. Special thanks to Nicolas Travers who led the practice and organized the feedback. What was shared offered useful insights that were considered throughout the writing of this essay.

Gravity and the Ear of the Body

Gravity is a mystery. For all our wild intelligence, for all our brightest scientific minds, it remains so. Alongside the contributions of Galileo, of Einstein, of Newton, the perspectives of scientific revolution, gravity does exist to some of us as a god—Eros, the god of Love, of Attraction, the god of Longing. Through gravity, all things with mass are attracted one to the other. The center of Earth's mass is drawn to the center of the Sun's mass. The Eros between them holds us in this spiraling galaxy. I love that the invitation of Eros, gravity, its forces, and counterforces, are what we play with in CI.

Gravity is something we invariably must negotiate in our lives on earth, all of our growth and development happening in relation to gravity. The spiraling forms of the vessels, bones, and muscles of our extremities, the vorticial shapes of our organs—all forged by the dialogue between gravity and the fluid we are formed of and within. The child, before birth, develops in a spherical fluid-filled envelope. The baby's form is itself primarily liquid, which gradually becomes more and more condensed. Upon being born, under the directional forces of the earth and the developmental processes of growth, body gradually becomes denser, and the internal forces become more able to support our uprightness in gravity. These rough and delicate negotiations toward standing are supported, in part, by the tiny organs of our inner ears.

From a physiological point of view, our ears have two distinct sensory functions, auditory and vestibular—what otolaryngologist Alfred Tomatis describes as the ear of hearing and the ear of the body. The cochlea, as the ear of hearing, helps us in the processing of sound. The vestibular mechanism, or ear of the body, helps us listen for our internal body states, particularly in relation to space, motion, gravity (Tomatis and Prada 2005). The ear of hearing is one way of translating incoming vibrational information from our environment through the spiraling fluid-filled cochlea of the internal ear, helping us to metabolize sound. Detecting gravity, being upright, moving, having an experience of ourselves in relation to other—are all rooted in a small, elegant structure within the inner vesicle of the ear. Here, three curving fluid-filled semicircular canals intersect at right angles, appearing to have been themselves formed from spiraling movement. This vestibular mechanism—the ear of the body—receives information regarding our position in space, our movements, our uprightness, as well as the motion of those we are in contact with. The vestibular mechanism functions via the spiraling motion of its fluid as it passes through these canals to detect horizontal, vertical, and back-and-forth body motion (Schwenk 1996). This helps us distinguish velocity and change of direction, working with gravity to identify where we are in space and in establishing the postural tone reflected in the quality of our movement. The vestibular mechanism helps us listen in on the ongoing dialogue between gravity, the counter-gravity contact forces of the ground, and the internal suspensory/tensile processes supporting our architecture in uprightness and motion.

From birth, there has been a quiet conversation between body and gravity happening just under my awareness. Today, as I turn my attention toward this small dance, I'm especially interested in my center of mass that is dynamically balancing over my base of support—in this case, my pelvic bowl over my feet. Interference from my conscious mind is minimal. I listen for the quality of movement flowing between my feet and my center of mass, for the quality of communication between my tail and my head. My body is like a standing river. Where is the water flowing? Where are the boulders? The river banks? Where does motion pool and

Self-Organizing Perceptual Systems

spiral? Listening in this sense is an inquiry about relationships—movement relationships. Habitual ways of perceiving are allowed to rest, inviting a direct sensory experience that is silent and felt. I listen for the small dance of self-organization.

Self-Organizing Perceptual Systems

Looking through a neurobiological lens, the information that our vestibular mechanism receives is coordinated in our vestibular system, which is a wider neurobiological network conducting sensory information from the inner ear, vision, proprioceptive, kinesthetic, and touch receptors. Our vestibular system relates the information coming from outside (what we see, hear smell, taste, touch) with information arising from our internal body (heartbeat, proprioception, sensations of digestion, and so on). The vestibular system feeds information directly to the cerebellum, which helps us to determine whether or not our intended action matches our actual action.

The vestibular system and the information it coordinates seem to be foundational to our kinesthetic intelligence, contributing to our sense of self, and helping to distinguish self from other and environment. Offering an uncommon perspective, eco-psychologist James Jerome Gibson (1966) explores a notion of the senses functioning not only as passive receivers of information, but rather, as an *active perceptual system* in reciprocal relationship with one's environment. Gibson invites us to consider that when the senses function as a perceptual system, they are a way of paying attention, able to orient, explore, and receive information without necessarily involving the intellect. In his book *The Senses Considered as Perceptual Systems* (1966), Gibson proposes that we are receiving sensory information even if we are not experiencing a sensation consciously—our active perceptual systems informing us on a non-conscious level.

The Stand can be one way of listening in on our self-organizing perceptual systems and an opportunity to become aware of how we habitually engage our attention. It is a practice that can help us creatively adapt and orient to something more than our survival reactions as we move and dance, particularly when circumstances are high stakes, as they often are in CI. Standing can be a meditation, a tedious necessity, a punishment, a privilege; it can reveal physical tension, painful memory, all depending on context, personal history, and perception. CI teacher (and contributing author to this volume) Guru Suraj points out that there are complex cultural contexts to consider when thinking about standing meditation. Guru describes his personal practice of standing meditation where one would pause and stand quietly for 15 minutes and simply observe or witness what is happening (as an aspect of Osho's Dynamic Meditation practice[5] [2023]). And yet Guru also recalls difficult memories of standing as a punishment in school growing up in India, memories which spontaneously arose while being led through the Stand during his CI residency at Oberlin in 2022. In a recent email exchange, Guru shared that he's since noticed it to be a common experience among his CI students in India as well. While the Stand appears to be a simple, uncomplicated physical practice, knowing that it is a powerful container in which

---

[5] Osho is a revolutionary Indian mystic whose work is described here: https://www.osho.com/read/osho/about-osho.

somatic histories or implicit memory can emerge unexpectedly, even within a seasoned practitioner, is a significant awareness to hold. Respectful of our own histories, limitations, and needs, the Stand could serve as one of the tools that someone navigating trauma can lean into. As an attentional training process, it's an opportunity to bring breath, motion, and attention all together into present-moment awareness. It can teach us to trust—again or for the first time—the self-organizational capacity of body in gravity. It is one way of supporting the organization of our perceptual systems and one way of navigating our position on earth.

Listening in Contact

To the newcomer and the uninitiated, Contact Improvisation may seem full of contradiction. In this movement form, there is an impetus to both attend to our internal body and have a heightened awareness of the world around us. Structure is prudent, but structure is flowing. To fly, I learn to fall. Moving at high speeds, a stillness often emerges. It's a lot to consider. CI is a world where flying is falling, where stillness is in motion, and the self and the other become a third. It is in the heart of this paradox that *listening* lives most vibrantly. Listening is a term often heard in the context of CI. It's a tricky concept to write about because it's a sensory experience that is silent and felt. Listening doesn't happen with the thinking mind—even though our thinking minds can be informed by listening and we can choose to listen—we can't think our way into the experience. To language a concept of listening, to make verbal the nonverbal, is a paradox—but, like CI, worthy of the challenge. The word "listen" is defined within the *Oxford English Dictionary* in this way:

> To hear attentively; to give ear; to pay attention to (a person speaking or what is said); to give attention with the ear to some sound or utterance; to make an effort to hear something; to give ear. (2000, 126)

While the contemporary use of the term *listen* commonly refers to the sense of hearing and aural perception, the origin of the word "listen" can be traced back to the old English "hlysnan," meaning simply, "pay attention to" (OED 2000). Why emphasize the word "listen" when what I mean is attention? Attention as a concept is excruciatingly complex and multimodal, and the word "listening" doesn't encompass the whole of it. Listening is a way of *engaging* attention. Allow me to offer a description of listening as I understand and the use the term here for you to consider:

> Listening is a metaphor for receiving information into awareness through our attention. Listening also implies that there is a biological response to the information being received.[6] (Greco 2021, 106)

Below, we will unbraid this concept of listening into three key principles in order to relate a concept of listening to a practice of standing, and standing into dancing.

---

[6] This description emerged through research for my osteopathic dissertation (Greco 2021).

Principle 1: Listening as Actively Receiving Information

How we engage our attention changes the information we receive; it changes our experience and our bodies. Attention in the most basic sense is bidirectional, efferent and afferent, flowing away, flowing toward. Attention directed outwardly in an efferent manner is a vital and functional mode of attention but differs from listening attention. A verbal listening exercise I've experienced in both osteopathic and improvisational training practices is to sit directly across from someone as a listener and to have all attention on them while they speak. The next part of the exercise is to reverse the flow of attention so that as a listener, your primary focus is resting in your own bodily sensations while allowing what the person is saying to flow toward you. Almost invariably, the person speaking would become physically uncomfortable and self-conscious when 100% of the listener's attention was flowing outward toward them. Likewise, it was common for the speaker to find it easier to rest within their own system when the listener was rooted in their own system and receiving them through a *receptive* quality of attention.

Staring is another example. Even from a distance, we can feel the impact of being stared at. An efferent or outwardly flowing mode of attention, staring acts as a force on the one being stared at, creating a subcortical biological influence on their systems.[7] In addressing the question of "Why standing?" Paxton refers to the fixated gaze of the predator and the effects of that gaze on the prey, comparing this to how the gaze of the audience in performance may potentially impact the dancer's ability to respond. He describes the Stand as a practice developed to help mitigate stage fright and the dangers that this form of paralysis could pose to the CI dancers in performance (Nelson 2015). It really is more than the performance context we need to consider. In a conversation between mayfield brooks and Karen Nelson published in *Contact Quarterly* (2016), brooks shares some of their experience of Improvising While Black (IWB), specifically in CI spaces. This conversation is an ongoing one in many communities highlighting a vital need to heighten awareness of how we're impacting each other through the ways we use attention. When attention is unexamined and directed in an outward manner, we are most often seeking information based on preconceived notions, unconscious bias, and inherited belief systems.

In contrast to this outwardly flowing mode, attention may be engaged in an afferent manner and oriented to *receive* information. When first learning to put my hands on someone as a teacher, they are not in a doing or fixing mode; in this context, my hands are sensory organs receiving information that this particular body is communicating in this moment in time. The first stage of listening touch,[8] as I'm understanding it from an osteopathic point of view,[9]

---

[7] Parapsychologist, researcher, and author William Braud PhD conducted extensive research on the effects of being stared at. In most cases the participants that were being stared at demonstrated significant changes in electrodermal activity, though they weren't consciously aware of when the staring was occurring. Further studies conducted by Marilyn Schlitz and William Braud showed statistically that one could potentially influence another's mind-body almost as much as they could influence their own. Another example of the influence of attention has been demonstrated in the classical double-slit experiments of quantum mechanics wherein the presence of an observer has been shown to alter the object of observation.

[8] In my teaching practice I draw on the work of osteopathic elders Rollin Becker and Viola Frymann, who explored at least four stages of listening touch, beginning with superficial touch of the sensory receptors developing through stages toward the skill of listening though the whole of ourselves (R. E. Brooks 1997; Frymann 1998).

[9] The point of view within this essay is shaped by an osteopathic understanding of the body and current interpersonal neurobiological research. Osteopathy is one lens, one philosophy through which we might consider the mystery of what this body is. The foundations of osteopathy appear to have been deeply informed by traditional wisdom of the Cherokee and Shawnee medicine peoples of the American Midwest, passed on to frontier doctor,

is a superficial contact involving sensory receptors in my skin and connective tissue matrix. With this initial contact, I'm receiving information about this body's tone, temperature, texture, shape, density, motion, and volume, in this moment. Listening touch may then increase in complexity, receiving information from my proprioceptive system that tells me something about the motion of your body and our bodies in contact, as well from the feedback processes of my sensory-motor system and so on through to an experience of listening with the whole of myself to the whole of the person that I'm in contact with. I do this through the shifting of my attention to receive present-moment information arising from various and distinct sources. As my listening skills develop over time, I put my hands on someone and receive the direct communication of their body without thinking through all of these stages.

When I refer to the term "information," I'm drawing on a frame proposed by Daniel J. Siegel in his research in the field of interpersonal neurobiology. He describes information as "Patterns of energy that carry meaning . . . a verb in that it gives rise to further processing in cascades of associations and linked meanings that emerge over time" (2012, A1-38, 39)—in other words, information as dynamic, everchanging, and flowing from various sources. Siegel identifies four distinct sources or fields of information that one may listen for or receive into awareness (2020a, 65–69):

1. **External sources** (exteroceptive system): information about the external world available through sense receptors; seeing, hearing, tasting, touching, smelling;
2. **Internal sources** (interoceptive system): information from the internal body senses.
3. **Cognitive sources** (higher cortical processes): cognitive level information, such as thinking, remembering, planning, imagining, narrative, language, and image;
4. **Interrelational sources** (mirror neuronal systems, somatic simulations, resonance circuits, polyvagal, neuroceptive systems): information available through relationships, self/other/environment.

Distinguishing between these four categories is an exercise in differentiation. Differentiating between the various sources of information available to our awareness can be a process and a practice. To separate these sources of information, one from the other, may seem arbitrary or artificial given our interconnectedness. The point is not to keep them separated, but to become aware of them, to study them, to notice the relationships between them and to invite the separated parts to integrate back into the whole with new awareness. Many of us grew up in a five-sensory oriented world where the five senses of seeing, hearing, tasting, touching, and smelling were all we were taught about the senses, and that the only valid way to know the world was through these five senses. The four categories of information described above are a conservative outline of what is known so far about information that we can sense; this outline recognizes the multi-sensory possibilities beyond five senses. We will learn much more in the years to come.

revolutionary thinker, and abolitionist Dr. Andrew Taylor Still in the late 1800s. The research within the field of interpersonal neurobiology is young research and quite incomplete. In a private exchange with cultural anthropologist, science and technology studies scholar and contributor to this volume Joe Dumit, it was pointed out to me that even though interpersonal neurobiology offers emergent and exciting insight, it is in no way a comprehensive or more sophisticated point of view than might be found within older, more mature systems of body understanding found in wisdom traditions around the world and throughout history. It is one point of view that offers some foundational language which may facilitate dialogue within the field of Contact Improvisation and in cross-disciplinary exchange.

166 Resistance and Support

J. J. Gibson (1966) notes two distinct meanings of the verb "to sense": the first meaning, to detect something; the second meaning, to have a sensation. Perception, he writes, is based on the first meaning (to detect something). Gibson points out that perception can't happen without receiving information via the stimulation of one's sensory receptors. The stimulation of the sensory receptors, however, may not be strong enough to reach conscious awareness. It is something Gibson refers to as "sensationless perception," even as he states that it isn't possible to have *information-less* perception. The information we receive from our inner and outer environments may not register as a sensation, yet it is influencing our perceptual systems. Perhaps Gibson's concept helps us make sense of the times we've reached out mid-fall and steadied ourselves even though we weren't consciously aware of where the supports were around us. We are receiving sensory information even if we are not experiencing a sensation consciously. Our active perceptual system is informing us on a non-conscious level. In this sense, Contact Improvisation has been, for me, a practice of physical self-trust and relational discernment, particularly in the early days of my practice.

Discomfort-Disorientation-Safety and the Influences of Information

In July 2022, Oberlin College in Ohio hosted *Critical Mass*, a four-day CI conference organized by Ann Cooper Albright. We gathered to honor, celebrate, and begin to untangle the 50-year history of Contact Improvisation, to examine the current expressions of the form, and to discourse about the directions that CI seems to be moving in.

The week at the conference has been volatile. It's been wild and beautiful and difficult. This is one of my first ventures out since the beginning of the pandemic and two years of immersion in mostly solo research. I'd left the contact jam context years ago in favor of more intimate, focused cohorts—there are more than 280 people here—my system is disoriented. I'm spiraling downward toward the worn wooden floor of Warner Main. The studio is hot and the windows are wide. Sounds of whale song are washing through and around us. mayfield brooks is teaching us about falling, attunement, and our vestibular systems. What I'm learning from them is about being human together, about disorientation and how to navigate with curiosity and skill, about being uncomfortable and moving through, about ways of listening and responding through our vestibular systems in motion. I'm relearning how to fall and how to rise up again. There is hope here, and Love.

Following a concussion, I developed a fear of falling. It was a great creative adaptation that protected my central nervous system, yet it really limited my CI experience. My protective filters eventually became habitual, preventing me from orienting my attention in ways where I could take calculated risks like falling into my back space and falling into flying, even after I had healed enough to do so. Once that reflex became conscious to me, I began relearning to fall, to break down and practice the components of falling through standing meditation and focused training with martial arts and movement teachers. I was learning how to receive new kinds of information that became available through disorientation. I was relearning to make contact with others in this state.

As we make contact with one another and move together, we are navigating not only our own unconscious filters and attentional habits, but also those of others and of the third system being formed between us. That third system is unique to our interchange. Stephen Porges,

Ph.D., explores this interrelatedness of experience through Polyvagal Theory. Building on the research of neuroscientist Paul D. Mclean, Porges (1995) proposes a bidirectional vagal system connecting one's patterns of social engagement with one's physical states. Porges uses the term "neuroception," which he defines as "the process through which the nervous system evaluates risk without requiring awareness" (2017, 19). Writing in the context of trauma experience, Porges describes neuroception as an automatic and ongoing scanning of one's environment to identify when danger is present and is related to trust building and social engagement. Neuroception occurs without awareness, yet produces changes in physiological states according to the context of the environment. What is the difference between safety and comfort? How do you discern between feelings of discomfort and the internal signals that you are unsafe?

Neuroception, Porges points out, is not always accurate, and our physiology may react in a defensive manner even when no danger is actually present, influenced perhaps by factors such as our trauma histories (2004, 2007). Listening for one's own shifting cognitive and sensorial states while being influenced by the shifting states of our partners and the environment is by no means a simple skill set, but appears to be imperative in learning to discern the accuracy of neuroception and developing choice in response. Porges distinguishes between neuroception and perception, adamantly separating the concepts to clarify that *suffering abuse does not mean we are to blame for not having picked up the signals that we were in danger.* Perception implies choice, and neuroception, in Porges's view, is bodily response that does not involve conscious choosing.

I've been playing with listening practices and sharpening this discernment for myself. If I enter a space that feels unsafe, my attention seems to automatically tune to receive specific types of information. Where are the doors? Who is in the room? Where is that sound coming from? How is my body responding? I often notice a grip throughout my system and a tightness of expression. When I'm at ease, I naturally turn my attention toward things that I'm curious about and that I find pleasure in. Without thinking a lot about it, noticing the way my attention is moving tells me a lot about the environment I'm in and my relationship to it.

Listening On-Balance and Off-Balance

A primary source of information we might draw on in CI is sensory kinesthetic information. Our awareness of kinesthetic information depends largely on the nature of our conscious relationship with gravity. In the Stand, we have the opportunity to observe a relatively steady dynamic between centers of mass and bases of support, to observe minute on-balance and off-balance navigations of our body in gravity. Moving from standing practice into partnering often invites unpredictable and precarious dialogue with gravity as we purposefully move off-balance and begin to share a center of gravity with increasing speed and momentum. Paying attention to these changes of orientation and accompanying sensations is a way of learning to discern between feelings of discomfort and actually being unsafe. Is my partner moving faster than my thinking mind can keep up with? That can be uncomfortable. That can challenge and stretch me in my developing CI practice. Is my partner moving faster than they or I have skill at moving in? That may be unsafe. If we are aware we are unsafe, we take measures to protect ourselves when we are able to do so. If I am feeling uncomfortable, maybe I can consider that improvisation and skill

168 Resistance and Support

development aren't necessarily about comfort, and also that I get to choose how I want to respond today.

Humans have an unconscious survival reflex to keep from falling that allows us to be upright without having to think much about it, provided we are moderately balanced. CI teacher, dancer, and activist Pam Johnson points out that because humans are typically adapted to maintain physiological balance, being off-balance for more than brief moments may naturally create a sense of *kinesthetic dissonance*. The experience of kinesthetic dissonance can feel anxiety-inducing and uncomfortable so that one will reflexively and unconsciously seek to rebalance, thus limiting choice and an array of sensory information. In the article "Theorizing Off-Balance" (2015), Johnson draws distinctions between a relatively balanced center of mass with a ground of support and a conscious, stable, organized off-balance state that allows us to receive a spectrum of information that is different from the information available to us in a "balanced" state. Renegotiating our inherent reflex not to fall requires rigorous attention and physical practice.

Physical tension can arise when we fear falling or haven't practiced moving in a stable off-balance state. Excessive physical tension can inhibit us from receiving the moment-to-moment sensory information required to safely and competently move with momentum. Moving off-balance with a partner, we are each surrendering some control over our physical directive. Unpracticed, unskilled, and unconscious, this state may easily become rigid or chaotic, endangering both partners. Standing together, forehead to forehead, for example, is one way to begin to play in the territory of being off-balance and to negotiate the experience of a shared physiology in the off-balance state. Consciously attending to the micro experience of standing can lay a foundation for the dynamic, larger movements of CI.

As many of us have experienced in the world of CI, opening our attention to the influences of so much information can become overwhelming and chaotic, or can put us at the mercy of unchecked, preconditioned patterning, bias, judgment, and rigidity. Yes, our brain is a predictive system and we all have unconscious biases—but that's not the only story. A listening practice such as the Stand is an opportunity to develop awareness, to distinguish between sources of information, offering the space to observe the relationships between them so that we can forget about it and dance, allowing our natural self-organizational intelligence to integrate partnered movement in ways our thinking or sensing minds alone are not capable of. Awareness seems to be a key.

Principle 2: Attention as a Conduit Delivering Information into Awareness

In a forest off the highway quite near my home is an old stand of Eastern Hemlock.[10] Since the start of the pandemic, I find myself there most days. It's late afternoon and I'm standing, quietly distinguishing between downward streaming sensations of gravity and this newer sensation of a simultaneous upward motion, like a bidirectional river—like a tree. The trees are teaching me this. They look like standing rivers today, swooning in the wind. The sensations are a source of information that I'm receiving into my awareness by turning my

---

[10] Traditional territory of the Attawandron, Chonnonton, and Neutral Peoples. Treaty land of the Mississaugas of the New Credit and part of the Dish with One Spoon Territory.

attention toward them. As is the visual information I'm receiving from the trees, so too the far and close calls of the great horned owl pair that live here—the memories that flush through me, the poetry that comes, a whole other source of information that I can receive into my awareness if I allow the light of my attention to hover there. The knowing and the knowns. The internal and the external. The upward and the downward. They are all moving now as a whole experience, awareness organizing the shifts of attention. I can separate out the various sources of information, distinguish between them as a practice, but it is the integration of all of this information and the consciousness that is receiving it that is the thing.

Attention, Intention, and Awareness

Awareness may be described from the most basic, brainstem-mediated sensory awareness to the experience of consciousness itself (Wallace 2016, 321). It's a huge concept with more theories, connotations, and historical and cultural perspectives than we are able to consider here. Awareness appears to be an agent of choice, enabling one to move from automatic, reactive, unconscious bias and behaviors toward a more conscious and reciprocal engagement. There are compelling relationships to consider between attention and awareness. While awareness seems to include states of knowing and that which is known, attention is being considered here as a relational process that influences the flow of information and delivers different types of information into awareness (Siegel 2020a).

We are immersed in an astonishing amount of information all the time. By default, some information may be received within awareness, and a great deal of information is received unconsciously. A lot depends on what we pay attention to, and stabilizing attention can be a massive challenge. Distractions, dissociative tendencies, fixations, and obsessions are some of the attentional challenges described and commonly experienced by people moving through trauma and in some experiences of neurodiversity. Ideally, attention would be adaptive, alert, and able to be modulated consciously (Ogden and Pain 2006). From a neurobiological perspective, two main factors seem to be involved in the stabilizing of attention. The first factor is knowing what one is aware of, and the second is attending to *intention* (Siegel 2012, 2020b).

If listening attention is actively receptive, the active part of that statement implies that we are choosing; it implies intention. Choosing to listen as a foundation for dancing together is an intentional act. Intention is a mental level activity that seems to set up the mind to function in a particular and ongoing manner. An intention to listen as we move and partner doesn't necessarily need to be held in conscious awareness. As a starting point, an intention to listen can help organize and influence the quality and content of sensory information we receive from ourselves, our partners, and our environment. In partnered motion, as we navigate simple and complex movement puzzles, what might it be to allow listening to serve as a mutually agreed-upon home base? The place into which all of our motion settles and from which all motion extends.

The Stand can be approached as an attentional practice where we play with being intentional with our modes of perception, as opposed to being in a default or habitual state of passive attention. Intention can direct one's attentional focus. With practice, this purposefully cultivated state may become innate. We intentionally train our attention to follow our rapidly self-organizing system in motion. We may practice listening within the Stand and then let

170   Resistance and Support

it go—we dance—attention is being organized by our intention to listen and our cultivated states of awareness. Within a listening practice like the Stand, we have an opportunity to slow the tempo of our listening[11] and practice intentionally focusing our sensory organs to receive information from various sources: sensations of weight from limbs and organs, the variable sensations of heartbeat and breath, the soundscape of our environment, sensations of motion, of gravity streaming through our form. Both conscious and non-conscious sources are informing our perception. Our perceptual system organizes our response—the action we take or don't take.

In a neurobiological frame to date, the brain, by default, is a predictive system. It's handy for bike riding and many activities of daily life. Our pattern-making predictive system is an effective survival mechanism. When improvising, when moving off-balance in unpredictable ways with a partner who is doing the same, the brain's predictive system is limited. If I acknowledge that my brain operates through predictive coding based on bias, judgment, and previous experience, then there is more choice and opportunity to listen and respond from current experience based on real-time information—listening for things as they are. Typically, this requires practice. I practice this by intentionally focusing my sensory organs to receive present-moment information. Through the organizing capacity of our perceptual system, we respond to that information. As we respond, we receive new information, we change focus and receive new information. Our sensory-perceptual system appears to function as a complex feedback system.[12]

Complex Systems and Self-Organization

Humans are complex systems. When we stand together, and move together, we are creating a third, living system by our interaction. We exist and develop in relationship. Neuroscientist and physician Antonio Damasio, in the book *The Strange Order of Things: Life, Feeling, and the Meaning of Cultures* (2018), points out that complex biological systems existed and interacted before brains and nervous systems developed. Nervous systems and brains emerged as a regulatory byproduct in highly complex self-organizing biological systems. The brain and nervous system, in this sense, function as a coordinator, arising from and serving the body proper—a very different point of view from a common Western understanding of the brain as the origin of the mind and ruler of the system. Damasio describes the necessary interrelationship between nervous system and body as the conditions from which mind emerged and that "minds occurred not to isolated organisms but to organisms that were part of a social setting" (2018, 71).

Complex biological systems (like our bodies) have been considered within the biological sciences to be open, adaptive systems that are nonlinear, chaos-capable, and able to self-organize. Not organized like a rigidly ordered office environment might be considered organized, self-organization is a process that emerges naturally within complex systems, shaping and adapting that system within its environment, moving toward increasing complexity. Rather than being pre-programmed into a system, self-organization emerges

---

[11] Concept shared by Bonnie Ginits DO (2007).
[12] Our sensory-perceptual system functioning as a deeply complex feedback system is written about in relation to CI by Bonnie Bainbridge Cohen in the book *Sensing Feeling and Action: The Experiential Anatomy of Body-Mind Centering* (Cohen, Nelson, and Smith 2012).

through relationship between the elements of that system/environment. Self-organization is a process that can be *supported* or that can be *inhibited*. When self-organization is supported, the system tends to express health, adaptability, coherence, and flexible stability, flowing harmoniously between order and chaos. When self-organization is inhibited, the expression tends toward either rigidity or chaos, rather than flowing easily between them (Siegel 2020b). In our movement form, in Contact Improvisation, the effects of a rigid or chaotic system are physically immediate.

As a practice, the Stand may invite the organization, integration, and coherence of our systems to arise and flow in original, spontaneous, responsive, and adaptive ways. How? Self-organization is supported through processes of unbraiding and distinguishing between all these various threads of information that are available to us, by examining the relationships between them and weaving it all together into an integrated whole. Imagine a weaver working with a huge, tangled ball of thread—all the colors mixed up and blending together. Separating the threads into piles of similar colors (differentiation) and placing them on the warp and the weft of the loom (relating) allow the weaver to weave a coherent tapestry (integration). An integrated system is capable of greater complexity, nuance, and choice. An integrated system has a greater capacity of discerning between resonance and enmeshment, meaning, connecting with others while retaining a sense of oneself, of choosing to move toward each other and to move away—of responding to the necessity of the moment.

Principle 3: Listening Implies a Biological Response to What Is Received

In the days and weeks after birth, as the caregiver imitates the expressions of the child, the infant's mirror neuronal and resonance systems begin to activate (Oostenbroek et al. 2016). Human beings seem to learn and to develop social cognition through the ability to absorb one another's internal states. At least this is what we understand about the neurobiology so far. Christov-Moore and Iacoboni (2016) point out that the observations of a person's emotional expression, sensations, and behaviors are processed by the observer in much the same way as one would process one's own. In a sense, we absorb and are influenced by what I would describe as one another's *atmospheres*. In other words, there may be both conscious and nonconscious imitation of one another's internal states, which Christov-Moore and Iacoboni refer to as "self-other resonance" (2016, 1545).

Siegel defines resonance as "[t]he mutual influence in interacting systems on each other that allows two or more entities to become a part of a functional whole" (2012, A1-69). When two or more systems come into contact, as we do in CI, they not only influence one another, but appear to function as a unified system. Resonance is the capacity to listen for and co-experience another's feeling state via neurobiological resonance circuits. Herein lies the beauty and risk in our form. Resonance is a co-experiencing—a reciprocity and an interchange between distinct yet integrated systems. It implies the choice to come together and the freedom to separate while keeping one's own sense of self. Siegel distinguishes resonance from the emmeshed, confusing state of "excessive linkage without differentiation" (2012, 19)—something we risk when we enter the dance without being able to clearly distinguish one source of information from another.

172   Resistance and Support

I love noticing how my body responds in another's atmosphere—how it slows or enlivens or grows playful. It's unique to our interchange. How we move together is specific to this exchange. It's one of the things that can be so hard about endings and so exciting about dancing with strangers and such an interesting thing to notice as relationships change over time. There are risks here and opportunities. How do I know that I'm not mistaking *the influence of you* for my own self-sense? Aside from the obvious physical risks we navigate, the potential for emmeshed, confused, and fraught interactions in the form of CI is massive. Listening can be a way of locating ourselves at the center of our experience and of our environment—like being in the eye of the storm rather than being blown around in the hurricane. What does it mean for each of us to be a center of experience as we dance together? What is the relationship between your center of experience and mine?

In the field of osteopathy, there is a quality of listening and responding described by some as balanced reciprocal interchange. Paxton (2020) describes coexisting states of mutual freedom and dependence. By relating concepts from neurologist Oliver Sacks to listening in CI, Bigé and Godard distinguish between listening through the mind of reason and listening through physical attention:

> I can include or exclude you. For instance, when I listen to you, I can listen to what you are saying, to the meaning of what you are saying, through the aerial transmission of the sound to my ears—in that case, you are kept at a certain distance, which allows me to approach your ideas through reasoning. But I can also listen to the vibrato of your voice, through the reverberations of your voice into my bones and viscera: in that case, I allow you into my territory, I let myself be affected not only by what you are saying, but also by how you are saying it. (Bigé 2019, 97)

What are the implications of allowing each other this intimately into our respective internal worlds? How do we discern when that is safe to do, and when we need to maintain distance as we negotiate a dance? If our instincts have been injured through cultural conditioning, education, trauma—how do we learn to hear and trust our own internal sense of yes and no? When we reach toward another person, how do we first establish connection within ourselves and with our own ground? How do we decide for ourselves who and what is trustworthy?

Biological frames of reference teach that we receive our outer world through our sensory system, and our body is influenced by and responds to that information. That response is silent, felt, and occurring prior to languaging, prior to perception, prior to conceptualization, and is sometimes referred to in neurobiology as a bottom-up process. In this way, listening implies that there is a direct biological response to information that is being received. The response of our bodily intelligence is a vital source of information, something we may become aware of and inquire into. It is something we can listen for. If we consider listening to be an active receiving of the Other into our awareness, it is a simultaneous receiving of ourselves. It is a choice and a process of discernment. How is my body responding here? What am I willing to allow into myself in this moment? What is not permitted? It is a state that is relational, alert, and responsive. If I am listening for you, I am simultaneously listening for my biological response to you and to our environment. To be a listening presence, I allow information to flow through my biology, to flow through awareness—*flow through*. I'm not a perpetually open receptacle. I open and close, inhale and exhale. I pause and listen for my own bottom-up input. I make choices informed by this.

Listening is a way, not by magically thinking that if we just listen everything will be okay, but by pragmatically establishing a practice that invites the organization and coherence of our systems to arise and flow in spontaneous, responsive, and adaptive ways. In other words, to increase access to our improvisational intelligence and choice, rather than be limited to our survival responses only. Listening together, standing together, invites a space to open between our immediate sensory experience and our habits of perception—a space from which uncommon perspectives, spontaneous gesture, startling beginnings, abrupt endings, and unexpected changes of direction emerge. Such is improvisation where listening is the fulcrum.

Standing practice, learning to listen for my biological intelligence and response, learning to differentiate, learning to inquire—am I thinking, or am I sensing? Is this information coming from inside of me or outside of me? Am I identifying more with the information than with my own sense of self? These inquiries may point us toward the freedom of integrated self-other resonance. Integration of the information we've differentiated seems to be the crux.

Integration

Thinking and sensing are each part of an integrated whole. The question for me is not necessarily whether to prioritize sensory information or cognitive information, but is rather a matter of integrating top-down and bottom-up information as we dance. Considered as a whole, the sensory-perceptual system includes both top-down and bottom-up processing—thinking *and* sensing. For many of us, by default of immersion in Western culture, the emphasis is predominantly on top-down processes of the higher cognitive centers: thinking, observing, describing, interpreting, judging, and evaluating experience. Perhaps because of this, or out of some other necessity, some will come to CI and saturate themselves in the sensory world exclusively and without discernment. Others may remain primarily in an evaluative state of mind, strategizing, evaluating, and planning. Most of us live more comfortably in one mode or the other.

In a seasoned practice of CI there are nuances of experiencing, of knowing when one is receiving sensory information or cognitive information—of integrating sensing and thinking, sensing and perceiving. The ability to draw on integrated sensory-perceptual experience is a vital CI skill set. Why? The capacity to distinguish between sensing and thinking is foundational to the integration of experience. How? Sensing and thinking seem to be processes that modulate each other.[13] When we are thinking, evaluating, and constructing narrative, there is typically less access to sensory experience. Likewise, to turn attention toward the direct sensory experience tends to quiet the thinking mind. Thinking and sensing coexist, they dance together yet are distinct strands of information. When integrated they become like voices in a choir that retain their full originality and integrity; together they create the *one voice*. Bonnie Bainbridge Cohen (2012) describes CI as a way of integrating experience. We acknowledge different sources of information in standing practice and let that go as we dance. We use our eyes, seeing our environment and each other, we touch with our backs, our feet, our skin as a sensory organ. We move, act, and make choices based on our perception.

---

[13] In neurobiological terms, the midline cortical structures which are active during cognitive processes dampen the lateral cortical sensory circuits of sensing (Siegel 2012).

174   Resistance and Support

We are informed by our partner's state, by each other's physiology. We speed up, slow down, pause, change direction. We fall. We learn.

Integration is being considered here as a process that strengthens the capacity to contact another person while maintaining a sense of oneself and a process that supports self-organization—something that often requires practice and a faculty for listening to discern one's own internal information and biological responses from information coming from an external source. Interoception, or sensing of the internal body, is often a key focus of the Stand, and a major element in developing the self-awareness necessary to carry self-other resonance consciously and in an integrated manner. A practice of the Stand may support an integrated negotiation with gravity in an upright stance, likewise in the complex movement of CI. Perhaps it could help us navigate the gravity between us as well.

What Causes you to Listen?

Pauline Oliveros (1932–2016) was a composer, performer, and founder of the Deep Listening Institute (now The Center for Deep Listening) at Rensselaer Polytechnic Institute, NY (2020) who's practice of Deep Listening involves the creation and performance of music centered around the listening state in improvisation[14]. In the text score Ear Piece (2005, p. 34), Oliveros asks "What causes you to listen?" It's a question that has lived in me through these years of navigating change in our CI communities and it underpins the writing of this piece. My standing practice is also a practice of reflecting on this question.

The Stand, as I'm understanding so far, is an opportunity to rest in and listen for my own nonverbal biological responses—in this instance, my body's biological response to the influence of gravity—to observe myself organizing in motion-pause-motion, in the tiny falling flights of standing. It's a skill I want, especially if I'm partnering—to hear my own biology as it responds to you, and yours to mine. This takes practice and stamina for many of us and can form a foundation of consent.

The elegance of the Stand, the complexity we are invited to experience, could be underestimated considering how simple it is. In standing, we attend to the self-organizational intelligence of this body, of Nature. It's humbling. We give over, however briefly, the insistence of our higher cortical centers in order to appreciate the natural intelligence of our system within its web of relationships. We invite a quality of internal dialogue wherein we partner with body, not dictate to it.

If we haven't listened, can you tell me what we've done? We've constrained expression and choice. We have imposed our will onto our body or the body of another. We've overridden relationship.

We can burden each other so deeply. We can lift one another, fly together. We are responsible for ourselves—for the atmosphere we carry. We are responsible to and for each other. When we make appropriate contact as a listening presence, we come into relation with ourselves and others and our world *as they are*—not as we wish or hope or fear, but as they are. This causes me to listen when I dance with you.

---

[14] I studied with Oliveros between 2007 and 2010 receiving direct mentoring and participating in intensive residency programs. My essay on listening, touch and voice was published in The Anthology of Essays on Deep Listening in 2012.

What causes me to listen is remembering that when we move toward each other and come into contact, we move into and are permeated by one another's atmosphere. We affect each other, change each other, we learn our humanity together. We move and are moved within the small dances of listening. What causes you to listen?

References

Bigé, R., and H. Godard. (2019). Moving-moved. In R. Bige (ed.), *Steve Paxton: Drafting Interior Techniques* (pp. 89–104). Lisboa: Culturgest

brooks, m. (2016). IWB = Improvising While Black. *Contact Quarterly Dance & Improvisation Journal* 41(1): 33–39.

Brooks, R. E. (1997). *Life in Motion: The Osteopathic Vision of Rollin E. Becker, DO*. Portland, OR: Stillness Press.

Carson, R. (2003). *The Sea around Us*. New York: Oxford University Press.

Christov-Moore, L., and M. Iacoboni. (2016). Self-Other Resonance, Its Control and Prosocial Inclinations: Brain–Behavior Relationships. *Human Brain Mapping* 37(4): 1544–1558.

Cohen, B. B., L. Nelson, and N. S. Smith. (2012). *Sensing, Feeling, and Action: The Experiential Anatomy of Body-Mind Centering*®. Northampton, MA: Contact Editions.

Damasio, A. (2018). *The Strange Order of Things: Life, Feeling, and the Making of Cultures* (Kindle ed.). New York: Pantheon Books.

Dudeja, J. P. (2019). Benefits of Tadasana, Zhan Zhuang and Other Standing Meditation Techniques. *International Journal of Research and Analytical Reviews* 6(2): 607–618.

Foundation, O. I. (2023). OSHO Dynamic Meditation. Osho International Foundation, New York. Retrieved from https://www.osho.com/meditation/osho-active-meditations/osho-dynamic-meditation

Frymann, V. M. (1998). *The Collected Papers of Viola M. Frymann: Legacy of Osteopathy to Children*. Indianapolis, IN: American Academy of Osteopathy.

Gibson, J. J., and Carmichael, L. (1966). *The Senses Considered as Perceptual Systems* (Vol. 2). Boston: Houghton Mifflin.

Gintis, B. (2007). *Engaging the Movement of Life: Exploring Health and Embodiment through Osteopathy and Continuum*. Berkeley, CA: North Atlantic Books.

Greco, L. (2021). *An Osteopathic Concept and Practice of Listening*. Thesis, Canadian College of Osteopathy. Toronto, ON.

Johnson, P. (2015). Theorizing Off-Balance: Movement Training for Actors. *Association of Theatre Movement Educators* 23(1): 12–14.

Kimmerer, R. W. (2013). *Braiding Sweetgrass: Indigenous Wisdom, Scientific Knowledge and the Teachings of Plants*. Minneapolis, MN: Milkweed Editions.

Manheimer, K. (2020). Steve Paxton's 1977 Small Dance Guidance. *Contact Improvisation*. Retrieved from https://myriadicity.net/contact-improvisation/learning-contact-improvisation/steve-paxton-s-1977-small-dance-guidance.

Nelson, K. (2015). Why Standing? Steve Paxton Talks about How the Stand Relates to Stage Fright and Entrainment in Contact Improvisation. *Contact Quarterly Dance & Improvisation Journal* 40(1): 37–40. Retrieved from https://contactquarterly.com/cq/article-gallery/view/CQ-40-1-Paxtoncompressed.pdf.

OED. (2000). *Oxford English Dictionary*. Retrieved from https://www-oed-com.subzero.lib.uofgueph.ca/.

176   Resistance and Support

Oliveros, P. (2005). *Deep listening: A composer's sound practice*. Lincon, NE: IUniverse.

Ogden, P. M., and C. K. Pain. (2006). *Trauma and the Body: A Sensorimotor Approach to Psychotherapy*. New York: W.W. Norton.

Oostenbroek, J., T. Suddendorf, M. Nielsen, J. Redshaw, S. Kennedy-Costantini, J. Davis, . . . V. Slaughter. (2016). Comprehensive Longitudinal Study Challenges the Existence of Neonatal Imitation in Humans. *Current Biology* 26(10); 1334–1338. doi:https://doi.org/10.1016/j.cub.2016.03.047

Paxton, S. (2020). *Gravity*. Bruxelles: Contradanse Editions.

Porges, S. W. (1995). Orienting in a Defensive World: Mammalian Modifications of Our Evolutionary Heritage. A Polyvagal Theory. *Psychophysiology* 32(4): 301–318. doi:10.1111/j.1469-8986.1995.tb01213.x.

Porges, S. W. (2004). Neuroception: A Subconscious System for Detecting Threats and Safety. *ZERO TO THREE* 24: 19–24.

Porges, S. W. (2007). The Polyvagal Perspective. *Biological Psychology* 74(2): 116–143. doi:https://doi.org/10.1016/j.biopsycho.2006.06.009.

Porges, S. W. (2017). *The Pocket Guide to the Polyvagal Theory: The Transformative Power of Feeling Safe*. New York: W. W. Norton.

Schwenk, T. (1996). *Sensitive Chaos: The Creation of Flowing Forms in Water and Air*. Hillside, UK: Rudolf Steiner Press.

Siegel, D. J. (2012). *Pocket Guide to Interpersonal Neurobiology: An Integrative Handbook of the Mind (Norton Series on Interpersonal Neurobiology)*. New York: W. W. Norton.

Siegel, D. J. (2020a). *Aware: The science and practice of presence--the groundbreaking meditation practice*: TarcherPerigee.

Siegel, D. J. (2020b). *The Developing Mind: How Relationships and the Brain Interact to Shape Who We Are* (3rd ed.). New York, NY: Guilford Press.

Stark Smith, N. (1979). Editor's Note. *Contact Quarterly Dance & Improvisation Journal* 5(1).

Stark Smith, N. (1987). Editor's Note. *Contact Quarterly Dance & Improvisation Journal* 12(2).

Tomatis, A., and R. Prada. (2005). *The Ear and the Voice*. Lanham, MD: Scarecrow Press.

Wallace, R. K. (2016). *The Neurophysiology of Enlightenment: How the Transcendental Meditation and TM-Sidhi Program Transform the Functioning of the Human Body* (Kindle ed.). Fairfield, IA: Dharma Publications.

Yunkaporta, T. (2020). *Sand Talk: How Indigenous Thinking Can Save the World* (1st ed.). New York: HarperOne.

9
Listening Touch

Rosalind Holgate Smith

Introduction

"touch that is not wanting"
"touch that is not asking or expecting anything"
"touch that is just receiving and reading information"[1]

In 2020 I began asking what kinds of touch dancers had learned through practicing Contact Improvisation (CI). From over 50 interviews, 90% described a type of touch that is *not wanting or expecting anything*, but rather is focused on *receiving information*.[2] Adopting a popular phrase, I called this "listening touch" and decided to further investigate how listening affects dancers and what it means as a skill and technique in dance improvisation.

In this chapter I build on somatic listening practices and hands-on therapies that have influenced CI and contemporary dance since the 1970s postmodern period. Through investigating these foundational practices, I propose new listening touch techniques that also integrate new materialist theory. I have drawn particularly on the molecular thinking of Jane Bennett (2009, 2020) and the quantum philosophies of Karen Barad (2003, 2012, 2017, 2018), where touch implies entanglement, and bodies and matter are to be understood as animate collections of force, continuously intra-acting, colliding, and coalescing. These lively perspectives that concern the complexity of all material relations have led me to reflect on touch as a way of being in the world, and listening as a haptic practice that enables encounters with Otherness—an Otherness that might include disturbing emotions and images, emergent arousal, numbness, overwhelm, and confrontations with the unknown. The most key techniques I introduce include *hovering, accompanying*, and *listening in action*, which are proposed as practices for dancers to navigate and embrace such encounters with Otherness. In these techniques, I also take inspiration from the political scholar Leah Bassel, in her notion of stewardship (2017), where enhanced spatial awareness is considered to support ethical and sustainable ways of relating and co-becoming with diverse cultures and differences. Broadening the scope of more introspective somatic models of listening, *hovering, accompanying*, and *listening in action* embody an expansive awareness of space to get in and feel among forces. I reflect on Bassel's contribution of space as a means of enhancing empathy and compassion toward experiences of Otherness, which in my techniques makes possible a deep environmental form of listening from within that can zoom in on micro sensations and zoom out to be with Others on more macro terms.

---

[1] Interview responses from Contact Improvisors describing touch learned through practicing Contact Improvisation. Survey conducted between August 2019 and December 2020; results: https://touchinfinities.wordpress.com/2020/12/01/what-kinds-of-touch-are-in-contact-improvisation/.
[2] Ibid.

Rosalind Holgate Smith, *Listening Touch* In: *Resistance and Support*. Edited by: Ann Cooper Albright, Oxford University Press.
© Oxford University Press 2024. DOI: 10.1093/9780197776308.003.0010

178   Resistance and Support

In style, the written form of this essay means to invite the feeling of listening. Differing from more punchy and entertaining literature, it remains in many places open and includes shifts from sections of discursive reflection to more poetic and illustrative accounts of experience. The various voices and accounts of experience that are included represent a series of lab[3] research exchanges with CI colleagues, which I hosted in Berlin (between September 2021 and January 2022). I describe and refer also to experiences of dancing with earth matter, including soil and trees. This research that has involved dancing with humans and separately with environmental matter reflects my expanded CI practice that over the past 15 years has included extensive outdoor dancing as well as traditional, in-studio CI teaching and practice. I invite your reading with patience, and with attention not only to the words but what arises between them. For readers interested in exploring listening touch more practically, the appendix to the chapter offers a concluding set of guidelines.

Models and Foundations of Listening

Since CI emerged in 1972, it has cultivated a language of listening through the skin. The small dance, developed by Steve Paxton, can be seen to foreground an early somatic practice of training listening (Novak 1990, 64). Also known as the Stand, the practice is typically performed in an upright standing position, where the touch between the dancer's feet and the ground features as the primary point of contact. This contact provides reference for registering bodily sensations and the subtle adjustments that dancers make within their body to maintain a balanced posture. Becoming aware of subtle weight shifts and the nature of one's alignment makes it possible to make minor modifications that create ease in one's posture. Paxton emphasized the small dance as a key training practice, as he found that by developing their inner awareness, dancers could expand their ability to make choices and finer structural adjustments when engaged in dynamic, high-speed dancing, involving flying and falling. Listening in the small dance, as such, primes dancers to recognize bigger and more complex forces at play.

Cellular Touch represents a further foundational model of listening used in CI, which comes from Body-Mind Centering®, a somatic practice founded by occupational therapist Bonnie Bainbridge Cohen,[4] which developed in parallel with CI since the early 1970s. In *Cellular Touch*, the full palms of the hands are used in a wholly receptive way. Whether in movement or at rest, the idea is that touch is applied to cultivate proprioceptive awareness and not to guide or manipulate a receiving partner, as is often the case in massage or manual therapy. Given that many Body-Mind Centering® practitioners practice CI, many cross-over techniques have developed. *Unwanting Hands* is a training exercise taught by CI teachers Kirstie Simson and Charlie Morrissey[5] in which the principles of *Cellular Touch* are very much present. In *Unwanting Hands*, dancers are instructed to similarly use their hands to follow and accompany a partner's movement. The exercise is called *Unwanting Hands*

---

[3] Lab (from the term *laboratory*) refers to a focused group research format used by Contact Improvisation dancers that embraces collaboration, experimentation, knowledge exchange, and discussion. A select topic is typically investigated and various formats can be used.

[4] Body-Mind Centering® (BMC), founded by Bonnie Bainbridge Cohen, is a somatic practice involving exploration and embodiment of the human anatomy through movement, touch, imagery, and voice.

[5] *Unwanting Hands* was introduced to me in a workshop entitled *Move, Touch & Be Moved*, taught by Charlie Morrissey and Kirstie Simson at Yorkshire Dance in 2015.

because it is about just sensing-being with, and not guiding, changing, taking, or attempting to achieve something. As two partners move through space, the hands-on follower may change the position of their hands to accommodate their partners' speed, and range of movement. The proprioceptive feedback may be used by both dancers to build awareness of how they are holding their structure, and identify opportunities to release tension, attune more closely with themselves and each other, attend to the direction in which movement is unfolding, and generally become more efficient in their movement.

A point often overlooked in hands-on practices such as *Unwanting Hands* and *Cellular Touch* is the way in which, by establishing roles of touch, givers and receivers can create imbalanced power dynamics between partners that ultimately prevent mutual forms of improvisation from evolving. In a lab series in Berlin,[6] I investigated *Unwanting Hands* and *Cellular Touch* with experienced CI dancers and colleagues. Through repeated and close exploration of these exercises, which involved follow-up feedback sessions, touch-givers and even experienced somatic practitioners reported giving touch as a form of service, and reflected upon experiences of going out of their way to oversee and provide affection to receiving partners. Some touch-givers also noted losing a sense of feeling in touch with themselves, while touch-receivers commented on losing a sense of agency. From witnessing these explorations, it was evident that when touch-givers assumed a holding kind of responsibility as being *in charge*, they in effect dampened and disempowered their partner's ability to communicate their needs and feelings. These imbalanced relationship dynamics seemed to be most disempowering for receivers when the bodywork exercises were performed at rest, as the passive receiver, often assuming also a nonverbal state, appeared to provoke their touch-giving partner to adopt more responsibility. Practicing bodywork lying down and from seated positions of stillness does equate to movement appearing subtler and less visible, which requires that touch-givers are especially attentive to pick up on fine cues, such as fluctuations in breathing that become essential to gauging whether what they are doing is consensual. It is hard to escape these entangled, hierarchical dynamics, and in somatic dance pedagogy, maternal caregiving dynamics are particularly evident.

The fact that practices such as *Cellular Touch* and *Unwanting Hands* come from and have shared applications in therapy suggests some evidence of where such maternal caregiving dynamics come from. In examining these cross-overs, it is worth recognizing how therapy necessitates a different setup to dance training. In one-to-one therapy sessions, touch-givers tend typically to supportively hold an overarching sense of their client's process and contain to some extent the experience of this receiver. With this holding dynamic, receptive touch has been found to activate the relational infant-caregiver dynamic which, as developmental psychologist Aline LaPierre discusses, can unlock childhood memories of how touch was experienced in infancy (LaPierre 2003). Somatic or receptive touch has consequently been incorporated into various forms of therapy as a valuable tool for addressing breaches in the development of the relational matrix which cannot be reached by verbal means alone (2003, 2). In CI jams, that are fundamental training spaces, the premise is mutuality (Paxton 2018), and dancers, regardless of experience, ideally meet on equal grounds. Mutuality is of course an ideal premise, intended to incite equality and collaborative forms of dancing and exchange. To not only support mutuality as an ideal, but more importantly to establish

---

[6] Between January and March 2022 I hosted a weekly series of touch labs, with dancers, somatic practitioners, and performers in Berlin to investigate the effects of specific touch practices.

ethical relationships, dancers need to move beyond giving and receiving and instead recognize touch as a part of their ongoing enmeshment in the world. Through and with receptivity to this touch, dancers need to develop listening as a skill to recognize from within how the roles they assume play out. Given the global growth of CI, 50 years on, which brings with it greater diversity, dancers now more than ever must come to appreciate how their positions, cultural backgrounds, and current needs and desires affect and contribute to the dances they attract and develop. Recognizing our interdependence cannot be done alone.

In the current dialogues and increasing guidelines addressing consent and boundaries (Beaulieux 2019; Rea 2020), Michele Beaulieux raises the fact that CI's first principle, of so-called *self-care and self-responsibility*, is fundamentally insufficient for solving situations in which dancers experience violence and boundary-crossing because this self-care principle "tends to side with privilege and can promote victim blaming" (2019, 47). Dancers who are new to CI spaces and are members of minority groups are most at risk of experiencing inhibitions or of conversely overstepping boundaries because they bring in new and different understandings of touch that are often under-acknowledged. Newcomers in jams often alone must navigate CI's ubiquitous codes of practice and learn for themselves what is acceptable and what is not. The first-principle notion of *self-care*, which emphasizes individual subjectivity, is often not enough for dancers to feel ethically included and may be seen to have come from the interoceptive focus established in most forms of somatic training. Karen Barad's new materialist thinking offers some quantum ways of recognizing the complexity of our entangled interdependence, which I have found valuable for revising this principle and building more inclusive modes of listening practice.

Applying Barad's concept of *intra-action* to listening models, including *The Small Dance*, *Cellular Touch*, and *Unwanting Hands*, has led me to develop a broader, more environmental, or eco-somatic sense of listening. As a concept deriving from quantum physics, intra-action, as Barad proposes, describes the way in which independent entities do not and cannot exist a priori, but rather only come to exist through their encounters (Barad 2003, 815). Intra-action consequently disturbs all possibility of thinking subjectively and objectively of contained bodies, material objects, and beings. Given intra-action, attention that concerns consciousness and the aliveness of existence must be reconceived as shared, volatile, and constantly shifting.

The Politics of Listening

Leah Bassel's concept of listening as stewardship (2017, 71–87) has further contributed to developing a more atmospheric perspective of listening that veers away from notions of containing others' experiences and overtaking caregiving dynamics. In her concept of listening as stewardship, Bassel proposes that space is brought into awareness as a relational field of solidarity which makes it possible to recognize and accompany differences from a distance. While Bassel's writing addresses immigration, racial, and colonial conflict, it has provided inspiration for thinking about how space can support the appreciation of differences and enhance human compassion. This idea of creating space relates to Barad's notion of intra-action and new materialist understandings of matter as made up of subatomic collections of force (Barad 2012; Bennett 2009). Assimilating these philosophies has led me to develop an atmospheric perspective and technique of listening that involves inhabiting an expanded sense of space. This technique, which I call *hovering*, involves allowing space to infiltrate into my awareness as a medium of suspension and delay that can support processing and communication. In *hovering* I may touch with my hands or other surfaces of my skin, and while sustaining physical touch, I lighten it and bring in more distance, which diffuses and softens the focus at the point of contact. By expanding my spatial awareness and bringing distance into my touch, I can find opportunities to release tension throughout my body, which enhances my capacity to stay open and receptive to my wider surroundings. The atmospheric embodied perspective of this work helps me to look beyond the containment of the skin that can come with a feeling of holding myself lightly, which can mean also holding judgments and projections lightly, and not getting assertively involved in specific issues. Through exploring this expanded sense of space, I have found my experience of time stretch and also my sense of patience, and my ability and acceptance to stay and reconcile with disturbing feelings. In practice, it is not about stepping away from the touch or disturbing encounters, but developing a deeper environmental sense of listening from within. As a perspective, it compares to auditory listening which occurs from a position of being already embedded within surrounding and fluctuating atmospheres of sound. When musicians train their hearing, they do so from within environments of sound to listen for "those exact kinds of tiny, invisible, modulations that no one else can hear" (Buhner 2014, 39). It is a kind of listening that does not go out to claim exposure, but is constantly receptive. For musicians and CI dancers alike, being able to identify tiny modulations provides opportunities to respond and adjust their instrument. In the lively case of jamming contexts, where dancers' bodies are their instruments, moving in and out of contact with one another, their environment is similarly complex and ever-changing. With multiple passing bodies, touches, grazes, as well as changing conditions of weather and light, haptic intra-actions occur ongoingly. Listening for one's safety cannot be an interoceptive choice or examination, and it is here that *hovering* can be brought in to broaden the scope of one's awareness and ability to respond.

CI dancers still need to train their attention to focus through specific points of contact. As Nita Little explains, training attention to the point of contact is an important way for dancers to learn to limit, organize attention, and refine their presence (Little, personal email communication, December 13, 2020). Such organizational skills are especially important in jams, where there is so much stimulation. *Hovering* adds to CI's attentional training by diffusing the focus and encouraging greater release through the body, which can make it possible to suspend habituated patterns of behavior. In practice, *hovering* involves training one's attention to zoom in through the point of contact and zoom out to feel for and embody a wider awareness of space. This zooming in and out can both facilitate the effect of diffusion and heighten a sense of clarity. My experience in training is that it is also best approached without the hands, to inhibit functional associations and implications of intent. As Professor Michael Banissy, a social neuroscientist and touch expert, points out, our hands are hardwired with very fast sensory receptors, which makes communication with the central cortex of the brain much quicker than when touch occurs on different places of the body (Banissy 2022). This is effectively what makes actions such as switching on the kettle, or driving, precise and efficient. In CI, learning to listen from all surfaces of the skin encourages practitioners to slow down. Through the embodiment of space, *hovering* also supports an extended sense of taking time that is valuable for recognizing and letting go of the many social, sexual, and functional associations people often hold in relation to their bodies, which are not relevant in CI. There can ironically be more intimacy in *hovering* as dancers tend to become more sensitive to one another's personal space and how they approach contact.

182 Resistance and Support

Listening on the Earth

In CI, lying on the earth is a key way of understanding and relating to gravity that is foundational to the practice. I have learned this practice of lying on the earth as a way of arriving in my body, and I have taken it from the studio into outdoor locations. More than anywhere, being outdoors has led me to incorporate a vaster awareness of space in my body, which has significantly contributed to *hovering* as a listening touch technique. In my words below I reflect on an instance of lying on the earth, beneath large trees and upon fallen leaves in a cemetery called St. Mariens, in Berlin (Figure 9.1).[7]

> *As we rest, I am falling*
> *Falling apart*
> *Focused thoughts disperse*
> *My mind fluctuates*
> *Contracting to release*
> *As I let go*
> *All sense of myself, I am becoming less apparent*
> *no longer at the centre parts of me hover and dissolve*
> *Space is everywhere and I am still falling.*
> (Holgate Smith, journal extract, December 22, 2021)

Figure 9.1. *Lying on Earth*, Holgate Smith, drawing, 2021.

---

[7] In October 2021 I danced in St. Mariens Cemetery in Berlin, and presented a performance called *Trees*, in "Walking through the Woods," an exhibition commissioned by the Verwalterhaus fur Aktuelle Kunst und Kultur. Documentation available at https://rosalindholgate-smith.com/trees.

In this act of lying on the earth, I observed my weight gravitate not just down, but also spread horizontally. As in my journal extract, I describe falling into a kind of void; a place I found not to be empty but, much like Barad's quantum void, that I discovered to be full with the liveliness of indeterminate possibilities (Barad 2012). With attention to yielding in and through my contact with the earth, that being in this instance, my back surface, I witnessed my awareness stretch further outwardly. Gradually I found space expand inside me and all around, and this feeling of diffusion and hovering progressed. In Jane Bennett's book *Influx & Efflux* (2020), she describes "hovering" as a valuable position from which to encourage the vital potency of feeling states to develop. Hovering, for Bennett, takes place among emerging forces to "reveal the ontological multiplicity of an I" (Bennett 2020, 55). When brought into embodiment, Bennett's ideas about hovering imply a kind of separating out of affixed contents. As a perspective of being among an indeterminate array of phenomena, forces, and possibilities, Bennett proposes hovering as "a method by which moral subjects may take their time with the evidence they have to make better decisions" (2020, 55). In lying on the earth, as I let my mind spread out, I noticed more thoughts, emotions, and information flooding in. This influx of information created a feeling of speeding up, which I found I could counter by staying still. In this staying still, I could observe my reflexes and suspend my agitational tendencies to react to thoughts and ideas. Here, in lying on the earth, I was resting into *hovering* as an atmospheric quality through which I could experience a lighter feeling of correspondence with aggressive thought patterns and emotions.

Because *hovering* expands the attention widely and sensitizes the body to becoming more porous, it can activate experiences of overwhelm. When it comes to macro and global issues such as climate catastrophes and rapid advances in technology, heightening receptivity and provoking overwhelm can be considered problematic. It is here important to recognize *hovering* as a perspective among influences that emphasizes being supported by space to *observe* what is already happening. Environmental catastrophes, such as forest fires, represent complex information that has amassed, that can feel chaotic, devastating, and intense. We need not shy away from complexity, and in *hovering* I propose one approach that involves slowing down to accompany it. Through widening one's perception, *hovering* becomes about experiencing oneself as a part of the macro picture. Sensing with an infiltrating awareness of space tends to expose more clearly areas of tension and also can facilitate ease and fluidity to accompany the disturbances we experience, whether in movement or at rest.

Embodying this expanded spatial awareness can be understood as an act of generosity. In her manifesto, "Touch Revolution," the CI dancer Karen Nelson suggests that, to open to the effects of touch, takes generosity with oneself (1996). Commonly, people protect themselves from being touched, which manifests in gestures of resistance and pushing away. For CI dancers, developing skills to finely moderate the tone of their tissues by, for example, falling and consciously relaxing parts of the body, can be seen as ways to open the body. With the infiltrating perception of space, *hovering* can support dancers to more expansively conceive of themselves as a multiplicity, existing among other collections of mass and density. To encompass oneself together with one's surroundings as more collectively composed can eliminate gripping to concerns over whether thoughts, ideas, sensations, and disturbances belong to me as entities or someone else. Under new-materialist terms, things do not need to belong, but are fundamentally there to be experienced. Spreading oneself into a multiple state can cultivate a porosity that supports sensations and disturbances to be experienced as more nuanced. As Barad describes, touch always involves stimulating multiple layers and multiple

184 Resistance and Support

intra-actions. To be without containing and holding one's thoughts and experience means to open to this complexity, to be open to being with difference, Otherness, and the unknown. To experience oneself as a multiplicity means being open to meet an Otherness within. Where touch always implies self-touching (Barad 2012) and we as bodies are made up of multiple collections of force, there will always be the possibility of meeting infinite alterity within.

> *Are you still with me?*
> *This poetic chaos is confusing*
> *. . . because touch affects our state of being*
> *. . . who we are is challenged.*
> *Who am I?*
> *Becomes impossible to understand.*
> (Holgate Smith, journal extract, December 22, 2021)

Exploring oneself as a multiplicity within the environment, and with multiple others, is a CI training perspective that has begun to be used by CI teachers, including Nita Little (2014). In my technique of *hovering*, thinking and moving as a multiplicity prepare dancers to pick up on collective and gathering forces, so that they may identify when to merge with and follow waves of momentum. *Hovering* and being a multiplicity are perspectives to be held lightly, as in jam situations dancers' attention will regularly need to shift in response to the fluctuations of other moving dancers and the unpredictable changes in the environment. In all situations, improvisors' attention will be called to their immediate needs and surrounding stimuli. Training perspectives for improvisation I propose as not absolutely fixed, but intentionally held within one's field of awareness and temporally to come more and less to the fore. For dancers conjoining with collective waves of momentum can be considered a shift to a more conglomerate form of becoming. This moving into and with momentum often happens when dancers join and develop partner exchanges, which can feel to be an intimate and visceral experience for dancers, perhaps because where momentum is concerned, the movement of fluids are always involved. When and through intra-action, new forms emerge. Performance theorist Hypatia Vourloumis suggests there to be "a kind of oscillation . . . where merging and the dissolution of subject and object take place" (2014, 233). When dancers conjoin in partnership with forces of momentum, such oscillations become present. *Hovering* can support dancers to withhold a wider perspective in these merging situations where they develop the ability to witness precisely where forces are accumulating, and emerging entities are integrating and establishing boundaries so that choices can be made. Zooming out to conceive of being a multiplicity makes it possible to oscillate and dive into interweaving forms with spatial porosity. Being able to feel the forces of these patterns from within and above can help sustain flow and the fluid ability to express oneself, which creates freedom for dancers in their relationships and can prevent contracting in intimate exchanges or otherwise intimidating situations.

Listening in Nature

The entanglement of outdoor elements—the way in which the trees are, for example, moved by the wind, and the wind is shaped by the trees—represents the interdependent complexity of huge collections of substance and force that are always in flux. Nature's entangled relationships belong to a much more than human world. Given the correspondence of these elements, belonging cannot be thought of as some staid concept or ideal, but rather as unpredictable, as ontologically only existing because of receptivity, responsivity, and *with* the consistency of change. In my improvisation practice outdoors, I have found the entangled nature of the environment to act as a model for listening that has taught me to recognize belonging amidst forces and elements that continuously transform. Miriam-Rose Ungunmerr, an aboriginal artist and activist from the Daly river region of Australia, proposes that simply going out into nature and waiting helps to recover people's ability to listen "to the deep inner spring inside us" (1988, n.p.). Ungunmerr uses the term *Dadirri* "to describe inner deep listening, that quiet, silent, still awareness based on nature." This notion of Dadirri implies that nature knows and is listening. Through dancing outdoors, I have realized that I am often able to hear and feel my thoughts more clearly, which has led me to choose rural and discrete places, where uninterrupted, I have discovered deep emotions that I tend to hold back in the presence of people. Such solo experiences have created opportunities to appreciate my existence with these emotions, without feeling alone but always among others, and given the expansiveness of outdoor surroundings I have found ways to come to term with them.

In the image "Dancing in Big Pats Creek" (Figure 9.2), I was in a logging site among burning cinders, a part of the Yarra Valley and native forest in Victoria, Australia. When I first encountered the Creek I remember shock, numbness, and a feeling of horror. Unsure of myself and my humanity, I also recall rage rising in me. I found myself witness to a scene of colonial destruction and capitalist chaos that came with questions of what might constitute responsible action. In many of my first visits to the site, I was simply overwhelmed and agitated, as I found myself among gaps and absences that I was unable to feel. Listening, passively and receptively, just seemed to aggravate the overwhelming disturbances. Interestingly, Barad proposes that at "perhaps it takes facing the inhuman within us before com-passion-suffering together with,

Figure 9.2. Holgate Smith, April 2020, "Dancing in Big Pats Creek," logging site, Victoria, Australia. Photograph: Paul Colcheedas.

186   Resistance and Support

participating with, feeling with, being moved by—can be lived" (2012, 214). Before all this dynamic agency, Barad suggests that we need to confront what we cannot feel, our inhumanity that refers to our actions lacking compassion. From the initial shock and numbness that had brought me to stillness in the Creek, I did gradually discover agency to move, which only became possible by deeply gravitating in and limiting my attention through my feet that were my primary contact with the land. In this treacherous site, where the ground was still burning and laden with fallen logs, maintaining a rooted connection was essential to my safety, and I consequently committed to channel my attention through my feet. As I danced, I encountered images that I sensed were coming from a collective field of experience: of Black African women, unable to feed their children. These images connected me to my white British origins, my ancestral lineage steeped in colonialism, and my place there as a foreigner. They brought to mind stories and strong emotions of anger and rage. Rather than getting overwhelmed by these stories and emotions, zooming my attention in through touch anchored me to stay connected to my emotions and express my experience in the present moment.

Listening with Dancers

Like outdoor environments, CI jams present also unstable, risky contexts, not only because of the ongoing flux and unpredictability of dancers improvising and perpetually falling through space, but also because the intimate nature of the dance can provoke social projections and judgments. Self-criticism and presupposing what others think and feel can quite easily be overwhelming. Having realized through my outdoor dance practice that I censor and hold back many emotions in social settings, this has led me to further investigate ways of cultivating confidence to experience and express my discomforts and challenging emotions in shared spaces with dancers. During my lab research on listening with CI colleagues in Berlin, one dancer called Marius reflected on the difficulty of experiencing social shut down:

> Listening—I hardly felt myself properly, in an emotional way. Physically it's quite easy, I don't feel myself emotionally, so I can't feel other people in the moment. Like are you having fun? are you okay? or are you in pain? I can only use my obvious senses. (Marius)

In these situations, Marius applied also the strategy of anchoring his attention into touch, touch being together without movement, one of his "obvious senses." This homing-in and through the body as an anchor brings me to recall the proprioceptive, micro awareness cultivated through the feet in the small dance. This same anchoring strategy that I had used in Big Pats Creek, Marius was applying in the context of being with people, not to bypass the chatter of his social stories, questions, and concerns, but as a tool to become more present with his local sensations and his state of embodiment. Given that both Marius and I had been encountering numbness and edging through and around experiences of not feeling, albeit in different locations, our technique of anchoring in and observing subtler sensations may be seen to have also calmed our nervous system and prevented us from completely shutting down. Below is a further extract from Marius, reflecting upon his experience.

> I know there is more, but I can't force it and that makes me mad
> There is no crvvmmh! Crashing through

So I can only, be gentle
It is going to come up
when it will come up, and that's it
There is nothing I can do.

At one point I was ahhh, almost bored . . .
And now I am lost in the now. (Marius, Focus Group reflection, October 6, 2021)

Dancers practicing listening and making themselves receptive do appear to heighten their exposure to more volatile feelings. The recurring surges of anger and rage that I encountered in the Big Pats Creek logging site represent a prime example of this. Improvisors and especially performers need to find ways to deal with such disturbing strong emotions, as well as sensational images and wild and erotic feelings that can be thought to hold some sense of Otherness or the unknown. For Black feminist philosopher Audre Lorde, the erotic can show up as disturbing, arousing, and as a strange or even frightening kind of Otherness because it has been oppressed. Appearing in emergent energies, emotions, images, and thoughts, the erotic is not necessarily sexual, but represents a vital, powerful creative life force that emerges from complexity. Both the rage I encountered in the logging site and the "crashing" surges of energy that Marius experienced can be considered as representations of such erotic forces that are yet to establish shape or integrated tangible forms. Examining experiences of the erotic represents a valuable way of understanding Otherness and how we might be with differences that, as Lorde underlines, behold social knowledge.

As she suggests, when accepted and allowed, the oppressed power of erotic forces represents deep knowledge, a provocative creative life force, a guide, an illumination that is social (Lorde 1978). In Bennett's *Vibrant Matter* (2009), she offers some further valuable considerations concerning how vital forms of energy and erotic forces might manifest. Under what Bennett calls "causality," agential forces swarm and swerve, and forces collide and coalesce. In causality, becoming appears as "more emergent than efficient, more fractal than linear" and "effect and cause may alternate position and redound on each other" (Bennett 2009, 33). Causality provides a good explanation for how dancers and people in all kinds of social interactions relate and communicate through the chemical reactions of their hormones that lucidly swarm, disperse, and collocate into feeling states. Ideally in CI, where listening touch is effectively being practiced, the nervous system can drop back to play a less active and more parasympathetic role in processing haptic information. Not all information is processed along the nervous system's linear pathways of motor and sensory neurons, and perhaps when the nervous system is less reliant on sympathetic patterns and habits, I experience the chemical interactions of the endocrine system that are also involved in social communication becoming more apparent. In Body Mind Centering®, the endocrine system is understood as much older than the nervous system in its evolutionary development and is considered to have "a profound effect on both physiological functioning and feeling states" (Hartley 1989, 207–8). Secreted from endocrine glands, hormones disperse on indeterminate pathways through the blood and fluids. As these chemicals react, they can very quickly excite new feeling states and behavioral shifts (207). With the interactions of hormones, unique forms of interplay and behavior are possible, both within one's body experience and between dancers as they meet and partner. In the following and concluding sections of this chapter, I propose a technique I call *listening in action*, in which I argue for methods of staying with

188 Resistance and Support

the emergence and development of feeling states. Although sometimes disturbing, accompanying the evolution of feelings states I equate to accompanying an Otherness or the erotic forces that, as Lorde suggests, behold deep knowledge and a creative life force that is social (Lorde 1978).

Listening in Action

Listening in action builds on *accompanying* the point of contact and also *hovering* above surfaces in touch. Again, it is not about acting upon disturbing or arousing forces, emotions, or images, but in suspension spreading out to recognize their contextual existence. We cannot know other people's experiences, and we often do not understand our sensations; it is here that *listening in action* sets the proposal to move with and begin to get to know our disturbances and oppressed tensions-ideas, which I began to put across in describing experiences of following, and conjoining with momentum (see above).

In the listening-lab research sessions, headaches proved to be recurring among participants. While headaches may seem minor compared to the traumatic situations already referred to in this essay, they exemplify a common psychosomatic pain which, under Lorde's definition, might represent an erotic repression of vital energy. One dancer called Jenny described, accompanying her headaches, an experience of "being with critical voices" that was what she realized and named listening to be about (Jenny, focus group reflection, October 6, 2021). For me, having headaches represented a disturbance I would normally deal with by going outdoors and/or by taking time alone. My first strategy was, for example, to move away from others, as I did not want to bother or inflict pain on other people. By socially distancing myself, I realized I was also containing myself and my tension, shutting down, and developing a feeling of shame that caused me also to inhibit my outward movement. When disturbing feelings arise, commonly people's ability to stay is challenged. *Listening in action* involves recognizing when disturbances are present, widening one's perception to explore the nature of these distances within the given context.

Psychosocial theorist Lisa Baraister suggests that in circumstances that demand transformation and imply rapid change, suspending action and resting with other people are needed to find new ways of moving on. Given traumatic events and times driven by capitalist production, Baraister argues that we essentially need rest in order to grieve our losses. I have alluded to rest in lying on the earth and methods of quieting the nervous system that are significant aspects of listening, concerned with developing the ability to stay with the trouble, as Donna Haraway puts it, that includes recognizing our part and power to harm (2016, 2). Learning to stay present, as Haraway emphasizes, is necessary to recognize the trouble of our existence on a damaged earth. Colonial enslavement, deforestation, and climate catastrophes represent some reasons to grieve. In capitalist economies, people may also experience grief in accepting and giving in to everyday pressures of needing to produce an income and deliver what is deemed socially acceptable, which can distract from deeper self-presence. Stopping together when performed voluntarily, Baraister suggests, could be a means to endure otherwise unbearable experiences of depression and exhaustion that are a result of our capitalist times (2017). In dance and somatic psychotherapy, research also evidences that restful, listening touch can support pain tolerance, where through attuning, and passively co-regulating, bodies experiencing disorder and dysfunction can find support to move and reorganize themselves toward a state of dynamic equilibrium (Dymoke 2014, 214). In my listening labs, I observed the group's tendency to begin at rest and thereafter intermittently return to periods of pause. These pauses came about through dancers subconsciously attuning to collective shifts in atmosphere and rhythm. Although I struggled to rest initially, gradually I realized that resting in contact with others was a way of co-regulating that was softening and releasing my awareness. These diffusive effects seemed to make it possible for me to move. As I noted in my journal, "I get up and move with my full head" (Holgate Smith, lab journal extract, October 6, 2021), and slowly I began to experience more nuanced micro sensations throughout my body and to identify choices.

A key and further aspect of *listening in action* is the act of decidedly following emergent sensations and feelings and supporting them with momentum to evolve and grow. In the text below I reflect on dancing with a tree and identifying and taking grasp of a particular call to action.

> *What is taking place?*
> *I wonder*
> *Reaching I am moving now.*
> *Down*
> *and a certain surge reverberates back up through my feet, legs and spine*
> *something grips as I commit to follow.*
> (Holgate Smith, journal extract, December 22, 2021)

In "reaching down," I moved consciously into synthesis with my sensations. In dancing upon this tree, my receptive and embodied experience of touch informed my decided action to follow. I was acutely aware that something was emerging. As Erin Manning describes, touch interacts, confounding memories, imagination, and present experiences of time. As bodies in process, "senses fold into one-another creating an in-folding and out-folding, an exfoliation of experience" (Manning 2007, 141). From dispersed hormones and alchemical information, there is absorption and there becomes expression. In the act of reaching down, I conjoined with the textures I was sensing and feeling in a definite gesture. Continuously *listening in action* can be understood as sequentially getting on board with sensations and momentum, without grabbing or holding these accumulations of force tightly. The skill of listening notably involves staying receptive to touch as a reciprocal intra-action. As in my gestural "reach down," I used motor and sensory nerve receptors to feel my way through my pathway and continuously I identified further sensations that I committed to follow.

Improvisor and Authentic Movement specialist Shaun McLeod would use here "discernment," as a term to describe "the ability to bring into consciousness awareness aspects of what our bodies feel and produce in their inter-action between proprioception, movement and social-relations" (McLeod 2020, 196). In Authentic Movement, discernment is usually understood as a highly attentive form of tracking by which practitioners pick out, get to know, and learn to control sensations. In my study and development of listening touch techniques, I have tended toward less vigilance, taking on board Bennett's proposal of *hovering* and favoring McLeod's suggestion of "a softer, cradling of attention" (McLeod 2020, 202) to hold all that comes up in improvisation. Attending with less vigilance is not about reducing presence, or denying the identification of thoughts or feelings, but using attention sustainably. Without such a piercing quality, McLeod proposes that discernment may be better described as a quality of awareness that can encourage and sustain "experiences of free form curiosity and flow for dancers" (2020, 203). In Contact Improvisation, attending through the skin with a kind of hovering, cradling porosity makes it possible to readily lighten one's touch when needed and conversely dive deep into giving weight. These adaptive responsive skills are essential for CI dancers to alleviate collisions and hard conflicts that may be applied also in situations beyond the dance, such as on public transportation at rush hour.

Hovering remains an essential component of *listening in action* that as an observational perspective in CI jams can make it possible to also notice patterns, and discover new pathways in and out: ways to commingle, reassemble, assimilate, or altogether resist participation. Jams are themselves pluripotent spaces where dancers need to decide whether to follow and encourage collective waves of force. Passing waves of momentum can be understood to possess collected agency. Getting on board with momentum involves dancers trusting their feeling of agency in contact with others and relying on their immediate senses to stay safe and present. When already in mid-flow with a partner, *hovering* one's awareness more widely can create the opportunity to step out of dances fueled by momentum and can also enhance receptivity to meet what is emerging in the current, with less control and more spacious compassion. *Listening in action* is about training listening as a skill while moving, which means, for dancers, maintaining an overview of the pathway they take, while entering and simultaneously driving the pathway. *Hovering* supports as a perspective that which can move down with gravity, rise up, and spread horizontally. Combined and applied with *listening in action*, these techniques make it possible to travel through space with others, with the ability to always zoom out, to generously see others and allow movement to expand, and conversely to zoom in to acuities of placement and moving directions of force.

In *listening in action*, I take from Lorde's suggestion, and propose to "attend to how acutely and fully we can feel in the doing" (Lorde 1978, 2). Nonvigilance and nonjudgmental witnessing serve within this approach to acknowledge sensations and tensions and disturbances. Through accompanying such sensations and disturbances, I find feeling states develop and swell, and I notice gestures that appear with surprising lightness. These gestures do not overextend me or come at a great cost. They may be familiar or unfamiliar actions and tend mostly to reside nearby, just within reach, reflecting clearly disposable options. Listening for subtle and micro shifts helps build awareness of these disposable options before actively engaging in gestures and exploring their outward expression. Dancing and exploring local actions can suggest a sustainable approach to movement, which involves staying within one's range and not overextending, that might reduce the risk of injury and help dancers sustain healthy forms of mobility and articulation. In CI spaces and in social interactions beyond dance, moving within one's range might also prevent boundaries being surpassed between people. This is much like Caroline McCalman's environmental sustainability research proposal, in which she promotes taking simple localized actions that respond to the environment one is in. This means disengaging from spectacular or activistic action and moving away from the so-called environmental movement that is often associated with occupations of power. McCalman instead promotes a practical stewardship reoriented toward the mundane (2019). Inspired by McCalman, I propose *listening in action* as an approach of ongoing curiosity and responsivity to what is emerging, whether the sensations or encounters be familiar or foreign.

Given situations of sensory overload, staying open and curious is not always possible, and it is here that I underline *listening in action* as a method concerned with maintaining the ability to feel in the doing, which may be used to recognize and build awareness of overstepping one's boundaries. If dancers are to keep a measure on their availability, and feel through their movement pathways, they may remain responsive and present in and to others in their local surroundings. Catching signs of numbness and not feeling may be signs of becoming less available for listening in outward actions and partnering engagements. In instances of exhaustion and shutting down, *listening in action* is also underpinned by calling upon the techniques of anchoring into one point of contact to harness safety and ground, staying with, resting with, and *hovering* one's attention, whether more intero- or exteroceptive. These I propose as foundational techniques that involve zooming states of consciousness in and out to empower the connection between sensual experiences and their expression. As a practice of building receptivity and skills to reconcile with disturbances, *listening in action* is considered a proposal not only for dancers, but a way of being with challenges and moving through the world that is concerned with cultivating full-bodied acceptance, compassion for oneself and others, and expressive and clear communication.

Appendix: Guidelines for Practice

These step-by-step guidelines outline a bodywork practice for training listening touch and *listening in action* as receptive ways of being and moving. Informed by *Cellular Touch* and Authentic Movement, I have developed and shared the practice in many workshop contexts and performances with dancers and non-dancers.[8]

1. Arrive with a partner, adjust to find a comfortable place to find stillness. In this practice, one of you will rest, and move following sensations as you feel, while the other will accompany giving touch.
2. For the partner giving touch, before starting out, ask your partner if there are places they want and don't want to be touched. Practice that they remove and change the placement of your hand and suggest that they verbalize any discomforts and can suggest changes.
3. Before making touch, take again time to relieve unnecessary tension, feel your breath, and see your partner.
4. Place your full palms onto your partner's body where you observe movement; this may be very subtle, as in the breath. If you see no movement, place your hands intuitively. Telescope your awareness in, to feel the landscape of your hands, and back out, to take in your whole body's sensations. Zoom out to see also your partner's whole body. What do you notice? Try to avoid changing the position of your hands unless your position becomes uncomfortable. If your partner signals to move, ready yourself, adjusting your position to follow their movement. Maintain a light full touch and try not to disturb or get in the way of the emerging movement. Track their center of weight—this can help predict where their movement will go. If your partner moves a lot, you may step further back and observe from a distance, later returning to touch. Ensure that you continuously stay visually present with your partner and aware of your relationship. You can

[8] Video documentation of my listening touch performances is available at https://rosalindholgate-smith.com/listening-touch-2.

192 Resistance and Support

always reconnect with the ground to release tension so that you maintain a supported sense of well-being.

5. You may, after some time, offer different surfaces of touch. Continue to listen with the same presence of your hands.

6. Should your partner appear to invite pressure or counterbalance, examine whether you can meet them equally in this. Can you support with resistance? Watch your partner's responses and be sensitive to ensure the weight you offer is balanced.

7. You may at some point let go of your roles and explore how a dance can evolve together.

This essay draws on Rosalind Holgate Smith's PhD dissertation that investigates "How touch facilitates encounters with Otherness and the vocabulary from Contact Improvisation," due for publication, spring 2025 at Kingston University, London. Further information about Rosalind's artistic research and practice can be found at https://rosalindholgate-smith.com.

References

Banissy, M. (2022). *Why Do We Touch? The New Science of Our Most Underappreciated Sense.* [PowerPoint Presentation] Touching Matters with Charlotte Spence Projects, Siobhan Davies Dance, London, January 16, 2022.

Barad, K. (2003). "Posthumanist Performativity: Toward an Understanding of How Matter Comes to Matter." *Signs: Journal of Women in Culture and Society* 28(3): 801–831.

Barad, K. (2012) "On Touching: The Inhuman That Therefore I Am." *Differences* 23(3): 206–223.

Barad, K. (2017). "Troubling Time/s and Ecologies of Nothingness: Re-Turning, Re-Membering, and Facing the Incalculable." *New Formations* 92(92): 56–86.

Barad, K. (2018). *On Touching: The Alterity Within.* [Conference presentation] Hold Me Now: Feel and Touch in and Unreal World , March 24, 2018. Amsterdam: Gerrit Rietveld Academie at Stedelijk Museum. Available at: https://www.youtube.com/watch?v=u7LvXswj EBY (Accessed: June 30, 2024).

Baraitser, L. (2017). *Enduring Time* (1st ed.). London: Bloomsbury.

Bassel, L. (2017). *The Politics of Listening: Possibilities and Challenges for Democratic Life.* London: Palgrave.

Beaulieux, M. (2019) "How the first rule brought #metoo to Contact Improvisation". *Contact Quarterly* 44(1): 48–50.

Bennett, J. (2009). *Vibrant Matter: A Political Ecology of Things.* Durham, NC: Duke University Press.

Bennett, J. (2020). *Influx and Efflux: Writing up with Whitman.* Durham, NC: Duke University Press.

Buhner, S. H. (2014). *Plant Intelligence and the Imaginal Realm: Beyond the Doors of Perception into the Dreaming of Earth.* Rochester, VT: Bear & Company.

Dymoke, K. (2014). "Contact Improvisation, the Non-Eroticized Touch in an 'Art-Sport.'" *Journal of Dance & Somatic Practices* 6(2): 205–218.

Eddy, M. (2017). *Mindful Movement.* Chicago; Bristol, UK: Intellect Books.

Haraway, D. (2016) *Staying with the Trouble: Making Kin in the Chthulucene.* Durham, NC: Duke University Press.

Hartley, Linda. (1989). *Wisdom of the Body Moving: An Introduction to Body-Mind Centering*. Berkeley, CA: North Atlantic Books.

Holgate Smith, R. (2021). "Poetry Extracts from the Artists Journals." Published for Techne podcast and Re-Enchantment Conference (2022) at Kingston University, London. Available at https://soundcloud.com/technecast/re-enchantment (accessed October 5, 2022).

LaPierre, A. (2003). "From Felt-Sense to Felt-Self: Neuro-Affective Touch and the Relational Matrix." *Psychologist-Psychoanalyst* 23(4): 43–46.

Little, N. (2014). "Articulating Presence: Creative Actions of Embodied Attention in Contemporary Dance." PhD thesis, University of California, Davis.

Lorde, A. (1978). *Uses of the Erotic: The Erotic as Power*. Brooklyn, NY: Out & Out Books.

Manning, E. (2007). *The Politics of Touch: Sense Movement and Sovereignty*. Minneapolis: University of Minnesota Press.

McCalman, C. (2019). "Nuclear Heresy: Environmentalism as Implicit Religion." PhD thesis, University of Sheffield. Available at https://etheses.whiterose.ac.uk/22794/ (accessed: January 17, 2022).

Mcleod, S. (2020). "Dance Improvisation through Authentic Movement: A Practice of Discernment." *Journal of Dance & Somatic Practices* 12(2): 191–205.

Mitra, R. (2018). "Talking Politics of Contact Improvisation with Steve Paxton." *Dance Research Journal* 50(3): 5–18.

Mitra, R. (2022). "Unmaking Contact: Choreographic Touch at the Intersections of Race, Caste and Gender." *Dance Research Journal* 53(3): 6–24.

Neimanis, A. (2019). "The Weather Underwater: Blackness, White Feminism, and the Breathless Sea." *Australian Feminist Studies* 34(102): 490–508.

Nelson, K. (1996). "Still Moving: Touch Revolution Giving Dance." *Contact Quarterly* 21(1): 65–67.

Novak, S. J. (1990). *Sharing the Dance: Contact improvisation and American Culture*. Madison: University of Wisconsin Press.

Rea, K. (2020). *Contact Improv Consent Culture* [website]. https://contactimprovconsentculture.com (accessed May 22, 2021).

Paxton, S., and N. Stark Smith. (2018). "The Politics of Mutuality a Conversation with Steve Paxton at the Kitchen Table with Nancy Stark Smith." *Contact Quarterly Unbound*. Available at: https://contactquarterly.com/cq/unbound/view/the-politics-of-mutuality#$ (accessed: June 30, 2024).

Stark Smith, N., K. Hennessy, A. Cooper Albright, G. Cron-Riger, D. Schwartz, K. Alexander, Z. Arfa, T. Will, K. Rea, and M. Brooks. (2018). "Intersections: Frictions and Illuminations." *Contact Quarterly* 43(2): 34–39.

Ungunmerr, M. R. (1988). "Dadirri Inner Deep Listening and Quiet Still Awareness" [online]. Available at https://www.miriamrosefoundation.org.au/dadirri/ (accessed June 8, 2022).

Vourloumis, H. (2015). "Ten Theses on Touch, or, Writing Touch." *Women & Performance* 24(2–3): 1–11.

10
Therapeutic Applications of Contact Improvisation

Aaron Brandes (Brando) and Gabrielle Revlock

Introduction

From our most common gestures of high-fives, pats on the back, handshakes, and hugs, we rely on touch to form meaningful bonds with other people. A tangible reminder that we are not alone, these connections (physical and emotional) bolster us as we weather the unpredictable ups and downs of life. Many people recognize the importance of touch in their lives, and yet they encounter barriers to access. They might not have a person with whom they have a touch-based relationship. If they do, the touch might be fraught, inconsistent, harmful, anxiety-producing, or otherwise limited. As longtime practitioners of Contact Improvisation (CI) we (Gabrielle and Brando) count ourselves among the many dancers who will testify to the benefits of engaging in this partner dance form. There are myriad ways in which CI contributes to our well-being. In this chapter, we will hone our focus on how the evolving CI pedagogy scaffolds multiple levels, depths, and qualities of touch, thus creating a container to safely explore nonsexual interpersonal body-to-body contact.

Drawing from our unique career pathways combining movement, choreography, fascial bodywork, psychotherapy, and evidence-based mindfulness practices, we have developed therapeutic material inspired by CI that articulates safety, empathy, mutuality, and agency through touch. Our aim in suggesting ways that CI might be adapted and bolstered is to make the benefits of touch accessible to a wider range of people who may or may not (ever) identify as Contact Improvisors. In this chapter, we will be offering insight from our two different contexts: Aaron is a licensed psychotherapist and Gabrielle is a professional dancer and educator.

Our Stories

Brando

For two years, I lived at the Kripalu Center for Yoga in Lenox, Massachusetts, and participated in the intensive Ashram-based lifestyle program where I would practice breathwork (*pranayama*) and yoga several hours each day. I remember during the evening concerts, while the guests would sit complacently on BackJacks enjoying the music, some of my cohort and I would dance ecstatically in the back of the chapel. It was during that time that I met one of the musicians who encouraged me to visit Earthdance.

That was over 20 years ago, when I took my friend's suggestion and attended my first CI jam. I witnessed in amazement dancers transforming their legs into ramps and their shoulders and spines into launching and/or landing pads. Dancers were mutually supporting each other via rolling and sliding on and off each other's bodies. I remember sensing the childlike play as people collaboratively curved, contorted, and remolded themselves to fit into the negative spaces and the contours of each other's body shapes. Upon an invitation, I was whisked into the percolating dance activity. The energy that I was so rigorously building in my yoga practice at Kripalu exploded in my dancing. That jam opened a new paradigm, and allowed me to re-examine what is possible in human play and connection. This began my lifetime love and dedication to Contact Improvisation.

Six months later, I moved out of Kripalu and into Earthdance. During my early years of training in CI, I had the great fortune to learn from masters of the craft, including Steve Paxton, Nancy Stark Smith, Karen Nelson, Nita Little, Kirstie Simson, Keith Hennessey, Andrew Hardwood, and Chris Aiken. In a workshop Aiken was teaching, he guided us in imagery and movement that engaged the fascia of the body.

Aiken provided an anatomical framework for us to experience how fascia encompasses muscles, muscle groups, bones, blood vessels, organs, and nerves, binding certain structures together (often indicating stagnation), while allowing others to smoothly glide over each other (indicative of healthy tissue). As I danced, I felt the elasticity of my fascia allow for the lengthening, stretching, and softening of my tissues. This embodied practice liberated my movement and I became fascinated with fascia! Sometime after that, at a weekend CI jam in Boston, I attended a lecture by Tom Myers, a renowned fascia expert. In his presentation, Myers showed a slide of an early photograph of Steve Paxton and Nancy Stark Smith dancing. Myers commented that in his opinion, Contact Improvisation was the most perfect movement form for experiencing the myriad of the body's fascial connections. I was sold! I enrolled in the Anatomy Trains Structural Integration Certification Program in Maine, under the tutelage of Myers.

Figure 10.1. Photo taken at Brown University; Institute for the Study of Environment and Society Conference performance. Image courtesy of Nikki Lee.

196 Resistance and Support

I feel blessed to have participated as an original member of Nancy Stark Smith's Underscore dance/research group, which met weekly for over 10 years. The Underscore is a long-form dance improvisation structure developed by Nancy Stark Smith. It has been evolving since 1990 and is practiced all over the globe. This opportunity was another foundational influence in my CI career. The physical state Stark Smith named, "Bonding with the Earth," is a section within the Underscore practice where practitioners lie on the floor, surrender to the forces of gravity, and tune into their internal embodied experience. This often leads to another aspect of the practice that she named "Overlapping Skinepheres," which includes sustained moving compression between two dancers. Each of these states allowed for me to stretch beyond my normal perception of time. Sinking into a depth of awareness of my embodied experience, I noticed the profound therapeutic effects on my nervous system.

CI-informed movement had a significant influence on my career as a bodyworker; and it continues to shape my work as a psychotherapist. My research continues along a lineage of improvisors and thinkers that celebrate pushing CI in new directions. It focuses on how I can maintain health and longevity in my dancing. Subsequently, this form can be practiced as a healing technique that is engaged in an ongoing exploration of how to help people discover the somatic and emotional tools to handle the complex problems of our current world.

Gabrielle Revlock

My introduction to CI was through a workshop with improvisor KJ Holmes at the American Dance Festival in 2003. It activated in me a sensation of pure joy and a feeling of interconnectivity that was lacking in my other dance class experiences. Years later, when living in New York City, I found myself diving deeper into CI and attending either a class or a jam nearly every day. CI provided me with not only an outlet for dancing, but also community, touch, play, and growth during a particularly challenging period of my life.

My interest in CI as a therapeutic practice developed out of a performance I created in early 2019, a slow-moving duet where my partner and I stayed in contact with one another for nearly an hour. I was interested in touch as a physical manifestation of care, but was troubled that it was almost exclusively in the context of a romantic relationship, instead of with friends who were my anchors of long-lasting support. To reimagine what friendship could look and feel like, I videotaped a chaste yet intimate encounter with a new male lover and then I took that "choreography" to my friend Michele (whom I had known for over 10 years), and we meticulously recreated it. I soon noticed that the act of performing the choreography made my skin vibrate. I felt relaxed and at times lightheaded. Michele had a similar reaction. Although we were good friends, we approached the learning of the choreography from a professional distance. We studied the video for details with the attempt to recreate it as technically accurate as possible. Disentangling touch from emotional and relational contexts (which existed in the original encounter) and replacing it with attention to the task, including an awareness of sensation, made the power of touch to change one's physical and mental state undeniable to me.

In January 2020, inspired by both my study of CI and my experience of creating the duet with Michele, I developed and began teaching "Restorative Contact," a partner touch-based mindfulness practice. A crucial part of Restorative Contact was an investment in slowness and stillness. One early participant reflected to me that the practice gave structure to something she had witnessed around the edges of jams—people lounging on each other in pairs or piles. This observation resonated with me and clarified that I wanted to create a formal structure for a casual body—a body relaxed and unshaped by technique—a body at rest.

Shortly thereafter, in March 2020, we went into COVID-19 lockdown and I shifted to teaching online, primarily through Airbnb Experiences, which connected me with people around the world, the majority of whom were utterly unfamiliar with Contact Improvisation. Wrote one participant, "My wife and I are not really the sorts to engage in this sort of experience, but we both felt extraordinarily calm and at peace after the session" (Airbnb Experiences). These people craved intentionality and connection; a deepening into the awareness of their body-mind through a process of co-regulation. The feedback I received was overwhelmingly positive. "Eye opening," wrote another participant, "I know the title is 'restorative' but I have never been at such an awareness and yearning for the bonding that physical touch with my partner can bring, than after this experience" (Airbnb Experiences). People appreciated having a space where they could take a break from their otherwise hectic routines and reconnect, physically with another person, and mentally with themselves.

The Value of CI-Informed Touch

One of the most radical perspectives offered by CI is the conceptualization of touching and being touched as a concurrent exchange. Think of hugging your best friend or shaking hands with a new colleague. These actions are symbolic gestures of mutual goodwill. When it comes to asymmetrical contact, specifically involving hands, the interpretation usually shifts. For example, when I rest my hand on your shoulder, many people would interpret this as: me touching you. However, your shoulder can receive, as well as energetically return, that subtle pressure. From this perspective, your shoulder is just as much touching my hand as my hand is touching your shoulder. This can be a challenging concept to grasp (no pun intended) because most able-bodied people rely on the dexterity of their hands to accomplish everyday tasks. Therefore, both touching someone's shoulder and opening a door are perceived as acts of "doing," devoid of reciprocity. CI disrupts the habituated use of the hands, as the primary tool for initiation. Body parts such as the back, torso, shoulders, legs, and so on, are just as likely to be points of contact. To maintain the connection, both partners engage in a subtle reaching toward one another at the point of contact. Should one person decide to shift or end the contact, they only need to reroute the orientation of their reaching. The use of touch via all surfaces of the body is a unique feature of CI, and as a result, this specific mode of utilizing and perceiving touch has not been researched extensively within the field of psychology (Jackson 2022, 26). Recognizing ourselves as active agents capable of both giving and receiving simultaneously can be a profoundly empowering realization in any situation, but particularly when it comes to physical contact. More research evaluating the benefits of reciprocal touch is long overdue.

Unlike most other touch-based modalities, such as bodywork, CI uses compression as a reciprocal activity in the form of weight sharing. Weight sharing can take many forms. Some examples of weight sharing include body surfing—this is when the dancer who is above "rides" the momentum of the dancer underneath who is in rolling motion. Another is counterbalance—this is when both dancers are pulling away from each other and if one were to let go, the structure would collapse and one or both people would fall. Bridging involves simultaneous pushing, where two body surfaces are pressed against each other. Finally, lifting describes one dancer holding the entire weight of another. Often our culture associates taking weight as a burden; however, many people enjoy compression because it engages the parasympathetic system, bringing a sense of calm and relaxation. The technique of swaddling an infant or the use of weighted blankets are examples of the use of compression as calming mechanisms. Nancy Stark Smith, the mother of CI, lovingly referred to compression as "Vitamin C." It increases endorphins, blood circulation, and immune functions while reducing heart rate, blood pressure, and tension in the body.

Spiraling, rolling, and sliding from one connection point to another using any and all surfaces of the body, dancers begin to release an attachment to "front." Steve Paxton refers to this conceptual orientation, where moving in any direction becomes possible, as "spherical space" (Paxton 2008). This is a distinctive feature of CI that has valuable applications within a therapeutic context. This 360-degree awareness increases a client's embodied intelligence by bringing cognizance to parts of themselves that they were unaware of—parts of the body that may be holding physical or emotional pain. With practice utilizing the concept of spherical space, one's peripheral vision is strengthened, and the perception of the space overhead, underneath, and the "backspace," or the unseen area behind you, becomes more vivid in one's field of awareness. Generally, when we are in our frontal orientation, able-bodied people tend to rely on their vision. When we are oriented toward spherical space, we pay more attention to physical sensations and sounds.

Parallels between Mindfulness and CI

Paxton's 1972 performance of *Magnesium* is considered to be the catalyst for the development of Contact Improvisation. In that work, the dancers are in a flux of dynamic movements, hurling their bodies through space and absorbing each other's impact. The performance ends with a demonstration of the Stand, otherwise known as the Small Dance. Maintaining the integrity of the spine while engaging in a relaxed standing posture, the Small Dance brings our attention to the nuanced self-corrections from our reflexes as gravity gently tips us off our center of balance. This standing meditation quiets the mind and reduces extraneous movement so that we become more aware of the intelligence of the body. "Tension masks sensation," is an oft-cited quote from Nancy Stark-Smith (Koteen 2008, 51). The Stand, through its easy posture, prepares the dancer for high-risk dynamic transitional moments because their ability to notice and respond quickly to stimuli has been sharpened. When contact with another is introduced, it is not advised to dive into one's fastest and most daring dance, but rather to take the time to attune to your partner. Observing your own small dance, that skill of "listening" with curiosity to your personal body experience, including your mass in relation to gravity, and the tiny weight shifts that keep you upright, can then be applied to your partner's body through the points of contact. As evidenced by the Stand, mindfulness is at the core of CI and has been since its early development.

"Beginner's Mind" is a concept from Zen Buddhism that eloquently describes a mode of perceiving devoid of preconceptions. For many people, this involves slowing down to reduce the likelihood of falling into the groove of reactivity. Nita Little, a founding collaborator of CI, offers her students the prompt to "move at the speed of your attention." Little's instruction directs her students to slow down their movement in order to notice and feel more. There is no *one* way to respond to a partner's touch, so the more you notice, the more choices you have for how to respond. Instead of leaping to interpret or create a story about the emotional subtext of touch, in CI we learn to investigate the physically based attributes of touch, such as deep or light compression, moving versus static, and so on, as they shift over time. Gabrielle likes to say that CI is a "series of missed opportunities." Throughout the dance there are countless invitations that present themselves and just as quickly disappear. There is no striving in CI. While it is typical for beginning dancers to have an attachment to achieving certain moves, for instance a lift, the seasoned dancer is constantly working to orient toward the unknown, having gained comfort with disorientation and trust in their reflexes. We would argue that *all* of the seven Attitudinal Foundations of Mindfulness-Based Stress Reduction—non-judging, patience, beginner's mind, trust, non-striving, acceptance, and letting go—relate directly to CI pedagogy (Kabat-Zinn 2013, 21).

In 1979, around the same time that Contact Improvisation was emerging through the body-based research of Paxton and his collaborators, Jon Kabat-Zinn was developing Mindfulness-Based Stress Reduction (MBSR). MBSR, a widely practiced, evidence-based therapeutic modality, is defined by Kabat-Zinn as "the awareness that arises through paying attention, on purpose, in the present moment, and non-judgmentally to the unfolding of experience moment by moment" (Kabat-Zinn 2003, 145). Daniel Lepkoff, another founding CI collaborator, offers insights that correlate to this definition of MBSR:

> My own fascination in dancing contact improvisation was the discovery that through my physical senses I can gather information directly from my environment, that using my own powers of observation I can shift my perspective, have new perceptions, and free myself from my own conventional/habitual ways of seeing. (2011, 40)

Here, Lepkoff sees CI as an exercise in paying attention, being present, and staying curious.

Applications of Touch

Body & Being Psychotherapy (Brando)

Prior to embarking on my career in psychotherapy, I had already begun incorporating CI-informed touch into my bodywork practice. The profound moments of release and expansion I witnessed during these specific sessions made a lasting impact on me. My training in improvisation influenced how I worked with clients, guiding and encouraging a much wider range of choice-making in their movements as I would work with them. The improvisational movement provided certain clients with a unique opportunity to discover newfound freedom and agency in their bodies. I approached the unconventional aspects of weight exchange and improvisation within my practice with caution. The notions of rolling over my client, or positioning myself beneath them, or encouraging spontaneous movement choices, felt somewhat eccentric within the context of a therapeutic setting. However, it was precisely these elements that proved to be potent and beneficial in my practice. Many clients expressed how unique and beneficial the experience was for them when we engaged in these

CI-informed practices. We ventured into something that was beyond traditional bodywork, and the noticeable benefits inspired further exploration.

These moments could come from larger ranges of motion and could also be felt within the micro-movements when we tuned our attention to those subtleties. Paxton compels us in the Small Dance to sharpen our focus with meticulous precision and refine our awareness of the subtlest nuances in our body's movements. This informed my bodywork. For example, by carefully positioning my hands beneath the client's shoulder blade and applying gentle upward pressure to the scapula, I could guide clients to engage and feel the subtle movements in that area. As the pads of my fingers respond to their minute shifts, we engage in a tiny dance together. In this process, we establish a reciprocal listening and responsiveness to each other's movements, pressure, and pauses, deriving delight from the exploration of new pathways within the tissues.

It is crucial for me to approach the application of touch with utmost care, considering the disparities influenced by factors such as gender, race, age, class, and ability. As a middle-aged, middle-class, able-bodied, cisgender white male, I am mindful of the potential impact of these factors when it comes to the introduction of touch in my sessions. This level of physical connection may not be appropriate due to various reasons. In such cases, significant benefits can still be achieved through guided movement exploration without direct physical contact from the therapist.

The Social Work Code of Ethics states:

> Social workers should not engage in physical contact with clients when there is a possibility of psychological harm to the client as a result of the contact (such as cradling or caressing clients). Social workers who engage in appropriate physical contact with clients are responsible for setting clear, appropriate, and culturally sensitive boundaries that govern such physical contact. (National Association of Social Workers [NASW], 2017)

Many psychotherapists avoid touch and refer to professionals in other disciplines (such as massage therapy) if they believe touch would be integral to their healing. However, there is a rich tradition of body-based psychotherapy that dates back to Freud, who described the ego as being first and foremost a body ego (Caldwell 1997, cited in Zur 2023). The use of psychotherapies that utilized touch continued with Reichian, Bioenergetics, Gestalt, and hypnotherapy, among others (Zur 2023, par 15).

Many who argue against the use of touch in psychotherapy do so on the basis that it will inevitably lead to sexual intimacy between therapist and client (Zur 2023). However, this is not the case. Well-trained therapists learn to manage erotic transference and countertransference while maintaining professional boundaries. Furthermore, the norms of Contact Improvisation dance disentangled physical touch from sexual intimacy by creating a language that emphasizes physics over chemistry. Paxton writes:

> I tried to create CI as (using the current linguistic codes) sex-neutral, or sex-agnostic. . . .
> I tried to present objective mutual physicality. I was mindful of the infinite subjective
> varieties of feeling that intimacy may conjure, so as a spokesperson in early CI I tried to
> present the view that touch need not be considered only from the perspectives culturally
> and perhaps genetically inculcated for us, but as a vehicle leading only to a form of dance.
> (1993, 257)

Therapeutic Applications of Contact Improvisation 201

Through its diverse vocabulary, CI has broadened our perspective of touch beyond societal norms. As Jackson states, "The core skills needed to make contact, both intra- and inter-personally, support a multitude of relational skills such as building trust (of self and others), increasing secure attachment, and building intimacy" (Jackson 2022, 39).

The following case study with "Clarissa" (a composite of a few clients) illustrates the application of CI-informed touch in psychotherapy. Clarissa was a graduate student with a history of sexual trauma who sought treatment to relieve intense anxiety and isolation. During our first session, Clarissa shared that she was dissatisfied with talk therapy and sought me out because my professional bio describes somatic and dance-based methods. As is my standard practice, in my initial orientation, I explained the potential benefits and risks of psychotherapy. I explained how I incorporate elements of Internal Family Systems, Dance Movement Therapy, somatic psychology, and CI-informed touch. I stated that as a social worker, my ethics prohibit me from having dual relationships, including sexual relationships, with clients.

For clients like Clarissa, who are eager to explore CI-informed touch, we typically begin our sessions with verbal processing. This initial phase allows us to build rapport, gain insight into the challenging narratives in the person's life, and establish a strong foundation before introducing touch. Before we choose to incorporate CI-informed techniques, I provide the clinical rationale behind each approach, discussing their potential benefits or drawbacks in relation to the client's treatment goals. We take the necessary time within this conversation to explore the client's comfort level and willingness to engage in this particular form of touch, ensuring their ongoing and active consent.

In my initial verbal assessment, I learned that Clarissa had internalized pressure to succeed academically from her parents and that fear of rejection contributed to hesitancy to advocate for herself within her academic program. This general fear of asserting herself, along with her history of sexual trauma, made her avoid dating, even though she wanted partnership. I saw how she became dysregulated as she attempted to describe her fears, leading her to avoid talking about them in detail.

Before we explored any form of interpersonal contact, I guided an individually based warm-up that highlighted the importance of tuning into her body's signals and connecting with its wisdom. This sets a framework for Clarissa to have a visceral experience of consent and choice-making. The embodied meditation also helps with calming the nervous system and anchoring the chaotic energy from the outside world. We began by finding a comfortable position on the floor. I invited Clarissa to choose whether she preferred to lie on her back, side, or belly, and continually invited her to shift as desired.

Our brains spend a large amount of time processing, deciphering, interpreting, and making sense of the visual stimulation within our environment. So I encouraged Clarissa to close her eyes in order to eliminate these distractions and take all that processing power to focus inward—it can be helpful to rest the palms of the hands gently on the eye sockets or just below on the top ridge of the cheekbones. Our hands are supremely adept at conveying and receiving information. From a neuro-receptor standpoint, they are some of the most sensitive and intelligent parts of the body. Together, we took time here to rest and acclimate to this new way of being, with our other senses opening up.

After a period of silence, I asked Clarissa about her experience. She commented that she felt more relaxed and somehow closer to the ground, with the tension in her body and in her thought patterns releasing. I instructed Clarissa to continue communicating

202   Resistance and Support

through her hands over various contours of her body, and feeling how this has an impact on her nervous system. This is a time to notice what feels comfortable, what parts of the body feel like they need more attention, and perhaps any feelings or sensations that are challenging.

It can be a radical act to experience the full range of sensations in the body. In her seminal essay, Audre Lorde (1978) writes about the radical act of feeling our pleasure in the face of a patriarchy that is trying to condemn and erase this experience—especially from women. She claims that to feel pleasure in the body and to embrace this more intuitive sense is a significant form of our liberating power. This can feel especially vulnerable while someone else is sharing this intimate space, yet this can be a powerful part of the process in building the therapeutic relationship. I convey to Clarissa that this is *her* practice. She has agency to reclaim the power of her embodied self, of her sensual experience within this movement exercise—and any vulnerability that might enter in is welcome. This process can have the same level of intimacy as writing a journal entry. Clarissa's body becomes her diary as she has an authentic embodied conversation through movement.

We transition into more expanded movement through exploring a deeper connection with the floor. I model movement patterns such as reaching out into space and then curling back into the body. I also demonstrate how to use resistance against gravity by pushing away from the floor or softening tone and yielding back into the floor. Using these tools, I encourage Clarissa's solo improvisational choice-making—listening to her body's authentic impulses, trusting its innate wisdom, its sense of timing, and knowing when or how her movements might want to change and evolve. In reflection, Clarissa commented that her movement revealed deeper emotional blocks. She felt a mix of resistance and exhilaration. It reminded her of times when she tried to assert herself but held back because of fear.

Through fostering this environment of ongoing learning and reflection, Clarissa was gaining agency over her sensations and emotions. She felt equipped to communicate her awareness about how she holds on to certain thoughts and feelings. This translates to clients being able to make more empowered choices in their lives. In our session, this skill enabled Clarissa to advocate for the support she needed and served as a healthy foundation for exploring CI-informed touch.

I introduced the concept of sitting back-to-back while sharing our experiences verbally. The back, supported by the spine, is often a more shielded area of our bodies, which can make it feel less vulnerable to start with. In this exercise, while sitting back-to-back and feeling each other's spines, we focus on our breath and movement. I guided Clarissa to observe her breath and see how it impacts both of us as we breathe together. For many people, it can be a relief to connect without facing each other. Sometimes the frontal orientation can feel intimidating or even confrontational. This actually dates back to Freud, who had clients lie down on a couch during sessions to encourage open sharing without eye contact. Also the ease and comfort we might experience sitting with this mutual support is similar to Freud working with his clients as they lay on a couch. Dr. Ofer Zur comments that Freud felt this position relaxed tense musculature and regressed clients to earlier states of development by lowering their defenses. (2023).

Leaning into each other, we noticed the shared warmth and observed how our breath expanded into each other's spine. We then leaned in with more weight to provide additional support and create different sensations. We each played with comfort and discovered how this interaction was a physical conversation. It's a way to experience connection and mutual support in a different way than what we are normally used to—and thus can be a profound awakening. When we were reflecting about the back-to-back exercise, I noticed Clarissa's demeanor shift as she spoke in a lower and clearer voice, continually expressing a sense of being more grounded. I asserted that her regulation was facilitated by her active participation, as she could push her energy into my back. Additionally, I believe that our mutual focus on this larger area of the body, coupled with the sustained physical contact, allowed her to experience herself within a stronger container.

During the session, while maintaining ongoing consent through pausing and checking in about the experience, Clarissa was able to express a boundary relating to her history of abuse. Clarissa expressed some confusion and disorientation during the mutual pushing. She thought I was pushing too aggressively, and part of her felt like she couldn't assert herself. She expressed her fear and hope that I wouldn't be angry with her for speaking honestly. I expressed appreciation and relief in hearing Clarissa share her vulnerability so openly and assured her that I don't take it personally. I explained how this is welcome in our sessions and is a path toward establishing trust. With Clarissa's request, we continued to stay in back-to-back physical contact. She was visibly emotional and expressed that it was remarkable that she could express her boundaries and provide feedback. Rather than reacting negatively or dismissively, I listened and acknowledged Clarissa's experience. This exploration helped Clarissa rewrite her narrative. While in the past, she felt helpless, this session offered the freedom to make choices with support rather than abandonment. Clarissa's voice was heard and respected.

This example illustrates how embodied nonjudgmental presence fosters client empowerment and healing. CI can help teach the concept of different kinds of relational support; and the practice of CI reminds us to feel and acknowledge the support around us, which can be transformative. Through a combination of CI-informed movement and exploring her feelings through talk, Clarissa was increasingly able to maintain emotional regulation while exploring her trauma and anxiety within this session. As time went on, Clarissa reported that during times of stress between sessions, she practiced embodiment and emotional regulation techniques learned in therapy, which helped reduce her overall anxiety. She reported greater willingness to speak up for herself at school and became more comfortable tolerating the anxiety that came with doing so.

Clarissa expressed her frustration with the emphasis on academic subjects rather than learning how to relate through touch. We both recognized the significance of finding a home within oneself and of re-establishing the connection with the earth as a way to help address the isolation she felt. We further reflected that this can allow for a deeper understanding of ourselves in relation to our world. It can cultivate awareness and gratitude for the earth and the force of its omnipresent gravitational embrace. When we reacquaint ourselves with our bodies in relation to gravity, it can be a grounding and healing antidote to the existential crises we face.

Susan McConnel, somatic psychologist writes, "When I am open to be impacted by my clients at all levels—cognitively, emotionally, physically, energetically, psychically—this strongly attuned state bumps us up another quantum level, where we are held in a relational field that has surprising transcendent potential" (2020, 96). CI-informed touch has the potential to create conditions so that we have direct access to immediate physical feedback and communication, and where our comfort is both dependent on our own abilities to take care of ourselves in a relationship that is also collaborative. As a therapist, I recognize that the art of my therapeutic practice involves striking a delicate balance between providing un-wavering support for the client and creating a physical space that offers honest and direct feedback. I believe that by doing so, clients can connect with their authentic humanity and establish a genuine connection with me.

Restorative Contact (Gabrielle Revlock)

This past winter I was contacted by a previous client. "Dear Gabrielle," she wrote,

> When my husband and I look back at 2020, taking a few of your virtual Couples Restorative Contact classes was one of the most meaningful experiences we shared. One of your classes literally helped reach into my depression and let it surface in a way nothing else could at the time.

There is evidence that mindfulness and touch work synergistically. Mindfulness begins with the cognitive decision to pay attention to the present moment and results in a shift in body state. Touch directly affects the body and sends signals to the brain, changing a person's mood. "Mindfulness practices and mindfulness-based touch interventions thus work from opposite ends of the information-processing hierarchy, resulting in the integration of immediate bodily experience with mindful cognitive self-awareness" (Stotter 2013, 186). I have seen firsthand how reciprocal mindful touch positively affects people who are struggling with depression, intimacy, conflict, and anxiety. Restorative Contact offers an adaptable practice for integrating touch into peoples' lives in a way that can be accessed and sustained throughout a lifetime.

As I've developed material for Restorative Contact, I've realized the importance of simple structures and guidance for making the exploration of interpersonal touch welcoming and empowering. Kellyn Jackson, a licensed professional counselor and dance/movement therapist, has recommended that within a therapeutic setting a "focusing effort" on the part of the facilitator is paramount (2022, 36). In an initial Restorative Contact session, I talk slowly, taking brief moments of silence. I direct the client's attention to different sensations, reminding them that their only task is to be a witness, taking in the information that is there. Improvisation is introduced in small doses. I often provide a starting and ending position and encourage them to "take the scenic route" in order to follow their curiosity rather than worrying about arriving at the destination. I let them know that they can always remove themselves from the practice, no questions asked, or make eye contact with me if they need additional support.

In the beginning of a session, I might introduce clients to "bridging," a CI skill where partners reach from the top of their heads and then lean toward each other, pouring their weight through their palms. I remind them that it isn't about giving or taking the maximum amount of weight, but rather about cultivating responsiveness and finding balance. Shifting only 5 percent of your weight toward your partner can be enough to establish a shared center. When we meet each other with the appropriate amount of resistance, we become available to making fresh choices in relationship. As the pair becomes comfortable with the technique, they often begin to play—changing the timing, the amount of weight

Therapeutic Applications of Contact Improvisation   **205**

shared, and using supports other than their hands. Mindfulness can take on a seriousness, yet I have noticed that some of the times when I feel most present are when I am having fun. As a creative facilitator and educator, I have more allowance to uplift play in my therapeutic work, which primes people to view our shared space as a place of enjoyment. While I have had pairs that come to me to work through difficulties, there is the understanding that we're not going to pick at those issues. Restorative Contact is about being, not doing; exploring, not fixing.

After an icebreaker such as bridging, I begin the contemplative component by having pairs sit back-to-back—similar to Aaron's practice. This is a more protected position because it reduces the potential of confrontation or exaggerated intimacy that can occur from eye contact when we are facing each other, particularly when we are moving at a slower pace, which is encouraged. Moving them through a sequence of postures, I unfold my sessions with evolving invitations that help people balance their individual embodied experience with the sensation of being in contact with another person. For example, in a session I might suggest the following:

After settling into a comfortable back-to-back position, I invite you to close your eyes and take a few breaths with me. Breathe slowly in through the nose and out through the mouth. On your next exhale see if you can make it slower . . . and longer. On the following deep, full, luxurious breath you might try coloring your exhale with a bit of sound. Now, without trying to change anything, follow your breath just as it is. Notice its rhythm and tempo. Is it steady or shifting? Observe how your breath expands and contracts your torso. Notice where your body connects with your partner. Can you feel the heat from their body? What about the texture of clothing or hair? If it feels right, gently sway your body side-to-side or forward and back. As you do so, what are you learning about the landscape of your partner's body? And how does their structure give you feedback on your own body? Notice how the touch goes both ways.

One of the biggest adjustments to the Restorative Contact pedagogy was catalyzed by COVID-19. During the lockdown I didn't want to stop offering Restorative Contact as a partner practice (although I did offer a solo variation), so I found myself working online with pairs who were quarantining together. Prior to the pandemic, I had participants work at random with whoever was in the room, a system common in CI classes. I personally find the task of dancing with anyone and everyone to be a valuable tool for community and resilience building, but I have come to the realization that for many people, working with a stranger is only a barrier to engagement. As a result, I offer one-on-two sessions (frequently with romantic couples) and teach drop-in workshops that people can attend with or without a chosen partner. I view my role as a guide, a collaborator, and a witness, championing mindful touch as a practice that can be accessed peer-to-peer. There are instances when a professional (massage therapist, somatic therapist, sex worker, etc.) is the best and most appropriate provider of touch. At other times, what is most healing is contact with an important person in your life. Early in 2020, I had a father and daughter practice with me for months. One day the father offered this reflection in an email: "You've helped open possibilities for communication that had gotten covered over. I appreciate the structure you've given us for embodied interactions. I think it's something both of us have wanted and neither knew how to initiate."

Figure 10.2. Smith College students participating in a Restorative Contact workshop organized by the Office of Disability Services in Spring 2023. Photo credit: E. J. Seibert.

Attunement

Healthy relationships are based on attunement, or the harmony that arises from being aware of and responding to the physical and emotional state of another person. It is a form of empathy and creates a mutual experience of connectedness. Attunement allows for babies to form attachment bonds with their caregivers and plays an important role in recovery from illness. A doctor who shows genuine empathy contributes to the speed of their patient's recovery (Siegel 2011). Expressing empathy verbally can be elusive, and from my personal experience is often replaced with commiserating, advising, analyzing, interrogating, or minimizing. Kinesthetic empathy is a concept proposed by Dee Reynolds and Matthew Reason, that names the phenomenon of experiencing empathy by observing the movement of another person (2012). I hypothesize that for some people, kinesthetic empathy can be more profoundly achieved through touch and avoids some of the pitfalls of verbal empathy.

Companionship is one of the tenets of Restorative Contact—showing up without expectations, to share space with another person. Clients are released from having to "do" something for their partner. Their primary job is to be a witness—to pay attention to sensations in their *own* body. By sitting quietly in contact with another person, they are positioned to feel if that person is fidgety, relaxed, tense, or at ease. Paying attention to our own experience is the foundation for noticing what is happening around us, including with our partner. I guide my clients to slowly release the tension in their body. Since they are doing this while in contact with another person, they are automatically sharing that state with their partner, creating a feedback loop where each can benefit from the relaxed state of the other.

Restorative Contact differs from CI in that it is weighted toward slowness and stillness and primarily uses passive body weight. When I guide clients in draping, for example, one person's belly draped over the other person's legs, I encourage them to yield at the places where their bodies connect with each other and/or the floor. At any point they are welcome to make adjustments to their posture, including incorporating pillows or blankets. It is important that they begin to distinguish when they are experiencing physical discomfort and to feel supported in making the changes to alleviate it. The goal of Restorative Contact is to create a container where people feel safe enough to be still. The ability to quiet one's movement without fear creates the possibility for intimacy and is the antithesis of the freeze response born from trauma. "When you think about it, isn't immobilization without fear really a goal of therapy?" poses trauma expert, Dr. Steven Porges:

> You don't want your clients to remain "tightly wrapped," anxious and defensive. You want your clients to be able to sit quietly, to be embraced without fear, and to be hugged and to hug others, to conform physically when embraced, and to be reciprocal in their relationships. (2011, 4–5)

As someone who has struggled with seated meditations, I discovered that it is much easier for me to be still when I am in contact with another person. When I feel the structure of another's body, their warmth and weight in a seemingly abstract way (as opposed to a symbolically charged action such as a hug or kiss), it helps me stay present and open because there is no pressure to have an emotional response.

The concept of draping extends to the use of the hands. Instead of engaging in manipulative touch, I instruct my clients to let their hands rest on their partner's body. This can be an unusual sensation for some, as many people have the impulse to start massaging their partner, which encourages the binary perspective of giving versus receiving. I have found that the more "active" the touch, the more likely it is for someone to attach a particular meaning to it—good or bad. The task is not to create meaning (e.g., demonstrate your affection) but to notice how your body is affected by contact with another human. Many pairs end up feeling relaxed or connected, but this arises organically—sometimes to their surprise. The skin and the brain both developed from the ectoderm, the outermost layer of cells in the embryo. What we experience through our sense of touch impacts how we feel mentally and vice versa (Juhan 2003, 34).

No matter if I am coaching a couple or working directly with a client, I stress the importance of mutuality. The goal is to enter a mode of embodied listening where leadership is fluid and at times imperceptible. This is a radical concept for people who have been habituated to be in a docile agreement with authority. The meaning of pulling (counterbalance) and pushing (bridging) changes when we no longer view it exclusively an act of aggression. For example, if someone pushes us on our left side, we move to the right because we assume they want us to get out of the way. If someone takes our hand, we often expect to be led somewhere. This automatic response to directional touch can obscure awareness of our agency. For the instances when we choose to disobey, it usually means conflict. But what if we experienced pushing and pulling as their CI equivalents: bridging and counterbalance? Might the encounter transform into a negotiation or, even better, a dance where there is no one right outcome, only the evolving relationship between two or more bodies. Philosopher Martin Buber in his 1970 publication, *I and Thou*, asserted a relational concept of existence. He states that there is no I, only I-You and I-It. I-It describes a transactional relationship, whereas an I-You relationship is one that involves genuine presence and the acknowledgment of the immensity and depth of the other entity (Benedikt 2020). In our touch-deprived culture, it is crucial to relearn, through experience and practice, the ability to attune, which can only be

Depth of Touch

Part of my guidance involves giving clients vocabulary to describe depths of touch. This can aid them in identifying their preferences and distinguishing variations in compression, some of which they may not have been conscious of. Drawing from CI pedagogy, I describe the depths of compression as skin, muscle, and bone. If beginning at the level of skin, I will instruct a client to rest a hand lightly on their partner's body with as little pressure as possible. If relaxed, the hand will naturally mold to the shape of that body part. It might be tempting for a client to begin using light stroking motions, either out of familiarity or to demonstrate that they are *doing* something. Instead of moving, I advise them to let their hands find stillness and imagine listening through the palms. I had a client who immediately began a caressing motion, so I stopped and demonstrated to him what I perceived him doing versus what I was asking. He reflected back that the moving touch felt like it was asking for something and the constant touch felt grounding.

Paxton uses the phrase "deformation of the skin" to describe how pushing into tissue temporarily changes its shape (Paxton 2008). In doing so, we access the second depth of touch, muscle. Many people will equate this level of touch with massage. Again, I advise them to put those associations aside because it encourages them to fixate on themselves as the active worker, and their partner as the passive receiver. The task is not to massage your partner, it is to listen at the level of muscle. Both partners are tracking changes to sensation.

A client can deepen their touch further by shifting their pelvis above and toward their partner, while listening through their palms. Here they can imagine their touch extending toward their partner's skeletal structure. Now we are working at the layer of bone. (Care should be taken when pouring the weight into certain body parts, such as the knees, where heavy pressure should be avoided.) Through our partner's bones, we can miraculously feel the ground on the opposite side! Our partner becomes a conduit to the environment.

In my practice I have followed this depth of touch exploration with a consent exercise borrowed from Betty Martin, author and developer of "The Wheel of Consent" (2014). In the exercise, partners take turns asking each other two questions: (1) How would you like me to touch you? and (2) How would you like to touch me? A request can be accepted, denied, or negotiated until both are satisfied with the agreement. Informed by the previous depth of touch exercise, I ask them to keep a couple of things in mind: (1) How does depth of touch factor into your preferences? and (2) When asked to provide touch to your partner, how might you continue to stay invested in your own felt experience?

Touch as Vehicle for Differentiation

It is nearly impossible to imagine how it would be to go through the world without a sense of touch. Every time we make contact with something or someone, it gives us immediate feedback on our physical existence. This basis for differentiation begins in utero as the embryo floats in amniotic fluid and presses up against the uterine wall. This encounter allows the embryo to develop awareness of the boundary of their skin, separating who they are from who they are not (Bainbridge Cohen, cited in McConnell 2020, 219). In a 2022 study conducted by Ariane Puhr on "The Effect of Touch in Contact Improvisation on Affect, Stress, Sense of Connectedness and Sense of Self," she compared the benefits of solo dance improvisation to Contact Improvisation. The results of her study indicated that CI caused the participants to experience a greater sense of self versus solo improvisation. (They also reported more happiness and a sense of connectedness.) In describing how partner touch enhanced her sense of differentiation, a participant reflected, "When you feel boundaries, you sense yourself better than when you don't have boundaries, and there the other body was my boundary and led me to be able to sense myself well" (2022, 21). Since I frequently work with romantic couples where boundaries are prone to becoming blurred, focusing on differentiation is essential. As a couple engages in co-resting, I direct them to sense into the contact, while also following and monitoring their own felt reality. Each person is having a unique experience simultaneous to, and supported by, their partner. They are attuned but not homogenized. Rather, they are together in a state of companionship. After our workshop at *CI @ 50*, one of the participants shared that the most impactful part of the workshop for her was when I stated, "everything that you feel belongs to you." Sometimes when we're upset, it's easy to put the blame on someone else (e.g., you made me feel this way!) but when we take responsibility for our own feelings and actions, we free ourselves of the burden of trying to change people or things we have no control over. Negative patterns of behavior can be triggered before we are even aware of what's happening. These automatic responses are coded into the body. When we slow down and pay attention to body sensations, our perspective is widened and this is the foundation for considered choice-making. A partner's touch has the ability to tether us to the present moment, and support our core values and intentions.

Conclusion

In our practices, we have experienced that people need far more than just a pat on the back, or an affirming squeeze of the hand. James Prescott, a developmental neurophysiologist at the National Institute of Child Health and Human Development, states: "The deprivation of body touch, contact, and movement are the basic causes of a number of emotional disturbances which include depressive . . . behavior, hyperactivity, sexual aberrations, drug abuse, violence, and aggression" (Juhan 2003, 54). From early childhood and continuing throughout one's life, touch plays a crucial role in a human being's development. Intentional positive touch is a necessary ingredient for healthy social integration and contributes to a stable psyche. We are social beings, and there is no modern invention (weighted blanket, sleep pod, hug shirt, etc.) that can substitute for the deep-seated attachment benefits that come with physical contact with another person.

Navigating touch among a population impacted by COVID-19 has its challenges. Certain people are more fearful of touch, and even innocuous contact can be construed as threatening or dangerous. Consequently, it is uncommon for mental health therapists to focus on touch as part of their practice. However, it is reductive to assume that touch itself is what creates harm—it is far more complex, with a myriad of contributing factors. As Janet Moursund, PhD, and Richard Erskine, PhD, explain, "while the no-touch rule may provide legal safety to the therapist, it could be depriving the client of precisely the thing that would most help them

210 Resistance and Support

heal" (Mousund and Erskine 2004, 33). We are acutely aware of the need for more resources to explore interpersonal contact within a framework of safety and collaboration. Our therapeutic work, informed by CI, lays the groundwork for reciprocal touch to become a welcome component to wellness. We advocate connecting mind and body, mental health, and somatic intelligence, and we believe that a grounded self helps generate a bonded community and a better world.

References

Airbnb Experiences. 2020. "Restorative Contact for Pairs & Groups." Airbnb. https://www.airbnb.com/experiences/1698043.

Albright, Ann Cooper. 2019. *How to Land: Finding Ground in an Unstable World*. Oxford: Oxford University Press.

American Psychological Association. 2019, October 30. *Mindfulness Meditation: A Research-Proven Way to Reduce Stress*. https://www.apa.org/topics/mindfulness/meditation.

Benedikt, Michael. 2020. *Architecture beyond Experience*. 1st edition. San Francisco, CA: Applied Research and Design.

Caldwell, C. 1997. *Getting in Touch: The Guide to New Body-Centered Therapies*. Wheaton, IL: Quest Books.

Jackson, Kellyn. 2022. "Where Contact Improvisation Meets Dance/Movement Therapy: An Embodied Group Artistic Inquiry." *American Journal of Dance Therapy* 44 (May): 21–44. https://link.springer.com/article/10.1007/s10465-022-09360-7.

Juhan, Deane. 2003. *Job's Body: A Handbook for Bodywork*. 3rd edition. Barrytown: Station Hill.

Kabat-Zinn, Jon. "Mindfulness-Based Interventions in Context: Past, Present, and Future." *Clinical Psychology: Science & Practice* 10, no. 2 (June 2003): 144–156.

Kabat-Zinn, Jon. 2013. *Full Catastrophe Living: Using the Wisdom of Your Body and Mind to Face Stress, Pain, and Illness*. Revised and updated edition. New York: Bantam Dell.

Koteen, David, Nancy Stark Smith. 2008. *Caught Falling: The Confluence of Contact Improvisation, Nancy Stark Smith, and Other Moving Ideas*. Northampton, MA: Contact Editions.

Lepkoff, Daniel. "Contact Improvisation: A Question." *Contact Quarterly* 36, no. 1 (2011): 42–44.

Levine, Paul. 2010. *In an Unspoken Voice: How the Body Releases Trauma and Restores Goodness*. Berkeley, CA: North Atlantic Books.

Lorde, A. 1978. *Uses of the Erotic: The Erotic as Power*. Brooklyn, NY: Out & Out Books.

Martin, Betty. "How to Play the 3-Minute Game." BettyMartin.org, November 29, 2015. https://bettymartin.org/how-to-play-the-3-minute-game/.

Masten, A. S., and A. J. Barnes. 2018. "Resilience in Children: Developmental Perspectives." *Children (Basel, Switzerland)* 5(7): 98. https://doi.org/10.3390/children5070098; https://www.ncbi.nlm.nih.gov/pmc/articles/PMC6069421/.

McConnell, S. (2020). *Somatic Internal Family Systems Therapy: Awareness, Breath, Resonance, Movement, and Touch in Practice*. Berkeley, CA: North Atlantic Books.

Moursund, J. P., and Erskine, R. G. 2004. *Integrative Psychotherapy: The Art and Science of Relationship*. Belmont, CA: Thompson/Brooks Cole.

National Association of Social Workers. 2017. *NASW Code of Ethics*. https://www.socialworkers.org/About/Ethics/Code-of-Ethics/Code-of-Ethics-English. (Retrieved 01/10/2020).

Paxton, Steve. 1993. "Drafting Interior Techniques-Paxton." *Contact Quarterly* 18: 72–77.

Paxton, Steve. 2008. *Material for the Spine. [Videorecording]: A Movement Study = Une Étude Du Mouvement.* Brussels: Contredanse.

Pike, G., Edgar, G., and Edgar, H. (2012). "Perception," in *Cognitive Psychology*, eds N. Braisby and A. Gellatly (Oxford: Oxford University Press), 65–99. Quoted in Fabian Hutmacher. 2019. "Why Is There So Much More Research on Vision Than on Any Other Sensory Modality?" *Frontiers in Psychology* 10 (October).

Puhr, Ariane. "The Effect of Touch in Contact Improvisation on Affect, Stress, Sense of Connectedness and Sense of Self." Unpublished Thesis, Netherlands, Open Universiteit Nederland, 2022.

Reynolds, Dee, and Matthew Reason. 2012. *Kinesthetic Empathy in Creative and Cultural Practices.* Intellect.

Siegel, Daniel J. 2011. *Mindsight: A New Approach to Psychotherapy.* PESI Inc. https://video.alex anderstreet.com/watch/mindsight-a-new-approach-to-psychotherapy.

Smith, Nancy Stark. "The Underscore." May 3, 2023. https://nancystarksmith.com/underscore/.

Stötter, A., M. Mitsche, P. Christian Endler, P. Oleksy, D. Kamenschek, W. Mosgoeller, and C. Haring. 2013. "Mindfulness-Based Touch Therapy and Mindfulness Practice in Persons with Moderate Depression." *Body, Movement and Dance in Psychotherapy* 8(3): 183–198.

Van der Kolk, Bessel A. 2015. *The Body Keeps the Score: Brain, Mind, and Body in the Healing of Trauma.* New York: Penguin Books.

Zur, Ofer. 2023. "To Touch or Not to Touch: Exploring Prohibition on Touch in Psychotherapy and Counseling and the Ethical Considerations of Touch." January 5, 2023. https://drzur.com/touch-in-therapy/.

11

XCI

Intimacy in Contact Improvisation

Aramo Olaya

I'm committed to taking Contact Improvisation (CI) as a movement language beyond the practice of CI as a dance form. This chapter explores some non-heteronormative practices I have developed in the past 15 years in the space between CI and queer sexuality. It's a personal search for shared intimacy, for an embodied sexual physicality outside the norm of genitality, a nonbinary ontology, a practice that undoes sex and gender as the sites from which to unfold people's body experience. In this journey, intimacy and improvisation came to be the particles with which any future compositions of more complex contacts between dance and sexual practices and identities were to be composed. XCI tries to embrace this quest for intimacy beyond the social power dynamics embedded in traditional notions of sex and gender. This "X" in XCI stands for the unknown in the interstitial space between queer sexuality and CI, or an understanding of CI as a language of flesh that is at least partially capable of untying itself from the symbolic order of gendered norm. I am interested in the bodily knowing that comes from sensitive, sensual, and sexual development, before our mastery of verbal language. This knowledge is related to the lack of adult intervention, the possibilities of movement and curiosity in the body languages and qualities of perception in childhood. A focus practice of CI can resemble and reminisce some of these qualities in adulthood.

What I have called XCI for this essay is not a commodifiable product that can be spread as a form independent from CI among any given community of practitioners. To generate XCI, it is necessary to deeply commit in developing CI/somatic-specific skills that can add layers of nuance to touch, learning to listen to the desires and boundaries of other bodies. It must be grounded in feminist and queer politics and practices; otherwise, it could turn out to be masked sexual aggression. It is not a standardizable practice to be multiplied voluntarily, but a research process that I have been able to develop only at very specific moments with the closest collaborators with whom one can cultivate a consensual and intersubjective exchange.

The Quest for Intimacy

I was a queer and feminist activist interested in intimacy, desire, and sexuality before becoming a dancer. I was part of the feminist/queer anarchist social movements in Spain in the first decade of the twenty-first century, and I was particularly interested in sexual activism. There was a big influence from the BDSM/kink scene, and postporn. It was hard for me to

Aramo Olaya, *XCI* In: *Resistance and Support.* Edited by: Ann Cooper Albright, Oxford University Press. © Oxford University Press 2024. DOI: 10.1093/9780197776308.003.0012

fully engage in that scene because I had concerns about the role of violence and what I saw as a narrow understanding of sexual practices and their political implications. I felt that the desire to be sex-positive led folks to embrace performative practices that, while consensual, still focused on performing violence in a safe space. I felt like I was in the middle, trying to think about nonviolent sexual practices from a queer sexual activism framework. I wanted to find a desire that did not reproduce heteronormative sexuality. Perhaps I was not as daring as other friends, nor was I very attracted to the aesthetic of BDSM. There were some discourses about non-genital or post-genital practices, but I felt a lack of an alternative epistemology and a political framework to address them.

During that decade, there was a common trope in feminist and (even more in) queer activism in Spain: "We need to bring the body to the center of the debate."[1] There we were, sitting in a circle, speaking, and talking *about* the body, which we felt was the place from which to unfold politics. But the center was empty, and the body was not there. We were trapped in discourse. I felt that we lacked a practice that reached the body from within. I wanted to find a queer practice that allowed me to resist or forget the omnipresent heteronormative sexual and gender scores we all learn as adults. Queer people often fail in performing gender roles and defy social expectations of normative sexualities. Because of this misalignment with social discourse, queer people can develop a somatic sensibility that exists outside of normative behaviors. Movement styles and patterns have been a source of constant self-consciousness for many queers, solved in many different creative or frustrating ways. Many queer people are especially sensitive to the politics of consent in sexual touch and can be particularly perceptive when engaging in physical relationality.

Because of both pleasant and unpleasant experiences that I had in childhood, I was looking for a way to access a transformative practice of desire that could engage in sociopolitical and anthropological transformation. For some unknown reason (maybe because what kids do is not always the result of pure imitation), I always felt that such a force was to be found in improvisation. I had some childhood memories about dancing, and some consensual early sexual experiences that felt like dancing, or that I could only describe as dancing. As an adult, some shared somatic sensing-touch-breathing-moving experiences drew me into dance. I imagined that improvised partnered dance might be the ideal site to practice bodies' relationality beyond what I had found in other kinds of embodied encounters. When I started dancing queer tango and CI, I discovered that somatic awareness was trainable: The possibilities of relation and sensation between bodies were much broader than what I had been practicing until then. I knew from the very first day that I had found the methodology I was looking for. Dance was for me the discovery of a place in which to embody the sensuous curiosity I had about intimacy that I couldn't meet in the context of queer sexual activism.

I engaged in deeper learning of CI at Espacio Formación Contact Improvisación Madrid (EspacioFCI)[2] with Cristiane Boullosa and Diana Bonilla, and other teachers like Patricia Gracia, whose approach to Contact Improvisation is informed by Body Mind Centering®. Cristiane's approach to CI is inspired by Shiatsu and Chinese medicine energy movements

---

[1] A sentence I heard many times in Madrid in the first decade of the twenty-first century, and that I heard again in 2019 from Teo Pardo, a queer activist friend from Barcelona, as a common trope there, too, at the workshop "El arte queer de bailar mal," held at II Congreso Internacional de Filosofía de la Danza 2019. https://congresofilosofiadelada nza.wordpress.com/. Videos from the second edition: https://canal.uned.es/series/5cf7d416a3eeb0812c8b4569?fbc lid=IwAR3i2MP3c45Vbamtl_9k2ThXkiSp2PbcP_uBq7rFOjEhlZ4_HFe_rxvfm8E.

[2] espaciofci.com.

214 Resistance and Support

and has been absolutely fundamental to my own understanding of CI. It confirmed the existence of a complex non-isolating grammar of intimacy. During my first training years, some
spontaneous dance encounters in classes and jams unfolded a world of nuances and sensations of connection, and possibilities of communication, reminding me of those consensual
early experiences. I am also a queer tango dancer, and I was explicitly researching gender embodiment and gendered movement roles in queer tango. I was always able to clearly see the
heteronorm functioning in CI spaces and dancing bodies, and I was worried about predatory
and abusive behavior happening in jams. I created a small reflection group on CI and gender
with some classmates at EspacioFCI. I also approached the broader yet small European and
Latin American queer CI community. In both queer tango and CI, my interest was always to
tackle queerness as a movement form. Thanks to CI, I had already created a methodology
to teach queer tango without movement roles. I started to wonder if it was possible to move
beyond gender roles and identities in movement through improvisation and energy-sharing
in the liminal space between CI and sexuality. Along with my own personal identity, I understood this as a nonbinary ontology. Did such a space exist? Was it possible to systematize it?

In the past years there has been an incipient debate about the role of sexuality in CI among
the queer CI community. Some people understand that a queer practice of CI refers to bringing into CI the problem of intersectional inclusivity, identity, and the accumulated political
experience of the queer movement, keeping CI inside the definition of a dance technique or
form. Others think that queerness could also bring a reflection and practice on sexual positivity to CI. I believe that this is what I and co-writer Wiktor Skrzypczak suggested in our
article in *Contact Quarterly*, "Queer Contact Improvisation (QCI): Alliance and Disruption.
Experiences and Reflections from the QCI Symposium and Festival Hamburg 2018."[3] Since
then, I have shifted to talk of addressing sexuality in CI rather than bringing sexual positivity to CI. My goal is to delve into CI as a queer practice. Although there may be some
incompatibilities between understanding queerness in CI as intersectional inclusivity and as
a queer practice, primarily due to their distinct interpretations of CI in relation to sexuality,
I believe that both perspectives are essential for a comprehensive understanding of CI within
queer activism. Addressing sexuality in CI from a queer perspective could be a very unsafe
space without an intersectional inclusivity and enthusiastic consent approach. Even taking in
these constraints, exploring CI as a queer practice might still be possible under very specific
conditions.

For some time, I was curious about the work of those intersecting CI and sexual feelings, as for example the Touch & Play or Explore projects. I engaged with sex-positive CI-
related spaces and participated in the organization of Touch & Play in Barcelona in 2019.
I proposed a debate space there in which the participants expressed profound and beautiful
utopian desires for community and sexuality. However, during the event, I felt the need for
more somatic experience within the space. Consent was practiced explicitly and elaborately,
resembling the practices found in the kink scene, relying on verbal refusal of an action or the
absence of a "no" as a form of tacit physical agreement.[4] This discursive-contractual approach

---

[3] https://contactquarterly.com/cq/article-gallery/view/queer-contact-improvisation-qci-alliance-and-dis
ruption#.

[4] For an explanation of Touch & Play guidelines on the space as a sex-positive space and their practices of con-
sent/somatic consensus-making: https://docs.google.com/document/d/10ayW8-sZq2w5beVD94IjreyWWRQW
SCILtsCinCGqt8U/edit#heading=h.8qe5maevo8x1.

to consent resembled the consensual practices I had previously distanced myself from during my involvement in queer sexual activism in the previous decade.

After this experience and through conversations with some queer friends in the CI scene, I resolved that if I wanted to find a solid ground for a queer approach to intimacy and CI, first I had to resign from my desire of starting by building community. That would take a long-term commitment with a complex set of skills and political practices in a world in which such a community could exist. I don't think we are there yet. Finding one person with shared interests with whom I could undertake such a process safely in this particular world was already a big challenge—a never-ending quest for intimacy that is still ongoing.

In the past 15 years, I have had some previous personal experiences and artistic collaborations that dwelled in the space in between the somatic and the sexual with a few queer dancer/collaborators. In 2021, I had the chance to engage specifically with a practice as research of what I have partly jokingly called "XCI." I collaborated with Ilda Freire, a queer contact improvisation dancer I met at EspacioFCI, who had just come back from dynamizing the CI scene in Beijing because of the pandemic. Ilda perfectly understood what I was looking for as soon as I explained it. These encounters were consensual and co-sensed, in a place of shared intimacy and shared CI language and methodologies in which we could be in control of the situation. We were not crossing previous boundaries through the practice, we were in a queer relationship already, and there was no significant socioeconomic-political power imbalance between us. These characteristics constituted a rare space for building a community of two questioning touch.

XCI as Practice as Research

Ilda and I programmed sessions with no decided specific scores beforehand, each of which stressed different qualities and dimensions of the interactions between CI and (queer) sexuality. Each session shaped our curiosities for the next one, until we came up with the resolution of creating an explanatory framework for the practice. We found four different dimensions in the practice of XCI: the XCI duet, the space in between for improvisation, the back-and-forth between sex and CI, and the occurrence of gender performativity within CI. Each of them unfolded different qualities of relationality between CI and sexuality, between CI and queerness, and between CI and language and the creation of meaning.

XCI and the CI Duet

The first session was initiated as a shared practice of a touched-based CI duet, rolling-sliding, sharing surfaces in fluid movement in the space, sensing different qualities of weight, mass, skin, speed, sight, and so on, alongside allowing sexual arousal to lead the movement. It rapidly led to a practice very close to CI from the outside, with a lot of weight sharing and agile movement, the sensation of two bodies acting as one, and the quality of body parts acting around freely and independently. Allowing shared arousal led to micro-decisions taken about directions, points of contact, and qualities of touch and pressure. We found that it helped with de-patterning, resulting in a highly energetic sensation of spontaneity and complicity in the improvisation. It really felt like the kids' sexual playing that I still remember from my childhood: sensations of spontaneity, of being led by the arousal with no particular goal, the interplay between grabbing, doing, going together, expecting, finding, and undefining of the rules of the game. When the sexual arousal is diffused, moving in contact without leading to specific sexual goals, it can happen that it fuels and potentiates the sensation of togetherness or communion.

We agreed that this skill is easy to perform if both partners are already engaged in this kind of relationship, with no significant imbalance in power and experience in Contact Improvisation. We also concluded that a sensitive body can receive the unblocking of sexual energy circulating in between and around the bodies and spread the capacity of sensing erogenously through the whole body. Erogeneity is detached from the places it has traditionally occupied, both externally and internally. The challenge is finding a balance between the sexual and CI languages, looking for a common ground or space in between, not succumbing to one or the other. This is done by never missing the presence of spiraling, sliding, rolling, and the everchanging qualities of touch and proprioception; avoiding highly culturally charged sexual practices like kissing or touching the genitals; avoiding being totally led by arousal, recycling that energy into dancing language, moving the excitement/arousal through the body. This is about de-genitalizing, de-hierarchizing "erogenous zones"; also, cultivating an attitude of no expectations to keep movement between those boundaries.

This leads to a practice of sexuality that happens in a place of movement significantly unrelated to sexual or gender roles, or any kind of sensation of sexual achievement or goal. As a sexual practice, it feels like it has no beginning and no end or ends. We found that this practice is profoundly related to non-hierarchy principles: between people, body parts, parts of a process, or goals.

XCI in the Space-in-Between of Improvisation

In the second session, we introduced skills related to *improvisation* (more than to *contact*) as a broader practice within CI. Some of them were: playing with distances, pauses, playing with entering and going out from the other body, gazing, pausing, running, crashing into each other, while letting sexual feelings be present and potentiated by the movement practices again. That brought some narrative. Training sight is a basic skill in CI for spatial awareness and spherical orientation, but when adding the possibility of XCI, sight easily becomes a gaze. The gaze is strongly symbolically charged, and it opens up a more performative space, because in it, participants elaborate roles. Gazing in space is by itself an open possibility for seductive or aggressive language, and there is the risk of it dragging us completely out from CI. How can we be in this gaze that speaks of desire, but at the same time stay in the space of the trained spherical sight of CI?

This was done by the use of the gaze, pause, speeds, and distances with the presence of sexual feelings and sensations, training to keep an open gaze to the space and embodiment, constantly attaching gaze to sight. A wider sphere of movement and play appeared, instead of focusing on the bodies and the encounter. The poetics of approaching closer and moving away in space were associated with different physical sensations and emotions like heat and cold, fear and trust, joke and seriousness, disregard and commitment, depth and poignancy, and so on. A dialogue was opened about the spaciousness and separation and the endearment of desire, therefore starting to step into the symbolic, but with the chance of not being completely captured by it.

We could detach the gaze from the duet form and the poetics of heteronormative narratives of seduction, opening up a wider body language for desire and encounter, and bringing sensual/sexual sensitivity and desire into the space. We perceived that the main difference with the first practice was that we entered a space of performance, in which culturally charged meaning is thrown into the space, rather than focusing on the technical aspects of CI's use of space. However, it was always possible to redirect this performative language to CI, by referring meaning to the somatic experience, keeping the arousal out in the space instead of focusing it on bodies and specific parts of bodies, and letting go of judgment, instead of making decisions about a sensual or sexual score to follow. XCI in this stage could have the power of widening our narratives of desire into energetic flows in space, broadening the attunement of all the senses.

CI and Sex

It is important to stress that XCI is not just about switching between CI moments and sexual practices. Sexual practices can be placed between moments of CI dancing, bringing another quality to the performance of sexual practices by, for example, using direct contact with and between genitals, kissing, and moaning during CI practice; or spiraling, sliding, and perceiving different qualities of touch during a sexual practice. But my understanding is that just switching between CI and sexual practices, although playful and good, does not constitute the practice I was seeking for. This feels more like bouncing between two poles, or switching to speak in two different languages that both parties know how to speak. But it is definitely *not* inventing a new language together. When we found ourselves practicing this, it became evident that we had moved beyond the realm of research we had agreed to explore together.

CI and Gender (Somatic) Performativity

If our first practice felt quite released from gender roles, we found ourselves delving more and more into questions of gendered meaning and behaviors. What happens when gender performance shows up? Including queer sexual practices in CI brings up gender performativity in the dance. Both heteronormative and queer sexuality are powerful sites for the staging of gender roles and symbolically charged gendered practices. Gender performance has a very important role in (lesbian and) queer sexuality. The conscious experience of gender performance in queer sexuality is related to the training and failing in gender performativity experienced by queer people. Queer people can't make the symbolic invisible by identifying it with the biological or the embodied norm because it doesn't align with our own bodies and identities. This includes the embodiment of organs, body features, gender identities and roles, that might or might not be those we inhabit most of the time. For example, having psychic penises or cunts is an embodied experience quite common among queer people. The experience of prosthetic or phantasmatic organs can take a significant role in queer lives and identities. Other common queer sexual practices (this varies a lot among different people)

218 Resistance and Support

are: imagining yourself or your partner as a woman, a man, or a trans or nonbinary person; performing power dynamics; the use of consensual pain and violence, and so on.

We found that gender performance in sex and CI are deeply linked to the inquiry about the limits of violence and tenderness, activity and passivity, and drive and resistance, at least. The appearance of the symbolic in the dance leads immediately to existing language: familiar movement patterns, assumptions about roles, body parts, attitudes. It feels like gendered sexual performance is an important source of meaning: up/down, giving/receiving, passive/active, soft/strong, doing/feeling, pleasure/violence, inside/outside, surface/interior, rough/tender, and many other basic markers of meaning rely on it. The most interesting finding was feeling how gender performance creates meaning: rather than the feminine or masculine being symbolically related to the actions (e.g., to succumb is feminine), it appears that the symbolically feminine or masculine is constituted by the actions (to be feminine is to succumb). This could explain how gender becomes ontologically ingrained in bodies through repetitive behavior (if I like to succumb, I must be feminine). Is it possible to escape this inscription of gender through nongendered sexual practices?

The CI language can help dissipate these meanings during the practice, bringing them to other places, or combining them anarchically, thus getting to transfigure or decontextualize them. Although learned forms of desire tend to bring us deep into existing layers of sexual meaning, XCI is a practice that can help bodies surface back into a somatic experience where these meanings are not so powerful, opening up new narratives of pleasure and shared intimacy, like the inscription of a nonbinary ontology through the repetition of nongendered sexual practices. However, in this stage of the research, I felt that it was especially difficult not to step on the symbolic order of existing language.

Conclusion about Our Research Practice of XCI

My search when dancing in the space in between CI and the sexual has been for a sexuality that is not governed by the symbolic, because the symbolic is the psychic erosion of cultural tradition, and our tradition is strongly embedded in sexual hierarchy. I want to obtain transformative performativity (Hunter 2019, 40–50) from XCI, detaching these meanings from existing language into new directions. Can we get rid of the symbolic? Could a somatic quality (for example, the pleasure of touch, or succumbing) be explained/practiced without reference to the symbolic: the gaze not leading to a specific politics of desire, the pleasure of touch not being necessarily attached to engaging in a deeper physical relationship, succumbing not being considered feminine? I would say that the first stage of our research was pointing in that direction, but we gradually abandoned that somatic quality and stepped more and more into preexisting regimes of meaning as we ventured into what is commonly understood as sexual practices.

Co-Sensing Queer Non-Intentionality in XCI

The process of practice as research in which Ilda and I engaged those months covered the non-intentional XCI qualities of touch, presence, and energy in the CI duet, the performance of desire in the space of improvisation, the mixing of CI and sex languages, the performativity of gender and power dynamics between CI, and some queer and BDSM sexual practices. Which somatic perspective could encompass this diversity? The concept of non-intentionality has had an important impact in my CI training. Ilda's and my CI school in Madrid, EspacioFCI, directed by dancers Cristiane Boullosa and Diana Bonilla, gives great importance to the idea of non-intentionality, referring it to qualities of movement and touch that are not committed with a specific formal goal, nor do they try to lead movement. They are focused on observation rather than on action, creating a movement or touch that is not governed by these behaviors (Boullosa 2022)[5]. Non-intentional is not unconscious behavior. It involves specific layers of attention and energetic flows in the space in between body-minds, tissues, physical forces, and modes of relationality.

Ilda and I developed some practices around different qualities of touch, especially from the first stage of our XCI research, the space in which we felt away from the symbolic charges of sexuality. These different qualities of touch can be practiced toward CI or just toward touch research. They consist in practicing how different attentional states affect the touch: paying attention to what I'm offering to the other body or to what I receive from the offering; focusing on the tactility of the other person's tissue, or on the tactility of my own physical sensations when doing or receiving the touch, and how all of this is expressed energetically. We felt that this detachment between the sensations of touching and being touched allows for a sensation analysis that embodies the idea of non-intentionality. Non-intentionality happens when we drop touching purposefully, plans and decisions about the touch, and the will to affect the other body in a specific way, but still we are fully aware of the actions taking place. It is the place in which the knowledge of improvisation emerges. For Boullosa, in this non-intentional space energy flows are manifested:

> The sensation of non-intentionality is to find the place in which you let the body resolve . . . it's not acquired patterns, or social and cultural behavior . . . you need to observe all of that constantly unraveling at the mental and automatic physical levels that is not allowing the body to resolve in the moment by itself. . . . I realized this thanks to the energy movements: We can gain awareness about this, but we cannot just put those patterns aside, because we are a whole. But we can train that they not take the lead of our decisions. . . . It allows us to see other colors we can't see when that information is guiding my conduct. (Boullosa 2022)

Therefore, for Boullosa the concept of non-intentionality links the practice of improvisation with the possibility of personal and political transformation. This might also be what Nita Little points at when she speaks of oscillating attention: "Oscillating attention rolls awareness from this to that in rapid cycles of shifting concern, from the general to the particular, from a diffuse awareness to a clarifying one, or from emphasizing actions of perception to emphasizing actions of thought, etc." For Little, touch manifests humans' sense-ability, and through it we are, following Barad: ' "intra-acting' in that we change the very thing we are observing" (2013, 287). Little stresses as well that attentional activities alter what we get as a world, and she also links this phenomenological attitude with the possibility of political transformation: "These ideas are the foundation for another politics of attention that the dance brings to life through real people actualizing their worlds in motion" (2013, 289).

---

[5] Interview with Cristiane Boullosa on June 29, 2022.

220 Resistance and Support

Non-intentionality unfolds ambiguous sensations in the middle in which no touching roles, body parts, body or mind, seem to be clearly taking the lead or being completely passive. In our practice, we found that non-intentional touching was helpful to enter into an intense somatic sensation of being led by embodied movement and sensation, by the other's body, and by the space, into a state of soft presence, communion, and undifferentiation of bodies. In the end, this is very close to the somatically aware practice of CI in general. This is not a practice about crossing boundaries or exploring other people's bodies. It is about softening and turning off the dispositives of intention and will to find out what remains of movement and sensation when we purposefully let movement release from specific goals and mind control. There is space for pleasure, and there is also space for the subconscious. It is certainly a risky space, but so far it seems that this does not lead to aggressive behavior more than a highly intentional dancing space. Could training non-intentionality deactivate the possibility of aggression by creating a shared space of intimacy in between will and boundaries?

Is sexual touch just an intention that occurs (or not) along with any touch interaction? Or is it an outcome of some kind of shared quality of presence in touch? The idea that sexual intention exists as a separate internal state of mind might underpin the belief that CI is primarily a de-sexualized or de-erotized practice. I believe that sexuality and sexual feelings (as understood from this broad framework in XCI) do happen very often in CI practice and spaces, the same as gender performativity does, for example. Acknowledging the role of the politics of desire in CI might be necessary to widen understanding of consent, somatic consensus, or co-sensed practices in CI. Reducing the sexual to an intention that comes along with movement can lead to masking aggression and abuse. Abuse and aggression can happen even when there is no sexual intention if the victim's boundaries are crossed, and they can also happen even when a person consents, if the other person intends to cross their conscious or unconscious boundaries. Also, passivity and activity are not always aligned with feeling aggressive or inoffensive. We can feel passive and aggressive, for example, if we are feeling uncomfortable and we are experiencing a freezing response. We can also feel active and inoffensive, for example, when we unknowingly cross another person's boundaries. There is a lot of learning in this wide space in between that becomes narrowed down when speaking just of intention or lack of it.

XCI as a practice of non-intentionality in the interstices of CI and sexuality constitutes one possible queer sexuality perspective on touch that could detach the sexual and violence. This excludes consensual practices that involve playing with *the idea* of violence, though of course they play in a liminal yet hard angled space. Researching touch could be a laboratory to try the possibilities of reaching out, as Erin Manning puts it:

> To touch is not to manipulate. I cannot force you to touch. I can coerce you, I can take your body against your will, but I cannot evoke purposefully, in you, the response of my reaching out toward you. To touch is to tender, to be tender, to reach out tenderly. Perhaps this tendering is always, in some sense, a violence. It does violence to my subjectivity, to the idea that I am One. (Manning 2006, 36)

I think that Manning wants to limit the concept of touch to the shared space of the desire and pleasure in reaching toward. Violence in contact would fall out beyond the act of touching. This unknowability of the other person's response to our touching and the lack of transparency about the drive that pushes us to touch are at the base of any practice as research of touching and responsive movement. Following this trail of thought, XCI would only happen when participants are not experiencing aggression. If there is aggression, then participants are not engaging in a practice of touch in the interstices between queer sexuality and CI.

Queer activists in the CI scene have pointed out the mirage of consensus in CI. Michele Beaulieux talks of how claiming self-responsibility in CI, what has been called "the first rule": "'Take care of yourself'—is insufficient and, as the first priority, actively harmful . . . amplifies privilege, is difficult to invoke in the moment, fails to prevent violations, promotes victim blaming, and impacts who participates" (2019, 47). Sarah Gottlieb asserts that:

> What I'm proposing around consent, sexism, and ethical communication is actually not such a radical extension of the form. CI already develops skills related to consent and ethical communication. The concepts of listening and shared agency in a dance are considered fundamental. (2018)

A commitment with CI as a dance technique does help in solidifying a consensual and ethical approach to the relationship between bodies. But *saying* that consent/consensus is happening or that it is important, or bringing discourses about it to CI, is not enough. A community-oriented constant dialogue and questioning is also needed: "*contact improvisation includes developing social responsibility.* And so, part of being concerned with how we affect others means that we talk about ethical sexuality, boundary setting, and power dynamics" (Gottlieb 2018). Agreeing in setting boundaries collectively, creating all sorts of protocols, and training somatic specific skills around attunement and consent are crucial.

XCI is aligned with the idea of moving: "From an ecology of (immune) *consent* to an ecology of (exposed) *co-sense*" (Novella 2019, 141). Caro Novella, thinking from dance movement activism and feminist and queer scientific and sexual practices, proposes the concept of *co-sensing* as a mode of being in rehearsal that consists of: "Softening: staying tender while owning our actions; Permeating: making porous the practices and bodies we inhabit; and Arousing: animating unspoken and unimagined intimacies" (2019, 149–50). XCI would be a practice as research of co-sensing specific to the intersection of CI and queer sexuality. Like Manning's tendering, co-sensing is different from consensus and the threat of aggression, aiming to discover pathways for: "Working together across difference that does not require agreement or consensus on what is, and that, instead, attends to how we attune." Cosensing and consensus-making practices are complementary: "Cosensing . . . that does not throw away 'consent' as a tool to make visible power differentials between people and to engage with human-centered structural forces. This is not an either/or; it is a kind of training in holding difference together" (2019, 149–50).

Queer sexuality has delved into the boundaries and pleasures of consent, but co-sensing in XCI can unfold the qualities of presence of a nonviolent understanding of queer sexuality. XCI can open up a broader understanding of the sexual as intimate somatic experience: Elizabeth Povinelli's definition of an intimate encounter points in the direction of the undifferentiation we can experience through XCI (and CI): "We know it happened because it happened to both of us, and the sign that it happened is that we have been transformed. Its happening made us; it made one out of two" (2006, 188). This intimacy is related to the transformation of individual and collective identity. This is also what Manning seems to point at

222 Resistance and Support

when talking of touch as a tendering that makes violence to the idea that I am one. Boullosa's non-intentionality and Little's oscillating attention also gravitate toward that possibility. Seemingly, touch and intimacy in XCI connect the sexual with the idea of fading identity and fostering transformation.

XCI understands the sexual as a non-intentional quality of presence that fades gender identity and relations of domination, a nonviolent means of intimate communication unfolded by human-alive flesh in touch: a non-imitative language of flesh that comes from the growth of matter and movement in human life. We learn perception and movement from our own body, and it is life itself that moves a body. Many forms of knowledge that are in the genealogy of somatics, like some radical pedagogies of movement development[6] (Pikler 1968), BMC°, and other somatic techniques, attend to non-acquired movement patterns like primitive reflexes. (Bainbridge-Cohen 1993) Wilhelm Reich's[7] (1927) early reflections about the relationship between the psychic and the somatic are inspired by a non-imitational model of learning and thinking about the body. Somatics and CI's quest for understanding the body from within is connected to early life experience and the knowledge of improvisation over formal imitative training. Somatics and CI share the leitmotiv of releasing movement and gaining body autonomy, which entails a process of dis-identification from external authority. XCI wants to harvest these knowledges to practice what this process could entail in human sexuality.

In her book *The Bonds of Love*, feminist psychoanalyst Jessica Benjamin argues that Winnicott's "transitional space,"[8] especially its earliest manifestation (Sander's "open space"), allows for the solidification of personhood in the spatial exchanges of movement and touch, primarily with the adult caregiver, and potentially with other animated and inanimate bodies:

> The early representation of self and other evolves in part through a play of distance and closeness, a shifting of spatial boundaries between two bodies. When this play is successful, it is as if both partners are following the same score. The "dance" becomes the mediating element between the two subjects, the movement in the space between them. It is this quality of "in-between" that so often recurs in the spatial metaphor. (Benjamin 1988, 225)

This open space resembles the one opened by non-intentionality, in which identity is negotiated and yet flexible and transformable. I believe that CI and XCI re-create this transitional open space of play, which potentially unfolds a relational spatial touch and movement

---

[6] "Long years of experience have led the author to the conviction that children who have reached the stages of sitting and walking on their own initiative, through their own independent efforts, move more steadily, less spasmodically, with more adroitness and harmony than do other children. Though children uninstructed in motor skills are very courageous in practicing movements, they are less prone to accidents under normal circumstances. For example, from among 1400 children in the Institute since its founding 20 years ago, there has been no case of fracture, either in the Institute or later, among children whose motor development took place in the Institute." E. Pikler (1968), "Some Contributions to the Study of the Gross Motor Development of Children," *The Journal of Genetic Psychology* 113(1): 27–39. https://doi.org/10.1080/00221325.1968.10533806.

[7] "It never ceases to be surprising how the loosening of a muscular spasm not only releases the vegetative energy, but, over and above this, reproduces a memory of that situation in infancy in which the repression of the instinct occurred. It can be said *that every muscular rigidity contains the history and the meaning of its origin*. It is not as if we had to derive from dreams or associations how the muscular armor developed ; the armor is the form in which the infantile experience is preserved as an impairment of functioning" (Reich 1973, 300).

[8] "I have introduced the terms 'transitional object' and 'transitional phenomena' for designation of the intermediate area of experience, between the thumb and the teddy bear, between the oral erotism and true objectrelationship, between primary creative activity and projection of what has already been introjected" (Winnicott 1953, 90).

communication language. This space in between bodies opens up beyond the identities that become unsharpened and malleable, transforming it. In the practice of XCI, this transformation moves toward a practice of non-heteronormative and nonviolent sexual embodied communication.

Conclusion

XCI is a quest for intimacy within queer and feminist sexuality (though anti-ableist, neurodivergent, BIPOC, and other perspectives should also be included). XCI without these perspectives would be a form of violence. This makes XCI aspirational. I was specifically drawn to CI because of some early life experiences of playful practices of movement and intimate touch with same-age childhood peers. In the same period, I also experienced some abusive touch. Both sides of touch stayed with me and pushed me to research in touch. I believe that a deep somatic practice of CI can lessen the issues and enhance the sensations of mattering within the intimacy of porousness between bodies, intensifying perception and expanding it throughout all tissues and states of embody-mind-ment and relationality. This kind of experience is something many CI dancers report that they have experienced at least once, and normally a handful of times. Is this experience reproducible? Researching how sexual intimacy is embedded in CI could help to access some somatic aspects that are consistently repeated in these experiences.

What can XCI contribute to CI? Sexuality, CI, queer practices, and social spaces in general are affected by a pervasiveness of heteronormative poetics. In CI's social scene, these poetics are often taken for CI itself. This hampers CI in multiple ways. By imposing excessive intentionality and downgrading somatic experience, it prompts public display or excessive passivity. It rewards social status and one-to-one heteronormative interactions. Consequently, rather than fostering a practice of improvised embodied relationality within the space, CI resembles a couples dancing salon. Also, sometimes in CI contexts we use expressions like "emptying or draining of mass, lymphatic or blood fluxes," treating the practice of touch in CI like massage. We speak of "manipulation" about the interactions between bodies that are moving and bodies that are still. Or we hear about ethereal (sometimes even gendered as "feminine" and "masculine") "energies" that populate the space. By acknowledging that these instances may sometimes be sexual, we could move beyond heteronormativity capturing the CI space. This could contribute to explicitly stating power dynamics, boundaries, and desires that do happen in the CI space, instead of putting them aside or ignoring them. XCI shows that isolating the sexual from the CI space hinders the chance to research about sexual touch and can perpetuate power dynamics, because the sexual is reduced to private mental states that come along with neutral actions, instead of being a genuine quality of presence. The sexual becomes silenced and taboo. XCI can offer some practices which could help to be responsible and nuanced toward this reality while acknowledging it, making the sexual present and accountable in the space.

What can be XCI's contribution beyond CI? XCI allows us to expand notions and practices of sexual and political consent and consensus, and opens up the possibility of articulating sexual co-sensing and somatic communication and relationality in theory and practice. XCI delves into how political awareness constitutes sexual somatic awareness. It delves into the possibility of accessing a de-gendered sexuality through CI and whether such an experience can be cultivated and shared. XCI allows a process of softening our sexual and gender identity in which we also face some difficulties: our attachment to the symbolic order and heteronormative sexuality; the existence of other axes of oppression we might not be paying attention to; and the existence of violence. But XCI is not limited to an identarian queer inquiry in the context of CI. XCI understands the sexual as a quality of touch that is only present when there is no aggression and no need for consent. It points at those scarce experiences of radical porousness between bodies embracing the fleshiness and diffuseness of sexuality as a driving force of life in which desire and curiosity for human bodies could eventually destabilize performative, symbolic practices. This co-sensed sexuality could open access to a nonviolent sexual somatically embodied communication. XCI might be one research strategy to materialize a language of flesh yet to be articulated.

References

Bainbridge Cohen, B. (1993). *Sensing, Feeling, and Action: The Experiential Anatomy of Body-Mind Centering.* Northampton, Mass: Contact Editions.

Beaulieux, M. (2019). *How the First Rule Brought #MeToo to Contact Improvisation. Contact Quarterly* Vol. 44.1 (Winter/Spring): 46–49. https://contactquarterly.com/cq/article-gallery/view/how-the-first-rule-brought-metoo-to-contact-improvisation.

Benjamin, J. (1988). *The Bonds of Love: Psychoanalysis, Feminism, and the Problem of Domination.* New York: Pantheon Books. http://archive.org/details/bondsoflovepsych00benj.

Boullosa, C. (2022). Interview by Aramo Olaya.

Butler, J. (1999). *Gender Trouble: Feminism and the Subversion of Identity.* New York: Routledge.

Gottlieb, S. (2018). *Myths to Break Down: Moving toward Ethical Communication and Ethical Sexuality in CI. Contact Improvisation* (blog). http://contactimprovblog.com/myths-to-break-down-moving-toward-ethical-communication-and-ethical-sexuality-in-ci/.

Hunter, L. (2019). *Politics of Practice: A Rhetoric of Performativity* (1st ed.). Palgrave Macmillan.

Hunter, L. (2022). "Seminario Internacional de Estudios Artísticos en La Universidad Distrital Francisco José de Caldas," Facultad de Artes ASAB, Bogotá, Colombia.

Intro to Touch&Play. (n.d.). Google Docs. Retrieved May 31, 2022, from https://docs.google.com/document/d/10ayW8sZq2w5beVD94IjreyWWRQWSCILtsCinCGqt8U/edit?usp=embed_facebook.

Manning, E. (2006). *Politics of Touch: Sense, Movement, Sovereignty.* First edition. Minneapolis, MN: University Of Minnesota Press.

Manning, E. (2013). *Always More than One: Individuation's Dance.* Durham, NC: Duke University Press.

Nelson, N. L. (2014). *Articulating presence: creative actions of embodied attention in contemporary dance.* (unpublished dissertation) University of California, Davis.

Novella, C. (2019). "From Consent to Cosense: Rehearsing Ecologies of Exposure within Quimera Rosa's Trans*Plant, My Disease is an Artistic Creation* / Del Consentimiento al Cosentir: Ensayando Ecologías del Estar Expuesta en Trans*Plant, mi enfermedad es una creación artística de Quimera Rosa Do consentimento ao Cosentir: Ensaiando Ecologias de Ser Exposta na Trans* Plant, minha doença é uma criação artística da Quimera Rosa." *Revista Corpo-grafías, Estudios críticos de y desde los cuerpos* 6(6): 135–152. https://doi.org/10.14483/25909398.14234.

Olaya, A. y Skrzypczak, W. (2019) "Queer Contact Improvisation (QCI): Alliance and Disruption Experiences and Reflections from the QCI Symposium and Festival Hamburg 2018." *Contact Quarterly* 44(2) (Summer–Fall): 50–53. https://contactquarterly.com/cq/article-gallery/view/queer-contact-improvisation-qci-alliance-and-disruption#

Pikler, E. (1968). "Some Contributions to the Study of the Gross Motor Development of Children." *The Journal of Genetic Psychology* 113(1): 27–39. https://doi.org/10.1080/00221325.1968.10533806

Povinelli, E. A. (2006). *The Empire of Love: Toward a Theory of Intimacy, Genealogy, and Carnality.* Durham, NC: Duke University Press.

Reich, W. (1973). *The Function of the Orgasm: Sex-economic Problems of Biological Energy.* New York, Farrar, Straus and Giroux. Available at: http://archive.org/details/functionoforgas01reic (accessed October 31, 2022).

Winnicott, D. W. (1953). "Transitional Objects and Transitional Phenomena: A Study of the First Not-me Possession." *The International Journal of Psycho-Analysis* 34(2): 89–97.

12

Rolling and Knowing

Reflections on the Endurance of the CI Event

Brian Schultis

My first CI dance after the COVID pandemic shut everything down is in late summer 2021, in an athletic field on the campus of Oberlin College. My partner is Sophie, a student whom I used to dance with before the pandemic. They're here as part of a summer term and organized this as a jam, but the two of us were the only ones who showed up. The dancing feels awkward, difficult. I'm rusty from the time off, but we're dancing. Gradually, my body readjusts to the sensations of another body, to following the impulses that come from it. Torsos connected, I roll on the dry grass and feel the compression of my body against the ground as Sophie slides onto me. I keep rolling and feel the compression of each part of my body in turn—my soft under-belly supported by sternum and the points of my ischial crests, the high structure of my side body, riding high on the trochanter and shoulder, following the curve of bone down to my back, spine-tail-glutes-scapulae. At the same time, I feel the parts of Sophie's body in similar succession as they ride my roll, perpendicular. First come the shoulder and ribs, then a little dip into the softness of the kidney/belly, then the bony structure of pelvis, which takes most of their weight with it as it rolls off me, leaving still to come the linear thighs and calves. Sophie curls to end up next to me as they come off, and once we're side by side in the grass they begin to roll, and I extend my arm over them to change roles. Now I am on top, riding the changes from front, to side, to back to side along my own verticality. We continue, the world spinning in soft focus as I come over, under, upside down, right side up, and soon these lose meaning and there is only blue sky, brown-green grass, and sun-heated skin.

Come fall, a few more dancers arrive in Oberlin. The dance department teaches an introductory class. Regular jams happen again. Come January, an international residency assembles at Oberlin. We dance almost every day. We grow and change and struggle. In July, almost 300 dancers are here for the Critical Mass: CI @ 50 *event. People leave pretty quickly after that, but there are a few who stick around. We keep dancing together. Now it's late August, the only dancer still here is Sophie. They're not a student anymore, graduated in May, but working in town for the summer, forestalling their return home. We dance together in the athletic field, and it doesn't hit me until we are going that it's almost exactly a year since that previous dance. It feels like the end of a cycle—the tentative first dance, all the people and dances that followed, and then back to me and this single partner in this same field. It's almost like we rolled together and got back to the same point of contact. The year of spinning and sliding and rolling a macrocosm of the simple yet profound shared movement that had started it. So, there it is . . . a year of dancing.*

I find myself struck dumb by the monumental accumulation of this movement: a tangle of sensations, the press of ribs and tailbones, wood floors and grass and sand, the smell of sweat and dust and grass, the heat of bodies, the passage from soft flesh to hard bone and back, wispy electrified body hair, fabrics, visions of rooms swirling, kaleidoscopic, lying in bed and feeling my body still moving—like on a ship. There is nothing to write about this. I can only write after it—this great density of sensation—the emptying of my language from which something else might emerge.

Faced with this inarticulate mass of sensation, I have a few options:

1. I can simply be silent, move on with my life, let it be.
2. I can articulate things that I learned from it. These could be technical things, for example, I learned to respond to different stimuli from my partner in a more varied ways, to execute CI "skills" with more ease and clarity; or they could be more abstract things, for example, I learned to trust myself, to be comfortable with instability and change, to set clear physical and psychological boundaries with others. These things-that-I-learned could be described as embodied knowledge—things which I couldn't explain but have as part of a physical vocabulary or embodied memory, or they could be further articulated as "insights"—things that I could explain or create a series of images to help someone else understand.
3. I could attempt to describe some of the things that happened, either in a technical way ("with a strong-quick-indirect move up and toward my right side I spread onto my partner's lower back") or in a much more metaphorical and imagistic way ("we swirled into the serenity of simple and subtle movement").

All of these responses have much to recommend them, and in the course of this essay, I will engage in all of them (including the first—leaving certain parts unmentioned). Other chapters in this volume explore them in greater detail. I bring them up in this way, though, because my intention in this chapter is not actually to give a report on my year of CI dancing, but to show some of the questions, difficulties, and possibilities around doing so. In this effort, this year of dancing becomes a case study which I hope will make these issues clear to both other dancers and to anyone who undergoes rich, complex, physical processes.

Here's the fundamental problem I'd like to address: with the possible exception of the first option (silence), these possibilities are predicated on a transition from something that actualized over time (the dancing) to something that endures through time (an insight, an embodied association, a description). This transition takes place at both the social-discursive level I've been discussing (what I say to others) and the personal level (what I say to myself— the structure of my memory). It has a politics and an economics. Typically, what institutions call knowledge and have given a requisite value is what endures through time—what is actualized over time can only attain value by undergoing the transition to this form.

Anthropologist Tim Ingold calls this valuation based on a transition from actualization to endurance a "logic of inversion," a process which "turns the pathways along which life is lived into boundaries within which it enclosed" (2011, 146). This logic is so pervasive that it seems almost self-evident. It is based on the idea that even as we know that life proceeds along pathways of movement and change over time, that the way we *know* it is by a series of representations of points along it. What we call a fact might be true for all time and everywhere, or it might be true in relation to a particular context, but it is always contained outside of the embodied events in which it is embedded. We read about it in a book or article or see it in an image. It is contained somewhere—on a hard drive, in the library, in your brain. To attempt to *know* life otherwise, to know it along pathways, feels very foreign. Ingold, an anthropologist, sees this possibility in "the understandings of the lifeworld professed by peoples commonly characterized in ethnographic literature as animists" (2011, 63).

To know life outside the logic of inversion requires another idea of what knowledge is and how it forms, another logic of knowing. Yet it is precisely such an alternative logic that would be necessary to speak after this year of dancing, because as Ingold points out, the logic of inversion is ultimately reductive. The meaning, the knowledge, the value of my dancing comes not only from what endures after it in memories, words, documentation, and insights, but in the ephemeral unfolding of the dancing in its own time. An alternative logic would need to honor *that* and include it in the conception of knowledge. And it is this that this essay seeks to describe.

Here I go back to the movement itself—not to say what it "meant," but to attest that a logic of knowledge-in-formation was happening that is perhaps continued but not validated or justified by these words-that-come-after it. I go back to that movement where my partner and I rolled together across the field and see in it the physicalization of Ingold's metaphor of inversion. Here our bodies are continually inverting, going upside-down, but significantly, they are also coming back. The motion of inversion is not final, not reductive, but generative of an ongoing flow of movement and relationship. In making this connection between the inversion of my body in dance and Ingold's inversion of pathways and their representations, I've blithely skipped between the metaphorical and the literal, the discursive and the embodied, the abstract and the specific, and that's the point. To right the inversion which values the enduring and abstract over the ephemeral event of movement, it is necessary to put these registers—metaphor, movement, memory, idea, action, pathway—into harmonic dialogue, just as my rolling puts my back body in harmonic dialogue with my front, and Sophie's body in harmonic dialogue with mine.

In this way I will propose the act of rolling itself as a logic for the production of knowledge which operates as an alternative to the logic of inversion described by Ingold. By a logic for the production of knowledge, I mean a way of thinking about the problem I posed in relation to my year of dancing at Oberlin—about the relationship between what took place over that stretch of time and what remains and endures after it. To do this, I will describe the way rolling affects the appearance of space. This is important because the production of knowledge is based on the idea of space as a ground for events to endure. This spatialization might take a variety of forms. It involves the localization of a past event in geography ("the dance happened on the athletic field at Oberlin college") or on the body ("my head, my back," etc.). It also involves locating the knowledge in a spatial container where it can endure—books, brains, and so on. Following such philosophers as Henri Bergson and Gilles Deleuze, I will argue here that this space that underlies the enduring character of knowledge is not a neutral container, but appears differently according to the logics of production we enact. So I will discuss rolling as producing knowledge according to two tensions in the appearance of space. First, I will discuss the tension between extensive and intensive space, and then between smooth and striated space, as described by Gilles Deleuze and Félix Guattari. I will argue that the logic of inversion recognizes and values only extensive and striated space, which fundamentally excludes the movement itself from its appearance as knowledge. Rolling does not simply replace extensive and striated space with intensive and smooth, but interjects these forms of spatialization into the production of knowledge in a way that values the event in its temporality and ongoing-ness.

Intensity: Individuality and Knowledge

It is spring break at Oberlin College. Most of the students are gone and so a few of the international dancers here for a six-month residency have the achingly beautiful Warner Main Space to "ourselves." It's evening and the lights are low. I lie on the softly glowing wood floor and breathe. The breathing makes my body subtly grow and shrink. Gradually that growing and shrinking expands from my torso to my whole body, my limbs participating. I find myself next to Gabi and slowly we begin to roll together like Sophie and I did that summer afternoon—it's a common pattern in CI. First, I shorten and curl toward him, then I lengthen again across his body, my earlier curl having taken us from parallel to perpendicular. As I come across, I curl and shorten again as I reach the other side and we return to parallel. We roll together across the space—huge for only a handful of dancers—maintaining this fundamental technique, but also delighting in all the variations that lead to new positions and discoveries, sometimes bringing us up off the floor but usually back down again. We keep going—around and around the space and around and around each other. Through all of this, the initial growing and shrinking I did by myself continues, echoing and building on my breathing. But through my rolling with the floor and with Gabi, it has transformed from something internal to something that explores the whole vast space.

Two important characteristics from this episode stand out for a discussion of a logic of rolling. First is the character of the growing and shrinking of my body in the warm-up, which I will argue works in intensive space, and subsequently how this intensive movement is incorporated into, but also transformed, by my rolling with Gabi.

The logic of inversion works in extensive space which can be divided into units. Objects within it may have positions which can be expressed in relation to each other, but fundamentally their position is expressible within a matrix that is independent of the relative position of things in it. Your GPS unit helps you find a specific house not by measuring a relationship between your position and that of the house, but by independently measuring your position and the house's relative to coordinates interposed on the earth by a satellite, expressible numerically, and then comparing those values. It doesn't matter what is next to the house on the ground, all that matters is the relationship to the matrix.

Intensity works differently. A level of intensity can be measured and quantified—as the intensity of heat is measured and quantified by temperature—but the frames of reference are internal to the intensity. Thus, the value of a certain temperature is meaningful only in terms of how it is different from other degrees of heat. Whereas it really doesn't matter what is next to your house when the GPS finds it, with intensities it does matter what is next to any point that can be pulled out of it; 80 degrees is only meaningful in relation to 79 and 81, the qualitative difference between them, and the necessity of passing through every possible degree of temperature when it changes. This relativity within intensity necessarily folds in a duration. The expression of a certain degree of heat is not abstract, it is indivisible from the entire intensive system of heating and cooling whose endurance provides the coherence of any degree within it. Even what appear to be fixed points, such as the freezing point of water, are thresholds which mark where the dynamic change of a system can be registered. Intensity implies disequilibrium, change, movement. It is defined not in terms of absolute values, but by its difference from the extremes. It implies repetition, not an impossible repetition of the same, but the resonance or reference of an earlier time in the later one. Human movement, such as my warm-up before rolling with Gabi, is intensive. Our muscles tense and release incrementally,

230 Resistance and Support

toward and away from the ends of our range of motion. You could artificially fix a point of my movement by taking a photograph with a fast shutter speed, but that position would be definable only in relation to the larger flow of movement which led into and out of it. This intensity is characteristic not only of CI warm-ups, but all human movement, perhaps finding a precarious equilibrium in stillness and sleep, but never ceasing the fundamental intensive movement, the growing and shrinking of our lungs and torso as we breathe, until death.

Identifying the movement of the human individual as intensively growing and shrinking is an important first gesture in our logic of rolling. A concept of an individual can function as a kind of containment par excellence. An individual, in this way of thinking, is *at* a certain place. It changes its location and then is *at* another place. The pathways it took are completely subordinated to the places where it ends up. You could take a single snapshot of that movement at any moment and, because the individual is distinct from the flow of their movement, say *where* that individual is at that moment. By reframing the individual as intensive growing and shrinking, I'm interrupting this view of individual as enclosure. An individual is not a point in space. It is an intensive *movement* involved in an indivisible flow of time. The life of that individual is not something it *has*, but is integral to its being and appearance in the world.

Yet we don't only move in place, we also move *through* space, and here it is not enough to be an individual. We need a partner. A rocket can travel through the vacuum of space by discharging fuel in the opposite direction of where its scientist steerers want it to go. It essentially gives itself a partner to push off of—makes itself two. We humans can't do that— we need a partner outside—the floor or ground or another body. Our movement through space is always a shared dance, as Steve Paxton says: "solo dancing does not exist: the dancer dances with the floor" (1977, 3). This partner transforms our growing and shrinking. Try this movement—or if you can't where you are, imagine it. Lie on your back and lengthen your body, as you shorten again, yield into the floor and enclose your right side over your left so that you roll onto your left side. Lengthen and spread again, yield into the floor, shorten and enclose as you roll onto your stomach. Repeat this rolling, paying attention to all the ways in which your individual vitality—your growing and shrinking—works periodically, and also observe how you've traveled through space. This rolling is the fundamental action which takes us from being an individual grower-shrinker into being a *mover*. Sure, we can push off a surface perpendicularly, and move through space without technical rolling, but this possibility is limited. Almost every movement we make in relation to another body (and I'm counting the earth as a body here) involves at least some rolling. Bipedal walking, that paradigmatic movement of the human through space, is predicated on the roll between the foot and the ground. Running shortens this rolling surface but doesn't eliminate it. Our rolling and the mutuality on which it depends bring our life (growing-shrinking) into the world.

The place where bodies roll against each other—what is often referred to in CI as the rolling point of contact—is therefore an important place. We might conventionally view the skin as a kind of interface between an individual and the environment, but the skin, so conceived, is actually very different from the rolling point of contact as I'm developing it here. Skin-as-interface is a container which locates the body in extensive space. The rolling point of contact is the place along which the body comes into being as intensity in relationship. It has no meaning outside the lived duration of the dance. Although we call it a point, it is locatable only in the abstract—if you artificially froze the movement, you could give it a place. It is always moving, and the play of intensities happens *along* it.

For philosopher Gilles Deleuze, it is the relationship between intensive series that constitutes the ontological difference that makes the universe come to be. This is an important and radical idea in that it shifts our perspective on both being and movement. In this view, neither being nor movement can be seen as properties of things. Movement is not something which things do, it is something that they are. Being happens along the edges between intensities, in their rolling points of contact, which are themselves the source of both intensive series and the "forced movement" which keeps them in development:

> Once communication between heterogeneous series is established, all sorts of consequences follow within the system. Something "passes" between the borders, events explode, phenomenon flash, like thunder and lightning. Spatio-temporal dynamisms fill the system, expressing simultaneously the resonance of the coupled series and the amplitude of the forced movement which exceeds them. (Deleuze 1994 [1968], 118)

Contact dancers participate in these "spatio-temporal dynamisms" in their dancing, not only in the sense of experiencing and illustration of an abstract idea, but because they work and live along the creative edges between intensive series.

This ontological idea of a resonance between intensive series is useful for thinking of knowledge as an event which works between duration and spatiality. It creates an edge or boundary not through spreading or separating bodies in abstract space, but through the emergence of a set of phenomena that functions as an edge because of the way it conditions the intensities that participate in it. Rolling is never generic. It is always particular to the bodies rolling (still including the earth as a body). The floors of many dance studios aspire to a kind of generic neutrality. They are usually flat and smooth. Yet any dancer who has danced on many knows that they all have a particular character. So too, of course, with human bodies. In his studies on the Aikido Roll, Crescent Roll (first developed by Simone Forti), and Helix Roll, Steve Paxton has pushed the limits of a body's uniform rolling surface, exploring how to roll with the absolute minimum effort or change in shape (2008). This is an interesting experiment and a valuable training, but no matter how perfectly spherical one makes oneself in an Aikido Roll, there is still a difference between rolling over the outside of the arm and the small of the back. Linked by the action of rolling, these differences become intensive—the hardness of your rolling partner's bone takes meaning in relation to the softness of their more muscled parts. Rolling, as I have argued, transforms oscillatory intensities into open-ended ones. This applies to the way rolling acts as an interface between the individual and world, but it also applies to the way in which the characteristics of the contact between two bodies carries into the future. As Heraclitus might remind us, we can't roll over the same point twice, but rolling puts what does repeat (my shoulder again, this spot on the floor again) and what is new into tension. Along the lines we roll, we encounter a history of bodies rolling together which actualized and transformed in each new turn of the body—time transformed into ongoing intensive space: a space at the edge of duration. A site of knowledge in-formation.

Rolling and Sensation: Smooth and Striated Space

The sun is streaming through windows of the slightly smaller dance studio next to Warner Main Space on this warm spring day, but I can't see the individual windows as my soft gaze

232   Resistance and Support

flies around the room, only a bright blur. My head is too far out on the end of these spiral movements to be much use as a steady guide. At times I find the ground, but even this is transitory, passing. I roll through it, taking energy and a moment of support from it and then moving on, around to another body part up into the air. The constant that I am oriented to is the rolling point of contact on Becca's body. This is, of course, not constant at all. It changes as we shift orientations with each other, exchange support, roll across backs, stomachs, and thighs; come into and out of the ground. Yet this, along with my body's sense of gravity, is enough to orient me. We keep enough peripheral awareness to avoid crashing into the walls or other dances, but I'm guided not by where I am in the room but by where I am in relation to Becca, and not even Becca as a totality, but the transitions between one sensation and another as the area of contact changes—from hard ribs to soft belly, from the extreme angle of the shoulder into the recessed neck and the sweat-moistened hardness of the head, from the bonier mass of the coccyx into the more precarious lumbar and thoracic vertebrae, from the narrow, rigid extended arms and legs to the denser, more complex and massive torso. The identity of the body parts doesn't even register, I use them here only to help you understand. What matters is the shifting sensations.

Two aspects of my perception of space in my dance with Becca stand out. The first is my orientation through the successive stimulus of touch over time, rather than an overarching visual perspective. The second is the way that my movements break the pattern of maintaining a visual orientation on the horizon in a way that takes my body into circular and spiral geometries. Both of these relations to space bring about what Gilles Deleuze and Félix Guattari would call "smooth space," which they put into tension with "striated space" (1989 [1980], 474–500). Deleuze and Guattari describe the geometry which underpins the logic of inversion as "striated space." Striated space is an open container. It exists prior to and independently of the things which may come to be located in it. It is navigated according to real or virtual lines which striate Cartesian coordinates, urban grids, longitude and latitude, GPS waypoints. The fundamental unit of this kind of space is the point—the location where something *is*. This locating within open space effects is what Ingold calls "enclosure." As a contrast, Deleuze and Guattari offer "smooth space," in which locations are determined not by reference to an external overlaid grid which opens the space, but to the durational trajectories of movement that pass through them. There are echoes here of the extensive-intensive tension I described earlier. Where that language spoke to the spatial component of my body's differentiation from and joining with the broader world, this language speaks to these ideas through the perspective of a sensing being.

An important feature of Deleuze and Guattari's concept of smooth and striated space is that it conceptually links the form of space with the perception and action of bodies within it. Neither smooth nor striated space is a default which exists in the world to be encountered. They are brought about by embodied actions, by conscious and unconscious perceptions, and by the interpretations and concepts which are drawn from them. This principle underpins my argument that the way we move underlies the way space appears, which underlies the way knowledge is produced.

One way in which Deleuze and Guattari describe smooth space is by associating it with what they call "close vision." While Deleuze and Guattari stay with vision as the primary sense mode in this description because they base it on the art-history writing of Aloïs Riegl, they directly relate this kind of vision to touch in ways that are relevant to CI: "The first aspect of the haptic, smooth space of close-vision is that its orientations, landmarks, and linkages are in continuous variation; it operates step by step" (Deleuze and Guattari 1989 [1980], 493). Rather than taking in an entire vantage at once, it works along a line or trajectory.

In the history of discourse on CI, particularly in the work of Steve Paxton, this step-by-step experience has been explored through the distinction between perception and sensation. Paxton introduced his study *Material for the Spine* by stating that it "takes as given that the palette of the dancer exists as sensations of the body" (Paxton 2008). His interest in sensation appears throughout his written and verbal statements and seems to be a touchpoint of his career, but it is a slippery concept. For sensations to be a "palette," they must be not only something that the body experiences, but something expressive. Elsewhere in *Material for the Spine*, Paxton discusses sensation as working in relation to desire and action—as a kind of link between them—suggesting that for him, sensations carry with them an embodied understanding of how to physically realize a certain form. So why does he call these "sensations" as opposed to, say, "skills"? Why the emphasis on a conscious awareness of what the body is doing and experiencing which pervades much of *Material for the Spine* and his entire body of work?

To help answer these questions, we might look to an important reference for Paxton— James Gibson, whose 1966 book, *The Senses Considered as Perceptual Systems*, Paxton considered an important discovery when he read it in 1972 (Paxton 2018). Surprisingly, though, Gibson appears to be somewhat anti-sensation. The thesis of *The Senses Considered as Perceptual Systems* is that rather than a series of discreet senses providing the brain with a string of discreet sensations which it must then process and coordinate to make judgments about what is happening in the environment, many sense organs coordinate as a system to furnish information that is integrated into an awareness of the environment without intermediary "sensations." The eyes don't send the brain an image of a cat from which it concludes that there is one there—a whole system of senses picks up a variety of stimuli that corroborate the idea of a cat in the environment and you recognize the cat's presence pre-consciously. Paxton's insistence on sensations as the palette of the dancer reads against Gibson, and this idea is supported by the theme in Paxton's work of attending to typically unconscious processes. Take the "Stand," for example (see Greco, Chapter 8 in this volume), in which the doer makes no consciously chosen movements but attends to the "small dance" which the body does automatically in order to maintain upright posture. The purpose here is not to teach the body to stand—it already knows how to do that—but to be aware of the usually unconscious play of stimulus and response which maintains that standing: the sensations.

Sensations in this sense are a kind of inhibiting or slowing down the process by which information from our sense organs is translated into information about our environment. This does give them a kind of creative openness. Where perception synthesizes a variety sense input into a broad overall experience, sensation keeps experience in its progressive pieces, experienced "step-by-step" over time. Sensation is thus not only a creative technique within CI, but fundamental to the way it shifts the appearance of space toward smoothness. The relationship between sensation and rolling doubles the relationship between growing-shrinking and movement in that the progressive ongoing movement from and along the rolling point of contact develops the sensation of the mover over time, giving it concrete duration in the absence of an overall spectacle.

Smooth Geometries: Spherical and Spiral Spaces

Another way in which rolling generates smooth space is by orienting the body into geometries that are curvilinear rather than gridded. The concept of "spherical space" has had wide circulation in CI discourse, and it is one way in which intervention can be conceived. CI practitioners describe a spherical space within CI, in contrast to a view of space that is oriented by a horizontal horizon. Again, following the concept of perceptual systems from Gibson, this visual confirmation of the horizontal is combined with the sensation of gravity to construct a three-dimensional perceptual matrix of the environment. The disorienting inversions of my dance with Becca prevented me from orienting on the horizon and opened my perception to spherical space. Unlike horizon-space, spherical space implies motion inasmuch as humans can only see a certain part of a spherical field at any one time. True spherical space requires movement to establish visual contact with the spherical range. Thus, the perception of spherical space is inherently smooth. It is not something that can be located, but something which you establish by moving through it.

The human body is adapted to moving through space while maintaining a vertical axis in relation to the horizon. This is walking. We do this by rolling on the relatively small area of the base of the feet and exchanging one foot for the other. This exchange of feet replaces the continuation of the roll along a circular arc with a fall forward which the next foot catches—translating a circular trajectory into a lateral one. The eyes face forward and can be held level. When we roll on other surfaces of our body, we exchange this coordination of falls and catches which allow us to keep a steady horizon with a continuous roll which cycles around a circular shape such as the ribcage or pelvis, or a pathway we can make circular such as the spine or the diagonal from the pinky finger through to the opposite ischium. Rolling along these circular or spheroid surfaces takes the eyes off the horizontal into corresponding circular paths through the environment.

In addition to the spherical field of perception, rolling also spatializes in spirals around an axis. Any rolling has two components—the surfaces which roll across each other, and the axis or axes around which the bodies rotate. To this point we've discussed the rolling surface to some extent, but less this axis. Its importance lies as a sensory point of reference. Anatomists and somatic practitioners often refer to an individual body's axis as a central vertical line around which it might rotate. In CI, however, rolling often involves multiple bodies, in which case the axis around which the rolling takes place is often not at the center of any of the individual bodies (the center of mass of multiple bodies dancing together shifts in similar ways). Rolling across the floor, I can feel the axis of rotation just a little bit off the ground and moving through space. As I spiraled around Becca, I could feel the axis of this rotation changing and moving in relation to our movement. When our bodies spiraled together and we rolled as a single unit, then the axis could actually be touched—it corresponded to the point of contact between our two bodies. In the disorientation of spiraling and rolling, the axis provides a reference which emerges from the movement. It is not there waiting to be discovered, but comes about in the rolling, is a product of that rolling. Following Deleuze's idea of the emergence of space of resonance between intensive series—it is an edge created by the unfolding of the movement. The axis of the roll sets up an intensive space in that things and events spatialize relative to it—toward the axis or away from it, a distinction or progression which also relates to speed and ease of the rotation.

These sensed geometries are important because they set up the spatial structure along which intensive rolling knowledge emerges. They bring about the tension between the new and repeated. They build along the geometries of the human bodies, the characteristics of physical spaces, and the styles and personalities of individual dancers. CI dancers don't learn so much as maintain this knowledge as each new sphere and spiral builds on and relates back to all those that came before.

Conclusion: Rolling with Language

The warm wood of the floor lights up in the small yoga studio in Cleveland where I've come to a jam. It contrasts the winter darkness outside the windows. This essay has gone through several drafts. My year of dancing feels distant in my memory. I find Emily next to me and I extend my leg over her, rotating the thigh slightly to allow it to connect to her hip joint as she rolls, my body rotating and sliding across hers and then into the floor again to accept her weight as she rides across me as I continue the roll. I'm still rolling—not again but still. To pull out a year—the time between one sticky summer dance and another—is like noticing that you've come back to a similar point—from my back to my back again. Yet that's not the end. Nor do I take something from it with me to these new dances, these new rolls. The resonance I can feel between my dance with Emily now and all that year of dancing is a glimmer of meaning that shimmers above the texture of a continuing movement.

In these last two sections I've discussed the ways in which the physical action of rolling establishes space in a way that can underpin a logic of knowledge production. With this established, it's time to turn directly to my original question: What can I and should I say after a period of dancing? This essay could provide an argument for my first option—to not say anything, to insist that the way the movement endures is in its continuation in future movement, in my dance with Emily and not this essay. Yet I have said things about this year of movement, from the very beginning when I recalled those year-apart dances. How does this relate to rolling, which now must move back from literal rolling, to taking the term to mean something more figurative? One way in which this year of rolling has appeared in this essay is through examples. An example straddles the particular and the general. The themes of my essay were general, but the examples were particular. They referred to specific moments of dance, and I signaled that by naming Sophie, Gabi, Becca, and Emily (and attaining their permission to do so) and specifying details about the place and context of the dances. I could have made my point by referring to many dances I have had or by invoking common CI patterns. I didn't. I chose *these* dances to illustrate my ideas. I think of these examples as points of contact between the physical and the conceptual, where through a linguistic gesture the singularity of the movement relates to the conceptual world without being consumed by it. I see this as a similar structure to the way the intensive growing and shrinking of an individual body is brought into relation with broader space by rolling against a surface. The examples offer a kind of rolling point of contact between the concepts and the events in a way which I hope productively destabilizes the ideas of the essay.

Another way I have attempted to incorporate rolling into my writing after dancing is to focus on places where I find myself located as waypoints within a smooth, intensive system. This entails a certain humility in the writing. I do not offer a holistic overview, but a perspective from the middle. I did this by writing a series of poems that spoke not of whole dances,

236 Resistance and Support

but of specific pauses or points of clarity within them. I'll finish this essay with two of them. I hope they not only express something about that particular pause, but also evoke the unspoken pathways of movement which led into and out of them. These poems are the final example, illustrating my ideas about writing on dancing, but of course they are also particular images which have the capacity to take your imagination in many directions, rolling across your own memories and experiences toward the future.

> *A hard bump into the ground wakes us up*
> *From this dream of heat*
> *And taut muscles*
> *And sliding releases*
> *And fast spins*
> *And going and going again and going again and going again*
> *Wakes us up*
> *To the blinking fireflies and buzzing mosquitoes*
>
> *I've lost all sense of direction*
> *Or orientation on your body*
> *A shoulder? A knee?*
> *Intervals of smooth melting interrupted by shocks of strength*
> *Only the floor, bones, and flesh hold constant*
> *Until a pause*
> *I find . . . yes, your head*
> *On my slightly twisted torso*
> *The stillness is like a center—the eye of this galaxy*
> *The pause stretches long*
> *Cosmic time*
> *Yet the slightest impulse*
> *Will set us swirling again.*

References

Deleuze, Gilles. 1994 [1968]. *Difference and Repetition*. Trans. Paul Patton. New York: Columbia University Press.

Deleuze, Gilles, and Felix Guattari. 1989 [1980]. *A Thousand Plateaus: Capitalism and Schizophrenia*. Trans. Brian Massumi. Minneapolis: University of Minnesota Press.

Gibson, James J. 1966. *The Senses Considered as Perceptual Systems*. Boston: Houghton Mifflin.

Ingold, Tim. 2011. *Being Alive: Essays on Knowledge, Movement, Description*. New York: Routledge.

Paxton, Steve. 1977. *Contact Quarterly* 2, no. 3 (Spring), 24.

Paxton, Steve. 2008. *Material for the Spine*. DVD-ROM. Brussels: Contredanse.

Paxton, Steve. 2018. *Gravity*. Brussels: Contredanse.

13

Something We Touch or That Touches Us

A Newcomer Locating Themselves in Contact

Lisa Claire Greene

I am relatively new to Contact Improvisation (CI), having started dancing the form in September 2021 with no prior knowledge of it whatsoever. In order to unpack this entrance and make sense of what happened in my body, there are two main intertwining threads of experience that I want to trace here. One has to do with what felt like a personally transformative initiation into Contact which led me to examine how such processes can occur in CI via a framework of neuroplasticity and integrated awareness. The other is how this transformation was contrasted by a sobering and maddeningly slow reveal of CI's own history that included exclusionary narratives. For our purposes, both are important for unpacking what can happen in the body when we start engaging with this form, and what kind of effects that exposure can have.

In June 2021, I began practicing Aikido. Having grown up doing Tae Kwon Do and Tai Chi, I loved returning to martial arts; the discipline, the attention to a mind/body connection, the new pathways that were opened during training as both the *uke* and *torinage*.[1] However, I felt an interest in exploring these elements in a more free-form way, and it was with this intention that I reached out to a friend to visit her dance community. She mentioned "CI," but I thought this was the name of the person who had started the group and was surprised to learn it was the name of a dance form that had been around for almost 50 years. In that humorous and uncannily perfect way, I stumbled upon CI as a dance form that gave me a vocabulary to explore the connection I had to my own body, in a way that was complementary to Aikido.

Almost immediately—and in a way I have heard many other CI dancers describe—I felt the personal transformative potential in dancing this form. Being prompted to turn inward, to close my eyes and pay attention to the sensation of another person tapping up my arms and legs with their fingers, putting light pressure on my limbs, and sweeping their hands in considerate arcs over my body. Being offered the first tiny impulse of a rolling point of contact, and observing where it took me in my first duet with a partner; being reintroduced to gravity. Noticing these multiple flows of information in my awareness created a double feedback loop of what was being sensed by my body, and the manner in which my mind tried to interpret this data in real time. I felt clear clues as to how my body operates as a vibrational organism, allowing me to find a seat to observe physical awareness alongside a mental interpretation. I found it remarkable that Contact seemed to have this inherent potential to crack open a physical experience of the body, as well as how that body relates to other bodies in real time.

I dove into the form and learning more about it. A friend shared with me their Contact YouTube playlist, which mainly featured Steve Paxton, Nancy Stark Smith, and Itay Yatuv.

---

[1] Names of the partner roles in Aikido; receiving the technique or performing it, respectively.

Lisa Claire Greene, *Something We Touch or That Touches Us* In: *Resistance and Support*. Edited by: Ann Cooper Albright,
Oxford University Press. © Oxford University Press 2024. DOI: 10.1093/9780197776308.003.0014

238　Resistance and Support

I appreciated Paxton's questions, the softness and frankness they posed, and continued to be prompted to notice things I had taken for granted before: "hanging by my skin," noticing the feeling of clothes, my weight in a chair; understanding with the body, rather than (or in addition to) the mind. When I heard Paxton say, "memories of past judgments tell me that pre-judging is not secure," I recognized that a key factor in the dancing for me was the novelty of interacting with another person in a manner that was entirely physical.[2] Rather than communicate intellectually, on a mental/verbal level, I was encouraged to tune my senses to what could be heard or felt, my entire body the receiver for call and response.

I immediately became intoxicated by, if not addicted to, this mode of interaction; it was so different from anything I had experienced before. The body was the primary focal point for interacting with my experience, rather than my mind or the observation of thoughts. I was able to connect with people in a physical, almost animal kind of way, allowing me to briefly forget my mental interpretation of the interaction. The newness of this experience, coupled with my own willingness to jump straight into this form, offered an opportunity for me to explore myself in a way that I had not previously. Once this possibility opened up, I craved it more and began seeking out spaces in which to continue the engagement.

Right after that first experience, I traveled with the Chicago CI pod to Oberlin College for a multi-jam event and class with Ann Cooper Albright. All of the programming took place in Warner Gymnasium, with Warner Main the primary location for the class and jams. I was introduced to body surfing, round robins, and the concept of harvesting and integration as an important individual and communal tool for processing what took place during Contact. In a manner that for me was wholly unique to CI, there was an emphasis on bringing the awareness we hone in workshops and jams into the non-dance spaces of our daily lives.

As a result of these events, I began noticing significant ways that my relationship to myself and others was changing. For instance, I had a long-held belief that I was other or less than, which was rooted in a history of behavioral disorders that had alienated me from social groups. Because I had grown up with severe attention deficit disorder (ADD), I was often too hyper to engage with others and had a difficult time reading social cues. My behavior irked adults around me, and based on the extremely negative manner in which they responded, I believed myself unrelatable, socially undesirable, and weird. What I believed about myself hinged on a feeling of disconnect between what was happening internally (inside my mind and body) and what was happening externally in the social world of grown-ups and peers. I felt that I could not make myself understood by those around me, because I lacked the vocabulary or social skills to communicate how I was feeling in a meaningful or true way. When I began dancing Contact, however, I experienced something altogether different, which I believe was a function of interacting socially in a manner that was entirely physical. Even though I felt that I had largely integrated my personality during my adolescence and had grown out of most of my ADD symptoms, I had never felt as accepted as I was by those I was dancing with in Chicago. At the time, I reflected:

I'm not used to feeling accepted in a group or communal setting. For so long, I embraced the identity of an outsider who couldn't be affirmed by external groups. For what feels like the first time, I feel widely accepted for who I am—by a pre-formed group—that I am liked and valued

---

[2] Klubki. *Contact Improvisation 1972.* YouTube, September 3, 2011, https://www.youtube.com/watch?v=9FeS DsmIeHA&list=PL6OwFWVZrRwWGfSoOzurwlUAUKAoQ2ggp&index=8.

for both who I am and the contribution that makes to the whole. Letting go of the limitation that I'm a burden. (November 15, 2021)

Shortly thereafter, I returned to Oberlin in January 2022 to participate in the winter term program taught by Jurij Konjar. The focus was to explore fundamentals of CI movement in relation to the Grand Union winter term of 1972 which culminated in the performance *Magnesium*. The session was part of a longer, six-month residency with dancers from around the world that would culminate with a summer festival to celebrate the fiftieth anniversary of CI. As this process of unfolding continued, I began to wonder what exactly was taking place in my body to produce the changes I was experiencing. At the time, I found what I was doing personally therapeutic, and I started to unpack what was happening to me in those terms, specifically via neuroplasticity and cognitive behavioral therapy (CBT). I have a history with both, since CBT was the primary treatment my parents elected to address my behavioral disorders. Rather than put me on five different kinds of medication at five years old, they put me in individual and group therapy, with the intention that I would learn to redirect my impulses. In my case, this was quite effective, and in revisiting the available data to describe this modality, I noticed strong parallels with what I have observed in Contact jams and how neuroplasticity provides a basis for what I was seeing.

Human brains are incredibly plastic, meaning they are capable of changing over time, and they do so in a manner that is reflective of what they are experiencing. Whatever kind of circumstance a person is born into, the shape of that environment is physically implanted into the body and consciousness as neuronal connections in the brain. The topography of our brains reflect the world that we come to know, and it is through these links that we develop frameworks by which we might navigate our lives. In mechanical terms, these neuronal connections are a reflection of what we perceive and therefore determine how we think (cognition), with these cognitions in turn determining our behaviors (who and how we are). In neuroscience, it is widely accepted that who we are is the result of how we perceive, and how that energetic information is catalogued in the patterns of how the neurons in our brains fire (Doidge 2016).

Part of how this works is that our bodies have perceptual systems, including nerve centers not located in the brain, that are constantly extracting information about the environment from the flowing array of ambient energy. We can phrase it this way because elements of perception, such as light, colors, sounds, smells, tastes, and pressures, are described as types of energy that can be quantified in a lab and measured (Gibson 1983). From a Western scientific point of view:

> any act of perception requires three essential elements—a stimulus such as a visual form, a sound, a smell, a taste, or something we touch or that touches us; a sensory organ; and a set of neuronal circuits in the brain that organize and make sense of the signals received from the sense organ. (Rinpoche et al. 2007, 78)

We perceive both variant information, such as a stimulus, and invariant information, which describes the permanent environment. Our brains take this information and catalogue it, represented by the order in which certain neurons fire.

However, these connections between the neurons in our brains are not fixed, but competitive, meaning that pathways that fire frequently become stronger, while ones that fire

240 Resistance and Support

rarely become weak and are reabsorbed. While humans go through critical periods of brain development early in life when they are building these neural maps, these maps also continue to change throughout our lives. These changes can be adaptive, indicating an improvement in function, or maladaptive, leading to a loss of function in a very "use it or lose it" kind of manner (Weyandt et al. 2020).

I saw this contextualized in my own experience of how I was changing beyond Contact or even dancing spaces. Roughly five months after I started doing CI, I traveled to Bogotá, Colombia, with my partner to visit with their family. I had never been there before, was not yet fluent in Spanish, and was basically along for the ride as far as planning our itinerary was concerned. Historically, this would have filled me with anxiety, necessitating copious alone time, but I was surprised to discover that I was completely unbothered and was able to meet the situation with calmness and ease. I felt little to no anxiety in being around so many unfamiliar people, and was open and willing to explore every opportunity that was presented to me. At the time, I was mildly shocked, because I had not known myself to respond this way to situations with so many uncontrolled variables. In light of what I had learned about neuroplasticity, I attributed this change to the embracing of disorientation that has been such a large part of my experience dancing Contact. Extended physical disorientation of my body in a dance space seemed to increase my tolerance for disorientation in general, and since physical activity can greatly increase neuroplasticity (Huang et al. 2021), a picture began to form of how this change could take place so rapidly.

In the space of a Contact dance, I seemed to be tracing my own neural patterns, and juxtaposing them against an awareness of what I could observe with my senses in real time. The relief this view offered could allow me to change my perceptions, because I could weigh past self-talk against new information that was coming in. Since my experience of Contact made physical perception the focal point of interaction, rather than a previous mental or emotional interpretation, I seemed to be able to bypass familiar behavioral patterns by relating to myself, others, and space differently. I could become simultaneously aware of how I was used to perceiving via a familiar mental interpretation alongside more up-to-date sensory information during the dance. The awareness of my own cognitions that this provided allowed me to prune ways of addressing myself that were no longer accurate with what I was currently perceiving: I was used to feeling like an outsider, but now I felt accepted within my Contact community; I was uncomfortable with environmental disorientation, but now I felt more comfortable with it in general. The topography of my brain seemed to be changing.

CBT uses these concepts in an applied sense in order to explore the links between thoughts, emotions, and behaviors (Fenn et al. 2013). If neuroplasticity describes the settings menu of our brains, then CBT allows us to toggle those settings, with widely documented positive results, particularly in groups. In a remarkable parallel to Contact jams, the group function here is critically important, because when a group is fully bonded, it creates a "group ego" entity that is the sum of its parts. The way that CBT sessions hold a container with clear expectations of what is allowed within the group, compare how individual experience is perceived internally versus externally, and seek to integrate these new perspectives into existing awareness, directly describes the orientation of the Contact spaces I had been in. There are a lot of other ways to structure CI spaces depending on what the intention of the dancers or facilitating bodies are, but when the intention of the group and expectations of its participants are clear, there is tremendous power for the group to function together (Schachter 2011).

I have witnessed this executed harmoniously and discordantly at various jams, and the difference can be staggering. In the case of the Chicago jam where everyone is required to arrive on time for the opening circle, going over community agreements and setting expectations have allowed the attendees to be on the same page. Usually this leads to an elated jam where people express feeling bonded and affirmed in the closing circle. In contrast, when I have attended other large jams where there is no opening circle and well over a hundred bodies in the space, the vibe has been more chaotic and often makes me wary of who is dancing there and why. In those instances, I have tended to keep to myself or only dance with folks whom I know I can trust, because otherwise the vulnerability is too great.

As these parallels became apparent, a hypothesis started to form: if CBT is a therapy by which we can develop the functions of our brains, and CBT and CI have strong similarities, then there is a potential for CI to develop the functions of our brains. Intentionality is key here, both in CBT and CI. If the goal is to integrate a mind/body connection and bring the sensory awareness often honed in Contact to non-dance spaces, then that would explain the stark changes I experienced almost immediately. My interpretation is that both practices can result in an altered relationship to the present, where perceptions are dictated by the physical interpretation of environmental factors. In this vein, there is a clear potential for CI to alter how someone relates to their environment, and it is directly because of the plasticity of our brains that this mechanism is able to occur.

Not included in this view—and in a break from CBT—is that a practice of Contact may not be trying to get anywhere. There are ever more ways to explore Contact movement with different interests or goals in mind, depending on who is practicing it and where. When participating in a workshop led by Guru Suraj and Adrianna Michalska, who have also contributed an essay to this volume, I resonated with the idea they put forward that Contact has an inherently questioning nature. In contrast, CBT uses a specific, time-directed approach to address what is referred to as "common health disorders." In this modality, the nature of our own cognitions is explored in order to prune experiences that are less desired and to cultivate behaviors that are more so. There is a prescriptive function around an outcome that puts the onus on addressing an unwanted behavior. However, an issue that emerged in both CI and CBT was that such behaviors could be trauma responses due to systemic factors, such as colonialism and institutional racism, and that mitigating the response does not address the larger context that precipitated it (assuming it could be addressed at all).

This point took a while to dawn on me, and I think that the environment in which I entered into Contact, as well as my own whiteness, contributed to the latency of this awareness. My primary exposure was to what I have come to understand as "core" spaces or teachers that presuppose a hierarchy of Contact, centering the voices of Steve Paxton, Nancy Stark Smith, the development and performance of *Magnesium*, as well as Oberlin as a site unto itself. I do not mean to suggest that these humans and spaces were not weighty in the development of the form Contact has come to be, but that their presence and the exclusion of others did not prepare me for the reality that I encountered reading the other essays in this volume. The process of writing this essay, attending the *CI @ 50* festival, and workshopping these written works demonstrated to me the myopia of how I had been exposed.

Initially, I had assumed that there was some kind of neutral point of awareness that could be arrived at through these kinds of therapies, a truly "objective" way to look at the world that could somehow be taught in a psychology manual. My view failed to take into account the inherent impossibility of a neutral worldview, predicated as it is upon the direct perception of the environment. From a biological standpoint, what we are exposed to during critical periods of brain development create a framework of behaviors by which we might survive (Schachter 2011). Having grown up in the United States, systems of colonialism and white supremacy are codified in the neural interpretations of my environment, woven as they are into the history of how it came to be a country. Since birth, I have been conditioned from the point of view of the colonizing culture, making it ingrained and difficult to dismantle without the intervention of other modes of awareness. I could not dance with these environmental forces without encountering where they surfaced within my own perceptual systems, and for me this racist or colonial conditioning would fall under the purview of "undesirable behaviors."

A difficulty I have encountered is that even though I reject the ideological concepts that colonialism and white supremacy are grounded in, their performance is still in my body because they are codified in my neural network. One of the things that really struck me at the *CI @ 50* festival was the apparent functioning of these societal structures in our bodies, and how they seemed to hijack the weekend's proceedings. By way of example, the opening circle began in Warner Main with acknowledging the historic cis-het-whiteness of centered Contact narratives. Shortly thereafter, a breakout space was offered for BIPOC dancers in an adjacent studio. Almost immediately, this space was interrupted by another attendee who burst in and deemed that the affinity space was racist. Accounts of this event began spreading, and those reverberations were felt for the rest of the weekend, leading to an informal multi-day class for white people, increased tensions around racial topics during panels, and an exceptionally charged closing town hall. There is a lot more there to unpack, really deserving its own essay, but I bring it up briefly here to underscore how there can be such a huge disconnect between what is said and what happens in Contact spaces, and how even an acknowledgment of that did not feel integrated at *CI @ 50*.

Attending this event furthered my awareness of Contact as a practice with a diverse history that has not always been true to its own international variability—how there was a lack of visibility of more diverse histories of CI that communicated how multidimensional and intersectional it can be all over the world. Their absence demonstrated how conversations about Contact happening around me often left out people of color, queer or transgendered bodies, as well as those teaching or practicing in communities that were not white, especially outside the United States and Europe. I was becoming aware that the manner in which I was introduced to CI lent itself to a hierarchized view that did not include the diversity of how Contact has developed, a misrepresentation by omission. Other voices simply were not there. Instead, I heard about Paxton, Smith, other "first- and second-generation teachers," and Oberlin, leading to my own perception of CI's history being grounded in whiteness and heteronormativity.

Other essays in this volume critique these driving concepts, for example Robin Prichard's essay on the natural body. During the writing group post–*CI @ 50*, there was a push to include even more diverse voices to better represent the multiplicity of how Contact is practiced worldwide, and how dancers and teachers have adapted a framework for dancing CI in their specific communities and contexts. At the time of this iteration, my essay has undergone several major rewrites to accommodate my own ongoing confrontations with these histories: how a rosy newcomer's view was tempered by an asymmetrical explanation of Contact.

Rather than consider these forces as opposing each other, I think they are complementary elements of the same process. A sustained relationship with a practice of Contact, which for

Something We Touch or That Touches Us   243

Figure 13.1. Lisa Claire Greene, "Queer Joy Fountain," watercolor and pencil on paper, September 19, 2022.

me has been characterized by noticing what can be felt by my body, has lent itself to addressing these unconscious biases that make their way into my neural pathways via environmental experience. An increased participation with these myriad communities has offered me an opportunity to extract this environmental programming from what I actually agree with. We will not always like what we are confronted with, but becoming aware allows for different choices to be made that would not have been available otherwise, for the lack of perspective. In that way, my view is that CI is not an ideological absolute, but more a method of questioning, with the potential to continue expanding.

In that sense, it led me back to a drawing practice that I had almost forgotten about, that allows me to continue exploring these ideas through visual work. This art practice was catalyzed by my experience of dancing Contact, and began just as *CI @ 50* was coming to a close. While these drawings are not explicitly about CI, they examine the experience of having a body within and without familiar identity narratives (Figure 13.1).[3] In my drawings, I describe what can be felt in states of embodiment and deep listening, and what those demonstrate about human existence. As an example, it shows how coming into Contact is generative and that the awareness made available through engaging with the form brought me to the place where I am now. It has helped circumvent "toxic positivity" that strives to only see the "light" side that I have often encountered in CI, and instead acknowledges that within us and these spaces are a range of forces that contribute to who is dancing there and why. Without

---

[3] The sketches that became this final scene were made during a performance by artist Catie Rutledge at the 2022 MDW Art Fair at Mana Contemporary in Chicago. They were invited by William Amaya Torres of No Nation Art Laboratory, and their piece included performers Grace Devies, Melon Sprout, and Clark Woods, with additional support. I want to credit them with inspiration, as their performance filled me with so much joy, and inspired me to make this drawing that intersects with my own experience in Contact.

that engagement, I do not know when or how I would have had the opportunity to observe these internal and social states of awareness; it has allowed me to grow and choose behavior that I can agree with, rather than just what is environmentally ingrained.

As I am wrapping up the writing of this essay in the spring of 2023, I am still dancing and working with these forces. As the newly revived Chicago jam continues to grow, I have noticed how we grapple with these themes as a community, while facilitating space for new and returning dancers. We consider the experiences we have had individually and collectively, especially in the wake of closing and reopening the Chicago jam (see Michele Beaulieux's chapter in this volume) and the *CI @ 50* festival which some of us were able to attend. We continue to learn from these experiences, stay present with ourselves, and hold each other accountable, with the intention that we foster a community where those who are connected to it feel welcome and supported. I am finding that this process is expansive, prompting individual and communal progress that seeks to take our experiences together into account and integrate them. I am still exploring my own neural pathways, dancing with all these levels of awareness and bringing them into how I maneuver through these dynamics.

Some of this is a process of unfolding that happens in real time, in a state of presence, and it is not always possible to notice what is being observed in a manner separate from the doing that characterizes it. However, engaging with CI can help us integrate these experiences by getting into the meat of them and becoming more aware of what is happening in our bodies during those moments. I no longer have a rosy newcomer's view of Contact, but I do hope that these skills that are continuing to be developed lend themselves to more inclusivity that lays down new ways of thinking, rather than perpetuating the inequitable legacies we have inherited.

References

Doidge, Norman. 2016. *The Brain's Way of Healing: Stories of Remarkable Recoveries and Discoveries*. New York: Viking Penguin Books.

Fenn, Kristina, and Majella Byrne. 2013. "The Key Principles of Cognitive Behavioural Therapy." *InnovAiT: Education and Inspiration for General Practice* 6, no. 9: 579–585, https://journals.sagepub.com/doi/full/10.1177/1755738012471029.

Gibson, James Jerome. 1983. *The Senses Considered as Perceptual Systems*. Westport, CT: Greenwood.

Huang, Z., Y. Zhang, R. Zhou, L. Yang, and H. Pan. 2021. "Lactate as Potential Mediators for Exercise-Induced Positive Effects on Neuroplasticity and Cerebrovascular Plasticity." *Frontiers in Physiology* Jul 5, no. 12: 656455. https://doi.org/10.3389/fphys.2021.656455.

Rinpoche, Yongey Mingyur, and Eric Swanson. 2007. *The Joy of Living: Unlocking the Secret and Science of Happiness*. New York: Harmony Books.

Schachter, Robert. 2011. "Using the Group in Cognitive Group Therapy." *Eastern Group Psychotherapy Society* 35, no. 2 (June): 135–149, https://www.jstor.org/stable/41716126.

Schwenk, Theodor. 1976. *Sensitive Chaos*. New York: Schocken.

Weyandt, Lisa L., et al. 2020. "Neuroplasticity in Children and Adolescents in Response to Treatment Intervention: A Systematic Review of the Literature." *Clinical and Translational Neuroscience* 4, no. 2, https://doi.org/10.1177/2514183X20974231.

14
The Religious Function of Contact Improvisation

Carol Laursen

Contact Improvisation (CI) found me in 1979 as I was about to drop out of college in the Pacific Northwest of the United States. In the first semester of sophomore year, I studied calculus, physics, and organic chemistry. I had gazed longingly at the arts curriculum, but couldn't put family finances on the line for something so intangible. During what would have been the second semester, I worked as a cook in a tavern and audited modern dance, acting, Aikido, and a life drawing class. Looking back, I think I was trying to find a path toward authentic, embodied experience—to find a home in myself through connecting the life of the mind with the body. A CI workshop came to our campus, and I was introduced to the small dance and was shown a way to enter conversations with others through my skin and joints. I was awkward and overeager, and, true to my upbringing, wanted to please. My body blundered, yet incorporating the impulses of another dancer into my own movement patterns engaged both my intellectual and somatic curiosity, and focused attention on the parts of myself that I had been taught to ignore and keep still in order to think. A link was tentatively drawn between the abstract intellect perceived in the head, and the biological structures that generated life. This process awakened an intelligent, moving body, along with a capacity to witness itself in an ever-changing environment.

Over the next several decades, I sought out more opportunities to ripen my relationship with CI at various jams and longer workshops such as A Capella Motion. The practice itself challenges conventional social norms, and began to dissolve my conditioned physical boundaries, giving me a chance to construct new ways of connecting with other people. Then a new quality began to emerge from learning lifts and finding a shifting fulcrum as we spun around, or as we rested, intently focusing on connection through our skin into fascia and muscle. After hours, days, and weeks of witnessing part of my psyche staying present with my body and the bodies of others, unusual states would enfold me and seem to lift my perceptions out of habitual patterns. My sense of being rigidly separate began to loosen, then might drop away for brief moments. These states might be expansive, explosive, or feel like an ocean of sweet weeping, but would usually present a tangible quality of otherness, or even an impression that there are no others. Sometimes returning to a distinct separate self felt surprising, a bit too tight, but usually a sense that I was at home in the world would persist.

The taste of these experiences sent me searching. I have come to consider these states to be pointers, but not the point. Over the last several decades, I have been engaged with several spiritual and religious forms, and now find a rich internal conversation among various practices as I understand them. In this essay, I explore CI's potential to facilitate a dancer's ability to perceive their connection with a mystery larger than any individual and what we might

Carol Laursen, *The Religious Function of Contact Improvisation* In: *Resistance and Support*. Edited by: Ann Cooper Albright, Oxford University Press. © Oxford University Press 2024. DOI: 10.1093/9780197776308.003.0015

246 Resistance and Support

learn from other traditions with these explicit intentions. I am interested in how a visceral connection has the power to change who we think we are and how we relate to the world. Here are some findings as I brought my contact-informed self into the spheres of Aikido, Quakerism, and Buddhism.

Each religion is made from stories and practices, a wide variety of origin myths and professed beliefs, along with techniques designed to help a believer manifest their beliefs. The Dalai Lama often says, "My religion is very simple. Kindness is my religion." This statement is a story of sorts. To support and honor this short creed, each morning he wakes at 3:30 to engage in study and meditation techniques which open him to loving-kindness. This one simple example shows the relationship between the two, as story encourages the practices which enforce the story. A virtuous cause-and-effect loop develops if the story and practice are well chosen.

Another type of story about the Dalai Lama came to me from a friend whose brother worked for a while as his private secretary. Reporters often pressured the secretary to reveal if he ever saw anything miraculous in the Dalai Lama's presence, perhaps levitation or mind reading. Mostly, he would laugh them off, but one day he responded to the question by saying he had. The reporters leaned in, recorders turned on, and he told them that in the several years he had worked in this position, the Dalai Lama listened deeply to everyone he met. He brought the same respectful attention that he used for prime ministers to the person who was cleaning his room. The reporters lost interest; this presumably was not the miracle they sought, but I have been experimenting with the possibility of manifesting this remarkable capacity since I heard of it 25 years ago. I don't know if this event actually happened, or even if I am remembering it correctly, but this anecdote is alive in me when I enter a Contact jam. It lingers as an aspiration as I ponder how to bring the same respectful attention to each dance I find and each dance that finds me. The person cleaning the room and the person elected prime minister may have very different things to say, just as every new dance partner brings different experiences to the dance encounter. Each dance becomes an opportunity to explore a new version of who I am and who we become together. These co-arising dances sometimes exhibit wild contrast, yet I aspire to bring consistency in attentive respect. When respect is present, the dance opens to more possibilities, and whatever dance is present can be more fully entered, be it playful, percussive, flowing, or filled with grief. I can offer what is arising in me when I wholeheartedly receive what is arising from others.

While the stated functions of religion vary greatly, I suggest that facilitating this authentic communication is one of the most vital. Some see the function of religion as a force to stabilize society, a way to impart or enforce ethical codes. Others see it as a way to transform the self into a more spiritual being. Certainly, religion pertains to things considered sacred or holy. If you trace the word "holy" to its Proto-Indo-European roots, its original meaning is "wholeness." For me, religious activity has become a way to gather all the parts that have been exiled, including that which is rejected in the name of religion. In each moment, all that is actually arising can be welcomed, which supports a broader perspective than the ego alone will typically provide. The attendant subjective state that accompanies this practice of widening perspectives opens a way of knowing about the transpersonal through the personal psyche.

For Carl Jung, religion is a human instinct which exists in each of us, as fundamental as eating and sex. He described this religious instinct as:

> a peculiar attitude of mind which could be formulated in accordance with the original use of
> the word religion, which means a careful consideration and observation of certain dynamic

The Religious Function of Contact Improvisation   **247**

factors that are conceived as "powers": spirits, daemons, gods, laws, ideas, Ideals, or whatever name man has given to such factors in his world as he has found powerful, dangerous, or helpful enough to be taken into careful consideration, or grand, beautiful, and meaningful enough to be devoutly worshiped and loved. (1958, 8)

For Jung, these "powers" are parts of the psyche, either individual or collective. Jungian psychology uses many techniques to discover estranged parts of ourselves that have been relegated to the shadow, and reintegrate them. Artistic expression was regularly depended on as a means to grapple with rising images and impulses. Dance was one pathway used to engage the active imagination during the process of individuation. During the process of looking into our psychological depths, where "spirits, daemons, [and] gods" are encountered, a sensibility develops which takes notice of intuition and shifting internal perceptions. A religious sensibility underlays religious belief and facilitates investigation of the sacred. The Buddha said we are not to take anything on the authority of another without trying the teaching out and seeing the results for ourselves. This is the aspect of religion that I wish to consider in relation to CI. In the dance, we can explore many concepts that elude a strictly intellectual religious approach in order to find a lived answer, an experiential communion. When the dancer is given to the dance, a sacred mystery is directly engaged.

I think religions, at their best, grew out of a desire to examine and perhaps repeat spontaneously arising sacred states. CI provides a set of circumstances conducive to exploring religious teachings and, as such, fulfills a religious function. I recognize that Steve Paxton might disagree. In *Drafting Interior Techniques*, he wrote that in the development of CI, "there should be no mention of sexuality, psychology, spirituality. I would leave these in the hands of the experts and proceed with what seemed more immediate—the senses and the physical body" (2003, 176). I can appreciate not wanting to be pulled into the quagmire of various psychological and spiritual theories while fine-tuning an ability to perceive fine-grained shifts of the physical body. However, not mentioning these aspects does not stop them from arising. I have heard from others, and find in myself, a sense of the sacred rising from the immediate senses and physical body during CI dancing. Of course, this is not the only, nor even the most prominent frame for this practice. However, I want to suggest that one can dance CI with intentional religious questions, and even talk about them, without harming the integrity of the practice.

But perhaps I am wrong in my guess about Paxton's opinion. In the special CI 50th Anniversary 2022 edition of the *Contact Quarterly*, he wrote a piece entitled "The Initiation of Contact Improvisation for Me." In this lovely article, he tells of dancing with Grand Union sometime before 1972 when he and Douglas Dunn entered a duet that was filled with waiting:

It proceeded in this expectant way for a moment, then one of us faltered. Maybe a shift of weight, or a wobble in the touch. It was enough. The equilibrium was cracked. It was a change by one that the other could take as a message. What followed has become familiar to tens of thousands by now, but what had begun all this was that first moment. It was a most abstract intimacy. Doug was the perfect gentleman. I felt I was being honored by his subtle pause. And I tried to honor him in kind. (2022, n.p.)

Quakers practice expectant waiting, Zen Buddhists sit upright with abstract intimacy, and two humans honoring one another can unfold a new practice. While reflecting on this dance

248 Resistance and Support

from over 50 years ago, Paxton says that when people ask him how to Contact Improvise, he should have said:

> Go beyond small to the place where no message is being given. Start there. Let small be the first of the pleasures to come. Accept the first perturbation of that emptiness as the focus of the next moments. It is not a dance about you, or your partner. It is a dance about its movement. (2022, n.p.)

This speaks to me of a practice that relaxes the habitual constrictions of the ego to allow the possibility of entering more open reality. Finding the place where no message is given has been a doorway and a discipline for me. In the religious traditions that I investigate, teachings have developed which point beyond the small and beneath the conditioning.

Aikido and Invisible Connection

Aikido originated as a mixture of martial arts techniques and the founder's philosophy and religious beliefs. These practices are some of the tributaries that flow through Steve Paxton's development of CI. He studied the form throughout the 1960s, first in Tokyo and then in New York. Initially, he considered dance and Aikido to be separate and was not interested in merging them. "I put a big taboo against that, you know. Aikido was Aikido and dance was dance. Then I somehow forgot that I did that. And by '72 Aikido was coming into my dance just because it was in my body" (2020, n.p.). He found the information he had gleaned in the Aikido dojo to be necessary for the safety of the dancers he was training in this new improvisational form:

> It's like . . . an embrace, that kind of energy, light, really sensitive, extended. And that seems from Aikido to be a real message of, of extension and stretch as a safety factor. And if you have that or if you learn it, then instead of falling and contracting and presenting bony bits to hit the floor, you're extending toward it, you're presenting curves and you're able . . . in just falling, toppling and rolling, you're able to harmonize with the inevitable plane that you're going to have to contend with. (2020, n.p.)

This speaks of Aikido as a way to develop a fresh response. Instead of following the conditioned habits of contraction and pulling back when threatened, the Aikido student slows things down in order to practice extending and entering. Instead of being stuck at the point of conflict, a student can learn to spin and pivot and find freedom within the constraints of being grabbed. Instead of receiving a strike with a direct block in an attempt to repel the force, the arms or body can swing, rolling under and away from potential injury. These are some of the physical lessons in Aikido that found their way into CI, but what of Aikido's stories?

Aikido was developed by Morihei Ueshiba in the 1920s when he was already a master of several martial art styles. As an experienced samurai, he tired of domination and longed for something different. Using new insights, hard linear movements transform into soft circular movements. In this new form, the energy of the attacker is rendered harmless so the violence hurts neither the attacker (*uke*) nor the attacked (*nage*). A punch is rerouted in a spiral, often ending with the *uke* face down on the ground or rolling propelled away from

The Religious Function of Contact Improvisation   249

the situation. Finding a way to take the throwing technique is known as *ukemi*, or receiving body. Often, we think the important parts of a martial art are the throws, but Paxton saw the profound usefulness of learning the falls and creating a receptive body that responds to the throws. He used these discoveries of Aikido in order to fall safely by using the spiral rolls which spread the force over a larger surface area, reducing the possibility of injury. But Aikido is based not only on the mechanics of the physical. Instead, students are taught that the energy of the spirals extend beyond the physical body, allowing practitioners to perceive invisible lines of connection between attacker and attacked in the context of relating to the whole universe. Morihei said, "The secret of Aikido is to harmonize ourselves with the movement of the universe and bring ourselves into accord with the universe itself" (1963, 9).

Even the name "Aikido" holds the meaning of an explicitly spiritual pursuit and is often translated as "the Way of unifying life energy," or "the Way of harmonious spirit." The first *kanji* "Ai" means harmony, and "Do" means path or way. However, the central *kanji*, "Ki," is not translatable into English as a single word, since the concept was not in the European lexicon. *Ki* is a palpable life force, and the equivalent word in Chinese is *chi*, and in Sanskrit is *prana*. This concept and perception are central to Tai Chi and yoga, both of which function to connect a practitioner to the subtle elements within and beyond their small being. The utilization of *ki* is equally important in CI. How we move follows lines of energy, and how we connect with others is from center to center.

Ki develops in practice. In order to respond in a new way to fearful situations, Aikido students train in the dojo to meet aggression with a powerful gentleness. Again, and again, *nage* is punched and grabbed, pulled and pushed, in order to apply principles of relaxation and extension during a violent encounter. Indeed, Morihei taught his students to touch their opponent as if cradling a baby. Using this tender connection, students then apply a studied technique in order to feel new possibilities in the face of danger. The *uke* is also always practicing and merging with the energy of the one that throws. As *uke*'s balance is taken during the throw, it is important to stay awake to the changing circumstances moment by moment, just as a Contact dance offers surprises in each instant and opportunities to find a skillful response. *Nage* also is receiving in each moment, while allowing a practiced form to flow through them. Each encounter is different and needs to be adapted to. This brings everyone involved into a receptive state, while at the same time engaged in great activity.

In *The Art of Peace*, Morihei writes: "Everyone has a spirit that can be refined, a body that can be trained in some manner, a suitable path to follow. You are here for no other purpose than to realize your inner divinity and manifest your innate enlightenment" (2002, 3). There are several implications in this statement that I wish to highlight. First, in following a path, one discovers a purpose, and finding purpose is often mentioned as a function of religion. Second, we have an inner divinity, and our enlightenment is innate. The practice of Aikido points us toward a direct, immediate wholeness because "Aiki reflects the grand design of the cosmos; it is the life force and irresistible power that binds the material and spiritual aspects of creation" (Stevens 1995, 3). What happens when we enter our Contact jams with the intention of bringing harmony to the whole cosmos? We begin finding our relationship to gravity and the ground, then extend this harmonizing awareness to the room and everyone in the space. While a CI jam may seem chaotic at first, there is a complex reconciliation of many movement impulses. We learn to take multiple distinct influences and include them all, rather than force a truncated unity. When a need to dominate shifted to a desire to join spirit and body, the martial forms began to support the development of a different kind of person. When working directly with *ki*, the invisible force capable of transforming aggression into innate divinity, the practitioner naturally evolves. Just as Aikido came into what Paxton did physically because it was in his body, perhaps the more-than-physical aspects of these practices had also entered him. When the principles of falling and spiral lines of connection were brought into the CI teaching arena, I suspect the spiritual aspects of Aikido came quietly along.

Quakerism and Group Listening

Quakerism began in England in the 1600s as a protest and response to the hierarchical structures of other Christian churches of the time. In some ways, CI mirrors this impulse to shift from a vertical hierarchy in the modern dance world to a more egalitarian expression. The central form in Quakerism is expectant waiting in worship, which requires looking inward to find "that of God" which is in each of us. This is done collectively, and the group that regularly gathers is called a Meeting. Some folks say you can't have a Quaker without a Meeting, and I wonder if you can have a Contact dancer without the existence of jams. A Contact dancer is born from the immersion in a group of dancers practicing together. Something new arises when people come together with the intention of opening to one another, and in the case of the Quaker, to God, or the Light. Those originating Quakerism were known as "friends of the truth" and referred to each other using that intimate term. Early Friends made a bedrock of the biblical quote "wherever two or more of you are gathered in my name, I am there." The inward-dwelling Christ is felt and considered to be present, both as a part of each and somehow joining each together in a collective whole.

Through this shared inward and open search, the worshipper can touch a sense of "continuing revelation" which condenses into language. Rather than scripted or doctrinal, Quaker worship is improvisational in nature, allowing the spoken word to surprise and enliven. Insights bubble up with a fresh quality. Reinterpreting the past may co-arise with a new idea, or an emotional floodgate might open as a parched place in the psyche finally gets what it needs. Or there can be a reaction of resistance since our comfortable identity is often challenged. In silence, Quakers seek images or ideas that run counter to the habitual personality and put faith in the possibility of guidance coming through their most inward states. Of course, it takes familiarity with the habits of the mind in order to discern what is new or outside of conventional thought patterns. In order to investigate our inner landscape, it is necessary to hold our fleeting thoughts in kind enough regard so they can be seen. Then an ability to witness develops and our internal life can be directly perceived. Coming together in this worship container supports the development of this ability.

In the same way, during a CI jam we can get stuck in the habitual patterns of the body. I remember someone asking why all his dances were starting to look alike, and why did it feel like his partners were trying to dance their own dance upon him. This sort of unsatisfying dance comes about when we are unwilling to surrender our habit bodies, even if we are particularly athletically skilled, maybe especially if we are particularly athletically skilled. The genius of CI is manifest when a fresh new dance is born of the moment between and beyond two or more dancers willing to be danced through. Sometimes, while sitting

The Religious Function of Contact Improvisation   **251**

together in Quaker worship, one member might have language coming into their internal world that is meant for another. The results of that deep sense of inner searching in a collective setting can then be shared with other members during worship through what is called a message. Each member surrenders to being used in this way, to being spoken through by "promptings of spirit" which can be seen as a parallel to a dance that is about "movement itself."

But these subtle promptings of spirit can only be felt if we clear the space. Early one morning at CI @ 50, I watched mayfield brooks strike Oberlin's beautiful main dance space after the Underscore of the night before. They were teaching the first class of the day. Slowly, and with respect, brooks cleared the detritus of the previous night's infinitude of experience in order to restore an uncluttered space that could welcome whatever arose with freshness. The course description said the class was designed to evoke dance while:

> . . . attuning the body and voice to the inner, middle and outer ear. These investigations into attunement will be the basis of moving in and out of different frequencies of sound, vibration, momentum, disorientation, decomposition, stillness and quietude. Listening is the basis of this work. (https://sites.google.com/oberlin.edu/criticalmassci50)

While the focus of brooks's teaching was on the literal ear and our aural connections to that which is inside and outside us, I found that their teaching evoked a state similar to Quaker worship. Turning attention to the subtleties of inner and outer sound, I found myself seeking what Quakers call the "still small voice" which is heard within and comes from silence. As we attuned to increasingly more refined perceptions, the witness was engaged, and along with it a tolerance for not knowing. While we each had our own experience, a palpable unity filled the space.

Quakers also come together in unadorned rooms to await the unexpected. Sometimes the Meeting for Worship becomes so powerful that all are drawn into a numinous state at which point it is called "gathered." This is the central ritual enactment of the Quaker tenets. In *Four Doors to Meeting for Worship*, Bill Tabor, a modern Quaker, has described the gathered meeting in this way:

> In this living Presence it becomes safe for the ego to relax, allowing us to realize that the sharp boundaries of the self can become blurred and blended as we feel ourselves more and more united with fellow worshipers and with the Spirit of God. This sense of corporate reality can become so strong that we can almost touch it, and we are reminded that Friends have traditionally referred to the meeting as "the body." (1992, 12)

This description of a gathered meeting could equally be applied to the state of the collective during brooks's workshop, where we became one body with many points of experience.

There is an often-repeated story in Quaker circles about a non-English speaker who consistently came to a small Meeting for Worship. Eventually, the attender was asked why they came if they didn't understand the words. They replied that they love to listen to the place where the words come from. Listening underneath the words is similar to listening for a movement impulse. Engaging practices that allow receptivity to this preverbal source opens a wider field, that can then be used creatively or spiritually. There is something about the presence of others similarly committed which amplifies grounding and opening. It takes a

252   Resistance and Support

while to come to a place of stillness and silence under the usual stream of conditioned associations in order to access where the words come form, and sometimes it takes a collected group to make this place available. Quaker practice is to draw guidance from that source.

These observations help free me from my tendency to reside solely in rationality. In her book *Listening Spirituality*, Quaker author Patricia Loring states that:

> those who discount the intimations of their intuitive nature, or subject their experiences to the reductionist exercises of rationalism, might unwittingly brush aside the overtures of the Spirit that seems to pass from Friend to Friend in a gathered or covered meeting. For many, there is an almost palpable, electric sense of Presence, of Life, of Power, of spiritual movement among them. (2009, 27)

When exploring with the listening body, as one does in dance improvisation or in Quaker worship, the intuitive nature can wake up and open the door when Spirit knocks, brushing away our conditioning, and allowing a trans-rational viewpoint. If we can patiently stay in the not-knowing with the awareness of the witness engaged, we can also begin to perceive shadow elements and know them as us. The exiled and exalted begin to interact. The collective nature of these forms allows us to draw on the wisdom of each of us, building an integrated whole greater than any of us. Those mature in the practice or naturally inclined can help create an environment where those new to the work can taste these rich expressions developed in collected gathering.

And then we discern how to move forward. Group discernment is perhaps one of the most difficult processes in a Quaker meeting, as we practice setting aside our individual opinions and attempt to listen for direction beyond any small self-identity. Preference is laid down as we attend to one another's words and attempt to hear what needs to happen in order to align with the will of God or source of goodness. Aikido practitioners might consider this harmonizing with the cosmos. We make many mistakes, but hopefully continue. I think of the dance structure of a round robin as a way to practice decision-making. As we sit in the circle, we listen/watch what is before us, at the same time opening to an inward prompting. When are we called in? How do we connect? What moves us in and out of the center, and how do we understand these impulses? It is a wonderful opportunity to study layers of our inner life in intimate interaction with the whole.

The whole is made of all of us who are guided to be in the space together. Although we may not all agree, we all belong. On his webpage, Martin Keogh generously shares some of his last communication with Nancy Stark Smith. As she expounds on the Underscore, she mentions the principle of being all in, all the time.

> That whole decision that people have in jams or even in life of do I belong? Am I in or am I out, and what makes me in? If you just say you are in, you are always in. You can't not be in. You are here. Whatever it is that you are doing—if you are sleeping in the corner, if you are crying, if you are bored—that doesn't matter, I mean it matters, it changes the composition, but it is no question that you are in. And you have an effect on other people, also. (2020, n.p.)

The jam and the Quaker meeting both arise from all of us who are present, and if any of us is missing, the whole is not the same.

Zen Practice/Realization

One of the most famous quotes of Zen Buddhism comes from Dogen Zenji, a monk who lived in thirteenth-century Japan. In his essay, the *Genjokoan*, he prods his followers with the insight, "To study the Buddha Way is to study the self; to study the self is to forget the self; to forget the self is to be actualized by myriad things." Sitting meditation is a form that encourages self-study through watching the ever-changing inner landscape, and allows the absence of a solid independent self to be directly experienced. Those deeply engaged with these teachings begin to see the way all things are conditioned by the existence of all other things, known as dependent co-arising. In a similar way, Dogen also taught that practice and realization are not separate. One doesn't practice in order to get realization, but rather the wholehearted practice is the realization. There is no goal, no grasping for that which isn't here right now. Zen practice is not transactional, not doing this to get that.

The Underscore also encourages self-study in this expansive non-grasping way. In a 2012 interview, Nancy Stark Smith describes the Underscore as a research tool to study phenomenon in dance improvisation and changes in state in the mind and body. Articulating this practice began as a way to describe sections that often occurred during a jam, and has evolved into a focused, yet open structure that allows a group to go through these various states uninterrupted. She points out that the Underscore provides a structure which both protects and challenges the dancer: "There is a protection in that you can go deeply into these states, but you're going to be asked to encounter things that you don't necessarily expect, and hopefully meet them" (2012, n.p.).

In my experience with Soto Zen, the group practice of extended sitting and walking meditation builds a container which functions much like the Underscore. CI's parallel to Zen practice, while not initially obvious, is striking when looking at Zen literary and lived traditions. In the popular imagination, Zen is often seen either as an individualistic, heady practice, or as a synonym for relaxed states. However, from within the tradition, the practice is collective, deeply embodied, and rigorous. Its extreme formalism protects the psyche to allow an experience of the totality of what is before us. Governed by the schedule, we enter the *zendo* walking slowly, and with awareness. We enter with the foot closest to the door hinge. We proceed to our seat, noticing the relationship to our neighbors. If they arrive first, they bow to welcome us as we bow to our sitting space, our two-foot by three-foot domain where we can practice essential dignity. If we are seated first, we bow with them on their arrival. Then as we sit in silence and stillness (that is rarely silent and never still), we join body and mind imperceptibly with all in the room. We honor one another.

The central form of Zen Buddhism is sitting upright and experiencing directly what is before us, just this. Nothing is added, just this is it. According to Zen teacher and scholar Taigen Dan Leighton, "This just sitting is not a meditation technique or practice, or any thing at all. 'Just sitting' is a verb rather than a noun, the dynamic activity of being fully present" (2002, 1). Just sitting can be seen as the small dance writ even smaller. Rather than feet, the pelvic floor is now the base. As in many beginning Contact classes, the novice meditator is instructed to follow their breath. The breath is a portal for awareness to enter the body. And then we watch. We watch the rising and falling of sensations. We watch the rising and falling of emotions. We watch the rising and falling of mind states and stories. Through this investigation we begin to notice that which holds all of these fluctuations. By directly touching the

254   Resistance and Support

moment that holds us all, we can experience how we are supported by all beings, and that we support all beings.

I remember Reb Anderson, former abbot of San Francisco Zen Center, once explained in a Dharma talk that our central delusion is thinking we are separate from everything else. We develop a story of an isolated self and then buy into it. Somehow we feel that there is the whole universe plus something else, and that something else is us. We fantasize that we are separate, sealed off, and then the mind tells us this is so. In fact, we are always interacting fundamentally with the environment in an action of co-creation. In each moment, we exchange our air with all living beings around us. Water enters as we drink and exits through evaporation or through kidneys or is being incorporated into this inherited structure for a short time. There may be good reason in our evolutionary past to create a sense of separate identity in order to survive, but at a certain point of ripening we can recognize that separateness as a fiction.

When entering a jam, there is a chance to explore this delusion. At first, I may see the jam as everyone else with myself added to it. As I begin to roll on the floor or drape over a chair, I come to realize myself in relation to the inanimate world. In order to awaken intimately to ourselves, Dogen encourages us to engage directly with earth, grass, trees, walls, tiles, and pebbles (1231). The dance floor itself becomes fascinating as the grain of the wood tells of former life, whispering tales of sunshine and rainfall long past. Our very bodies exist as an expression of non-living elements. Then, as we come into contact with other living beings, there is an opportunity to hear and tell stories unimpeded by words and concepts. We can come out of a cage built of preconceptions and can risk knowing others in their complete and unexpected forms. In revealing ourselves, we can discover our own unexpectedness. Zen priest Zenju Earthlyn Manuel writes, in her book *The Way of Tenderness: Awakening Through Race, Sexually, and Gender*, "we must look our embodiment in the face in order to attend to the challenge it presents. Only then will we come to engage each other with all of what we are—both the relative and the absolute, the physical and the formless" (2011, 27).

Over the past 50 years, those dancing CI have struggled to articulate the fruits of their practice. Buddhist teachers have struggled with the same imperfection of language for several thousand years. Hongzhi, a Chinese Zen teacher who lived a generation before Dogen, was known for his teaching of silent illumination, and his poems are filled with metaphor. In *Cultivating the Empty Field*, one of his verses is titled "The Original Dwelling":

> A person practicing the Way subtly goes beyond words and thoughts. Instantly authentic, one is on the affirmed path and does not attach to reasoning. Extensively intermingled, the moon flows in all the waters, the wind blows through the supreme emptiness. . . . Then you can enter Samādhi in every sense dust and gather the ten thousand forms in the single seal." (2000, 48)

The term *Samādhi* has various definitions and is hard to pin down. It refers to a concentration of the mind that is effortless, where the knower and known are united. In Hongzhi's verse, it is suggested that we can enter a state where we know our unity with all things, even through a speck of dust, or any other sensation or cognition. And we can realize that the ten thousand forms, which we perceive as outside, come together as us. This is the single seal: all things coming together to make up our actual self, which consolidates in this moment and has no permanence. Our true nature is empty except for a wind blowing or the reflected moon. Steve Paxton tells us to "accept the first perturbation of that emptiness as the focus" (2022, n.p.). Only metaphor can point to these momentary flashes of insight.

Some of the states that emerge during extended sitting practice (or the Underscore) feel transcendent, but the point of Zen practice isn't about non-ordinary states. Rather, it is about waking up in the ordinary and to the everyday. Sitting upright is a ritual enactment of Buddha's realization. As such, the practice and the realization are one. We do not sit in order to become something else, but to acknowledge what we already are. Each of us fundamentally has Buddha nature. Although this may not be apparent, it is part of Buddha's teaching. Buddhism also teaches about the three poisons that keep us from expressing our inherent awakened nature: greed, hate, and delusion. These three negative qualities of the mind originate the actions that bring about non-beneficial situations. We see them moving through the world now, as they have for some time. They create and bind us to suffering. The only way I have found to negotiate this difficult teaching is to come together in small groups, put up ethical guardrails, and intentionally explore together. I need the friction of intimate communication with other bodies and minds to knock off my encrusted selfishness. This is usually uncomfortable. The three poisons function by justifying any unwholesome action I may take, such as grabbing what I want or pushing away what bothers me, without regard for the needs of others. The antidote to greed, hate, and delusion is to abide in discomfort while learning to express our innate generosity and kindness; and to build a capacity to tolerate not-knowing. Embracing not-knowing comes with the disorientation that results from questioning the certainty of our positions. Those dancing CI develop a great tolerance for disorientation. As we care for our dance partners, we directly know generosity and kindness. The tender concern we offer and receive on the dance floor is a manifestation of Buddha nature. In this improvisational arena, certainty can be replaced with curiosity, and we can explore together with more openness and subtlety. The community builds trust by calling forth and re-entering Hongzui's original dwelling.

CI dancers share an implicit question with many Zen practitioners: What is the nature of reality as perceived within and by this body/mind? Both our lineages interpret experience and relay voices of the past which offer hard-won insights which can be used to help pry us out of current societal blind spots. Since those from different times were conditioned by different events, wrestling with their insights can help us see our situation with fresh eyes. Bodhidharma, who initiated Zen Buddhism in China, is supposed to have said, "If you use your mind to study reality, you won't understand either your mind or reality. If you study reality without using your mind, you'll understand both." In CI we are given an unusual set of circumstances to study reality: the surface of the skin, our sense of self in space, and our soft-focused visual impressions of a rapidly shifting field, to name only a few. All these points of information pour in all the time during a dance, while the mind comes along for a ride. The universe speaks to us through the laws of physics and our partner's touch. We listen by being falling, spiraling, rolling bodies, and we can study the mind as we find a way into this dance about movement itself.

Dance Improvisation as Embodiment of Mystery

As we dance together using improvisation, new possibilities enter the world. In each listening situation we have a chance to see and feel multiple lines forward. When choices are made, bodies collide, flow together, pull apart, bounce, leap, rest; and we emerge as changed beings. The person coming out of a duet is not the same one that went in. There is a mysterious exchange and enlargement. Aldous Huxley once observed: "Ritual dances provide a religious experience that seems more satisfying and convincing than any other. . . . It is with their muscles that humans most easily obtain knowledge of the divine" (Ehrenreich 2007, 33). There are many examples of dance used for explicitly religious ends. Many of them utilize a detailed choreography to unify a group, or use repeated movements to induce a trance state. But there are forms of improvisational devotion expressed through movement which break the trance and keep awareness rooted in the senses. When deep inner awareness is linked to nuanced perception of the outer world, an individual is stretched in both directions. Expanding and exploring this inside/outside exchange is one of CI's great gifts, and produces a spaciousness that invites the unknown and unknowable.

Early in their history, Quakers got their name, in part, because when they felt Spirit move, they moved. As time went on, physical stillness became the norm and was enforced during Meeting for Worship. Movement was exiled, yet not everyone welcomed this truncated form, and the Shakers came out of this rift. In the mid-1700s, those in disagreement with the new norm founded a new Society where they could keep dancing their worship. In her article *Enlivening Spirits*, Kimerer LaMothe further stated, "The United Society of Believers began with dance. There was no moment at the beginning of the movement when members came together and decided to start dancing. The movement formed among a group of people who refused to stop dancing" (2017, 106). Shaker historian Edward Andrews describes the earliest Shaker practice as beginning in silence. Then worshipers would be:

> seized by such ecstasy of spirit that, like leaves in the wind, they were moved into the most disordered exercises: running about the room, jumping, shaking, whirling, reeling, and at the same time shouting, laughing or singing snatches of song. No form existed: someone would impulsively cry out a line from the psalms, part of a hymn, or a phrase—perhaps in an unknown tongue— . . . another might suddenly start whirling like a dervish; then, as in a Quaker meeting, all for a time would be silent." (Andrews 1953, 7)

While this description doesn't directly follow the Underscore, I am struck by the similarities given the distance in time and culture. It reminds me of parallel evolution when the same form is generated in different species for a similar function. Using intertwined movement is a vehicle to know ourselves and the nature of reality in a fundamental way. Children do this through play. Andrews's description comes from detractors of Shaker practice and doesn't take a perspective from within the dance, but it sounds like the possibility of play was included for the worshippers. In his book *The Art of Is: Improvising as a Way of Life*, Nachmanovitch offers that "voice and body are the oldest toys. In an age of high technology, they remain the ultimate toys. Artistic experience that seems frivolous may also allow people entry into states of being profoundly present with each other and themselves" (2019, 76). From events that may first appear chaotic, group improvisation self-organizes in a vital and meaningful way. I wonder about this organizing force.

Clearly, CI circles and Shaker theology differ in their description of this dynamic organization, but both use the body to investigate and express something from a deep somatic source. Nancy Stark Smith said that through practicing the Underscore "experience is revealing knowledge" (2012, n.p.). LaMothe contends that by Shakers using spontaneous dance as

The Religious Function of Contact Improvisation 257

> their key theological treatise, dance garners praise not only as an expression of Shaker beliefs, but as their authorizing source. . . . For the Shakers, dancing is the medium through which the God that the dancing enables them to conceive, becomes real for them. Dance, in this sense, is "theopraxis" where theopraxis refers to bodily actions that educate the senses of those who do them, to feel and know a given conception of the divine. (2017, 103)

The dance makes it possible to perceive a thought form about divinity through the moving body. It is an investigation and a realization.

But there is a danger when we begin with a concept of some higher power. The divine that interests me is sought not only out-there as a describable entity, but is immanent and living at the core of each of us. In many religious traditions there is a tendency to superimpose an ideal over who we actually are and then suppress what doesn't fit the ideal. Perhaps there is excessive infatuation with the Light as a metaphor for God, as it may exclude what is outside an idealized framework without embracing the shadow; too much Spirit and not enough Body. Marion Woodman, Jungian analyst and one of the early influences in the development of Authentic movement, spoke about the battle between spirit and matter in a lecture entitled *Holding the Tension of the Opposites*. She contends that there is a seductive quality of Light as an ideal that resonates in us and creates a desire to "transcend this terrible earth." She continues, "Spirit when it is just allowed to float in a disembodied way can be murderous, because it is judgmental [and] self righteous." She identifies the rejected side as in and of the body which is considered to be "opaque, dense and less than spirit." But if we can come close to our darkness, a "pearl light" can emerge to rejoin the parts we have been taught were incompatible (1991, n.p.).

In CI practice, our awareness awakens in the spaces internal to us, where there is little actual light. We enter the places where the eyes cannot follow, and ears, nose, and tongue have limited range. In our explorations on the dance floor, so many gradations of touch have been found and named. By including the brush of wrist, the scrape of the floor, pounding heart, cold air, peristalsis, and pain, we open to a mysterious life force which tends toward care and harmony. We knowingly enter a collective field that calls forth a palpable Presence that hums with vitality. Our truest self is available in this larger field when we bow to one another. When we bow to the body, we stitch together spirit and matter. In this way, CI can offer an antidote to spiritual traditions that might impose a cramped vision of what it means to be a good human. The possibilities for physical expression of this electric sense of presence are vast. Through our imperfect and authentic corporeal selves, we can be wholehearted and full-bodied manifestations of the unconditioned source. In this way, we can discover what we want and what makes sense for each of us.

The religion I want holds both the actuality of the body and the metaphoric aspects of spirit and links them. Neither is superior, yet I don't want them to merge. The tension that arises from simultaneous inward focus and outward perception creates space which allows growth. Dancing with the specificity and quirkiness of others while experiencing my own unfolding mystery is where I come to know my gods. These encounters knock off the elements that deny who I am. Through these multilayered conversations, I come to know a more inclusive truth at the intersection of form and formlessness. My rib cage on your instep may hold the secret to embodied enlightenment, indeed must hold it, since awakening can be entered through every sensation. This secret is being shouted by every plank, blade of grass, and rotating spine, if we only have ears to hear.

References

Andrews, Edward. 1953. *A People Called Shakers*. New York: Dover Publications.

Dogen, Eihei. 1231. *Self-Receiving and Employing Samadhi*. https://www.sfzc.org/files/daily_sutras_Self-Receiving_and_Employing_Samadhi.

Dogen, Eihei. 1233. *Genjokoan*. https://www.sfzc.org/files/daily_sutras_Genjo_Koan.

Ehrenreich, Barbara. 2007. *Dancing in the Streets: A History of Collective Joy*. New York, NY: Metropolitan Books, Henry Hold and Company.

Jung, C. G. 1958. *Collected Works*, Vol. 11. Princeton, NJ: Princeton University Press.

LaMothe, Kimerer L. 2017." Enlivening Spirits: Shaker Dance Ritual as Theopraxis." *Théologiques* 25/1: 103.

Leighton, Taigen Dan. 2000. *Cultivating the Empty Field: The Silent Illumination of Zen Buddhist Master Hongzhi*. San Francisco, CA: North Point Press.

Leighton, Taigen Dan. 2002. "Introduction: Hongzui, Dogen, and the Background of Shikantaza." In *The Art of Just Sitting*, edited by John Daido Loori. Boston: Wisdom Publications, 1–10.

Loring, Patricia. 1997. *Listening Spirituality*, Vol. 2. New York: Openings Press.

Manuel, Zenju Earthlyn. 2011. *The Way of Tenderness: Awakening through Race, Sexually, and Gender*. Boston: Wisdom Publications.

Paxton, Steve. 2003. "Drafting Interior Techniques." In *Taken by Surprise*, edited by Ann Cooper Albright and David Gere. Middletown, CT: Wesleyan University Press, 175–183.

Paxton, Steve. 2020. "Pillow Voices Podcast: The Origins and Value of Contact Improvisation in the Words of Steve Paxton." Posted August 22, 2020, accessed April 9, 2023. https://pillowvoices.org/episodes/the-origins-and-value-of-contact-improvisation-in-the-words-of-steve-paxton/transcript.

Paxton, Steve. 2022. "CQ Special Edition CI@50: The Initiation of Contact Improvisation for Me." Posted May 14, 2022, accessed April 9, 2023. https://contactquarterly.com/contact-improvisation/newsletter/view/the-initiation-of-contact-improvisation#$.

Smith, Nancy Stark. 2012. "An Emergent Underscore: A Conversation with Nancy Stark Smith, London." Posted by dancetechtv on June 12, 2013, accessed April 9, 2023. https://m.youtube.com/watch?v=gzG609NWp1Y.

Smith, Nancy Stark. 2020. "Conversation with Nancy Stark Smith." Martin Keogh's blog. Posted September 14, 2020, accessed April 9, 2023. https://martinkeogh.com/?page_id=1557.

Stevens, John. 1995. *The Secrets of Aikido*. Boston: Shambhala Press.

Tabor, William. 1991. *Four Doors to Meeting for Worship* (Pendle Hill Pamphlets, Book 306). Wallingford, PA: Pendle Hill Publications.

Ueshiba, Morihei, 1963. *Memoir of the Master*. Scotts Valley, CA: CreateSpace Publishing.

Ueshiba, Morihei. 2005. *The Art of Peace*. Translated and edited by John Stevens. Boston: Shambhala.

Woodman, Marion, 1991. *Holding the Tension of the Opposites*. Boulder, CO: Sounds True.

Local Communities/Global Contexts

Ann Cooper Albright

From its beginnings, Contact Improvisation developed as a peripatetic form. Early dancers traveled back and forth between Oberlin College in Ohio and Bennington College in Vermont, between New York City and Northampton, Massachusetts, from the East Coast to the West Coast (often with stops at Naropa Institute in Colorado on the way), and in Canada, from Montreal and Toronto to Vancouver. Traveling and teaching workshops, sometimes with informal performances along the route, was a way of life, a way of sharing the dance. By the early 1980s, those cross-country treks expanded to include England, where Steve Paxton taught regularly at Dartington College, and Europe, where institutions such as the Theatre School in Amsterdam and Tanzfabrik in Berlin frequently hosted contemporary American dancers steeped in CI. Students from all over the world began to travel to these hubs for intensive workshops or big festivals with several day-long jams. They would then return to their hometowns and share their experiences with friends. As an improvisational form, Contact can be adapted to many different circumstances and the interests of the local community. Reports from Brazil, Denmark, Oregon, and Texas, among other places, fill the CI newsletters published in *Contact Quarterly*. Two decades into the twenty-first century, there are thriving communities of Contact practitioners in many countries all over the world. Like any global phenomenon, however, this spread of the form included unspoken gendered, racial, and class hierarchies. The essays in this section take stock of these pathways of influence and inspiration, charting the implications of their uneven exchanges while also recognizing the ways in which this form fosters community.

As Contact gained popularity at the end of the twentieth century, it was not unusual for American teachers to offer intensive workshops in exotic places such as Costa Rica or beach towns in Mexico and even India. Rarely did these (often male) teachers consider the emotional and economic impact of these events on the local dance community whose members were structurally locked out by the high cost of the workshops. In their provocative essay, "Resistances and Horizons: EPIICO, Community, and Self-Organization," Chapter 15, the Mexican feminist collective EPIICO takes this privileged cluelessness to task, fiercely calling out the uneven system of work-study and arguing for a recognition of their participation as critical and valuable. This writing began as an intervention during a panel at the *Critical Mass: CI @ 50* conference and then was revised to include their experiences during the 7th Gathering of CI in Mexico two months later. In their piece, the collective insists that their experience—the places where they live, work, take care of their families and one another— is a critical foundation for their dancing. This acknowledgment of national histories, economic contexts, and environmental impact is just as important as learning new skills and hosting well-known teachers. Through the process of decolonizing CI by embracing a potent form of "communitarian-territorial feminism" influenced by their Zapatista sisters, these women reclaimed their unique corporealities as the ground for growing their own movement practice.

As the first major CI event in Latin America after the pandemic, the 7th Gathering of CI in Patzcuaro, Michoacán, was framed as a "return" to dancing together. The themes of this event included Self-Care and Collective Care, Diversity and Inclusion, as well as Community and Globality. EPIICO's discussion of this profoundly healing event begins with a litany of "re's." "Returning, rethinking, rediscovering, reliving, re-encountering, revolving, reflowing, reflecting, reclassifying, reproducing, restructuring, resisting, renaming, regrouping." Participants in that gathering reflected on the power of a CI event that was attuned to their needs—affordable, in Spanish, and non-hierarchical in its organization. They were able to create a new paradigm for coming together, a way for dancing and co-creating in an equitable space that was environmentally and energetically sustainable.

Chapter 16, "Making Contact: Presenting and Creating Spaces of Contact Improvisation in India," by Guru Suraj and Adrianna Michalska, explores some of the same themes of the previous essay. Certainly, the example of the Goa Contact Festival, which began in 2010 and was primarily curated by European teachers, echoes some of the same cultural insensitivities. Suraj, who is a Tamil CI dancer, and Michalska, who is originally from Poland but now is based in India, explain the complexities of introducing a dance form based in physical touch in a huge country with deeply ingrained separations—both physical and metaphysical—between people. The intersecting threads of colonial legacies, territorial disputes, and religious, economic, and caste divisions create a veritable minefield of negotiations about where, when, and for whom this dance practice exists.

In 2011, a group of people, including the authors, formed the InContact collective, with the goal of making CI sustainable in India. They found that CI can be a hard sell in a country where there are many reservations about touching across gender and caste. The authors relate stories of the many difficulties they encountered, including having a planned workshop canceled due to sectarian violence. And yet, for each moment of frustration, there were powerful moments of breaking through restrictions. Their workshops were often received with enthusiasm by the participants, if not by the local authorities. Navigating intimacy in Contact is always fraught, as many of the essays in this volume attest. This is especially true in India, where the facilitators of workshops and jams have had to be very clear about the fact that this is not a sexual space. Much of the collective's focus in the past few years has been on integrating participants from different backgrounds, proactively reaching out to lower caste or economically disadvantaged communities. They have worked with a Dalit theater group in Chennai and public-school children in Kerala. As the authors make clear, facilitating cross-caste participation is a radical proposition in India and it is important to "listen to the space" while introducing physical contact. Sometimes, the best approach is to interject some humor and make sure folks are having fun.

During the months before *Critical Mass*, I was asked to lead two Zoom events in China, one in Beijing and one in Shanghai. This was a moment when the country was in COVID lockdown. Hearing people's enthusiasm for Contact Improvisation and their interest in the 50th anniversary celebrations (even if they could not travel) inspired me to include a discussion about CI in East Asia in these pages. Fortunately, Yuting Wang, a former student, was able to help organize the panel, and I am grateful for her help, including her transcription and translation of the roundtable discussion. To give some context for the growth of the form in East Asia, Huichao Ge wrote an introduction to Chapter 17, "Contact Improvisation in China and

Taiwan," which details the beginnings of CI in Taiwan and Hong Kong in the 1990s. This was a moment when dancers like Ming-Shen Ku and Mui Chak-Yin were able to live and study in the United States. Ming-Shen's first exposure to the form was at the University of Illinois, Urbana-Champaign. Like so many early CI dancers across the world, when she returned to Taiwan in 1992, she needed people with whom to dance, so she began to teach Contact, eventually hosting Steve Paxton and other American teachers. Her company, KU & Dancers, is one of the few groups to center their creative work in Contact Improvisation.

It seems that right from the beginning, an important focus of CI in East Asia was its open, public nature. This was particularly true for the facilitators of China's TOUCH Contact Improvisation Festival in 2016, whose theme was "Body Empowerment for the Body." Similarly, Alito Alessi's Dance Ability work inspired another dancer, Maru, to become certified in its pedagogy and to introduce CI to people with autism and debilitating diseases. Maru has studied extensively with Nancy Stark Smith, as well as co-teaching with Alessi in Hong Kong, and founded Symbiosis Dance to work with populations across diverse medical conditions. As Contact spread throughout mainland China in the first decade of the twenty-first century, dancers formed the iDance Network to share resources and envision what a distinctly Asian approach to the form might be. Recently, a CI research group was convened to translate articles from *Contact Quarterly* and other important sources for the growing readership in China.

The intersection of Contact Improvisation and mixed-ability dancing is also a focus of the next two essays in this section. Ana Carolina Bezerra Teixeira's Chapter 18, "Deviant Bodies: Improvising Survival in Brazil," documents her experience as a disabled performer in Brazil. In the 1990s, Alito Alessi's Dance Ability work found a very receptive audience in South and Central America. For instance, the 25th anniversary of Contact (held at Oberlin College in 1997) featured a mixed-ability weekend with the Brazilian Compania 100 Habilidades performing. Teixeira danced for 11 years with Roda Viva Dance Company, eventually taking over its leadership from 2004 to 2007. While directing the company, she shifted the emphasis on using CI as a way to generate movement to using CI as a political practice. Not only did Contact inform their movement training, but CI became the pathway for reaching other communities, including disabled communities. Taking to the streets, the company crafted actions that, in her words, "foregrounded the perception of our bodies in their spasms, tensions, fractures, amputations, and all their deviations." In this compelling and provocative narrative, Teixeira questions the neoliberal bias toward "efficient" bodies, employing CI to re-envision disability as a creative perspective, rather than an identity grounded in limitation or lack.

Chapter 19, "Queering Contact Improvisation with Sara Ahmed (and the Wheelchair)," centers the wheelchair as an object that elicits Mª Paz Brozas Polo's own moving, thinking, and writing. Drawing on Ahmed's theoretical interventions in phenomenology, Polo argues that disability (as signified by the wheelchair) offers an opportunity to queer CI. Like Teixeira, but speaking from her perspective as a professor of dance in Spain, Polo is interested in collective navigation. She uses Sara Ahmed's book *Queer Phenomenology* to chart the possibilities of dancing with and through disorientation. Queer can be an identity ("I am queer") or it can be a verb ("to queer"). In Contact, dancing (with or without a wheelchair) is a practice of risk. Leaning toward a partner, we necessarily give up our physical stability in order to share a center with another person. This merging is wonderfully unstable and offers the opportunity to think beyond the binaries of self and other, able-bodied and disabled, individual

262 Resistance and Support

and community. After describing her experiences working with Isabelle Brunaud and her company, ANQA Danse avec les Roues, Polo critiques the physical inaccessibility of many Contact workshops and festival venues. Nonetheless, propelled by Ahmed's thinking, she affirms a queer and crip vision of bodies and wheelchairs dancing side by side.

The final essay in this section is staged as a conversation between two Contact teachers, one from Davis, California, and one from Copenhagan, Denmark. Chapter 20, "Intensive Curiosity: A Dialogue about Teaching CI," by Joseph Dumit and Dorte Bjerre Jensen, acknowledges that Contact Improvisation classes and jams can be porous, noting that some instruction is often offered before a jam and that moments of open dancing can be integral to many formal class situations. Nonetheless, they want to pose the question: How does one teach Contact Improvisation? Their discussion parses the question of emphasis: Do we teach a set of physical exercises or open explorations? While it is true that certain skills can help make the form safer for everyone involved, there is always the danger that certain activities can quickly become "dogma," especially for beginners, who frequently try to copy directly what they see the teachers doing. Much of the authors' interest is in the ways that teachers engage students' curiosity, empowering them to explore variations on a theme rather than steps in a sequence. This allows for attention to the subtler aspects of dancing intimately with another human being in all their complexities.

Drawing from various conversations with other teachers and from their survey of teaching strategies published in *Contact Quarterly*, Dumit and Jensen present different facets of the form. One important section discusses how "labbing" operates in the context of CI, with many workshop situations structured as investigative labs where folks share the responsibility for leading explorations. This is a model of practice as research, in which the roles of teacher and student are porous. Even in a more traditional setting in which there is a designated instructor, the class itself may be improvised, with the teacher following the mood of the class rather than the syllabus on the page. Quoting Simone Forti, the authors discuss her desire to "create a structure that the people [in the workshop] can transcend." In the end, this essay argues that teaching Contact Improvisation is most often a question of setting up the conditions for dancers to pursue their own curiosity.

15

Resistances and Horizons

EPIICO, Community, and Self-Organization

EPIICO: Ariadna Franco Martínez, Esmeralda Padilla García, Elisa Romero Morato, Mariana Torres Juárez, and Laura Villeda Aguirre; translated by Caroline Tracey

Introduction

This essay is not an academic article, but rather a collective writing based in our experience. For that reason, we do not cite other authors. We believe that we don't need to justify our experiences by basing them in authors who are not from our region, who enjoy a diversity of privileges (free time, access to creative spaces, economic resources), and who don't share our experiences as subalterns (racialized, peripheral, and precarious), because their voices don't represent our realities.

The bodily experience is a valid source of knowledge that is capable of sustaining the experiences spilled into this essay. We situate ourselves from our geographies, life histories, and corporealities as a political posture.

In Mexico and Central America, the written record about Contact Improvisation (CI) is scarce, since it has been disseminated [*socializado*] very little outside the spheres that have produced it. The present text is an effort to condense our knowledge-experience, and it contains fragments of texts gathered in the Seventh Gathering of Contact Improvisation in Mexico, whose central theme was the decolonization of the practice. This writing is the result of a chaotic collective process among the current members of the collective, who also take up the voices of other members of the CI community of Mexico and Latin America.

The necessity of a text to express and recognize ourselves from our particularities came about after having participated in the Panel "Global and Local: Facilitating Contact in Different Communities" at Oberlin College in Ohio, part of *Critical Mass: CI @ 50*, one of the celebrations of the 50th anniversary of Contact Improvisation.

After presenting the document at *Critical Mass: CI @ 50*, we noticed the resonance that the text had with other practitioners from Latin America and India, who identified and felt moved by what we described. For that reason, we received requests to share the text that we had presented during the panel. This document is also a response to those requests.

After the panel, some teachers from other countries approached us, asking what would be the "correct" way to relate to Mexico and our collective; there were also questions about our lived experiences. We have no pretentions of answering all the questions that we received, since we believe that it should be left to privileged white bodies to find new ways to relate to us and to share their knowledge without extractive and colonial practices.

Ariadna Franco Martínez, Esmeralda Padilla García, Elisa Romero Morato, Mariana Torres Juárez, Laura Villeda Aguirre, and Caroline Tracey
Resistances and Horizons In: *Resistance and Support*. Edited by: Ann Cooper Albright, Oxford University Press. © Oxford University Press 2024. DOI: 10.1093/9780197776308.003.0016

We also offer the clarification that we do not position ourselves against people with white skin, but against whiteness [*blanquitud*], understood as a historical structure of privileges granted since colonization to certain groups with certain physical characteristics. Thinking from this understanding of whiteness does not exclude the possibility that there are dark-skinned people who experience privileges, or that there could be white people experiencing forms of oppression.

In the original text in Spanish, we mainly write using the feminine forms of words because those of us writing are women; we also play with the use of the *x*, the combination of the two forms, masculine and feminine, and with the duplication of the final syllable of the words. All of these forms coexist in the text, and we believe that diversity, far from causing confusion, enriches the reading by naturalizing the varied use of feminist forms of resistance, including those that have to do with the uses of language.

The essay is composed of the following parts: "About our Collective, EPIICO"; "The Appropriation of the Practice"; "On the COVID-19 Pandemic"; "The Seventh Gathering of CI in Mexico"; "A Politics of Our Own"; "Ideas, Philosophies, and Thoughts That Accompany and Inspire Our Manner of Doing Contact Improvisation"; and "Conclusions and Final Questions."

About our Collective: EPIICO

The work that we have done is that of resisting and building a possible world based on our tools and possibilities. To create and sustain our collective space, we have taken inspiration from diverse philosophical and countercultural movements: the Zapatistas, feminism, communitarian-territorial feminism, agroecology, constructive spaces such as EIMCILA (The International Conference of Teachers of Contact Improvisation of Latin America), and the continual conversation with our Latin American sisters.

All of this thought has allowed us to listen and give space to our **mixed-race body** [*cuerpo mestizo*], a body that resists conquest, that resists Western impositions, and that recalls in its memory the ancestral wisdom that comes from our ancestry and that appears to mediate and discern between the exploration of certain physical principles and the imposition of a certain way of doing CI and of conceptualizing its principles.

The *mestizo* body is one that has wisdom regarding how to move itself, to resolve and create in the conditions at hand, that does not stop dreaming because it has learned to work, to fight, and to construct new possibilities to dance and create in collective. This mixed body that is also so rejected and denigrated and that for many people (including Mexicans) is not the type of body that should be practicing or teaching CI.

We are a collective of Mexican women—*mestizas*, racialized (dark-skinned), lower-middle class; we come from the periphery of the city. Moving ourselves anywhere implies an hour commute. We do not live in the white, privileged neighborhoods; we combine our corporal investigation with diverse employments like working in cafeterias, giving workshops, dance classes, and other types of classes in independent spaces. Most of us have multiple jobs to survive, because in Mexico, for our social class, it is not easy to survive being only a dancer, performer, or dance teacher.

In July 2014 we began to organize ourselves to start a group to regularly practice Contact Improvisation. Previously, some of us had attended a workshop at the UVA (the Artistic

Liaison Entity of the Tlatelolco Cultural Center) where they had done CI. Some of us come from the contemporary dance world; some of us graduated from dance schools; others have received our education outside of institutional settings. And we must recognize that in our country being able to get a college degree and study arts is a class privilege, so we are fortunate in that sense.

Our objective was to come together to dance, explore, and oversee our own practice, simultaneously as apprentices and as comrades. Almost all of us wanted to share and explore, in a laboratory format, ideas that hadn't fit into other spaces and that resonated with the language of Contact Improvisation (see Figure 15.1).

The majority of the initial practices were guided by members who had studied with professors outside of Mexico, principally in Europe and the United States, and who had a clearer understanding of the principles of CI. By that time, there had been various attempts to create a CI community in Mexico City and there were some people teaching it; however, none of those spaces was what we were looking for.

When we started to gather, we had the expectation of creating a large community as existed in other countries, with the desire to dance CI "well," that is, to learn its principles correctly. When we heard that a foreign teacher was going to be in the city, we found a way to invite them to the space. Some members dedicated themselves particularly to organize classes and workshops, without being remunerated in any way for that work.

Over the course of the years that have ensued, we realized that there was not just one way to dance CI, and that our country and our contexts are very different from those of the other countries where CI has flourished, and thus that our bodies, dances, and community are also distinct and singular.

Figure 15.1. One of the first collective practices at Piso 7 as EPIICO in 2013. Printed with permission from the participants in the practice. Photographer EPIICO.

In Mexico the spaces where CI is recognized as a practice that are legitimated by the art and dance worlds are few. Among them are the aforementioned UVA, which is attached to the National Autonomous University of Mexico; and the Center for Choreographic Research of the Institute of Beaux-Arts, where some of us first encountered the practice of CI and which for a long time offered us the use of dance studios for our laboratories and open jams. Although we have received some economic assistance for presentations, most of our activities have been realized in independent spaces or public spaces such as parks and plazas.

During the years that we have existed as a group, the members of the collective have changed; and we have nourished our practice by taking courses, workshops, classes, attending festivals, networking, interweaving with the CI communities of Mexico and the world, and studying related corporal practices.

It is also worth acknowledging the affective ties that have grown between us, turning partnership into friendship and holding the dance practice. Dialogue, reflection, and discussion are pillars of our collectivity. We recognize the importance of continually questioning in our practice what we do, from where, for whom, and why.

The Appropriation of the Practice

From the start, we have understood ourselves to be a space of practice open to anyone who would like to train and practice this confusing somatic language that makes us feel dance like none other. For a few years EPIICO (Space of Practice and Investigation into Contact Improvisation, by its initials in Spanish) maintained a weekly practice and jam; any curious person was welcome to the laboratory, and the rental fee for the spaces was shared among all the participants.

However, with the passage of time we realized the necessity of excluding certain forms of masculinity in order to cultivate safe spaces for women to dance. We encountered men who entered dance spaces with intentions of coming on to women, men who refused to renounce their privileges, who did not listen, who wanted to direct or instruct us all the time, who danced exclusively with women, and who took advantage of their experience in the practice.

Despite the context of Mexico, where we have high rates of femicide and violence against women, and despite the fact that from the start we have sought safe spaces, it took us time to recognize that some forms of patriarchal violence had filtered into our spaces; we continue to learn to identify and take actions regarding them. For example, we created filters for entry into the activities we organized, and we have denied entry to certain masculine bodies that reproduce macho attitudes in the spaces we create—listening and dialogue have been part of the process.

We also saw the necessity to exclude interests that diverged from the exploration of the physical principles of CI—therapeutic-type interests that ended up limiting our exploration of movement, rather than enriching it. There were individuals who during the practices had findings that had to do more with their internal processes—psychic, relational, or emotional—and for whom we did not have the tools or the interest to offer the support they were looking for. We recognize that the practice can take us to deep places, and we decided to invite individuals to inhabit those spaces with responsibility and listening, but without letting the practice overflow into therapy. We saw that our experiences transform constantly to mold our collective approach to CI, just as the characteristics of the practice spaces do.

Now we see ourselves as a collective that has had changes in its composition due to the exit, entry, and return of some of its members. The activities that we have organized have been transformed as well; in the beginning we developed our work in regular classes, workshops, jams, performances, and meetups/conferences in the style that we observed taking place in the United States and Europe (always with a view to our own context). Later, we opened our listening to the Latin American context, and as a result of the COVID-19 pandemic we were able to listen to our own voice with greater clarity, and it made us situate our practice and reflection within our own context.

On the COVID-19 Pandemic

The COVID-19 pandemic is another event that has modified our personal and collective practice. In March 2020 the pandemic was declared in Mexico; we had many activities in progress, and like the rest of the world, we had to stop—stop to understand what was going on, to evaluate how to continue our practice that we love so much, our life-giving practice. During the pause we maintained a continual dialogue about possibilities, responsibilities, self-care, and collective care.

From the starting point of the particularities of the members of the collective, and from the care of the social and affective connections that each maintains, we generated accords regarding the conditions for continuing our practice of CI. Some of the decisions were to generate weekly practices only for the core of the collective, to personally take on the risks of meeting up, to each practice self-care according to the way we understood it, to collectively cover the rent of the dance studios, to take a collective responsibility in the event that one of us caught COVID-19, and to support one another in the management of the illness.

In addition to the practice space for the core group, in October 2020 we organized a virtual meetup, the Fifth Gathering of Contact Improvisation in Mexico, followed by an in-person, self-organized retreat limited to a small number of participants from the CI community in Mexico. The virtual meetup took place in collaboration with dancers from Mexico and other countries, with whom we dared to explore movement mediated by virtuality, discovering limitations and possibilities for Contact Improvisation and some related corporeal practices. We appreciated that the virtual medium allowed us to dance synchronously with people who inhabit other geographies, that we could connect with them in a way that maintained distance while also sustaining and keeping the community active.

For two years we maintained a closed weekly practice while simultaneously holding conversations about the conditions of continuing our practice in the pandemic, about how and when to open it to others, and whom to invite when the public health conditions permitted it. The words *self-care*, *collective care*, and *security* were very present in our reflections, conversations, and dances. We recognized that the individual is also part of the collective.

During the pandemic some foreign teachers (male and female) came to Mexico with the intention to give workshops and to organize retreats and workshops in natural areas of the country. Partially this was because the mobility restrictions here were less drastic than in other countries. This increased the number of retreats, festivals, and workshops that were offered in paradisiacal sites, at costs inaccessible to most Mexicans, especially in a context in which many people had lost their employment due to the pandemic. In addition, various of these events were advertised only in English, while the linguistic majority of Mexico is

Spanish. We observed that these teachers were not interested in what was happening in the Mexican community, nor in how we were experiencing the pandemic. Thus, it appeared that the activities they were offering were directed only at foreigners, which was very impactful for us; we experienced it as an extractivist and colonialist practice at the height of a global pandemic. These practices reaffirmed that this is not the CI we hope to reproduce, and that we do not want to attend or create events from such a completely mercenary logic.

In May 2022, we decided to continue with the weekly CI laboratory for the core group and to open a weekly open jam to the rest of the community. We devised the jams for a small group of people, and incorporated recommendations for preventing the spread of COVID-19.

The Seventh Gathering of CI in Mexico

Returning, reflecting, rethinking, rediscovering, reliving, re-encountering, revolving, re-flowing, reflecting, reclassifying, reproducing, restructuring, resisting, renaming, regrouping.

In July 2022 we returned from the conference in Oberlin vibrating with what had been expressed by our comrades from Latin America and India, with the desire to put all our reflections into action as we prepared for the Seventh Gathering of CI in Mexico, which was to take place in September. To our surprise, our invitation to gathering echoed across Latin America: Costa Rica, El Salvador, Guatemala, Uruguay, Argentina, and with fellow Mexican comrades in Monterrey, Puebla, Morelia, Hermosillo, and Mexico City.

The Seventh Gathering was framed as a return, given that due to the pandemic it had not taken place in an in-person format for two years and that we were coming out of a long confinement. The question was: a return to what? The themes that gave life to the 2022 CI Gathering were: Contact after and in Pandemic, Self-care and Collective Care, Diversity and Inclusion, Community and Globality, and Intersectionality. All of these were products of the questioning and reflection that we had undertaken during our trajectory as a collective.

In this iteration we worked in collaboration with Casa Werma and the Jesuit College Cultural Center in Patzcuaro, Michoacán. We selected these places due to the fact that both are spaces that open themselves up to distinct forms of exchange, where the main goal was not the money we could bring in, nor attracting tourism, nor using the lands of Patzcuaro in an extractivist manner.

The Gathering was nonprofit. If we were going to encounter one another again, it was not going to be to repeat what we had done before, but to find new ways to relate to one another. The invitation was an open one, but we did undertake a selection of participants, so that only those with kindred goals and who wanted to join in the questioning that we had framed would be welcome. The conference would be in Spanish, and those who spoke other languages would be supported with some translations, but being in Mexico, the discussions would be in Spanish. The cost would be equal for everyone, we would all pay according to our abilities from an agreed minimum for room and board, with the option to contribute, or not, something extra for the organizers (see Figure 15.2).

This cost was an accessible price for people in social conditions similar to ours, and we had the openness to make attendance possible for anyone who felt called to participate but who could not afford the fee. The group was organized between rooms, cabins, and campsites, divided according to the needs of each person; we all received the same, and we all received abundance. The commitment of the conference was to a collaborative process equally in the

Figure 15.2. The 4th Gathering of Contact Improvisation in Mexico, itinerant meetup celebrated in CDM, Mexico. Printed with permission from the participants in the gathering. Photographer Dalia Ju.

practice of CI as in the sustaining of life; thus it was expected that everyone involved herself equally in the organization of dance activities, as well as in kitchen duties, food preparation, and the cleaning of the spaces during our stay. Here we will share a reflection by Alí Salguero, a participant in the gathering:

> *I wondered how a retreat with a Latin American majority, with such an accessible cost and a decolonial aim, would be. I wondered how we would manage to achieve that decolonial endeavor. What implications does the word "achieve" have? Is it a goal, a standard, a fixed destination to which one aspires? Does "to achieve" imply a dichotomist (and therefore colonial) line of thought: it was achieved, or it wasn't? What other word can we use to refer to the teachings that emerge from Contact Improvisation and from this 7th Conference? I think of "approach," in a transit around and through strategies. Achievements are external and quantifiable manifestations; what one learns are approaches to an expanse of behaviors.*
>
> *The open spaces in the schedule permitted an appropriation of our time and our interests. Asking about the concerns of the participants and for opening the possibility of the collective generation of practices that address those interests was one route that can work for decolonizing Contact Improvisation conferences, dissolving the notion of "teacher" and "learner," transcending linear learning measured by achievements in favor of learning that is spiral, expansive, never-ending...*
> *BEING instead of DOING*

The same Latinas accustomed to going to festivals on scholarship, with discounts, to working extra hours, to sleeping in basements or in student dorms, now received the same,

270 Resistance and Support

worked the same, and danced the same, as Alejandra Garavito Aguilar (Guatemala) wrote in her reflection about the conference:

What do I reflect on? What do I say about being here? What happened, what hit me? I found my spine again and the non-space that supports me from behind; everything fits in the empty space and in the silences of what still has not yet been brought to my reality; my eyes guided between the yellow tatamis, the red bricks, the green leaves; I heard the dismembering voices of Spanish, that ancient imposition now decorated with generations of idiom, multidimensional wounds, multigenerational pleasures. I found myself with the earth tones, the dancing mestizes. How to dance this dance, how to hold this conversation without words? Vocabulary in construction in front of each body. What is (are) identity(ies)? Mine or what you know of me? Fluctuating membranes. . . . The risk of accepting myself in my now, paused, majestic, and monstrous, body, vessel, nucleus, and periphery, individual and collective at the same time. To let go of lack and embrace abundance. A thousand times mantra, a thousand times spiral, a thousand times the fall as the start of the flight to transform knowledge and experience into wisdom.

The Seventh Conference was a success, the first after various attempts. With the desire to see ourselves, to dance, to create something truly as a collective, 25 people came together to create a new, different way of being, dancing, and co-creating. But what happened for it to be possible? We believe that EPIICO has matured, over eight years of practice, and what happened is that we now know the importance of creating among ourselves, of sustaining a space, of valuing our bodies, of validating our ideas and knowledge-experience, and of not minimizing our efforts.

We add fragments of writings by some of the participants in the Seventh Gathering of CI in Mexico:

A world into which many worlds fit, the horizontality and decoloniality as formulations for the practice of Contact Improvisation in this seventh conference, where dance is in all the plans, all the shared quotidian tasks, where all of us are teachers and students, where we are hinge-bodies, a collective body, a contact body. We are arriving one by one to the house where we would live during the following days, like Tetris embedded by the gravitational dance of curiosity. I confess that I frowned at seeing that the dance spaces were one tight space of tatami mats and a wide field of grass . . . there was no dancing sliding on smooth wood like at Earthdance. We got along well with the living wood of the trees, the perfume of the flowers, insects, birds, rain, and even two earthquakes.

In particular, I was called to the conference by questions that have surrounded my being and my practice for a long time. The members of EPIICO put words to these feelings, which within the invitation was the common feeling. The firmness and clarity of the proposal generated a filter and a weight to a conference that could have repeated the common power dynamics and formulas that infringe upon us without being questioned. But in this occasion, time, energy, and space were taken to do it differently, inspired by the way it was done at the EMCILA in Uruguay from a few years earlier. (Andrea Scheel, Mexico)

I find in the textures of the grass that I step on a vegetal, vascular, and playful fascia that responds with great patience to my own fascia, which is more tight and viscous. Both are equally alive. Both form part of the same dance. By re-creating ourselves in the beautiful site of the seventh conference of Contact Improvisation in Mexico, the spaces of Casa Werma also recreate themselves in us, opening the possibility of reinventing themselves so that they, in their time, reinvent us. (Esteban Fredin, Mexico)

There is a horizontal proposal intervened in and co-created from the same group, without hierarchies nor judgments of the results. Decolonization begins to be seen where power is exercised from an exercised authority. Every community should feel how it should organize itself, every community is a collection of individuals with multiple thoughts and cultures, to construct "a world into which many worlds fit" where the integration and the uniting of the micro and macro worlds, where we weave ourselves as Latin American hinge-bodies, weaving, constructing, dreaming, smiling, and building together, improvisationally contacting our creation, rooting ourselves and recognizing our being, co-creating our own identity that we inhabit in the great and rich diversity that connects us to the living and pure earth, breathing. (Ricardo Azofeifa, Costa Rica)

We touched something of the alive in that conference. . . .
Something of the alive touched, spiraled, melted, moved, de-centralized structures and reorganized worlds.
We intuited something of the open, or we caught sight of it. We sensed it, perhaps; pacifying the curious and beauty-obsessed gaze I felt us awash in the oceanic beauty of the bodies.
We touched infinity and we intuited that it is impossible to define, to define it, to define us.
We touched something of the subtlety of Presence, too. . . .
(Carolina Fernández, Uruguay)

My body is a witness because it holds as traces and fissures the rubbings, the weights, the involuntary caress, the unknown spine, a multiplicity of fingers, hands, arms, elbows, hairs, smells. Hinge-skin, rhizomatic skin, that makes me lose the beginning of myself and extend myself and end 2,3,4 bodies away. Dear complicity, indifferent tenderness.

*My body remembers the fleeting rain, the foot merged with the eye, a thousand eyes, the crow that sings our meditation, the yawns that stretch, the hollow of the couches, the itch of the grass, the heat of the fireplace, the humid verdure, the surprises in the tastes that nourish us, the **bebitas** of wild and pristine liberty, the cold that gets into the bones, the head-hip that is an axis and a decentering, the swarm-mass-multitude-pack that sustains and rubs and weighs and sweats and envelops and embraces and dances and let me go.* (Yunuen Moreno, Mexico)

A Politics of Our Own

Even after 50 years of CI, we feel that a form of thought from a place of whiteness and colonization still permeates the practice. We believe that it is necessary to question from where CI is taught and reproduced.

Here we mention the three points that we named in the panel at Oberlin:

1. For Latin Americans of our social class, it is very difficult to come to a national or international conference. The majority of the time we cannot afford it, and we cannot leave

work for so much time. The practice of *helpers* is something that should change and/or disappear. We who are writing this essay have been *helpers* in various festivals in order to receive a lower cost that we can pay. We had to clean bathrooms, help in the kitchen, clean the studios, and so on, and at some festivals we slept in places that were not bedrooms or did not even have beds. At first, we thought that this was the way that we could attend these festivals given our conditions, but now, we know that we deserve to be in the same bedroom and in the same conditions as someone who has the privilege to pay for it. We reject that the tasks of cleaning and organization should be optional only for those who can pay the full cost, as though preparing food, washing dishes, or washing a floor were not part of the dance itself and even distanced us from the experience of coming together to dance. Once again, dance is seen as a merely pleasurable art.

2. Teaching, creating festivals, and giving workshops in Mexico: At first, our knowledge was limited to our experience, so we thought that it was a good idea to organize workshops to give more tools to the people who were starting to come to the practices. There were people who offered their work in a friendly way, who helped us understand what we were doing. And there were people who took advantage of their power, who charged the same prices as they charge in Europe where the economy is completely different, and we did work for them without receiving any compensation, perhaps because of inexperience or perhaps because of a complete normalization of the economic power that whiteness continually exercises in Mexico. In contrast, those who could pay those costs were in the majority foreigners and travelers, not locals. Fortunately, this did not last long.

We are not saying that foreigners should not come and teach, but we believe that it is important that they come with an understanding of the economic reality of the country they are visiting, and based on that, decide whether it will work or not for their interests. It is rather insensitive to look at the invitations posted in Facebook groups or in certain spaces in the city by North American or European teachers with costs that aren't at all related to our economy and with the message "join us." It's offensive to see teachers organizing workshops and festivals in beautiful and paradisiacal locations, in retreat centers were only people of the upper class and foreigners of sufficient means live, and that aren't places where local people can be. It's offensive to see workshops or retreats announced only in English, making clear that they presume that only people for whom it is their native language, or who speak it because they have had the privilege to learn and speak it, will sign up. We observe that many of these teachers and organizers expect that people from the Global North, as it is called, will come, because if it were truly for Mexicans, it would have a different cost.

Some teachers have implemented a practice of offering one or two scholarships to people from the locality or community or country where the retreat or festival is taking place; however, we believe that this does not solve the root of the problem and that it accentuates the rift by using terms like "dancers," "local people," and "connect with the community." We believe that this mode continues to perpetuate the hierarchical and paternalistic model that defines colonialism, where the teacher, generally a man, who is in possession of knowledge, chooses whom to help, instead of finding other ways to generate exchanges that de-articulate those structures. These other ways perhaps will involve less economic profit, but they will give space to listening, to conversation, and to exchange, which define CI.

In manifesting this point in the panel, we received comments and above all unsolicited advice, for example that we should do fundraising campaigns in order to attend national and international festivals, and we believe that this is not the solution either. It is necessary to create a different logic by which these events are organized, one that is decentralized from whiteness, that is inclusive and sensitive to other cultures and global economies.

3. The final point that we share is that if you come to Mexico, to our conference, or to the jams or classes that we organize, don't expect to have the same conditions that you have in Europe or North America. We work in spaces that we can afford, many of which are in the periphery of the city, which don't have a stave floor and aren't dance studios. We work in places that are interested in us and our practices and not only in collecting rent. The majority of these places are independent spaces.

Over the course of our experience, we have received comments from people from the United States as well as Mexico, with better economic conditions than we have, regarding why we work in spaces that are so ugly; we have been told that there are many dance studios in better neighborhoods and that if we moved, we could charge more. Obviously, they did not take into account that we—the people who dance—for the most part live on minimum wage; that for us it is a luxury to dedicate two or three hours of our time to the practice of CI; and that if we increase the price of our activities, we will make them inaccessible to people like us, who do not have a lot of disposable income. Also, in the classes we have received comments from North Americans who, when they arrive, ask where the teacher is—to us who are the teachers—because it seems that in their conception of CI, our small, brown bodies do not correspond with the phenotype of those who commonly teach/guide in their places of origin. Finally, there are those who have written on social media that Mexico City has no CI community because there isn't a jam when they are passing through the city, making invisible the work that we have been doing for eight years, at our own rhythm and possibility.

After sharing these points, we want to enunciate some postures that we have adopted in the spaces we maintain:

- To deny entry to masculine bodies that reproduce patriarchal activities in the spaces we construct, in the service of generating safe spaces for women to dance in.
- No longer organizing workshops and courses for foreign, heterosexual male teachers. We decided to stop working for men who do not question their privileges, and who use their power with personal intentions alien to the practice of CI.
- To not participate in organizing, nor in teaching, in festivals or events that take place in Mexico whose philosophical principles do not coincide with ours.

Ideas, Philosophies, and Thoughts That Accompany and Inspire Our Manner of Doing Contact Improvisation

Communitarian-Territorial Feminism and Why the Earth Should Be Respected

There is a type of feminism that emerged in Guatemala that speaks about the idea that we women are the earth, and that the earth is women. By taking care of the earth, we take care of our women, and by taking care of our women, we take care of the earth. The body [*cuerpa cuerpo*] turns once again into earth. Many of us found in CI a creative space of encounter and possibility. With the passage of time, we discovered that we started this collective because there was nothing like it in our lands, and it fell upon us to create the space. This space more and more takes care of women and distances itself from the masculine bodies that do not share our vision and care. This feminism speaks of territorial gathering, which implies a positioning from where women are, feel, act, and come together to defend in a collective manner their bodies and lands. We, as city-dwellers, want to take care of our earth from the locality that we inhabit.

To use the earth to obtain something is to turn it into an object; to come to our land because it is cheaper or because it offers better conditions at lower prices is to make it into merchandise, and when the earth becomes objectified or becomes merchandise, women also become objects and merchandise. Those who tend to clean rooms, studios, those who cook in retreat spaces, normally are women, and they do it for rather low pay. To create with the land is to create with the women of this territory; if those women do not have the resources or the interest to participate in such a practice, festival, or workshop, then that practice does not have a place in that setting. If it resonates with the women of a place, if they come together and become part of the proposal, then the earth welcomes that practice. Conversely, if you facilitate a workshop in a place where the women of those lands cannot access it, you are causing violence to that land.

Zapatismo, a "World in Which Many Worlds Fit," a Fight for Life

We believe, like our Zapatista sisters, in the necessity of imagining and constructing a different world: imagining and constructing other forms of doing politics and of being in society. The Zapatista project inspires us because it shows us the way of the communities that fight from below and to the left, against capitalism and the patriarchy, toward the construction of a new world, where many worlds fit, where many dances fit. We believe and we take up the seven Zapatista principles of the National Indigenous Council:

1. Propose and do not impose.
2. Convince and do not conquer.
3. Obey and do not direct.
4. Represent and do not replace.
5. Descend and do not ascend.
6. Serve and do not be served.
7. Construct and do not destroy.

We believe that these forms of political life are very relevant, and for that reason we want a horizontal organization that goes against patriarchal, hierarchical, and vertical practices.

We have shared practices of CI in rural meetups, self-organized festivals, and in support of political demands and struggles. We have danced at marches and offered our bodies when a given political event resonates with us. Our CI has taken place in the streets, in markets, parks, plazas, universities, and in any place where we feel we can contribute something. In the same way, when it is important to listen or to give space, we give it, which is to say, when it falls on us to bear witness to other voices, we support them with our presence, our listening.

Because *we want a world into which many worlds fit*, it's necessary to learn to listen, to give space, and to learn to recognize ourselves in difference. That phrase resonated in the Seventh Conference and continued echoing with various participants.

Our Zapatista sisters have also taught us to organize gatherings "from below and for all"; they have taught us that the struggle is for life, for dignified life; and they remind us of our responsibility to construct the world that we want and need. In the Seventh Gathering these voices of our Zapatista sisters kept resonating, and now those resonances are traveling throughout Central America, and perhaps after this text is read their ideas will travel through many more geographies.

Conclusions and Final Questions

We took the space to put into words the path we have taken as a collective over the course of eight years of reunions, of coming together and moving apart, from the open score that Contact Improvisation has been. In its origin, this practice represented a space of exploration where bodies [*las cuerpas*] could play with the physical forces that affect all of us. But with the passage of time, and in deepening our somatic practices, we noticed that not only gravity weighed on our bones, but also oppressions and fights that are not only ours, but those of other corporealities that have preceded us. The dance is not universal, it is a dance that transforms us and that we transform. We reject dancing without context: on the dance floor we dance with and even despite it. We consider that by problematizing the practice with our lived experience, the space of dance can become a potential site of shared, collective pleasure and creativity, where we can exercise the liberty with which we want to live our relationships in the present moment and, with any luck, in the future.

In the Panel at *CI @ 50*, we concluded with some questions that we would like to share in this paragraph:

- If at any point you have thought of coming to Mexico, where did that desire come from?
- What do you hope to offer the community with your presence?
- Have you thought of the community and the bodies that will come to your classes, or with what kind of bodies you will be dancing? Are you expecting white bodies?
- Would you teach the same material as you would in your own country? Would you teach it in the same way?

16

Making Contact

Practicing and Creating Spaces of Contact Improvisation in India

Guru Suraj and Adrianna Michalska

The year 2023 marked 51 years since movement research, which later developed into Contact Improvisation (CI), was initiated by Steve Paxton in the United States. Since then, the practice of CI reached India through traveling Indian and international dancers and developed significantly when a community of Indian CI teachers was formed in 2016 to travel and teach across India. This act of taking a movement practice that originated in a specific context (in the case of Contact Improvisation, in the 1970s in the United States) and then introducing it into a very different context brings many questions of cultural influences, power dynamics, and so on. The context of India is also extremely diverse and complex—social and economic divisions are influenced by ongoing colonial practices of power and policing, which are part of life. There are deeply ingrained partitions in touch, which are underlined by many legacies of violence and hatred from colonial, social, and religious separation. Practice of Contact Improvisation in India is therefore a radical proposition that has a potential to challenge the multiple layers of divisions and categories. To bring nonverbal communication and physical contact between groups of people that are extremely far from each other in the social context means to practice something that is productively anti-segregation and potentially revolutionary.

In this essay we will discuss and reflect on some of the implications of the practice of Contact Improvisation in India from our perspective as CI facilitators and community co-creators. We—Guru Suraj and Adrianna Michalska—work together to share the art of Contact Improvisation in India through residencies, workshops, classes, jams, intensives, and different forms of improvised performances. Guru Suraj is a Tamil Contact Improvisation dancer, facilitator, and one of the first Indian CI practitioners to start teaching in India. In his 13 years of experience of dancing and facilitating Contact Improvisation, he has been dedicated to researching ways of including different groups of people in the CI practice. Adrianna Michalska is a Contact Improvisation facilitator from Poland, based in India from 2019. Her teaching and study of movement revolves around understanding movement as a culturally and socially influenced activity with a potential for conversations across cultural and social categories. In this essay we will reflect on the question: "How do we do that?" to look at how we have molded, shaped, improvised, and adapted ways of facilitating Contact Improvisation to the context of India. Our starting point for writing this essay is the awareness of our identities, origins, and collective and individual histories. We are curious to untangle the implications of these lived experiences to use our embodied experience of dancing and facilitating CI in India and written and recorded reflections as sources of knowledge.

Guru Suraj and Adrianna Michalska, *Making Contact* In: *Resistance and Support*. Edited by: Ann Cooper Albright, Oxford University Press.
© Oxford University Press 2024. DOI: 10.1093/9780197776308.003.0017

We will first briefly address some aspects of living in India that are crucial for general understanding of the implications of introducing the practice of Contact Improvisation: the extensive diversity, casteism, and certain norms that regulate ways of relating and interacting in the society. We will then briefly outline how Contact Improvisation was introduced to India and how the first Indian CI teachers emerged and started to teach. Using examples from our work of traveling, organizing, and facilitating CI events across India, we will discuss how the social norms related to race, caste, economic and social status, and gender become a form of improvisational scores to explore different ways of teaching and adapting Contact Improvisation as an evolving movement practice. We will consider ways that allow us to create spaces where inclusion and equality can be researched and embodied in the movement, reclaiming personal agency and a sense of ownership of one's embodied experience of living and interacting with others. From the point of view that these social dynamics and norms are specific, but not exceptional to India, we will look at Contact Improvisation as a practice that can potentially expand the boundaries and structures of the society, starting the revolution from our skin.

The Diverse Context of India and the Introduction of Contact Improvisation

India has the second-largest population in the world, which stretches across historically, culturally, traditionally, and socially diverse communities. From cities to villages, the people, mindsets, customs, languages (with 22 officially recognized regional languages), and behaviors are vastly different. Every state is a completely new world of gestures, movements, attitudes, and nuances. Indian society is further systematically fragmented through the caste system—a form of social stratification classified by one's birth. Although the caste system has existed in India for centuries, it continuously evolved in its ways of functioning. British, Portuguese, Dutch, and French colonialism sedimented the caste system by contributing to the accumulation of wealth and privilege among certain castes (especially those who collaborated in colonial governance) and other regulations. Currently, casteism is greatly shaped by the political climate in India. The ruling party (Bharatiya Janata Party, BJP) is a far-right, ethnonationalist, conservative party, which favors Hinduism as a religious system and related traditional practices by censoring and infiltrating many institutions of education, art, politics, and media. The system of the BJP governance is supported by a tight bond with the minority of the upper castes that share the influence, resources, and power, while the overwhelming majority of the lower castes are kept at a distance.

The evolving and ungraspable caste system pervades all aspects of life in India in complex ways. Bhimrao Ramji Ambedkar, a member of the Dalits (the lowest stratum of Indian caste system, previously known as "Untouchables") and politician famous for being an anti-oppression advocate for Dalits, describes in "Annihilation of Caste" (1990) the depth of the caste system: "Caste is not a physical object like a wall of bricks or a line of barbed wire which prevents the Hindus from co-mingling and which has, therefore, to be pulled down. Caste is a notion, it is a state of the mind." To add to Ambedkar's statement, caste can be understood as an embodied practice of segregation, discrimination, and partition in terms of social interactions, especially in terms of physical contact. The complexity of the caste system

278 Resistance and Support

is in how it continuously adapts itself to the changing political scene. Performance studies scholar Brahma Prakash (2019, 19) outlines:

> Beyond texts, caste is a living practice in Indian society with each caste having its own customs, practices and rituals. . . . Until recently, there was a belief that caste would gradually disappear with the vanishing of traditional social institutions. But the caste system has been reinventing its structure, even so, to fit into the cosmopolitan society.

Ambedkar and Prakash both point out the difficulty in eradicating the caste system because of how it evolves to maintain the power and privilege structures that separate Indian society.

Caste is written on the body and the way that people interact. Traditionally, the skin of people from lower castes, or Untouchables, was considered dirty because of the jobs they did around cleaning or working with dead or sick bodies. Nowadays it is engraved in how people function and interact with each other—simply nobody is touching or staying in close proximity with people of lower castes. In our practice of Contact Improvisation, we bring a lot of attention to the embodiment of the values of diversity, inclusivity, non-separation, and mutual respect. With this approach, we continuously investigate if this body-to-body movement conversation can become a counterbalance to what is being practiced daily. Can the state of mind, as in Ambedkar's words, be altered through movement practice? Can Contact Improvisation be more effective than laws and official regulations?

Another extensive influence on shaping norms around social interactions in India is colonial history, especially British colonialism. The hierarchical cultures of modern schools, including corporal punishment of students (based on the British colonial model), the criminalization of homosexuality, the state's policing of public sexuality or indecency, and the valuing of white, foreign teachers over local teachers are examples of these influences. Therefore, when it comes to physical contact in India, the matter is ambiguous, politicized, and controlled by the government and society. According to the law, obscene public display of affection is punishable for up to three months in jail. Since "obscene" was never defined, many police officers often take advantage of various situations and abuse their power. Public displays of affection are also not socially approved—hugging and kissing are not often seen. Women and men are frequently separated in public—there are separate cars for women in metros and trains, and separate seats in buses. In most families, touch is also not practiced as a way of showing affection, but rather as a display of respect—for example, greeting elders by touching their feet. Many of our friends and students expressed that they have not been embraced or touched by their families or partners and therefore have never embodied much knowledge about touch. The case of same-gender physical contact is often different, though—young men hold hands, embrace each other, or even sleep together in trains and different public spaces. However, at the same time, being a homosexual until 2018 was a punishable offense (under section 377 of Indian Penal Code introduced by the British in 1861). Even though decriminalizing homosexuality was a great success for the LGBTQ+ community, the perception of many in Indian society remains the same.

Given these constraints, it was possible to introduce the practice of Contact Improvisation only to specific spaces. Contact Improvisation was taught from the first decade of the twenty-first century in contemporary dance schools and studios in cities (Delhi, Bangalore, Mumbai, and others) by various European and American teachers. A group of European organizers and facilitators, who created the Goa Contact Festival, had an important impact on the CI scene. In 2009 they arrived in Goa—a state by the Arabian Sea on the west coast of India and a former Portuguese colony. Goa became synonymous with hippie culture from the 1970s, when large populations of European and American travelers arrived on the coastline, making it one of the end points of the hippie trail. The already existing subculture of artists and travelers (both international and Indian) was a very fertile ground for Contact Improvisation, and the team created an international CI festival a year later. The festival grew into an event of almost 200 people, with participants and teachers from around the world, but mostly from Europe and the United States.

Even though the Goa Contact Festival has been the biggest influence on sharing the form in India, the CI events were only periodical. Workshops, jams, intensives, and the festival itself took place during the tourist season in Goa, which lasts from December to February. The festival organizers made some efforts to assimilate Indian participants—they offered them positions such as helpers, artists in residence, class teachers, jam holders, and scholarship students, and so on, but the vast majority of people in the festival were always foreign and it was not a priority to create a continuum of CI events in India or to develop a community. It is also notable that the organizers of the Goa Contact Festival established a high level of control over other events during the season—they made decisions about classes and jams and about who could facilitate Contact Improvisation workshops or intensives. Therefore, until 2016, local CI practitioners did not build a sustainable CI scene, and the practice was associated with the periodical activities of the international community. Given this tendency, the activities of the Goa Contact Festival in certain ways perpetuate colonial mindsets: bringing a foreign community to a new site or land, exploiting its resources (space, favorable costs of living, permeable tax structure, avoidable law enforcement system, etc.), repeatedly coming back to draw on the resources and establishing the colony—a certain authority, hierarchy, and exclusivity for teaching CI as the movement art form.

The practice of Contact Improvisation developed differently in big cities of India. It was also influenced by traveling international teachers, but the practice was not continuous and functioned mostly as a complimentary training for contemporary dance students, rather than an open practice for everyone to experience. Later, Indian contemporary dance teachers, who had a background of studying dance in either Europe or the United States, also started to incorporate Contact Improvisation into the contemporary dance curriculum. The work of Ahilash Ningappa, Ashutosh Muhanty (Shifu Ash), and others continues to strongly influence the CI scene in India.

An important shift in understanding who can teach and practice the form of Contact Improvisation happened in 2016, when a group of Indian CI practitioners gathered and made a commitment to travel and teach Contact Improvisation to as many people as possible. The newly formed Contact Improv India community included: Swapnashree Bhasi, Aditya Sasidharan, Guru Suraj, Hari Chaudhary, Akshay Murarka, Lional Lishoy, Niranjan Harish, and Karthik Rajmohan. The first workshop and jam took place in Bangalore under the name "Play Support Explore." The community then traveled and taught in cities of Delhi, Jaipur, Dharamshala, Mumbai, Pune, Chennai, Udaipur, Chandigarh, and others. Since then, new generations of facilitators have emerged as a result of training offered by Indian teachers through workshops and intensives. There is now a significant number of CI dancers in India who were introduced to and learned CI only from Indian teachers. The collaborative work of the CI India community mostly continued until 2020, when the COVID-19 pandemic started. Currently, the CI events are organized in different places as non-regular

280 Resistance and Support

collaborations between various members of the expanded community of teachers. In 2021, Guru Suraj, Harmandeep Singh, and Adrianna Michalska formed InContact collective—a registered organization that became a platform for CI projects and collaborations with individual Indian and international CI facilitators. With the goal of making the Contact Improvisation practice sustainable in India, the Indian community started and continues to navigate the deeply rooted historical issues of colonialism and racism, reinforced by some of the legacy of the Goa Contact Festival, to ensure that the creative and artistic practices remain respectful and foster genuine cross-cultural understanding.

The Beginnings of the Indian Contact Improvisation Community

When the CI India community was formed, the vision was clear—to dedicate time and effort to introduce Contact Improvisation in as many places as possible. It would have been easier to keep running events in spaces like Goa, where the constant flux of international travelers creates a continuous possibility for securing a crowd interested in joining the practice. But it was clear that the sustainability of the CI scene could not rely on the small hubs of international practitioners. Therefore, the community decided to travel, live, study, and teach together for a couple of months. Looking at the possibilities of teaching Contact Improvisation in India, a plan was formed to start the journey from large cities. Large cities in India, especially Bangalore and Mumbai, are centers for different forms of arts and communities that engage in experimental and alternative practices in the field of dance and theater. That is also where members of the newly formed CI India community had connections with different dance studios and a network of people who could help with promoting the events in their circles. Therefore, the way the events were conducted was often spontaneous and improvised and the information was spread through word of mouth. The community realized that every time different people participated in the workshops—with their movement across India, the demographics of participants started to become very diverse.

The organization of events was difficult and there were reservations toward Contact Improvisation. As expected by the community, touch and physical proximity created suspicions and unease of cross-gender connections. One of the main immediate obstacles was securing the workshop spaces without foreign teachers. Dance studios and schools were more interested in having foreign teachers as guest facilitators. Workshops offered by a foreign facilitator inherently seemed more attractive, worthwhile, and safe to attend. International teachers easily secured spaces to conduct workshops, often regardless of their level of experience. For Indian teachers, it was required to have documented years of experience in teaching. Unless there was a personal connection with the studio owner or director, there was no understanding that this was the first generation of Indian CI teachers that were emerging and who needed the space to gain that experience. Major dance schools would either not respond to the proposals made by the community, or claim that there was no need for exploration of improvisation because they already had their choreographies. When presented with video recordings of CI, they responded that this did not count as a dance practice that would be useful in terms of either skills or possibilities of gaining financial outcomes.

Even when the space for the workshop was secured, there were other issues. As mentioned, public display of intimacy is a punishable offense in India. CI India community members were very aware and ready to take the consequences of proposing Contact Improvisation workshops. There was one instance of cancellation of a workshop planned in 2017 in Ravindra Manch Art and Culture Center in Jaipur. An Indian right-wing group vandalized semi-nude paintings and injured the artist during the Jaipur Art Summit in December 2016, a couple of months before the planned workshop. The story attracted a lot of attention and was widely covered by the media. When the poster of the workshop (a white woman sitting and balancing on an Indian man's shoulder) was published, the management of the center canceled the workshop because it looked "too intimate." An official note was issued, but privately a representative of the management explained that the political climate in Jaipur was tense, and they feared hosting an event that had the potential to attract another intervention from the public or the authorities and to cause one more scandal in the venue. The workshop eventually took place in another studio, which was privately owned, and the promotion of the event was based on word of mouth.

Despite the challenges, the work shared by the CI India community was also received with a lot of enthusiasm. In the same year, 2017, a first performance of Contact Improvisation took place also in Jaipur in Jawahar Kala Kendra—a government-build multi-arts center. The performance was created spontaneously by CI India members and musicians who were friends of the community (see Figure 16.1). At the beginning of the performance, as the audience was walking in, Guru decided to ask them to stay on the stage. From there, the performers improvised the verbally guided exploration of sensing the gravity, seeing each other, and introducing touch through fingers or hands—all while continuously walking on the stage, blurring the roles of performers and audience, and establishing a different perception of experiencing and witnessing each other. The audience was then invited to their seats and the performance continued with improvised scores. Toward the end, one of the performers suddenly invited the audience to join again. In the audience there were community friends and CI practitioners, so they responded to the call. And gradually the rest of the audience

Figure 16.1. Guru Suraj and Swapna Shree with the audience during the performance in Jaipur in 2017. Photography by Kishore Kumar.

282 Resistance and Support

spontaneously joined, transforming the performance into a space of jamming—children and adults of all ages, different backgrounds, and ranges of physical ability.

This experience confirmed the vision of the CI India community—that when facilitated gradually and with openness and clarity, CI was accessible to everyone who had an interest. The performance was followed by the workshop—a structure that was then often repeated by the community. It became clear that verbal explanations, videos, or pictures of people dancing Contact Improvisation were not effective. The practice had to be witnessed and felt kinesthetically for newcomers to become interested. And it was an easier step to invite new people to a performance than to directly involve them in the practice. Often the audience members felt inspired by the performance, but had doubts whether or not the practice was suitable for them. One female participant approached right after the performance in Chandigarh in 2019, sharing that she was sexually abused as a child and was afraid that the space would be too triggering for her. It was explained to her that in the workshop everyone is encouraged to engage according to their own boundaries, and it is possible to also come and only witness. She joined both days and later described how the experience started to transform her relationship with touch.

Introducing and Working with Touch: The Question of Boundaries

Given the implication of social norms revolving around physical contact and the diversity and unpredictability of the participants, the question remained how to create spaces that were flexible and inviting for everyone. We started to develop different strategies of teaching and to create new exercises by exploring the possibilities of teaching. Rather than dramatically opposing the culturally derived reservations, we respect them and strive to gradually invite participants to the space of opening the boundaries. When we introduce physical contact to beginners, it is very limited. If we work with people who also have no movement background, we spend a lot of time with solo movement study. The sessions often start from the ground with a guided exploration to focus attention on the sensation of weight and gravity—for example, scanning or traveling with attention through different body parts and encouraging the sensation of releasing tension and falling into the gravity. The practice of relaxation and grounding allows the mutual arriving into the practice, which is continued with the exploration of walking and noticing the orientation of oneself in the space, opening the peripheral vision, and engaging in the kinesphere of others.

Touch is introduced after participants have had time to get familiar with who is in the room and to explore their own movement. One of the often-practiced ways of beginning the exploration of touch is the finger-to-finger exercise—two people join fingers and keep the connection while starting to move together. From slow to more dynamic movement, the whole attention is on this minimal point of contact, understanding the shared moment of movement and the possibilities that arise while dancing together. With this exploration we open up the idea of dancing without set roles and also emphasize the continuity of the movement—rather than standing in one place, there is a constant shift in the space.

We often notice a dropping of the focus when the physical contact is introduced, so by inviting the movers to keep traveling through space, we keep the practice of expanding attention to others, beyond the duet. We also realized that by keeping the participants engaged in the flow of movement, the experience of dancing with physical contact is less intimidating and more accessible. This exercise often progresses to finger-to-back exploration—in this version, one person leads the other by communicating the direction through a finger (or a hand) pressed on the other person's back. If we find it suitable, we propose to the person who is led to close their eyes. In this development we invite the research of trusting and listening to the proposed direction, as well as focusing the attention simultaneously on the point of communication through the touch and moving through the space. One of the scholarship participants of the CI Facilitators Training organized by InContact, Geethi Priya, commented how important this exercise was when she started to teach Contact Improvisation in her rural area. She specifically focused on working with communities of Dalits and teenagers and young women who had been sexually abused and locked in an asylum by the authorities for their safety. Geethi wrote:

> Finger to finger is always asked again by children who don't feel safe to dance, touch or are too tired to move. I guess it's because the intense focus on one specific small point of contact gives them deep rest within the mind. . . . This is asked by teenagers and kids who went through very uninspiring circumstances and they really felt we didn't ask too much of them. I adore the person who found this small little task of exploration because . . . tired people also get to connect without tiring themselves and can get a feeling of community and yet not feel they are being dragged into something when they are not ready.

Even with the finger-to-finger exploration, we often keep the movement dynamic playful. Especially with participants with no previous experience of Contact Improvisation, we avoid very slow and extended explorations. We create the spirit of playfulness through our demonstrations and music, which we use on and off to build the momentum of the classes. One of our most popular workshop series is "Fall to Fly"—a workshop open to all levels, which explores different variations of flights and transitions with weight sharing. By focusing on the physicality of learning about falling and flying, the perspective of movement exploration is more exciting, and the participants are less suspicious or uncomfortable about the idea of being in physical contact with each other. The ways of advertising classes are also very specific—we do not choose any pictures for posters that would potentially imply intimacy. The promotional materials mostly represent dynamic movement, and the elements of support and exploration are highlighted. During the workshops, or even when handling registrations, we often refer to martial arts, especially Aikido. We highlight the difference, but by keeping the connection to practices that are more known, established, and clear with the content, there is more ease in deciding to explore something that is new.

Another key decision we made as facilitators was to create spaces of Contact Improvisation that are not open for sexual exploration. This decision was also the point of separating the activities of CI India and InContact. Some members of the community did not wish to make the spaces of CI strict about limiting the exploration of sexuality. The way that Contact Improvisation was introduced in Goa through the Goa Contact Festival led to assumptions that CI can become a space where participants search for intimate partners to explore sexuality. And gradually many people were deciding to join with this intention. When the CI India community started to travel and teach together, there were different opinions about how to approach this aspect. At some point we realized that the question of sexuality was too important to compromise the ideas, and we decided to separate and create a new organization—InContact. By setting the intention to not have sexual exploration as part of our practice of Contact Improvisation, we had to develop ways of creating clear guidelines, understanding the shared responsibility to uphold them and respond to situations when participants would violate them. When we collaborate with different teachers, the aspect of sexuality and intimacy is addressed as a primary rule—no tolerance for teacher-student intimate relations for the duration of the project.

Participants are also informed beforehand that, according to our facilitation of Contact Improvisation, the space is not intended for researching sexuality. In the opening circle of events, we reinforce this statement and discuss the idea of consent and respecting everyone's boundaries, as well as informing that we have the right to cancel anyone's participation if the guidelines are violated. These guidelines are often challenged, and it is a continuous effort of both facilitators and participants to respond to situations of violations. When we scan the room of the class or jam, we already recognize which participants might encounter difficulties or might openly oppose our proposed boundaries of exploration of physical contact. People who are new to the form sometimes do not have much experience of touch beyond the hands—when more skin and other body parts are involved, the dance can become challenging. A simple note, a reminder, or a demonstration is usually enough to direct the exploration away from something that could be potentially confusing or misleading. Then there are both Indian and international people who are known in the local communities for their attitudes or activities. They are not regular to jams so we would suspect that they are looking for "something" when they appear in the space. Usually such cases go through a certain process: a demonstration, a note, a reminder. If this does not work, then we ask them to leave the space. If they come back and still continue doing what we consider as harmful to others and to the practice, we ask them not to come again in the future.

Opening circle is also vital for each jam, class, and workshop, as this is the space where we speak and demonstrate behaviors that are not welcomed in the space. We found out that different ways of doing it bring different effects into the space. Since many first-time participants were often almost completely blocked with fear of physical proximity, we realized that being very serious as facilitators was uninviting for participants to try to move in the jam. At times, humor would bring the message across and simultaneously make the possibilities of dancing more encouraging. Some of our other practices are to pause during the classes and ask for reflections or thoughts—many times, participants found it useful to ask questions of what would seem confusing in the unspoken spaces, especially if someone is questioning the use of touch and the difference between, for example, sensing with skin and being intimate. During those brief conversations we encourage the participants to give themselves permission to take care of their state and say "no" when they need to. Another example of our practice is to keep attention to the constellations of dances and how participants partner up—especially when it comes to the delicate subject of gender. If we notice that someone purposefully chooses partners from their gender of interest, we start to partner up with them or ask someone from the experienced dancers to work with them or suggest to all participants to choose a partner they have not danced with yet. If the behavior of a participant is not affected by any of these suggestions, we open a private conversation with them.

The guidelines and approach toward sharing the art of Contact Improvisation were greatly shaped by the decision to bring the practice to as many people in India as possible. Introducing physical contact and holding spaces that are focused on the research of nonverbal communication, physical principles of dancing together, mutual respect, and listening became crucial to our way of practicing and sharing Contact Improvisation. Since CI is not a strictly defined practice, it allows a variety of philosophies and ideas to be incorporated into it. To be able to share it with very diverse groups of people, we began to shape the core of our practice. We decided to focus on the physical principles of movement—gravity, momentum, inertia, and the aspect of nonverbal communication that is based on mutual respect, listening, and consent. Although asked many times, we did not wish to offer CI as a healing practice, spiritual practice, or movement therapy. Neither did we focus on the emotional aspects of the practice or sexuality. We acknowledge that these things can emerge while moving together with physical contact, but we made it clear that in our approach to Contact Improvisation, this is not the foreground of the practice.

Who Joins Contact Improvisation

From the beginning, the CI India community was dedicated to actively reaching out and integrating participants from different social backgrounds into the practice of Contact Improvisation. When the community of Indian CI teachers started to extend their CI events to new groups of people across India, the privilege of race, class, or caste would emerge during workshops. Between the core members of the CI India community, the caste background was never asked or questioned in any circumstances (although when writing this essay we noted that majority of the initial core members were coming from the lower castes). The community had a clear intention to share Contact Improvisation as an inclusive space where caste does not define how people interact with each other, and to embody practices that disrupt the codified ways of being. The work of Indian CI teachers, however, is not yet well known, and there are often misconceptions about the CI practice in India.

Royona Mitra, Indian scholar of dance and performance studies based in the United Kingdom, offers a valuable critique of CI, and its "deemed democratizing principles as a movement practice" in her recent article "Unmaking Contact" (2021). Based on her experience as an Indian female scholar and dancer and on interviews with four other dancers and scholars from India and the Indian diaspora, she points that "CI can be a violent practice in its inherent invisibilization of the different power asymmetries that it harbors and perpetuates in the guise of democracy." Referring to one of the interviews, she states: "Tavag mentions that, although she is not fully certain, she wonders whether CI spaces in India may well operate in exclusionary ways because of India's inherent and internalized practice of discrimination via colorism, excluding participants with darker skin from the practice." However, Mitra does not recognize the work of Indian teachers and facilitators who themselves come from the lower castes, and who build the practice of Contact Improvisation with the specific intention of inviting the participants from all backgrounds. The South Indian origin, dark skin, and lower-caste definitions which could all be attributed to Guru already defy the above statement. We further provide examples of our work to reflect on the inclusive potential of the practice of Contact Improvisation. Main areas of our practice include reaching out to lower-caste or underprivileged communities, the flexibility to make our events affordable for whoever is interested, sharing the practice of CI spontaneously with coincidental groups of people, collaborating with intercultural projects, and focusing on the practices that embody the principles of inclusivity and equality.

286 Resistance and Support

Integrating participants from different backgrounds is an active intention of pre-planning workshops that specifically include these groups. Some examples of such collaborations include workshops with nongovernmental organizations (NGOs) that work with lower-caste young adults in Delhi (2018–2019), workshops with a Dalit and LGBTQ+ theater group in Chennai (2014), classes for government school children in Kerala (2010), intensive workshops with alternative schooling Yatra participants (teenagers and adults) and teenage male school dropouts from lower castes in Dharamshala (2019), and more. We also offer support to other facilitators (for example, the above-mentioned work of Geethi Priya) who have the possibility to share the practice of Contact Improvisation with the lower-caste communities. Sometimes, however, the inclusion of diverse practitioners in the sessions of CI is a matter of spontaneous reaction to a situation. In one of the projects organized by InContact, the Art of Improvisation residency in Udaipur in 2021 in the deserts of Rajasthan, two lower-caste young men who were working on the premises of the venue were continuously curious to witness our practice. Before the event they hand-made the floor of the studio, using some of the traditional techniques of mixing cow dung with water and mud. When our group started the workshop, we noticed how they became interested in the practice, gradually approaching the space. At some point we invited them to join. Working with the language barrier, we slowly encouraged them to explore the movement—they were visibly awkward but curious to dance with each other and at times with other participants. Eventually they asked to play their own music and integrated their street-style movement into improvisation during the jam.

Inviting the lower-caste people into the space of physical contact and into the space shared with participants from other castes is a radical proposition—an opportunity for people from very different backgrounds to communicate through movement that is outside of their habitual ways of interacting. However, there were also instances in which the owners of the spaces of workshops rejected our invitation for the workers to join, reminding us that the categorization of the society and people's roles is a strong boundary for the integration of participants. Similarly to what Mitra points out, in certain circumstances the practice becomes exclusionary—not necessarily because of the interests or intentions of organizers and facilitators, but because of the wider structures of the society.

We also put a lot of effort into making events accessible to the groups that usually would not even consider joining such workshops due to financial constraints. When announcing the event, we always state that financial struggle should not stop anyone from participating in CI events. We often get inquiries from people from all backgrounds. We developed a few options to offer possibilities of attending: scholarships, volunteering positions, exchange, or paying later. Our approach is to not offer free attendance, but rather an exchange of work (from logistics to advertising, photography, archiving, documenting, etc.). Together with our own involvement in other activities apart from teaching, this creates an environment of community, mutual exchange, and support—values that we find in the practice of Contact Improvisation itself, and which transgress into the fabrics of the group. Also on occasions, we conduct free workshops or donation-based workshops. This approach to sharing Contact Improvisation is not practical for sustaining ourselves as CI facilitators, but at the same time, it grows a sense of mutuality and community.

The spaces of sharing Contact Improvisation are also spontaneous and have porous boundaries, just like the practice of opening one's skin is in CI. A similar principle—expanding boundaries, pouring the experience from one to another—guides many CI performances or city interventions organized throughout India. We engaged with various audiences through participatory performances—for example, the above-mentioned Jaipur performance in 2017, the "Connect Two" participatory piece in Chandigarh in 2019, and many others. We also performed in outdoor spaces, open for anyone to stop by and ask about the practice. Often follow-up workshops are organized, engaging the accidental, passing audience in the embodied experience of the practice. A constant gesture of inviting anyone who shows interest allows bringing the practice closer to different demographics.

We also continuously search for many different cross-cultural collaborations to challenge and keep our practice of sharing CI adaptable. In 2021 we had an opportunity to collaborate with the Ziarat Project—an intercultural project that brought together us as CI facilitators and three classical Tibetan opera artists and teachers from TIPA (Tibetan Institute of Performing Arts) to work with a group of participants for a week (see Figure 16.2). The hall of Tara (the Buddhist deity of compassion and wisdom) was the space of our meeting. We arrived, pondering on how we can use Contact Improvisation as an artistic bridge between our backgrounds, stories, cultures, and experiences. Throughout the week, every session was an experimentation of co-creating across our differences. The set choreographies of Tibetan classical dance and tones of traditional songs contrasted strongly with the improvisational scores of CI movement. However, there were common themes that we realized were engraved in our practices—the sense of an ensemble, listening to each other, communicating through movement, and mutual respect. We found out that creative and open scores, rather than movement skills (for example, rolling or inversions) were serving well the space of this collaboration.

We practiced many group improvisation tasks, for example, flocking, copying the movement of a person standing at the front of the group, or finding stillness and movement

Figure 16.2. Samten Dhondup, Kelsang Chukie, Lhakpa La, Guru Suraj, Adrianna Michalska, Gerush Bahal with participants after the final performance of the Ziarat Project. Photography by Dhriti Bahal.

together. We also introduced physical contact through scores that included touch but did not primarily focus on it—for example, working with movement and stillness in duets and passing the movement to the next person through touch. Being in the constant flux of improvisation, letting go of planning, and allowing the unexpected to happen created an atmosphere of communication and mutual understanding. We were immersed in the perplexing and rich process of translating our expressions despite the immense cultural differences. At the end of the residency, one of the reflections shared by the classical Tibetan opera teacher was that he was inspired by the atmosphere of the sessions and decided to incorporate the opening and reflection circles in classes with his students at the Tibetan Institute of Performing Arts to encourage a more personal approach to the learning of the art form. For us, this residency was an inspiration to continue refining our particular approach toward Contact Improvisation and the values of compassion, respect, and mutual joy that we wish to transmit through the practice.

Finally, there are practices of inclusivity and equality that we continue to include on a regular basis in all CI sessions. For example, a way to create a common ground for practice, regardless of social status, is through the opening circle—when we ask participants to introduce themselves, we would not ask questions such as "What is your job?" or "What is your last name?" which could be indicative of their status or caste. We facilitate a more neutral sharing by asking questions such as "What is your favorite fruit?" Using the floor to dance and to roll is another example of a practice that becomes a radical act on its own. We have been observing that people from upper castes mostly are not comfortable with the floor. The upper-caste lifestyle is symbolically away from the floor—in sharp opposition to how lower-caste people (cleaners, cooks) relate to the ground. For example, in India mopping the floor is mostly done on the knees, and cooking (peeling vegetables or grounding spices) is often done while sitting on the floor or squatting. Therefore, coming closer to the ground and sharing the ground with others, regardless of their background, is awkward yet potentially transformative. Through shared movement experience, a new concept and understanding of bodies are developed. When observing participants in the workshop, there is a certain shift from what we named the "hesitant body" into an "ease body." It comes with a realization that there are more possibilities for interaction with each other. However, we also note that these moments of practice in the studio are impermanent—some participants go back to their habitual ways of being as soon as we end the closing circle, and some stay within the practice, continuously shifting their perspectives.

Reflecting on these practices, we are curious to look into how CI events happen worldwide. In the increasingly woven structures of CI events and hierarchies of teachers and facilitators, we question: Are CI teachers and organizers open enough to invite a bystander to the workshop? Can they improvise in any given situation to share the space?

Teacher-Student Power Dynamics

Diminishing the social barriers and hierarchies is also embedded in our practice of blurring the lines of student-teacher power dynamics. In the majority of Indian schools, students do not have individual choices, questions, and opinions. Different forms of corporal punishment are used when students don't pay attention during class. When sharing Contact Improvisation, we understood that we cannot demand attention or force someone to move when their attention is distracted. It became very important to us to make it clear from the beginning that participants can say "no" to what we propose at any point in time. We often explain that our proposed explorations could be beyond their boundaries, and it is vital to practice sensing one's limits. We encourage participants to question these boundaries, to deconstruct them, to work with them, to explore them, but also to respect them and stay within them when needed, to honor themselves in the state they are in. We had many students who, for example, took naps or completely fell asleep in our classes. Many people have approached us to thank us for this possibility of resting. These situations are possible because we create an environment in which taking care of the body-mind is more valuable than following the teacher's instructions.

Deconstructing the student-teacher power dynamics is not to say that there is no hierarchy in our events. When looking at CI events worldwide, it is also evident that the myth of no hierarchy in CI is a utopian dream. Embracing the ideal, we set the intention to create the ground in our practice, where the vast distance between teachers and students is diminished and the perception of self-teacher is encouraged. Through conversation, the embodiment of each other's role—student-teacher, worker-facilitator, on and off the floor—we sweep, shake, reverse, question, and reflect on the collective social conditioning. The valuing of foreign teachers over local teachers also often comes into the picture, especially when organizing the CI events with new studios. As mentioned before, this social norm could be pointed to the heritage of British colonial influences. However, ways in which Contact Improvisation was introduced and developed by foreign teachers in India also reinforced this dynamic. Throughout the years, various CI practitioners and organizers supported the learning and development of Indian CI dancers. The Goa Contact Festival offered multiple scholarships, exchange and volunteer positions, as well as some teaching positions. The work of Erica Kaufman—her continuous effort to conduct workshops in different cities and her involvement in organizing and gathering Indian CI teachers in a week-long ICITE (Indian Contact Improvisation Teacher Exchange) in 2019—contributed to the individual growth of Indian CI dancers and the development of the community.

However, even though these activities made the training and emergence of Indian CI teachers possible, they also created an image of Contact Improvisation as being a "white practice" taught by "white people," who create the space of movement and then disappear. Since we are a combination of Polish and Indian teachers, the myth of foreign teachers having more expertise or power also appears in our classes. We take these situations as a playground for researching expectations and unveiling the still existing supremacy of foreign teachers. For example, during one of the workshops in Delhi, many questions during the opening circle were asked to Adrianna, all heads pointing at her, although we introduced both of us as teachers. At some point, Guru suddenly stated: "But you know, you can also ask me a question. I'm also a teacher even though I have dark skin." The statement was followed by laughter and embarrassed looks, but gradually participants started to ask for information and interact with both of us equally. Our identities related to gender and race offer us possibilities to untangle the power dynamics of personal and collective histories that are embodied, deeply rooted, and carried in codified social interactions. To be aware of them and to deconstruct the social conditioning is to be present and responsive to any given situation, in conversation as well as in actions and in dance—constantly exchanging roles of teaching and supporting each other. By challenging the student-teacher hierarchy, we encourage people to engage in a self-driven study, reclaiming their personal agency to learn, investigate, explore, and experience living and interacting with others.

The Practice of Listening to the Space

To summarize, in this chapter we have presented some practical examples of caring, observing, and sharing the space of Contact Improvisation in India as facilitators and community co-creators. The intention behind our work is to create more spaces that bring people together, rather than separating them. By considering the implications of the power dynamics at the intersection of race, gender, and castes, and social conditioning in relation to physical contact and ways of interacting in the society, we strive to support every individual who joins the practice. Sharing Contact Improvisation in India is both about researching the form and about expanding the nuances of living. Learning how to communicate and how to touch each other is a revolution that starts with the sensation on the skin of every individual.

On a larger scale, we adopted a practice of "listening to the space" as a metaphor for meeting with the possibilities or needs of a specific group, sensing the group energy and the kind of practice that is suitable moment to moment. This changes instantly and again requires a specific practice of attention, proposing, and letting go of any plans or ideas. Sensing the fabrics of the space of classes or jams as they emerge is an art on its own and a unique space of conversation—to listen, to propose, to respect, and finally to melt the roles in the dance that exists in the unique space of each meeting. Sometimes the teaching exists in space, and when we are aware and present, the role of a facilitator disappears. When this happens, there is a deep sense of the spirit of improvisation.

References

Ambedkar, B. R. 1990. *Annihilation of the Caste*. London: Arnold Publishers.

Mitra, Royona. 2021. "Unmaking Contact: Choreographic Touch at the Intersections of Race, Caste, and Gender." *Dance Research Journal* 53(3): 6–24.

Prakash, Brahma. 2019. *Cultural Labour: Conceptualizing the "Folk Performance" in India*. New York and London: Oxford University Press.

17
Contact Improvisation in China and Taiwan

Roundtable discussion with Ming-Shen Ku, Shuyi (Candy) Liao, Xiao Zhang, Huichao (Dew) Ge; introduction by Ge; transcription and translation by Yuting (Elsie) Wang

Introduction

Contact Improvisation (CI) in East Asia began in the 1990s in Taiwan and Hong Kong, and then spread in the mainland in a scattered manner. It is a human-to-human dance, so the teaching and dissemination of CI is based on direct physical communication between practitioners and practitioners. Since the 1990s, CI founders and CI teachers from all over the world have visited China, leaving behind the collision, growth, and memory of Contact Improvisation in China. At the same time, the mutual teaching, support, community building, and public facilitation that took place between local Chinese practitioners and organizers is a continuation of the practice and integration of this endless physical experiment, this non-hierarchical river, by members of the global CI community. The exploration of Contact Improvisation happening in China is also engaging with important questions about the ideological roots of CI, the democratic construction of the form, and its relevance to people in our time.

Seeds

Dancer Ming-Shen Ku was an important driving force behind the promotion of Contact Improvisation in Taiwan. In 1992, she returned to Taiwan from the United States and began teaching Contact Improvisation, offering free classes to the public at the Crown Theater, Grotto, and Yunmen, where participants included not only dancers, but also members of the public. In the same year, Ku invited Paxton to Taiwan for a workshop and a joint performance of "New Journey Dance Exhibition." This was Paxton's first trip to Asia. In 2011, her company began to organize the i-dance Taipei International Dance Improvisation Festival, an international arts event with dance as its main focus. Ku & Dancers is one of the few groups in the Chinese-speaking region that uses Contact Improvisation as a creative method, physical practice, and even a way of life. Over the years, Ku & Dancers has nurtured a group of experienced CI teachers and dancers, including instructors Xinglang Zhu and Chengwei Xu, who often come to the mainland to teach, and Iris Cheng, who later founded the Shanghai Contact Improvisation Community and the Shanghai Improvisation Festival in Shanghai.

Hong Kong dancer Mui Cheuk-yin studied in the United States around the same time as Ming-Shen Ku, and in 1990, Mui received a grant from the Asian Cultural Council to

---

Ming-Shen Ku, Shuyi (Candy) Liao, Xiao Zhang, Huichao (Dew) Ge and Yuting (Elsie) Wang, *Contact Improvisation in China and Taiwan* In: *Resistance and Support.* Edited by: Ann Cooper Albright, Oxford University Press. © Oxford University Press 2024. DOI: 10.1093/9780197776308.003.0018

292 Resistance and Support

study Contact Improvisation and postmodern dance techniques in New York City, where she attended Paxton's workshops and met first-generation dancers Daniel Lepkoff and Lisa Nelson. After returning to Hong Kong, Mui Cheuk-yin taught Contact Improvisation at the Hong Kong Academy for Performing Arts and the Arts Centre, where dancers and students of the Academy became the first practitioners of CI in Hong Kong. In 1998, Mui started the community "Contact Point" in Hong Kong, which included the current acting artistic director of City Contemporary Dance Company of Hong Kong, Dickman Wong, and dancer Ka Nang Leung. Contact Point developed a three-year plan for Contact Improvisation. In the year of its inception, Mui Cheuk-yin invited Lisa Nelson, Karen Nelson, K. J. Holmes, and Scott Smith to come to Hong Kong to teach and perform together. Nancy Stark Smith also taught in Hong Kong and went to Guangzhou, where she worked with the Guangzhou Ballet as well as some dancers of the Guangdong Modern Dance Company.

Pioneering choreographer Hou Ying joined China's first modern dance company, Guangdong Modern Dance Company, in 1993. The first full Contact Improvisation class that Hou Ying took was in 1995, when Mingxin Gu came to Guangdong Modern Dance Company to teach Contact Improvisation. With the financial support of the Asian Cultural Council, she traveled to New York City in 2001 where she took various postmodern dance classes, as well as CI classes. She returned to China in 2011 to establish Hou Ying Dance Theatre, and since then CI classes have been offered at almost all of the annual summer and winter dance camps.

Shuyi Liao, one of the initiators of Contact Improv Beijing, was introduced to Contact Improvisation through dancer Hou Ying's workshop in 2009, which opened up a new world of dance for her, and in 2013, Shuyi Liao met Junhao Shi at the workshop of Italian CI instructor Irene Sposetti, an early European instructor who lived in China to teach CI and taught many practitioners. In December 2013, Liao and Shi started to organize a jam together every Sunday, so in December 2013, Liao and Shi launched Beijing Contact Improvisation (BJCI), which gradually gathered a group of members who love movement research, body exploration, and the joy of CI. In 2015, Andy Wang joined and was responsible for both organizing and promoting its events. Around the same time, Bo Shi from Beijing Dance Academy, Benny Yan from Beijing Normal University, and Xi Zhao from Central University for Nationalities also began to explore improvisation. With the increasing interest, Shuyi Liao began to go to Europe and the United States to participate in CI dance festivals, including the 2016 Italy Contact Improvisation Festival, and in 2017–2018 to the United States to participate in one of Nancy's intensive training camps.

In 2015, Huichao Ge (the author of this introduction) became the producer of Hou Ying Dance Theatre and participated in the CI training class of the dance company. In 2016, Hou Ying Dance Theatre was invited by New York University to perform in New York, and after the performance, Guanglei Hui, who was living in New York at that time, invited us to join the regular dance jam of 100 Street, which became the starting point of the birth of TOUCH Contact Improvisation Festival. After returning to China, the author and Hou Ying Dance Theatre performed in various cities and presented public workshops based on Contact Improvisation in major art museums, including Beijing Minsheng Art Museum, UCCA Ullens Center for Contemporary Art, and Long Museum of Art, among others. After this early exploration, TOUCH Contact Improvisation festival introduced the form with an eye toward diversity and engaging the public.

The first TOUCH Contact Improvisation Festival was based on the theme of "Body Empowerment for the Body," inviting everyone to re-perceive their own bodies, their relationships with others, and the reality that comes through physical movement, and inviting everyone to dance together regardless of their previous experiences or abilities. The first festival took place in five cities, Beijing, Shanghai, Guangzhou, Chengdu, and Yinchuan, with international instructors Martin Keogh, Elise Knudson, Irene Sposetti, Daniel Aschwanden, Daniele Sardella, and others. Each teacher guided workshops in at least two cities during this trip, which was certainly exciting and challenging for the instructors who were in China for the first time. For the next two festivals, we continued to follow this multi-city, multi-tutor approach, with limited travel support, to maintain the initial public phase of CI as a participant experience and urban community development. In terms of topics of discussion, TOUCH has maintained the opening forum and has started to do some literature translation, including discussions on the development of Contact Improvisation in Asia, the discussion of gravity, the comparison of Eastern body methods (we have invited *taijiquan* masters and classical yoga teachers to teach), symbiotic dance with people with disabilities, and so on.

In 2018, TOUCH team and Beijing Contact Improvisation launched the first Mainland teacher exchange. In that year, there were fewer than 10 teachers in the mainland who focused on teaching Contact Improvisation, and most of them were mainly engaged in modern dance, incorporating CI. In the past two years, the Teacher Exchange Conference has also evolved into the TOUCH Community Conference, with two days of teacher exchange and two days of public participation. When the COVID-19 epidemic broke out in 2020, TOUCH had to choose an adaptable way to move on. What this unprecedented quarantine, social distance, and other medical and epidemic prevention policies triggered was a worldwide collapse and a reconstruction of collective consciousness. In that year, TOUCH formed a domestic mentorship and took the initiative to go nomadic in five cities to face the world's disasters and grief with the theme of "New Neighbors." "New Neighbors" is about the trust between people and the possibility of creating self-organized relationships based on this trust. And, in 2021, under the pressure of multiple uncertainties, TOUCH has held its fifth festival in Beijing.

In mainland China, stemming from the persistence of early practitioners, communities have gradually taken shape in multiple cities in the past five or six years. The earliest was BJCI, initiated by Shuyi Liao and Junhao Shi at the end of 2013, and then in 2016 Shan Chen initiated Chengdu Contact Improv; Ixian Zheng initiated Shanghai Contact Improv; Yuehong initiated Guangzhou Contact Improv; Xiaoling Xu, Dan Yi, and Xiaolei Xu initiated Hangzhou Contact Improv; Tiger launched Xi'an Contact Improv; and so on. The various teaching and dance jam activities loosely organized by the academy and individual practitioners are also happening with their own frequency. Communities that can persist for a long time have basically completed the establishment of the initial "container," with core members, enthusiasts, openness to communicate with the public, the injection of mentors, and the team spirit to constantly solve organizational problems; on this basis, the community can enter the active exploration of body technique and creation.

The Chengdu Contact Improvisation Community is an organization that practices a high degree of democracy. Founder Shan Chen started Contact Improvisation in 2014 while studying at the University of Bedfordshire in Luton, United Kingdom, where she studied under CI scholar Tamara Ashley as part of her graduate studies, as well as with Hiroko Takahashi, Yasukichi Suzuki, Seki Juntaro, and a group of friends from Contact Improv Japan. After that,

294 Resistance and Support

she traveled back and forth from Japan to Europe and the United States, and to CI festivals in India and Thailand. The Chengdu community started with only Shan Chen, but now the core members have grown to nine, with the nine members forming a network of equal resolutions and rotating leadership. Chengdu Contact Improv had compiled a list of over 100 rules in the Contact Improv Dance Jam to respond to the questions new dancers have when facing the dance jam, for example: What do I need to prepare? What do I pay attention to? Whom can I dance with? How do I say no? Based on the frequency of questions from local dancers, and in conjunction with the Contact Improv Quarterly Dance Jam Guide, Chengdu Contact Improv has compiled this set of Chinese version of the "Dance Jam Tips" that many other communities are currently learning from, which covers everything from preparing the body and consciousness upon entering the venue, to finishing up the space together after the dance jam, including the dance jam neutral boundaries/respect and safety.

Beijing Contact Improvisation is the first community to crowdfund to develop a larger community. Since the end of 2013, the core members have grown from the earliest Shuyi Liao, Junhao Shi, and Andy Wang to a committee of more than 20 people who work together to plan events. In the beginning, the community was supported by a venue and was run on a drop-in basis. Later, as costs increased and more and more local teachers started teaching, the committee discussed monthly crowdfunding as the basis of the community's operation in order to keep the community sustainable. The community initially focused on a regular dance jam every Sunday night, but later had regular classes, invited domestic and international instructors to teach in Beijing, organized performances and impromptu themed gatherings for Contact in the community, and so on. In Liao's latest review of the community, she found that as the teachers improved and the number of participants increased, some interest groups gradually emerged in the community, some of which are keen on philosophical discussions around Contact Improvisation, some focus on the relationship between Contact Improvisation and lifestyle, some expand Contact Improvisation to other fields of mind-body science, and some communicate on creative work.

In 1987, Alito Alessi applied the concept of "danceability" in Contact Improvisation to people with any type of physical limitation and found it to be effective. He and his dance partner Karen Nelson began exploring mixed-ability dancing, creating the Dance Ability methodology. Dance Ability works to create opportunities for people with and without disabilities to dance and move together, to bring people from different backgrounds together to experience the arts, and to reduce prejudice and misconceptions about the field of dance and the diversity of society.

Maru, the founder of Symbiosis Dance, is a teacher and creator in China's Contact Improvisation who focuses on the integration of differently able bodies ("dance for all") and promotes accessible dance spaces. In 2005, Maru participated in a workshop that Alito Alessi was invited to in Hong Kong, and in 2006, Maru was invited to Hong Kong again as an assistant teacher for Alito's "Dance for All Community Dance: A New Era of Dance for the Disabled" project. In 2012, Maru went to Bogotá, Colombia, to take the Dance for Empowerment Teacher Certification Program, becoming the first Asian Chinese to receive this certification. As an early practitioner of improvisation in Hong Kong, Maruzi also attended Nancy's lectures in Hong Kong in 1999, participated in the Hong Kong Regular Dance Jam, and has studied with Nancy many times since then. Nancy's latent movement score (one of the detailed formats of dance music developed by Nancy for global CI), Mike Vargas's four principles of improvisation (Be Aware, Be Available, Be Responsive, Be Clear),

Alito's Dance What You Can, and Ancient Dance Company have all contributed to his work. He has had a positive influence through his exposure to improvisation and symbiotic dance.

In 2007, Maru created his own "On-Grid-Line Moving" dance for autistic people, which he first named "symbiotic dance" after the lines and grids posted on the floor. The meaning of symbiosis is that Maru wanted to change the idea of "volunteer dancers" to "help people." In 2012, after Maru was certified in Dance to Be Able, the Beijing Porcelain Doll Rare Disease Care Center invited Maru to conduct a symbiotic dance at the I Can Collaborative Camp in the same year. Almost every year since then, symbiotic dance has been a designated program at I Can Camp, because it is so effective in empowering people with rare diseases (some of whom use wheelchairs). So far, Symbiosis Dance has conducted programs in Shijiazhuang, Wuhan, Chengdu, and Nanning, among other locales. Maru has touched almost 200 patients with rare diseases. Among them, the series of workshops and the "Symbiosis Dance Training Camp" conducted by Symbiosis Dance in Guangzhou's Hopwood Innovation Center directly led to the establishment of China's first fusion dance company, "Symbiosis Nice Dance Company," in Guangzhou in 2018. The leader and core members of Symbiosis Dance Company are all people with disabilities, and Symbiosis Dance itself is about practicing equality for all people through dance, sharing connection, inclusion, and gaining dignity and respect. Maru has practised and taught Symbiotic Dance for more than 10 years. Currently, he is developing what he calls "Barrier-Free Contact Improvisation dance sauce" which adheres to the original intention of "dance for all."

Since 2017, TOUCH Contact Improvisation Festival has been trying to do special workshops with autistic children in the form of Contact Improvisation. At that time, there were relatively few studies and cases of intervention and healing in the direction of autism dance in China. In 2018, TOUCH invited Maru and Mimi Lo to lead wheelchair users and autistic young adults to do symbiotic dance together. As a result, Body and Soul began in 2019 to focus on disability and inclusive arts practices. This author also began to think more deeply about the diversity of the body, how neglected and even discriminated groups can participate more equally in public culture and art, and what kind of dance process can heal the body and mind.

The Contact Improvisation Chinese Research Group began to take shape in 2021, when veteran practitioners of CI in China began to collaborate on their own to translate articles from *Contact Quarterly*. Yin Haolong spent a year in China in 2021 and felt that the information in the Chinese context was too empty and white. Although Contact Improvisation is now 50 years old, in China we have just begun to explore its potential. As Haolong states, "being behind does not mean a disadvantage, it is just our reality now, and how to find our voice in the present moment as a third-generation practitioner is what I am thinking about." Another core organizer of the Contact Improvisation Chinese Research Group is Shuyi Liao, a frequent resident of Beijing. She began to translate some of the early literature on her own initiative six years ago, and with the research group, she has deepened her personal research. She has recently returned to the practice of the Small Dance, first introduced by Paxton, the founder of Contact Improvisation. In March 2021, Yin Haolong, together with healer Angie and mobile artist couple Fire Nomad, launched the Dali Contact Improvisation Festival, which invited all participants to live and practice together for a period of time in a Dali village close to nature.

Building on previous TOUCH Contact Improvisation festivals, the Contact Improvisation Chinese Research Group has translated a large number of articles by early practitioners, such

296 Resistance and Support

as Paxton, Nancy Stark Smith, Barbara Dilley, Daniel Lepkoff, Lisa Nelson, Hubert Godard, and others. These ideas and discussions around the experiences, confusions, and different aspects of the practice are encouraging Chinese Contact Improvisers to move to a subtler exploration, from physical practice to everyday life, or to the transition to mind-body practice, the study of other mind-body disciplines, and a variety of socially oriented applications and dialogues.

Transcript of the Roundtable "Contact Improvisation in China and Taiwan"

With Yutian (Elsie) Wang, Huichao (Dew) Ge, Shuyi (Candy) Liao, Xiao Zhang, and Ming-Shen Ku; recorded February 18, 2023

ANN COOPER ALBRIGHT: I want to start by thanking you all very much for showing up to this roundtable and particularly thank Elsie for being willing to gather you together on Zoom and undertake the translation and transcriptions.

Let me provide a bit of context for this roundtable. When I organized *CI @ 50*, one of the events was a three-day writing workshop where attendees proposed essays on the practice of CI in the contemporary context. These essays will be compiled into a collection titled *Resistance and Support: Contact Improvisation @ 50*. I've been in contact with several people who are writing essays, and their work is coming along well. The essays contain provocative and rigorous thinking from a diverse range of locations, including India, Brazil, Argentina, Canada, the United States, and Europe. However, I also wanted to make sure that we include perspectives from China. I thought the best way to do it was to do a roundtable.

ELSIE WANG: Let's start from the beginning and talk about how Contact Improvisation took root in East Asia. I believe Ming-Shen has been one of the earliest to bring Contact Improvisation to Taiwan. Could you share with us the process of how you first brought it to Taiwan?

MING-SHEN KU: I started getting to know Contact Improvisation in a history class at the University of Illinois Urbana-Champaign. And then in 1988, I attended the American Dance Festival. I didn't get a chance to take a class in Contact Improvisation, but I went to a jam and happened to dance with a Contact Improviser. We danced for a few hours straight, and I felt like my body just wanted to keep going. I was put into a trance and we danced for the whole evening. I felt like it was something right and natural for me, so I decided to live in New York in 1991 and 1992 to get to know this dance form better.

When I returned to Taiwan in 1992, I realized I needed someone to dance with me, so I started offering free Sunday classes. The class lasted for five years until 1997. People came and went without any restrictions, and only those who truly loved it stayed, and eventually, I accumulated a big group of people. At the same time, I began teaching CI at the National Institute of Art. The chairperson valued this art form very much, and back then, I was the only one who could teach it. Ever since then, we have had several teachers teaching this dance form at the university.

CANDY LIAO: For me, I started Contact Improvisation in 2009. I first learned about it from a contemporary dance artist during a modern dance technique workshop. I began to enjoy the feeling of flying and the force of the leverage. This aspect of Contact Improvisation attracted me a lot.

Later, I started to learn CI from a European Contact teacher. Through her class, I started to realize that, in addition to partnering techniques in the modern dance world, Contact Improvisation has many layers to discover. So, in 2013, I started a community by holding Sunday evening workshops and jams, and this has continued for 10 years.

I first started the community with another partner, Roselyn Shih, and then later other members joined. The community is membership-based, and we discussed how to sustain it along the way. As for my personal learning, the very important years are 2017 and 2018. Back then I felt a strong desire to learn more about the roots of Contact Improvisation, so I went to Nancy Stark Smith and took her three-week January intensive at Earthdance for two years. After that, COVID started, and it gave us a lot of time on our own. Because teachers from the outside world were unable to travel to China, we had to teach ourselves. As a result, my attitude toward CI became more serious. Before, I played and learned, but I never thought about teaching seriously. But in the past three years I have realized that I need to delve more deeply and take teaching and sharing more seriously.

DEW GE: I first encountered Contact Improvisation when I was working as a producer for the contemporary choreographer Hou Ying, whom Candy also took a CI workshop with. Hou Ying has given some CI workshops in China, which gave me some exposure to this art form. However, I had never jammed in this context before. In 2016, I went to New York because Hou Ying's dance troupe was performing there. While I was there, I had the opportunity to participate in a CI jam, and that was the first time I had ever jammed. I immediately fell in love with that feeling.

When I returned to China, I began promoting CI by organizing workshops, and most of these workshops were given by choreographers. In 2017, I organized the first TOUCH CI festival in China, and have been working to promote this art form by organizing different kinds of events ever since. So that's how I came to know about CI from both a producer's and a practitioner's perspective.

ELSIE: Could you talk more about the TOUCH CI Festival since you're the only one with a producer's perspective?

DEW: Sure. To provide some context, TOUCH was initiated by me, Candy, and three other friends, each with different backgrounds and interests. For example, Candy is particularly interested in exploring the origins of CI. Personally, I value the public value of CI. Another friend, Roselyn, places great emphasis on the communal development of CI. And then there is the director, Yang Rui, who explores the dissemination of CI through dance film. So, in fact, we all have different individual directions of exploration that collectively converge into a shared passion for organizing this festival.

From my personal perspective, I am always very passionate about promoting Contact Improvisation in China. Firstly, I feel that it is a very physical art form. I have always been interested in exploring the physicality of the body, its public existence, and its narrative. Secondly, it creates a sense of connection. Why are people able to establish this kind of trust and let go of their judgments in such a context? I feel that Contact Improvisation is very much needed in Chinese society, where we lack this kind of connection and trust beyond the body. Thirdly, it also holds important aesthetic and artistic value as a form of postmodern art. When we hold events in art museums, we also consider exploring

298 Resistance and Support

its artistic values and historical background, such as how it developed into an art form through a group of artists' experiments.

XIAO ZHANG: Let me share my experience with CI. In December 2016, some people in Hangzhou organized a jam and invited Irene Sposetti, the dancer that Candy mentioned earlier, to come to Hangzhou to give a workshop. I did not participate in the workshop, but I did participate in the jam. At first, I didn't know what it was, but it felt very familiar to me and I enjoyed the feeling of touch. Starting in 2017, I began attending more workshops, including one taught by Xu Chengwei from Ku & Dancers, one given by two Ukrainian dancers, and later I met Ming-Shen in person. This was roughly my learning experience. Since 2019, I have been leading some workshops and jams in Hangzhou myself. Last year, I also began creating some performance pieces. In 2020, I attended the Touch CI Festival in Beijing, where I felt connected with the whole Contact community in China for the first time. That is my experience with CI. Beyond CI, I am also an individual photographer.

MING-SHEN: There's something I would like to add. As I mentioned earlier, I gathered a large group of people in the 1990s, and at that time, we had all kinds of teachers who taught in Taiwan, such as Steve Paxton, Nancy Stark Smith, Julyen Hamilton, and Lisa Nelson, among others. In fact, my first improvisation performance was with Steve Paxton in Taiwan in 1992. After we had gathered this group of people, I started my own company in 1993, and this year marks our 30th anniversary. Over the years, my company has slowly transitioned from being a contemporary/modern dance company into a more improvisation-oriented company, and we now tour around the world and teach, among other things. We currently have 15 members, and we are also starting to establish more connections in Asia.

When I first became involved in the Contact community, I thought it was very Westernized, and I felt that we needed to do something from an Asian perspective. So in 2011, we created the iDance Network between Taiwan, Hong Kong, Japan, and Korea. In this network, each country can hold its own festival, but we also share artists and engage in more and more communication. It is a biennial festival, and this year will be our seventh year. The festival in Taiwan is called iDance, and it usually includes a nine-day workshop, which features what we call an improvisational banquet. This is an ongoing performance in which anyone who wants to perform can do so. We have participants at all levels, and we offer workshops, jams, site-specific improvisation works, theater performances, and a roundtable discussion. The festival also features a five-day theater performance.

ANN: One thing that struck me as I was listening is that there are two distinct aspects of Contact: the movement form and technique, and the aspect of improvisation that requires participants to let go of their expectations and be open to moving with another person. I would like to hear your thoughts on this latter aspect, particularly in terms of its value for Chinese dancers.

XIAO: Recently, I have been watching video clips of Contact Improvisation online. I studied the videos and what was happening in them, and I found that there were two types of physical appearances. In one type of video, there is a flow similar to Tai Chi, while the other type is more physical, involving a lot of crossing, crushing, and falling, and it is more about going with the unknown. I have been watching videos of Ku & Dancers, and I feel it falls more into the second type. It has a different quality, flow, and appearance of movement.

ELSIE: So what exactly are the differences between those two types of movements?

MING-SHEN: If you didn't see the video, it may be difficult to understand what Xiao is saying, but I can help clarify his message. As a dance company, Ku & Dancers' performers have received many forms of physical training, not limited to Contact Improvisation. They may have received training in other styles in the past, which explains the different physical appearances Xiao noticed. Such physical appearance comes from years of practice and training, as the body accumulates memories that eventually manifest in movement.

And because the Ku dancers have been dancing together weekly for 10 to 20 years, we have developed a deep understanding of each other's bodies. Therefore, we are always trying to break through what we already know about ourselves and about each other. Our practice is very different from other improvisational performances that just require a short period of rehearsal before the performance. We dedicate a significant amount of time to exploring our bodies and generating physical data, which we can draw on during performances. As a result, our bodies develop differently in terms of texture and movement choices. These differences are not necessarily good or bad, but simply unique. As the saying goes, "you are what you eat."

CANDY: Besides practicing CI, I also have professional training in theater performance. A few friends and I started a small experimental performance group where we try out some improvisation or CI performances. We're all professional dancers or actors, and we all have more than five years of CI experience. As trained performers, we're really aware of how to keep the audience engaged when we're on stage. Therefore, we think a lot about how to organize the space and direct the audience's attention, which isn't solely about CI. In CI, there's this flow—it's hard to describe, but we somehow just know where our body should go. This flow might sometimes conflict with or fit in with the training and aesthetic style we pursued as performers before.

Lately, I've been really interested in exploring how to balance these two aspects in my practice. In the performance group, we sometimes chat about whether we feel influenced by the audience's attention and respond accordingly, or if we keep our own style and try not to be affected by the audience. There's a lot to balance in this process.

I don't think Contact Improvisation performance has taken off in China yet, maybe because people still think that when talking about improvisation, it's about dancing as you want or showcasing personal style. The term *improvisation* is very broad in this sense. However, at the subtle level of observing one's consciousness and the different relationships with space, partners, and the audience at every moment, there's still so much room for discussion.

ELSIE: Thank you.

DEW: I would like to follow up on Candy's thoughts. To start, I'll share my experience as an audience member. I have seen many different performances, such as contemporary dance and theater, but I especially enjoy watching CI jams. I could watch people jam for hours and find the flow of their bodies particularly captivating. Even though they may not be professional dancers and their physical skills may not be strong, I can see a lot of their personalities in their dance, which is why I find watching jams so fascinating.

I believe it's wonderful to be in contact with the body, but for many participants from Chinese cultural backgrounds, they need a long period of mental preparation before they can naturally enter into the flow of contact without too much judgment or intention. Once they can enter into contact smoothly, they may enjoy it very much. In the workshops we have done in the past, some participants have been deeply touched by being touched, hugged, or having their weight supported by another person. Some may even cry.

I'd also like to expand on what Candy said about different forms of improvisation. We often have discussions about the quality or texture of improvisation. Not all improvisations are comfortable or of good quality. Many contemporary dance performances also use improvisation, but the improvisation they use is not always relaxed or comfortable. Dancers may think about presenting their bodies to the audience in a certain form, and they may not be attending to their bodies. However, there is a different quality or texture to the improvisation we talk about in CI. A good Contact Improviser must notice what their body wants to do at every moment and attend to their body's choices. That quality is what makes improvisation good. These are some of my additional thoughts.

ANN: Thank you. Moving to a contemporary context, I guess my question is: When people have been separated and in lockdown in China, what is the role of Contact Improvisation in getting people in touch again, both with themselves and with one another?

MING-SHEN: I believe that COVID did slow down the momentum of what was happening, but I haven't noticed a significant difference since jams continued to take place. In 2021, we held a three-hour-long super jam with over 100 participants dancing together in a large hall. Everyone wore a mask for the entire duration of the event, and nobody complained or removed their mask. Overall, I didn't observe any major changes. Taiwan is a small place, which makes it easy for people to connect with one another. Transportation is also very convenient, so it seems that people can easily get to know each other without Contact Improvisation.

In the long run, I never feel I have to convince everyone to practice Contact Improvisation. Although the world will be an ideal place if everyone practices CI, and there would be no wars or invasions, we can't force everyone to be interested. Everyone's sense of bodily boundaries is different, even among people with similar backgrounds. I think the most important thing is that we really want to do this, and we want to continue to share it. Some people who are destined to meet us will come and stay. I have always approached this matter with this mindset.

This is also why it took me more than 20 years to finally start the iDance festival. I'm not someone who plans things in advance, so I only take the next step when I feel it's the right time.

DEW: We held the TOUCH festival in 2020 and 2021, but not in 2022. I didn't dance much myself, either, and it was very challenging to organize events in China last year. However, during the first few years, many people were enthusiastic and signed up for it. We held the TOUCH festival in the fall, followed by the TOUCH community meeting in the winter, where teachers came to Beijing to dance and exchange ideas. My memory of TOUCH halted in 2021.

But I think things will be different this year after the country opens up. I feel that people will be more enthusiastic about traveling and attending events, and I imagine there will be a lot of people coming to this year's festival. We are also planning to invite different international artists to China this year, so I think there may be a large TOUCH event this year.

I feel that the name TOUCH contains a sense of connection that people living in the city really need. There is still a big gap between cities and rural areas in China, and Contact Improvisation is more likely to happen in cities.

I love what Ming-Shen said before, "When you dance more, you may love humanity a little more." Although I didn't dance much this year, I touched my dog every day at home, and now I love my dog even more. So, I believe that touch is also a form of love.

XIAO: I actually think the pandemic has had some positive effects, as it has brought people closer together. Because of the pandemic, people cannot leave the city easily. They are confined to their current location, and they are only able to dance and socialize with those around them, and this has resulted in the CI community in Hangzhou becoming closer. The impact of the pandemic on Hangzhou doesn't seem to have been too significant, as there have been continuous jams and regular classes. Although there were occasional temporary pauses during the pandemic, these only lasted for about a week before classes resumed. However, I do feel that after the pandemic is over, the community was not as close as before. It seems that after reopening, people become attracted to other things and are less in need of contact.

CANDY: I feel like once people meet, all their fears and sense of alienation disappear. The CI community is just a place that allows this kind of meeting to happen. When we dance with one another, all of our worries fade away. Despite the pandemic, the CI community in Beijing is still going strong, and the impact of the pandemic has not been particularly significant. However, promotional events have been affected a lot. Many of the theater projects I worked on were also greatly affected, as they require specific time and space, which were always disrupted due to COVID regulations. On the other hand, the CI community has been less affected. It operates in a natural way, relying on the community members' commitment instead of a specific time and location, so it's able to adapt to different circumstances.

ANN: Great, thank you. I guess my final question is: What do you think the future of CI in China will be?

DEW: I am generally an optimistic person, and when I have the passion to continue doing something, I strongly believe in its future potential. In mainland China, most of us who practice Contact Improvisation are young people born in the 1980s and 1990s, so I believe there are still many unexplored possibilities in this field. Moreover, I think China is in the middle of a trend where many people are starting to explore the field of spirituality. At the same time, many people are getting interested in Contact Improvisation because it is a very open and authentic way of moving the mind and body. I don't know if there will be a greater convergence between Contact Improvisation and the trend of spirituality, but I believe that this trend has already begun in China.

CANDY: Following up on Dew, I believe that CI can take on many meanings. It can be used for spiritual exploration, building trust, and exploring intimate relationships. For example, some people find trust the first time they dance CI and believe that this is what CI is all about. Therefore, we can see CI as an empty container that can hold many things. However, at the same time, it cannot give you any promises. If you develop in a certain direction, you may find that it could turn into something completely different. This doesn't mean that the other thing is not good. It's just that CI is not goal-oriented and doesn't give you any promises. So, it's hard to say what a person can get out of practicing CI.

But even without any promises, CI has developed for many years, thanks to its openness and inclusivity, which are values that are very much needed in contemporary times. Because it has an empty middle, anything can come into it, and it can continue to evolve.

302 Resistance and Support

It may not become wildly popular, or it may be used for other purposes, but its empty nature will allow it to keep nourishing us.

MING-SHEN: I am also optimistic about the future of CI, just like Dew. For the past decades, I have been promoting CI all by myself, but nobody really understood it. However, in the last 10 years, it seems that the seeds that were planted have slowly germinated, and more people have started to dance CI, and we also received more outside support.

Currently, the dancers in Ku & Dancers range from their twenties to their sixties, so there is already generational continuity, and each generation of dancers has their own style and cares about different aspects of CI. I'm actually very curious about how future generations will continue to dance CI, and whether the things they care about will change. I also really understand what Candy said, that everyone wants different things from CI, so I will just watch quietly and happily what happens next.

I also have a feeling that I want to express, even though there is no answer to it. In the past few decades, language has always been a barrier for me to get enough connection with people from the Western world, where the major CI communities are located. Even though I have a close connection with the older generation of CI dancers, there were always some obstacles whenever I tried to put things into writing. Many developments in CI have occurred over the past 50 years, but they are often recorded in writing, which is in English.

Every year, we place a little advertisement about Taiwan CI in *CQ* [*Contact Quarterly*]. Sometimes, we receive phone calls from people who saw the ad and want to dance with us when they visit Taiwan. However, the language barrier still creates many challenges. I know that many Asian countries, such as mainland China, Taiwan, Japan, and South Korea, are making great efforts to promote CI, but regarding language, there is still a significant gap between Asia and the rest of the world. I don't have any opinion; I just think it would be great if we could have more opportunities to interact with different people.

ANN: That's one great reason to have this roundtable and translate it. Hopefully, once we have a presence of China and Taiwan in this book, more people will be able to travel and exchange.

DEW: I have a final suggestion. I have written an article that outlines the historical development of Contact Improvisation in the Greater China region, and it will be published by the Dance Research Institute of the Chinese National Academy of Arts. If this article can be translated and published in English, it can provide a lot of useful information about the practice of CI in Asia.

ELSIE: I also want to add something. As we know, CI has roots in many Asian martial arts such as Tai Chi and Aikido. Therefore, I believe it would be very meaningful to contribute an Asian perspective to it. I am aware that many people have been committed to this mission for decades, and I am glad to participate in it.

ANN: Definitely, I think this could be the first step, and we can continue our conversation on this topic. I would like to thank you very much for coming in and thank Elsie for organizing this roundtable and doing the translation.

18

Deviant Bodies

Improvising Survival in Brazil

Ana Carolina Bezerra Teixeira

> I dance due to the cruel improvisations of my social persistence. Exclusion, indifference, and underestimation are situations that happen in my life even when I am out of the picture.
> —Carolina Teixeira

This essay is an interweaving of experiences, perceptions, and historiographies about the practice of Contact Improvisation (CI) in Brazil since the 1990s. I intend here to reflect on the development of CI in relation to its accessibility for bodies with some kind of disability. I document the emergence of mixed-ability dance companies in Brazil, arguing that the ideology of social inclusiveness in bringing differently abled bodies to the stage does not necessarily disrupt the overarching neoliberal logic of economic productivity that situates bodies in terms of productive and unproductive within the nation-state. Drawing on my experience with CI as both a social and an artistic practice, I suggest that we re-envision disability as a creative perspective, rather than an identity grounded in physical limitations or a perceived lack of an "efficient" body.

That dance, with its aesthetic legacies of a virtuosic, ideal body, would become the route to my physical and imaginative liberation from the normative standards of bodies imposed by contemporary society, is both counterintuitive and extraordinary. From the time that I first set my foot on a stage, I would never have imagined I would be working as an artist/scholar within the fields of Dance and Performance Studies. The story of that journey interweaves the histories of Contact Improvisation, disability activism, and the tricky tactics of everyday survival in Brazil. Even though I am currently a professor in the Dance Department at the Federal University of Paraiba in Brazil, my academic career has been characterized by hardships and obstacles, which are, unfortunately, a common pattern for many Brazilian professors, educators, and researchers, disabled or not.

In 1988, I suffered a cerebral vascular accident (CVA) at the age of nine, an episode that profoundly marked my relationship with my body and with a society used to policing all the deviant bodies in its midst. The stroke left me with a slight paralysis and threw me into a medical establishment (both a place and an ideology) predicated on "rehabilitating" a body back to "normal"—buying into a mechanized model of an efficiently functioning and productive body. Among the numerous disciplinary regimes to which I was subjected, traditional physical therapy was the most enduring of them. These body rehabilitation exercises were limited to isolated body parts, numbingly repetitive, and keyed to a motor-mechanistic result that met a functionalist perspective of bodily gain. Hooked up to machines that measured range of motion in terms of numbers, without any attention to what I was feeling or

---

Ana Carolina Bezerra Teixeira, *Deviant Bodies* In: *Resistance and Support*. Edited by: Ann Cooper Albright, Oxford University Press.
© Oxford University Press 2024. DOI: 10.1093/9780197776308.003.0019

304   Resistance and Support

experiencing, made me realize how systems of state, medical, and economic power operate on both our bodies and our souls.

My first exposure to dance was in a Contact Improvisation class, which I felt was a more organic experience than my previous physical practice in rehabilitation. This CI class happened during the staging process for a choreography by the Argentinian Luis Arrieta. It was July 1996, and he was creating a work for the renowned Roda Viva Company Dance. The class was always held before rehearsals as a form of experimentation with the mobilities and sensibilities of each body. Coming from a physical therapy model where the only touch was with cold metal, I was at first surprised and then relieved to experience a body-to-body contact based on sensation from skin to bone. This experience of knowing other bodies through CI provided a suspension of the usual fear, often the greatest barrier that existed on the part of people without disabilities who were experiencing their first contact with people with disabilities. The possibility of moving with another, to feel their singularities and their limitations, encouraged respect for the bodies that moved differently from one's own. It is important to highlight that Roda Viva had in its cast bodies with diverse disabilities such as Down syndrome, paraplegic, hemiplegic, visual impairment, amputees, and people with cerebral palsy and poliomyelitis.

The sensitivity to tactile perception that is a foundation of CI allowed the participants to experience a dialogue between their bodies and other bodies that moved in different ways. Even when no physical contact was present, it was possible to create an emotional connection while we discovered unique patterns of moving together. CI facilitated the building of community spirit within our group, and this is partly what we shared in lectures, workshops, and performances of Roda Viva Company Dance. We were aware of the importance of this somatic exchange between bodies, and we sought to share what we developed in our dance studio in the educational events we performed throughout Brazil.

For 11 years, I was a dancer for Roda Viva Company Dance, created by the choreographer Henrique Amoedo in 1995. His work enshrined the presence of bodies with and without disabilities in its choreographic repertory and was generally well received. Working together, we forged a sense of inclusion within the group, even if the economic reality of our lives was shaped by the extreme exclusion of atypical bodies in our society. This diversity of body experiences allowed the group to investigate the possibilities of movement, dialogues between bodies, and, above all, to change the prevailing aesthetics of dance on stage. Contact Improvisation practices were the basis for the discovery of movements and choreographic actions that emerged from the relationships generated in collective or individual exercises, which revealed unique characteristics of each disability and each person's particular way of moving. Roda Viva also used CI as an educational format in schools, universities, and other institutions where we performed. There were open workshops which provided contact between our bodies and the community with whom we were engaging. Students, educators, researchers, and professionals from different areas had access to the techniques of CI through these events held throughout Brazil.

This experience was extremely relevant for my formation as an educator and artist. Through this work weaving arts and disability activism, I came to understand Contact Improvisation as a political practice of reaffirmation and engagement of all bodies in a relationship that respects and rebuilds from the multiplicity in each participant. The composition at that moment was no longer vertically and hierarchically defined, but rather it exhibited a horizontality of shared knowledge of all our differences. However, the choreographer's work did not always fit into the process required by the diversity of bodies present there. Although CI was essential to our process of movement research and kinesiological knowledge about our own different corporealities, it was not the basis for our artistic creations because the company tended to commission choreographers who were often used to working with normative bodies. In other words, while there was at that time (and still is) a kind of curiosity about what bodies with disabilities are able to do in dance, this manifested as movement investigations in the studio, not as legitimate performances for the stage.

For this reason, when I assumed the direction of the company between 2004 and 2007, I aimed at an aesthetic change that firmly grounded CI and Performance Studies as the artistic basis of our work. Contact Improvisation classes were held daily and influenced the creation and construction not only of abstract choreographies, but also of performances that foregrounded the perception of our bodies in their spasms, tensions, fractures, amputations, and all their deviations. As a community, we started to occupy the streets and to improvise with what the urban space offered us, from the architecture to the prejudiced look of people to our own way of facing limits, situating our impossibilities as propellers of creation and existence in a period so invisible for bodies considered outside the normative standards of contemporary Brazilian dance.

In Brazil, there was also another place of affinity with the experience of disability beyond the veiled or overly polite forms of the term. All of us were very aware of the exclusionary reality that was experienced there, either through the direct experience of limited physical function or in terms of the limits that society, family, public spaces, and the inaccessible architecture of the places where we worked imposed on us. Indeed, when we talked about improvising, the concept itself was already part of our palpable, everyday reality of living. The power to make the best of what is available only gained in potential when we applied these skills to making art. Many of us improvised our housing, food, transport, orthotics, and prostheses to continue rehearsing and maintaining the group—sometimes selling tickets, managing the company's production, and mobilizing support within the local community to make the ongoing project operational. The group's economic diversity reflects the way our bodies act in this artistic context. In this sense, even the greatest names of Brazilian dance with whom we worked committed themselves to rethinking their choreographic aesthetic projects in order to achieve a canonical change in the processes of creation in dance.

Thinking about the history of Contact Improvisation in Brazil is also thinking about a practice that was based on community actions in dance. This includes an attempt to break the patterns of social judgment based on deviance from a normative, efficient body. In this sense, the work of Maria Duschenes is an example of CI as an inclusive practice aimed at the affirmation of collective existences. Maria Duschenes was a choreographer and educator who was a former student of Rudolf Laban. Born in Hungary in 1922, she migrated to Brazil at a young age, fleeing persecution against Jews during World War II. She brought the first references of the Laban system to Brazil from the perspective of understanding it through Brazilian bodies, undertaking what I understand as a political project of emancipation through corporeality. Inspired by what Laban called Choral Dance, she involved dozens to hundreds of participants with different bodily experiences, performing in conventional and unconventional spaces.

Parks, squares, and urban centers were used by Duschenes as real spaces for the practice of dance as a space in which to create a broader understanding of community and collective coexistence. Her work was very similar to the community dance practices developed by Anna

Halprin during the 1960s and 1970s, which connected diverse and multiple bodies based on the idea of building group improvisational scores, as well as a kinesthetic awareness based on connections with the environment. Dona Maria, as she was known, experienced a physical disability when she acquired polio at the age of 22, a fact that did not prevent her from choreographing and acting as an educator in the city of São Paulo. Through Educational Dance, she encouraged the participation of bodies considered deviant in form and productivity— her practice was designed for the participation of all.

Bodies of elementary school teachers, dancers, therapists, lawyers, doctors, students, psychologists, and children mingled in their collective practices, whether in open or closed spaces such as rehearsal rooms in theaters. Her contribution was fundamental to dance investigations in Brazil, especially during the 1970s and 1980s, and to the generations of dance educators who followed her teachings. Whether in the artistic, educational, or therapeutic space, entire generations of professionals were influenced by the work of Dona Maria. This includes educators such as Maria Mommensohn and Cassia Navas, who were Dona Maria's students between the 1970s and 1980s. Angel Vianna was also someone who was deeply influenced by her work. Dona Maria's focus went beyond the teaching of dance, but allowed the understanding of subtle body practices within an identity perspective that considered the differences and singularities of each body (Itaú Cultural Encyclopedia, 2020).

Dance performances involving people with disabilities in Brazil developed between the second half of the 1990s and the beginning of the twenty-first century. Interestingly and ironically, this period was also dominated by professional companies that stood out for the extreme virtuosity of the dancing on stage, such as Deborah Colker Company, Grupo Corpo, and Quasar Dance Company. Concurrent with this scenario, the emergence of companies that mixed dancers with and without disabilities inaugurated a different and unimaginable scenario for the Brazilian public, who were accustomed to artistic presentations whose aesthetic priority was to stage amazing feats of acrobatics and high-energy dancing. In the same way, much of what was built in Brazil on the relationship between dance and disability was due to the therapeutic area, rehabilitation practices, as well as the study of CI techniques based on the activities of teachers such as Steve Paxton and Alito Alessi.

The history of improvisation related to bodies with disabilities in Brazil has promoted the construction of different approaches to the work. One especially important intervention was that of DanceAbility, based on the work of the American choreographer Alito Alessi, who consolidated in Brazil a work perspective aimed at the integration of bodies with and without disabilities. The dancer Neca Zarvos was primarily responsible for the first courses in Brazil and for Alessi's first visit to the country in 1997. The groundbreaking work of Alessi was offered at two institutions: the Association of Friends of People with Disabilities (AACD), and the Vergueiro Rehabilitation Center, both in the city of São Paulo. Along with Alito, the dancer Emery Blackwell (who uses a motorized wheelchair) was also present. In 2007 Alessi would return to Brazil to hold workshops for dancers and teachers, and also for a show involving bodies with and without disabilities entitled Joy LAB Research. The following year, Neca would hold one of the country's largest workshops ever made, with the DanceAbility Brazil project involving more than 200 people from various regions of the country (Núcleo Dança Aberta Brasil, 2007).

This work was so important for that period that in 2009 and 2010 it became part of the Contact in Rio festival program. It is critical to emphasize that Alessi's methodology aimed to encourage the development of mixed skills between dancers with and without disabilities.

In these workshops, most participants were from different regions of Brazil. Cia Pulsar, in Rio de Janeiro, also stood out in the 1990s and the following decade for connecting Rudolf Laban's research methodologies to the pedagogy of Angel and Klauss Vianna—both dancers and movement scholars. The Viannas were pioneers in the practice of dance as a mechanism for self-knowledge, beyond mere technical reproduction. The work developed by them did not adopt the therapeutic label, but instead searched for cultivating bodily responsibility connected to understanding gesture/gesturality as a way of expressing oneself.

To exist as a disabled body in Brazil is to confront views that are still stereotyped, fetishistic, and discriminatory. While our bodies may have helped to explore more inclusive methodologies and different approaches to the teaching of movement and dance, we are still living in a society where we are forced to confront prevailing systems of normative representation. From the perspective of improvisation as a practice of the body's possibilities, we resist traditional models of identity representation because we are already inserted in ways of seeing that are associated with refusal and denial. Although much progress has been made in the discussion of disability, difference, and diversity, we have not managed to consolidate a social policy for true access to culture, education, and employment. Even in professional dance performance, we are still objectified by scientific research or by excessive compartmentalization of capitalist art systems, which see in our practices the tidy commodification of our struggles and subjectivities. We have not yet constituted improvisation as a practice of political emancipation of the body—everyone's bodies.

Since colonial times, the Brazilian people have incorporated improvisation as a survival practice. This kind of social practice helped to cope with the historical traumas of socioeconomic discrimination that consolidated the effects of poverty, criminality, institutional racism, and other exclusionary practices that have not yet allowed the advancement of public policies to the mentally marginalized in Brazil. In our country, we have adopted the expression "to get by" (*se virar* in Brazilian Portuguese) to designate the ability to get around a problem and solve it most appropriately, aside from institutional structures. Turning around or pivoting becomes incorporated as a way of creating action, of "finding a way" in the face of degrading situations such as hunger, poverty, and lack of hope.

Faced with this reality, we learn to improvise as a kind of dissent that can mark the Brazilian figure as a *malandro*, an unreliable, crooked, or a smart aleck who takes advantage of another person. These labels consolidate a cruel typification, totally disconnected from the harsh reality of bodies that climb hills, that must dodge stray bullets, hunger, femicide, racism, ableism, and institutional violence in an attempt to stay alive or "sub-live" to reality. At the same time, we Brazilians are so often represented in the international media as a kind of happy and partying people, placed in the shadow of a false ideology in which the body's status quo of living precariously is seen as "overcoming adversity," like an eternal buffoon giving joy to the world.

The Brazilian body learned from the shackles of colonialism how to survive on the margins. Whether it was our sensuality artificially commercialized for the sake of tourism, or even a mythical idea of a welcoming people living on a kind of fantasy island, we were portrayed as poor but happy. And yet, climbing the favela's hill requires more than navigating the narrow gaps of the community's alleys. It is undertaken in a courageous act of existence, solidarity, and engagement that acts, sometimes, in the field of the unknown; a corporeity permanently subject to states of deviation and always falling toward the marginalized high of the marginalized areas. One example of how bodily and racial segregation in Brazil created

308 Resistance and Support

niches of appropriation and fetishization is the Funk movement in the Brazilian peripheries (where the ruling class only goes to dance Funk). Those bodies were forced to create their own musical cultures, improvising forms of survival outside the dominant ideology that demands production, control, economic and moral stability, without recognizing their humanity or offering any living support.

Improvising in dance is mixed up with the idea of exploring, investigating, and discovering the impossible-possibility of other bodies and ways of moving, welcoming in the vulnerabilities, fatigue, and folds of each body's characteristic movement. Improvising insists on the unique experience of discovering oneself in the forms and anti-forms of action—bodies as defined by Nancy, who asserts:

> Who else in the world knows anything like the body? It is the latest product, the longest decanted, refined, dismantled, and reassembled of our old culture. If the West is a fall (as its name suggests), the body is the ultimate weight, the extremity of the weight that is oscillating in that fall. The body is the fact of weighing. The laws of gravitation concern bodies in space. But first of all, the body already weighs on itself: it has descended on itself, under the law of its own gravity, which has pushed it to the point where it is confused with its load. (2008, 8)

This weight of feeling excluded in the idealized inclusion of colonialism reminds me of the phenomenon of "double-consciousness" advocated by W. E. B. Dubois in his book *The Souls of Black Folk*, when referring to the identity condition of North American Black people. In Dubois's words:

> It is peculiar sensation, this double-consciousness, this sense of always looking at one's self through the eyes of others, of measuring one's soul by the tape of world that looks on in amused contempt and pity. One ever feels his two-ness, an American, a Negro: two souls, two thoughts, two unreconciled strivings; two warring ideals in one dark body, whose dogged strength alone keeps it from being torn asunder. The history of American Negro is the history of this stuff—this longing to attain self-conscious manhood, to merge his double self into a better and truer self. In this merging he wishes neither of the older selves to be lost. He does not wish to Africanize America, for America has too much to teach the world and Africa. (1987, 2–3)

In my doctoral thesis I approached this feeling of belonging to the world through the demarcation of the eyes of others as being a condition also common to people with disabilities, because we too are divided between two realities, creating our own sense of "double-consciousness." The first concerns the disability marked on the body, one's pathological condition, the clinical diagnosis, and the daily processes of exclusion. The second is the reality of efficiency translated into the obligation of production, of individual achievement. The issues involving the processes of discrimination intersect not in the sense of recognizing who is more or less marginalized, but of alerting us to the phenomenon of exclusion as something already naturalized. In the case of disabled bodies in Brazil, there is a false sensation of being included in a country that refuses our humanity, except when others speak for us, intercede for us, or assist us amidst the multiple crossroads of social exclusion that involve gender, race, and ability issues across the land. I claim this from my position as a woman with a disability, a dancer, born in the poor North-East of Brazil, a Latin American and underemployed woman at a public university that is still far from instituting an inclusive educational perspective. I recognize myself in what authors like DuBois advocate regarding dual states of social jurisdiction of our citizenship, whose demand imposes itself under our daily practices of existence and resistance.

In my view, the CI practice is still organized under an integrating veil for its apparent access to multiple bodies and their singularities, despite having been consolidated in fact in body practices of extreme physicality, performance, and creation of communities distanced from the body-political reality of thousands of people who live the experience of disability, especially in Brazil.

> It is a fact that the plural aspect of contemporary dance, especially since the 1980s, has promoted corporal "diversity" and political activism, but it is still limited to the participation of bodies that even in their physical multiplicities (fat, mestizo, elderly, and sick bodies) reproduced the culture of ability. I reflect and ask myself: what would be the role of the artist in these frontiers of exhaustion of mobilities? I draw attention to the significant aesthetic change that wheelchairs, crutches, prostheses, orthosis, hearing aids and blindness inaugurated in the contemporary dance context of the late 1980s and 1990s. (Teixeira 2021, 174)

The history of people with disabilities in Brazil is always told by other voices that mostly do not live or have lived the experience of disability. This phenomenon has also been repeated in the verticalized way in which we have had access to the arts. Often our bodies were only included or endorsed by slogans of opportunity and with dance and even improvisational Contact it was not much different. We were first included for an appropriation of our corporal powers to only then be included artistically.

In 2019, I created a dance solo entitled *Extrema Direita* ("Far Right"), a form of protest against the political crisis faced in Brazil, with the ascension of a reactionary right wing influenced by the rise of European right-wing and neo-Nazi ideologies. Civil society was divided as never before by populist and radical discourses, by discriminatory postures that revealed a country whose identity has always been known as cordial and glorious in its diversity. The artistic project was a desire of mine to deal with these phenomena that had occurred between right and left wings, having my body as a kind of tragicomic support. We performed some exercises through CI, and we used objects and texts that I wrote on walls of the dance studio. Words, objects that were spread on the floor, danced with me and dialogued with my disability and the excess of mobility on the right side of my body.

Beyond showing my abilities on stage, I was interested in sharing with the audience a creative exercise of will and of political action with the disability that I live in my body. My experience with CI mobilized contrary forces of my hemiplegic body, forces that already materialized in my daily relations with society and in the artistic space. At the same time, I offer them my incarnated experience with disability, with prostheses and orthoses, and with the poetry shared throughout the process of the performance. Although I am dancing alone, I do not remain alone. The audience (including my director) are invited to participate almost the entire time of the performance, interacting and intervening in all the events. The idea of improvisation in this event was to blur the line between the figure on stage and the private person behind the person on stage. In this sense, it is a way of freeing myself from preconceptions. The notion of improvisation in this case is its use as a tool of *crippin*, the reality that was made manifest in this work. The director Mauricio Motta and I explore the audience all the time—my body leads and is led by the audience and in its relationship with my disabilities, my prostheses and orthoses placed on the scenery.

The generation of dancers with disabilities active during the 1990s was, in my view, responsible for a profound aesthetic rupture in the ways of doing and thinking about dance in Brazil. Somewhat later, schools, universities, and non-formal dance spaces also began to recognize this work as an important area in the field of performing arts. Nonetheless, the population of artists, producers, directors, and educators who worked in the field of dance and who live the experience of dance and disability is still incipient. While the motricities, the abilities, and the potentialities of our bodies may be recognized, there is not an effective training of dancers with disabilities or a pathway to find a place in the professional dance market. Our generation learned the CI techniques as a process of individual and collective investigation, rather than within a pedagogical formation that would consider our contributions as professional dancers. In Brazil, we continue to be isolated, welcomed only in specific festivals aimed expressly for bodies with disabilities. For instance, in the case of CI festivals, the participation of people with some type of disability is still very rare, which makes the practice still restricted to specific groups that can easily travel to events across the country. Often these events happen in places with little accessibility, both structurally and economically. This creates a de facto culture of exclusion, even exposing a rhetoric of inclusivity.

During my years as a dancer with Roda Viva Company Dance, I was able to experience moving with people who had various disabilities, be they visual, physical, congenital, acquired, syndrome-related, or otherwise. This diversity of disabilities was what made the difference in my training for understanding disability not only as a given of my existence, but also as a political and artistic resistance. Dancing was, for me, the first space that allowed me to understand the word *improvisation* as a strategy not only for movement, but also for survival in a Latin American culture riddled by colonialism and a neoliberal economic standard that passes over most of the Brazilian population. Improvisation recognizes the precarious states of existence reinvented every day as a resilient poiesis.

References

Du Bois, W. E. B. 1987. *The Souls of Black Folk*, in his *Writings* (Library of America). New York: Random House, 2–3.

Enciclopédia Itaú Cultural de Arte e Cultura Brasileira. 2001. Maria Duschenes. São Paulo: Itaú Cultural. Viewed May 31, 2023. http://enciclopedia.itaucultural.org.br/pessoa252508/maria-duschenes.

Nancy, Jean-Luc. 2008. *Corpus*. New York: Fordham University Press, 8.

Núcleo Dança Aberta Brasil. 2008. https://nucleodancaaberta.com/quem-somos/

Núcleo Dança Aberta: Danceability Brasil. 2007. Viewed May 12, 2023. https://nucleodancaaberta.com/

Teixeira, Carolina. 2021. *Deficiência em Cena: a ciência excluída e outras Estéticas*. Natal: Offset Ed., 174.

19

Queering Contact Improvisation with Sara Ahmed (and the Wheelchair)

Mª Paz Brozas Polo

Reading Sara Ahmed's book about how the spatial and the social are implicated in objects and orientations, I began a Contact Improvisation duo with her. She pushed me and my thinking as I was moved again and again to consider CI as a practice of disorientation, co-perception, and inclination. I began to imagine the idea of queering as an aspect of the dancing itself. At one point, an object, the wheelchair, joined our duo, so the duet became a trio. This is the story of that dance.

In her book on *Queer Phenomenology*, Ahmed, following Husserl, chooses the table as a referent object, the primordial object of writing and thinking, an object that gathers bodies and that in turn invites many other smaller objects to be placed upon it.[1] In addition to highlighting the historical peculiarities of its patriarchal construction, she offers us a somatic approach to the table, as one could do with any object within reach: "Phenomenology for Husserl means apprehending the object as if it were unfamiliar, so that we can attend to the flow of perception itself" (2006, 35–37). Ahmed turned toward the table quite by chance and decided to stay with it: "Once I caught sight of the table in Husserl's writing, which is revealed just for a moment, I could not help but follow tables around" (2006, 22). In my case, I turned toward the wheelchair when I ran into it several times—casually, but insistently. I had been finding it in the faculty warehouse piled on top of the German wheels[2] since 1997, and every time I wanted to use those props, I had to remove the wheelchairs one by one, so I came to know its shape and its weight. I danced for the first time with a wheelchair user in 2009 at the Contact Improvisation Festival in Freiburg and since 2014, I collaborated regularly with Isabelle Brunaud and her company *ANQA Danse avec les Roues*[3] (ANQA Dance with Wheelchairs) which is based in Contact Improvisation (Bruneau and Lamoine 2014). Then, in September 2020, I broke a metatarsal bone and so I took a wheelchair home, where I became intimate with its singular way of moving.

---

[1] Sara Ahmed (1969) is a British-Australian writer whose study area includes the intersection of feminist theory, queer theory, diversity, critical race theory, and postcolonialism. Within the framework of a prolific work, *Queer Phenomenology: Orientations, Objects, Others*, published in 2006, is one of her first books.

[2] The German Wheel is a gymnastic object used in circus performances. It is the size of the human body and inside a German Wheel we can put several wheelchairs. In 2019 we started an ongoing exploration project between wheelchairs and German Wheels, two displacement objects that refer to different contexts and imaginaries. Placing in the same space and in the same game a support object—which refers to bodies unable to walk—and a spectacular object that refers to wonder is one of the purposes of this collective experience. Perhaps risk and even marginality or queerness inhabit both objects.

[3] In her last choreographic piece TAKAMASHI, which I witnessed in April 2022 in Palaiseau (close to Paris), there are six bodies on stage and a wheelchair that houses one of them. Other orthopedic objects also inhabit space and the encounters are all mediatized; bodies and foreign objects approach, enlarge each other.

Mª Paz Brozas Polo, *Queering Contact Improvisation with Sara Ahmed (and the Wheelchair)* In: *Resistance and Support*. Edited by: Ann Cooper Albright, Oxford University Press. © Oxford University Press 2024. DOI: 10.1093/9780197776308.003.0020

312 Resistance and Support

I choose the wheelchair instead of the table—Husserl and Ahmed's object of study—to reflect on the interactions between bodies and objects, but above all to reflect on the interaction between bodies and bodies.[4] The wheelchair is not as familiar an object as the table; it is not in every home. It is a dynamic object that refers to the fragility of our bodies and the need for assistance. It is an object created to receive, support, and move a body; it is an object that often has handlebars which a second body holds, but it also has the possibility of being manipulated directly from the wheels by whoever sits on it.[5] The wheelchair allows us to observe the co-perception of the relationships between bodies and nearby objects proposed by Husserl (Ahmed 2006, 39). Also, in this kind of chair we can indeed experience how two bodies coincide and move at the same time in proximity, much like Contact Improvisation. Yet they do not walk side by side. Rather, they do it one in front of the other, but it is not known who is following whom. It may be that it is the body that is positioned in front which guides and decides the path and the speed, while the body behind merely accompanies or pushes. But it is also possible that it is the one behind who decides the trajectory and the body in front is simply carried along for the ride, so to speak. Sometimes these power relations of dominance or submission are self-evident, but sometimes they can be subtler, as when the wheelchair becomes an object that mediates their partnered dancing in a way that disorients the usual pathways.

In Contact Improvisation, the roles of leader and follower dissolve into a common trajectory. Based on a study of Paxton's writings in *Contact Quarterly*, the philosopher José Gil asks, "How can Contact Improvisation dance avoid the small and unconscious captures or manipulations that take place across the contact and instead support a democratic ideal" (2001, 156).[6] We can't completely avoid power dynamics inside the dancing, but we can learn to subvert them. Phenomenology offers some important tools to understand bodies in contact: it reveals to us a body that is present in its own surfaces and borders; by showing us its limits, it also shows us its possibilities of becoming space or merging with other objects or bodies. Alluding to *Nausea* by Sartre (1988/1938), Ahmed meditates on the meanings of touch and its reciprocity, on touching and being touched. She also underlines the role of contact and touch in the generation of both space and desire (Ahmed 2006, 23).[7] José Gil—with Deleuze—proposed:

> to consider the body no longer as a "phenomenon," no longer as a visible and concrete
> perception moving in the objective Cartesian space, but rather, . . . to consider the body
> as a metaphenomenon, simultaneously visible and virtual, both emitter of signs and

---

[4] About crutches as body extensions, one could also to refer to the Cunningham, Curtis, and Pell (2019) Project on Differences: *The Way You Look at Me*.

[5] The International Symbol of Accessibility created in the 1960s is a schematic and static image of a body in a wheelchair (https://www.riglobal.org/about/intl-symbol-of-access/). In 2010, a more dynamic alternative image to this icon was created, where the wheelchair is maintained but the body itself is perceived as self-propelled. A debate between these two icons continues to unfold (https://accessibleicon.org/#an-icon-is-a-verb). In any case, the wheelchair continues to be the symbol associated with disability.

[6] The democratic self-respect in Contact Improvisation is also the focus of criticism by Mitra: "far from being a practice of liberation, CI can be a violent practice in its inherent invisibilization of the different power asymmetries that it harbors and perpetuates in the guise of democracy" (Mitra 2021, 21).

[7] Even if more recent theories have surpassed to a certain extent the relational presuppositions of Phenomenology, it is still valid and in continuous revision (Fraleigh 2018). What Ahmed does in fact is to put forward a new perspective in which Phenomenology is somehow questioned as it is traversed by cultural theory.

trans-semiotic, endowed by an organic interior ready to be dissolved as soon as it reaches the surface. (2009, 94)

Taking into account that living is different from thinking, we can invite Ahmed's proposal to queer phenomenology by inviting cultural studies to be thinking together. Although Sara Ahmed does not write about Contact Improvisation per se, she writes about the improvisation—how spontaneous actions can diverge from well-worn pathways without ever completely escaping their matrix. Her attention to space and to the individual and collective actions and decisions that shape our lives is revealing.

In this essay, I draw on the ideas and even the structure of Ahmed's book to address the concepts of disorientation and collective navigation in Contact Improvisation as a form of queering. Between the introduction and the conclusion, Ahmed has included three chapters: the first dedicated to orientation toward objects, the second to sexual orientation, and the third to orientation in relation to the relative East Orient. Where Ahmed raises the orientation toward objects, I propose the orientation between the bodies; second, with her, I address the issue of sexual orientation and gender as a primary aspect of the debate on the term *queer* in Contact Improvisation, and finally, about Orient otherness, I recover Ahmed's idea of otherness as a form of bodily extension and the concept of following as a form of commitment to the other. Here, I add the presence of the wheelchair within the framework of Contact Improvisation to explore how physical differences can be problematic and at the same time generative. I have fallen into the mesh of the book, fascinated by the coincidences between the terms used by Ahmed and my own conception of Contact Improvisation. I am also interested in the breadth and complexity with which Ahmed approaches queerness, not only in relation to identity (I am queer), but also as a verb—to queer. I will address the issue of disability in dance as an aspect of diversity (related to disabilities, illness, age, or other more or less transitory states of fragility) as part of the spectrum of alterity around gender and queerness[8] and disorientation.

Inspired by Ahmed's book, *Queer Phenomenology*, I proposed a performance experiment with the *Armadanzas* choreographic group from the University of León, that we called *Triádico entre líneas*—Triadic between the lines—for which we rehearsed with Ahmed's book in hand, reading and dancing, in January and February 2021. We addressed the issues of disorientation and mutual guidance. It was a game of spatial improvisation in which three bodies moved in three different ways: drawing on their own trajectory, following the direction of one another, that is, an external direction, or following a collective path—determined by the wheelchair itself. As an extension of our bodies, we used music, voice, and objects. In this way, we made a small nod to Oskar Schlemmer's *Triadic Ballet* (1922), created just 50 years before Steve Paxton gave Contact Improvisation its name. We developed a design of 12 scores

---

[8] The intersection between gender and race chosen by Ahmed already has a recognized track record: "Il me semble que le dialogue entre les corps racisés et les corps queer (l'un n'excluant pas l'autre) est puissamment porteur pour l'ensemble des corps qui composent les espaces du Contact Improvisation. Ce dialogue affine et reforcé le regard que l'on peut porter sur les corporéités dans la practique. Il permet d'ériger en exigence l'inclusivité à l'égard des marges et de ne jamais se satisfaire ce qui est confortable pour le centre" (Rabah-Konaté and Bigé 2021, 198). A perhaps lesser-known queer and crip alliance exists (McRuer 2006) and therefore I propose its consideration in the context of Contact Improvisation. Other approaches have been also developed, such as Shildrick's (2012) book, to critically engage disability and instability at the center of a feminist thinking about intersubjectivities.

Figure 19.1. Wheelchairs at the FCAFD ULE Warehouse. Photo courtesy of the author.

based on orientation—a central topic in Schlemmer's work—and walking, an action very present also in Paxton's Research.[9] The open improvisations illuminated the choreography itself, but also revealed other possibilities of play, contact, and tensions between bodies and objects.[10] The experiment has continued in 2022 with another performance called *Triádico sobre papel*—Triadic on paper—that is composed with the presence on a big paper of three bodies, three wheelchairs, and three German wheels (see Figure 19.1). The choreography is articulated with the progressive use of space from the ground; a paper as a ground could be perceived as a queer surface.[11] While in the *Triadic Ballet* the objects operated by limiting the possibilities of bodily movement, in this improvisation on paper the objects—with the bodies—are mainly supports that superimpose different—almost antagonistic—imaginaries loaded with limits and powers, ability and disability.

[9] Véase, https://www.artforum.com/interviews/judson-at-50-steve-paxton-31419. This reflection on the walk is also published in Hayes, Marisa (2018), Témoignages des danseurs sur la marche. *Repères* 42, 16–18.

[10] Fernando Ballarín, Ruth Oblanca García, and Adrián Pérez Aller participated in the experience and acted in the choreographic piece. It was presented at the El Albéitar Theater on February 24, 2021. https://blogs.unileon.es/danzaule/triadico-entre-lineas/. This piece is part of a broader research called Se Rueda beginning in 2019.

[11] It is a piece made with "walker" dancers Ruth Oblanca García, Adrián Pérez Aller, Pablo Parra, and Lou Guerrero (https://blogs.unileon.es/danzaule/triadico-sobre-papel/) at FCAFD. It can be performed by those who can roll on the floor and get into a wheelchair.

Contact Improvisation: Disorientation and Orientation between Bodies

> I suggest above that disorientation happens when the ground no longer supports an action. We lose ground, we lose our sense of how we stand; we might even lose our standing. It is not only that queer surface support actions, but also that the action they support involves shifting grounds, or even clearing a new ground, which allow us to tread a different path. (Ahmed 2006, 170)

As Ahmed defines it in the above quote, disorientation involves the appearance or use of different pathways and changes in support surface. When dancing Contact Improvisation we constantly adopt unknown paths and continuously change the support surface, and so it is the weight and the displacement of the point of contact that give direction to the movement. Contact Improvisation can be considered, in this sense, a practice of disorientation. Disorientation implies different paths and shifting grounds and also the loss of straight verticality. Dancing Contact Improvisation—that is, moving shared weight in contact—is only possible by falling (toward the other), losing contact with the ground, experiencing disorientation, which leaves us open to changing trajectories and patterns of movement. In Contact Improvisation, the other is also a ground, but a shifting ground, a moving and sensing ground that could be understood as a *queer surface* to meet, discover, melt into, or cross over. We could understand bodies as moving identities or moving objects. Sara Ahmed reminds us that "What makes bodies different is how they inhabit space: space is not a container for the body . . . they become the space they inhabit, they move, they move the space . . ." (2006, 53). When we improvise in Contact, we experience disorientation because we move in a three-dimensional spherical space. Using all the axes of rotation, we do not have a stable horizontal visual reference. Instead, we rely on other moving bodies.[12] It is not a single body falling or losing its vertical axis and its horizon, but rather two (or more) bodies, both orientated toward one another, that become the ground on which we move. "Bodies as well as objects take shape through being oriented towards each other" (Ahmed 2006, 54).

In Contact Improvisation, therefore, there is not an absolute disorientation, but a relative orientation toward another body or several bodies and gravity. It is this attention to another body and its weight that allows me to disorient myself regarding my own path and my own vertical axis. In his early writings Paxton explained that "orientation to space has to do with knowing where one is and, more importantly, where down is" and "training consists of encouraging the improvisers to explore the edge of their disorientation" (1975, 41). I have been impressed to read again these old definitions by Paxton after discovering the same terms in Ahmed's book. Above all, I appreciate how Paxton also placed orientation together

---

[12] The ground—flat, horizontal, rigid surface that affords support—is the basis of our visual perception and space perception in general. The earth at the scale of the human animal is flat, not round, and the earth is separated from the sky by a horizon that can be seen and felt, "in the sense that any surface one touches is experienced in relation to the horizontal plane" (Gibson 2015, 124). Godard proposes another ground, the second ground, which allows us to be oriented. "There are perhaps several senses of weight. . . . A radical foundational sense of weight grounded in response to gravitational attraction, as well as another, more subjective, sense of weight given by the orientation of the face through the eyes, the sense of smell and the vestibular system of the inner ear. The latter is composed of gelatinous surfaces upon which rest little crystals subject to the pull of gravity. Our subjective position orients these surfaces. The vertical dynamic draws up the vertebral column which thus serves as a support point for the ribs involved in exhalation to let go. Without this subjective ground, oriented by the head, the abandonment involved in exhaling would be like being in free fall" (Godard 2021, 23).

with disorientation and how he refers to training in both as complementary aspects. In this process of destabilization and this approach to another body, the encounter is creative and allows for the expansion of the usual social-individual patterns of movement that so constrain or condition us. "For Husserl while orientations also do not simply involve differentiating left from right sides of the body, they do involve the question of sides" (Ahmed 2006, 8). According to Ahmed, we encounter "things" as coming from different sides, as well as having different sides, and we can say that by dancing Contact Improvisation we encounter bodies coming from different sides and having and offering different sides—coming also from different geographies and cultures. As we orientate to others while dancing, we extend the reach of our body reaching the other (from different sides), touching and sharing our weight and our common axis as a deep way to connect.

From a general point of view, orientation of a body is constructed in relation to the placement of the face or the front of our body, which points toward something or someone, toward where or to whom we are heading. Something that I love about practicing Contact Improvisation is that all the combinations of orientation are possible since orienting toward another body implies a displacement of one's own weight toward it, rather than an offer of our frontal side. It can be offered by the front, side, or back; that is, if you lean toward it, you are to some extent oriented. Dancing Contact Improvisation, we learn to use the whole circumference of our body, sensitizing the surfaces of our back and our sides. We learn to attenuate this hierarchy of the visual that our face imposes on us by developing perceptual strategies with our whole body and communicating through contact and through weight. It is by approaching and tilting our weight toward the other body that we dance together. For Sara Ahmed, it is also this closeness—or approach—that allows us to create new directions and reaches.

"Moments of disorientation are vital. They are bodily experiences that throw the world up. Or throw the body from its ground" (2006, 157). In the conclusions of her *Queer Phenomenology*, Ahmed recapitulates the relationship between disorientation and queer experience or queer objects: she proposes a learning of disorientation, a reflection on this experience that can offer some hope in the sense that it offers, despite the crisis of instability that it causes, new directions. This encouraging proposal of Ahmed and its relationship with bodily practices have been collected and explored also by Albright (2019) in her book *How to Land*, in a chapter dedicated precisely to disorientation. By dancing Contact Improvisation, we experience our vulnerability and the possibilities of losing contact with the ground that supports us, but at the same time, we can discover the opening of the movement of our body in the encounter with other supports: the bodies become mobile supports that support and are sustained during the experience of disorientation.

In Contact Improvisation, leaning toward the other implies a transfer of weight, a distribution of one's own forces and an acknowledgment of the other. Could this distribution of forces also have a social meaning? An inclination, leaning, means staggering, losing the shaft, falling, losing balance, losing strength. Leaning toward the other, something we do necessarily when dancing Contact Improvisation, can acquire other meanings, such as greeting the other—the inclination as a form of greeting that is generalized in various cultures—recognizing their difference, approaching, coming into contact, using their mass and strength. But it can also be a way to support the other or receive their weight, sharing one's own mass and strength. "Through orientation we might allow the moments of disorientation to gather. . . . Indeed to live out a politics of disorientation might be to sustain wonder about the very forms of social gathering" (Ahmed 2006, 24). While dancing, the other could be identified not only as a partner, but also as a witness, a director, a choreographer, or a teacher. In addition, in a Contact Improvisation class, jam, or performance, the other's gaze could be supportive or disorienting. According to Sara Ahmed, disorientation is something experienced by queer people, but disorientation could be also understood as something experienced in queer practices. Could we then consider Contact Improvisation a queer practice? In what senses could we say that Contact Improvisation is a queer practice, only in a spatial sense? How are the spatial and the social intertwined, in the practice and in the theory of Contact Improvisation? Spatial orientation means for Ahmed (2006, 23) relations of proximity and distance that are shaped by other social orientations such as gender, race, or class, and we could also add ability and disability.

What Does It Mean to Queer Contact Improvisation?

"What does it mean to queer Phenomenology?" (Ahmed 2006, 23).

Sara Ahmed uses the word *queer* in at least two senses:[13] on the one hand, queer is a way to describe that which is oblique or diverges form the norm. She describes, for example, the presence of bodies of color in white spaces as disorienting and working to "queer" those spaces; on the other hand, she uses *queer* to describe specific sexual practices, and so queer in this case would refer to those who practice non-normative sexualities. In Ahmed's approach, queerness affects people who are different due to their sexuality, skin color, or geographical location. These singular bodies are pushed out toward the margins; they are sometimes unable to fully occupy the center of normative spaces. She writes: "they have no place at the table." I also wonder about (other) bodies that stay away from the table: there are multiple reasons why a person may not be welcome at the table. Who are the other others that Ahmed also alludes to (2018, 221)? Are shy bodies queer? Are queer bodies shy? The question is to observe the difficulties that different bodies experience trying to occupy the space, trying to share the space, trying to jointly create dance or improvisation spaces. In what ways is the Contact *jam/performance/class* a normative space? We can also observe in the jam "how bodies come to have certain orientations over time and that they come to be shaped by taking some directions rather than others and towards some objects rather than others" (Ahmed 2006, 58).

Of course, from the very first decades of Contact Improvisation discourses (ideological, pedagogical, or aesthetic), there has been a complex debate regarding gender, including the questioning of masculinity, ideas concerning the neutral body, and efforts to minimize sexuality while emphasizing sensuality, not to mention discussions of various feminist and queer approaches to the form (Brozas 2020). These are documented in *Contact Quarterly*, the journal in which there have been special issues focused on sexuality and identity. On the *Contact Improvisation Facilitators Worldwide Networking & Discussion Group*, jam guidelines are shared and a "Compendium of CI Guidelines from around the world" is curated

---

[13] I agree with Bietti (2013) that Ahmed invites us to a broad understanding of the term *queer*. The term *queer* cannot belong to any political movement, feminism or the LGBTI, or anti-racists . . . it must be a meeting point to forge alliances for difference.

by Benjamin Pierce.[14] These guidelines are meant to address the often-invisible norms of heteronormativity, whiteness, physical ability, class, and so on, that structure the space. It is a delicate issue that has become more prominent recently as the community begins to have a greater awareness about implicit hierarchies, and accessibility policies are launched from feminist and/or queer perspectives. Complaints about unequal and even abusive practices have been very publicly expressed in recent meetings such as the *Future of CI Conference* (April 2021 in Earthdance), the European Contact Improvisation Teacher Exchange (ECITE, October 2021, London), and *Critical Mass* (July 2022, Oberlin). This has led to a certain segregation of affinity groups creating their own BIPOC or queer jams. This move has not been well perceived or understood by everyone who practices Contact Improvisation. Indeed, many people think that Contact Improvisation is already an egalitarian and accessible—even queer—practice.

In the past decade, the relationship between Contact Improvisation and queer has been analyzed and written from queer perspectives (e.g., Aramo and Skrzypczak 2019; Papineau and Engelman 2019). I agree with Papineau and Engelman (2019) that we must insist on the interest of accentuating the queer quality of Contact Improvisation. This accent is something claimed perhaps more strongly by women, often affected more directly by the latent patriarchal culture also in the dynamics of dance. Queer groups have underscored the prevalence of heterosexual "coupling" dynamics in certain jam spaces, inviting us not only to reflect upon, but also to queer, the organization or the activities within a form of dance that could be considered queer itself (Horringan, 2017).[15] However, following Ahmed (2006, 170), it must be observed that there is also a homonormativity, which can become equally oppressive for those who consider themselves queer. For these reasons, I want to propose the term *queer* as a utopian action, a verb that is always insufficient and imperfect but equally necessary. I think that to queer Contact Improvisation could be a way to sustain wonder, to keep questioning it: the choreographic and social questions raised at the origin of the form are not enough, but must be maintained, updated, and regenerated.[16] To queer CI, using Emma Bigé's terms, could also mean that sometimes, in some contexts, it is necessary to do "*du mauvais CI*" or to do Contact Improvisation "*de travers.*" We need to refuse the flow and the evidence (Rabah-Konaté and Bigé, 2021).

Following as a Form of Body Extension

"A following in which one is not left behind" (Ahmed 2006, 117).

In her third and final chapter, Ahmed points to the encounter with otherness as a form of extension of the body itself. This approach is what allows new perceptions—co-perceptions—and new scopes.

---

[14] https://www.google.com/url?q=https://docs.google.com/document/d/1Os8c2ukZRS5cnJhJv0SuBX5Mr pGKAMZk6U3i-Pbfezk/edit%23&sa=D&source=docs&ust=1658519392508907&usg=AOvVaw0rxCsoLHQxN DJSEoxpxjHj.

[15] To develop *discursive practices* is already a way of queer Contact Improvisation, as Aramo and Skrzypczak (2019) propose.

[16] Questioning Contact Improvisation is also an insistent invitation coming from Keith Hennessy (2018), and as Sarco-Thomas (2014, 189) points out, "a practice of questioning is significant to improvisational modalities in dance as well as wider practices of relating to social, mental and physical spheres of thought."

What is other than me is also what allows me to extend the reach of my body. Rather than othering being a simple form of negation, it can also be described as a form of extension. The body extends its reach by taking in that which is "not" it, where the "not" involves the acquisition of new capacities and directions. (2006, 115)

The act of following other bodies, a crucial aspect in the learning and practice of the Contact Improvisation technique, has, from a social point of view, two polarized interpretations. We can focus on the benefits, such as augmenting social skills in approaching, listening, adapting, accompanying, empathizing, and so on. But another reading alerts us to the risks, the bodily traces or the submission, dependency, or loss of identity of the action of following the other, and especially if the other in turn follows a path predetermined by tradition.[17] With social networks, this sense of group could be further underlined where some follow others and where the risks and perversions of the action of following are clearly manifested. These two readings have a direct application in Contact Improvisation. Learning to follow the other is important, but learning to follow the shared weight, the collective center of gravity, is essential in the dancing. The listening inherent in following is also critical (Chung 2006; Hassmann 2017.) Ahmed refers to the act of following as a form of commitment or social involvement that requires time, energy, and resources. At the same time, the social pressure to follow a certain path—the line that is followed by others—can be felt as a physical pressure on the surface of the body, as something that creates a lasting impression on one's skin (Ahmed 2006, 17).

Ahmed describes two bodies placed side by side, and she explicitly refers to the act of walking "in unison" or "arm in arm"; this act requires, according to her, a certain effort to stay (2006, 169). To walk together you have to resort to the gesture of following each other, a following in which one is not left behind: maybe an important slogan in the practice of Contact Improvisation! For Ahmed, the simple gesture of keeping the bodies side by side implies a radicalization of the side, that part of the body that is so important during the dance, the one that allows us to perceive or imagine the body as a cylinder which dissolves the front/back hierarchy—when the opposite side becomes side by side; when one side is not against the other side. Sarah Ahmed (2006, 115) reminds me that otherness allows me to do something, create something, that otherness allows me to dance with her. Contact Improvisation could be understood also as a practice of migration, in which you have to leave your dance home (your own patterns, your own space, your support base, your center . . .) and move with a degree of uncertainty. Ideally, you are moving thanks to the listening and support of another body, which implies not only co-perception but also co-migration. You are not walking alone.[18] Other bodies, and also other objects, could be walking with you.

---

[17] The following is questioned in other dances, such as tango argentino, because it is an action assigned to a particular gender (Brozas 2022).

[18] Although the migratory processes among those who dance CI has been something not only inevitable but enriching and it is what has allowed expansion, learning, and exchange (Brozas and García 2014), these processes can be analyzed from the experience of colonization and the North-South gap (Rabah-Konaté and Bigé 2021), and there is an urgent need to recognize the inequalities and difficulties of those who emigrate, especially those traveling in difficult economic conditions, those who have to move in order to study or work, or those who flee from armed conflicts or vital tragedies.

320 Resistance and Support

A Wheelchair in Contact Improvisation

At this point I return to the wheelchair, an object that walks and dances. I recover here the experience of sitting, pushing, carrying, and being carried along. An object whose footprint is a continuous line, well, rather two continuous, parallel lines. It's an object that minimizes the effort of the walk and allows for speed and a smooth ride. The wheelchair knows how to roll.[19] Can we learn to roll with it? The wheelchair already has a place in the history of Contact Improvisation, and its presence has contributed to making the form not only more accessible for diverse bodies, but perhaps queer as well. The wheelchair was introduced in the late 1980s in the practice of Contact Improvisation thanks to the initiative of some dancers with various disabilities (Bruce Curtis, Emery Blackwell, Patty Overland, Charlene Curtiss, etc.) and to its confluence and encounter with pioneering improvisers such as Alan Ptashek, Alito Alessi, Karen Nelson, and others. Perhaps it was Alito Alessi who in "Wheels of Fortune" with Emery Blackwell in 1988 (Ashwill 1992/1997) was one of the first dancers to appropriate with humor and freedom this object designed for people with disabilities. In this pioneering performance, the wheelchair is already revealed to us as an object—along with others—that is shared and that transforms the motor skills and the images of the bodies that interact: the chair leaves in some way the body to which it was assigned.

Bruce Curtis is a dancer with paraplegia who moves, teaches, and dances in a wheelchair. In "Exposed to Gravity," one of the first joint educational research projects between dancers with and without physical disabilities, Curtis and Ptashek (1988/1997) revealed their fears, difficulties, discoveries, and the different perception and relationship that each establishes with the wheelchair during learning and improvisation. In the case of Bruce Curtis, the wheelchair not only expands the range of movement in his dance and everyday life, but amplifies the perceptive possibilities—also affected by his spinal cord injury: "It has movements, sounds and rhythms that describe the texture of the ground that I am moving across, defining the space that I am passing through" (Curtis and Ptashek 1988/1997, 157). Ptashek underlines the extreme sensitivity of the chair to subtle weight changes and explains how this precision and dynamism of the object, together with the receptivity and responses of Curtis's condition, form the organization of his own body with respect to the chair: "Bruce's wheelchair is surprisingly light and responsive to subtle degrees of weight and momentum, although it is Bruce's receptivity to those subtleties that determines how my body and movement can shape itself with his chair" (Curtis and Ptashek 1988/1997, 161). Are they a duo, a trio, or a whole? I imagine the dance being a duo of two bodies—one of them in chair—or a trio of one object and two bodies as three bodies—objects in interaction, or perhaps as a whole where bodies and object are confused. In the case of two wheelchair dancers the panorama is another; the objects, chairs, take on even more prominence. Curtis details the explorations and learnings of his first duets with Patty Overland, each in their own wheelchair:

> It is difficult to stay in close contact with each other because the chairs are rigid[20] and don't wrap around each other like bodies do. Both of us have limited use of our waist muscles, so it has forced us to experiment a lot. We have to lean out away from our chairs to remain in

---

[19] Rolling is a contact way of moving forward, to dance in continuous touch, to follow a body or a surface, to create new pathways ... it is a main practice in Contact Improvisation and it is the way a wheelchair moves.

[20] "Hard metal, soft bodies" is the title of one of the sections of Adam Benjamin's book (2002) on ability and disability in dance.

contact while allowing enough space for our chairs to move off the momentum from the shifting balance between us. We have also started working off each other's chairs like they were bodies. Since we feel that our chairs are part of ourselves, it feels natural to grab hold of or push off of a chair if it is in front of us at the moment. Last week, I discovered that she could get out of her chair, down to the floor and then back into her chair fairly easily, so we started incorporating this into our dancing. (Curtis and Ptashek 1988/1997, 159)

One of the first and most promising actions experienced in Contact Improvisation, where rolling over the body of the other and rolling on the floor are common skills, is precisely the descent and ascent from the wheelchair to the floor or to another body. This fact allows some users of the wheelchair to discover other possibilities of movement outside the chair without walking (see Figure 19.2).

But, in addition, when the descent of the chair occurs, sometimes, the object is available to other dancers, also for those who do not usually use it in everyday life. On the one hand, it occurs in the user who dances the separation of this support object, of this extension of the body itself which is changed by the contact and extension of the body itself with another body which is followed, on which it rests and at the same time serves as support, toward which it is necessary to orient and with which it is possible to disorient oneself. On the other hand, from another point of view, the orientation of "walker" bodies toward such an object occurs, an object in some mysterious measure, sometimes unknown to them.

I was able to witness in the ANQA company how a wheelchair broke when it was used by a dancer other than its owner. Fortunately, it was secured, and the mishap was solved quickly—the company already has an experience of a couple of decades dancing with chairs!—but the user was scared, and it was an emotional and expectant moment for the whole group. Whoever enters the dance space with their chair, an object that can be almost as precious as

Figure 19.2. Marie Laure Kaminski (left) dancing with the author (right). ANQA Courtesy Paris 2016.

322 Resistance and Support

the body itself when living with them and in them, usually develops that double generosity, that of the delivery of the object along with the delivery of the body in dance. But beware, in neither case are there unlimited and unconditional deliveries; it is always necessary to define and negotiate to what extent, at what times, and in what way they are shared. This is a responsibility not only of each dancer, but of the organizing community that supports the activity and of the entire participating group. We would enter here into the realm of the intersections of gender, skill, and social class, as well as the question of respect and consent. It is not uncommon for a person in a wheelchair in the street to feel run over or invaded by an external contact that affects his chair or body, and that often responds to a well-intentioned ignorance in the few daily encounters between bodies with and without a chair. "For a person in a wheelchair, control over your own body's safety is never easily relinquished to someone else's judgement. My life is full of people who want to help me by grabbing my body or my chair and dragging me somewhere in an unsafe manner" (Curtis and Ptashek 1988/1997, 158).[21]

What would an able or disabled dancer with a wheelchair be expected to do? Besides a functional use, perhaps it also holds an exploratory use, one you would make of any other object appearing in the dance space? We may wonder if in these choreographic actions we do not run the risk of banishing or trivializing the object by deviating from the important use for which it was conceived. I understand rather that the use—sui generis—of the wheelchair does not stop being another way of recognizing it: facing it, leaning toward it, using it, and making it visible can be an invitation to take it into account, to learn to use it, and to learn with it. One of the learnings surrounding the chair is about taking care—care of the object, the other objects, the other bodies.[22] It should be stressed that the wheelchair is also an object of play and an object of improvisation very attractive to any curious person; I have witnessed, on several occasions, how children request its use to have fun climbing or pushing the chair, openly transgressing the function and taboo of the object.

My didactic experience with wheelchairs began in the early 1990s in the framework of the degree in Physical Education where you could take a couple of optional subjects related to disability: "Special Physical Education for Physically Disabled" and "Special Physical Education for the Sensory Disabled." There was a final practical part in each subject in specific centers of "special education" where we carried out a didactic project, but in which we did not have real references, so we had to start experimenting directly without any clear orientation: in my case in the Association of the Deaf and Dumb of León and in ASPACE (Association of Cerebral Palsy). In ASPACE there was a team of physiotherapists and monitors who practiced sports adapted for wheelchairs. I was clear that my field of action was not

---

[21] Also, Lila Derridj comments on her experience with the chair in daily life and in dance and warns us that when we touch her chair it is as if we were touching her (Fertier 2015).

[22] In an open workshop we organized at the University of León in 2016 on Contact Improvisation and disability, Marisa Brugarolas, director of the project "Ruedapies" (https:/ruedapies.org/), raised the problem of the dissemination of images with wheelchairs. We had not registered people with disabilities, most of us were middle-aged women dance teachers (https://blogs.unileon.es/danzaule/marisa/). Brugarolas preferred not to expose images of people without disabilities using the chair; one of their arguments is that it can be misleading and can scare someone known to relate the use of the wheelchair with an accident or injury. I am not sure of the possible repercussions, but this debate invited at least careful use. I have always considered the chair as a very valuable object: the presence of wheelchairs in my faculty responds to the pedagogical objective of knowing its operation for sports or artistic activities and in fact there are several modalities of specific basketball chairs or other modalities which are particularly expensive. We can never lose sight of the economic point of view—the price of wheelchairs—nor what it can mean to access or not be able to access such chairs when you need them or they would make your life or work easier. This ethical question generates a certain conflict and to a certain extent I am conditioned sometimes by the collective research of the chair that I am raising.

that of competition or rehabilitation, but that of learning and playful body experimentation. I didn't know Contact Improvisation then, but I set out to introduce choreographic games. What impressed me most at the beginning about those people in wheelchairs were the difficulties of verbal communication and a high muscle tone that years later has been revealed to me as a valuable resource in dance. I found totally unknown bodies, which I was afraid to hurt with contact; I had barely met or seen people with cerebral palsy in my daily life. We began to dance together, inspired by the popular dances where participants weave colored ribbons for which I proposed some rolls of toilet paper. I just remember the somewhat run-down crossing of wheelchairs in the narrow space and the festive atmosphere we created.

In Choreographing Difference (1997), Ann Cooper Albright analyzed and compared the different ways in which some pioneering companies summoned dancers with and without disabilities (Cleveland Ballet Dancing Wheels, Candoco, Light Motion) through their performances. In them—in each company and in each artistic composition—different ways of understanding dance are manifested, as well as several models of interaction between the bodies that dance. Contact Improvisation is presented in her review as the most open dance form to physical differences, a form where the wheelchair object occupies a unique and paradoxical place when it was introduced in the late 1980s, at a time of acrobatic development of dance, in which it suffers, by the way, a kind of shrinking in its movement patterns. "Instead of privileging an ideal type of body or movement style, Contact Improvisation privileges a willingness to take physical and emotional risks, producing a certain psychic disorientation in which the seemingly stable categories of able and disabled are dislodged" (Albright 1997, 85). The attention to diversity, which was being demanded at the time from the collectives with disabilities, comes as a fresh air to the communities of CI, and at the same time comes to reveal a certain polarity between an elite CI and an accessible CI. Is it true that within Contact Improvisation there is an eviction of categories of able and disabled, as well as of leader and follower, or female and male?

In her chapter "Moving across Difference," Albright (1997) alludes to the secondary place of women in these processes of inclusion of disability in the practice of Contact Improvisation, and invites us to address the relationship between gender and disability. The historical moment she analyzes, when the wheelchair begins to appear in the dynamics of dance, is presented as a moment of little performance or female visibility. Certainly, at the end of the twentieth century, Contact Improvisation and other experimental dance were developed also in the European scene looking for difference; for example, the policies of contact seem to have leaked in the choreographic and audiovisual production of Lloyd Newson and his company DV8. In *The Cost of Living*, in addition to exploring the margins with different approaches about masculinities and their sexualities, disability manages to integrate into this framework of questions about normative sexuality. In this film the differences of class, gender, color, and ability are constantly crossed, but the female presence is rather discreet. Only the female legs are hypervisibilized, associated with the classical ballet they question. They also call attention to various gadgets such as cars, chairs, skates, and so on, and how they are combined with the different ways of carrying, integrating, or merging a "body without legs" with other "walker bodies."[23] Other objects, such as a hoop and a stereo, are

---

[23] This game of prolongation of the bodies is also developed with the participation of the actor, already deceased, Dave Toole with Stopgap Dance Company and can be seen in *Artificial Things* (2014), in particular in minute 19 that reminds us of the final minute of *The Cost of Living*—the scene in which two bodies walk together, more than one following the other, one on another or one inside another?

324 Resistance and Support

used to expand the space or voice of timid bodies and contribute to their spatial expansion and interaction with other bodies.

In my most recent experience with wheelchairs in Contact Improvisation, over the past decade, I was able to approach myself to the didactics of Alito Alessi and DanceAbility method (Ibiza 2013),[24] but what would stand out most are the initiatives and experiences of some women who fortunately, in a more or less direct and prolonged way, have crossed my path: wheelchair dancers like Lila Derridj and Marie-Laure Kaminski, and pedagogues and artists such as Isabelle Brunaud, Carolina Becker, Andrea Fernández,[25] Marisa Brugarolas,[26] and Laura Jones.[27] I also want to mention the piece *Lines Forces* by choreographer Roser López Espinosa, presented in the framework of the Europe Beyond Access (https:/www.disabilityartsinternational.org/europe-beyond-access/), because it pushes us energetically toward other possible scenarios[28] (with and without wheelchairs). Contact Improvisation occupies an important place in the dance community that we have built since 2010—el Aula de Artes del Cuerpo—in León. One of our first guest teachers was Carolina Becker, who shared with us the pedagogical experience she had developed in Mallorca with a wheelchair user dancer named Paquita Ferragut Carbonell. The chair is witness and protagonist of their learning processes in the film *Danza sin fin*.[29] We can see the wheelchair dancing, extending, accompanying, appearing, and disappearing among other objects and bodies, crossing multiple daily and CI landscapes.

Gathering Bodies and Objects

I wonder where we are now, if we are really advancing in CI communities in a process of progressive accessibility. At the last ECITE[30] organized in Portugal in October 2022, the spacious and luminous venue that welcomed us was not even a space suitable for wheelchairs. I was puzzled by this. In my community in León, our practice room is not a fully accessible space either, no wheelchair-using dancers have joined our composition processes or classes, jams, or other improvisational practices, although for years people with other disabilities have (Brozas 2016).[31] We often characterize the practice of Contact Improvisation as a practice that allows for housing body diversity and access to bodies with mixed abilities (Brozas 2013; Brozas and Vicente 2017). But how many CI spaces are accessible? To what extent are we looking for such spaces?

---

[24] And other approach such as Jess Curtis (Madrid 2019).

[25] Andrea Fernández, Marina Gubbay, and Gabriela Gebber founded the project *Danza sin Límites* (https://danzasinlimites.ar/) in Buenos Aires in 1997. Recently, after the death of Marina Gubbay in 2021, Carolina Becker has joined the team.

[26] Together with Marisa Brugarola, we invited Enikö Szilágyi, a member of Tánceánia Company—a mixability dance company in Budapest—but a broken bone finally prevented her from traveling to León.

[27] I only know Laura Jones because of her online classes I was able to attend during the pandemic when I was injured, and I could also see her performances with the StopGapDance Company: https://www.stopgapdance.com/biographies/laura-jones/.

[28] Another Catalan choreographer working with wheelchairs is Jordi Cortés, who has been organizing training and choreographic activities with his group with and without disabilities *Liant la Troca* since 2011 (https://liantlatroca.com/).

[29] *Danza sin fin* (2011/2012) https://vimeo.com/44572972.

[30] European Contact Improvisation Teachers Exchange.

[31] In the project with wheelchairs and German wheels that we started in 2019, mentioned at the beginning of this text, most of the participating artists have an indirect experience in the daily use of the wheelchair, for having family members with disabilities or working with users, but we are not users.

Ahmed points out that when we have to follow a line, we are making a straight dance. I wonder if dancing Contact Improvisation does not follow an invisible line? Is it true that there are no movement patterns or visible forms to imitate? Could we say that what the CI technique offers us is to un-choreograph the space and break down the pedagogy of dance? The original proposal of a dialogue in Contact between the weights of bodies could have ceased to exist as figures of movement and postures to be learned, and through which we have learned to listen to other bodies or discover our own dance, our own path. After 50 years of development stemming from this proposal, we can however, recognize that the didactic hierarchy continues to exist and that some tendencies of movement within it have been consolidated, although they have evolved within the form itself. The form has acquired certain shapes over the time that we follow while dancing. As Ahmed reminds us, time tends to consolidate patterns or figures. The wheelchair object invites us to alter tradition and the imitation procedure as a didactic and vital strategy. What are the ways in which other bodies and our interactions with them configure us? This is the central question of this meditation by Sara Ahmed on directionality, disorientation, and queer experience. How can the emphasis on the perception of movement—one's own and the other's—be associated with political or social consciousness: is this determination in the physical consciousness of the body compatible with other forms of consciousness? How are they involved in each other?[32]

If we look through Ahmed's *Queer Phenomenology*, Contact Improvisation is revealed to us as a paradoxical practice, which is clearly outlined as a choreographic gemstone, not only cooperative, but almost religious. But the mutual support, displacement side by side, the fall toward the other, and the loss of the vertical that encompass its notion of queer allow us to observe the dance also as a risk practice: the miracle of the collective body that implies the fusion of identities, a porous practice in which cracks breathe not only camaraderie and maximum empathy, but other power games. What bodies are at the borders of the group? What differences are visible or invisible in the collective disorientation? What social practices prevent discouragement or distancing? Which objects should queer the dance? The wheelchair is just one of them.

> For me the table is just such a supporting device for queer gatherings, which is what makes the table itself a rather queer device. It is not surprising that a queer phenomenology, one that is orientated toward queer, will be full of tables. (2006, 179)

As Ahmed ends her book claiming the table for queer gatherings, suggesting this dream of a queer phenomenology full of tables, I imagine that a queer (and crip) dance and a Contact Improvisation jam, class, or performance would be full of wheelchairs! I can imagine also in the dance space one single wheelchair full of bodies since it is an object that gathers bodies! Even an empty wheelchair holds some potential to transform the dance space and to queer it.

References

Ahmed, S. (2006). *Queer Phenomenology. Orientations, Objects, Others* . Durham, NC, and London: Duke University Press.

---

[32] These are questions that I have raised when thinking also about gender in Contact Improvisation (Brozas 2020, 143).

Ahmed, S. (2018). *La política cultural de las emociones*. México: Universidad Autónoma de México.

Albright, A. C. (1997). *Choreographing Difference: The Body and Identity in Contemporary Dance*. Middletown, CT: Wesleyan University Press.

Albright, A. C. (2019). *How to Land: Finding Ground in an Unstable World*. New York: Oxford University Press.

Aramo, O., and Skrzypczak, W. (2019). Queer Contact Improvisation (QCI): Alliance and Disruption. Experiences and Reflections from the QCI Symposium and Festival Hamburg 2018. *Contact Quarterly*, 44(2), 50–53.

Ashwill, B. (1992/1997). Emery Blackwell, a Dancer Becoming. In *Contact Quarterly's Contact Improvisation Sourcebook: Collected Writings and Graphics from Contact Quarterly Dance Journal 1975–1992*, (edited by Nancy Stark Smith and Lisa Nelson). Northampton, MA: Contact Editions, pp. 238–241.

Benjamin, A. (2002). *Making an Entrance. Theory and Practice for Disable and Non-Disable Dancers*. Oxon: Routledge.

Bigé, E., Falcone, F.; Godfroy, A.; and Sini, A. (Eds.). (2021). *La perspective de la pomme. Histoires, politiques et pratiques du Contact Improvisation*. Rome: Piretti Editore.

Bietti, F. U. (2013). La ética del desvío, la fenomenología queer de Sara Ahmed. Hacia una política de la desorientación. In *X Jornadas de Sociología*. Facultad de Ciencias Sociales. Buenos Aires: Universidad de Buenos Aires. https://www.aacademica.org/000-038/546.

Brozas, M. P. (2016). Danza Contact Improvisation en la Universidad. Análisis de un proceso didáctico inclusivo con una alumna invidente. *Tándem. Didáctica de la Educación Física*, 51, 50–54.

Brozas, M. P. (2017). Pedagogía del cuerpo sensible: Tacto y visión en la danza Contact Improvisation. *Movimento*, 23(3), 1039–1052.

Brozas, M. P. (2020). Discursos de género en Contact Improvisation. Deliberación y acción coreográfica en torno a la revista Contact Quarterly. *Co-herencia*, 17(33), 133–164.

Brozas, M. P. (2022). Llevar o ser llevada. Construcciones de género en tango argentino y Contact Improvisation. *Movimento*, 22, e28053.

Brozas Polo, M. P. (2013). La accesibilidad en la danza contact improvisation. *Arte Y Movimiento*, 8, 33–44. https://revistaselectronicas.ujaen.es/index.php/artymov/article/view/919.

Brozas, M. P., and García, T. (2014). Contact Improvisation in Spain: The Beginning (1980-1990). *Revista Internacional de Medicina y Ciencias de la Actividad Física y del Deporte*, 14(53), 169–181. http://cdeporte.rediris.es/revista/revista53/artcomienzos433e.pdf

Brozas, M. P., and Vicente, M. (2017). La diversidad en la danza contemporánea. Una mirada retrospectiva al siglo XX. *Arte, individuo y sociedad*, 29(1), 71–87.

Bruneau, I., and Lamoine, J. (2014). De l'empêchement comme appui. *Repères. Cahier de danse*, 33, 17–18.

Butler, J. (2018). Acerca del término "queer." In *Cuerpos que importan*. Paidós: Barcelona, pp. 313–339 (translated by Alcira Bixio).

Claid, E. (2021). *Falling through Dance and Life*. London: Bloomsbury.

Croft, C. (Ed.). (2017). *Queer Dance: Meanings and Makings*. Oxford University Press.

Cunningham, C.; Curtis, J.; and Pell, L. (2019). Differences: Creating a Cultural Shift toward Embedded Access and Artistry. *Contact Quarterly*, 44(1), 32–37.

Chung, R. (2006). Listening. *Contact Quarterly*, 31(1), 54.

Curtis, B., and Ptashek, A. (1988/1997). *Contact Quarterly's Contact Improvisation Sourcebook: Collected Writings and Graphics from Contact Quarterly Dance Journal 1975–1992.* Northampton: Contact Editions, pp. 156–162.

Fertier, A. (Ed.). (2015). *Danse & handicap moteur. Pour une accessibilité des pratiques choréographiques*, vol 2. Paris: Centre National de la Danse.

Fraleigh, S. (Ed.). (2018). *Back to the Dance Itself: Phenomenologies of the Body in Performance.* Champaign, IL: University of Illinois Press.

Gibson, J. (2015). *The ecological approach to visual perception.* New York: Psychology Press.

Gil, J. (2001). A comunicação dos corpos: Steve Paxton. In *Movimento Total. O corpo e a dança.* Lisboa: Relógio D'Agua, pp. 131–156.

Godard, H. (2021). *A breath.* Brussels: Contredanse Editions.

Hassmann, J. (2017). Leading and Following: Focusing on the Communication in and under the Skin. *Contact Quarterly*, 42(1), 44.

Hennessy, K. (2018). *Questioning Contact Improvisation.* San Francisco: Circo Zero.

Horringan, K. (2017). Queering Contact Improvisation: Addressing Gender in CI Practice and Community. *Contact Quarterly*, 42(1), 39–43.

McRuer, R. (2006). *Crip Theory: Cultural Signs of Queerness and Disability.* New York: New York University Press.

Mitra, R. (2021). Unmaking Contact: Choreographic Touch at the Intersections of Race, Caste, and Gender. *Dance Research Journal*, 53(3), 6–24.

Nelson, K. (2008 [1996]). Touch Revolution: Giving Dance. In N. Stark Smith and L. Nelson (Eds.), *Contact Quarterly's Contact Improvisation Sourcebook II: Collected Writings and Graphics from Contact Quarterly Dance Journal 1993–2007.* Northampton: Contact Editions, pp. 103–105.

Papineau, E., and Engelman, S. (2019). Creating Space for Queer Contact Improvisation. *Contact Quarterly*, 44 (1).

Paxton, S. (1975). Contact Improvisation. *The Drama Review*, 19(1), 40–42.

Paxton, S. (1993). Drafting Interior Techniques. *Contact Quarterly*, 18(1), 64–78.

Paxton, S. (1996). To Touch. *Contact Quarterly*, 21(2), 50–51.

Paxton, S. (2015). Why Standing: Contact Quarterly Still Moving, Contact Shoptalk (edited by Karen Nelson). https://contactquarterly.com/cq/article-gallery/view/why-standing#.

Rabah-Konaté, M., and Bigé, E. (2021). Ce qui nous retient de nous toucher. In E. Bigé, Francesca Falcone, Alice Godfroy, and A. Sini (Eds.), *La perspective de la pomme. Histoires, politiques et pratiques du Contact Improvisation.* Rome: Piretti Editore, p. 204.

Sarco-Thomas, M. (2014). Touch + Talk: Ecologies of Questioning in Contact and Improvisation. *Journal of Dance & Somatic Practices*, 6(2), 189–204.

Sarco-Thomas, M. (Ed.). (2020). *Thinking Touch in Partnering and Contact Improvisation.* Newcastle: Cambridge Scholars.

Sartre, J. P. (1988/1938). *La Náusea.* Madrid: Alianza Losada.

Shildrick, M. (2009). Queer Phenomenology: Orientations, Objects, Others. A Review. *International Journal of Philosophical Studies*, 17(4), 632–635.

Shildrick, M. (2012). *Dangerous Discourses of Disability, Subjectivity and Sexuality.* London: Palgrave.

20

Intensive Curiosity

A Dialogue about Teaching CI

Joseph Dumit and Dorte Bjerre Jensen

Contact Improvisation (CI) has hundreds of definitions! From art-sport to an open form of "shared responsibility for one another's weight" while in physical touch (Albright 2013, 214, 221). Most of these take the Contact jam as the site for defining the form—hours-long to all-day sessions of movement exploration, research, and togetherness. At the same time, there are many people who say they are not really into jams. Instead, they go to classes, workshops, and intensives as their CI practice. They don't see these as training or preparation for how to be in jams, but rather seem to make a study of studying CI. And there are people who do both for decades!

As longtime CI practitioners and researchers who are also teachers, we find the idea of a life of CI classes and not jams fascinating. In this chapter, we make a deep dive into CI from the point of view of teaching. We assume for purposes of argument that classes and jams are different kinds of things. We oppose them even though those holding space for a jam are sometimes like teachers, and guided jams are like classes. Similarly, individuals and sometimes groups come to jams with focused research and scores in mind that they are practicing. It is also true that classes are sometimes so open-ended that they could be called jams, and indeed, they often seamlessly transition into jamming. Nonetheless, here we seek to learn about CI through treating classes as the point. Our interest is in the insights that CI classes provide about teaching, and teaching improvisation in particular, and in turn what teaching CI lets us see about CI as a particular kind of collective focused research into body-mind curiosity.

Our primary method has been to survey *Contact Quarterly* and pull out the accounts of classes by practitioners and teachers, to collect stories from fellow teachers, and to draw on our own experience in classes and teaching them. Cofounder of CI, performer, and co-editor of *CQ*, Lisa Nelson has described awakening to CI through realizing, "This is a form that teaches itself!" But what is clear from the beginning and throughout CI's history is the paradox of teaching improvisation, between open exploration and forms that hold this exploration. Cofounder Steve Paxton described his recognition that teaching in a martial arts way was counterproductive to improvisation with others; instead, he had to learn to "instigate" this exploration with his "students." He said, "I felt that the exercises had to somehow present to the students the final form that we would have before we knew what the form was. The dancing head-to-head exercise is a conceptual version of it. You stand there until you feel the other person's small dance" (Paxton 2018, 37). This approach to teaching is an example of setting up the conditions to become curious: to attend differently and intensively to what is happening in oneself, in the other, and in the space in-between and around.

Joseph Dumit and Dorte Bjerre Jensen, *Intensive Curiosity* In: *Resistance and Support*. Edited by: Ann Cooper Albright, Oxford University Press. © Oxford University Press 2024. DOI: 10.1093/9780197776308.003.0021

A set of themes emerged for us around this practice of learning to teach curiosity intensively, which we present in the form of a dialogue:

- CI teaching is a continual balancing between showing and telling and instigating.
- CI can be teaching "practice as research" together, including teaching collective research and researching togetherness.
- CI teachers are often able to explore their own curiosity through teaching, through sharing the edge of their curiosity; they often improvise teaching in order to teach improvisation.
- CI uses words to push practice and practice to push language. Not only is reflection time critical in teaching CI, but words are also a necessary part of this "practice as research."

CI Teaching is a Continual Balancing between Showing and Telling and Instigating

JOE: There are many accounts in *CQ* of people who started teaching for the same reason: to have more people and more time to dance! Anthropologist Cynthia Novak, in her ethnographic history of CI, describes early classes as arising from the need to create co-investigators to practice it:

> However, those individuals who wanted to continue investigating and practicing contact improvisation began to teach what they knew to other people in order to have partners with whom to dance. Contact improvisers take pride in the process of "passing the dance on," seeing this process as part of the "folk" nature of the form and as a demonstration of how the form itself requires that the dance be shared. (Novack 1990, 69–70)

DORTE: Exactly! The beauty of "passing on the dance," and the beauty of how important it is as an already established teacher to create the space and opportunity for others to taste the role of being a facilitator/teacher. I remember how I encouraged some students to join festivals and then, next time, apply for teaching a class. Or if there is a class I cannot teach, I hand it over to someone I know is ready to give it a go.

JOE: In the early issues of *CQ* there are many moments where people are trying to figure out what to offer in classes and workshops—the question of whether there could be fundamentals that were codified. What *should* be taught? What should not be taught? What is Contact Improvisation, what is not? But answering that question formally meant codifying or standardizing CI.

DORTE: It's an interesting struggle. What to teach and what not to teach? How much to show and tell and how much to leave it up to the students/participants to figure out. I like the struggle, it keeps me at the edge of my role as a facilitator, it demands that I keep asking the question: How do I choose to deal with this endeavor? (Bjerre Jensen 2020).

JOE: It seems to me that one way or another, codification or certification would restrict the inquiry of teaching curiosity itself—there would of course be innovators, as there are in yoga and bodywork, but the emphasis would be on learning it properly, and learning to teach in the right way. This isn't to say that there weren't fundamentals to teach (physics,

330   Resistance and Support

safety, consent) but that there were always more fundamentals within those fundamentals (psychology, affect, approach) and within those (what is teaching, research, curiosity). In some sense, fundamentals are always being taught, even if not named, and names can get in the way, become dogma.

DORTE: Yes, there is a kind of common material/fundamentals/vocabulary, I think we have all accepted: point of contact, rolling point of contact, and so forth. All dance forms have their own fundamental vocabulary, they are a kind of stepping stone, a starting point, and then it is all about how we present those. I think we as teachers execute the show and tell very differently. The important and interesting thing is *how* people are thinking and moving with the proposal. Are they copying or exploring? Are they so afraid not to get it right and do it in the right way, that they don't allow themselves to explore and make mistakes? Sometimes the goal can get in the way, and we tend to skip these very important layers/steps.

JOE: When I teach people for the first time, I emphasize slowness. I encourage people to roll over another as slowly as possible, almost to the point of stillness. It sometimes seems boring, but then something else emerges. I like the curiosity that emerges from letting go of where you are going next. A kind of research starts happening in that curiosity: What if I let this arm let go of its tension? I'm most interested in having these kinds of questions show up without having suggested them myself.

DORTE: Sometimes I think it can be nice to show a certain way to move, and then it is all about how I speak about it, and how I let the participant explore it. It can be nice to watch someone demonstrating an idea, it can inspire, but it can also trick people to think that they are not good enough. At one point, I was a bit hard on myself as a teacher, I felt stuck in my demo-model, and decided to not demonstrate with my own body at all. But it quickly became the feeling of all or nothing. I think it's blurred lines. And it is all about context: space, people, and the situation!

JOE: Do you talk about teaching "skills"?

DORTE: Hmmm, no I don't think so, I never actually call it that. Yeah, and then again, everything is a skill, no? But I think we have divided things into certain categories, like, a skill is that I can lift you high up in the air and spin you around the neck, then the rest is preparations for that skill. But listening is a hardcore skill; noticing where your body is in space is an ongoing demanding practice. And being present is a skill. Sometimes people freeze up with the word "improvisation" so I have them just walk, sit down, and get up—but to notice how they are doing each thing—that movement is really complex. Taking the time to realize that they are experimenting with motion as they slow down and as they pause.

Sensing gravity and letting it do its thing is a hardcore skill. I like to have conversations with people about the topic. Some students want "technique," a concept defined by its end-state, which implies that there can be shortcuts, rather than inquiry. I am always curious to hear how and in what way they define skills. Trusting your own way of exploring and researching is maybe the most valuable skill.

JOE: We will get to research as a skill. One of the main issues that teachers talk about is how many students have a very strict idea of teaching. They want to learn how to do something *right*. And even if they know it is improvisation, they still feel like there is a right and wrong way. The philosopher Jacques Rancière suggested that most European (and American) teaching is based on a model of teacher verification. The student needs to

Intensive Curiosity **331**

check with the teacher to see whether what they have done is correct or not. This continually reinforces the notion that verification is up to others.

DORTE: Exactly. I remember way back when I was a schoolteacher, and some kids showed me their drawings and asked: Is it good enough, is it done? I remember clearly being taught what was a right or wrong way to learn. Sometimes when I teach at a movement place, the roles are quite ingrained. There is a place where I am teaching at the moment, where it took me a while to get CI going. A lot of the other classes were yoga, or dancing by yourselves. People were a bit scared. I needed to guide them a lot more than I wanted. They were used to following yoga instructions, and their yoga mat was their safe haven. I had to bridge it somehow.

JOE: Yes, but how do you hand it over then? How do you get from playing on an imaginary mat to improvising together, to not trying to follow you? By being silly?

DORTE: Yes, sometimes. I use humor a lot, to be honest. It's good if they can laugh a bit. I can show that it is okay to be silly, awkward, and not perfect. Awkward especially. I think we all feel that when we try out something new. But I think there is a tendency to delete "the awkwardness," because it makes you feel a bit vulnerable, it is messing with your comfort zone. Walking is also a way to bridge the familiar with the unfamiliar. Walking makes us travel in space. And walking in itself carries all the material for spiraling, falling, and moving in space. When I can sense they feel a bit more relaxed, I make them travel a bit in space by slowly letting walking transform itself by the way I guide them.

It also calls up the tension in improvisation: how to let go of trying to do things, how to arrive? Arriving could be the theme for an entire class. What does it mean to arrive? I always give people a bit of time to tune in/arrive with their body-mind on their own. It is also a way for me to sense how they are doing and what is needed individually and as a group. And people arrive in so many different ways. I can see a lot in just those few minutes: if they are new to the form and space, if they are stressed, tired, happy, and/or ready to move. It is an important moment because a lot of things are happening already. When people arrive, I always tell them that it is their time and space, and attending the class already started when they were thinking about going. I soften the space with suggestions such as if you need to take a nap for one minute, do so, or go for a run or jump if needed, rolling or whatever is needed right now. Different people with different lives. It's a way to give agency and space for arriving, and also a way to start to move their bodies on their own.

JOE: This reminds me of Peter Ryan's comment that CI shows you the "difference between your real body and your idealized body by asking what your body can do, not what you can make it do" (Ryan cited in Novack 1990, 181).

DORTE: I often start with asking people, "What kind of body do you have today? How is your breath, your walking, how do you feel the weight into your feet?" I ask this because I want them to feel themselves *right now*, tight because of sitting at a computer in the afternoon. It disrupts the notion that they can know their body without checking in. It resonates with Erin Manning's proposal (using a concept developed by Deleuze thinking with Spinoza): it is not so much about what the body is, but what the body can do! So, it's not about the idea of our bodies, but about paying attention to the now-body, the body you are right now and its current potential. The first preparation for improvisation is to have everyone arrive with the body they have that day. It is the first score of the day. It is also for them slowly to figure out that there is an openness to how things are running. And I'm

332 Resistance and Support

checking: how comfortable are they with this open space? This is a way of having us arrive together, physically and mentally.

JOE: This seems like it takes a lot of time to get to the rest of the class.

DORTE: Yes, and that is why classes are often too short. An hour never feels like enough time. I think arriving is the first skill that I need to teach. Once I've given them time to arrive, my first instruction is: Okay, everybody, let's come to standing. I always ask if there's anything they need to share, which creates a shift from the individual to the collective body. We talk about the individual, but when you share, you don't carry it all by yourself. And it's also good for people to know if you just had knee surgery, or a hurt shoulder or toe. Or maybe you have a broken heart. I bring this up: My "broken heart thing" is always this bridge from the physical to the emotional. A broken heart feels like both: physical and emotional. These minutes arriving and sharing together are of importance for them and for me to check in and start to sense the space and how our time together will unfold. We keep beginning.

JOE: This reminds me of Fred Moten in conversation with Stefano Harney, talking about how to acknowledge that there is no outside of the classroom, and that it has already begun:

> Let's just see what happens if I don't make that gesture of calling the class to order—just that little moment in which my tone of voice turns and becomes slightly more authoritative so that everyone will know that class has begun. What if I just say, "well, we're here. Here we are now." Instead of announcing that class has begun, just acknowledge that class began. (2013, 126)

DORTE: I like that one. Some places it works, and some places it doesn't. Should I call to order or not? When people are arriving, I often mention that it has already begun: it begins at that moment, when you decided to join the class and booked it online, or sometimes it begins when you pack your bag! And you're here, when you step into this room, you have already started. It makes me think of a phrase I got from Emma Bigé (who got it from Fred Moten and Stefano Harney, *Undercommons Fugitive Planning and Black Study*), "What if study is everything that happens before the class begins," continued by me and Bigé: the thoughts about the class, the conversations, the ideas, feelings, passions that precede the moment when the teacher starts to speak. I will let it linger! So, it's your time, it's your space. It's about starting to let people understand that they also have to take agency of this time and space also. And if people need to speak a lot, they can go out and do that! I also say that if you're really stressed and you think about this text message that you have to send, please go out and do it. Right now. They will actually always laugh. One person ran out and did it and came back all relieved and then continued.

CI Is Research: CI Teaching Is Teaching Practice as Research

JOE: A recent paper by CI teacher, artist, and *CQ* co-editor Colleen Bartley and performer and CI cofounder Nita Little (2023) insists that CI is research. I love this because it draws attention to ongoing intentional body-mind learning. Using Nita Little's version of body-mind as attention in motion, I hear her narrate a continuous history of CI as a reflective body-mind practice, one in which improvisation is not just doing something new, but noticing what is new in what one is doing.

DORTE: "What is new in what you are doing," love it, this phrase is stretching the idea of repetition. I want to emphasize that it is about what you are doing with your today-body here and now. Sometimes people say, "How do I do what you did?" and I have to say, "No, no, no, no, no, it's your body, it is not your body trying to do my body." You can never do it as I do. That's not the purpose. But that you get inspired and want to explore the suggestion with the body you have. It's super important that people get that. Many of us are trained in schools as kids, you know, you have to write what I have written on the blackboard, or in ballet classes. So we have to relearn that, we have to learn (again) to trust our own research, *even though something is being proposed*. I think that's a nice situation. It helps us see when people do not trust their own research and keep asking, am I doing it right?

JOE: After facilitating a workshop in Beijing, Yeong Wen Lee wrote, " 'Someone asked, 'How can I improve?' I responded, 'Practice. Discover your own and not just "do" the learned' " (Lee 2018, 47). What I find special about classes, and especially intensives, are how they densify time through focused repetition. To be given time to do something again and again is to create the context where the deep discovery of inquiry itself becomes visible, it smacks you. CI classes offer time, they point to duration as a space of enjoyment, they teach curiosity.

DORTE: That is beautiful, this hanging out in process, allowing an openness to noticing. Repeating and practicing and focusing curiosity lead to insights. For instance, when I teach a multi-day intensive, I have us revisit what we did the day before with the body we have today. Researching through this kind of repetition opens up a door to another way of doing it. I call this a "recap" to name the familiarity we have with something that is also new. Now we know how to slide and then suddenly, whoa, I did something else. Wow, that made me suddenly create a new pathway, taking us to a place we haven't been before, while being in physical contact.

JOE: Nancy Stark Smith, *CQ* editor and one of the early instigators of CI, described this kind of instigation as creating the conditions for having a consciously new experience. She was deeply in dialogue with the founder of the experiential anatomy practice Body-Mind Centering, Bonnie Bainbridge Cohen, and they spent many interviews finding words for body investigation together:

> This pointing to experience, this kind of provocation that you [Bonnie Bainbridge Cohen] are creating, is the environment, the condition, in which I have my experience. Creating that condition is an essential and important factor in the evolution of our consciousness. People in your workshops aren't just wandering around the room without any direction. I mean, your presence gives a lot of direction, but that's not always quite enough. You give more orientation than that. I feel like the condition that you set up—and that we all set up in our teaching and structuring of improvisations and our relationship to our communities—is very influential and crucial in what happens among people. (Cohen and Stark Smith 2020, 54)

I love this almost constant refrain in CI teaching that is practice as research. Doing something again is never doing the same thing, you almost can't help but learn! And

334   Resistance and Support

the delight when students discover that they are the ones running the experiment. Postmodern dancer, choreographer, and teacher Simone Forti described this approach to teaching: "The problem is to create a structure that people can transcend. Something else happens beyond the structure" (cited in Lassiter 1984, 30).

DORTE: I like this idea that doing something again is a form of extended "more-ness." Of course, it is not on the order of days or weeks or months, but years in CI. This is deep research. Repeating is deep, it iterates through our bodies, it has its own paradigms.

JOE: One of my favorite philosophers, Isabelle Stengers, thinking with Alfred North Whitehead, pointed out that science itself is the practice of looking again, sensing what else might be happening, listening more, deepening one's ongoing relation to a phenomenon. The more you attend, the more you find. CI extends this very intentionally to movement: the more you move with awareness, the more you find in movement. It is not unique to CI by any means. *CQ* is full of dialogues with many different bodywork and movement teachers.

DORTE: There is something quite profound in this approach to collaborative practice as research. It is research into practice and into togetherness. Paxton named the necessity of collaboration for the very politics of CI:

> I couldn't progress without collaboration. It's a mutual form. . . . The politics of mutuality suggests collaboration; it doesn't suggest monitoring the correctness of anybody's behavior . . . there was to be a mutual listening to the movement. There was to be the creation of a third entity in the dance, which was the mutual movement paths and timing and all of that. That's the way it was defined. So what we were doing was essentially defining power as not applicable. (Paxton and Stark Smith 2018, 36–37)

At one point I was teaching at a dance theater with its own dance troupe. They were all highly trained professional dancers. And what I found important for them to learn was noticing what they were not noticing: to not skip what was being offered right in front of them, not to fix anything, but to welcome the always already that was being presented. Without thinking about it, we have a tendency to skip and or erase opportunities that don't come from our own doing and thinking. How can you move with another person as if you have no clue, and listen to what they say and not predict or think you know what they're going to say, or think you know who they are.

JOE: This effect on students, according to Christina Svane, was the "most wonderful attitude of making each of us feel that our perceptions and our experiments were all of equal value as research" (Svane cited in Bartley and Little, 6).

DORTE: How can you move with someone (in contact or not) and allow that to open up for you, the mutuality of moving together? It's much smarter than we are. Yes, the human mind can be very creative, but we are not as creative as the mutual space that is being created between us. Mutuality as a relational space creates this third space between two sensing moving bodies, and it is quite fascinating how it unfolds in negotiation and presence—if we let it!

JOE: This is a special kind of research, one that does not result in insight per se, but in a new way of being, of unlearning: Yeong Wen Lee described, "Hugging the awkwardness. . . . Learning and unlearning. Letting the questions be questions. Allowing the answer to pass through" (Lee 2018, 47).

DORTE: Yes, hugging the awkwardness, staying with the trouble! Asking questions with questions instead of having to seek the answers. Daniel Lepkoff wrote an article in 2008. For me, it's a classic, "Contact Improvisation: A Question?" He argues:

> The underlying technique needed to prepare for and survive the surprises of a Contact Improvisation duet is to pose and maintain a question: When I believe I know where down is, I am always wrong! Only gravity has that information. If I am not asking gravity for the direction of down, my idea cannot be correct. In this work knowledge can only be a question! What a relief! This questioning, rather than formulated within one's verbal mind is formulated and resides within the tissues of the body: bones, muscles, organs, nerves, and brain. (Lepkoff 2011, 39)

It is almost like an abstract form of moving meditation, and what they have in common is not getting attached to anything. I'm not saying Contact Improvisation can heal the world, or it can save everything. I don't think the form itself can, but it's how we share, teach, and practice the form. This third entity that's happening between two bodies who are trying to be present, I think it is a hardcore way of training your awareness and intention. It is different from meditation, which is often sitting down, not being in touch with anyone.

JOE: It is interesting to temporarily contrast CI with modalities like yoga, meditation, and even individual movement practice. Sometimes you create a very static environment to hold you, so that the only thing that's moving is your mind. And maybe you feel little things happening in your body. Or you focus on how your body interacts with a relatively predictable environment so that you can dive into your bodily (and body-mind) experience. But CI throws you into responsivity (see Myers and Dumit 2011). Being in contact, in touch with someone else, there's no stepping back, no time to reflect, because each movement back or each pause is itself part of the dance. You are (trying to be) aware of how you're affecting them, and they are aware of the mutual affecting as well. Nita Little calls this "enminding," and she'd remind me that this is happening whether or not your skin is touching their skin. We can be across the room from each other.

DORTE: Yes, interaction requires something from us, and it can be a bit overwhelming. So, when I teach, I point out that the connection we create is not about you or not about me, but the third space we create. Or, when standing and sensing the support from your partner's body, is not so much about them, but their connection to the earth that you feel through their body and the connection is bridging how we correspond with the earth. It takes a bit of pressure off the shoulders and enhances the sense of responsivity. I think it resonates with Glissant's notion that in exchange, we change (Glissant 1997, cf. 154).

JOE: The power of exchange, I like that! It reminds me of Albright's insight that "[t]he sensitivity to another's experience also creates an awareness of subtle differences, differences that can be celebrated within the improvisation" (Albright 2013, 271).

DORTE: Yes, I like Albright's insight. Glissant also talks about difference in a "creolizing of Being," approaching being from the perspectives of difference, relation, and immanence: I don't need to understand you to be with you, it's our differences (and the acceptance of difference as an entity in itself) that change can happen!

JOE: Thinking back to this collective research as a kind of science: it really plays with the moreness. You realize that you can't run a scientific experiment on this, since you can't

336 Resistance and Support

hold anything steady. If you try to do something again, it is not a repetition, because now you're doing it the second time.

DORTE: As researchers we are not separate from the research, and this gets us back to Nancy's suggestion that it is an experiment in community making! As such, it requires "holding space" for the practices of curiosity to unfold, and that is not easy.[1]

CI Teachers Are Exploring Their Own Curiosity through Teaching

DORTE: Another way we can think of practice as research in CI is through *labbing*, the verb for having laboratories to explore in common. Emerging through early practices in movement, dance, and performance, we use the phrase to denote a time for practitioners to get together and co-inspire each other with proposals that we can take extended time with. Sometimes people take turns leading, other times there is a circle and proposals are made: "I'd like to work with eyes closed," or "I'm really curious about using the top of the foot as a support."

JOE: Reading *CQ*, it's clear that teachers often actively use classes as labs to deepen their research. Lily Kiara said:

So the images are developing continuously through my daily practice. I also taught workshops where I used images that I developed further, from the practice and my teaching. This is something I do to be in tune with my body and with the world, with the reality of the imagination: the experience of expansion. (Dean et al. 2020, 50)

Similarly, working with costumes, Dean notes how learning from costumes provided new ways to perform, and she could share this exploration with others in workshops: "These Somatic Costumes have led to performances, talks, workshops, films, and more" (Dean 2019, 33).

DORTE: Yes! I think CI allows this research-driven teaching because it does not have a structured curriculum. Teachers are encouraged to share the edge of their curiosity; they bring their research to the class. And weirdly, in CI, this doesn't depend on students having done lots of CI. I mean, it could, but it overall doesn't. You can still teach most of the things you're interested in with some beginners in the class. This also means that almost all workshops are "all levels welcome." Many teachers describe the value of having many

---

[1] Many in CI have pointed out however, that many people do not feel welcomed to CI jams and classes because they reinforce other structures of hierarchy, violence, and exclusion. *CQ* has been one site for discussing this problem and especially the fantasy of CI being an inherently safe space (Brooks and Nelson 2016; Taja Will in CQ Editors 2018, 38; see also others in this volume). Another has been festivals in their role of curating teachers and topics. These can change quickly, though it has required interventions to shift who gets to teach and what topics are put forward. Classes, workshops, and intensives can offer the possibility to make whiteness, heteronormativity, sexual harassment, trauma relations to touch, and improvisation's critical history into guided engagement with social body-minds (Alexander, Albright, and Hennessey's comments in CQ Editors 2018, 35). The public context of classes can enable experimentation with reactivity and practical forms of somatic training. Elias explained one aspect of this, "Contact is intimate, but it is public; you need other people there for legitimacy, for reinforcing the set of values connected to doing the form. Without the presence of a class and teacher emphasizing touch as a means of generating the dance, the social, sexual aspects of touching became too predominant" (Novack 1990, 168).

different people with different bodies and different experience with CI to dance with. Research begins in this diversity.

One of my favorite experiences was when I worked with non-dancers for eight weeks. In order to not become the leader, I chose to use the lab format and importantly to call it a lab, so that we could find the experiments together. "Let's work with sliding." This gave us space for each person to try out their own interpretations of sliding. It meant that there were no failures, only weird inventions that others could take up. It took a few weeks (of frustration) for the students to accept their role as co-creators, but it also truly built a collective sense of investigation (Bjerre Jensen 2020).

At another class, one student asked me, "So Dorte, how planned are you before you come to teach a class?" I could have answered, "I have prepared myself for 20 years!" I always have a plan, I just never tend to follow it. I need to be able to change and adapt due to what is needed, due to the group constellation and so forth. If I never improvise myself, what am I teaching? Improvising is being attentive to the moment. Like right now, what am I seeing, what am I noticing? And of course, it has to be a part of what I am doing.

JOE: And this lets classes themselves be an example of improvisation.

DORTE: Exactly!

JOE: *CQ* has many examples of this. For instance, Lassiter described how "Forti continually seeks new structures for improvisation. She may plan them ahead of time or make them up on the spot in class" (Lassiter 1984, 26). Classes are sometimes proposed on the fly and they certainly are adjusted on the fly. "Each meeting, though carefully structured by Forti, has a life of its own. Forti acknowledges the possibility that one exercise or event may transform into something else" (Lassiter 1984, 26).

DORTE: The fact that the classes have this openness to them also helps prevent, maybe, students from thinking that there's a right thing to do. So, the fact that the teacher is, in the moment, out loud changing the plan is actually a really good way of holding space for improvisation.

JOE: Yes. I've been thinking about it this way: Because CI is not about curriculum, but continually introducing the idea of inquiry, the question arises: Can you teach love of research, curiosity, how to move by being moved by what is moving you? Anthropologist of science Sharon Traweek found that this took years in physics. Curiosity and wonder may have drawn undergraduates to the major, but then they spent years learning not to be so curious, learning equations, then years learning to do experiments, and even postdocs being given questions. Only the most successful scientists reached the assistant professor level where they could formulate their own questions to research.

DORTE: So, if CI *is research*, if it is not about control, then it requires a meta-teaching: the teacher must not only transmit curiosity and improvisation, but the teacher must also be genuinely curious and improvising in the moment.

CI Uses Words to Push Practice, and Practice to Push Language

JOE: One critical part of CI teaching is active reflection using words and demonstrations. These include sharing with a partner after a score, coming up with scores to share, popcorning words or comments at the end of a day, demonstrating and witnessing, and

338 Resistance and Support

round robins as sharing ideas. A notable thing is that these forms of feedback are barely recorded. Documentation is not the point. The sharing in classes is about seeds that are embodied, the words shed phenomenological insight to self and others—by offering aspects of experience that had been missed the first time (distracted with others), and distinctions that had not been made are now made retroactively (micro-phenomenology). These are seeds that grow in the jam that follows the class, in other classes, in life.

In many ways, the classes are the seeding, pollinating, cross-fertilization of CI—really the ongoing mutations in practice and meta-practice, in ideas, scores, affects, and so on, transmission of curiosities. These classes also provide many of the descriptions that are shared in *CQ* as well. Teacher Jerry Zientara reflected on the importance of words and drawings in trying and failing to capture the immediacy of CI:

> At the best of these moments, the principles that live within our process emerge momentarily, and some of the phrases stay around repeating definitions describing the same moment several times, feeding our words and gestures into the common experience keeps refining and redefining and refinding the same old gravity and change. (Zientara 1979, 9)

DORTE: What I love about this description is that the words aren't sacred! They are a means, seeds, temporary instruments for provoking and developing practice.

JOE: I love too Bonnie Bainbridge Cohen's explanation of the power of words and *CQ*'s role in circulating them:

> In discussions after an exploration, people will say, "I don't know what to say"—because it's preverbal. That's one of our challenges in the field of somatics—how do we create verbal and written language. You and Lisa, through *CQ*, have been at the forefront of that. How does experience come back to words? How do we create a vocabulary of preverbal experience that then goes back to the experience? So that the verbal isn't what is being transmitted but rather transmits back to original experience. It's another seed. (Cohen and Stark Smith 2020, 55)

To academic ears, however, this use of words as seeds is almost backward. Typically, words are understood as the goal, as knowledge's end. Practical experiments, as in science, are needed when words need improvement, and the goal again is to end back at better words. In CI research, however, the inverse is true. We start with doing things, and this can lead to new distinctions that we put into words. Those words are not the final say, however; they are merely springboards for more movement research.

DORTE: Your approach to words has really struck me. As an academic writing mentor, you realized that CI practitioners often think most clearly while teaching (or I do!).

JOE: I've always encouraged students to tape sessions and still think if you need to make a paper, a transcript of a class is a most-lively document. Class transcripts are live-taught, they are audience specific, most CI teachers become incredibly sensitive to the room, to the people in the room, adjust the class on the fly, because of course, they are the point. In teaching, words are not endpoints but "sendpoints"; they provoke. Words are provoked by the situation and in turn they provoke future selves.

DORTE: And sometimes words name habits that we then want to change! Nancy Stark Smith once narrated her own shift in curiosity, in *CQ*:

Intensive Curiosity 339

I've learned a lot from doing Contact Improvisation about coordinating with the forces-that-be: Accepting gravity, falling, following momentum, blending with a partner's movements—i.e., "going with the flow." But lately, I've been feeling feisty. I'm a little too comfortable now with the dizzy of flipping horizons, torquing pathways and unexpected chutes, and more and more I find myself playing against the forces—making myself heavy instead of light when a lift starts, adding a splash to the easy pouring of weight, insisting instead of yielding, adding fierce to gentle, no to yes. It's a start. I've been in the harmony business a long time now.

It might take a while to really get the hang of holding my ground instead of so gladly letting it slip out from under me. As much as I love running around, I think I'm going to try running into things more often, or at least up against them. (Stark Smith 1984, 3)

JOE: I really like Nancy's phenomenological engagement with CI as research here. She is noticing how she is becoming resistant to her practice, as if a paradigm has set in, and her affect is activated—"lately, I've been feeling feisty." The passive voice is a clue, she is dissociating, but reflectively. Always more, but my curiosity is flagging. A more-ness seems to have exhausted itself. How do I know this? Because "I find myself. . . ." This lovely phrasing notes a not choosing, but another within me is going in a different direction, against a previous focus. The mark of a CI researcher is this deep engagement with body-mind curiosity itself. Where is this curiosity going, where is it losing steam, what is it telling me? This is a way of learning how to be bored creatively.

DORTE: Writing an intensive description is putting words on your practice as they are now. So, it's an archive of what we're doing in that certain time and place and period of our lives and history and everything. And then it's also a way of what am I actually doing, what I am interested in now, but how do I put it into words? I'm trying to get closer to what I'm actually interested in, even though I sometimes feel that words make me stumble. But step one is to try to find some words and then maybe I come closer to words that are more exciting, that move me creatively and physically.

JOE: Words move us, as descriptions they catch us initially, but in reflective movement, we notice words as forces and not descriptions. Words play with other words, connecting, prompting connections inside life, and in CI they can prompt new forms of inquiry. Whole intensives and workshops start with a single word (attention, body-mind, a body part, form of energy, thing, animal, sound) and implode it, so by the end the word has become a multiplicity. Research takes off along many lines.

Last year I was teaching a class on "traversing tables" in which students were to practice being side-by-side on all fours and finding new ways for one to roll up on over the other. But I realized that they were super focused on getting to the other side. So, I instead asked them to find their way onto the other and then explore being up there, find ways to play slowly, and for the base (the person on the bottom) to enjoy the sense that the other was playing, even if it felt like they weren't moving. Traversing was my own provocation, but "tabletop play" was the outcome.

DORTE: This is one reason why CI class descriptions can be dropped, because they are means and not ends. The class is not supposed to meet the description, the description provokes people to show up and the teacher to have a starting point. Workshop descriptions are often described as questions and are often full of questions. Or they can be!

340 Resistance and Support

JOE: Yes. They are written six months to a year before the actual event, they are a record of what the teacher was curious about at the time, in the words that showed up then, and as questions they can always be deepened. Questions here are portals: orientations to universes in which these body-minds learn to do/ask, learn to change themselves. The teaching words can themselves help hold space for curiosity and research. In talking with teachers, they often laugh as they say that they do not actually follow their workshop description. Even if they tried to, they would not get through half their material.

DORTE: Yes, writing is a peculiar doing. It makes this bridge between what you've just been doing and a wish for the future. I think it helps you to come closer to something that is maybe not super clear for you, but that's not supposed to be. Maybe this practice-word-wish becomes something you're curious about in a new way. And so that's why I think it's good that we have to write these descriptions. Even though I have this love and hate relationship with writing, because it takes so much time away from my body and my kid. But it also forces me to think and reflect upon my current interest. My writing really affects the way I also teach.

JOE: Let's leave it here for now, with these words that will hopefully provoke us all to play, contact, and improvise more.

References

Albright, Ann Cooper. 2013. *Engaging Bodies: The Politics and Poetics of Corporeality*. Middletown, CT: Wesleyan University Press.

Ashley, Tamara. 2020. "Janis Claxton October 6, 1964–September 7, 2018." *Contact Quarterly* 45, no. 1 (Winter-Spring): 17.

Bigé, Romain, and Charlie Morrissey. 2017. "Mind-Fucking and Other Uncertainties." *Contact Quarterly* 42, no. 2 (Summer-Fall): 19–22.

brooks, mayfield, and Karen Nelson. 2016. "IWB = Improvising While Black: Writings, Interventions, Interruptions, Questions. With Conversation between mayfield brooks and Karen Nelson." *Contact Quarterly* 41, no. 1 (Winter-Spring): 33–39.

Carney, Kay. 1985. "Opening the Actor's Creative Unconscious through Psychophysical Awareness Exercises." *Contact Quarterly* 10, no. 3 (Fall): 12–18.

Chung, Ray, and Kevin O'Connor. 2020. "Moving and Thinking with Fascia: Interview with Ray Chung on the Intersection of Fascia and Contact Improvisation Training." *Contact Quarterly* 45, no. 1: 66–71.

Cohen, Bonnie Bainbridge, and Nancy Stark Smith. 2017. "A Certain Kind of Knowing: Interview with Bonnie Bainbridge Cohen." *Contact Quarterly* 42, no. 2 (Summer-Fall): 30–33.

Cohen, Bonnie Bainbridge, and Nancy Stark Smith. 2020. "Self and Other, SelfOther: Bonnie Bainbridge Cohen in Conversation with Nancy Stark Smith for CQ." *Contact Quarterly* 45, no. 1: 51–56.

CQ Editors. 2018. "On CI Intersections: A Question from CQ, and a Round of Responses." *Contact Quarterly* 43, no. 2 (Summer-Fall): 35–39.

Dean, Sally E. 2019. "Somatic Costumes: A Teaching Resource and Performance Generator." *Contact Quarterly* 9, no. 2 (Summer-Fall): 33–37.

Dean, Sally E., Margit Galanter, Lily Kiara, and Julie Nathanielsz. 2019. "An Image That's Alive: Conversation on the Image Worlds of Skinner Releasing Technique and Amerta Movement." *Contact Quarterly* 45, no. 1 (Winter-Spring): 44–50.

Dowd, Irene. 1984. "On Metaphor." *Contact Quarterly* 9, no. 3 (Fall): 18–22.

Forti, Simone. 1984. "Full Moves: Thoughts on Dance Behavior." *Contact Quarterly* 9, no. 3 (Fall): 7–14.

Glissant, Édouard. 1997. *Poetics of Relation*. Ann Arbor: University of Michigan Press.

Harney, Stefano, and Fred Moten. 2013. *The Undercommons: Fugitive Planning and Black Study*. New York: Autonomedia.

Jensen, Dorte Bjerre. 2020. "Facilitating Thinking-Touch through Process Philosophy and Contact Improvisation." In *Thinking Touch: Philosophical pedagogy and practice. Perspectives on Partnering and Contact Improvisation*, edited by Malaika Sarco-Thomas. Cambridge: Cambridge Scholars: 104–125.

Lassiter, Laurie. 1984. "Movement Research Inc. and the Workshop Process." *Contact Quarterly* 9, no. 3 (Fall): 23–24.

Lee, Yeong Wen. 2018. "Embracing the Unknown in Beijing." *Contact Quarterly* 43, no. 1 (Winter-Spring): 47.

Lepkoff, Daniel. 2011. "Contact Improvisation: A Question?" *Contact Quarterly* 36, no. 1 (Annual): 38–40.

Little, Nita, and Colleen Bartley. 2023. "Cultivating Emergence in Contact Improvisation: A Path of Research." Manuscript.

Myers, Natasha, and Joseph Dumit. 2011. "Haptic Creativity and the Mid-Embodiments of Experimental Life." In *A Companion to the Anthropology of the Body and Embodiment*, edited by Frances E. Mascia-Lees. Hoboken, NY: Wiley-Blackwell: 239–261.

Novack, Cynthia Jean. 1990. *Sharing the Dance: Contact Improvisation and American Culture*. New Directions in Anthropological Writing. Madison: University of Wisconsin Press.

Paxton, Steve, and Nancy Stark Smith. 2018. "The Politics of Mutuality: A Conversation with Steve Paxton at the Kitchen Table." *Contact Quarterly* 43, no. 1 (Winter-Spring): 36–38.

Soto, Merián. 2019. "How Does This Body Want to Move: Dancing the Legacy of Elaine Summers." *Contact Quarterly* 44, no. 2 (Summer-Fall): 44–49.

Stark Smith, Nancy. 1984. "Dealing with the Heat. Editor Note." *Contact Quarterly* 9, no. 3 (Fall): 3.

Stark Smith, Nancy. 2018. "'Causing It Only a Little'? Editor Note." *Contact Quarterly* 43, no. 1 (Winter-Spring): 3.

Zientara, Jerry. 1979. "Junior! How Jump Can You Far?" *Contact Quarterly* 4, no. 3 (Summer): 8–10.

Index

For the benefit of digital users, indexed terms that span two pages (e.g., 52–53) may, on occasion, appear on only one of those pages.

Tables and figures are indicated by an italic *t* and *f* following the page number.

Afro-Caribbean dance, 115
agency (feelings of), 15, 41, 67–68, 88, 179, 185–86, 194, 199–200, 202, 221, 277, 289, 332
Agitating the Underscore, 143, 144, 144n.3. *See also* Akiyama, Jun; Ver, Ronja
Ahmed, Sara, 20, 115, 261–62, 311, 311n.1, 312n.7, 313–17, 313n.8, 318–19. *See also* Contact Improvisation and queer sexuality
"desire lines," 77
disorientation and queer experience, 325
"Feminist Killjoys (and Other Willful Subjects)," 106
queer duet with Mª Paz Brozas Polo, 311
Queer Phenomenology: Orientations, Objects, Others, 261–62, 311, 311n.1, 313–14, 316, 317, 325
Aiken, Chris, 140–41, 195. *See also* teaching Contact Improvisation
Aikido, 13, 156–57, 231, 237, 248–50, 302. *See also* Contact Improvisation and spirituality; Ueshiba, Morihei
bringing harmony to the whole cosmos, 249–50
Ki, 249
ukemi (receiving body), 248–49
unifying life energy, 249
Akiyama, Jun, 143, 144n.3, 146–47. See also *Agitating the Underscore*; Underscore; Ver, Ronja; teaching Contact Improvisation
Albright, Ann Cooper, 110, 136, 147, 328, 335
Choreographing Difference, 323–24
How to Land, 316
"Open Bodies: (X)changes of identity in Capoeira and Contact Improvisation," 109–10
organizing CI25 and Critical Mass CI @ 50 109–10, 166
teaching CI at Oberlin College, 238
Alessi, Alito, 261, 294–95, 306, 324. *See also* DanceAbility; teaching Contact Improvisation; wheelchair, the
"Dance for All Community Dance: A New Era of Dance for the Disabled" project, 294–95
"Wheels of Fortune," 320 (*see* Blackwell, Emery)
Alexander, F. M, 16. *See also* the natural body; Duncan, Isadora
Alexander technique, 126–27
connection with eugenics, 126–27 (*see* Saleeby, Caleb Williams)
focus on the head position as evolution, 127
Man's Supreme Inheritance, 127

Ambedkar, Bhimrao Ramji, 277–78. *See also* Contact Improvisation in India, caste
American Dance Festival, 196, 296
Amoedo, Henrique, 304. *See also* Roda Viva Company; teaching Contact Improvisation
Anatomy Trains Structural Integration Certification Program, 195. *See also* Myers, Tom
Anderson, Reb, 254. *See also* Contact Improvisation and spirituality, Zen
Andrews, Edward, 256. *See also* Shakers, the
ANQA Danse avec les Roues, 261–62, 311, 321–22. *See also* Brunaud, Isabelle
Appel, David, 108. *See also* teaching Contact Improvisation
Arisman, Jolyn, 6. See also *The Future of Contact Improvisation* conference
The Art of Is: Improvising as a Way of Life, 256. *See also* Nachmanovitch, Stephen
The Art of Peace, 249–50. *See also* Ueshiba, Morihei
Authentic Movement, 154, 189–90, 191–92, 257. See also *Holding the Tension of the Opposites*; McLeod, Shaun; Woodman, Marion

Banes, Sally (1950–2020), 21, 28, 34–35. See also *Democracy's Body*; Judson Dance Theater
Banissy, Michael, 181
Barad, Karen, 154, 177, 180–81, 183–84, 185–86, 219. *See also* Bennett, Jane; new materialist theories
Baraister, Lisa, 188–89
Bartley, Colleen, 332–33. See also *Contact Quarterly*; teaching Contact Improvisation, CI as research
Bassel, Leah, 154, 177, 180–81
The Beaulieu Test, 14, 45, 46*b*, 46, 47, 48*b*, 48. See Beaulieux, Michele
Beaulieux, Michele, 14, 56, 75, 180, 221. *See also* The Beaulieu Test; Contact Improvisation jams, Chicago jam, the; safe space(s)/safer brave spaces
Beavers, Wendell, 134. *See also* teaching Contact Improvisation
Becker, Carolina, 324, 324n.25. *See also* Carbonell, Paquita Ferragut
Benjamin, Jessica, 222. See *Bonds of Love*
Bennett, Jane, 154, 177, 183. *See also* Barad, Karen; *Influx & Efflux*; new materialist theories
Bigé, Emma, 15–16, 106–7, 108–14, 318. *See also* Godard, Hubert; Singh, Paul; teaching Contact Improvisation, CI as research; "Wrong Contact Manifesto"

344 Index

BIPOC participation in Contact Improvisation (Black, Indigenous and People of Color), 6, 9–10, 15, 55, 76–77, 83, 98, 107, 242, 317–18. *See also* Moving Rasa; XCI

Black/African-American Arts movement, the, 2. *See also* brooks, mayfield; Jackson, Jonathan David; Moten, Fred; Smith, Joy Mariama
  African-American music forms, 2
  Black radical tradition, the, 111–12, 113 (*see also* Moten, Fred)
  contribution to American dance, 132–33
  history, of the, 111
  "Improvisation in African American Vernacular Dancing," 104 (*see aslo* Jackson, Jonathan David)
  Improvising While Black, 16, 77, 104, 106, 113, 135, 164 (*see also* brooks, mayfield)
  jazz music, the jam session, 3
  sociopoetics of blackness, 113 (*see also* brooks, mayfield)

Black bodies, 84–85, 148n.7. *See also* contentious issues; NCI practice; Smith, Joy Mariama
  alienation, history of, 85
  honoring ancestry, 85
  in opposition to the neutral body, 127, 131, 132
  Whale Fall Cycle (*see* brooks, mayfield; *Whale Fall* Cycle)
  working definition of PoC/people of color, 103

Black feminism, 114. *See also* feminism

Blackwell, Emery, 320. *See also* Alessi, Alito; "Wheels of Fortune"; wheelchair, the

Bodhidharma, 255. *See also* Zen Buddhism in China

body, the. *See also* Black bodies; somatics
  complex biological systems, as, 170–71
  fascia, 195, 245, 270–71
  flesh, 114, 155–56, 212, 222
  fluids, 93, 94, 161, 208–9
  injury (*see* injury)
  mixed-race body, 264–20
  muscle, 160, 195, 208, 322–23
  natural body, the (*see* natural body, the)
  neutral body, the (*see* neutral body, the)
  primitive body, the, 125
  queerblind body, 130, 132, 133–34
  site for liberation/freedom, as a, 124, 125, 129, 133, 303 (*see also* Duncan, Isadora)

Body-Mind Centering® (BMC), 132, 178n.4, 213–14. *See also* Cohen, Bonnie Bainbridge
  annual conference, 7
  Bob Turner's critique, 132
  Cellular Touch, 178–79
  endocrine system, the, 187–88
  in dialogue with Nancy Stark Smith, 333
  re-patterning developmental movement patterns, 132
  published in *Contact Quarterly* (1980–1992), 132

Bolster, Gurney. *See also* Catpoto Dance Collective; teaching Contact Improvisation

Bonds of Love. See Benjamin, Jessica

Bonilla, Diana, 213–14. *See also* Espacio Formación Contact Improvisation Madrid; teaching Contact Improvisation

Boullosa, Cristiane, 213–14. *See also* Espacio Formación Contact Improvisation Madrid; teaching Contact Improvisation

brooks, mayfield, 7–8, 16, 113, 135–36, 251. *See also* Black/African-American Arts movement, the; Black bodies; teaching Contact Improvisation
  class at CI @ 50, 166, 251
  "Improvising While Black," 16, 104, 113
  in conversation with Karen Nelson, 164
  on practicing refusal, 114
  sociopoetics of blackness, 113
  teaching at Oberlin College, 8
  Whale Fall Cycle, 149n.9

Brown, Byron. *See also* Mangrove Dance Collective; teaching Contact Improvisation

Brugarolas, Marisa, 322n.22, 324. *See* Contact Improvisation in Spain; DanceAbility; teaching Contact Improvisation

Brunaud, Isabelle, 262, 311, 324. *See ANQA Danse avec les Roues;* teaching Contact Improvisation

Buber, Martin, 207–8. *See also I and Thou*

Buddhism, 111, 148n.7, 157, 198–99, 253–55. *See also* Andersen, Reb; Bodihidharma; Contact Improvisation and spirituality; Dalai Lama; Dogen, Zenji; Hongzhi; Leighton, Taigen Dan; Manuel, Zenju Earthlyn; Zen Buddhism
  breath as a portal for awareness, 253–54
  relation to inanimate world, 254
  Samādhi (concentration of the mind), 254–55
  self-study, 253
  sitting upright, 253–54

Bull, Richard, 2, 112. *See also* Foster, Susan; Novack, Cynthia

capitalism, 96, 106–7, 274. *See also* neoliberalism

capoeira, 109–10. *See also* Contact Improvisation in Brazil

Carbonell, Paquita Ferragut, 324. *See also* Becker, Carolina; *Danza sin fin* film

Carson, Rachel, 160

Casa Werma, 268, 270–71. *See also* Seventh Gathering of Contact Improvisation in Mexico

Catpoto Dance Collective, 13–14, 27–29. *See also* Bolster, Gurney; Davida, Dena; Ginzberg, Evelyn; Harwood, Carol; teaching Contact Improvisation
  contact-infused choreographies, 29
  performance with Mangrove Dance Collective, 29 (*see also* Mangrove)
  performances in galleries and museums, 28
  reciprocal CI touring network with colleagues, 28 (*see also* Banes, Sally)

Cellular Touch, 154, 178–80, 191–92. *See also* Body-Mind Centering®

Center for Deep Listening, 174. *See also* Oliveros, Pauline

Cerny, Mary, 23–25. *See also* teaching Contact Improvisation

Index

Chak-Lin, Mui, 260–61, 291–92. *See also* Contact Improvisation in Asia; teaching Contact Improvisation
Chan, Sze-Wei, 6, 107. See also *The Future of Contact Improvisation* conference
Chen, Shan Chengdu, 293–94. *See also* Contact Improvisation Community in Asia
Cheng, Iris, 291. *See also* Contact Improvisation conferences, Shanghai Contact Improvisation Community and Festival; Contact Improvisation in Asia; teaching Contact Improvisation
Chengwei, Xu, 291, 298. *See also* KU & Dancers; teaching Contact Improvisation
Cheuk-yin, Miu, 291–92. *See also* Contact Improvisation in Asia; "Contact Point" community; Hong Kong Academy for Performing Arts; teaching Contact Improvisation
Choral Dance, 305. *See also* Duschenes, Maria; Laban, Rudolf
CHUTE, the film (1972), 34, 65. *See also* John Weber Gallery in New York City
CI @ 50 zine, 8–9. *See also* Michalska, Adrianna
civil rights movement, the, 19, 111, 115–16
Cognitive Behavioral Therapy, 156, 239, 240, 241
Cohen, Bonnie Bainbridge, 173–74, 178–79, 333, 338. *See also* Body-Mind Centering®
Cohen Bull, Cynthia Jean (aka Cynthia Novack). *See* Novack, Cynthia
Collective Gestures: Experimental Performance at Oberlin College in the 1970s exhibition, 8, 147. *See also* Critical Mass: CI @ 50
colonialism, 185–86, 241–42, 272
    in Brazil, 29, 307–8
    da Silva, Denise, 103
    in India, 277, 278, 279–80
Color Block 2023 retreat, 15, 87f, 92f. *See also* BIPOC; Not Contact Improvisation (NCI) practice; Smith, Joy Mariama
Compania 100 Habilidades in Brazil mixed ability weekend, 261. *See* Contact Improvisation conferences
consent culture, 14, 37, 38–40, 39t, 44, 45, 51, 86, 91, 220–21. *See also* contentious issues; Vionnet, Claire
    Bechdel Test, 45
    Beaulieu Test, 14, 45
    Caro Novella's co-sensing, 221 (*see also* Novella, Caro)
    Consent Culture in CI Symposium, 74 (*see also* Contact Improvisation conferences; Kim, Richard)
    "The Wheel of Consent," 208 (*see also* Martin, Betty)
Contact at 10th and 2nd performance, 15–16, 105–6, 108. *See also* Holland, Fred; Houston-Jones, Ishmael
Contact Improvisation, contentious issues. *See also* Black bodies; "Doing It Wrong: Contact's Countercultures"; *The Future of Contact Improvisation conference*; Hennessey, Keith
    accessibility, 5–6, 56, 102, 303, 310, 312n.5, 318, 324

caste (*see* Contact Improvisation in India, caste)
    consent (culture) (*see* consent culture)
    cost accessibility (*see* EPIICO)
    equity, 5–6, 14, 62, 122, 130, 136, 147
    eroticism (*see* eroticism)
    ethics (*see* ethics)
    exclusion/ inclusivity (*see* exclusion/ inclusivity)
    "founders' lineage," 7
    gender identities (*see* gender)
    hierarchies, 6, 62, 66–67, 259, 271, 288–89, 318
    homogenous white spaces, 85, 113, 116, 317
    institutional racism, 109, 241, 307
    neutral body, the (*see* the body, neutral; Paxton, Steve)
    organizational structurelessness, 41t, 41, 42
    patenting Contact Improvisation, debate about, 4
    patriarchal violence, 266 (*see also* EPIICO)
    politics post-Paxton, 129 (*see also* Turner, Bob)
    power dynamics (*see* power dynamics in CI)
    racism (*see* racism)
    rape culture (*see* Beaulieux, Michele; rape culture)
    safety protocols, 14 (*see also* The Beaulieu Test)
    unwanted sexual contact, 14, 74, 75, 133–34 (*see also* Beaulieux, Michele; Vionnet, Claire)
    violating women's boundaries, 6, 14, 40–41, 43, 45, 47, 50 (*see also* Beaulieux, Michele; Vionnet, Claire)
    visibility of diverse histories of CI, 110, 242
Contact Improvisation and differently abled bodies, 20–21 See also Alessi, Alito; Dance in Brazil; Dance in Spain; DanceAbility; *Liant la Troca* group; Maru; Roda Viva Company Dance; Symbiosis Nice Dance Company and Training; Tàncenània Company in Budapest; Teixeira, Ana Carolina Bezerra
    autistic people, 295 (*see also* Maru; TOUCH Contact Improvisation Festival)
    Body and Soul, 295
    Choreographing Difference, 323 (*see also* Albright, Ann Cooper)
    The Cost of Living, 323–24 (*see also* DV8; Lloyd, Newson)
    culture of exclusion in Brazil, the, 305, 306–7, 308, 310
    dance companies in Brazil, 306
    re-envisioning disability, 261–62
    Symbiosis Dance, 294–95 (*see also* Maru)
    Zarvos, Neca, 306 (*see also* Contact Improvisation in Brazil)
Contact Improvisation and philosophical sources
    Alexander Weheliye's sociogeny of movement, 114
    Brian Schultis' rolling as knowledge production, 235
    Edmund Husserl's phenomenology, 311–12, 315–16
    Erin Manning's touch as tender, interacting, 189, 220
    Fred Moten's ani*materiality*, 109, 113–14, 332
    Gilles Deleuze's body as metaphenomenon, 228, 231, 232, 312–13, 331–32
    Hortense Spiller's flesh hieroglyphics, 114
    Jane Bennett's hovering, 154, 177
    Karen Barad's quantum philosophies, 154, 177
    Martin Buber's relational concept of existence, 207–8

346 Index

Contact Improvisation and power dynamics, 6, 13, 14, 312
  between dance partners, 179
  identity-based/gendered, 62, 66–67, 68, 72–73, 76–77
  India, in, 276, 288, 289, 290
  Seventh Gathering of CI in Mexico, at the, 270
  sexual touch, in, 212, 218–19, 221, 223
  within rape culture at jams, 40, 42
Contact Improvisation and queer sexuality. *See also* queerness
  BDSM, 44, 212–13, 218–19
  Contact Improvisation and sex, 217
  Espacio Formación Contact Improvisation Madrid, 155, 213–14
  "Queer Contact Improvisation (QCI)," 214 (*see also* Skrzypczak, Wiktor)
  queer jams, 317–18
  XCI (*see* XCI)
Contact Improvisation and sex, 66, 217. *See also* XCI
Contact Improvisation and spirituality, 156–57. *See also* Laursen, Carol
  Aikido (*see* Aikido; Paxton, Steve; Ueshiba, Morihei)
  Carl Jung's "powers," 246–47
  China, in, 301
  Quakerism, 157, 250
  Shakers, the, 256–57 (*see also* Shakers, the)
  Soto Zen/ Buddhism/the Buddha, 253 (*see also* Buddhism; Dalai Lama)
  Steve Paxton's perspective on, 129
  trance, 256
Contact Improvisation audiences, 32, 299, 300
  continuity between movers and watchers, 28
  engaging/facilitating the, 281–82, 299
  gaze, the (*see* gaze, the)
  non-manipulative approach to the, 23
  relationship with disability, 261, 309–10
  role in India, 281–82
  talk, post-performance, 29
  "You come, we'll show you what we do" tour, 3–4, 28
Contact Improvisation conferences. *See* Contact Improvisation events
Contact Improvisation events (conferences, festivals, teacher exchanges)
  CI@25, 7
  CI@36, 7
  Compania 100 Habilidades from Brazil, mixed ability weekend, 261
  Consent Culture in CI Symposium, 74 (*see also* consent culture; Kim, Richard)
  Contact Meets Contemporary festival in Goettingen, 110
  Critical Mass: CI @ 50 (*see* Critical Mass CI @ 50)
  Dali Contact Improvisation Festival, 295 (*see also* Contact Improvisation in India; Holong, Yin)
  European Contact Improvisation Teacher Exchange (2021), 317–18
  Fifth Gathering of Contact Improvisation in Mexico (2020), 267 (*see also* EPIICO)
  Freiburg Festival (2007), 70–71

The Future of Contact Improvisation conference, 6–7, 9 (*see also* Chan, Sze-Wei)
  Goa Contact Festival, 260, 278–80 (*see also* Contact Improvisation in India)
  i-dance Taipei International Dance Improvisation Festival, 291 (*see also* Contact Improvisation in Asia)
  Indian Contact Improvisation Teacher Exchange (2019), 289
  The International Conference of Teachers of Contact Improvisation of Latin America (EIMCILA), 264
  Moving Rasa, 77 (*see also* BIPOC; gender; Suseno, Andrew)
  QCI Symposium and Festival Hamburg 2018, 214 (*see also* "Queer Contact Improvisation")
  Seventh Gathering of Contact Improvisation in Mexico, 263
  Shanghai Contact Improvisation Festival, 291 (*see also* Contact Improvisation conferences, events, festivals; Cheng, Iris)
  Teacher Exchange Conference and Community Conference in Beijing (2018), 293 (*see also* Contact Improvisation in Asia; TOUCH Contact Improvisation Festival)
  TOUCH Contact Improvisation Festival (*see* TOUCH Contact Improvisation Festival)
Contact Improvisation Facilitators Worldwide Networking & Discussion Group, 317–18
Contact Improvisation festivals. *See* Contact Improvisation events
Contact Improvisation fundamentals (core concepts/ common skills), 4, 26, 83, 284–85. *See also* Ahmed, Sara; Paxton, Steve
  Aikido rolls, 231
  attention to internal sensation, 3, 4, 145, 160, 161, 162, 165, 171, 174, 196 (*see also* The Stand/ the small dance)
  axis/fulcrum, 155, 234, 315–16
  carrying, 20, 26, 30–31, 320, 323–24
  disorientation, 4, 15, 69, 92, 93, 135, 160, 166, 198–99, 234, 240, 255, 261–62, 313, 315–16
  falling, 3, 4, 166, 168, 183–84, 282, 315, 316–17
  flow, 13, 73, 94, 108–9, 131, 234, 299–300, 339
  following, 13, 178–79, 184, 189, 190, 319, 325
  gravity, 3, 4, 13, 26, 129, 139, 159–63, 167–69, 170, 174, 182, 196, 198, 202, 203, 249–50, 282, 293, 308, 330, 335, 339
  lifts/lifting, 14–15, 30–31, 61–62, 63, 68, 69, 110, 133, 197–98
  momentum, 4, 131, 167–68, 184, 189, 190, 197–98, 320–21, 339
  peripheral vision (soft focus), 4, 26, 198, 282
  physical forces, 3, 22, 25, 26, 95, 128–29, 153, 156, 161, 218–19, 275, 339
  reciprocity, 67, 91, 171
  riding, 26, 197–98, 226
  rolling/rolls, 13, 231, 248–49
  rolling/sliding point of contact, 25, 61, 181, 230, 233, 237, 330

round robin, 157, 252
sharing/sensing weight, 20–21, 25, 178, 197–98, 319
spherical space, 198, 234, 315
The Stand/ the small dance, 3, 23–25, 26, 153–54, 159–60, 159n.2, 160n.4, 161–63, 164, 167–68, 169–70, 171, 174, 178, 186, 198, 200, 233, 253–54, 295, 328
weight, 4, 11, 20–21, 25, 26, 61, 63, 64, 67–68, 70, 75–76, 109–10, 183, 190, 197–98, 204–5, 206–7, 308, 315n.12, 319
Contact Improvisation in Asia, 260–61, 291
Beijing Contact Improvisation, 292, 293, 294 (see also Liao, Shuyi; Shi, Junhao)
Chak-Yin, Mui, 261 (see also Hong Kong Academy for Performing Arts)
Chengdu Contact Improvisation Community, 293–94, 295 (see also Chen Shan)
Cheuk-yin, Mui, 291–92
CI communities across mainland China, 261, 293, 301
Contact Improv Beijing, 292 (see also Liao, Shuyi)
Contact Improvisation Chinese Research Group, 295 (see also Haolong, Yin)
"Contact Point" community, 291–92 (see also Cheuk-yin, Mui)
(English) language barrier, the, 302
first classes in 1992, 291 (see also Ku, Ming-Shen)
Ge, Huichao, 260–61, 292 (see also TOUCH Contact Improvisation Dance Festival
Gu, Mingxin, 292
iDance Network and Festival between China, Hong Kong, Japan, Korea and Taiwan, 261, 298, 300 (see also Ku, Ming-Shen)
i-dance Taipei International Dance Improvisation Festival, 291
Ki, 156–57, 249–50 (see also Ki)
Ku, Ming-Shen, 260–61, 291–92, 296 (see also KU & Dancers)
Liao, Shuyi, 292 (see also Contact Improv Beijing)
Maru, 261, 294–95 (see also DanceAbility; Symbiosis Nice Dance Company)
"New Journey Dance Exhibition" (1992) duet with Paxton, 291 (see also Ku, Ming-Shen)
Shanghai Contact Improvisation Community and Festival, 291 (see also Cheng, Iris)
Sposetti, Irene, 292, 293, 298
Tai Chi (see Tai Chi)
translating CQ writings into Chinese (see Haolong, Yin)
TOUCH Contact Improvisation Festival, Teacher Exchange Conference and Community Conference, 261, 292–93, 295 (see also Ge, Dew)
Wang, Yuting, 260–61
Ying, Hou/Hou Ying Dance Theater, 292, 297
Contact Improvisation in Brazil, 303. See also Contact Improvisation for the "differently-abled"
Capoeria, 109–10
Compandeia 100 Habilidades, 261
DanceAbility Brazil project, 306

disability activism, 303, 304–5
Duschenes, Maria, 305–6 (see also Duschenes, Maria; Laban)
Extrema Direita (Far Right), 309 (see also Teixeira, Ana Carolina Bezerra)
improvisation as a survival practice, 307
mixed-ability dance companies, 261, 303, 305
Roda Viva Company Dance, 261, 304, 310 (see also Amoedo, Henrique)
Vianna, Angel, 306–7
Zarvos, Neca, 306 (see also Alessi, Alito; DanceAbility)
Contact Improvisation in China. See Contact Improvisation in Asia
Contact Improvisation in India, 276–77. See also Michalska, Adrianna; Muhanty, Ashutosh; Ningappa, Shilash; Priya, Geethi; Suraj, Guru
Art of Improvisation residency, 286
British colonial influence, 278
caste, 9, 260, 277–78, 285–86, 288 (see also Ambedkar, Bhimrao Ramji; Mitra, Royona)
Contact Improv India (2016), 279–80, 285 (see also Suraj, Guru)
creating a CI community, 279–82
deconstructing student-teacher power dynamics, 288
early historiography and context, 277–80
financial accessibility, 286
first Contact Improvisation performance (2017), 281–82
Goa Contact Festival, 260, 278–80, 283–84, 289
inclusion and equality, 277, 286, 288
InContact collective (2021), 260, 279–80
Indian Contact Improvisation Teacher Exchange, 289 (see also Kaufman, Erica)
Jaipur Art Summit workshop vandalized, 280–81
Mitra, Royona, critique of, 285 (see also Mitra, Royona)
physical contact stigmatized, 282–83
question of sexuality, the, 283–84
teachers in India, 278, 280, 289
touching across gender and caste, 282
Untouchables, the/ Dalit caste, 260, 277–78, 282–83 (see also Priya, Geethi)
Ziarat Project with Tibetan opera artists, 287
Contact Improvisation in Mexico. See also EPIICO feminist collective
ancestral wisdom, 264
Artistic Liaison Entity of the Tlatelolco Cultural Center 264–65
Center for Choreographic Research of the Institute of Beaux-Arts, 266
"communitarian-territorial feminism," 259–60, 264
economic affordability, 266, 268–69, 271
Fifth Gathering of Contact Improvisation in Mexico (2020), 267
impact of COVID-19 pandemic, 267–68
Seventh Gathering of Contact Improvisation in Patzcuaro, 268–71
against whiteness (blanquitud), 264

348 Index

Contact Improvisation in Québec, 21, 25, 28, 34.
 See also Bolster, Gurney; Catpoto; Davida,
 Dena; Gaudreau, Stéphanie; Ginzberg, Evelyne;
 Godbout, Daniel; Harwood, Carole; Harwood,
 Andrew; teaching Contact Improvisation
Contact Improvisation jams, 51, 53, 100, 179–80, 186,
 190, 293–94, 299, 336n.1
 affinity jams (queer and BIPOC), 10–11, 76–77
 Burlington annual jam, 49
 A Capella Motion, 245
 Catpoto Montréal jams, 28
 Chicago Jam, 14, 42, 51, 52, 53, 54, 55–57, 241, 244
 focus on gender, 69–70
 jam guidelines, 46, 75, 317–18
 Mexico, in, 268
 open jams, 37, 38, 39t, 42, 266
 Philadelphia Thursday Jam, 46
 shared jam guidelines compendium, 46
 social spaces, as, 5–6
 wcciJam (2018), 41
Contact Improvisation practice
 artivism, as, 22, 25
 "a community of experience," as a, 21 (*see also*
  Novack, Cynthia)
 democratic ethos, as a, 5–6, 13
 feminist empowerment, as, 32
 form of postmodern dance, as a, 13, 29–30, 31
 fostering community building, 15, 82, 291
 migration, as a practice of, 319
 network, as a, 4, 28
 purely physical practice, as a, 26, 266 (*see also* neutral
  body, the; Paxton, Steve)
 recreation, as, 3–4, 38, 72
 skilled movement form, as a, 4, 100, 101
 spiritual form, as a, 245–48, 301 (*see also* Laursen, Carol)
 therapy/therapeutic practice, as, 3–4, 154, 194,
  196, 198, 209–10, 239 (*see also* Brandes, Aaron;
  Restorative Contact; Revlock, Gabrielle)
 touch revolution, as a, 111, 183–84 (*see also*
  Nelson, Karen)
 vehicle for social change, as a, 264
 white North American artsport, as a form of, 105
Contact Improvisation writing
 Contact Quarterly, in the (*see* Contact Quarterly)
 Contact Quarterly's set of books published, 112
 Encounters with Contact, 5n.4
 Gravity (see *Gravity*; Paxton, Steve)
 Nancy Stark Smith's writings/legacy in *Contact
  Quarterly*, 150
 research, 34
 Steve Paxton's early writings, 315–16
 Steve Paxton's writings in *Contact Quarterly*, 311, 312
Contact Meets Contemporary, 117–18. *See also* Contact
  Improvisation events
Contact Newsletter (*1975*), 4. See also *Contact
  Quarterly*; Smith, Nancy Stark
Contact Quarterly: A Vehicle for Moving Ideas, 140n.1.
  See also *Contact Newsletter*; Bartley, Coleen;
  Nelson, Lisa; Stark Smith, Nancy
 accounts of classes, 328

college issue, the, 5
CQ Unbound, 159n.2
creating a "contacts" list, 4
Dance Jam Guide, 142
discussing forum for the form, 26, 110
improvisation and philosophy folio, 111
mobilizing Black radical tradition, 113, 164 (*see also*
  Moten, Fred)
Nancy Stark Smith's writings/legacy, 5, 7, 150
newsletters in the, 259
publisher of a set of books, 112
publishing Body-Mind Centering® writing, 132 (*see
  also* Body-Mind Centering®)
sexuality and identity issues, 317–18
Steve Paxton's writings, 312, 315–16
survey of teaching issues, 262
translations for Chinese research group, 261, 295 (*see
  also* Haolong, Yin)
Contact touring network, 28. *See also* Banes, Sally
Cortés, Jordi, 324n.28. See also *Liant la Troca* group
The Cost of Living, 323–24. *See also* DV8;
  Newson, Lloyd
countercultures of the 1960s and 1970s 33, 65, 108, 111.
  See also hippie countercultures
COVID-19 pandemic (lockdown), 54, 106–7. *See also*
  Jackson, Kellyn
 adapting the TOUCH activities, 293 (*see also*
  TOUCH Improvisation Festival)
 Contact Improvisation with quarantining partners,
  205
 Critical Mass: CI @ 50, at, 4–5, 8
 effects on CI in China, 297, 300
 effects on the EPIICO collective, 267 (*see also* EPIICO)
 impact on Restorative Contact pedagogy, 205
 modifying the EPIICO practice, 267
 social distancing, 38
 teaching CI online, 197, 205, 209–10, 260–61
Crenshaw, Kimberlé, 64–65. *See also* intersectionality
Critical Mass: CI @ 50, 8–11, 166. See also Albright,
  Ann Cooper; CI events
 consent and diversity issues at, 9–10, 32–33, 226
 curation of, 4–6, 7–9, 11
 emergence of an anthology, 10–11
 exhibition on Nancy Stark Smith, 147
 reckoning with Contact Improvisation's past history,
  55, 136–37, 242
 Underscore at, 10, 143, 144n.3, 144n.4, 145–47
 workshops at, 20–21, 251 (*see also* Underscore)
 writers' workshop at, 2, 241–42, 296
Crowley, Patrick, 146–47. *See also* teaching Contact
  Improvisation; Underscore, the
Cultivating the Empty Field, 254. *See also* Hongzhi
Cunningham, Merce, 125–26, 130
 masculinist, as, 125–26
 neutral body, the, 16 (*see also* body, the)
 objectivist modernism of, 126
 repudiation of the natural body, 125–26 (*see also*
  body, the)
Curtis, Bruce, 320. *See also* "Exposed to Gravity";
  wheelchair, first performances

da Silva, Denise Ferreira, 91, 103. *See also* colonialism
Dalai Lama, 246
Daly, Ann, 16, 124. *See also* Duncan, Isadora; feminism
Damasio, Antonio, 170. See *The Strange Order of Things: Life, Feeling, and the Meaning of Cultures*
DanceAbility, 294, 324. *See also* Alessi, Alito; Contact Improvisation and differently abled bodies; Polo, Mª Paz Brozas; wheelchair
  classes in Brazil, in, 306 (*see also* Alessi, Alito; Zarvos, Neca)
  classes in China, in, 294–95 (*see also* Maru)
  creating a methodology, 294 (*see also* Alessi, Alito; Nelson, Karen)
  first explorations, 294
  wheelchair (*see* wheelchair, the)
Dance Studies Association annual conference (2022), 32–33
Dances That Describe Themselves, 111–12. *See also* Foster, Susan Leigh; Novack, Cynthia
Danza sin fin film, 324. *See also* Becker, Carolina; Carbonell, Paquita Ferragut; *el Aula de Artes del Cuerpo* dance community
Dartington College of Arts, 259. *See also* Fulkerson, Mary; Paxton, Steve
Davida, Dena. *See also* Catpoto Dance Collective; *Each Man for Herself*; New Age movement of the '70s; *Pièce de resistance*; teaching Contact Improvisation
  CI informal touring network, 28
  Contact Improvisation as a feminist practice, 20, 29–30
  formulating a framework for teaching CI, 26
  founding/curating Tangente (1980–2021), 25–26, 28
  hosting panel "Global and Local: Facilitating Contact Improvisation in Different Communities" at Critical Mass: CI @ 50, 33
  learning CI in Minnesota with Mary Cerny, 23
  performing in museums and galleries, 28
  shift from modern to postmodern dancing, 22–23
  teaching CI at the *Université du Québec*, 27n.6
  teaching first community CI classes in Québec, 26
Deleuze, Gilles, 155–56, 228, 231, 232–33. *See also* Schultis, Brian
  forms of spatialization, 228
  spatio-temporal dynamisms, 231
Democracy's Body, 21. *See also* Banes, Sally; Judson Dance Theater
Dowd, Irene, 127. *See also* somatics; Todd, Mabel
DuBois, W. E. B, 308–9. See also *The Souls of Black Folk*
Dumit, Joseph, 164–65n.9, 262. *See also* Jensen, Dorte Bjerre; teaching Contact Improvisation
Duncan, Isadora, 16, 122, 124. *See also* Alexander, F. M.
  claims for a "universal body," 124 (*see also* Daly, Ann)
  classical Greek sources, 16, 124
  derision for Black and Native American dances, 124–25
  natural dancing body, the, 16, 122, 124
  primitive body, the, 125
Duschenes, Maria, 305–6. *See also* Laban, Rudolf
DV8, 323–24. See also *The Cost of Living*; Newson, Lloyd

Each Man for Herself. See also Davida, Dena; Godbout, Daniel
Earthdance, 6, 140n.1, 195, 297. *See also* Young, Sarah
  founding principles, 140n.1
  Future of CI conference (April 2021), 318
  truth and reconciliation process (2019), 55
Ecstatic Dance, 37
"The Effect of Touch in Contact Improvisation on Affect, Stress, Sense of Connectedness and Sense of Self," 208–9. *See also* Puhr, Ariane
el Aula de Artes del Cuerpo dance community, 324. *See also Danza sin fin* film
Encounters with Contact, 5n.4
Enlivening Spirits, 256. *See also* LaMothe, Kimerer; Shakers, the
EPIICO feminist collective (acronym in Spanish for Space of Practice and Investigation into Contact Improvisation), 259–60, 264, 265f, 266, 270. *See also* Contact Improvisation in Mexico; teaching Contact Improvisation
  EPIICO collective profile, 264
  excluding certain forms of masculinity, 266
  mixed-race bodies (*cuerpo mestizo*), 264 (*see also* body, the)
  racialized, lower-middle class women from the city's periphery, 264
  taking care of women and the land, 273–74
  Zapatista principles, 259–60, 274 (*see also* National Indigenous Council)
eroticism, 15–16, 20–21, 110, 187–88, 200. *See also* Lorde, Audre; Vionnet, Claire
Espacio Formación Contact Improvisation Madrid (FCI), 155, 213–14. See also *Body-Mind Centering®*; Bonilla, Diana; Boullosa, Cristiane; Contact Improvisation and queer sexuality; Gracia, Patricia
Espinosa, Roser López, 324. *See also* Europe Beyond Access; *Lines Forces; wheelchair, the*
ethics, 20, 32–33, 103, 114, 141, 154, 177, 179–80, 200, 221, 246
Eugenics Education Society, 127. *See also* Alexander, F. M.; Saleeby, Caleb Williams
Europe Beyond Access, 324. *See also* Espinosa, Roser López; *Lines Forces*; wheelchair, the
exclusion/inclusivity, 16, 20–21, 77, 85, 108, 115, 122–23, 124–25, 135, 241, 303, 304, 308–9, 310
"Exposed to Gravity," 320. *See also* Curtis, Bruce; wheelchair, the

Feld, Robin, 108
feminism, 13–15, 16. *See also* Davida, Dena; gender; Vionnet, Claire
  Black feminism, 114 (*see also* Audre Lorde)
  communitarian-territorial feminism, 259–60, 264, 273–74 (*see also* EPIICO)
  consent (*see* consent culture)
  Duncan, Isadora (*see* Duncan, Isadora)
  EPIICO feminist collective (*see* EPIICO)
  feminist rage, 187
  feminist sexual/social revolutions, 25, 212–13

350   Index

feminism (*cont.*)
feminist studies, 5, 14–15
#Metoo movement/protests, 13, 20
Pièce de resistance (*see* Davida, Dena)
sexism, 69
white women in Second Wave feminism, 20
women lifting men, 29, 61–62, 71–72, 110, 133 (*see also* Davida, Dena; *Each Man for Herself*)
in XCI, 212, 221 (*see also* XCI)
"Feminist Killjoys (and Other Willful Subjects)," 106. *See also* Ahmed, Sara
foreign teachers, 267–68, 272, 278, 280, 289
Forti, Simone. *See also* postmodern dance
developed Crescent Roll study, 231
on teaching, 333–34
transcending the structure, 262
Foster, Susan. *See also* Bull, Richard
book on Richard Bull's improvisation, 2
Dances that Describe Themselves, 111–12 (*see also* Novack, Cynthia)
Four Doors to Meeting for Worship, 251. *See also* Tabor, Bill
Franco, Ariadna. *See* EPIICO; *The Future of Contact Improvisation* conference
Freiburg Festival. *See* Contact Improvisation events
Freud, Sigmund, 200, 202
Friere, Ilda. *See* Espacio Formación Contact Improvisation Madrid (FCI); teaching Contact Improvisation
Fulkerson, Mary (1920–2008), 23. *See also* Dartington College of Arts; teaching Contact Improvisation
The Future of Contact Improvisation conference, 6–7. *See also* Arisman, Jolyn; Chan, Sze-Wei; contentious issues; Franco, Ariadna; Harville, India; Horrigan, Kristin; Thielen, Diana

Gaudreau, Stéphanie, 34. *See also* Contact Improvisation in Québec; teaching Contact Improvisation
gaze, the. *See also* the audience
audience, 164
black body, of the, 84
male gaze, 31–32
predator, of the, 164
soft gaze (soft focus)
white gaze, 111–12
Ge, Huichao (Dew), 260–61, 292–93, 295, 297. *See also* Contact Improvisation in Asia, caste; TOUCH Contact Improvisation Festival, Teacher Exchange Conference and Community Conference in China; teaching Contact Improvisation; Ying, Hou
Geethi, Priya, 282–83. *See also* Contact Improvisation in India, the Untouchables; teaching Contact Improvisation
gender, 62, 63, 65. *See also* feminism; queering Contact Improvisation; XCI
CI as gender progressive in the 1970s, 65
discrimination, 72–73

embodiment, 64, 213–14 (*see also* queerness, Queer Tango)
expression, 14–15, 63–64, 67, 68
gender affirming choices, 66
gender embodiment, 67–68
gender identity, 14–15, 63, 71–72
gender socialization, 14–15, 63, 68
hetereonormative/ cisgender dynamics, 66, 69, 70–71
homophobia/ transphobia, 62, 69
intersectionality, 64 (*see also* Crenshaw, Kimberlé)
Moving Rasa, a BIPOC practice, 77 (*see also* Suseno, Andrew)
objectification, 69–70, 73 (*see also* Hannaford, Zara)
power dynamics, 66–67
trans/ non-binary/ transgender, 69–70
Genjokoan, 253. *See also* Zenji Dogen
Gibson, James Jerome
important reference for Steve Paxton, 233
sense organs as an active perceptual system, 162, 166, 234, 239
The Senses Considered as Perceptual Systems 162, 233
Ginzberg, Evelyn. *See* Catpoto Dance Collective; teaching Contact Improvisation
Glissant, Édouard
"creolizing of Being," 114, 335
"in exchange we change," 335
Global Underscore team, 8. *See also* Young, Sarah; Underscore
Goa Contact Festival in India (2010+). *See* Contact Improvisation in India, Goa Contact Festival
Godard, Hubert, 160. *See* Emma Bigé
Godbout, Daniel. *See* Davida, Dena; *Each Man for Herself*; teaching Contact Improvisation
Goldberg Variations. See Paxton, Steve
Goldman, Danielle, 114
Gottlieb, Sara, 221
Gottschild, Brenda Dixon, 2
Gracia, Patricia, 213–14. *See also* Body-Mind Centering®; Espacio Formación Contact Improvisation Madrid; teaching Contact Improvisation
Graham, Martha, 16, 125, 128, 130
Grand Union, 2, 3, 23, 239, 247. *See also* Judson Dance Theater; Paxton, Steve; postmodern dance; Siddall, Curt; Smith, Nancy Stark; Woodberry, David
Gravity, 160. *See also* Paxton, Steve
gravity, 3, 13–153, 159–60, 161, 167–68, 174, 182, 190, 196, 198, 202, 234, 282, 320, 330, 335. *See also* Paxton, Steve; small dance, the; Tomatis, Alfred
Greene, Lisa Claire, 156
CI and neuroplasticity, 237, 239, 240, 267
similarities between CI and CBT (*see* Cognitive Behavioral Therapy)
Guattari, Félix, 155–56, 228, 232–33. *See also* Deleuze, Gilles; Schultis, Brian

Halprin, Anna, 305–6
Hannaford, Zara, 73. *See also* gender, objectification

Haolong, Yin, 295. *See also* Contact Improvisation Chinese Research Group; Contact Improvisation conferences and festivals, Dali Contact Improvisation Festival; Contact Improvisation in Asia, translating CQ writings into Chinese; teaching Contact Improvisation

Haraway, Donna, 188–89

Harville, India, 6. See also *The Future of Contact Improvisation* conference

Harwood, Andrew, 26, 28n.7. *See also* Contact Improvisation in Québec; teaching Contact Improvisation

Harwood, Carol, 26–27. *See also* Catpoto Dance Collective; teaching Contact Improvisation

H'Doubler, Margaret, 127. *See also* body, the natural body and the primitive body

Hennessey, Keith, 20–21, 195, 336n.1. See also *Questioning Contact Improvisation*; teaching Contact Improvisation

hippie counterculture, 2, 101, 111, 278–79. *See also* Davida, Dena; Goa Contact Festival

Holding the Tension of the Opposites lecture, 257. *See also* Authentic movement; Woodman, Marion

Holland, Fred, 15–16, 105–6, 108–9. See also *Contact at 10th and 2nd* performance; Houston-Jones, Ishmael; St. Mark's Church Performance Space; *Untitled (Oo-Ga-La)*; Wrong Contact Manifesto; teaching Contact Improvisation

hong, elle, DJ for Underscore, 145. *See also* Underscore

Hong Kong Academy for Performing Arts, 291–92. *See also* Chak-yin, Mui

Hongzhi, 254. See also *Cultivating the Empty Field*; Zen Buddhism

Horrigan, Kristin, 6, 14–15, 107. *See also* Earthdance; *The Future of Contact Improvisation* conference; teaching Contact Improvisation

Houston-Jones, Ishmael, 15–16, 105–6, 108–9. See also *Contact at 10th and 2nd* performance; Holland, Fred; St. Mark's Church Performance Space; *Untitled (Oo-Ga-La)*; Wrong Contact Manifesto; teaching Contact Improvisation

"How touch facilitates encounters with Otherness and the vocabulary from Contact Improvisation" PhD dissertation, 192. *See also* Smith, Rosalind Holgate

Huxley, Aldous, 256

I and Thou, 207–8. *See also* Buber, Martin

Ideokinesis, 127, 128. *See also* Dowd, Irene; Todd, Mabel Elsworth; Sweigard, Lulu

Improvising While Black, 16, 77, 106, 113, 135, 164. *See also* brooks, mayfield

InContact collective, 260, 279–80. *See also* Contact Improvisation in India

Influx & Efflux, 183. *See also* Bennett, Jane

Ingold, Tim, 155–56, 227–28, 232

injury, 4, 22–23, 131, 153–54, 190, 320

intersectionality, 64–65, 268. *See also* Crenshaw, Kimberlé

Jackson, Kellyn, 144, 144n.4. *See also* Critical Mass CI @ 50; *Underscore Unwound*; teaching Contact Improvisation

Jensen, Dorte Bjerre, 262. *See also* Dumit, Joseph; teaching Contact Improvisation

John Weber Gallery in New York City, 15–16, 34, 65. *See also* CHUTE, the film (1972)

Johnson, Pam, 168. *See also* "Theorizing Off-Balance"

Jonathan David, 104. *See also* "Improvisation in African American Vernacular Dancing"

Judson Dance Theatre, 2, 21, 34. *See also* Grand Union; Judson Memorial Church, at; postmodern dance; Rainer, Yvonne

Jung, Carl, 246–47

Kabat-Zinn, Jon, 199. *See also* Mindfulness-Based Stress Reduction (MBSR)

Kaufman, Erica, 289. *See also* Indian Contact Improvisation Teacher Exchange; teaching Contact Improvisation

Kelley, Prema, 146–47. *See also* Underscore, the; teaching Contact Improvisation

Keogh, Martin, 40–41, 252, 293. *See also* teaching Contact Improvisation

Ki, 156–57, 249–50

Kim, Richard, 38, 74. *See also* Contact Improvisation conferences, Consent Culture in CI Symposium; teaching Contact Improvisation

kinesthesia, 4, 19, 23, 162, 167–68, 305–6. *See also* kinesthetic empathy

kinesthetic empathy, 22, 206. *See also* Reynolds, Dee; Reason, Matthew

Konjar, Jurij, 7, 156, 239. *See also* teaching Contact Improvisation

Kreiter, Jo, 31. *See also* teaching Contact Improvisation

Kripalu Center for Yoga, 194–95

KU & Dancers, Taiwan, 261, 291, 298–99, 302. *See also* Chengwei, Xu; Contact Improvisation in Asia; Contact Improvisation in Asia, first classes in 1992; Ku, Ming-Shen

Laban, Rudolf, 305–6. *See also* Choral Dance; Duschenes, Maria

Laban Movement Analysis, 27

Laban's Kinesphere, 143

Nazi connection, and his, 143

LaMothe, Kimerer, 256–57. See also *Enlivening Spirits*; Shakers, the

Lapierre, Aline, 179–80

Laursen, Carole, 156–57. *See also* Contact Improvisation and spirituality

Lee, Rythea, 9, 75, 146–47. See also *Underscore Unwound*

LeFan, John, 29. *See also* Catpoto; Mangrove Dance Collective; teaching Contact Improvisation

Leighton, Taigen Dan, 253–54. *See also* Buddhism; Contact Improvisation and spirituality

Lepkoff, Daniel, 199, 291–92, 295–96, 335. *See also* teaching Contact Improvisation

352 Index

Liant la Troca group, 324n.28. *See also* Contact Improvisation in Spain; Cortés Jordi

Liao, Shyui, 292, 293, 294, 295. *See* Contact Improvisation in Asia, Contact Improv Beijing; teaching Contact Improvisation

Lines Forces, 324. *See also* Espinosa, Roser López; Europe Beyond Access; wheelchair, the

Listening Sprituality, 252. *See also* Loring, Patricia; Quakerism

listening touch, 154, 164–65, 177–78, 191. *See also* Bassel, Leah; Bennett, Jane
  accompanying, 192
  Cellular Touch (see *Cellular Touch*)
  hovering, 182, 190
  listening in action, 187–88, 190

Little, Nita, 3–4, 65, 181, 184, 195, 198–99, 219, 332–33, 335. *See also* teaching Contact Improvisation, CI as research; "You come. We'll show you what we do" tour (1973)
  body-mind as attention in motion, 332–33
  "enminding," 335
  oscillating attention, 219, 221–22

Lorde, Audre, 110, 187–88, 202. *See also* black body, the; Contact Improvisation, contentious issues; feminism

Loring, Patricia, 252. See also *Listening Sprituality*; Quakerism

Magnesium performance, 1, 3, 7, 34, 65, 148–49, 198, 239, 241. *See also* Oberlin College; Paxton, Steve

Mangrove Dance Collective, 28n.7, 29. *See also* Brown, Byron; LeFan, John; Siddall, Curt; Tyler, James

Manning, Erin, 189, 220–22

Manuel, Zenzu Earthlyn, 254. See also *The Way of Tenderness: Awakening Through Race, Sexuality, and Gender*

martial arts influence in Contact Improvisation, 3, 159n.3, 166, 237, 248, 283, 302, 328. *See also* Aikido

Martin, Betty, 208. *See also* "The Wheel of Consent"

Maru, 261, 294–95. *See also* Contact Improvisation in Asia; DanceAbility
  integration of differently abled bodies, 294–95
  Symbiosis Dance, 294–95

Marx, Karl, 109

Material for the Spine, 233. *See also* Paxton, Steve

#MeToo movement/protests, 13, 20–21, 33, 38, 43, 51, 56. *See also* feminism

McCalman, Caroline, 190. *See also* stewardship

McConnel, Susan, 203–4

McIntyre, Dianne, 3. *See also* Sounds in Motion

McLeod, Shaun, 189–90. *See also* Authentic Movement

Michalska, Adrianna, 7n.6, 8, 9, 66, 241, 260, 276, 279–80. *See also* Contact Improvisation in India; CI @ 50 zine; InContact collective; Suraj, Guru; teaching Contact Improvisation

Mitra, Royona, 20, 29, 33, 76, 285, 286, 312n.6. *See also* Contact Improvisation in India, Mitra, Royona, critique of; "Unmaking Contact: Choreographic Touch at the Intersection of Race, Caste, and Gender"

modern dance, 16, 19–20, 23–25, 128, 134, 293, 298. *See also* Cunningham, Merce; Duncan, Isadora; Graham, Martha; H'Doubler, Magaret; Shawn, Ted
  authoritarian, as, 22–23
  Eurocentrism, 122
  exclusionary and racist, as, 2
  freedom and liberation, as, 129–30
  as masculinist, 125–26
  natural body, the, 16, 122, 125, 127
  neutral body, the, 129
  somatics, and, 122–23, 127 (*see also* somatics)
  Steve Paxton and, 129–30

Morrissey, Charlie, 178–79, 178n.3. *See also* Simson, Kirstie; *Unwanting Hands* exercise

Moten, Fred, 16, 104, 109, 111–12, 113–14, 332. *See also* Black/African-American Arts movement, the

Moving Rasa, 77. *See also* BIPOC participation in Contact Improvisation; Suseno, Andrew

Muhanty, Ashutosh, 279. *See also* Contact Improvisation in India

Myers, Tom, 195. *See also* Anatomy Trains Structural Integration Certification Program

Nachmanovitch, Stephen, 256. See also *The Art of Is: Improvising as a Way of Life*

Nagrin, Daniel, 3. *See also* Workgroup

Naropa Institute, 259

National Indigenous Council, 274. *See also* EPIICO, Zapatista principles

natural body, the, 16, 122–23, 133, 134, 135–36. *See also* Alexander, F. M.; modern dance; neutral body, the; primitive body, the
  Contact Improvisation and the, 131
  Isadora Duncan's vision of the, 124–25 (*see also* Duncan, Isadora)
  Margaret H'Doubler's pure, non-sexualized, 127 (*see also* H'Doubler, Margaret)
  Merce Cunningham's repudiaton of, 125–26 (*see also* Cunningham, Merce)

NCI practice (Not Contact Improvisation), 82–83, 84, 86, 102. *See also* Smith, Joy Mariama
  connection, 98
  consent, 86
  fluids, 93
  questions, 90, 91, 93, 97
  resisting homogeneity, 100
  rest, 96
  safety, 89
  trust, 89

Nelson, Karen, 41, 195, 291–92, 320. *See also* teaching Contact Improvisation
  conversation with mayfield Brooks, in, 164
  teaching mixed-ability with Alito Alessi, 294
  "Touch Revolution," 111, 183–84 (*see also* Nelson, Karen)

Nelson, Lisa, 3, 4, 108, 140n.1, 291–92, 295–96, 298, 328. See also *Contact Quarterly*

neoliberalism, 261, 303, 310. *See also* capitalism

neurobiology, 153–54. *See also* Gibson, James Jerome; gravity
  co-experience/resonance, 171
  fields of information, 165 (*see also* Siegel, Daniel J.)
  interpersonal neurobiology, 164–65n.9, 165 (*see also* Siegal, Daniel J.)

neuroception, 166–67. *See also* Porges, Stephen

neurophysiology, 209. *See also* Prescott, James

neuroplasticity, 237, 239, 240

neutral body, the, 16, 122–23, 128–30, 131, 132, 133–36, 317–18. *See also* natural body, the; Paxton, Steve; primitive body, the; Todd, Mabel

new materialist theories, 154, 177, 180–81, 183–84. *See also* Barad, Karen; Bennet, Jane

Newson, Lloyd, 323–24. *See also* DV8; *The Cost of Living*

Ningappa, Ahilash, 279. *See also* Contact Improvisation in India; teaching Contact Improvisation

"No Manifesto," 23. *See also* postmodern dance; Rainer, Yvonne; Trio A

Novack, Cynthia (aka Cynthia Jean Cohen Bull) (1947–1996), 3–4, 19, 21, 111, 112, 129. *See also* Bull, Richard; Foster, Susan; *Sharing the Dance: Contact Improvisation and American Culture*; *Dances That Describe Themselves*
  Contact Improvisation's "community of experience," 21
  Contact Improvisation as a white American movement culture, 111, 112
  tradition of sharing the dance, 329

Novella, Caro, 221. *See also* XCI

Oberlin College, 1, 238. *See also* CI @ 25; *Critical Mass: CI @ 50*; *Magnesium*; Smith, Nancy Stark; Warner Main Space/ Warner gymnasium
  Ann Cooper Albright's teaching at, 5, 7
  CI@25 at, 7
  Collective Gestures: The Impact of Experimental Performance at Oberlin in the 1970s, 8 (see also *Critical Mass: CI @ 50*)
  Grand Union residency at, 3
  hosting Critical Mass: CI @ 50, 1–2, 8, 166 (*see also* Albright, Ann Cooper)
  Jurij Konjar's intensive workshop at, 156
  Magnesium (January 1972) performance at (see *Magnesium*; Paxton, Steve)
  Underscore performance at, 146, 147

Olaya, Aramo, 155. *See also* Freire, Ilda; queerness, Queer Tango; XCI
  created reflection group at Espacio Formación Contact Improvisation Madrid (FCI), 155
  organized Touch & Play Barcelona 2019, 214–15

Oliveros, Pauline 1932–2016), 104, 153, 174. *See also* Center for Deep Listening; *Quantum Listening*

"Open Bodies: (X)changes of identity in Capoeira and Contact Improvisation," 109–10. *See also* Albright, Ann Cooper

Orientations, Objects, Others, 311n.1 *See also* Ahmed, Sara

osteopathy, 164n.8, 164–65n.9. *See also* listening touch

Others/Otherness, 154, 177, 183–84, 187, 192, 313, 318–19

Overland, Patty, 320. *See also* Curtis, Bruce

Paxton, Steve (1939–2024), 237–38, 249, 254–55
  on aesthetic freedom, 129–30
  Aikido, Crescent and Helix rolls, 64, 248 (*see also* Forti, Simone)
  body's reflexive response to physical forces, 40, 129
  Contact at 10th and 2nd, 108
  Contact Improvisation as aesthetic freedom, 129–30
  Drafting Interior Techniques, 247
  early writings, 315–16
  "founder's lineage," 7
  Goldberg Variations, 7
  Grand Union, with, 3
  Gravity, 160
  "The Initiation of Contact Improvisation for Me," 245–47
  instigating Contact Improvisation, 19, 64
  Judson Dance Theater, with (*see* Judson Dance Theater)
  Magnesium performance (1972) (*see Magnesium*; Warner Main Space)
  Material for the Spine, 233
  neutral body, the, 40, 128, 129, 132 (*see also* neutral body, the)
  on power relations and politics, 129–30
  on predation, 74
  retrospective at Dia Beacon, NY, 7
  ReUnion tour (1975), 4
  rolling, 231 (*see also* Contact Improvisation fundamentals, rolling)
  "spherical space," 198
  The Stand/ the small dance (*see* The Stand/ the small dance)
  on teaching, 328
  teaching in Taiwan, 298
  teaching regularly at Dartington College of Arts, 259
  on women supporting men, on, 29
  writings in *Contact Quarterly*, 312, 315–16
  "You come. We'll show you what we do" tour, 3–4

Pièce de resistance, 29–30. *See also* Davida, Dena

Polo, Mª Paz Brozas, 261–62. *See also* Ahmed, Sara; ANQA Danse avec roues, Contact Improvisation and differently abled bodies; *Triàdico entre lineas* and *Triàdico sobre papel*; *Queer Phenomenology*

Porges, Stephen, 166–67. *See also* neuroception

postmodern dance, 2, 8, 13, 19, 21, 22–23, 29–30, 31, 34, 291–92. *See also* Banes, Sally; Gottschild, Brenda Dixon; Grand Union; Judson Dance Theater; Judson Memorial Church; Rainer, Yvonne

Povinelli, Elizabeth, 221–22. *See also* consent culture

Prakash, Brahma, 277–78. *See also* Contact Improvisation in India, caste

Prescott, James, 209. *See also* neurophysiology

354 Index

Ptashek, Alan, 108, 320. See also *Contact at 10th and 2nd*; Curtis, Bruce; wheelchair, the
Puhr, Ariane, 208–9. *See also* "The Effect of Touch in Contact Improvisation on Affect, Stress, Sense of Connectedness and Sense of Self"

Quakerism and Contact Improvisation, 250. *See also* Contact Improvisation and spirituality
  Doors to Meeting for Worship, 251 (*see also* Tabor, Bill)
  expectant waiting, 157, 247–48, 250
  "friends of the truth," 250
  improvisational worship, 250
  inner search in a collective setting, 250
  listening body, the, 252
  Listening Spirituality, 252 (*see also* Loring, Patricia)
Quantum Listening, 104. *See also* Oliveros, Pauline
"Queer Contact Improvisation (QCI)," 214. *See also* Skrzypczak, Wiktor
Queer Phenomenology: Orientations, Objects, Others, 223, 261–62, 311, 311n.1, 313–14, 316, 317, 325. *See also* Ahmed, Sara; queerness
queerness/ to queer, 13, 14–15, 66, 70, 71–73, 76–77, 313. *See also* Contact Improvisation, affinity jams; Ahmed, Sara; XCI; Touch & Play; *Queer Phenomenology: Orientations, Objects, Others*
  affinity spaces/ events/ jams, 9, 76–77, 317–18
  disorientation, as, 315
  queer activists in Contact Improvisarion, 221
  queer anarchist movements in Spain, 155, 212–13
  queer as a utopian action, 318
  queer as identity ("I am queer"), 261–62, 313
  queer cultural theory, 14–15 (*see also* Ahmed, Sara; gender)
  queer politics, 212
  queer sexuality, 155, 212–16, 217–19, 220–21 (*see also* XCI)
  Queer Tango, 155, 213–14
  queering Contact Improvisation, 317, 318
Questioning Contact Improvisation, 20, 126, 318n.16 *See also* Contact Improvisation critics/ critiques; Hennessey, Keith

racism, 3, 5–6, 10–11, 55, 62, 107, 109, 115, 116, 117, 133, 135, 241, 279–80, 307
Radler, Karen, 3–4. *See also* "You come. We'll show you what we do"
Rainer, Yvonne, 23. *See also* Judson Dance Theater; "No Manifesto"; postmodern dance; *Trio A*
rape culture, 38, 39*t*, 40, 41*t*, 41–42, 43, 44, 45, 47, 49, 51–52, 53
Reason, Matthew Reynolds, 206. *See also* kinesthetic empathy; Reynolds, Dee
Reich, William, 222, 222n.7. *See also* somatics
Respecting Boundaries/Co-existing Genders zine (2016), 74. *See also* gender
Response Protocol Working Group, 55–56. *See also* jams, Chicago Jam; Schaffer, Sarah
Restorative Contact, 154–55, 207–8. *See also* Revlock, Gabrielle
  attunement, 206
  during COVID-19 lockdown, 205

  depth of touch, 208
  embodied listening, 207–8
  kinesthetic empathy, 206
  passive body weight, 206–7
  reciprocal touch, 204–5
  relational existence, 207–8 (*see also* Buber, Martin)
  slowness and stillness, 196–97, 206–7
  sustained compression, 196, 197–99, 208
ReUnion Tour (1975), 4. *See also* Grand Union
Revlock, Gabrielle, 154–55. *See also* Restorative Contact
Reynolds, Dee, 206. *See also* kinesthetic empathy; Reason, Matthew
  Roda Viva Dance Company, 261, 304, 310. *See also* Teixeira, Ana Carolina
Royona, Mitra, 20, 29–30, 33, 76, 285–86, 312n.6. *See also* Contact Improvisation critics/critiques; "Unmaking Contact: Choreographic Touch at the Intersection of Race, Caste, and Gender"
Ryan, Peter, 108. *See also* teaching Contact Improvisation

safe space(s)/safer brave spaces for jams, 37–38, 46–47, 266, 273. *See also* Beaulieux, Michele
  Beaulieu Test, the, 14, 45, 46*b*, 46, 47, 48*b*, 48
  community accountability, 48, 49–51
  maintaining a democratic jam community, 49–50
  propagating new social norms, 51
  repairing (past) harm, 54–57
  reporters/reporting, inhibitions to, 51–52
Saleeby, Caleb Williams, 127. *See also* Eugenics Education Society; Alexander, F. M
Savage, Saliq, 146–47. *See also* Underscore
Schultis, Brian, 7n.6, 8, 15–16. *See also* Contact Improvisation and Philosophy
The Senses Considered as Perceptual Systems, 162, 233. *See* Gibson, James Jerome
Schaffer, Sarah, 55–56. *See also* Contact Improvisation jams, the Chicago Jam; Response Protocol Working Group .
Shakers, the, 256–57. *See also* Andrews, Edward; Enlivening Spirits; LaMothe, Kimerer; Nachmanovitch, Stephen
Sharing the Dance: Contact Improvisation and American Culture, 3–4, 3n.2, 19, 111, 112. *See also* Novack, Cynthia
Shawn, Ted, 125–26
Siddall, Curt, 3–4, 29. *See also* Mangrove Dance Collective; ReUnion tour (1975); "You come. We'll show you what we do" tour (1973)
Siegel, Daniel J, 164–65n.9, 165, 171. *See also* interpersonal neurobiology
Simson, Kirstie, 178–79, 195. *See also* Morrissey, Charlie; *Unwanting Hands* exercise
Singh, Paul, 15–16, 107, 108, 109, 115, 116–17. *See also* Bigé, Emma; "Wrong Contact Manifesto"
Skrzypczak, Wiktor, 214. *See also* "Queer Contact Improvisation (QCI)"
small dance, the, 3, 23–25, 26, 153–54, 159–60, 159n.2, 160n.4, 161–63, 164, 167–68, 169–70, 171, 174,

178, 186, 198, 200, 233, 253–54, 295, 328. *See also* Contact Improvisation fundamentals, The Stand/the small dance; Paxton, Steve

Smith, Joy Mariama, 15, 87*f*, 92*f*. *See also* BIPOC; Color Block 2023 retreat; Not Contact Improvisation (NCI) practice

Smith, Nancy Stark (1952–2020), 3, 5, 7, 17, 65, 111, 139, 140–41, 144, 198, 241, 252, 253, 291–92, 295–96, 298
  Caught Falling, 141n.2, 142, 144, 146, 150
  Contact at 10th and 2nd, 108
  defining Contact Improvisation, 146
  dialogue with Cohen, Bonnie Bainbridge, 333
  exhibition on Smith at Oberlin College, 7–8, 147
  on flow 330, 338–39
  founded/managed *Contact Quarterly*, 4, 5, 140n.1
  intensive at Earthdance, 6, 297
  memorial exhibition at *Critical Mass: CI @ 50*, 8
  published first *Contact Newsletter*, 4
  States of Grace, 142–43
  Underscore, the, 150 (*see also* Underscore, the)
  writings/legacy in *Contact Quarterly*, 150

Smith, Rosalind Holgate, 192. *See also* "How touch facilitates encounters with Otherness and the vocabulary from Contact Improvisation" PhD dissertation

somatics, 4, 7, 11, 83, 95, 153, 154, 220, 223–24, 338. *See also* Alexander, F. M.; Beaver, Wendell; body, the, neutral body, the; Dowd, Irene; H'Doubler, Margaret; Sweigard, Lulu; Reich, William; Todd, Mabel; XCI
  claims to evolution and universal humanity, 128, 135
  emergence of, 16, 126
  listening practices, 177, 178, 188–89
  natural body, and the, 122–23, 128, 133
  primitive patterns and reflexes, and, 134, 222
  queer people's sensibility of, 213, 214–15, 217, 221–22
  as related to freedom and liberation, 129
  release techniques, 122–23, 129, 131, 133, 134
  self-care, as, 180
  somatic identity, 15
  somatic intelligence, 15, 83, 87–210
  somatic psychotherapy, 188–89, 201, 203–4
  trans-Black practitioners, 117
  understanding from the body, 222

The Souls of Black Folk, 308. *See also* W. E. B. Dubois

Sounds in Motion, 3. *See also* McIntyre, Dianne

Sposetti, Irene, 292, 293, 298. *See also* Contact Improvisation in Asia; teaching Contact Improvisation

St. Mark's Church, 105. *See also* Contact at 10th and 2nd; Holland, Fred; Houston-Jones, Ishmael; *Untitled (Oo-Ga-La)*
  stewardship, 154, 170, 177, 180–81. *See also* Bassel, Leah; McCalman, Caroline

The Strange Order of Things: Life, Feeling, and the Meaning of Cultures, 170. *See also* Damasio, Antonio

Suraj, Guru, 7n.6, 162–63, 241, 260, 269*f*, 276, 279–80, 281*f*. *See also* Contact Improv India; Contact Improvisation in India; InContact Collective; Michalska, Adrianna

Suseno, Andrew, 77, 106, 148n.8. *See also* Contact Improvisation events, Moving Rasa

Svane, Christina, 108, 141–42, 334. *See also* teaching contact improvisation

Sweigard, Lulu, 127, 128. *See also* Ideokinesis; Todd, Mabel

Symbiosis Nice Dance Company and Training, 261, 294–95. *See also* Alessi, Alito; Dance in Asia, Maru; Maru

Tabor, Bill, 251. See also *Four Doors to Meeting for Worship*; Quakerism

Tai Chi, 3, 156–57, 237, 249, 298, 302

Tànceània Company in Budapest (mixed ability dance), 324n.26

Tangente dance presenting space, 25–26, 26n.4, 28. *See also* Davida, Dena

Tansey, Vicky, 26. *See also* Davida, Dena

Tanzfabrik in Berlin, 259. *See also* teaching Contact Improvisation

teaching Contact Improvisation, 5n.4, 262, 329. *See also* Contact Improvisation, fundamentals
  about what the body can do 331–32 (*see also* Manning, Erin)
  active reflexion, 337–38
  arriving (the first skill to teach), 10, 331, 332
  avoiding dogma, 262, 329–30
  awareness of subtle differences, 3, 153, 178, 190, 299, 320, 335
  in China, 293
  Contact Improvisation practice as research, 262, 329, 332, 339 (*see also* Bartley, Colleen; Little, Nita)
  collective body, the, 270, 325, 332, 336
  copying vs. exploring, 330
  creating a third space, 334, 335
  creating scores, 69, 77, 287–88, 305–6, 337–38
  Dance for Empowerment Teacher Certification Program, 294–95
  debating certification, codification, 329–30
  demonstrating or not, 284, 330
  humor, 260, 284, 331
  in India, 280
  investigative labs, labbing, 336
  listening more, 334 (*see also* Stengers, Isabelle)
  open explorations or physical exercises, 262
  porous roles of teacher and student, 262
  variations on a theme, 140–41, 141*f*, 262, 283

Teixeira, Ana Carolina Bezerra, 261, 303. *See also* Alessi, Alito; Contact Improvisation and differently abled bodies; Duschenes, Maria; teaching Contact Improvisation
  CI as a political practice, 304–5
  doctoral research on disability, 308–9
  Extrema Direita ("Far Right") solo, 309–10
  Roda Viva Dance Company, 261, 304, 310

The Stand. *see* small dance, the

Theatre of the Oppressed, 46

Theatre School in Amsterdam, 259. *See also* teaching Contact Improvisation

356 Index

"Theorizing Off-Balance," 168. *See also* Johnson, Pam
Thielen, Diana, 6, 107. See also *The Future of Contact Improvisation* conference
"Throwing Like a Girl," 67–68. *See also* Young, Iris Marion; feminism; gender
Tibetan Institute of Performing Arts, 287–88. *See also* Contact Improvisation in India, Ziarat Project
Todd, Mabel, 127. *See also* body, the, neutral, the; Cohen, Bonnie Bainbridge; somatics
  anatomical language of mechanical balance, 128
  influenced Lulu Sweigard, 128 (*see also* Ideokinesis)
  movement re-education, 128
  overcoming primitive mind and body, 128
  The Thinking Body, 134
  "Structural Hygiene" course, 128
  uprightness as moral goodness, 128
Tomatis, Alfred, 161. *See also* gravity
touch/ touching, 91, 154, 197, 312–13. *See also* Manning, Erin; psychotherapies using touch; Puhr, Ariane; Restorative Contact; Smith, Rosalind Holgate
  abusive, unwelcome touch, 20–21, 32–33, 40, 69–70, 74, 114–15, 223 (*see also* Beaulieux, Michele)
  across gender and caste in India, 260, 278
  being touched, 154, 183–84, 197, 219, 299–300, 312
  CI-informed, 197, 201, 203–4
  Cellular Touch (*see* Body-Mind Centering®; Cellular Touch)
  compression as weight-sharing, 197–98
  haptic practice, as a, 116, 153, 154, 177, 187–88
  intimate touch, 14, 33, 91, 155, 223
  listening touch (*see* listening touch)
  Mitra's critique of touch as liberation (*see* Mitra, Royonna)
  "non-intentional," 219–21 (*see also* XCI)
  psychotherapies using touch, 200
  tender touch, 220, 249 (*see also* Manning, Erin)
  way of being in the world, as a, 177
TOUCH Contact Improvisation Festival, Teacher Exchange Conference and Community Conference in China, 261, 292–93, 295. *See also* Ge, Huicho (Dew)
Touch and Play, 37, 74, 214–15. *See also* Olaya, Aramo
"Touch Revolution," 35, 111, 183–84. *See also* Nelson, Karen
Triàdico entre lineas and *Triàdico sobre papel,* 313–14. *See also* Polo, Mª Paz Brozas
Trio A/ The "No Manifesto," 23. *See also* Judson Dance Theater; Rainer, Yvonne
Turner, Bob, 130
Tyler, James, 29. *See also* Mangrove Dance Collective

Ueshiba, Morihei, 248–49. *See also* Aikido; *The Art of Peace*
Underscore, the, 17, 141n.2. See also Agitating the Underscore; Global Underscore team; Smith, Nancy Stark; Underscore Unwound; Young, Sarah
  Assembly (opening circle), 10, 49, 140–43, 141n.2, 146–47, 148
  Bonding with the Earth, 10, 141–42, 145, 149, 196

Critical Mass: CI @ 50, facilitating at, 10, 143, 144n.3, 144n.4, 145–47 (*see also* hong, elle, DJ)
  Final Resolution, 148–49
  Gap, the, 146, 148n.7
  Global Underscore, the, 139, 148n.7 (*see also* Young, Sarah)
  Global Underscore team, the, 8
  glyphs, the, 5, 141*f*, 143, 144, 148
  Harvesting, 139, 146, 148–49, 238
  Kinesphere (in Underscore), 142, 143, 148–49 (*see also* Laban, Rudolf)
  Northampton group, the, 17, 140–41, 145
  ongoing questions about the, 150
  Open Score, 139, 149
  Sharing/Thanksgiving (closing circle), 49
  Skinesphere, 140–42, 148–49
  soundscape for, 148–49 (*see also* Yermakova, Anya)
Underscore Unwound, 144, 144n.4. *See also* Crowley, Patrick; Kelley, Prema; Lee, Rythea; Savage, Saliq; Jackson, Kellyn; Young, Sarah
"Unmaking Contact: Choreographic Touch at the Intersection of Race, Caste, and Gender," 20, 32–33, 285. *See also* Mitra, Royona
Untitled (Oo-Ga-La), 105. *See also* Holland, Fred; Houston-Jones, Ishmael; St. Mark's Church Performance Space; *Wrong Contact Manifesto*
Unwanting Hands exercise, 178–79, 178n.5. *See also* Body-Mind Centering®, *Cellular Touch;* Morrissey, Charlie; Simson, Kirstie; touch

Vargas, Mike, composer, 10, 145
Ver, Ronja, 144n.3. *See also* teaching Contact Improvisation; Underscore, *Agitating the Underscore*
violence prevention and response paradigms, 44–45. *See also* Response Protocol Working Group
Vionnet, Claire, 20–21, 33. *See also* Contact Improvisation critics/critiques; contentious issues
Vourloumis, Hypatia, 104, 184

Warner Main Space, 1, 5, 11, 229, 231–32. See also *Critical Mass: CI @ 50; Magnesium;* Oberlin College gymnasium
The Way of Tenderness: Awakening Through Race, Sexuality, and Gender. See Manue, Zenju Earthlyn
Weber Gallery residency, the, 65. *See also* John Weber Gallery in New York City
Whale Fall Cycle, 149n.9. *See also* brooks, mayfield
wheelchair, the, 261–62, 306, 312n.5, 313, 320, 322. *See also* Ahmed, Sara; Alessi, Alito; *ANQA Danse avec les roues;* Cortés, Jordi; DanseAbility; Nelson, Karen; Polo, Mª Paz Brozas; Ptashek, Alan; Zarvos, Neca
  bodies and objects, 303, 322, 323–24
  Choreographing Difference, 323–24 (*see also* Albright, Ann Cooper)
  The Cost of Living, 323–24 (*see also* DV8; Newson, Lloyd)

descent and ascent from, 321

Exposed to Gravity, 320–21 (*see also* Curtis, Bruce; Ptashek, Alan)

Lines Forces, 324 (*see also* Espinosa, Roser López)

queering the wheelchair, 311 (*see also* Polo, Mª Paz Bronzas)

rolling, 320, 320n.19

"Ruedapies" workshop, 322n.22 (*see also* Brugarolas, Marisa)

TOUCH Contact Improvisation Festival, at, 295

Triàdico entre líneas and *Triàdico sobre papel*, 313–14, 314n.11 (*see also* Polo, Mª Paz Bronzas)

wheelchair dance companies, 323 (see also *ANQA Danse avec les roues*)

wheelchair dancers, 320, 322n.21, 324

"Wheels of Fortune," 320 (*see also* Alessi, Alito; Blackwell, Emery)

"The Wheel of Consent," 208. See also Martin, Betty

"Wheels of Fortune," 320. *See also* Alessi, Alito; Blackwell, Emery; wheelchair, the

Woodberry, David, 4. *See also* ReUnion tour (1975)

Woodman, Marion, 257. *See also* Authentic movement; *Holding the Tension of the Opposites*

Workgroup, 3. *See also* Nagrin, Daniel

Wrong Contact Manifesto, 15–16, 105–6, 108. See also *Untitled* (*Oo-Ga La*)

Wynter, Sylvia, 110

XCI ('X' Contact Improvisation), 77, 155, 212, 218. *See also* Manning, Erin; Olaya, Aramo; "Queer Contact Improvisation (QCI)"; queerism; Skrzypczak, Wiktor

Contact duet, and the, 215–16

co-sensing, 221

gendered meaning, 217–18

improvisation, and, 216–17

non-intentionality, 218–21, 222–23

politics of desire, 212–13, 220, 223

queer sexuality, 220, 221–22

violence and aggression, on, 220–21

Yermakova, Anya, 148–49. *See also* Underscore, soundscape

Ying, Hou/Hou Ying Dance Theater, 292, 297

yoga, 111, 194, 249, 331, 335. *See also* Kripalu Center for Yoga

"You come. We'll show you what we do" tour (1973), 3–4. *See also* Little, Nita; Paxton, Steve; Radler, Karen; Siddall, Curt; Stark Smith, Nancy

Young, Iris Marion, 67–68. *See also* feminism; "Throwing Like a Girl"

Young, Sarah, 8, 141*f. See also* Global Underscore team; Underscore

contemplating Stark Smith's legacy, 140, 147, 150

director of Earthdance, 140–41

Underscore at Oberlin College facilitation, 143

Underscore Unwound facilitation, 144n.4

Zarvos, Neca, 306. *See also* DanceAbility; Contact Improvisation in Brazil; teaching Contact Improvisation

Zen Buddhism, 198–99, 253–54. *See also* Bodhidharma; Buddhism; Leighton, Taigen Dan; Zenji, Dogen

Zenji, Dogen. See *Genjokoan*; Zen Buddhism

Zientara, Jerry. *See* teaching Contact Improvisation